CONSTRUCTION MANAGEMENT & ACCOUNTS

Other Related Books :

1.Construction Equipment and Its Management *by S.C.Sharma*

2.Construction Engineering & Management of Projects *By S.C.Sharma*

3.Construction Equipment & Job Planning *by S.V.Deodhar*

4.Construction & Foundation Engineering by *J.Jha & S.K.Sinha*

5.Construction Management of Industrial Projects *by S.K.Bhattacharjee*

6.Fundamentals of PERT/CPM & Project Management *by S.K.Bhattacharje*

7.Safety Management in Construction *by S.K.Bhattacharjee*

8.Safety in Building Construction,Health & Enviornment *by S.C.Sharma & B.Panda*

CONSTRUCTION MANAGEMENT & ACCOUNTS

V.N. VAZIRANI
S.P. CHANDOLA

Revised by

PROF. S.V. DEODHAR

Edited by

VINEET KUMAR

KHANNA PUBLISHERS
Operational Office
4575/15, Onkar House, Ground Floor,
Darya Ganj, New Delhi 110 002
Phones : 011-23243042, 011-23243043 & Mob. 9811541460
E-mail : contactus@khannapublishers.in

Published by :

Romesh Chander Khanna & Vineet Khanna
for **KHANNA PUBLISHERS**
2-B, Nath Market, Nai Sarak
Delhi- 110 006 (India)

Website : www.khannapublishers.in

Hologram & Description

To all readers of our books, from yourself if being defrauded by pirates to prevent, please make sure that there is an Hologram on the cover of our books with the below specifications. If you find any book without Hologram and Description, please mail us at contactus@khannapublishers.in

Thanking you

ISBN No. 978-81-7409-303-5

Eighth Edition : 2011

***Price :* ₹ 299.00**

Contents

Chapter *Pages*

PART I: CONSTRUCTION MANAGEMENT

PART II: ACCOUNTS

Chapter | Pages

PART–I

CONSTRUCTION MANAGEMENT

1. Construction Management
2. Construction Planning
3. Organisation
4. Site Organisation
5. Construction Labour
6. Control of Progress
7. Cost Control
8. Inspection and Quality Control
9. Miscellaneous Topics
10. Project Management with C.P.M. and PERT

1

Construction Management

1.0 INTRODUCTION

Food, shelter and clothing are the most essential needs of human being. The history of development of civilisation of mankind is in fact the history of development of shelter from time to time. For example the only shelter available to mankind was the "Caves". These formed natural shelter from the elements *i.e.*, storm, rain and sun. In the second stage, which some of the natives still adopt, was to build platforms on the trees with some type of roof which gave protection against natural elements as well as from the wild animals.

With the development of civilisation, the constructions were required not only to provide shelter for existence but for various activities associated with such development such as industries, installations, organisations etc. These developments called for specialised agencies for economical and organised management. For major construction activities proper management consists of the most economical construction using as far as possible local resources (labour, material and equipment) and consistent with the safety of the construction.

1.1 CONSTRUCTION IN INDIA

In order that the under-developed countries be able to improve their standard of living it is essential that the production within the country is increased with a view to its becoming not only self-sufficient in its most of the requirements but should be able to export its commodities. By undertaking a series of five year plans, India has already made outstanding improvement in the field of Industrial development, Agriculture, Education, Housing, Water

Supply, Irrigation, Multipurpose River Valley Projects, Sanitation, Science and Technology. As a result of these developments India has already become a developing nation from the underdeveloped category in which it was only three decades back. Out of the total five, 5-year plans which have been completed so far the amount spent on the various construction projects has been well above 50% of the total outlay. For ready reference the amount spent on construction projects during the various plan periods are shown in table 1.1.

Table 1.1. Construction : Content of Plants

Plan period	*Construction content as % of total development of plan outlay*
1st Plan (1951-56)	50.4
2nd Plan (1956-61)	42.6
3rd Plan (1961-66)	42.3
4th Plan (1966-74)	43.2
5th Plan (1974-79)	43.4
Annual Plan (1979-80)	46.1
6th Plan (1980-85)	36.2
7th Plan (1985-92)	40.0
8th Plan (1992-97)	43.5

1.2 CLASSIFICATION OF CONSTRUCTION WORK

Construction works in the construction industry are classified in a number of ways. The system of classification also varies from department to department. Some of the common system of classification are given below:

(*a*) **Minor works, Major works and Projects.** This is the most commonly used classification and is based on the cost of completion of the work. The various categories under this classification are briefly explained below:

(*i*) **Minor Works.** These are works for minor nature costing below say ` 20,000. The departmental heads are given bulk allotment for the financial year and works are sanctioned on as required basis.

(*ii*) **Major Works.** Works costing between rupees twenty thousand and one lac are treated as major works. Such works are carried out against specific proposals and allotment of funds by competent financial authority.

(*iii*) **Projects.** Works costing above rupees one lac are termed as projects. It may be noted that the financial limit of these works changes from time to time and from department to department.

(*b*) **Permanent, Semi-permanent and Temporary Works**

The terms used are self-explanatory.

(*c*) Original works, and repair works.

(*d*) Light, heavy and industrial construction.

(*i*) **Light construction.** This denotes comparatively light structure such as office and residential buildings, transist sheds, etc.

(*ii*) **Heavy construction.** Constructions which can be treated as complete projects in itself and involves use of heavy structural members such as multistoreyed construction, factories, highways, railways, airports, dams, tunnels etc., (where manpower and machines are used for the completion of work).

(*iii*) **Industrial construction.** Special projects needing highly specialised and skilled technique and requiring coordination of different branches of Engineering fall under this category. Examples of such works are fertiliser and chemical plants, power stations, steel plants, oil refineries etc.

1.3 STAGES IN CONSTRUCTION

The various stages of construction are:

1. Initiation of proposal.

2. Acceptance of the proposal in principle by the competent Administrative Authority on not exceeding basis estimate. Sometimes the report on which such sanction is accorded is termed as Feasibility Report.

3. Survey, Planning, Design, Drawings and preparation of estimate.

4. According of Administrative approval and allotment of funds.

5. Preparation of tender, documents and acquisition of land and inviting tenders.

6. Preparation of comparative statement and allotment of work.

7. Execution of work.

8. Completion report Part I (submitted on the completion of the work/project).

9. Completion report Part II (closing of accounts after disposal of surplus stores).

Broadly speaking the stages of construction may be divided into two major stages namely Pre-tender stage and Post-tender stage.

The pre-tender stage requires a coordinated effort on the part of the user (owner), Architect, Engineer, Administrative and Financial authority. It includes the following:

(*i*) Selection of site and finalisation of alignment of works,

(*ii*) Acquisition of land, and

(*iii*) Finalisation of designs, details including soil investigations and preparation of estimate.

(*iv*) Obtaining administrative approval and allotment of funds.

(*v*) Arranging resources (manpower, stores, equipment and money). The post-tender stage consists of the following:

(*a*) Assessment of work and expenditure during execution with a view to exercise proper quality control and financial control. It includes network planning (CPM) and other methods of ensuring completion in time.

(*b*) Finalisation of accounts and handing over the work to the user.

The selection of site is done normally by constituting Sitting Boards consisting of the following:

1. Representative of user (Department for which work is to be undertaken).

2. Representative of local civil Authority/Army authority in case of Cantonment Boards.

3. Representative of Engineer Authority.

4. Representative of Administration.

1.4 CONSTRUCTION TEAM

The term construction team denotes the various parties which have to coordinate on the ground with the common target of completing the work/project as per specifications, drawings and design details. These parties may be broadly classified into the following:

(*a*) User/owner.

(*b*) Engineer, Architect, Designer.

(*c*) The Contractor.

(*a*) **User/Owner.** The initiation of the proposal for a project may be from the user or from the owner. Sometimes both these functions may be performed by the same agency. For example, when a State or Central Government initiates a proposal say for the construction of an educational institution, or for the construction of a highway the owner would be the State or Central Government as the case may be but the users would be the staff and students in the case of educational institution or the public in the case of the highway. If on the other hand an industralist is getting a factory constructed he would be both the owner as well as the user.

(*b*) The Engineer is normally responsible for preparation of the estimate, design of structure and supervision of works during their execution. He also prepares design details of the outlines of the structure prepared by the architect. The roles between the engineer and architect are comparable with that of a physician and a beauty clinic. The beauty clinic would be interested in the external appearance whereas internal body structure is taken care of by the physician. In the same way the architect primarily prepares the drawings with external appearance of the structure whereas the engineer finalises the details. The engineer employed in the office work is responsible for the design whereas the engineer employed at site takes care of the progress of the project at site.

(*c*) The contractor is a person, firm or agency who undertakes to execute the work/project on the basis of agreed rates of payment and in accordance with the terms and conditions of contract agreement.

The various parties in the team described above have necessarily to work in perfect harmony and close cooperation. It is the responsibility of the engineer to see that to the best of his ability the structure is the most economical one in conformity with the requirements of structural safety. In some cases he is also responsible to arrange regular payments to the contractor. In some projects it is the architect who coordinates the work of the engineer and the contractor and arranges payments both to the contractor as well as to the engineer.

1.5 RESOURCES FOR CONSTRUCTION

Resources in a construction project are made up of:

1. Plant equipment and machinery required for the project.
2. Construction stores such as cement, bricks, steel, timber, aggregates and other fixtures and fittings etc.
3. Skilled and unskilled manpower.
4. Supervisory staff consisting of technicians and technocrats.

The above four categories of resources are directly responsible for the execution of the work. In addition to it the command and control of the project as a whole is exercised by the administrative cell.

1.6 OBJECTS OF CIVIL ENGINEERING MANAGEMENT

It is said that the best designed structure is one which would collapse at the applied loading such that this loading is safety factor times the loading that is expected on the structure and that when such a failure occurs all the components of the structure fail simultaneously. Such an ideal situation can only arise when each component of the structure has not only been properly designed but also suitably fabricated and assembled. This brings home the need of proper planning, design and execution of the work (*i.e.*, Modular Coordination).

The above observation to a large extent can be made applicable to any construction project as a whole with the additional rider that the project be executed in the most economical manner so that consistent with the safety and durability requirement, the total expenditure incurred would be the least under the circumstances. The engineer would design the structure and estimate the resources required for the project which would be the basis for the project management to plan its procurement and recruitment in a phased manner. To achieve this target a suitable organisation which would indicate the following is invariably needed:

1. Planning and procuring of resources including procurement of stores and recruiting of personnel.
2. Supervision and site inspection of the works to ensure quality and quantity control.
3. Exercising financial control over the expenditure.

Such as organisation is known as the Management or project administration.

As has already been stated the main purpose of having a proper orgnisation is to make the construction most economical. Apart from the part played by the project administration by controlling the finances (budget allotment, expenditure return, cost control relation etc.) the engineer and the contractor can also exercise financial control as detailed below:

Economy by the Engineer

1. By incorporating components in the design which are either locally available or made within the country.

2. By avoiding special equipment and technique not available in the country.

3. Using standard or similar section in concrete structure so that same shuttering may be used over and over again. (*i.e.*, modular coordination techniques).

4. Giving full and detailed specifications along with detailed working drawings to the contractor so as to eliminate chances of his procuring wrong parts.

5. Giving the details of tests of each component where required so that the contractor is aware of the requirement.

6. Having a trained and experienced supervisory staff who can give suitable guidance to the field workers. In case of large projects special training cells are organised to make the supervisory staff acquainted with the job requirement.

In order that the contractor fully knows the scope and requirement of the work so that he takes into consideration these factors at the time of bidding, it is desirable that the engineer-in-charge holds a conference with the bidding contractors, well before the date of receipt of tender, and acquaint them with the job requirments.

7. To provide all necessary documents to avoid any delay during execution of work (due to lack of decisions) or should not leave any work, decision to be done during the execution of project.

Economy by Contractor

The contractor can also plan his activities so that he also gets maximum output from the resources deployed by him. This may not affect the project directly as he would have already given his rates but it would help in bringing down his subsequent rates and at the same time eliminate disputes since a satisfied contractor would not create disputes. Some of the important steps in this direction are:

1. Proper choice of plant and equipments. As a rule larger capacity plant are more economical.

2. Provisioning adequate spares so that plant and machinery are kept in working order in arranging the stores/ materials well in advance to avoid delay.

3. Employing trained and experienced staff.

4. Giving liberal incentive for greater output. For example, paying the labour or group of labour on the basis of production.

5. Following proper safety precautions so that there are no accidents.

6. Initiating welfare scheme for the staff and the labour. This includes provision of medical facilities.

This additional expenditure would give high dividends.

1.7 FUNCTIONS OF CONSTRUCTION MANAGEMENT

This construction project administration/management carries out the following functions:

1. Phasing of project.
2. Exercising administrative, financial and technical control.
3. Planning and designing.
4. Procuring plant, machinery and equipment including workshop cover.
5. Procuring of construction stores.
6. Recruitment and training of staff and labour.
7. Arranging payment of salaries and wages.
8. Welfare of staff and labour.
9. Establishing round the clock communication between the administrative cell and field staff.

The above functions are briefly detailed below:

1. **Phasing of the Project.** This is based on the users requirement, availability of resources and availability of funds.

2. **Exercising Administrative, Financial and Technical control.** The administrative control is exercised by having the work administratively approved so that the expenditure incurred on various items is as per sanctioned estimate of work and also the

quantity of work done is not in excess of the quantity shown in the estimate for administrative approval of the work.

Financial control is exercised by providing budget allotment and obtaining the sanction for the expenditure for various projects and parts of projects and getting all the payment vouchers audited from time to time.

Technical control is exercised by ensuring that no item of any work is taken in hand without according technical sanction to avoid extra items/ substituted items, and excesses in the quantities of items.

3. **Planning and Designing.** The planning of various activities and designing the sequence of operation of a project/work are very essential. A considerable economy can be achieved by planning and designing. The construction period of project can be reduced which consequently reduces overheads thereby economising the construction cost. Planning of each activity in advance procuring construction material in advance, appointing subcontractor, labour etc., reduces construction time considerably. This all consist of planning and designing of various construction activities.

4. **Procuring Plant, Machinery and Equipment including Workshop cover.** Before taking the execution of any construction project in hand it is necessary that the resources such as machinery, plant and equipment are made available and that suitable arrangements for the maintenance and repairs as well as provision of POL (Petrol, Oil and Lubricants) including diesel are made. At the same time the project management has to see that the resources brought to the work site are not kept idle for want of operators or for having not started the work. This requires a very careful planning and coordination.

5. **Procurement of Construction Stores.** The construction administration or management has to ensure that the work is not held up at any stage for want of stores and construction material. A golden rule is that 2/3 of the construction stores should be at site (work site) and 1/3 in sight (procurement initiated).

6, 7, 8. Recruitment and training of staff and labour, arranging payment of salaries and wages and welfare of the staff.

These factors are of special importance in case of departmentally run projects. When the execution of the work is through contractors, major portion of this problem is eliminated, as this is arranged by the contractors.

9. **Establishing round the Clock Communication.** It is necessary that the project management is always in contact with site executives. This is best achieved by establishing telephone or wireless communications.

1.8 SCIENTIFIC METHODS IN CONSTRUCTION MANAGEMENT

This involves the use of modern technology, plant and equipment and scientific methods of exercising control on all the activities of the project. Main features of this are:

1. Proper planning, design and site investigations.
2. Use of scientific and mathematical instruments for quality control.
3. Training of skilled and supervisory field staff for specific jobs.
4. Use of CPM, PERT and bar charts for ensuring timely execution of different elements of the construction project.
5. Use of works diaries for recording day-to-day progress and output.
6. Use of log books to record consumption and output of plant, equipment, machinery and vehicles.
7. Introduction of usage rates for purpose of debiting the project in respect of the usage/hire charges of plant, equipment and machinery.
8. Cost control study to check the performance of the project as a whole.
9. Monthly expenditure return to check the position of expenditure with reference to budget allotment and administrative approval.
10. Arranging periodical audit of the expenditure incurred headwise (store, machines, labour and supervising staff).

1.9 PROJECT MANAGEMENT

Project management its widest sense includes both project formulation and its implementation. The project management would broadly cover such activities as preparation of feasibility report and obtaining sanctions, selection of proper technology, entering into foreign collaboration where necessary, construction of plant structures and utilities procuring and installation plant equipment and commissioning production. Construction of the factory structures has to be completed by the time plant and equipments arrive at site to avoid the problem of storage and delay in erection. The building of factory structure and utility services. Therefore, forms a pre-requisite of plant installation and as such construction activity requires the highest priority. There is increasing awareness by the top management of the need for adopting the latest technical know how and sophisticated design and construction techniques to optimise construction costs and reduced consumption of scares building materials. There are examples of Scooters India Ltd., at Lucknow and Bharat Heavy Electricals at Jhansi, that the old concept of steel factory structure has changed and has now given place to modern pre-fabricated, pre-stressed concrete construction, standardisation and modular co-ordination. Similarly, the traditional methods of organising project are being replaced by modern project management techniques including network programming and monitoring progress and inventory control to reduce time and cost over runs.

The broad stages of a project to plant construction are:

1. Project formulation on the basis of reconnaissance; funds available; market and need of the country and its future planning.

2. Preparation of Techno-economic feasibility report.

3. Preparation of detailed project report.

The first stage of planning of project formulation begins usually with the sectorial studies for the various planes based on government policies and market trend and ends with the commissioning of one or more feasibility studies. The actual investment decision is taken only after detailed consideration of the feasibility report. As soon as a decision to commission the feasibility study has been taken, a suitable and competent person has to be appointed, who could be associated with the preparation of the feasibility report and should ensure that the project is processed with speed. This ensures efficiency of working and would help in better coordination and faster decision making.

The task of Techno-economic feasibility report preparation should be done by an experienced professional consultant of that field. This report should contain the following information:

1. General information of exciting industries, their working conditions etc.

2. Preliminary analysis of alternatives.

3. Project description.
4. Market analysis.
5. Capital requirement and costs.
6. Operating requirements and costs.
7. Financial analysis.
8. Economic analysis.

The Techno-economic feasibility report must contain discussed in subsequent paragraphs. Adequate investigation, data collection and care at this stage lead to significant economics.

The most important factor governs is this study is the site selection. The choice of location of the project has a great bearing on the economy of construction and viability of the proposal. The traditional considerations for site selection are:

1. Prominity of the sources of raw materials.
2. Availability of a suitable distribution system and transport facilities.
3. Nearness of the center of demand.
4. Availability of adequate power and water.

It is a good practice to consider more sites and then to select on their merits. In some cases particularly in government projects, sites are selected not only on Techno-economic considerations but on the basis of social cost-benefit analysis. Sometimes political considerations also become the basis of selection of site. Whether or not the locations are technically the best. Only the minimum requirement of land including that needed for future expansion should be acquired at nominal cost. Given the choice, the most appropriate technology consistent with economy, profitability and the local conditions has to be selected. In some cases particularly in government projects or public undertaking project election of technology is tied up with loans and foreign assistance available to vital local conditions. Since process technology determines the design of the factory, the capital cost and the cost of production, the selection of technology is important for the success of the project.

It is always a good practice to prepare a master plan of all the structures and utility services including future expansion and indicating phasewise construction. If number of projects are coming in the same vicinity it will always be economical to have integrated planning in collaboration with surround industries. This will reduce the cost of services like water supply, sanitary, electrification etc.

The cost of plant and auxiliary structures form the main component of the cost of civil construction. A careful planning of these structures would lead to considerable economy and efficiency and better viability of a project. Adhoc provisions and without systematic and detailed space planning often results in over sized structures and higher capital investment.

Advancement of technology has also brought in its wake problem of environmental pollution. It is essential to study the effect of project on environment and to take preventive measures. Parliament has also legislated for control of environmental pollution. The time schedule for the completion of the project should be accessed realistically.

The cost estimates and the profitability calculations in the feasibility report are based on present cost of the inputs and selling prices of the output. However, since the project implementation extends usually over a period of several years, the financial calculations at the time of preparation of feasibility report often do not hold good at a later data due to escalation in the prices of material and labour. It is therefore essential to make provision for escalation of costs. While doing all these studies, it is essential to do scrutinity of certain board issues as:

(*a*) The contribution of the project to the economic and social objectives and adherence to the policies of the government.

(*b*) Availability of plan funds, desirability of division of plan, funds of the new project from those already in hands.

(*c*) Plant capacity and the dimensions of the investments in the light of demand and supply balance including export possibilities of the product services to be provided.

(*d*) Economic benefits of the project as distinct from financial return.

(*e*) Crucial assumptions in the feasibility report which are likely to affect the performance of the commissioned project in relation to the claims made thereon in the feasibility report.

(*f*) Major technological and structural aspects.

Once all these studies are made, preliminary reports are received and scrutinized, final and '*Detailed Project Report*' is prepared. All these preliminary reports, civil works reports etc., are arranged in a sequential order with the analysis of each and overall view of the project. This report is then submitted, approved and sanctioned finally for execution. Funds are made available and civil work starts, orders for machineries placed, recruitment's are made. Hereonward a manager has to administrate the whole work from this stage onward. He has to control all activities and has to see that the jobs are executed properly till final product comes to the market.

1.10 FINANCIAL MANAGEMENT

The management of finance means control on available financial resources in a manner such that there should be maximum use of it with a minimum unnecessary expenditure. It is essential to control the expenditure on almost all the stages right from its inception through its development and design, till its execution and payment of fine bill. This is essential required as the available resources are always limited and it is primary job of an engineer to utilise them in the best possible manner by proper planning, designing and on all the items of construction to ensure that project cost is not exceeded from estimated and sanctioned cost. Cost control and financial management are important aspects of construction management to almost all the persons involved in construction industry as well as to National Economy.

The basic object of cost control and financial management are to minimise the cost of project and to minimise the efficient use of available resources.

1.10.1 Stage where cost control and financial management is needed

Theoretically speaking cost control and financial management is needed at all the levels. But there are two major stages where it has effected as at these steps only if proper control is made, considerable financial resources can be saved. These stages are:

1. Planning and Design stage.
2. Execution stage.

1. Planning and Design Stage. The planning of any project can control the cost of a project to a considerable extent. Studies have revealed that efficient planning of any project can reduce the project cost by about 10 per cent. Similarly, specifications and design also affect a lot on project cost. If specifications are duly specified, local available materials used, it is possible to control the cost to a considerable extent.

Accurate and realistic estimation of a project is also vital for its successful implementation.

2. Construction Stage. Construction of any project consist of:

(*a*) Material cost including transportation cost.

(*b*) Labour cost including wages, accommodation and travels.

(*c*) Plant, machinery and equipment including cost of fuel, and lubricants.

(*d*) Overheads cost such as guarantee, supervision, insurance, liquidated damages agency charges, maintenance charges after completion, company taxes and engineers facilities, head quarter expenses.

There is a considerable scope to economise all these costs. Efficient use of material and efficient and effective use of machineries can control financial resources to a great extent. Wastage of material must be avoided and equipments must be maintained properly. Overhead cost also needs sufficient control.

1.10.2 Management of Estimation of Project

In the presence competitive environment, a construction company has to be able to execute the work at the least cost and for this, a systematic understanding of various cost components, which constitute the total cost is absolutely necessary. The accurate and realistic estimation of a project is very important for its successful implementation. The estimation of any project can be divided into two categories.

1. Preliminary Estimation. For inclusion of projects in the planning of the country and obtaining administrative sanctions for budget purpose. There may be a large time gap between this stage and the actual implementation stage.

2. Detailed Estimation for Project Implementation which precedes Execution of the Project. In respect of the project executed by the Governmental agencies such as Public Works Department and Railways, as also the Government undertaking in India, the detailed estimate is basically done on unit rates of work based on standard schedule of rates of various types of works, prepared and approved from time to time. These schedule of rates are prepared based on current market rates, mostly judged from tenders of work executed at the time of preparation of the standard schedule of rates. This type of detailed estimates does not consider the time element of execution. This if speedy construction is executed either by better site management planning and technique or by better methodology, one gets advantage but not reflected in the estimate, as such these estimates many times called as '*Execution Estimate*'. There should not be much time lag between time of preparation of this estimate and actual execution of work, otherwise there is always escalations in the cost of material, labour, machineries etc. These estimates generally remain valid for a period of four months in the intentional tenders. The execution estimate therefore must be accurate and should be prepared on actual basis not only on the basis of the unit rate of work.

The cost analysis is mainly based on 4 types of cost as given below:

(*a*) Material

(*b*) Labour

(*c*) Equipments and machineries

(*d*) Overheads.

The rate analysis must be carried out by an experienced person having thorough knowledge of various material cost, labour cost and other items. Provision for tools and plant must be made in rate analysis. There is a real need to analyse the overhead expense and their control. The overhead cost in the form of supervision includes the cost to higher level managers at sites, their accommodation, travel, site office costs, vehicle for inspection, maintenance office, stationary, telephones, telex, rest house facilities etc. These charges go on increasing if the work is delayed, consequently increase the project cost.

Various activities involved in proper estimation of cost of the project are:

(*a*) Study of tender documents: General and special conditions of contract specifications, study of drawings.

(*b*) Contradictions or ambiguous clauses in the condition of contract.

(*c*) Methodology for execution to achieve minimum cost.

(*d*) Quantities and scope of work, sequence of operation, bar charts, parallel activities.

(*e*) Assessment of quantum of materials of different items used in the work, their specifications, cost delivery schedule etc.

(*f*) Study of field data with advance planning of items with which information is to be collected.

(*g*) Calculation of operating cost in detailed manner, avoiding approximation keeping in view the machine oriented or labour oriented technique of execution adopted.

(*h*) Study of alternative design to minimise costs.

(*i*) Compare economics of cost by executing it yourself or through local subcontractors lists.

— Work done by contractors.

— Project supervision.

— Depreciation cost of equipment if purchased specifically for the project.

Indirect cost are those such as organisation overheads and management costs which are normally shared by various activities between the projects.

Time is an important element in some of these costs, particularly those relating to materials, services and sub-contracts. If the project manager is concerned with the money which may be available to him to pressure alternative courses of action, he needs to know the combined value of the committed costs and the actual costs.

1.11 MANAGEMENT OF CONTRACTS

Projects involving civil engineering construction and more so the large projects; are usually executed by engaging contractors. Even when turnkey contracts for large projects are awarded to big contractors; they are executed through sub-contractors; the prime contractor looking after only coordination activity and a part of the work on his own. As such management of contract is one of the important aspects of construction management. Since the agencies which deal with such contracts are government department; corporations or other semi-government agencies and also as large number of contracts are item rate contract; it becomes still essential to have good management of contract.

Foundations of contract management are laid early at the time of investigations of the project on analysis of rates for preparation of estimate. Natural situations are required to be taken into considerations while framing the contracts. Fairness or equity to both the parties of the contract is essential. Drafting of contract documents; especially the specifications; would need to be assigned by mature and experienced engineer. When works are of repetitive nature; adoption of standard specifications would be desirable.

Clarity or un-ambiguity is yet another attribute. The expression to the satisfaction of the engineer as well as the contractor; both should be taken into consideration. Avoidance of redundancy is desirable. It is a quality of good contract document. A standard model tender document should be used for all such purposes.

Every contractor is required to deposit some security money with the department as a guarantee of completion of work satisfactory. At the same time; contractor also need some seed money to start the work. If this seed money is not provided to him under contract; contractor has to borrow it at higher interest rate from some one else. He also looses interest on security at the same time, pays higher interest for money borrowed for starting the work. Hence instead of this; if a guarantee either in the form of bank guarantee or bonding companies bond are given; probably contractor as well as department; both will be satisfied. The concept of Bonding-companies is not prevalent in India so far and bank guarantee from nationalised bank is a factor that must be considered. Further price escalation should also be taken into consideration in contract document; as prices of each and every commodity is following a rising trend at present. Extra items should be avoided and arbitrations must be minimised for smooth working of a contract deed.

1.12 MANAGEMENT OF PROJECT CONTROL SYSTEMS (PCS)

The task of control is to ensure that plans succeed by detecting deviations from plans and furnishing a basis for taking timely action to correct potential or actual undesired deviations. The type of control system should be such that it measures in a verifiable way whether the plans under consideration are being accomplished or not. Control should be tailored to the specific needs of the project under execution. More the control techniques and information are understandable to individual managers, who must utilise them for results, the more they will be actually used and the more they will result in effective control.

Essential features required for proper and better functioning of project control system are:

1. A convenient framework to integrate time, cost and performance.
2. Ability to track progress according to defined parameters.

3. Ability to produce relevant, reliable and accurate data base to facilitate decision-making of various levels of management and

4. Capacity to anticipate pitfalls.

The key of successful management is monitoring. Monitoring performs a distinct function in PCS. It renders possible, timely identification of problems and a realistic evaluation of alternative methods of corrective action.

1.13 PERSONS REQUIRED ON-SITE

Once a work is allotted to a contractor, before he starts construction, various categories of persons are required to be recruited by contractor for smooth working of the work. Though contractor has his office staff well equipped with facilities, still some other persons are required to be deputed. Many contractors have their own permanent workers, but in absence of these he appoints a few. These personnels are:

1. Site Engineers
2. Site Supervisor
3. Watchmen, store clerks
4. Mistries and labour

Each of these personnels have their specific duties. The job of site engineer is to maintain quality control and to get work executed as per drawings. He is also to check the design. He is also required to prepare measuring books, running bills, and to maintain stock of materials. The basic job of site supervisor is to supervise the construction works as per schedule. He also assists site engineer for preparation of bills, maintaining stock etc. It is his duty to report the contractor through site engineer the progress of works, requirement of materials, labour problems if any, construction problems etc. The duty of watchmen is to have a close watch on the materials lying at site against any type of thefts. Unwanted persons should not allowed to enter the site. In many cases registers are maintained to note the name of persons visited the site including their time of arrival and departure. He should duly permitted by the contractor or his authorised representative. Store clerk maintain the daily stock of receipt and issue of materials to the construction works.

Contractor either appoints his own masons and labour paid either monthly or daily or sublets work to any known mistry as a reasonable rate as per that item. The later practice of appointing labour contractor *i.e.*, sub-letting labour work to mistries is most common maintain good progress of the work, moreover contractor gets relieved from dealing with labour class. The mistries and labour are generally belong the same family hence not only good amount, also being amount depending up work output; the progress of construction work is always speedy and fast. The drawbacks with this system is that the quality of work is not maintained many times. Contractor is always required to have a watch on quality of construction work as is the work is not approved by the engineer, his bill is likely to remain pending or unpaid.

Other personnels involved are electrical and mechanics. They are required on large sites if needed. In cases of constructions involving use of heavy machineries and equipments, these are always required so that in case of any fault, repairs and corrections can be undertaken immediately and down time could be reached to minimum. Many times the services of the persons are hired. Other personnels required depending upon type of construction and its extent are:

1. Plumber
2. Carpenter
3. Welder
4. Peons etc.

2

Construction Planning

2.1 JOB PLANNING

During the planning of a construction project it is usual to divide the entire project primarily for phasing out the sequence of construction and secondly for dividing the operation of one phase into a number of jobs or units of construction.

Each job has further to be planned with respect to the following:

1. **Manner of Execution of the Job (Work).** Whether it is to be executed departmentally, or through contractor. In case the work is done through the contractor, type of contract is to be finalised.

2. **Duration of the Job.** The following factors govern the duration of the job or the proposed period of its completion.

(*a*) Urgency of the work.

(*b*) Availability of resources.

(*c*) The position of the construction with reference to the *net-work*.

3. **Planning of Resources.** The following constitute the resources for any construction project.

(*a*) Plant, equipment and machinery.

(*b*) Construction stores.

(*c*) Supervisory technical and non-technical staff and skilled and unskilled labour.

(*d*) Construction stores.

The recruitment of personnel and procurement of plant, equipment and machinery and field staff should be such that all the resources are usefully deployed all the time and the recruitment of staff and labour is so phased that there is no wastage of manpower and material.

2.2 TECHNICAL PLANNING

As the name indicates technical planning is confined to the planning done by the engineer authority for economical execution of the construction project. It starts after the administrative approval of the work is obtained for giving technical sanction.

Technical planning is carried out for the following objects:

(*i*) Preparation of detailed drawings, finalization of design, details and specification.

(*ii*) Preparation of detailed estimate.

(*iii*) Finalising method of execution of work namely, departmental, contractor or any other system including type of contract and contract documents.

(*iv*) Planning resources and initiating procurement action.

(*v*) Continued checking of stages of securing resources required before commencement of the project.

(*vi*) To visualise bottleneck likely to arise during the execution of the project and to take remedial action for the same.

These objects are briefly described below:

(*i*) *Preparation of detailed drawings etc.* The estimate prepared for obtaining administrative approval does not cover working details of various structural members nor does it contain working drawings. These details would be infructuous in the event of the project not being sanctioned. However, after the sanction of the project, these details become necessary.

(*ii*) *Preparation of detailed estimate.* The estimate prepared for purpose of obtaining administrative approval, though fairly detailed in respect of the items of work to be executed is not a comprehensive one and therefore after the sanction of the work further details in respect of schedule of stores, general and particular specifications have to be incorporated within the framework of the approved estimate.

(*iii*) *Finalising method of execution.* The various methods open to the project management for getting the work executed are:

1. **Through Contractor.** This has been the most common method of getting the work executed as it is

administratively the easiest way of getting the work done. There is, however, a rethinking about this system and a number of projects requiring heavy construction machinery have been successfully executed departmentally. The main points in favour of executing the work departmentally are:

(*a*) Better quality control.

(*b*) In case of strategic installations and work, this is the only method available.

(*c*) Provides employment to larger section.

(*d*) Helps in preventing accumulation of wealth in the hands of a few capitalists.

(*e*) Difficulties in the execution of work are also known to the department.

(*iv*) *Planning resources and initiating procurement action.* This is particularly important in the case of departmentally run projects. Proper planning for procurement of construction stores, machinery and manpower is required well ahead of the start of the project. In addition to this, provision of spares for running repairs and workshop cover for plant, equipment, machinery and vehicles has to be made along with training of drivers and operators.

(*v*) *Continued checking etc.* It is not enough for the engineer authorities to initial procurement of resources. A continued check on the phased programme of procurement has to be exercised before and during the project.

(*vi*) *To visualise bottleneck etc.* Only highly experienced engineers are detailed to look after the execution of a civil engineering project. At the planning stages he makes an appreciation of the situation and visualises the likely obstacles during the execution of the project and takes remedial action to ensure that there are no holdups once the project has been started.

The following are some of the important points which have to be considered at the stage of technical planning:

1. **Resources.** The following points have to be considered

(*a*) Availability of site.

(*b*) Availability of stores.

(*c*) Availability of labour.

(*d*) Availability of equipment and plants.

2. **Works Plan.** A comprehensive plan showing the following particulars should be prepared:

(*a*) Various stages in planning.

(*b*) Fixing responsibilities for each stage and timing of these stages.

The work plan thus prepared should show logical development of the various stages.

The officer responsible for technical planning should further ensure that the various stages visualised in the project are adhered to. A CPM chart showing the various activities should be prepared and periodical review of the work done, undertaken by scrutiny of fornightly or monthly progress reports as the case may be.

2.3 PRE-TENDER AND CONTRACT PLANNING

Contract planning is divided into the following two categories:

1. Pre-tender planning.
2. Contract or post-tender planning.

The above two categories are explained below:

1. **Pre-tender planning.** The planning required for the time of inviting of tenders upto the receipt of the same is termed as pre-tender planning. It includes the following:

(*a*) *Finalisation and acquisition of site.* Before placing an order on the contractor for starting the same, it is necessary that not only the selection of site should be finalised but the same should be acquired as well.

(*b*) *Planning of resources.*

The resources required are:

1. ***Men:*** Skilled and unskilled, supervising staff, specialist personnels.

2. ***Materials:*** Such as cement; steel; bricks; timber; aluminium; aggregate; fittings and fixtures; scaffolding and shoring, oil and lubricants etc.

3. ***Machineries:*** Trucks and dampers, concrete mixer and vibrators, road rollers, scrappers, pile driving machines, earth moving machines etc.

4. ***Money:*** Almost all above items need financial resources without which nothing can be executed.

Resources in the form of labour (Men) material and machineries are essential for any civil construction work. No Civil engineering work can be started and executed unless resources are made available and therefore their planning is one of the important item of Civil engineering works. There are various cases that the projects have been delayed due to non-availability of resources and as and when required. It has been observed that many a times materials are ready at site but works could not be started due to non-availability of labour force. Therefore, planning of resources their availability and management are very essential for successful completion of works as her time schedule.

(*c*) *Determination of time limit of each work.* The requirement of resources and time limit are inter-related and both these aspects have to be taken together. In some cases the available resources are known and taking their output into consideration, time required for the completion of the job is decided. This is of particular importance when the work has to be executed departmentally. However, in the case of urgent work where the time limit for completion of the work is fixed, resources have necessarily to be planned and procured before commencement of the work so that the job is completed in time.

Even when the work has to be executed by the contract agency, the duration of the project has to be decided and notified before inviting tenders. If the time allotted for the work is comparatively short, the bids would invariably be comparatively higher.

When the contractor has to fill in the tender for any work, he has to plan the whole thing and consider the following:

(*i*) Site survey.
(*ii*) Availability of materials.
(*iii*) Equipment and plants (1. Hired, 2. Purchased).
(*iv*) Fuel.
(*v*) Labour.
(*vi*) Facilities for camp.
(*vii*) Study of Drawing/Design/Specifications.

Post Tender Planning

(*i*) Setting camp site office etc.
(*ii*) Welfare of staff/labour amenities.
(*iii*) Material required (use economically).
(*iv*) Labour required (minimum input for maximum output).
(*v*) Equipment (not to remain idle).
(*vi*) Safety measures to avoid accidents/theft.

(*vii*) Follow up of Drawing/Design/Specifications.

(*viii*) Billing etc., to record progress to calculate material/labour.

2. **Contract or Post-tender planning.** When the work is to be executed by contract agency the post tender planning consists of the following:

(*a*) Splitting the work in various stages and fixing responsibility for recording in the works diary the day-to-day details of work done. The planned progress in the form of bar charts or progress reports should be known to the contractor as well as to the engineer's representative.

(*b*) **Procurement of Construction stores.** It is normally the practice of all Civil Engineering projects to make controlled construction stores available to the contractor so that the work is not held up for want of the same. The rate at which such stores are to be issued to the contractor are also fixed before the issue of tender form. When the project is run departmentally the number of such stores increases considerably.

2.4 SCHEDULING

While planning the various events of any project it is necessary that the sequence in which the project is to develop should be known not only to the project administration but also to all the links in the system namely the engineers, supervisors, contractor and other site workers. The requirement is met in a systematic manner by scheduling or programming not only the main construction activity but also the supporting element such as labour, material, equipment and expenditure.

Once the scheduling for resources has been done it is comparatively easy to prepare time and progress chart also known as the Bar chart or Gantt chart or the modified Milestone chart and to prepare net work analysis in the form of Critical Path Method (C.P.M.) charts. The other advantages of preparing these schedules are:

1. Knowing the desired output of work along the various activities, the requirement of labour during different stages of construction can be worked out and phased recruitment/retrenchment interproject transfers of labour can be prepared well ahead of the actual occurrence.

2. Useful deployment of plant equipment and machinery can be ensured so that these costly machines do not remain idle for

want of skilled and unskilled labour or they are not off road for want of proper maintenance and repairs.

3. Cost control study of the project at different stages of construction can be periodically reviewed on the basis of expenditure, returns and progress of different items of work.

4. A phased programme of procurement of construction stores can be prepared.

5. Requirement of funds during the various stages of the project can be predicted fairly accurately.

The various schedules referred to above are given below:

1. Construction Schedule

The schedule is a time table showing proposed duration of construction of various items of work. Such a table can be prepared when the following data has been collected.

(*a*) Number of operation/activities.

(*b*) Output of labour and machinery.

(*c*) Quantity of various items of work involved.

(*d*) Number of field workers, and other resources (plant, equipment, machinery and construction stores) sequence.

(*e*) Sequence in which the various activities are to be taken in hand. Format of a typical construction schedule is given in table 2.1.

Table 2.1. Construction Schedules (Weekly)

Project Particulars......

Location

Administrative Approval.... No. ..... Date.....

Amount of administrative approval.

Sl. No.	*Item of work*	*Total quantity*	*Units*	*Month*								*Month*								
				Week								*Week*								
				1		2		3		4		1		2		3		4		
				Estim-ated prog-ress	A	E	A	E	A	E	A	E	A	E	A	E	A	E	A	

Note : E = Estimated progress
A = Actual progress

Alternately Construction Schedule may be prepared in the form of T and P chart or bar chart as shown in table 2.2.

Table 2.2 Construction schedule-1

Time and Progress Chart/Bar Chart/Gantt Chart

Name of project.....

Location....

Administrative No. ..... Date......

Amount of Administrative Approval.....

Progress as on....

	Part 1st		**Stores**					
	Item	*Quantity required*	*1st month*		*2nd month*		*3rd month*	
1	Cement	500 T	1	15	1	15	1	15
2	Steel	50 T						
3	Timber	20 C.M.						
	Part 2nd		**Construction Equipment**					
1	Dolers	4						
2	Road Rollers	4						
3	Concrete	2						
4	Bitumen mixers etc.	4						

An improvement in the bar chart is achieved by having a time schedule of the completion of various activities.

The Part III of the chart illustrated in table 2.2. is reproduced in table 2.3 and put in the form in which events on completion are identified. The completion of each activity is numbered in the sequence in which it should be completed. The estimated completion of an event is shown as whereas the activities actually completed are shown as on the date of reporting if all the activities on the left hand side of the reporting date line are shown as . It shows that the time schedule has been correctly followed. On the other hand, ends of activities denoted as on the left hand side indicate time lag in the completion of the target. Similary, if the right hand side contains certain activities shown as it indicates that the item of work has been completed ahead of schedule.

Table 2.2 (*Contd.*)
(Fortnightly Progress Report) ending 15th January

S. No.	*Item of work*	*Total quantity*	*1 January*		*February*		*March*	
			1	15	1	15	1	15
1	Earth work in excavation	C M						
2	Foundation concrete	C M						
3	Masonry up to plinth level	C M						
4	Masonry up to Intel level	C M						
5	Masonry up to roof level	C M						
6	Rooting	S M						
7	Doors & windows	S M						
8	Flooring	S M						
9	Plastering	S M						
10	Finishing white washing painting distemper	S M						
11	Approach road	km						
12	Site clearance	S M						

Reference: Actual progress / Estimated progress

2. **Labour Schedule.** The purpose of the labour schedule is to know well in advance the type of labour and their numbers required from time to time so that steps required for their recruitment are taken in advance. A typical labour schedule for a building project is given in table 2.4.

3. **Material Schedule.** The purpose of the material schedule is to know the requirement of various construction materials well ahead of the start of the project so that at no stage during the execution of the project, work is held up for want of stores. In the case of departmentally run projects storage of construction stores would not only result in the delay in the completion of the project but would result in resources being undeployed or under deployed which may call revision of the estimates along with disciplinary action against those responsible for delay in the procurement of store. (See Table 2.2 Part I).

Table 2.3. Milestone Chart

Name of the Project

Location

Administrative Approval No. ..... Date.....

Amount of Administrative Approval.

Progress report for the fortnight ending 15th January.

S.No.	*Item of*	*Total quantity*	*1st month Jan. 1 15* · *2nd month Feb. 1 15* · *3rd month Mar. 1 15* · *Apr. 1*
1	E.W. in		▼ 1
2	Foundation con		▼ 2
3	Masay after PL		▽ 3
4	Masay upto		▽ 4
5	Masay upto roof 1 leaf.		▽ 6
6	Roofing		▽ 7
7	Door & Window		▽ 5
8	Floor		▽ 8
9	Plaster		▽ 9
10	Finishing (white wash, painting, distemper)		▽ 11
11	App. road		▽ 10
12	Site clean		▽ 12

Estimated progress ▭

Planned events ▽

Complete events ▼

Table 2.4. Labour Schedule

Name of the Project ......

Location ......

Administrative Approval No. ...... Date.......

S. No.	Labour classification	*1st month* *Feb* *Weeks*				*2nd month* *Mar* *Weeks*				*3rd month* *Apr* *Weeks*				*4th month* *May* *Weeks*					
		1	2	3	4	5	6	7	8	9	10	11	12	13	14	15	16	17	
	Mason																		
	Carpenter																		
	Mixer operator																		
	Cement																		
	Truck driver																		
	Supervisors																		
	Labourers																		
	etc.																		

4. **Equipment Schedule.** The success of modern Civil Engineering Projects depends to a large extent on the proper use of construction equipment. The use of heavy equipment in construction projects is like having the *Allandin's* jin in ones possession, who if constantly deployed on some mission or the other would do wonders but might cause considerable damage if enough work is not found for him. The heavy equipment plays a similar rolo in a Civil Enginoering porjoct. If thc machincs arc properly maintained and usefully deployed they not only accelerate completion of the project but also bring down the expenditure on the project. If, however, their deployment is not properly planned, they can result in heavy financial burden on the project. The project management should therefore plan the use of construction equipment and machinery in such a way that they are usefully deployed all the time and taken out of the project at the earliest (See Table 2.2 Part II).

5. **Expenditure Schedule.** The engineer is primarily judged by his ability to provide most economical construction. It is, therefore, essential that the financial position of the work is reviewed at regular intervals to ensure the following:

(*a*) Expenditure during the financial year is kept within the allotment for the year.

(*b*) Expenditure on each item of administrative approval does not exceed the administratively approved amount.

The return is submitted in the beginning of the month and the expenditure shown therein is verified/reconciled with respect to the cash book entries.

A typical expenditure return chart is given in table 2.5.

Basic construction Networks and C.P.M. and Pert methods are given in chapter 10.

Table 2.5. Expenditure Schedule

Name of the Project ....

Location ....

Administrative Approval .... No. .... Date ....

Amount of Administrative Approval Allotment for the year.

Expenditure Return for the months of ....

Nature of Expenditure (As per item of Administrative Approval)	*Expenditure during the month*	*Expenditure upto the end of the year (During the year only)*	*Expenditure upto the end of the year including expenditure of previous*	*Liability*	*Total expenditure*	*Remarks*
(1)	*(2)*	*(3)*	*(4)*	*(5)*	*(6)*	*(7)*

3

ORGANISATION

3.1 TYPES OF ORGANISATION

For the most economical execution of any project it is necessary that it should be properly planned so that a planned development/ progress of the same is ensured. In the initial/pre-contract stage of the project therefore only the minimum personnel required for planning, phasing and designing should be established and other resources should be inducted into the work theatre on as required basis. An organised planning/design cell is therefore the first requirement of any project.

Once the project gets growing it has essentially to be divided into various sections. Each incharge of a section deals with the special technique of the section concerned. For example, a senior Civil Engineer could be incharge of Civil Constructions while a specialist in Water Supply and Public Health Engineering would be looking after the works of his field. Similarly, Senior Electrical and Mechanical engineers could be entrusted with electrical and mechanical installations. Depending upon the type of project the overall directions may be given by the Civil Engineer incharge and comparatively junior electrical/mechanical staff may be employed under him. It would thus be seen that there can be no hard and fast rule about the organisation in any construction project.

However, the project as a whole cannot be successfully executed unless each member of the team knows his work as well as the work of his associates, it is therefore necessary to have a format of organisation adopted giving duties, responsibilities and powers of every unit in the organisation. An organisation which has been developed to achieve the above would thus satisfy the following conditions:

1. The scope of the project is known to every one associated with it.
2. There should be a well-defined and demarcated sphere of duties of each group of workers engaged in any Construction Unit.
3. There is a proper coordination between the various working groups.

The overall organisation varies with the individual characteristics of any project and hence a rigid framework of universal nature cannot be laid down. However, some of the important types/patterns of organisations are given below:

1. Line Organisation.
2. Line and Staff Organisation.
3. Functional Organisation.

These organisations are briefly described below:

1. Line Organisation. This is the simplest form of organisation wherein the responsibility is distributed from top to bottom in a triangular pattern. The pattern has been borrowed from the military organisations where the general may be having three Lieutenant Generals under him looking after the three army commands. Each Lieutenant-General may be having three Corps-Commanders of the rank of major general and each major-general may have three brigadiers under him looking after the three brigades. Each brigadier may be having under him three Colonels/ Lieutenant-Colonels and so on till it trickles down to the level of a corporal who has three sections of 10 to 12 men under him. For this reason this type of organisation is known as *Military Organisation* as well. The salient features of this organisation are:

(*a*) The command and control is very effective.

(*b*) Responsibilities at all levels are defined and fixed.

(*c*) The system enables quick decision to be taken at all levels.

(*d*) Each individual carries out order of his next superior and this helps in maintaining rigid discipline.

While adopting this system, the following defects inherent in the system should be taken care of:

(*a*) Difficult to do interchange of work due to rigidity of the structure.

(b) Communications are routed through a number of intermediate channels.

(c) The top level executives get overworked as they have to look after other duties as well. This is partly rectified by having senior staff advisors.

(d) The persons doing important jobs are liable to get overworked. Figure 3.1 shows a typical line organisation.

Line Organisation

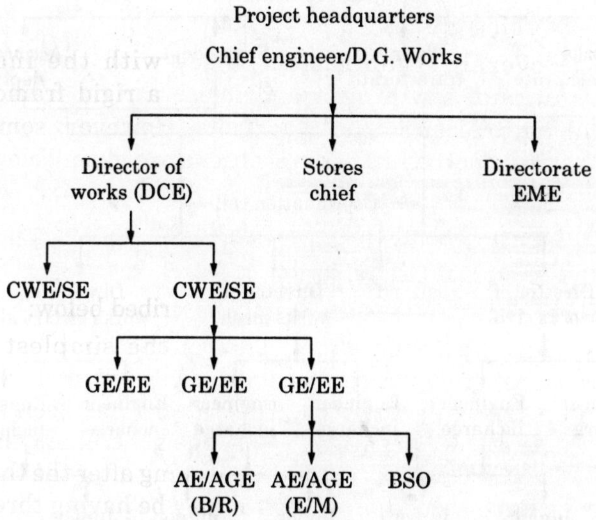

Fig. 3.1

DCE : Deputy Chief Engineer
CWE : Commander Works Engineer
SE : Superintending Engineer
GE : Garrison Engineer
AGE : Assistant Garrison Engineer
B/R : Buildings and Roads
E/M : Electrical/Mechanical
B.S.O. : Barracks and Stores Officer.

2. Line and Staff Organisation. The main disadvantage in the line organisation setup is that the top executive has to take decision in respect of all matters related to the project. The system is, therefore, not very suitable for large projects requiring specialist services; though for routine type projects it may be quite useful.

The line organisation system has, therefore, been modified in such a way that the benefits of line organisation such as rigidity in discipline and stability of the structure are retained and the expert knowledge of the specialist is added to it. Such an organisation is shown in Fig. 3.2. Figure 3.2 shows Line and staff organisation.

Line and staff organisation

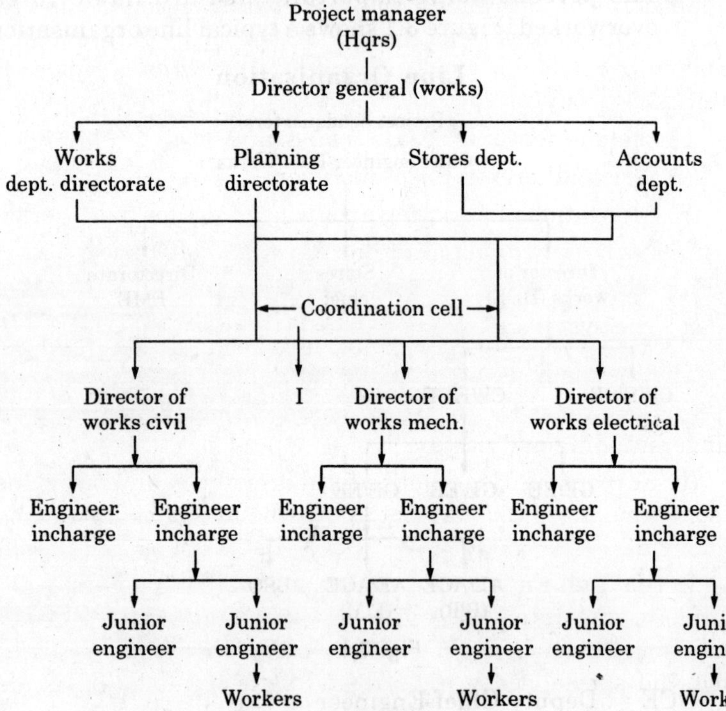

Fig. 3.2

The salient features of this set up are:

(*i*) Expert advice is available at all levels and maximum use of specialist is made.

(*ii*) The operations are efficient and hence the method economical inspite of additional expenditure on experts.

(*iii*) The staff at site is competent to take decisions and hence works is not delayed. The system however has the following short comings.

(*a*) If the duties of experts are not properly defined, there may be misunderstanding between staff and line workers.

(*b*) The expert advice given by specialists may get distorted by the time it is passed on to the field worker.

3. Functional Organisation. The line and staff organisation suffers from one serious handicap in respect of confining the sphere of work to the directly concerned channel. The group incharge tend to increase their authority resulting in partial disorganisation of the system. The shortcoming of the line and the line and staff organisations are taken care of by introducing a system of working known as "*Functional organisation*", evolved by **Frederick W. Taylor.**

The salient features of this system are:

(*i*) Strict adherence to specification.

(*ii*) Separation of planning and design part for field work.

(*iii*) Each individual maintains functional efficiency.

(*iv*) Work is properly planned and distributed.

(*v*) The system is based on knowledge of the experts.

The system however suffers from the following defects:

(*a*) Sometimes the functions overlap, which may give rise to misunderstanding and friction.

(*b*) Responsibility cannot be fixed directly on any individual and sometime a worker may not know who his immediate senior is.

In the Civil Engineering Construction, the line plan, which is simple to understand and operate is the most popular type of organisation though in projects of large magnitude requiring highly skilled and specialised work line and staff organisation is also sometimes used.

3.2 PRINCIPLES OF ORGANISATION

The primary and basic test of any construction organisation is that it should get the job completed in the specified time (period of completion) in the most economical manner. To achieve this aim certain guide lines, known as principles of organisation, evolved on scientific lines and developed after years of experience have been formulated.

Some of the important principles are:

1. Units of Command.
2. Cohegency.
3. Job to be well defined.

4. Effective Control at all levels.
5. Delegation of authority.
6. Flexibility in job assignments.
7. Interaction between executive and worker. These principles are briefly described below:

1. Unity of Command. A worker should not get orders/ instructions from more than one individual. Dual nature of such instructions create confusion and delay. In some cases the worker is likely to exploit the situation.

2. Cohegency. The organisation should afford coordination and cohegency between the different branches of the organisation. The work of subsidiary units should be correlated with the progress of the mass unit so that the resources are not under deployed.

3. Job to be well defined. In order that a job may be done well it should be well defined in respect of materials to be used, dimensions method of construction etc. There should not be ambiguity about the work to be executed. Otherwise there will be delay and may lead to dispute.

4. Effective Control at all levels. In order to have an effective control at all levels the ratio between the superior and supervisors should be properly arranged. For example, the top executive may have 3 to 5 advisers or assistants, whereas a foreman may have 15 to 20 workers. The executive engineer for example, may have three to four assistant engineers under him.

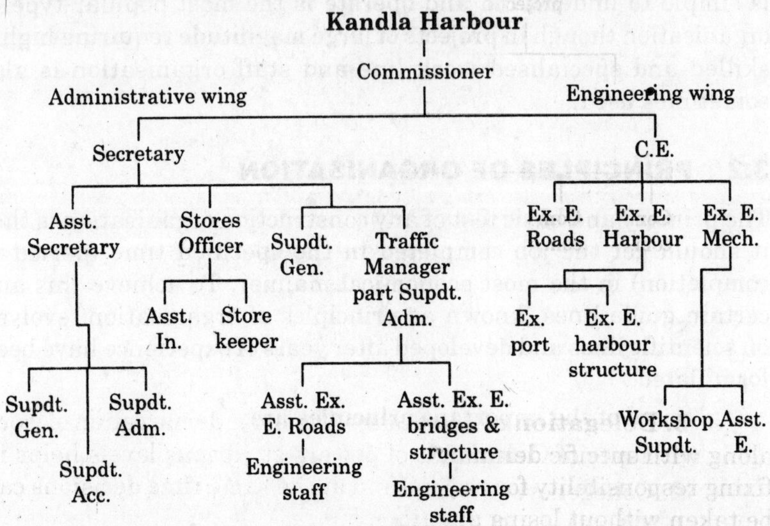

Fig. 3.3

Railways Organisation (Civil Eng.)

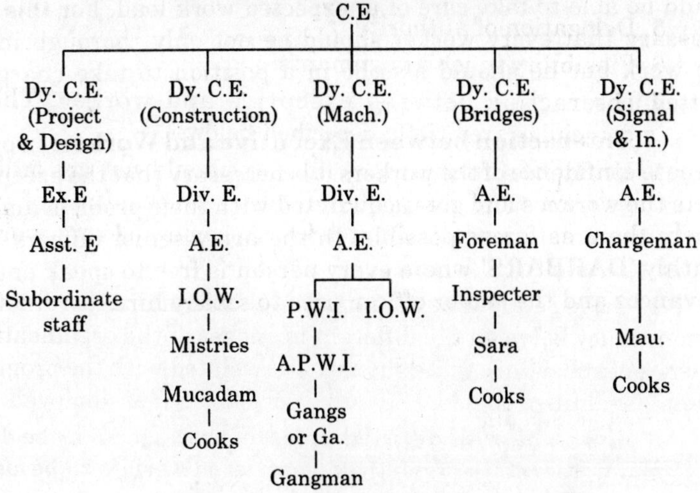

Fig. 3.4

Border Road Organisation

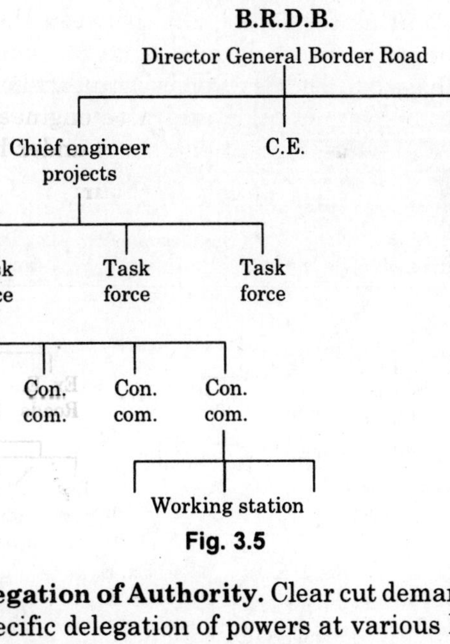

Fig. 3.5

5. Delegation of Authority. Clear cut demarcation of work along with specific delegation of powers at various levels helps in fixing responsibility for any job and at the same time decisions can be taken without losing any time.

6. Flexibility in Job Assignment. The organisation should be able to take care of unexpected work load. For this it is necessary that every worker should be not only thorough in his own work but he should also be in a position to take charge of allotted jobs.

7. Interaction between Executive and Worker. In order to create confidence of the workers it is necessary that the executive meets the workers and gets acquainted with their problem and try to help them as far as possible. In the army senior officers hold monthly **'DARBARS'** where every person is free to speak out his grievances and the senior officer tries to satisfy him.

4

SITE ORGANISATION

4.1 TECHNICAL CONTROL AND SITE ORGANISATION

Technical Control over any project is the most important function of the competent engineer authority. The engineer authority, being specialist in its own field has full powers for this control and is therefore directly responsible to see that all works executed are technically sound and at the same time the construction is most economical taking into consideration all the individual circumstances of the project.

The estimate of work is prepared at a stage at which it is not known whether the work would be approved or not and hence only the minimum required details of work are given therein. For example, based on empirical rules or rough calculations the size of the roofing having only T-Beam and slab construction may be fixed for purpose of estimate of cost which can be done from the overall dimensions of the slab and the beam. Before starting the construction further additional details such as details of reinforcement, schedule of bending and binding of bar, end anchorage of bars, camber of the beam and surface slope of the top of the floor have to be given to the contractors/workmen. These details are provided by according technical sanction to each item/ sub-item of the work.

The powers of according technical sanction by various officers of the department are different for different departments and are also changed from time to time. Thus the Engineer-in-charge (Assistant Engineer) may have powers varying for ₹ 10,000/- to ₹ 25,000/-, that of Executive Engineer/Garrison Engineer may be upto 2 lakhs that of Superintending Engineers (S.E)/G.W.E. be upto 5 lakhs.

The Chief Engineer of the project is the final technical authority and enjoys full powers.

The competent engineer authority has however to satisfy himself in respect of the following points before according such a sanction:

1. Items of work being sanctioned are in accordance to the administrative approval.

2. Approved scales have been followed.

3. Design, details and specifications are economical and confirm to sound engineering practice.

4. Rates are based on the correct schedule of rates.

5. Adequate working details and drawings are furnished.

6. Separate technical sanction is accorded for establishment charges. Amount sanctioned for establishment can not be utilised for any other purpose.

7. The sanctioning authority should be personally scrutinize the draft, technical sanction for the following items in particular:

(*a*) The main object of the technical sanction is to exercise a check on the engineering aspects of a work before the same is executed.

(*b*) The scope of the work should not be changed or modified.

(*c*) The amount of technical sanction for any item/items of the administrative approval should not exceed the items of the administrative approval under reference.

(*d*) The sanction is accorded for only authorised scales.

(*e*) Superior specification/fitting are not provided unless catered for in the administrative approval.

Table 4.1 shows a typical technical sanction.

The organisation at site responsible for the execution of Civil Works consists of the following:

1. Engineer incharge, overall in charge of the works at site.

2. **Junior Engineer.** The engineer incharge divides the work into various sections and each section is looked after by one Junior Engineer who is directly responsible to the engineer incharge for his section. He enters the work in measurement book and prepares bill for payment to the contractor.

Table 4.1 Typical Technical Sanction

Name of the Project ....
Administrative Approval No. .... Date .... Amount ....
Technical sanction No. ....
Amount provided in the A.A. in respect of items for which T.S. is given ....
Allotment of fund for the year ....

Sl. No.	*Description of work*	*Reference to authority for scales*	*Reference to drawing*	*Particular specification*	*Units of measurement*	*Name*	*Rate*	*Amount*	*Remarks*
1	2	3	4	5	6	7	8	9	10
								₹ ... ₹ ... ₹ ...	

Total cost as per Schedule of rates ₹ ...
Add for contractors percentage ₹ ...
Add for stores supplied free of cost (fixing only) ₹ ...
Add difference in cost of building materials ₹ ...
Prescribed in excess of issue rate ₹ ...
Total cost technically sanctioned ₹ ...

(Sd.) (Competent Engineer Authority)

3. **Sub-Overseer/Work Agent.** The Junior engineer further divides his work into sub-sections each incharge of a small unit. He maintains the works diary, attendances of muster roll and causal labour, handles receipts and issues of stores at work site. He is directly responsible for site and labour supervision.

4.2 SCRUTINY OF SITE DOCUMENTS

The site documents form the basis of the work executed at site and should be available at all times to the engineer's representative at work site. In the case of disputes between the contractor and the department, these documents form the basis of resolving such disputes.

The site documents consist of the following:

(*a*) Copy of the contract agreement and working drawings.

(*b*) Site order book.

(*c*) Record of receipt of stores to the work site and issues of stores to the contractor/labour.

(*d*) Muster roll and casual labour roll.

(*e*) Copies of all technical sanctions.

(*f*) Correspondence, if any with the engineer incharge and the contractor.

(*g*) Works Diary.

These documents are briefly described below :

(*a*) Copy of the contractor agreement and working drawing.

This the most important document and consists of the following:

(*i*) General conditions of contract

(*ii*) Site Plan of the land/area of construction

(*iii*) Details of structure showing plan, elevation, section elevation and other details

(*iv*) General and particular specifications

The specifications are further classified as:

(*i*) General/Standard Specifications to cover all types of works.

(*ii*) Particular Specifications or Project Specifications to cover special requirements of the progress.

(*iii*) Manufacturers specifications with respect to plant, equipment and machines supplied by the manufacturer.

(*v*) Schedule of items of work showing rates

(*vi*) Stores Schedule

(*vii*) Schedule of tools, plant, equipment and machinery.

(*b*) **Site order book.** Normally correspondence between engineer's executive staff and the field staff is done by noting instructions in the site order book. In the same way orders given to the contractor in respect of quality of work, passing of works etc. are recorded on the site order book.

(*c*) **Record of receipts and issues of stores.** Store is an important part of construction works. Various material purchased for construction are stored in store and issued as and when required. Major funds of any construction works are consumed by construction materials and therefore it is essential to maintain an account where in all materials purchased and then issued to construction are recorded. Store inchange under an engineer is inchange of these materials. He records all the materials regarding its receipt and issue date wise lot wise etc. The quantity received, issued and balance with store are recorded on register duly signed by store incharge. There is a set procedure to maintain record.

(*d*) **Muster rolls and casual labour rolls.** These are normally available with the sub-overseer/work agent/mate and the physical presence of the labour present at site is occasionally checked by supervising officer of the department.

(*e*) **Copies of technical sanction.** These sanctions form the basis of work on the ground.

(*f*) **Correspondence.** Record of all letters of correspondences are required to be maintained date swise. Letters received and issued to various departments are recorded. Inward number for letters received and outward number for letters dispatched with date are recorded.

(*g*) **Works Diary.** This is the most important document wherein the following information at work site is recorded in respect of the item of work every day.

A specimen Page of Work Diary is given in table 4.2.

Table 4.2

Works Diary

Name of the Project .....
Location .....
Item of Work .....
Date ......
Weather... Maximum/Minimum Temp. .... Clear/Cloudy/Rainy
No. of labour employed ....
Receipt of stores — Issue of stores to
(*i*) Contractor
(*ii*) DEL.

Progress of work done by
(*i*) Contractor/DEL
Signature of Incharge Site Works
Remarks by.... Inspecting/Visiting Officer.

4.3 JOB LAYOUT

The layout of a construction project camp is governed by the following factors:

1. Type of Project and its location.
2. Method of execution of the project.
3. Availability of resources (manpower, plant, machinery, equipment and construction stores).
4. Availability of water supply, electricity and sewage disposal works.
5. Availability of medical facilities.
6. Availability of welfare facilities such as mail service, fresh vegetables, newspaper, canteen facilities, recreation and religious facilities.

These factors are briefly described below:

1. **Type of Project and its Location.** The size of project camp and deployment of its resources in the project area is governed by the type of project and its location. For example, if the project consists of construction of multi-storeyed buildings in a localised area, it would be advantageous to have all the project units located in a central area. On the other hand, in case of a highway project a

number of construction centres have to be established and apart from the project headquarters a number of subordinate project headquarters or centres have to be established.

By the term location is meant the topography of the area, its distances from the rail head, and its special feature such as snow bond, subject to occasional heavy rainfall etc.

2. **Method of Execution of the Project.** The main methods of execution open to the project administration are:

(*a*) Contract agency and

(*b*) Departmental.

The layout of the project would be quite distinct in the two cases.

3. **Availability of Resources.** The project resources consist of plant, equipment, machinery, construction stores and manpower. When all or most of these resources are locally available the task of the project management is considerately simplified. For example, if labour has to be imported from outside the project theatre, a number of arrangements for food, accommodation and transport have to be made and incorporated in the layout.

4. **Availability of Watersupply, Electricity and Sewege Disposal Works.** In case these essential requirements are not locally available, considerable additional efforts for these facilities have to be made and incorporated in the layout.

5. **Availability of medical facilities.** It is not necessary to have a dispensary or hospital within the layout of the project if such facilities are available in the adjoining area. The project layout in such case would include only a field medical aid post.

6. **Availability of Welfare Facilities.** In the project theatre the workers are constantly overworked and it is the duty and responsibility of the project management that welfare, recreational and religious facilities are provided if they are not locally available.

A typical layout of a departmentally executed highway project is given in Fig. 4.1.

4.4 PRINCIPLES OF STORING MATERIALS

Project stores/materials, for purpose of storing include plant, equipment and machinery for the project. The analysis for storing construction equipment and other stores have necessarily to be dealt with separately.

It should be appreciated that fool proof arrangements for receipt, issue and holding are essential not only for general stores but also for equipment. Experience on construction projects shows that not only general stores are pilfered but also costly parts of equipment are very often replaced by cheap substitutes. Plant equipment and machines are therefore dealt with separately in the succeeding article (4.5).

The following basic factors should be taken in respect of receipt, storage and issue of stores:

1. There should be only one ingate and one out-gate for entry and exit of stores unless the stores themselves are classified into separate groups and are handled by separate sections such as iron and steel, timber, cement, brick and aggregrates and miscellaneous section in which case each group may have its own entry and exit gates and connected security arrangement.

2. Entry of all consignments is recorded at the in-gate.

3. No stores/consignments are taken out unless authorised by a supporting out pass/gate pass slip.

4. The total storage accommodation should be divided into the following three sections:

(*a*) Receipt Depot

(*b*) Holding Depot

(*c*) Issue Depot.

The following factors should be taken into consideration so that the stores are protected from the weathering action of elements such as wind, rain and sun and that the sequence of arrangement should provide first in first out principle so that stores do not deteriorate due to long storage.

1. Inflamable material (POL, explosive etc.), should be stored separately and storage licence for such commodities should be obtained and by-laws/storage regulation prescribed from time to time should be adhered to.

2. Stores more frequently required to be issued should be stored relatively near to the exit end.

3. Storage yard for timber and similar other materials should have adequate anti fire measures such as fire extinguishers, sand buckets etc.

4. Coarse and fine aggregates should be stacked in bins and underground pits respectively.

5. Materials like cement, lime should be protected from contact of moisture.

6. Cement bags should be stacked clear off the ground by providing donnge of stone slabs, steel girders or timber beams/ ballies. They should be stacked atleast 30 cm away from the wall and the height should be restricted to 12 bags.

7. Bricks should be stacked on prepared level ground. Heights of individual stacks should be restricted to 1.50 meters.

4.5 LOCATION OF EQUIPMENT

The following points should be considered while locating construction equipment:

1. Project owned equipment should be segregated from hired equipment. The arrangement in respect of hired equipment depends on this conditions of hire.

2. The project equipment should be provided permanent shed for static equipment and temporary garages for mobile equipment.

3. All equipments received in the project should have initial inspection carried out. In the case of new equipment this inspection is carried out jointly by the project workshop and the representative of the firm from which it is obtained. The equipment should be taken complete with history sheet, log books, maintenance manual and operation manual. A trial demonstration should invariably be insisted upon.

In the case of transfer from another project or department the initial inspection is carried out jointly by the field workshop of the project and representative of the source from which the equipment is obtained.

4. Adequate provision for fast moving parts as spares should be made along with the procurement.

5. Washing ramps, platform should be provided.

6. Responsibility of workshop cover and regular inspection should be fixed.

4.6 ORGANISATION OF LABOUR

The organisation of labour for a project involves the following:

1. Recruitment of labour.

2. Provision of accommodation and welfare activities including medical facilities.

3. Arrangement of training.
4. Deployment of labour.

The above factors are briefly described below:

1. **Recruitment of Labour.** This is particularly important in the case of departmentally run projects. If local labour is available, it saves considerable amount of expense and administrative arrangements. In projects in remote areas or in the forward areas where local labour is not possible labour recruiting zones have be established and a special training cell in the project to take care of the labour from the recruiting zone to the work site has to be established.

2. **Provision of Accommodation, and Welfare Activities including medical facilities.** When labour is an imported one, the transit cell makes the transit arrangement whereas the administrative cell makes arrangement for their living, eating and medical treatment. Sometime all such facilities consisting of transport, accommodation, messing and clothing are provided free as part of agreement with the workers and entire expenditure is debitted to the project.

3. **Arrangement for Training.** Labour is primarily classified into skilled and unskilled. Whereas the unskilled labour can be deployed directly on the job under supervision of technical supervisory personnel, the workers required to do specialised/skilled jobs such as carpenters, masons and other trades-men have to be trade tested at the time of recruitment. In case skilled trademen are not available semi-skilled are initially recruited on a lower grade, given training and then deployed on job on higher grade after qualifying in the trade test.

4. While deploying workmen on production jobs the following points should be considered:

(*a*) Work should be divided into a number of teams doing similar work.

(*b*) Production of such teams are regularly assessed and reasons for short-fall if any investigated.

(*c*) Work incentive for higher production is provided. A small incentive helps increase output considerably.

(*d*) Grievance/complaints of workers are heard from time to time by having open meetings (Darbar) where every individual can bring out his points.

(*e*) Proper welfare activities are provided.

4.7 PREPARATION OF JOB LAYOUT

The preparation of job layout of any project is decided on the individual project requirement and a hard and fast rule connot be laid.

Figure 4.1 gives a typical layout of a highway project (departmentally executed). This shows the layout of a project headquarters in the forward areas to which one of the authorities was associated. The numbers in Fig. 4.1 stand for:

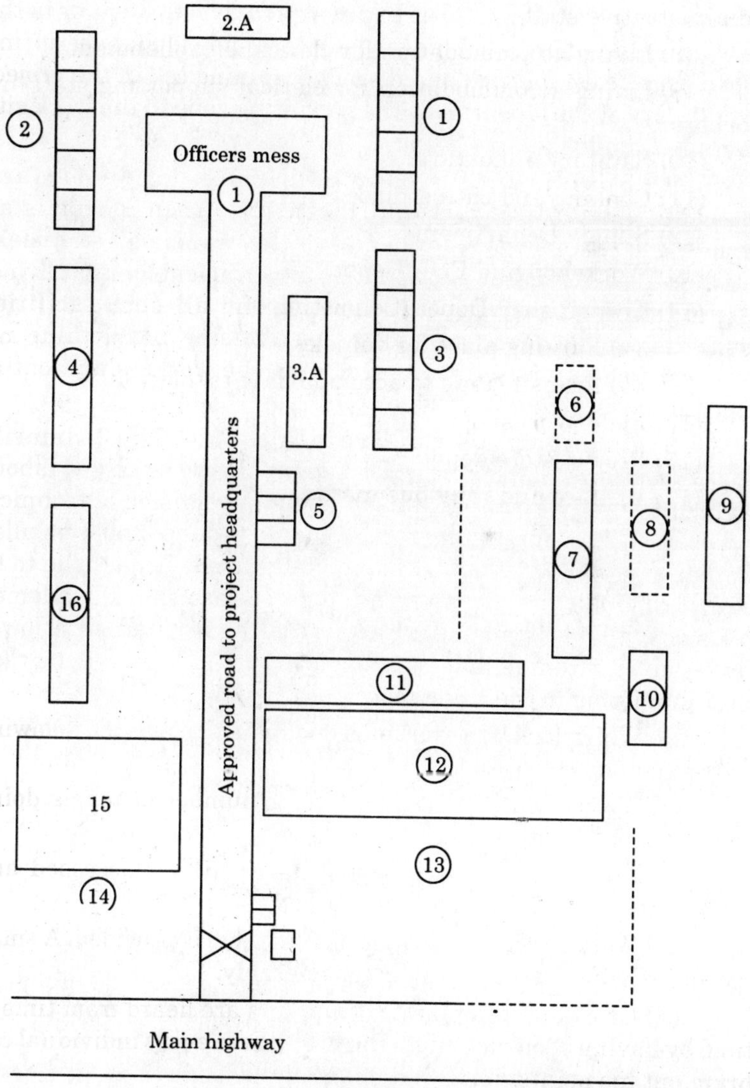

Fig. 4.1s

(1) Officers Mess

(2) Officers Quarters

(3) Servants Quarters.

(4) Administrative officers car parks

(5) Medical aid Post/Centre

(6) Reception and Enquiry

(7) Living accommodation (Supervisory and Subordinate Administrative staff).

(8) Living accommodation for clerical establishment.

(9) Living accommodation for clerical supporting staff and workers.

(10) Sanitary annexture.

(11) Cooking and eating place.

(12) Supply Department

(13) Workshop and POL Depot.

(14) Transit shed/Depot. Consisting of:

(*a*) Parking place for vehicles

(*b*) Transit camp to accommodate transients.

(15) Field Workshop

(16) Project store depot.

(17) Welfare and religious institutes.

5

CONSTRUCTION LABOUR

5.1 CONSTRUCTION WORKERS

Labour is defined as human efforts (physical, mental of both) which are directed towards production.

The condition of workers everywhere is dictated and governed by the normal law of supply and demand. In a country like India where manpower is available in plenty, and a large portion of population is in the poverty zone and wealth is confined in the hands of few capitalists the employer has so far been dictating service conditions of the workers resulting in less wages, longer hours of work, insecurity of job and in short exploitation of human beings. However, with the awakening around the world progressive labour regulation such as Trade Union Act, Labour Welfare Organisation, Payments of Wages Act, Minimum Wages Act, Workmen Compensation Act and Contract Labour Acts have gone a long way to reduce some of the handicaps to which labour had earlier been subjected to an exploitation of man by man has been considerably reduced if not altogether eliminated.

In Civil Engineering Projects there are two systems of employment of workers namely:

(*a*) Time work/Day work/Time rate system and

(*b*) Piece work/Piece rate system. These systems are briefly described below:

(*a*) Time work/Day work/Time rate system. This is most commonly used and is the oldest system of determination of labour unit and for payment of wages.

The salient features of this system are:

(*i*) Simple and easy method of determination of the unit of work done.

(*ii*) Unit of measurement for payment of wages is fixed on the basis of man hour, man day, man week or man months.

(*iii*) Rates of payment are fixed for different categories of work.

The system has the following advantages:

(*i*) Particularly suitable for jobs not suspectible to measurements.

(*ii*) The worker is not bothered about the quantity of work done and hence better quality of work results.

(*iii*) The worker has comparative sense of security.

It however has the following disadvantages:

(*i*) Good, bad and indifferent workers are treated at par and there is, therefore, no urge for improving quality or production.

(*ii*) Effective Cost Control cannot be exercised.

(*iii*) The system requires regular and constant supervision.

(*b*) Piece work/Piece rate System.

The important features of this system are:

(*i*) The payment is linked to the production.

(*ii*) Efficiency is rewarded as larger production results in higher remuneration.

(*iii*) A spirit of competition between groups of workers is introduced.

The resulting advantages are:

(*i*) Supervision can be considerably reduced.

(*ii*) Idle time is reduced if not eliminated.

(*iii*) Employers-employee relations are better.

(*iv*) Effective Cost Control is ensured.

The disadvantages are:

(*i*) The worker is liable to overstrain himself for increased production. This is likely to have adverse effect on his health.

(*ii*) A worker is paid according to production and regular payment is not assured.

(*iii*) The system does not take care of period of sickness or casual absence.

(*iv*) Linking production with payment requires careful study of unit production.

5.2 TRADE UNION ACT

Trade Unions are voluntary organisation of workers having the primary object of protecting the interests of the workers in respect of their conditions of service including wages and compensation. These unions also function as regular liason between the employer and employee. It benefits the employer as day to day problems are solved by negotiations. It helps the employer as such an organisation provides an umbrella and protects all round interests of the workers. The primary object of such unions are summarised below:

1. Improving of service conditions of workers such as wage structure, bonus, terminal benefits.

2. Promoting welfare activities such as recreation facilities, medical facilities, accommodation, education of children. Benevolent fund to needy workers at the time of death or injuries.

3. Struggling continuously for improvement of service conditions particularly increase in wages and reduction of working hours.

4. Providing legal aid.

5. Establishing and maintaining cordial relation between the employer and the employee.

The first trade union was established in a local textile mill at Ahmedabad in 1920. Presently there are four important trade unions in the country namely:

(*i*) All India Trade Union Congress (AITUC)
(Under Communist Party of India)

(*ii*) Indian National Trade Union Congress (INTUC)
(Backed by the Congress Party of India)
(Established in 1947)

(*iii*) Hind Mazdoor Sabha (HMS).
(Set-up by PSP of India in 1948)

(*iii*) United Trade Union Congress (UTUC).
(A leftist oriented union established in 1949)

In order to protect the unprivileged class of people, *i.e.*, the workers from the exploitation by the capatalists Indian Trade Union Act was passed in 1926.

Amendments to the act have been carried out in 1928, 1937, 1942, 1948, 1950, 1951, 1960, 1964 and 1970.

Salient features of the Act are:

(i) A minimum of seven workers is required to get them registered as members of a trade union under the Act. Certain conditions laid down in the act have to be satisfied before the Union can be registered by the Registrar. The Registrar on being satisfied that the Union under reference has completed with all requirements of the Act in regard to registration, registers the trade union and enters in the relevant register the particulars relating to the Trade Union.

(ii) Every registered Trade Union has to be a body corporate by the name under which it is registered along with perpetual succession and a common seal with power to acquire and hold its property.

(iii) The funds of the Registered Trade Union shall be spent only on the following:

1. Payment of salaries to office bearers.
2. Defence of legal proceedings.
3. Conduct of trade disputes.
4. Compensation to members.
5. Welfare activities of the members of the union.

(iv) Contribution for promotion of civil and political interests shall be made from a separate fund maintained for the purpose.

(v) No office bearer of a Registered Trade Union can be prosecuted/punished in respect of any agreement made between the members for purpose of furthering the object of the Trade Union.

(vi) Any person who has attained the age of fifteen years may be a member of registered Trade Union subject to any rules of the trade union to the contrary.

(vii) At least 50 per cent of the total number of the office bearers shall be persons actually employed in the concerned industry.

(viii) In the event of the dissolution of a Registered Trade Union, notice of such a dissolution duly signed by seven members and by the secretary of the Trade Union shall be sent to the Registrar concerned within fourteen days of the dissolution.

(ix) The appropriate Government may make regulation for the purpose of carrying into effect the provisions of the Act. Power to make such regulation is however subject to the condition of regulation being made after previous publication.

(*x*) In the event of a default on the part of any registered Trade Union in giving any notice or sending any statement or document required under any provision of this Act, the concerned person or officer bearer shall be punishable with fine which may extend to five rupees. In the case of continued default the additional fine of rupees five for each week after the first subject to the aggregate fine not exceeding rupees fifty.

(*xi*) No Court inferior to that of a presidency magistrate or I class Magistrate shall try any offence under the Act.

5.3 LABOUR WELFARE

Welfare of the workers is an essential requirement of any production organisation. A comparatively happy and satisfied worker would give much higher returns as compared to a dissatisfied and frustrated worker. It is for this reason that the Government appoints a labour welfare officer who looks after the following welfare activities:

1. Payment of salary on specified date.
2. Provision of Provident Fund and Life Insurance benefits.
3. Protection of seniority and allied service conditions of the workers.
4. Grant of maternity leave in case of female workers.
5. Arranges financial aid to needy employees.
6. Looks into general grievances of the workers.
7. Investigates cases of victimisation, if any, brought to his knowledge.

The other general welfare activities with which the labour officer of the establishment is associated are:

1. Educational facilities.
2. Medical facilities.
3. Transportation arrangement.
4. A provision of accomodations.
5. Canteen facilities at subsidised rates of payment.
6. Cooperative store facilities.
7. Recreation facilities: Games, cinemas, cultural activities, reading room and library facilities.
8. Sanitary Facilities: Separate latrines and bathrooms for male and female labour.
9. Provision of drinking water.

10. Safety arrangement for workers.
11. Provision of parking places and play grounds.
12. Provision of proper lighting and ventilation.
13. Institution for training of workers.
14. Provision of Insurance Scheme for Workers.

5.4 PAYMENT OF WAGES ACT

This Act is known as Payment of Wages Act 1936. The salient features of the Act are:

1. The Act applies to the payment of wages to persons employed in any factory or to persons in any railway whose wage is below ₹ 4000 per month.

2. Payment shall be made by 7th of the following month in case of the number of workers is below 1000, and by 10th of the following month where the number of workers is above 1000.

3. "Wages" means all remuneration (inclusive of salary, allowances or otherwise) expressed in terms of money.

4. Every employer shall be responsible for the payment to persons employed by him of all wages required to be paid under the Act.

5. The wages of an employed person shall be paid to him without deductions of any kind except those authorised by or under this Act.

6. No fine shall be imposed on any employed person except in respect of such acts and omissions on his part as the employer, with the prior approval of the prescribed authority, may have specified.

7. Deduction may, however, be made on account of absence of an employed person from the place of his employment.

8. An Inspector of Factories shall be an inspector in respect of all factories within the local limits assigned to him.

9. Employed persons are said to belong to the same unpaid group if they are borne on the same establishment and their wages for the same wage-period have remained unpaid after the fixed date of payment.

10. In the event of an appeal of non-payment of wages being filed by an employed person and the court referred to, is satisfied that the employer is likely to evade payment of any amount, the authority may direct the attachment of such property of the

employer which is adequate to meet the amount due for payment to the employer.

5.5 MINIMUM WAGES ACT

The Act is known as the Minimum Wages Act 1948. The salient features of the Act are:

1. The employer shall pay to every employee engaged in a scheduled employment under him wages at a rate not less than the minimum rate of wages fixed by such notifications for that class of employees in that employment without any deductions except as may be authorised within such time and subject to such conditions as may be prescribed.

2. If an employee whose minimum rate of wages has been fixed under this Act by the day works or any day on which he was employed for a period less than the requisite number of hours constituting a normal working day, he shall be entitled to recover wages for a full normal working day.

3. Every employer shall maintain records giving particulars of work performed by the employees, the wages paid to them, and the receipt given by them.

4. Amounts of an employee remaining unpaid on account of his death before payment or otherwise be deposited with the prescribed authority, who shall deal with the money so deposited in the prescribed manner.

5.6 WORKMEN COMPENSATION ACT

The Act is called Workmen's Compensation Act 1923. Workmen for the definition of this Act, the employment must be of a casual nature. The question whether the employment is of a casual nature or for employer's trade or business is essentially a question of fact and in no case should be considered a substantial question of law.

Wages. The term implies contract of service solely for the benefit of employers. The important features of the Act are:

1. If a personal injury is caused to a workman by accident arising out of and in the course of his employment, his employer shall be liable to pay compensation in accordance with the provision of the Act.

2. The term accident includes not only such occurrence such as collision, fall of roof etc., but also less obvious once causing injury such as internal accidents, heart failure etc., while the worker is doing his ordinary work.

Table 5.1
Schedule of compensation in case of death and permanent and temporary disablement

Monthly wages of workman injured		*Amount of compensation for*		*Hall-monthly payment as compensation for temporary disablement*
		Death	*Permanent total disablement*	
(1)		(2)	(3)	(4)
More than	But not more than			
0	60	7,200	10,080	Half his monthly wages.
60	90	9,720	14,608	36.60
90	120	11,520	16,128	42.00
120	150	13,500	18,900	48.75
150	200	16,800	23,520	60.00
200	300	18,000	25,200	82.50
300	400	19,200	26,800	100.00
400	500	21,000	29,400	118.75
500	600	21,600	30,240	135.00
600	700	23,100	32,340	148.75
700	800	24,000	33,600	160.00
800	900	27,000	37,800	168.75
900	1000	30,000	42,000	175.00

3. Personal injury means not only physical injury but also physiological injury caused by witnessing a total accident to a fellow workman.

4. **Amount of Compensation.** For purpose of compensation, the injuries are classified as:

(*a*) Injury resulting in deaths.

(*b*) Injury resulting in total disablement.

(*c*) Injury resulting in permanent partial disablement specified in the Act.

(*d*) Injury resulting in permanent partial disablement not specified in the Act.

The amount of compensation due in the above cases is explained below:

(*a*) **Injury resulting in death.** The amount of compensation is given in column (2) of table 5.1.

(*b*) **Injury resulting in permanent total disablement.** The amount of compensation is given in column (3) of total 5.1.

(*c*) Injury resulting in permanent partial disablement specified in the Act.

Table 5.2 gives the test of injuries deemed to result in permanent partial disablement along with the percentage of loss of earning capacity. The compensation due is such percentage of the compensation which would have been payable in the case of the permanent total disablement.

Table 5.2

List of injuries deemed to result in permanent partial disablement

Sl. No.	*Description of Injury*	*Percentage of loss of earning capacity*
(1)	(2)	(3)
	Amputation cases—upper limbs	
1.	Amputation through shoulder joint.	90
2.	Amputation below shoulder with stump less than 8″ from tip of acromin.	90
3.	Amputation from 8″ from tip of acromin to less than 4½″ below tip of olecranon.	70
4.	Loss of a hand or the thumb and fore-fingers of one hand or amputation from 4½″ below tip of olecranon	60
5.	Loss of thumb	30
6.	Loss of thumb and its metacarpal bone.	40
7.	Loss of forefinger of one hand.	50
8.	Loss of three fingers of one hand.	30
9.	Loss of two fingers of one hand.	20
10.	Loss of terminal phalanx of thumb.	20

(*Contd.*)

Sl. No.	*Description of Injury*	*Percentage of loss of earning capacity*
(1)	(2)	(3)
	Amputation Cases—Lower limbs	
11.	Amputation of both feet resulting in end-bearing stump.	90
12.	Amputation through both feet proximal to the metatarso-phalangeal joint.	80
13.	Loss of all toes of both feet through metatarso -phalangeal joint.	40
14.	Loss of toes of both feet proximal to the proximal inter-phalangeal joint.	30
15.	Loss of all toes both feet distal to the proximal inter-phalangeal joint.	20
16.	Amputation at hip	90
17.	Amputation below hip with stump not exceeding 3″ in length measured from tip of great trenchanter.	80
18.	Amputation below hip with stump exceeding 5″ length measured from tip of great trenchanter but not exceeding middle thigh.	70
19.	Amputation below middle thigh to 3½″ below knee.	60
20.	Amputation below knee with stump exceeding 3½″ but not exceeding 5″.	50
21.	Amputation below knee with stump exceeding 5″.	40
22.	Amputation of one foot resulting in end-bearing.	30
23.	Amputation through one foot proximal to the metatarso-phalangeal joint.	30
24.	Loss of all toes of one foot through the metatarso-phalangeal joint.	20
	Other Injuries	
25.	Loss of one eye, without complication, the other being normal.	40

(*Contd.*)

Sl. No.	*Description of Injury*	*Percentage of loss of earning capacity*
(1)	(2)	(3)
26.	Loss of vision of one eye without complications or disfigurement of eye-ball, the other being normal.	30
	Loss of	
	A—Fingers of Right or Left Hand Index Finger	
27.	Whole.	19
28.	Two phalanges.	11
29.	One phalanx.	9
30.	Guillotnie amputation of tip without loss of bone.	5
	Middle Finger	
31.	Whole.	12
32.	Two phalanges.	9
33.	One phalanx.	7
34.	Guillotine amputation of tip without loss of bone.	4
	Ring or Little Finger	
35.	Whole.	7
36.	Two phalanges.	6
37.	One phalanx.	5
38.	Guillotine amputation of tip without loss of bone.	2
	B—Toes of right or left foot Great Toe	
39.	Through metatarso-phalangeal joint.	14
40.	Part, with some loss of bone.	3
	Any Other Toe	
41.	Through metatarso-phalangeal joint.	3
42.	Part, with some loss of bone.	1

(Contd.)

Sl. No.	*Description of Injury*	*Percentage of loss of earning capacity*
(1)	(2)	(3)
	Two toes of one foot, excluding great toe	
43.	Through metatarso-phalangeal joint.	5
44.	Part, with some loss of bone.	2
	Three toes of one foot excluding great toe	
45.	Through metatarso-phalangeal joint	6
46.	Part, with some loss of bone.	3
	Four toes of one foot, excluding great toe	
47.	Through metatarso-phalangeal joint.	9
48.	Part, with some loss of bone.	3

(*d*) Injury resulting in permanent partial disablement not specified in the Act. The compensation payable in respect of permanent total disablement shall be proportional to the loss of earning capacity permanently caused by the injury.

Table 5.3 gives list of injuries deemed to result in permanent total disablement.

Table 5.3

Sl. No.	*Description of injury*
1.	Loss of both hands or amputation at higher sites
2.	Loss of hand and a foot.
3.	Double amputation through leg or thigh, or amputation through leg or thigh, on one side and loss of other foot.
4.	Loss of sight such to an extent as to render the claimant unable to perform any work for which sight is essential.
5.	Very severe facial disfigurement.
6.	Absolute deafness.

5. **Distribution of Compensation.** No payment of compensation shall be made otherwise than by deposits with the commissioner. No such payment made directly by an employer shall be deemed to be a payment of compensation.

6. **Non-attachment of Compensation.** No lumpsum or half monthly payment paid as compensation shall be liable to attachment except as provided in the Act.

7. **Reports of Fatal Accidents and Serious Bodily Injuries.** In the event of an accident occurring on the premises of the employer resulting in death or serious bodily injury, the employer shall notify within seven days the death or serious bodily injury to the commissioner for compensation, giving the circumstances attending the death or serious bodily injury.

8. **Reference to the Commissioner.** If any question arises in any proceedings under this act, such a question shall, in default of agreement, be settled by a commissioner.

No Civil Court has jurisdiction to settle such cases under the Act.

The appointment of the commissioner for worker's compensation is notified by the State Government in the Official Gazette.

5.7 CONTRACT LABOUR ACT

In the case of regular establishments such as factories, workshops and similar institutions the interests and welfare of the workers is protected by the various Acts of the Government such as Factories Act, Minimum Wages Act, Payment of Wages Act, Compensation Act etc. In the case of contractor's labour, which is employed on daily wages basis for the duration of a specific work, it is not possible to apply most of these Acts though some of them such as Minimum Wages Act and Compensation Act are applicable to such labour. The Government of India therefore passed an Act in 1970 which is known as 1970 Contract Act. The main provisions for the welfare of labour under this Act are to be made available by the contractor are:

1. Rest room and Canteen facilities when the number of labour exceeds 100.

2. Nursery facilities when number of female labour exceeds 20.

3. Well ventilated dewelling accommodation. The accommodation thus provided should not be less than 2.2 m high and 3 sq. metre in area for each worker family. The minimum spacing of such dwelling units shall be more than 6.1 metres spacing.

4. Cooking, Water and Sanitary arrangements.

6

CONTROL OF PROGRESS

6.1 PROJECT SUPERVISION

The purpose of the supervision of the project is to achieve the following:

(*a*) **To exercise quality control on the work.** This is achieved by ensuring the following:

(*i*) Only approved materials are incorporated in the work. In fact any material which is to be brought to the project theatre should be approved before it is brought.

(*ii*) Detailed specifications are prepared and strictly adhered to.

(*iii*) Working drawings are complete and comprehensive leaving no place for ambiguity.

(*iv*) The work is approved in stages and defective part dismantled/removed.

(*v*) Proper record of stores incorporated in the work is separately maintained to allow independent check on the quantity of material used in the work.

(*b*) **To exercise quantity control.** This is achieved by the following:

(*i*) Preparing construction schedule well ahead of the start of the project.

(*ii*) Regular checking of output of plant, machines equipment and labour.

(*iii*) Preparing CPM/bar charts and review the progress regularly.

(*iv*) Providing production incentives.

(*v*) Specifying period of completion of the project when it is executed through contract agency.

(*c*) **To exercise financial control.** This is exercised by the following:

(*i*) Administrative approval of the work. The expenditure on each item of work is restricted by its administrative approval.

(*ii*) Inviting open tenders/bids so that as far as possible only the bid involving minimum expenditure is accepted.

(*iii*) Keeping overheads or unproductive elements to the bare minimum.

(*iv*) Providing regular accounts sections and getting the expenditure audited at regular intervals.

6.2 METHODS OF RECORDING PROGRESS AND WORK DIARIES

The method of recording progress depend upon the agency of execution of work namely by:

(*a*) Contractor, and,

(*b*) Departmentally.

However, whatever be the mode of execution, the following documents form the backbone of recording progress:

(*i*) Work Diaries.

(*ii*) Site order books.

(*iii*) CPM/Bar charts/Progress Reports.

(*iv*) Project Report.

(*v*) Construction report.

(*i*) **Work Diaries.** The work diaries form the most important authenticated document which not only reflects the quantity of work done in respect of specific item/sub-item of the work at site but also gives additional and allied information associated with the project. For example, it very often happens that the contractor due to his own negligence is not able of complete the work in time and subsequently claims extension to time due to say harvesting season, excess rains, bad weather or so on. The works diary enables a proper scrutiny on the claim of the contractor and hence helps sloving disputes. In the same way the quantity of steel or cement incorporated in any portion of the work, an independent check on the same can be exercised. (See Table 4.2).

(*ii*) **Site Order Book.** This is the main channel of site correspondence between the representative of the engineer-in-charge and the contractor and compilation of the information contained therein serves an independent check on the quality and quantity of the work.

(*iii*) **CPM/Bar Chart/Progress Report.** (Refer Chapter 10).

(*iv*) **Project Report.** In addition to the progress tables/charts mentioned above, the engineer-in-charge prepares progress reports and progress charts at regular intervals the frequency of which may vary from daily to monthly.

(*v*) **Construction Report.** These are initiated by the engineer-staff at site on the basis of work diaries and sent to the engineer-in-charge for his record.

In the case of departmentally executed projects the following additional documents are used for recording progress of work:

(*a*) Labour slips,

(*b*) Cost control analysis of works/works study reports.

(*a*) **Labour Slips.** The labour slips are prepared daily by the Junior Engineer giving details of labour employed on each job and the quantity of work done. At the end of the fixed period of say a fortnight or a month, the total of work done is evaluated at the prevailing scheduled rates and compared with the amount of the pay roll. In case of large discrepancy, the matter is investigated and payment is delayed/withheld. The cumulative total of the daily work gives the quantity of work done in respect of the various items of work.

(*b*) **Cost Control Analysis of Works/Works Study Reports.** The quantity of work done against the various items of the administrative approval is evaluated from time to time against the total expenditure incurred which consists of the following:

(*i*) Expenditure on directly employed labour.

(*ii*) Expenditure on labour in making arrangement for the labour if the labour is imported and food, clothing, accommodation and transport is arranged by the project administration.

(*iii*) **Expenditure on Construction Stores.** This includes the cost of procurement of store at the site of procurement transport and storage cost.

(*iv*) **Contingent and Over-Heads.** The contingent and over-heads cannot be directly evaluated and hence the project management issues instructions from time to time intimating such as expenditure. Till such time as the actual details are made available the actual available and anticipated expenditure is increased by 1/3rd to cover such expenditure.

In the case of work executed through contract agencies apart from the documents giving progress of various items of work, the monthly running bills against the contract provides an independent check on the progress of the work.

6.3 ANALYSIS OF PROGRESS

The cost control analysis referred to Art. 6.2 has of late become a very important and effective parameter. This has been necessitated because of large projects executed departmentally in the country. The importance of the feature has lead to the establishment of School of Works Study. In the case of contract works such a study is of limited importance for controlling the expenditure on contingent expenditure not included in the contract as all the items of work are paid for at the rates specified in the contract agreement. In the case of departmentally executed works this study is done for the following purpose:

(*i*) To evaluate the work done against the various items of the administrative approval with the corresponding expenditure and thereby revise the overall expenditure of the project against the work done and its value at the prevalent schedule of rates.

(*ii*) In the event of expenditure exceeding the corresponding value of administrative approval, reasons for such an excess are investigated and timely and remedial actions are taken.

Some of the reasons which may be responsible for excess expenditure are:

1. **Lack of Supervision.** Such a study would awaken the staff concerned. In extreme case it may lead to disciplinary action and removal.

2. **Plant Equipment and Machinery and Dependent Labour Idle for want of Spares or Repairs.** The history sheet and log books would show the period during which the equipment such as stone crusher, concrete mixer, road roller was off road for want of spares. This results in idle labour which only increases cost of construction without any output.

3. Hold up for want of construction store.

6.4 CORRECTIVE ACTION

The analysis of work is used to correct the defects revealed from the study of such an analysis. This would lead to some or all of the corrective actions given below:

1. Adequate provision of fast moving spares.

2. Arranging preventive maintenance of plant, equipment and machine.

3. Procurement of construction stores well ahead of their requirement at site.

4. Tightening of security measures to eliminate chances of pilferage.

5. Providing incentive schemes which results in comparatively high additional production/output against comparatively small additional expenditure.

6.5 WORK STUDY

(*a*) **Method/Motion study and time study/work measurement.** The main purpose of the Works Study is to analyse the performance of project equipment and labour from time to time and compare their output with the standard/rated output. In the case of smaller output, the individual case is investigated in detail and corrective measures as specified in Art. 6.4 are taken.

The site data collected for such a study are:

(*a*) **Performance of Equipment.** The study of the equipment is carried out in two parts namelv.

(*i*) Expenditure and

(*ii*) Output.

Let us take for example, the case of a stone crusher. The expenditure incurred consists of the following:

1. Equipment, man-power and construction store used in quarrying operation including primary and secondary blasting.

2. Expenditure incurred on transporting, stacking and feeding the stone crusher.

3. Operating expenses consisting of:

(*i*) Hire/usage/depreciation of equipment.

(*ii*) P.O.L. charges. (Petrol, Oil and Lubricant)

(*iii*) Operating crew.

The output is the crushed stone on the ground.

(*b*) **Performance of Workers Employed on Manual labour.** Comparison of expenditure and output as well as comparison of output of labour with the standards specified or laid down as output constants.

(*c*) **Workcharged establishment.**

(*d*) **Overheads.**

Works study is further categoried as:

(*a*) Method/Motion study and

(*b*) Work measurement/Time study.

(*b*) **Method/Motion Study.** The analysis during the execution of the project would invariably show slackness or comparatively less output in certain fields. Such fields are specified and detailed study under the following heads in respect of each job/item thus selected is carried out.

Before during and after method study, the team should prepare a self-examining questionnaire and try to get satisfactory answer to the following:

(*a*) **Method adopted for the Job.** (*i*) Whether the particular method adopted is the only one available or more modern or cheaper alternatives are available.

(*ii*) Are there ways and means of reducing the expenditure.

(*b*) **Quality of finished Products.** (*i*) Whether the finished product satisfies the specifications.

(*ii*) Are there ways and means of reducing expenditure without sacrificing the quality.

(*c*) **Specification of Materials.** (*i*) Is the material specified suitable in conformity with the job requirement.

(*ii*) Is it to possible to water down the specification with the object of reducing cost without sacrificing the job requirement.

(*d*) **General** (*i*) Are workers deployed in such a way that free working space is available to everybody.

(*ii*) Is the output of workers daily checked and regularly supervised.

(*iii*) Are there incentive given to workers in larger per head production.

(*iv*) How often is the labour idle for want of construction stores, technical guidance or plant being off road.

The answers to these questions would reveal the extent and manner in which addition, alteration, replacement or improvements in the existing job organisation can be effected.

(*e*) **Work Measurement/Time Study.** The two operations of method study and time study have necessarily to go together. For example, while carrying out the method study the work done by any equipment has necessarily to be measured against time. The following additional data are however, collected to complete the time study. The observations are confined to each individual operation such as compaction by road roller, or group of operations such as battery of stone crushers.

(*i*) Details of working conditions *i.e.*, altitude of place, humidity of atmosphere, source of power etc.

(*ii*) Record of failures during collection of data/observation and cause of failure *i.e.*, due to want of electricity. P.O.L. want of adequate labour, absence of operator etc.

(*iii*) Record of actual hours of work done during the data collection or period of observation.

(*iv*) Specified time of continuous operation.

6.6 PROCESS CHART

This chart is prepared to ensure a smooth follow up of various operations involved in a job against time. It is analogous to the C.P.M. Chart for specified phase of the project as well as for the project as a whole. In the C.P.M. chart each activity is allotted a given time depending upon the magnitude of the operation and availability of resources to complete the job. The process chart may be considered critical chart for day-to-day work for a specified job of any activity. The main purpose of such a chart is to achieve economy in time without sacrificing its quality.

This chart represents comprehensive details of various steps of executing a project. The operational records available from the chart can be used for compairing with the output of similar operations in similar situations.

Once the process chart is finalised further site instructions are eliminated and there is no chance of any misinterpretation of instructions.

Thus a complete operation of laying foundation concrete of any structure starting from collection of materials at site upto finishing at site may be symbolically represented as

O—⊙—□—o—∇—L

where the various symbols which represent various activities associated with the job against allotted time are as below:

O—Collection of material at the mixing place.

⊙—Proportioning and mixing.

□—Inspecting the mix.

o—Transportation to work site.

∇—Laying and compacting in the foundation trench.

L—Levelling.

7 Cost Control

7.1 INTRODUCTION

The ultimate object of planning and supervising a project is to achieve maximum economy in the cost of its construction/execution consistent with the standards specified therein. In the case of work carried out by the contractor cost control is exercised at the pretender stage by having the most economical design. Maximum advantages of the locally available resources (plant, equipment, machinery and construction stores) should be taken and most economical section adopted. The overheads should be kept the minimum. In the post tender stage cost control is exercised by accepting as far as possible the lowest bid.

7.2 PURPOSE OF COST CONTROL

Cost Control serves the following purposes:

(*a*) Exercise overall financial control and relationship between value of the work completed and valuation of the work done every month.

(*b*) Revision of output constants in respect of plant, equipment and machines due to improved techniques.

(*c*) Providing basis of revision of rates in view of improvement in the output.

7.3 STAGES OF COST CONTROL

Important stages at which cost control can be exercised are given below:

(A) **Precontract Stages**

(*i*) **During the design stage.** Most economical section consistent with the job requirement should be adopted.

(*ii*) **Planning of specification.** Maximum use of locally available materials and their specification should be adopted.

(B) **Post Contract Stages**

(*i*) Inspecting construction material at source so that chances of defective material being incorporated in the work are eliminated.

(*ii*) Adopting suitable quantity buying policy so that infructious expenditure in transport is avoided.

(*iii*) Exercising proper supervision of labour.

(*iv*) Providing incentive for increase in output by labour.

(*v*) Continued valuation of output.

(*vi*) Avoiding idle hours of equipment.

(*vii*) Having a well-planned repair organisation and workshop cover so that equipment and associated labour is not kept idle for want of proper maintenance and repairs.

(*viii*) Keeping overheads to the minimum.

(*ix*) Taking safety measures to avoid accidents and security measures to avoid theft of materials.

7.4 ESTIMATING AND COST CONTROL

Before any project is accorded administrative approval a detailed estimate of the various items of works involved is prepared along with its supporting documents. The quantities of such items of work are arrived at from the dimensioned drawings of the various components of the structure. For example, the item of work namely excavation in trenches for foundation is arrived at on the basis of dimensions given on the trench plan and sectional details of the foundations. The rates on which the costing of the items of work are based are taken from the current standard schedule of rates. In the absense of any rate provided in the standard schedule the rates are analysed.

The preparation of the schedule of rates itself is a continuous exercise on account of the continuous change in the materials incorporated and the wages of workers.

The various elements which are considered in arriving at the rates provided in the standard schedule or rate are primarily three namely:

(*a*) Cost of Material.

(*b*) Cost of Labour.

(*c*) Contractor's Profit.

In the case of work executed through contract agency, the department does not have to exercise any cost control as irrespective of the operations and other costs, the payment to the contractor is made on the basis of the tendered rates. It would, however, be advisable for the contractor to analyse the rate for himself and record all the expenditure and thus arrive at the actual cost of production at various stages of construction. From such a data for each item of production the following questionnaire should be filled.

Output of Work

(*i*) Is the production/output constant in respect of manual work satisfactory as compared to standards available.

(*ii*) Is the production of skilled labour (artisians) satisfactory with respect to the rated constant.

(*iii*) Is the quantity of construction stores incorporated in the item as per standard calculations. For example, in the design of a R.C.C. beam of a given size the various raw materials required are:

1. Fine Aggregate
2. Coarse Aggregate
3. Cement
4. Steel.

The above quantities actually incorporated in the work can be compared with the designed quantity and the variation if any investigated. This information can be used by the contractor for his own bid in the subsequent work.

Expenditure on Work. Actual payment/expenditure for the corresponding items and quantity is recorded and the proportionate expenditure incurred by the contractor by the way of overhead charges is added and the overall expenditure on production of unit item arrived at. From this data the profit of the contractor is arrived at. In the subsequent bid for similar work the contractor would have to take the information of cost control study into consideration.

In the case of departmentally executed project, exercise of collection cost control data and its continuous valuation with respect to the item of administrative approval which is based on the estimated rate of the item is very essential since it is the primary responsibility of the engineer-in charge to ensure that the administratively approved amount in respect of each item of the estimate is not exceeded. The cost control data collected from the site is compared with the data provided in the analysis of rate and if necessary the analysis of rate of some of the items themselves can be revised. This study in itself would provide adequate grounds for engineer-in-charge in asking for a revised administrative approval of the work.

7.5 CLASSIFICATION OF COST CONTROL

The various ways during the execution of the project open to the engineer-in-charge/contractor of collection of site data collected by the cost control and work study item are:

(*a*) **Exercising cost control on components of the item of administrative approval.** For example, the item of administrative approval may be foundation concrete. The basic raw materials are fine and coarse aggregate and cement. There is not much that can be done in efficiency cost control on cement and fine aggregate and hence cost control study would be primarily for production of crushed coarse stone aggregates. The cost of production of crushed aggregate is then compared with the cost specified in the analysis of the rates, which serve as guidance for the engineer-in-charge and at the same time hourly production of the stone crusher can be compared with its rated capacity.

The engineer-in-charge can further make an appreciation whether it would be economical to get the material delivered at site through contract agency.

(*b*) **By comparing the cost of unit of administrative approval.** In the first case the cost control study was limited to one component, *i.e.*, production of store aggregate for the foundation concrete. The study can be carried out for other components namely cost at site of other stores and cost of mixing, placing and curing. The combined cost of the operation would give the actual production cost of the item of administrative approval and reasons for variation if any should be investigated.

(*c*) **By comparing the cost of unit of construction.** In this case the combined cost of the individual structure or construction is taken into consideration and the total actual cost of construction of the unit is arrived at.

(*d*) **By comparing the overall expenditure of the project.** At various stages of the construction, the physical progress is evaluated in terms of actual expenditure incurred and overall picture of the project is obtained. Even when the purpose is to arrive at the overall expenditure, it may sometime happen that although the overall financial position of the construction is satisfactory, particular items of work are not being carried out economically. Such items are then investigated in detail. Such a detailed analysis of a particular item is sometimes classified as "*Cost control by Detail of System.*"

(*e*) **Special System.** Under this category may be included other methods of increasing production at comparatively less increase in expenditure. One of the most commonly adopted system is the system of incentive in which benefit of additional output by worker or machines are shared by the project and the workers.

7.6 COST CONTROL CODES

The purpose of adopting codes in cost control study is to avoid repetition of description of any item/sub-item of the work. The essential requirements of such a code are:

(*i*) The system should be simple and leave no ambiguity about its interpretation.

(*ii*) Each item of work should have distinct code to avoid confusion amongst the workers.

(*iii*) The system should be flexible so that slight modification in the main item of work may be readily distinguished from the main item.

(*iv*) The system should be clearly explained to and understood by all the field workers associated with the study.

The engineer-in-charge or the cost study cell of the project is free to evolve its own coding system provided the above basic requirements are satisfied and the key to the code used is readily available and understood. However, as far as possible it is advisable to adopt one of the standard coding system so that the code adopted has universal application and does not have to undergo modification with the change of engineer-in-charge or the incharge work study and cost control team at work site. Two such systems are:

(1) The Decimal Coding System.

(2) The Simple Coding System.

The above two systems are briefly described below:

(1) **The Decimal Coding System.** In this system each unit of construction in the project is allotted a range say between 0–100 depending upon the component into which the unit may be classified. For example, the main project may be construction of an airport complex. The complex is primarily divided into functional units such as Administrative Block, Hangars and workshop complex, Taxiway, Landing strip, Take off area, Main runway and so on. Let us consider the cost coding system for the administrative block. The first digit of the code represents the construction unit under consideration while the second figure of the coding system pin points the specific part. The first and second digits would be codified as below.

00–Reception and Information centre.

10–Lounge.

20–Custom clearance.

30–Booking area.

40–Canteen.

and so on.

In other words, 0, 1, 2, 3, 4 represent the components of the main unit and is designated as first figure.

The second figure denotes the specific part of the component referred to by first figure. The coding of the second figure may be as below:

01–Superstructure.

02–Equipment.

03–Approach road.

04–Furniture.

05–Interior decoration.

06–Sanitary fitting.

07–Electrification.

Thus 41 represents superstructure of the canteen. The details of work in the various such-units of construction are classified as

Site Clearance	.1
Sub-Structure	.2

Flooring .3

Roofing .4

Thus 41.3 represents flooring work in the canteen area.

The second place of decimal may designate the particular work of the component. Thus

Excavation of foundation .01

Concreting plain .02

Concreting re-inforced .03

Brick work in cement masonry .04

and so on.

Thus 41.32 represent concrete work in the flooring of the canteen area.

There is no end to which the item may be further divided depending upon the individual merit of the case and depth to which the study is desired. The work of flooring of the concrete of the canteen designated by 41.32, concreting designated by (.02) may be further sub-divided into

.021–Collection of material

.022–Mixing of concrete.

.023–Placing of concrete.

.024–Compacting/vibrating of concrete.

.025–Curing of concrete.

The 41.325 could represent curing of cement work in the flooring of canteen area.

(2) **Sample coding system.** This system is based upon alphabetical coding as far as possible and the initial letter disignates the main operation. Thus.

B–Brick work

C–Concrete work

D–Drain work

E–Excavation/Earth work

F–Form work

G–Ground Levelling

F–Filling

S–Steel work

and so on.

The main trade may further be sub-divided as

G : Concreting

CB : Concreting of beam

CC : Concreting of column

F : Form work

FT : Form work using timber

FS : Form work using steel

and so on.

7.7 COLLECTION OF DATA FOR COST CONTROL

The data for the cost control is usually completed from the field notes or fields records maintained by the sub-overseer or the work agent who is specifically detailed for a specific job. In the case of equipment, the operator/driver records the details of work done and the POL used in the daily duty slips, log books and other documents. In the case of static plants sometimes hour meters are installed with the equipment to record the total hours for which the machine has been run while in the case of vehicle kilometrage is obtained directly from the reading of the vehicle meter.

In order to have a systematic and scientific record of the data a number of standard forms are devised by the project management in consultation with the staff specially trained in work study and cost control studies. These forms are given to operator, driver, incharge work section. Others are derived from weekly and monthly progress reports and expenditure returns.

Some of the common forms used on such jobs are:

1. Record of material and cost thereof in incorporated in the job.
2. Cost analysis of material
3. Details of labour deployed on the job.
4. Cost analysis and labour output/production.
5. Details of equipment used.
6. Cost analysis of equipment used.

Typical forms showing the above are given below.

Table 7.1 Record of material incorporated in the job

Name of item of work... Estimated quantity.... Rate.... cost

Date	*Source from which brought*	*Description of material brought to site*	*Previous balance*	*Incorporated in the work*	*Balance at the end of day*

Table 7.2 Cost analysis of material used in the job

Name of item of work.... Estimated Quantities of material... Rate Cost...

Date	*Quantity incorporated in the work*	*Actual cost of material*	*Estimated cost*

Table 7.3. Details of labour deployed on the job

Job No.... *Period from..... to.....*

S. No.	*Item of the administrative approval*	*Particulars of labour*	*Rate of payment*	*No. of days*	*Amount of payment due*

Table 7.4 Cost analysis of labour output/product

Job No.... *Period from..... to.....*

S. No.	Item of adminis-trative approval	Amount of payment due	Nature and type of work done	Cost of work done	Estimated cost of the work

Table 7.5. Details of equipment used

Job No.... *Period from..... to.....*

Name of the equipment

Item of adminis-trative approval	Hours or run	POL consumed	Details of manpower	Quantity produced

Table 7.6. Cost analysis of equipment used

Job No.... *Period from..... to.....*

Name of the equipment

Hire charges/rent/depre-ciation of equip-ment	Running charges			Total expen-diture	Quan-tity pro-duced	Rate of produc-tion	Esti-mated rate
	P.O.L.	Operat-ing ex-penses	Sup-porting labour				

8

INSPECTION AND QUALITY CONTROL

8.1 INTRODUCTION

It has been very often said that an engineer would get the work done in say ₹ 100, what any other person would probably do for ₹ 200 or so. There is, however, an equally if not more important aspect of the work namely exercise of quality control. What an engineer can produce in ₹ 100 may be produced by an other person for say ₹ 80 if provided the rigidity of inspection and the quality control is waived off. This in a nut shell explains the need of inspection of work from the source of supply upto the finished production.

8.2 FUNCTIONS OF INSPECTING DEPARTMENT

The normal inspection of work at various stages is primarily the responsibility of the engineer-in-charge and the inspecting officers associated with the project.

The various stages at which such inspections are carried out are:

(*a*) **Inspection at source.** It is a sound policy to check the materials at source so that inferior or defective material is not brought to the work site. Once such defective material is brought to work site there is a tendency on the part of contractor to incorporate the same in the work.

(*b*) **Inspection during the execution of the work.** It is better to inspect the work during the construction stage instead of carrying out the same after its completion.

In the Military Engineering Services and the Central Public Works Department, there is one Technical Examiner attached to each Chief Engineer who carries out scrutiny of the payment bills of the contractor. Although it is a sound policy to have an independent inspecting policy as it creates quality consciousness amongst the workers yet it is not as much effective as it could be if such independent inspections are carried out during the execution of the work.

An effective system which has been introduced by a number of construction departments is passing of work in stages. A clause is incorporated in the contract agreements according to which the contractor is required to get the work passed in stages. For example, in the construction of a building work, the contractor is bound to inform the site engineer about preparation of each work for excavation of the trenches. No concreting work can be taken in hand unless the foundation excavation is approved and an entry to this effect is recorded in the site order book and the works diary.

(*a*) **Inspection of the completed job.** The contractor has to complete the job within the specified period and his failure to stick to the schedule may result in one of the following actions:

(*i*) Imposition of a penalty to the extent of 10% of the contract amount.

(*ii*) Getting the incomplete work completed by debitable agency.

(*iii*) Getting the job completed by departmentally employed labour and debiting the cost thereof to the contractor.

Before the certificate of completion of the work in time is given to the contractor it is necessary that a thorough inspection of all components is carried out and short-comings/defects/rectifications are pointed out. 10% of the running payments made to the contractor is kept retained till such time that defects pointed out during the final inspection are rectified in time.

(*b*) **Inspection of Equipment.** There are two channels of obtaining equipment *i.e.*,:

(*i*) directly from the manufacturers, and

(*ii*) by transfer from other project/department. In the case of direct purchase the initial equipment inspection is carried out jointly by the representative of the firm and the workshop organisation of the project. Defects thus found are noted and rectified by the firm. A trial demonstration to check the ratings is also included in such an inspection.

In the case of transfer from other project/department a joint inspection is carried out between the two departments and agreed grading of the equipment is recorded. If the project workshop organisation feels that the equipment does not meet the project requirements, the transfer of such an equipment may be dropped.

8.3 INSPECTION PRACTICES

What has been discussed in Article 8.2 above is summed up in inspecting practices given below. Such inspection practices are:

(*a*) Inspection of raw material at source.

(*b*) Rejected material to be removed from worksite forthwith.

(*c*) Inspection of work in stages.

(*d*) Insist on rectification of defects before proceeding to the next stage.

(*e*) In the case of sanitary/electric and other fittings, approved samples, apart from contract specifications, should be exhibited in the project museum and supply checked against those specimens/samples.

(*f*) Stages of inspection of any work should be well defined and specific points to be looked for defined.

(*g*) The aim of the inspection is to exercise quality control of the work. This should be clearly understood by the entire supervisory project staff.

8.4 TECHNICAL SOURCES REQUIRED FOR INSPECTION

The various technical sources required before, during and after completion of a project are given in Table 8.1. The table gives only guideline and illustrates a typical case. In each project details of such services have to be finalised at the investigation stage itself.

Table 8.1 Technical Services Required for Inspection

Sl. No.	*Stage at which required*	*Inspection particular*	*Technical services required*	*Remarks*
1.	Before starts of project	Geological examination and sub soil borings	Geologist	
2.	”	Bearing capacity of soil	Foundation Engineer/Soil Mechanic expert	

(*Contd.*)

Table 8.1 Technical Services Required for Inspection *(Contd.)*

Sl. No.	*Stage at which required*	*Inspection particular*	*Technical services required*	*Remarks*
3.	Before starts of project	Climatic conditions	Meteorological Department	
4.	"	Checking of design	Design engineer	
5.	During execution or project	Testing of materials	Engineer-in-charge/ Material Testing Lab.	
6.	"	Passing an inspection of soil during actual execution	Engineer-in-charge/ surveyor of works	
7.	"	Passing of works in stages	Engineer-in-charge	
8.	"	Test check of completed work for final payment bills	Technical Examiner of works	

8.3 MAJOR ITEMS OF CONTROL

The major items of the project over which quality control is to be exercised have been discussed in detail in the preceeding articles. They are summed up below:

(*a*) **Controls before start of projects**

(*i*) Verification of bearing capacity of the soil with reference to the designed loads.

(*ii*) Verification of the design with respect to the job requirement, structural safety, durability and economy.

(*iii*) Checking the quality of materials to be incorporated in the project at source.

(*b*) **Control during construction**

(*i*) Execution of work as per specifications.

(*ii*) Preparing test cubes for strength of concrete and getting them tested on due dates.

(*iii*) Testing of other materials incorporated in the work as per I.S.I. Standards.

(*c*) **Testing of equipment supplied by the firm.** Initial workshop inspection and trial run of the equipment.

9

MISCELLANEOUS TOPICS

9.1 REPAIRS

Keeping the structures in useable state is a major function of the works department. Timely repair enhances the life and value of the structure and provides better comfort to the users.

The various types of repairs are given below:

1. **Buildings.** Buildings are required to be maintained in properly repaired condition to get the maximum benefit from the existing buildings. The national planning and financial stringency in a developing country like ours calls in stretching the resources to their maximum.

Repairs to buildings consist of the following:

(*i*) Petty replacements;

(*ii*) Renewals.

(*iii*) Periodical services consisting of whitewashing, distempering and painting.

(*iv*) Repairs to internal water supply system.

(*v*) Repairs to electrical installation.

(*vi*) Repairs to sanitary system.

2. **Roads.** Repairs to roads consist of the following:

(*i*) Patch and petty repairs.

(*ii*) Surface renewals.

(*iii*) Maintenance/renewals of drains, culverts, bridges and causeways.

(*iv*) Maintenance and renewals of sign posts, milestones and boundary pillars.

3. **Airfields.** Repairs to airfields consist of the following:

(*i*) Maintenance and renewals of runways.

(*ii*) Maintenance and renewals of taxi-tracks.

(*iii*) Maintenance and renewals of pathways.

(*iv*) Maintenance and renewals of aprons.

(*v*) Maintenance and renewals of cross drainage works.

4. **Installations.** Repair to installation consist of:

(*i*) Maintenance and renewals of water supply and electrical systems.

Funds for repairs of assets are provided on the basis of the following:

(*i*) Type of the building *i.e.*, permanent, semi-permanent, temporary, hutted.

(*ii*) Cost of construction.

(*iii*) Year of construction.

Percentage of the booked value of the building is provided as repair grant.

In the case of roads the maintenance grant is given on the basis of type of road and kilometrage. No separate proposal for administrative approval is required. The estimate of the planned repairs is however submitted to the Chief Engineer. The estimate of repair works is based on the following:

(*a*) Quarterly Inspection.

(*b*) Inspection by engineers/staff.

(*c*) Demand from users.

(*d*) Timed programme of periodical repairs.

(*e*) Storm damages to cover minor damages. In the case of severe damage special repairs are initiated. The repairs however are carried out under the maintenance head and the sum thus spent is reappropriated subsequently to the special repairs grants.

The following points should be examined while preparing estimate of repairs for the financial year.

(*i*) Only necessary and essential repairs are carried out.

(*ii*) Specifications adopted for carrying out repairs are technically sound.

(*iii*) Replacement of a fitting or portion of a building by one of better class necessary from engineering considerations constitutes repair only if the existing fitting/portion of a building is worn out and is to be replaced at any cost.

(*iv*) Quantities, rates and cost are correctly given.

(*v*) Correct percentage is added to the cost at scheduled rates.

(*vi*) No allowance is made for utilising demolition stores obtained from the repair items but the cost of demolition stores from other sources is allowed at the rates assessed by the Executive/ Garrison engineer.

(*vii*) While according technical sanction for repairs it should be ensured that allotments of funds has been adhered to.

To facilitate advance planning and achieve even flow of expenditures the following relaxations have been permitted in the M.E.S. and other works departments.

1. Liability on account of repairs for the next financial year can be incurred in the last financial quarter upto 25% of the present year's allotment.

2. Adjustment of cost of stores drawn for carrying out repairs as per (1) above could be postponed to the next financial year by marking them **"Not Adjustable Until 1st of April"** in red ink.

9.2 SPECIAL REPAIRS

A large number of temporary structures were constructed during the Second World War. The useful span of such structures was for 5 to 10 years but more durable or permanent structures could not replace such construction due to stringency of funds. A new procedure for carrying out such abnormal repair was therefore evolved, by which, no separate administrative approval was necessary. Such repairs, which form major works in themselves are termed as, '*Special Repairs*'.

When however, special repairs and additions and alterations to a structure become necessary at the same time, the work is taken up as a project and treated as original work for all purposes.

Estimates for such repairs are submitted to the Chief Engineer or equivalent authority supported by the questionnaire to support the necessity as given below:

Questionnaire to accompany all proposals for special repairs

1. Name of the station.
2. Reasons for initiating special repair.

3. Details giving plinth area of each building and plan of other structures showing type of structures (temporary/permanent) and the year of construction.

4. Type of original construction.

5. Plinth area/plan of each constructional unit based on:

(*a*) New specifications in respect of special repair.

(*b*) Existing specifications for the rest.

6. Have any special repairs been carried out to the structure earlier.

7. Brief description of proposed repair.

8. Estimated cost of repair.

9. Whether the amount involved in repairs would be within formwork of economical repair.

10. Whether Engineering appreciation of the repairs has been carried out.

11. Have superior specifications been prepared. If so, reasons therefore.

12. Estimated life of structure after the repair.

13. Whether the repairs can be done away with by making use of existing alternatives.

14. Amount proposed to be spent during current financial year.

15. Whether the requisite amount can be met from existing allotment for repairs.

16. Time required for completion of the special repairs.

9.3 RECORDS OF STRUCTURES

The purpose of maintaining records is to have a clear idea of the following:

(*a*) Details of assets owned by the department/owner.

(*b*) Capital cost of individual asset.

(*c*) Changes/alterations.

These serve as useful basis for handling/taking over of assets. At the same time the capital cost serves the following purpose:

(*i*) Demand for repairs.

(*ii*) Rent assessment.

(*iii*) Disposal Value.

(*iv*) Estimates for providing similar construction such as plinth area estimate for buildings, kilometrage for highways etc.

The following records are maintained in suitable forms which vary slightly from department to department.

1. **Buildings**

(*a*) Register of buildings.

(*b*) Completion drawings.

(*c*) Periodical services measurement books.

2. **Roads**

(*a*) Road Registers.

(*b*) Record plans.

(*c*) Metalling charts.

(*d*) Road inspection books.

These documents are briefly described below:

1. **Buildings**

(*a*) **Register of Buildings**

Separate registers are maintained for permanent and temporary buildings on any area/station.

Copies of such registers are kept with:

Executive Engineer/Garrison Engineer.

Superintending Engineer/Commander Works Engineer.

Chief Engineer.

Secretary to the Government.

The Executive Engineer/Garrison Engineer is responsible to ensure that all additions and alterations are recorded in the register.

(*b*) Completion drawings of a building are prepared as soon as possible after physical execution. Such drawings are maintained, in the Executive Engineer's/Garrison Engineers office.

(*c*) **Periodical Service Measurement Book, (P.S.M. Bs.)**

P.S.M.Bs are maintained for all buildings for purpose of periodical services (whitewashing, painting etc.).

2. **Roads**

(*a*) **Road Register.**

The following details are recorded in a road register:

(*i*) Length and class of road.

(*ii*) Capital Cost.

(*iii*) Annual maintenance expenditure.

The road registers are maintained by the Executive Engineer/ Garrison Engineer.

Typical Road Diagrams and Index sheet which form part of the road register are shown in Tables 9.1 and 9.2, respectively. A typical page of road register is shown in Table 9.3.

Table 9.1 Road Register

Name of Road ....

Class ....

Specifications ....

Bridges ....

Culverts ....

Description of importance crossings.

Year	*Expenditure in Rupees*		*Remarks*		*Year*	*Work and renewal chart*
	New work	*Renewal*				

INDEX

Metal Collect

Metal Consolidated

Concreting and filling expansion joints

Premix Carpet

Black topping

Table 9.2 Index Sheet (Road Register)

Corrected upto						
	1 2 3		4 5 6		7 8 9	

Table 9.2 *(Contd.)*

Sl. No.	*Name of Road*	*Reference to Plan*		*Page No. of Road Register*	*Classified*	*No. of*		*Length of Road*		*Width of Roads*	*Speci-fications*	*Remarks*
		No. of Road	*Colour*			*Bridge*	*Culverts*	*km.*	*M*			
(1)	(2)	(3)	(4)	(5)	(6)	(7)	(8)	(9)	(10)	(11)	(12)	(13)

Table 9.3 Specimen page of a Road Register

Name of the Highway ....
Year of Construction ....
Capital cost of Construction ....
Annual Maintenance Grant ....

S. No.	*kilometre age*		*Carriage way width*	*Carriage way surface (type)*	*Formation width*	*Road land width*	*Bridges gutter and culverts*	*Retaining wall*	*Breast wall*	*Parapet wall*	*Remarks*					
	From	*To*														
(1)	(2)	(3)	(4)	(5)	(6)	(7)	(8)	(9)	(10)	(11)	(12)	(13)	(14)	(15)	(16)	(17)
Remarks																

(b) **Roads Plan.** These plans are maintained by the drawing branch of the Executive Engineer or E—6 branch of the Garrison Engineer as the case may be.

These plans show the layout of the road along with the following details:

(i) Road gradients.

(ii) Curve radius.

(iii) Stacking places for road metal.

(iv) Location of catch water drains.

(v) Kilometre stones.

(vi) Road land boundary posts.

(vii) Bridges, culverts and causeways.

(viii) Retaining walls, breast wall and parapet walls.

(ix) Any other conspicuous object along the road.

(x) Inspection house, gang huts.

(c) **Metalling Charts.** Metalling chart is a graphical representation of the progress of metalling/remetalling year wise. It is valuable aid for preparing road repair/maintenance programme.

A typical road metalling record chart is shown in Fig. 9.1.

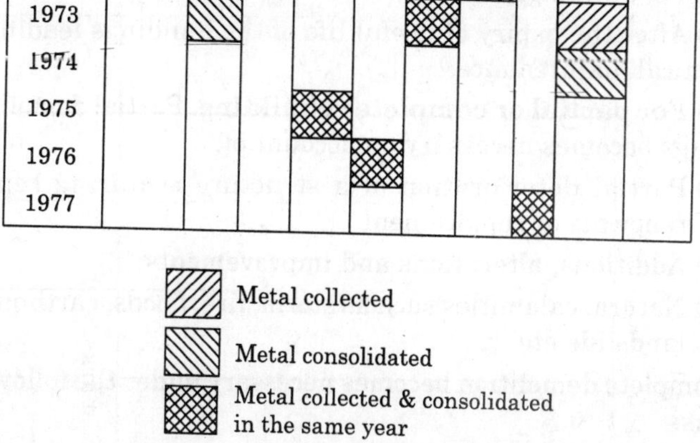

Fig. 9.1 Road metalling record chart

(*d*) **Road Inspection Book.** This book contains record of all road structures such as:

(*i*) Scuppers.

(*ii*) Culverts.

(*iii*) Causeways.

(*iv*) Bridges.

All such structures are numbered in series by kilometres (*e.g.,* 5/10 represents 5th culvert in 10th kilometre) for ready identification.

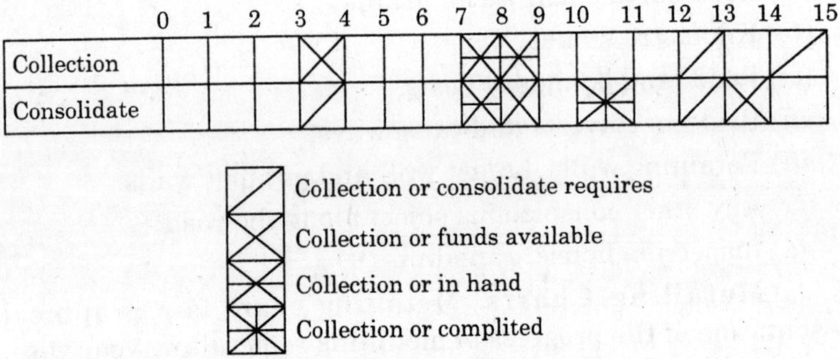

Fig. 9.2 Metalling progress chart

The book also contains Cross-Section of nalla, crossing, high flood levels (with date) and other relevant details. Such details are attached as appendices.

9.4 DEMOLITION OF BUILDINGS

The following causes call for initiation of partial or complete demolition of buildings:

(*a*) After the expiry of useful life of the buildings leading to uneconomical maintenance.

(*b*) **For partial or complete rebuilding.** Partial demolition of buildings becomes necessary on account of:

(*i*) Partial deterioration of a structure requiring repair, renewals or replacement.

(*ii*) Additions, alterations and improvements.

(*iii*) Natural calamities such as storm, fire, floods, earthquake landslide etc.

Complete demolition becomes necessary under the following situations:

(*i*) The maintenance of repair becomes uneconomical.

(*ii*) When land is required to provide space for new projects. Demolition in such cases is restricted to such cases where the buildings are temporary and would have to be demolished sooner or later. In the case of permanent buildings structures as far as possible efforts should be made to utilise the structures within or without the project complex.

(*iii*) When buildings are surplus to the requirements. This situation normally occurs only in the defence department.

(*iv*) When land has been hired/requisioned for a specific period is to be released.

(*v*) When the structure has been rendered completely unserviceable due to normal calamities.

The authority competent to sanction demolition is the administrative authority competent to sanction its construction. No attempt should be made to initiate separate demolition statements within an area with a view to get such statements sanctioned by a lower competent authority. In other words demolition statements in respect of a particular area should be initiated at one time and not piece-meal.

Demolitions are carried out to the best advantage of the state. Partial demolitions are generally entrusted to the agency carrying out repairs, renewals, replacements or alterations or departmentally. Complete structures are however normally disposed off by a public auctions through government approved agency.

All materials obtained from demolition of structures are accounted for in Demolition Register which contains a numerical account of stores. A demolition certificate is attached to contractors' bill to ensure that such stores have been properly accounted.

The relevant records such as Buildings Register, PSMB and layout plan must be amended immediately after demolition.

It should be borne in mind that demolitions involve '*assets*' and therefore their demolition must be based on the authority competent to create such an asset *i.e.*, the competent Administrative Authority.

10

PROJECT MANAGEMENT WITH C.P.M. AND PERT

10.1 INTRODUCTION

The engineer has been defined as one who provides in a penny what a layman produces in two pennies. This in a nutshell brings out the importance of the Engineer in the economic development of the nation.

In India a series of five year plans have been prepared for the socio-economic development of the country. Most of the expenditure on such development plans is incurred through Engineering Project. For example in the fifth year plan out of a total of ₹ 18,000 crores about ₹ 12,000 crores is envisaged to be spent on Engineering Projects which thus forms about seventy per cent of the capital outlay. About two-third of this amount that is ₹ 8,000 crores is to be dealt with by Civil Engineers.

If by planning and effective exercise of control at various stages even if one per cent economy is achieved, it will mean saving of ₹ 80 crores. Hence the need for proper planning and management in Civil Engineering Projects is self-evident.

From the inception of the project to its completion, the Civil Eginneer has to be face heavy tasks of management and administration. It is not sufficient only to be good professionally as an Engineer. It is very necessary that the Civil Engineer should be competent in management in various fields such as planning, engineering, staffing, directing, controlling and coordinating. He will have to take bold decisions on technical as well as management problems. Sound engineering management is an art backed by modern scientific tools. Linear Programming is one such tool which enables the engineer to arrive at an optimal solution to complete a project at the minimum of cost for a specified construction time. The Critical Path Method (C.P.M.) and Project Evalution and Review. Technique (PERT) have already proved their usefulness in many fields of Civil Engineer. The CPM has already replaced the old, familar bar chart, which used to be the engineer's tool so far as controlling, planning and scheduling of sequence was concerned.

The CPM is the schematic representation of a project by means of a diagram called network depicting the sequence and interplay of various component events that go to form the project. From this network, the most suitable programme for implementation of the project can be evaluted. The final programme is so selected so as to result in the lowest cost consistent with the time factor.

Though the CPM has been recently used way in late 50s, its advantages as a management tool has been established in countries abroad where large savings have been reported in time and cost of projects, by its use.

In India, there are a large number of constraints due to shortage of resources such as steel and cement, non-availability of skilled labour, seasonal availability of labour and climatic variations like monsoon, floods, the planning and execution of projects could be done in a more efficient manner by application of CPM. The CPM can reduce even a complex project plan to a simple graphical form which is basically free of ambiguity and is free of complex mathematical analysis. Such a graphical form or network provides a basis for ready analysis and communication of the plan and schedule.

10.2 PROJECT MANAGEMENT

A project is usually a one time effort. Although similar work may have been done previously, every project has its own features and therefore is of non-repetitive nature. In order to complete the project tasks efficiently, the project manager must plan and schedule largely on the basis of his experience with similar projects. During the course of the project, he will have to replan and schedule due to unexpected progress, delay or technical conditions.

In all these projects, one is concerned with developing an optimal plan of the activities that make up project including a specification of their interrelationships. One is also interested in scheduling these activities in an acceptable time span and finally with controlling the progress of the scheduled work. One should first plan the work and then work the plan.

With respect to planning and scheduling, one must consider the manpower and facilities required for carrying out the programme as its progresses in time. The aim should be to carry out the programme so that the cost and time required to complete the project are properly balanced. CPM has generally concentrated on time parameter and less on cost parameter, which is more difficult problem requiring technical judgement.

Therefore purpose of project management can be summarised as:

(*i*) Preparing plans of the various tasks involved.

(*ii*) Initiate the various tasks.

(*iii*) Review from time to time progress of the project and take suitable measures to accelerate the same in case it is behind schedule.

A delay in the time schedule not only reflects adversely on the administrative ability of the project manager but also upset the coordination of various phases. This results ultimately in underutilisation of the available resources and inflates the completion cost of the project.

10.3 TIME AND PROGRESS CHART, BAR CHART OR GANTT CHART

About 1919 Henry L. Gantt came forward with a method called *Gantt Chart*. The chart is essentially a graphic representation of programme of procurement of materials and time bound schedule of completion of various elements of the project. The scheduled programme of various activities is represented by a number of bars as shown in Fig. 10.1 and hence the method of scheduling is also called as *Bar Chart*.

Various construction activities are indicated on the left hand side and the proposed duration of its execution is represented by thick horizontal lines or bars. The portion of the work completed is shown by shading in between the bars. Therefore, this shaded portion will represent the percentage of work completed at a date (time). Therefore, the graph will show the progress of the various

	Item	Total quantity	Jan.	Feb.	Mar.	April	May	June	Remarks
A	Materials								
i	Cement								
ii	Steel								
iii	Timber etc.								
B	Machinery								
i	Road rollers								
ii	Stone crushers								
iii	Heavy transport etc.								
C	Physical tasks								
i	Excavation								
ii	Foundation & plinth								
iii	Super structure upto plinth								
iv	Super structure upto roof								
v	Roofing								
vi	Plastering								
vii	Flooring								
viii	Joinery/fitting								
ix	Internal services								
x	White washing & painting								
xi	External services								

elements of the project and hence known as *time and progress chart.*

10.4 SALIENT FEATURES OF BAR CHART

(*i*) The chart is simple to prepare and interpret.

(*ii*) Each item of work (activity) is shown separately.

(*iii*) Modifications to the chart on as required basis can be carried out easily.

Because of the above, the use of the chart has been very popular with construction departments and even after introduction of CPM network, the use of the chart has not been diminished.

The bar chart method has the following shortcomings.

(*i*) The sequence of activities is not clearly defined.

(*ii*) The various activities are interdependent.

(*iii*) Interdependence of tasks makes it necessary to pay equal attention to all the items of work or activities. The chart therefore does not reflect whether the completion ahead of the schedule of certain items would correspondingly accelerate or retard the project.

(*iv*) The chart is suitable only for simple and small jobs.

10.5 CRITICAL PATH METHOD (CPM)

On account of the shortcomings of the bar chart given above efforts were made to improve on the method. Thus in 1957-59 U.S. Navy Department developed a system of network for a submarine project which involved as many as 250 separate contracts. This new technique was called "*Programme Evaluation and Review Technique or briefly as* **PERT**. The introduction of this technique resulted in the project being completed two years ahead of schedule and corresponding reduction in cost.

During the same period an American firm E.I. Duyont developed another technique which was designated as "*Critical Path Method*" or **CPM**. Since the analysis is essentially in the form of networks the method is also known as "*Critical Path Analysis*", **CPA**. In some special cases it is termed as **RAMPS** (Resources Allocation for Multi-Project Scheduling).

Whereas the term PERT is normally applied to projects under research, the term CPM deals with the project of known magnitude. In such cases time can be assumed and the sum of the total time taken by the activities equals the schedule period of the project. In the case of construction industry therefore CPM is more suitable.

10.5 TERMS USED IN CPM

Before the procedure for constructing the network is discussed, some of the terms commonly used are defined as follows:

(*i*) **Network or Flow Diagram.** It is a diagrammatic representation of the entire project. In this diagram the various items of work are shown in order in which they are to be performed. Figure 10.2 shows one such network. The general flow of events is shown from left to right.

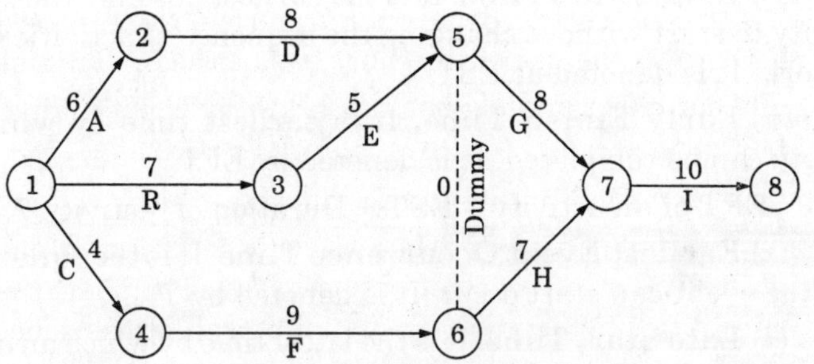

Fig. 10.2

(*ii*) **Activity.** An activity is a part of the project denoted by an arrow on the network. The tail of the arrow shows the start of the activity and the head the end of the activity. One and only one arrow can be used to represent one activity. Each activity has to have a given time. The arrows are not drawn to scale. This activity *A* is shown by arrow 1-2 and 6 on top shows the duration of time *i.e.*, 6 units of time.

(*iii*) **Event.** An event is a stage or point where all previous jobs merging in it are completed and all further jobs bursting out are still to be completed. Thus event (1) is the starting of the project. The bursting activities are *A*, *B*, and *C*. The event (5) has *D* and *E* as merging activities and activity *G* bursting. The activity *G* will be started only when the activities *D* and *E* have been completed. The event is represented on the network by a circle or mode at the junction of arrows. These events are numbered in their sequential order on the network.

(*iv*) **Duration.** Duration is the estimated time *T* required to complete an activity and is denoted on the activity in the network.

(*v*) **Dummy activity.** It is a fictitious activity with zero duration and no cost. It is used to maintain the sequential order of the activities in the network. It is represented by dotted lines on the network. The activity 6-5 is a dummy activity in Fig. 10.2. It show that all activities commencing from event (5) cannot start before completion of the event (6).

(*vi*) **Restraint.** It is a restriction very similar to a dummy activity but has a duration which can either be negative or positive. It is used to fix intermediate dates within the network and thereby fix the relative start or finish or the parallel activities when these activities are not coincident.

(*vii*) **Early Start Time.** It is the earliest possible time for the activity to start without changing the sequence of activities in the network. It is denoted as EST.

(*viii*) **Early Finish Time.** It is earliest time by which the activity can be completed. It is denoted by EFT.

EFT of an activity = **EST** + Duration of activity T.

(*ix*) **Earliest Event Occurrence Time.** It is the earliest time that the event can start occur. It is denoted by T_E.

(*x*) **Late Start Time.** It is the latest time by which an activity can be started without delaying the project. It is denoted as LST.

(*xi*) **Late Finish Time.** It is the latest time by which an activity can be completed without delaying the project. It is denoted as LET.

(*xii*) **Latest Allowable Event Occurrence Time.** It is the latest time the event can occur. It is denoted by T_L.

(*xiii*) **Total Float.** It is the difference between the maximum time allowed for an activity and its estimated duration. In other words it is the amount of time by which the activity can be started late without causing the project to last longer. It is also called total activity slack and is denoted by S.

$$S = LST - EST = LET - EFT = T_L - EFT$$

(*xi*) **Free Float.** The free float of an activity is the amount of time by which the activity completion time can be delayed without interfering with the start of succeeding activities. It is denoted by *SF*.

$$S_F = T_E - EFT$$

(*xv*) **Interfering Float.** It is the difference between the total float and the free float.

(*xvi*) **Critical Path.** The events which have no float or slack are the critical events *i.e.*, if $T_E = T_L$. These events must be completed on schedule if the project is to be completed in the minimum total time. The path joining such critical events is called the *critical path of the network*.

(*xvii*) **Critical Activities.** The activities lying on the critical path are called *critical activities*. Critical activity has a zero float.

10.7 MERITS OF CRITICAL PATH METHOD

The CMP has the following advantages:

(*i*) The sequence of operations is established.

(*ii*) In irrelativity of activities is shown.

(*iii*) The problems in the carrying out of the various activities can be readily solved by the executives.

(*iv*) Difficulties/bottlenecks associated with the activities are known well in advance.

(*v*) Proper coordination of activities is established.

(*vi*) Eliminates idle period and hence reduces project time and the cost.

(*vii*) Difficulties likely to occur during the execution are lime-lighted well in advance and therefore elimination of these results in satisfactory and smooth execution of the project.

(*viii*) Provides most economical deployment of project resources (Personnel, Equipment and Machinery) are best-utilised.

(*ix*) Provides an authentic record of the position of the project at any instant of time and hence facilitates smooth change-over of the command.

10.8 SEQUENCE OF PROJECT MANAGEMENT USING CPM

The various stages in the management of a project using CPM technique are:

(1) Planning of the task or activity.

(2) Forming the network.

(3) Allocation of Time to various activities.

(4) Scheduling of the activities and determination of Critical Path.

(5) Review of the network formed.

(6) Control of operations.

(7) Crash Programming.

(8) Maintenance of Management records.

10.9 PLANNING OF THE ACTIVITY

As a first step, the activities involved in the project are carefully listed out without regard to their order of occurrence. Care should be taken to list out all activities as any error at this stage would be a basic one and the network prepared would be wrong. The bill of quantities for the work will give a very good idea of the various feasible activities involved. Some of these items may be broken down further into smaller activities if necessary, depending upon the degree of refinement required.

10.10 FORMING THE NETWORK

Next step is to establish a logical sequence of the activities. In arranging the order of the activities. The following points should be kept in mind:

(*i*) Which are the activities that must be completed before the start of particular activity.

(*ii*) Which activities can occur simultaneously.

(*iii*) Which activities must succeed particular activity.

The few rules of networking may be classified as those common to all activity on arrow networking systems, and those rules imposed by the use of computers or tabular methods of CPM computation.

Basic Rules

(*Rule* 1) Before an activity may begin, all activities preceeding it must be completed.

(*Rule* 2) Arrows imply logical precedence only. Neither the length of the arrow nor its direction on the drawing have any significance, excepting in case of Time-Scaled Networks.

Rules imposed by computers or tabular methods.

(*Rule* 3) Any two events may be directly connected by no more than one activity.

(*Rule* 4) Event numbers must not be duplicated in a network.

(*Rule* 5) Networks may have only one initial even (with no predecessor) and one terminal event (with no successor).

Flow diagram has some logic as given below. In Fig. 10.3, the activities are shown in sequence. The activity B can be started only when activity A is completed. Similarly, activity C can be started only when activity B has been completed.

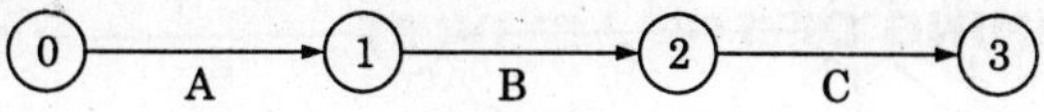

Fig. 10.3

In case it is to be shown that activity *C* can be started only when activities *A* and *B* have been completed but these activities have no bearings on each other and can be started independently then any one method as shown in Fig. 10.4, (*a*), (*b*), (*c*) can be used. The use has been made of dummies.

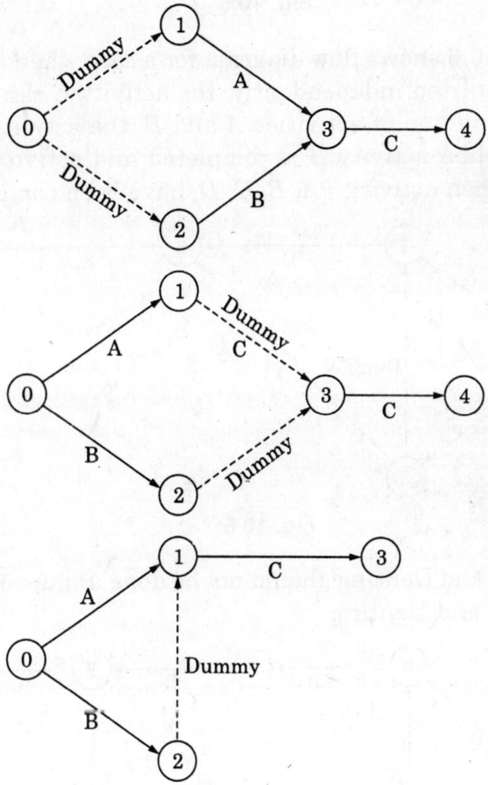

Fig. 10.4

Figure 10.5 shows flow diagram when it is required that activities *A* and *B* can be started independently and activities *C* and *D* being independent but can be started after *A* and *B* have been completed and activity *E* can be started only when all activities *A*, *B*, *C*, *D*, have been completed.

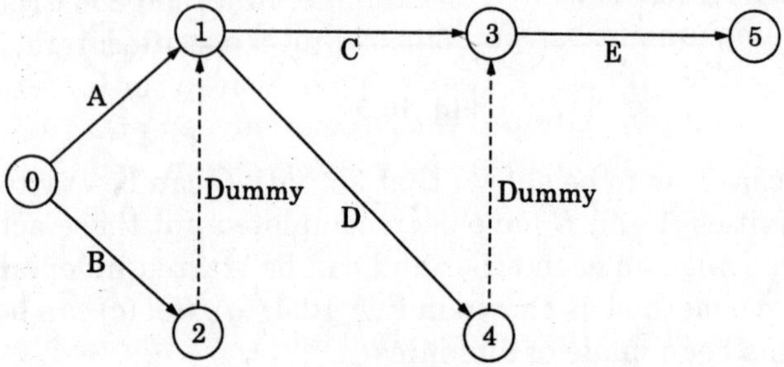

Fig. 10.5

Figure 10.6 shows flow diagram for a case when activities *A* and *B* can be started independently, the activity *C* can be started only after completion of activities *A* and *B*, the activity *D* can be started only when activity *B* is completed and activity *E* can be started only when activities *A*, *B*, *C*, *D*, have been completed.

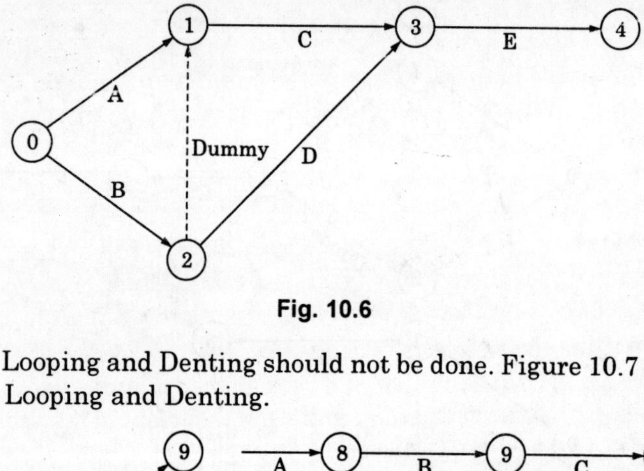

Fig. 10.6

Looping and Denting should not be done. Figure 10.7 (*a*), (*b*) shows Looping and Denting.

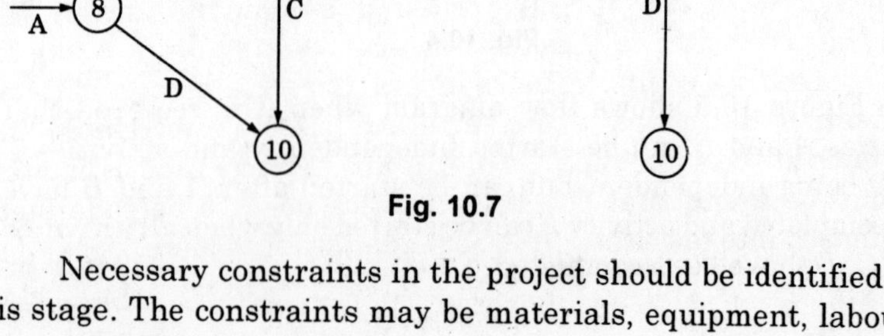

Fig. 10.7

Necessary constraints in the project should be identified at this stage. The constraints may be materials, equipment, labour, variation in seasons etc. For example, in a road construction job, the bitumen might be available only at a specified date. While all activities not requiring bitumen can be done prior to this date, the activities requiring bitumen can be done only after that date. Labour might not be available in the harvesting season, and this should be considered in the project scheduling. Heavy rain in monsoon period rule out the possibility of bituminous work and this is a seasonal limitation.

It is common to print several descriptive words of the activity on the arrow. This avoids the need for cross-reference with a separate list of activity descriptions.

The descriptions themselves must be unambiguous. They must mean the same thing to the project manager, the field superintendent, the various sub-contractors and others expected to use the network. Descriptions should be brief and should make use of reference points.

As networks become larger, consisting of hundreds of activities, it becomes more important to organise the activities into logical groupings and to locate the groupings in labelled areas of the drawing. Without a disciplined approach, the object of providing quick visibility of the project plan will not be possible to achieve.

The basic organisational approach is by physical subdivisions, of the project, for example, by the floors of a multi-storey building the spans of a bridge, kilometres of road. This organisation provides a ready correspondance between the physical progress of the work and the graphic progress on the network.

Within each physical subdivision the network may further be divided into responsibility groups. The responsibility groups aid the supervisor of the each group in the management of his activities.

10.11 ALLOCATION OF TIME TO VARIOUS ACTIVITIES

As explained in Article 10.10, one may develop the first draft of the project network. Now it will be required to refine the network and add time estimates to obtain a practical working draft, ready for the scheduling computations. In practice, the process of time estimation and network refinement are closely interrelated and are done at the same time. As one begins to make time estimates, it may be found that certain activities need to be redefined, condensed into fewer activities, or expanded into more.

The time estimate to be made for each activity is called the *activity duration*. The time may be expressed in units as working days. Weeks months etc. The same unit should be used throughout the network. Estimates of activity duration do not includes uncontrollable contigencies such as fires, floods, strikes or legal delays.

In estimating an activity's duration time, the acitivity should be considered independently of activities proceeding or succeeding it.

In case the activity is dependent on delivery of some material for example, R.C.C. Work is dependent on steel and if there is delay in delivery of steel, the two items procurement of steel and R.C.C. Work should be shown as separate activities. In procurement of steel the duration of time should take the realistic delivery time into account.

In case of duration by working days it is assumed that no work is carried out during week ends. But there are certain activities which are to be continuous like curing of concrete. In such cases the time estimate in working days will result in over estimation of the project duration. In such cases if the activity is carried out during week ends and holidays, the number of working days should be counted by deducting from total duration the week ends and holidays.

10.12 DETERMINATION OF PROJECT SCHEDULE AND CRITICAL PATH

At this stage the performance time for each activity has been estimated. Now scheduling of activities is begun to determine the network critical paths. The basic scheduling computations involve a forward and a backward pass through the network. Based on a specified occurrence for the initial network event, the forward pass computations give the earliest start and earliest finish times for each activity and also the earliest occurrence time for each event.

By specifying of the latest allowable occurrence time for the terminal network events, the backward pass computations will give the latest allowable start and finish time for each activity and the latest allowable occurrence time for each event. After the forward and backward pass computations are completed, the slack or float can be computed for each activity and thereby critical and subcritical paths through the network are determined. When an activity has slack, there is more time available to do it than it requires.

In initial stages it is convenient to begin with zero as the starting time of the initial project event and estimate the activity performance times in working days. Finally these computational results are converted to calender dates. It is also assumed that there is only one initial event and one terminal event and that the latest allowable finish time for the project is equal to the earliest finish time computed in the forward pass computations.

10.13 METHODS OF INDICATING *EST*, *LST*, *EFT*, *LFT*, T_E AND T_F OR T_L

The following four methods are used to indicate *EST*, *LST*, *EFT*, *LFT*, T_E and T_F or T_L (see Fig 10.8)

The purpose of forward pass is to compute the earliest start and finish times for each activity in the project. Forward pass computations start with an earliest occurrence time of zero for the initial project event and it is assumed that each activity starts as soon as possible *i.e.*, the instant its predecessor event occurs. In network logic, an event occurs when all of its predecessor activities are completed. Hence the earliest event occurrence time is equal to the largest of the finish time of the activities merging to the event in question. These rules can be summarised as:

10.14 FORWARD PASS COMPUTATIONS

(1) The earliest occurrence time of the single initial event of the network is taken as zero. $T_E = 0$

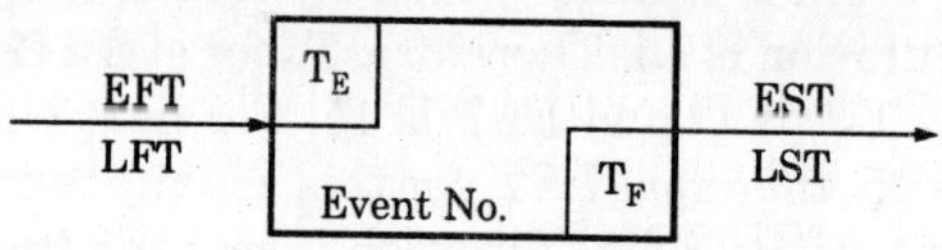

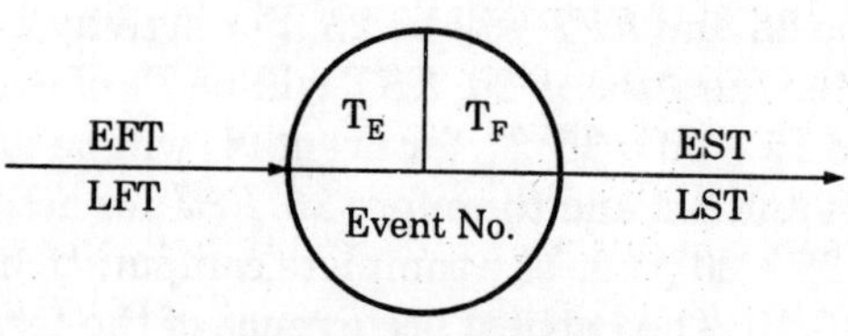

Fig. 10.8 *(Contd.)*

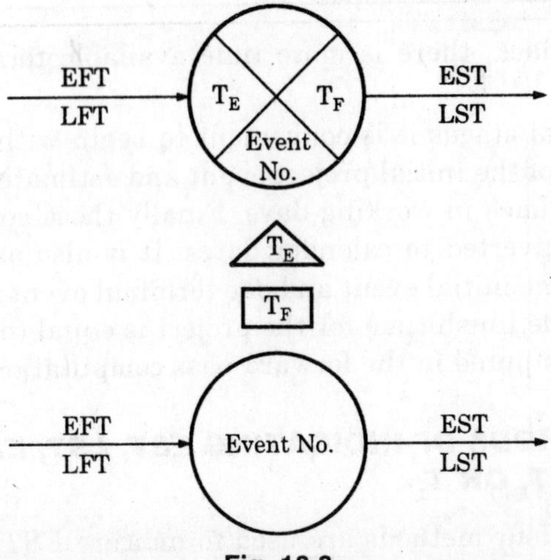

Fig. 10.8

(2) Each activity begins as soon as its predecessor event occurs.

$$EST = T_E \text{ for predecesser event.}$$
$$EFT = EST + T = T_E + T$$

(3) The earliest event occurrence time is the largest of the earliest finish times of the activities merging to the event in question.

$$T_E = \text{largest of } EFT_1, EFT_2....$$

The forward pass computations will be explained by taking problem 10.1.

Problem No. 10.1 The network gives activities for getting ready and reaching office in the morning.

The first event is start for which $T_E = o$. For activity 1-2, get up and wash, duration is 15. Therefore, T_E for event (2) is 15. *EST* for this activity 1-2, is *O* and *EST* is 15. For heat water activity 1-3, duration is 25, therefore *EST* for this activity is *O* and *EFT* is 25. For dummy acitivity 3.4 as duration is zero, *EST* will be T_E for (3) which will be 25 and *EFT* will be 25. For activity 2-4, for bring milk and have tea duration is 20, *EST* will be T_E of event 2 *i.e.*, 15 and *EFT* will be 15 + 20 = 35. T_E for event (4) will be larger of *EFT* for activities 2-4 and 3-4 and therefore 35. *EST* for activity 4-6 will be 35 and *EFT* 35 + 20 = 55. The complete computations have been shown in Fig. 10.10. The earliest occurrence of the terminal event 10 will be 120.

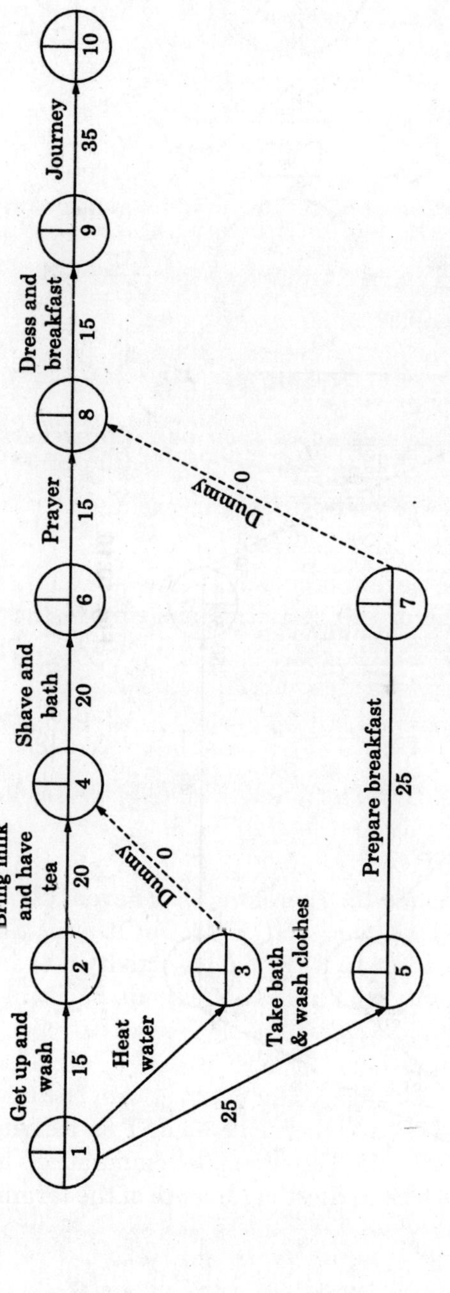

1
2
3
4
5
6
7
8
9
10
Get up and wash
15
Bring milk and have tea
20
Shave and bath
20
Prayer
15
Dress and breakfast
15
Journey
35
Heat water
Dummy
0
Take bath & wash clothes
25
Prepare breakfast
25
Dummy
0

Fig. 10.9

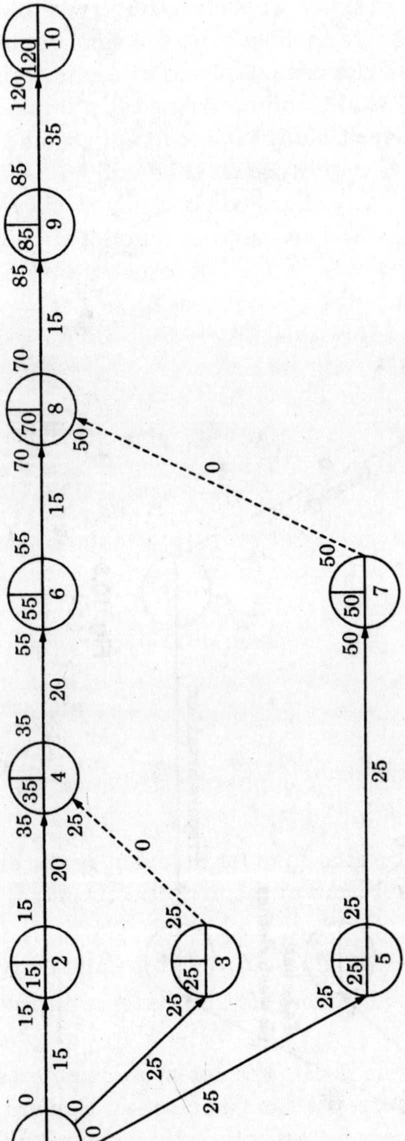

Fig. 10.10

10.15 BACKWARD PASS COMPUTATIONS

The purpose of backward computations is to compute the latest allowable start and finish times for each activity, which will permit the last event to occur at its earliest expected time as computed in the forward pass. The backward pass computations start with the single project terminal event and assigns to it a latest allowable occurrence time equal to its earliest occurrence time. Following this, the latest allowable activity start time will be defined as the time to which the start of an activity can be delayed without directly causing any increase in the total time to complet the project. For the terminal network event $T_L = T_E$. The latest allowable activity start times *LST* are computed by subtracting the activity duration times from and latest allowable finish time *LFT*. According to network logic, an event must occur before any succeeding activities commence. The latest allowable occurrence time for an event is equal to the smallest of the latest allowable start times of the activities bursting from the event in question. These rules can be summarised as:

(1) The latest allowable occurrence time of the single terminal event of the network is set equal to the earliest occurrence time computed in the forward pass.

$$T_L = T_E \text{ for terminal event}$$

(2) The latest allowable start time *LST* for an activity is its successor event latest allowable time minus the duration time of the activity in question.

$$L_O T = T_L, \text{ for successor event.}$$

$$LST = LFT - T = T_L - T$$

(3) The latest allowable time for an event is the smallest of the latest allowable start time of the activities bursting from the event in question.

$$T_L = \text{Smalest of } LST_1, LST_2 \ldots \text{ of bursting activities}$$

The backward pass computations are explained taking problem.

The terminal event is 10. The latest allowable occurrence time will be earliest occurrence time as given in forward pass *i.e.*, 120. The latest finish time for activity 9-10, journeys will be 120. The latest start time for activity 2-10 will be 120-35-85. The T_L for event 9 will be 85. Figure 10.11 shows the backward pass computations. The latest occurrence time for event 8 is 70,

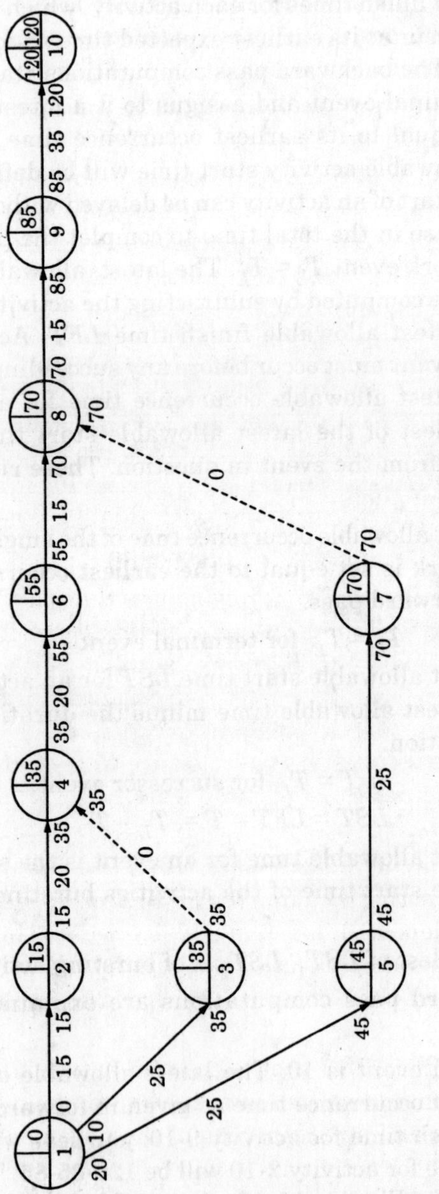

Fig. 10.11

Therefore, for both activities 6-8 and 7-8 merging in event 8, latest finish time will be 70. Now coming to event (1), the bursting activities are 1-2, 1-3, and 1-5 and their earliest latest starting times are 0, 10 and 20, therefore latest occurrence time for the event (*o*) will be minimum of these *i.e.*, *O*.

Figure 10.12 shows complete computations forward and backward and slacks or floats.

Total activity slack is equal to the latest allowable time of the activity's successor event minus the earliest finish of the activity in quession $S = T_L - EFT$. The total slack also is defined as the difference between the latest start and earliest start of the activity or latest finish and earliest finish of the activity

$$S = LST - EST = LFT - EFT.$$

In problem 10.1 the path 1-2-4-6-8-9-10 is the critical path and duration of project is 120. On this path the activities have no slack. The path 1-5-7-8-9-10 is a slack path having a slack of 20. The path 1-3-4-6-8-9-10 is also a slack path having a slack of 10.

For activity 5-7, $S = T_L - EFT = LST - EST = LFT - EFT$

$$\therefore \qquad S = 70 - 50 = 45 - 25 = 70 - 50 = 20$$

Free slack S_F can occur on merge point activities which lie along slack paths. Free slack is equal to the earliest expected time of the activity's successor event minus the earliest finish time of the activity in question $S_F = T_E - EFT$. It is also defined as the amount of time than the activity completion time can be delayed without affecting the earliest start or occurance time of any other activity or event in the network. Dummy activity 7-8 in problem 10.1, $S_F = 70 - 50 = 20$.

Free slack will occur in slack path when there is different total slack in different activities along the path. Thus in slack path 1-3-4-6-8-9-10 in problem 10.1, slack in activity 4-6 is 0 but slack in activity 3-4 is 10, therefore free slack in activity 3-4 will be 10. As there is same slack of 10 in activity 3-4 there is no free slack in activity 1-3.

Problem 10.2. Fig 10.13 shows skeleton network for road project. The project consists of widening the existing single lane pavement to two lanes and strengthening of the pavement at the same time.

The number of activities into which the project has been broken up and their normal durations are shown in the network.

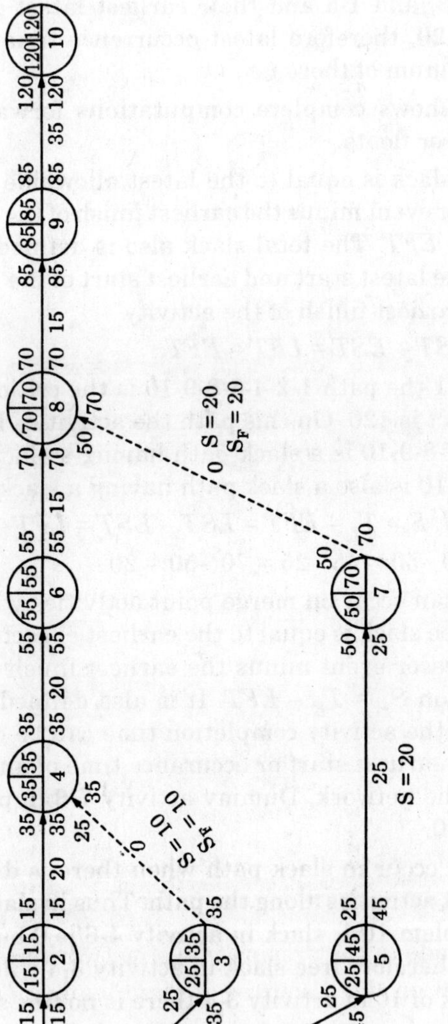

Fig. 10.12

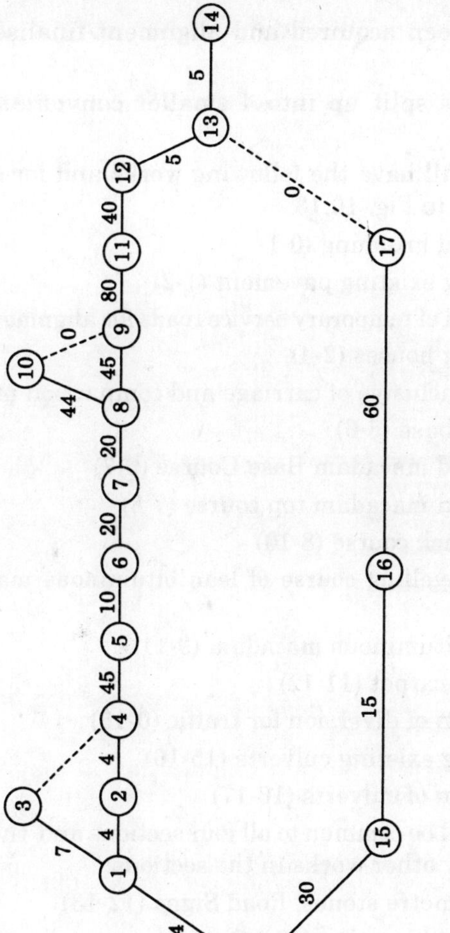

Fig. 10.13

Assumptions made in the preparation of network are :

(1) No constraint on the resources of plant, equipment and labour.

(2) The work can commence in the month of April. There is a slack period of about 1½ months (July and August) when due to monsoon, the only activity that can be carried on is the water bound macadam.

(3) The work is to be completed before the next monsoon starts.

(4) Land has been acquired and alignment finalised and traced.

(5) The work is split up into 4 smaller convenient sub-sections.

Each section will have the following works and for section (1) Network is shown in Fig. 10.13.

(*i*) Clearing and grubbing (0-1)

(*ii*) Dismantling existing pavement (1-2)

(*iii*) Construction of temporary service roads for alignment (1-3)

(*iv*) Dismantling houses (2-4)

(*v*) Earhwork inclusive of carriage and compaction (4-5)

(*vi*) Gravel sub-base (5-6)

(*vii*) Water bound macadam Base Course (6-7)

(*viii*) Water bound macadam top course (7 8)

(*ix*) Providing tack course (8-10)

(*x*) Providing levelling course of lean bituminous macadam (8-9)

(*xi*) Providing bituminous macadam (9-11)

(*xii*) Semi-dense carpet (11-12)

(*xiii*) Construction of diversion for traffic (0-15)

(*xiv*) Dismantling existing culverts (15-16)

(*xv*) Construction of culverts (16-17)

(*xiii*), (*xiv*) and (*xv*) will be common to all four sections and therefore will not be affected by other works in the sections.

(*xvi*) Fixing Kilometre stones, Road Signs (12-13)

(*xvii*) Finishing and opening (13-14)

(*xvii*) will commence only when all the sections have been completed.

Figure 10.13 shows works for sections (1) *i.e.*, 1-13 only and some ccmmon works *i.e.* 0-15-16-17-13-14.

Figure 10.14 shows network for all the four sections taking that all works can be done independently in all the four sections, materials, labour and equipment being separate.

Section (2) forms the critical path. Project time will be 292 days.

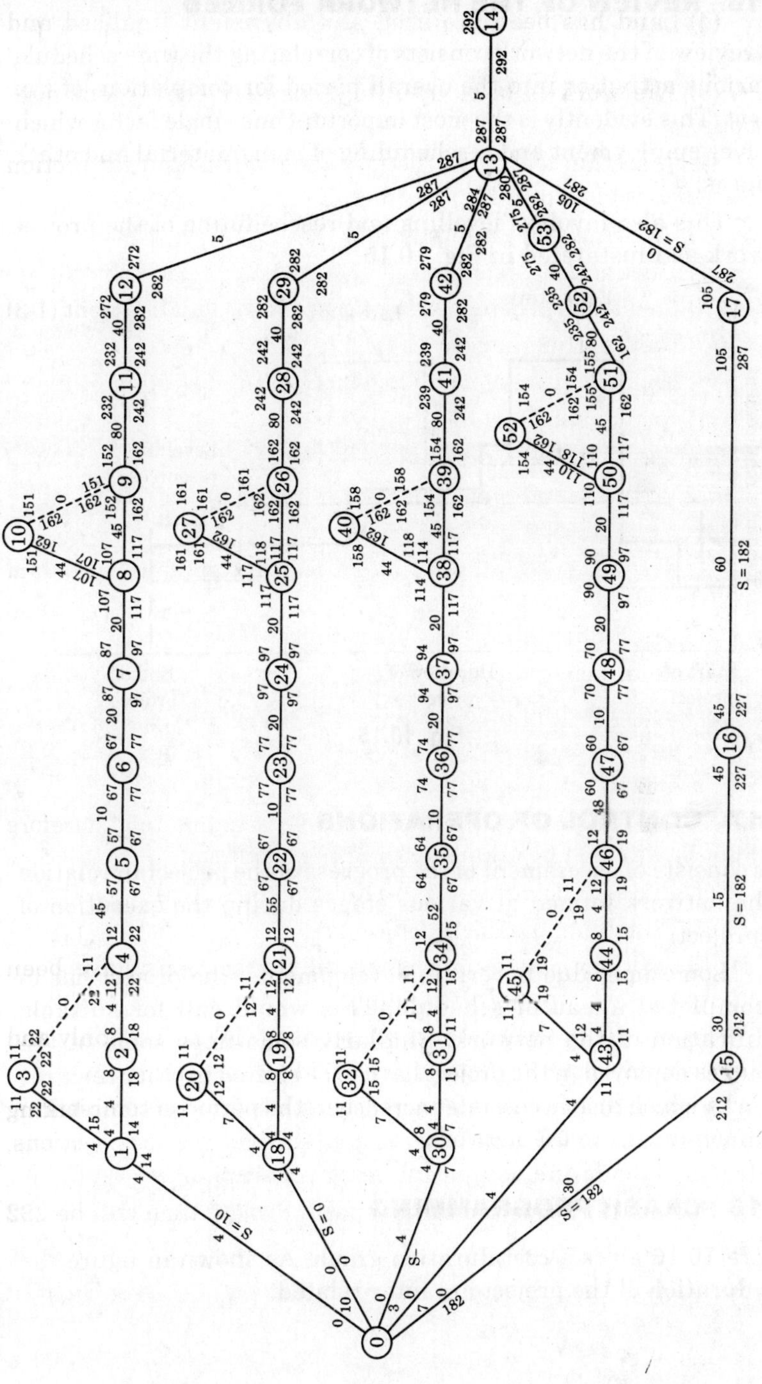

Fig. 10.14

10.16 REVIEW OF THE NETWORK FORMED

The review of the network consists of correlating the time schedule of various activities into the overall period for completion of the porject. This evidently is the most important one single factor which involves employment and rescheduling of men, material and other resoures.

This also involves levelling and rescheduling of the project network as illustareted in Fig. 10.15.

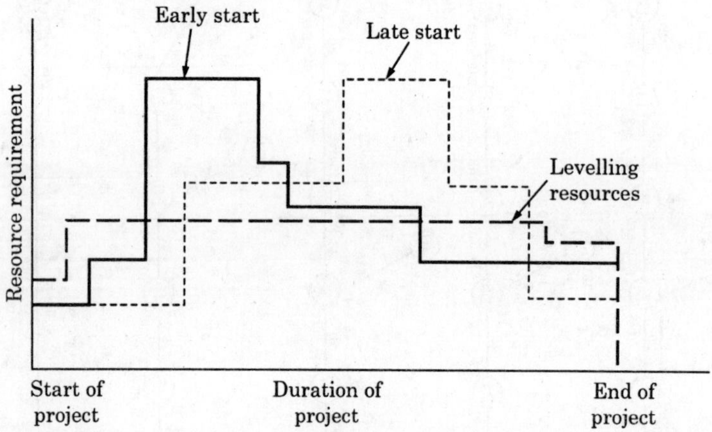

Fig. 10.15

10.17 CONTROL OF OPERATIONS

This consists of assessment of the progress of the project in relation to the network formed at various stages during the execution of the project.

Sometimes due to certain developments, the project has to be completed ahead of schedule. This would call for suitable modification of the network. Similarly sometimes some of the resources deployed in the project have to be shifted to other theatres of works which also necessiate increase in the period of completion and amendment to the network.

10.18 CRASH PROGRAMMING

Figure 10.16 gives a cost duration graph. As shown in figure the cost duration of the project are inter-related.

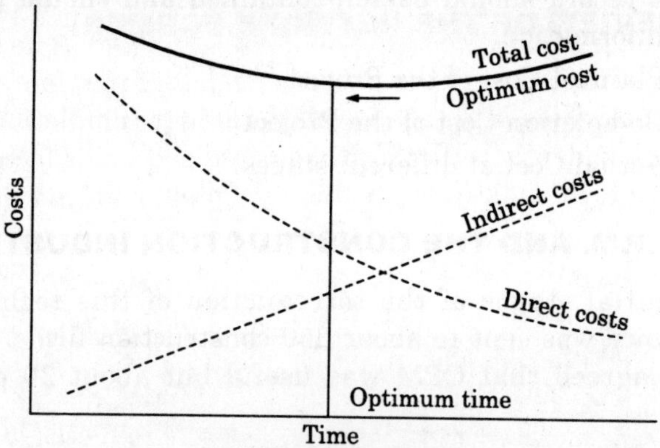

Cost duration graph

Fig. 10.16

The total cost of the project consists of:

(*i*) **Prime Cost or Direct Cost.** This consist of cost of labour, material and machinery used in the project.

(*ii*) **Secondary or Indirect Cost.** This consists of expenditure on the administrative and technical personnel for the project and forms the overheads.

As the project costs are a function of time, there is an optimum period for the most economical completion of the project. This ideal situation is very difficult to achieve in practice and therefore only an honest-effort is made to achieve this object.

10.19 MAINTENANCE OF MANAGEMENT RECORDS

The project records consists of:

(*a*) History of the project indicating how the proposal was initiated and administratively approved.

(*b*) Initial planning of network.

(*i*) Reasons for modifications/amendments to the network if any along with a comparative statement of the initial and revised network.

(*b*) Progress achieved at various stages.

(*e*) Important events in the history of the project. These record are prepared in the form of ready reckoner of the project flow and serve as a guide for similar projects to be executed in the future.

This record should be self-contained and should give the following information:

(*i*) Planned Cost of the Project.

(*ii*) Completion Cost of the Project

(*iii*) Actual Cost at different stages.

10.20 C.P.M. AND THE CONSTRUCTION INDUSTRY

At the rinitial stages of the introduction of this technique a questionnaire was sent to about 350 construction firms. Most of the firms agreed that CPM was useful but about 20 per cent opposed.

The following are some of the comments:

(*i*) The analysis helps being ahead of schedule.

(*ii*) Elements causing delay can be eliminated.

(*iii*) Small items which otherwise would be ignored are suitably attended.

(*iv*) Results in thorough and detailed planning.

(*v*) Period of construction can be reduced.

(*vi*) Considerable saving in project can be achieved.

(*vii*) Flaws/faults/defects are located and rectified in time.

10.21 LIMITATIONS OF C.P.M.

For small projects *T* and *P* or Bar Chart is more popular. Even for larger projects CPM is comparatively less used in India Inspite of the above fact, the usefulness of the technique is being realised and in time to come this method of programming would replace the present method of bar chart, particularly in the case of major projects.

10.22 ADVANTAGES OF CPM NETWORK IN EXECUTION OF A PROJECT

It has been generally seen that although considerable progress has been made in the country in the design of Engineering Projects, the progress in the planning or execution of the projects, has been far from satisfactory. In a majority of major projects the period of completion and the estimated cost change considerably. This type of shortcoming can only be overcome by ensuring that each and every activity that forms part of a project is considered logically and in the correct sequence. Likely bottlenecks should be foreseen well ahead and remedial action taken. The required control on the progress of the various activities can only be exercised by the CPM network system of analysis.

The CMP has the following advantages:

(*i*) The activities of the work are integated into the time schedule and hence calender-wise schedule of commencement and completion of each activity, manpower, machinery and resources can be drawn up.

(*ii*) Inter-relationship and sequence of performance of various activities/items of work are clear from the network.

(*iii*) Builder and Executive responsible for the conduct if the project can determine the time when various resources/men, material machines and equipments) are needed and procurement action can be taken accordingly.

(*iv*) From the schedule of procurement thus prepared, difficulties can be visualised will in time and timely action for removing them can be taken.

(*v*) In the event of the programme getting upset due to some unforeseen reason, a revised CPM chart can be prepared to avoid further loss of resources.

(*vi*) Realistic time to complete the project can be ascertained by going into the details of time required and sequence of each operation/activity.

(*vii*) During the execution of the project the output constants for various tasks can be revised in the light of the output experience gained during the execution of the project.

(*viii*) The network scheduliug ensures optimum use of the men, machines and materials.

(*ix*) The executive gets a reliable and valuable aid to asses progress of the work and exercise the required control.

Thus the network analysis helps in locating trouble spots and bottlenecks and adverse situations can be avoided by proper planning. Any delay in the period of completion adds considerably to cost and by CPM network analysis such expenditure can largely be avoided if not altogether eliminated.

PART–II

ACCOUNTS

1

ACCOUNTS

1.1 NECESSITY OF ACCOUNTS

In day to day working of an individual or a family so far as his expenses are concerned, they have necessarily to be related to his individual mean or that of his family. In the case of a State or Central Government the expenditure has to be planned well ahead of the financial year concerned so that an effective control is exercised on the expenditure of various departments of the Government. The expenditure has further to be related to the expected resume/receipts/income of the State. This exercise is known as budgeting and the session of the Centre or the State in which the budget is passed is known as budget session.

The system of maintaining the income from revenue, taxation and other sources of the various departments and the expenditure on various works and items of expenditure made by the respective departments is known as Accounting System. From the records of properly maintained accounts of the Government and from time to time to control the financial position of various ministries, departments and projects by scrutinising the receipts and expenditure in respect of the following:

(*i*) Are accounts of receipt and expenditure properly maintained.

(*ii*) Is the expenditure incurred the more economical for the particular work.

(*iii*) Has the entire expenditure incurred been spent for the item of work associated with sanction project/work.

(*iv*) Has expenditure on each item of the administrative approval been kept within the sanctioned amount.

(*v*) Has the expenditure been restricted to the allotted funds.

(*vi*) Has the expenditure allotted been utilised and no lapse of funds has taken place.

The above questionnaire can be answered only if accounts are kept properly.

(*vii*) Is there any requirement of appropriation or reappropriation of funds.

1.2 BOOKS OF REFERENCE AND CODE

Accounts are the backbones for the satisfactory execution of any project. Maintenance of accounts starts even before the project is taken in hand and the finalisation of accounts is the last item before closing the project.

Although upkeep of accounts is the responsibility of the representative of the accounts department of the Centre or the State concerned yet every executive associated with the construction project is required to control certain expenditure. Even the subordinate staff is frequently to be expowered to incur expenditure for the project. It is, therefore, necessary that every officer of the department should be conversant with the financial aspect of any construction work. It is not necessary that all the rules and regulations concerning financial transactions should be mugged up by the executive and the subordinate field workers and office staff but one must know the source of authentic guidance on the subject and hence the need for heavy reference books. The published references on the subject can be broadly classified under two main categories namely Central Government Publications and State Publications. Some of these reference books are given below:

(*A*) *Central Publications:*

1. Fundamental Rules
2. The Civil Service Rules
3. Minimum Wages Act
4. Trade Union Act
5. Payment and Wages Act
6. Payment of Gratuity Act and Central Rules
7. Employees Provident Funds and Miscellaneous Provident Act 1952.
8. Financial Rules and Treasury Rules
9. Public Works Department Code

10. Account Code Vol. I and Vol. II

11. Treasury Rules.

(*B*) *State Publications*

1. Departmental Financial Rules. The book contains financial and accounts procedure rules supplementary to the general financial rules.

2. Manual of orders. Each state P.W.D. and as well as each branch of such P.W.D. maintains its own Manual. These manuals are primarily supplementary to the code and provide detailed instructions particularly in matters peculiar to the department concerned.

3. Public Works Department Code

.......Compulsory to the Central Code on the subject each State has its own code which defines the functions of the executive and administrative ways of the department.

1.3 DIFFERENT CLASSES OF ESTABLISHMENT IN THE P.W.D.

The following are the different categories establishment in the Pubic Works Department.

1. Basic or Regular Establishment
2. Workcharged or Project Establishment.

These Establishments are briefly described below:

1. Basic or Regular Establishment. Division or the office of the Executive Engineer is the main executive unit. These divisions are primarily organised to look after the maintenance of the assets of the department such as buildings, roads, bridges, canals, etc. Since the requirement of such establishment is permanent and does not change from time to time it is known as basic or regular establishment. This category is further divided into three classes namely.

(*i*) Permanent

(*ii*) Quasi Permanent ; and

(*iii*) Temporary

(*i*) **Permanent Establishment.** This consists of the Divisional/Executive/Garrison Engineer under whom there are normally three subdivisions. The Divisional Accountant or the Unit Accountant is attached to the division who is responsible to the Divisional officer for the correct maintenance of the accounts of the division.

Table 1.1 gives the basic establishment of a division along with main duties of each branch.

Table 1.1

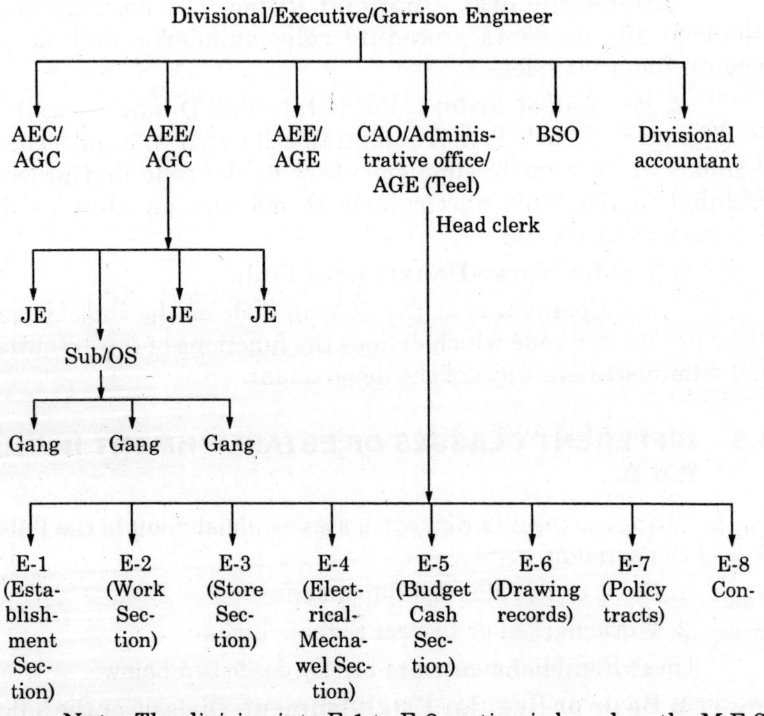

Note. The division into E-1 to E-8 section is based on the M.E.S. organisation but essentially other departments are also similarly organised and known as indicated within the brackets though the nomenclature E-1, E-2 etc., is not used.

E-7 section deals with policy and hence does not exist in the Divisional/Garrison Engineer's Officer.

In the above establishment persons holding substantive posts form the permanent establishment.

(*ii*) **Quasi Permanent Establishment.** Due to ever increasing work load of the divisional office, say on account of projects taken in hand from time to time, additional staff is, therefore, recruited to handle the increased load. Till such time that the basic cadre is recruited, this staffs remain as temporary establishment. However, such of the temporary staff whose work has been found satisfactory for at least three years and there is no likelihood of their being retrenched due to reduction in work load is appointed as Quasi Permanent. It is class between temporary and permanent establishment.

(*iii*) **Temporary.** This has been explained in 2 above.

The salaries of basic establishment are drawn monthly from the treasury or sub-treasury on which the office is based. The establishment is governed by Civil Service Rules of the Centre or State as the case may be. In the case of M.E.S. the staff governed is by Civil Service Rules as well as rules applicable to civilians in Defence Service. In the case of defence personnel working in the M.E.S. they are governed by the Army Act.

2. Work Charged Establishment. The Establishment recruited primarily for work associated with the project in the division is termed as work charged establishment. All personnel employed in addition to the basic establishment comes under this category. The various categories of workers which come under this category are:

(*i*) Additional Supervisory field staff as distinct from the regular staff for the supervision of jobs associated with the project.

(*ii*) Mates and mistries engaged in the project attached to junior engineer or other field workers.

(*iii*) Additional technical and non-technical staff engaged to take care of the increased work load in the basic establishment on account of the project works.

(*iv*) **Contingent Establishment.** This consists of field workers such as office–khalasis, dak runners, security staff etc., for which provision exists in the project under the head contingencies.

(*v*) Daily Labour or Casual Labour employed by the department for jobs associated with the project.

Except daily labour which is paid on muster rolls and the pay bills are prepared as for regular establishment but they are not required to be sent to the treasury. They are passed for payment by the Divisional/Garrison Engineer after proper scrutiny by the divisional/unit accountant.

Work charge establishment is not entitled to benefits like pension, leave or travelling allowance except when the journey is performed in connection with the project work in which case such expenditure is passed and paid under the contingency of the project.

The above description of work charged establishment is particularly applicable to additional work load caused by projects in the division. In the case of some of the major projects the entire establishment is workcharged and benefits applicable to regular temporary establishment are applicable to such personnel.

1.4 DIFFERENT METHODS OF CARRYING OUT WORKS.

Works executed by the Public Works Department can be broadly divided into two categories namely:

1. Original Works
2. Repairs or Maintenance Works (A.R.M.O. and S.R.)

1. Original Works. Depending upon the type of work original work falls under three categories, namely:

(*a*) Minor Works

(*b*) Major Works

(*c*) Projects

The classification into the above three types is governed primarily by the value of the work. This value however differs from State to State and department to department. It also changes from time to time in the same department. For example, above twenty years back work upto the value of ₹ 20,000 and 50,000 were classified as minor Works and major Works respectively. The present corresponding limit may be ₹ 50,000 and ₹ one lac respectively. Works which exceed the monetary limit of major works fall under the category of the project.

In some departments specific additions and alternations to existing structures costing say below ₹ 500 are termed as minor works chargeable to maintenance. This has been primarily done to overcome the difficulty experienced by the department and the users in making minor changes in the structure where such changes do not basically modify the original structure but add considerable living facility to the user. For example, if the bathroom is not connected directly with the bedroom but one has to enter the bathroom through the verandah, the provision of a small connecting door would fall under the category of a minor work chargeable to maintenance.

2. Repairs or Maintenance Works. This consists of the work executed for keeping the structure in proper working condition. No administrative approval is required for carrying out the maintenance works as funds are allotted on the basis of earlier budget grants, on percentages basis, on the total expenditure, year of construction and type of construction (temporary/permanent)

Whatever may be the category of work before any work is executed the following three conditions should be satisfied:

1. The work should be Administratively approved.
2. It must have a Technical sanction.
3. Funds should be available to meet the expenditure.

Note. As has already been stated above, no administrative approval is required in the case of maintenance work. An estimate of work has however to be prepared and approved by the Chief Engineer who holds bulk allotment for his zone and is competent to reappropriate the grant from one division to the other.

Works in the P.W.D. are executed by one of the following three agencies:

Contract Work. This is the standard form of carrying out all but petty works and routine maintenance. The contract is given out on the basis of open tender. The main types of such contracts are:

(*a*) **Item rate contract.** A schedule of item of work to be done under the contract is as in the form given in table 1.2.

S. No.	*Description of item with brief specification*	*Quantity*	*Unit*	*Value*	*Amount*
(1)	(2)	(3)	(4)	(5)	(6)
		Total			₹

All columns of the schedule are prepared by the department except columns 5 and 6 which are filled by the tendering party.

(*b*) **Lumpsum Contract.** In this type of contract full details of the work along with detailed drawings and specifications are given and the tendering party undertakes to complete the job within the specified period at the rate quoted.

(*c*) Combination of item rate and lumpsum. Where the contractor undertakes to get job done on the lumpsum contract basis and at the same time quotes the rate in the schedule of rates provided in the tender for to regulate the rate of payment in respect of additions and alterations.

(*d*) Contract based on fixed percentage above/below the current standard schedule of rates. Schedule of quantity is blank and the bidder only gives his bid as percentage above/below the standard schedule rates under reference.

2. **Piece Work System.** This system is adopted for small jobs at the current scheduled rates at the discretion of the Engineer-in-charge. In remote areas sometimes contractors to undertake a job are not forthcoming while local people are available for small jobs. Sometimes if this work is found economical (the rates tendered by bidder being higher) and the Piece Work is converted into a Bond or Contract Agreement.

3. **By Departmental Labour.** This is the only method available for carrying out mixed jobs, and maintenance. Some of the major projects (such as projects in Border Roads) are entirely carried out by departmentally engaged labour. Almost all the cement concrete work in the Highway departments is carried out departmentally. Most of the track laying and maintenance work in railways is carried out by departmental labour. The comparative cost is higher but proper quality control is easier. The system also saves time.

1.5 CORRELATION BETWEEN WORKS AND ACCOUNTS

Funds are allotted for the execution of works on the basis of the Administrative Approval of the work and the schedule of demand for the financial year under consideration. The financial year of the country is from 1st April to 31st March. The forecast for works in progress and expected to be taken in hand by the Works Departments is made in the month of July of the proceeding year. In October 1st changes in grants is initiated and in the month of December second and final change is made. The purpose of this is to enable the demands to be consolidated on the basis of overall availability during the budget session between February to April. It would thus be clear that the funds for any work are based on the works and overall control of expenditure can only be exercised by maintaining separate construction accounts for each work. This establishes the correlation between Works and Accounts.

Further control is exercised on the expenditure in respect of the various items of administrative approval by segregating the expenditure in respect of individual items of the Administrative Approval. Not only the overall expenditure should be within the sanctioned amount but also the expenditure on individual item of the Administrative Approval is controlled. So far as audit requirement is concerned control on these primary elements is not required. Moreover in the case of works executed through contract agencies a further division of expenditure is not feasible because the contractor is paid on the basis of the total quantities of each item of work of the Administrative approval and hence no further correlation between Works and Accounts is possible:

In the case of works executed departmentally expenditure is further split into the following sub-heads in respect of each item of the Administrative approval.

(*a*) **Stores (constructed material).** For work study and cost analysis purpose the quantity of each material incorporated in each item of work is recorded.

(*b*) **Labour.** The time spent by each type of labour is noted.

Maintenance of accounts under the sub-heads mentioned above thus serves the following purpose, particularly in works executed by departmental labour:

(*i*) For compilation of data for works study and cost control.

(*ii*) For verification of output constants leading to revision/modification of existing schedule or rates *i.e.*, for revision of analysis of rates.

(*iii*) To have an independent and permanent record of payment and production.

The above brings home the correlation which exists between Works and Accounts.

1.6 MANUAL OF ORDERS

In addition to Public Works Department Code, each branch of the P.W.D. maintains its own manual. The manuals serve as a supplement to the code. They contain the powers, jurisdiction and limits of expenditure of the various government officers. They also contains rules and orders on subjects peculiar to each department.

1.7 DEPARTMENTAL FINANCIAL RULES

This contains the financial and accounts procedure rules which are special to the Public Works Department. These rules are supplementary to the general financial rules of the Government.

In general it deals with the working procedure of P.W.D. It lays down the rules for maintaining records of work done and payments made. It also deals with the procedure of stores material.

2

Organisation of Public Work Department

2.1 INTRODUCTION

The various engineering departments of the government responsible for construction and maintenance of public works such as buildings, roads, canals, public health and electrical installations, are known as Public Works Department. The main branches of this department are:

1. **Public Works Department—Buildings and Roads Branch.** The department is responsible for construction of buildings and roads of the centre or state as the case may be.

2. **Public Works Department—Irrigation Branch.** The department is responsible for construction and maintenance of irrigation system of the state comprising of:

(*i*) Dams

(*ii*) Canal headworks

(*iii*) Irrigation channels.

Note. In the case of the construction of major dams autonomous boards are constituted where senior engineers of the department are sent on deputation.

3. **Public Works Department—Local-self Government.** (Engineering Department) also known as Public Health Department. The department deals with the water supply and sewage disposal works.

4. **Electricity Department.** The department deals with the construction of generation and distribution of electricity. On account of the large expansion in the production and distribution

system, this department now functions as Electricity Department, such as DESU (Delhi Electric Supply Undertaking) UPSED, HSEB, PSEB etc. The other departments of the Government are:

(*a*) **The Railway Department.** Though this engages the longest number of Engineer (Civil, Electrical and Mechanical) yet it does not strictly fall in the category of PWD. The accounting procedure is however, the same with slight modification to suit the needs of the department. For example, an imprest in the PWD means the standing advance given to Junior Engineer to meet his day today requirements and is recouped at regular intervals. The term *'imprest'* in the railways denotes the tool box containing specified number and types of track fittings from which the engineer draws his daily requirements. The fittings thus used are replaced/ recouped from time to time.

(*b*) **Military Engineering Services.** This engineering department of the Government is responsible to the Engineer-in-Chief for construction and maintenance of defence works. The working of the department is however very much similar to the working of other PWD's.

2.2 ADMINISTRATIVE SETUP OF PUBLIC WORKS DEPARTMENT

2.2.1 Organisation of P.W.D.

For the Administration of Public Works, each State is generally sub-divided into Circles, which are in the charge of Superintending Engineers. Circles are further subdivided into Divisions, and Divisions into Sub-divisions. Divisions are under the charge of Executive Engineers (also called *Divisional Officers, District Engineers, Divisional Engineers* etc.). Sub-divisions are in charge of Sub-divisional Officers (also called *Assistant Executive Engineers, Sub-divisional Engineers, Upper Subordinates* etc.) The department as a whole is again generally divided into three branches, namely, (*i*) *Buildings and Roads*, (*ii*) *Irrigation*, and (*iii*) *Public Health Engineering*. Each branch has Chief Engineers who control the activities of the branch through the Superintending Engineers.

2.2.2 Functions of CPWD

CPWD is an agency of the Central Government operating throughout the country for planning, construction, maintenance, and repair of all works and buildings financed from the budget of Civil Works (including renting and purchases of buildings). Civil Works means building works including air-conditioning, plumbing, sanitary works, compound walls, fire fighting, interiors, landscaping, renovation, rehabilitation and other Miscellaneous works.

2.2.3 Relation with Treasury/Bank

Divisional Officers of the CPWD draw money for works expenditure and for salaries by means of cheques on the Bank direct (In P.W.D. of some States, money for works expenditure is drawn by cheques. and for salary of staff by bills presented at treasury.)

2.2.4 Cheques

Cheques are drawn by Divisional Officers on bank, with which they are placed in account by their Accountant General (or Pay & Accounts Officer). In CPWD, the bank sends to the Divisional Officer daily-scrolls of cheques paid. In the States, at the end of the month, the Treasury Officer, coordinating with the bank, furnishes a certificate to the Divisional Officer showing the cheques paid during the month against his account. These documents help the Divisional Officer to make out a list of cheques issued by him but not yet encashed at the treasury/bank. He submits a list of uncashed cheques to the Pay and Accounts Officer (or Accountant General) in support of his account. This is known as Schedule of settlement with Treasury/Bank-Cheques.

2.2.5 Receipts

Receipts realised by the officers of the department are remitted as soon as possible in lump into the bank (in the case of CPWD) and into the treasury (in the case of State PWD). Each remittance is accompanied by the usual chalan. At the end of each month, the treasury officer sends to the Divisional Officer a consolidated receipt for all the remittances of the entire division during the month. For receipts deposited by CPWD Divisions in the bank, the bank sends its daily receipt-scroll to the division. Amounts deposited by the Division as per Cash Book is then reconciled with the amounts shown as received by the Treasury. This is known as *Schedule of Settlement with the Treasuries/Banks*-Receipts.

2.2.6 Divisional Offices and Sub-divisional Offices

Each Division, which includes one or more sub-divisions, is accounting unit of PWD. To each divisional office is attached a Divisional Accountant who is a subordinate of the A.G. (or Pay and Accounts Officer) but is posted to the divisional office to check and compile the divisional accounts under the supervision and responsibility of the Divisional Officer.

Table 2.1 gives the normal setup of the department of the centre or the state as the case may be.

Table 2.1

MINISTER

(There may be one or more ministers. For example, at the Centre, Works and Housing are under one minister, while Power is under the other and Water Resources under another.)

SECRETARY

(A Senior technical person or IAS/PCS Officer)

CHIEF ENGINEER

(Sometimes there are a number of Chief Engineers in which case the seniormost Chief Engineer who is responsible to the Government for all the works in his jurisdiction is designated as Engineer-in-Chief. In other cases other Chief Engineers are designated as Additional CEs)

Superintending Engineer Circle I — S.E. Circle II — S.E. Circle III etc.

(There are 3 to 4 SE's under a CE)

Divisional Engineer/EE/GE — EE/GE — EE/GE — EE/GE — EE/GE

(There are 4 to 6 divisions in a circle)

AEE/AE/SDO — AEE/AE/SDO — AEE/AE/SDO — AEE/AE/SDO

(There are 4 to 6 sub-divisions in a division)

JE (I) — JE (II) — JE (III) — JE (IV)

There are 4 to 6 Junior Engineers and Section Officers in a sub-division.

2.3 THE FUNCTION OF CHIEF ENGINEER

The Chief Engineer, who is the technical and administrative head of the department is responsible to the Secretary to Government for efficient running of the department. As a technical head he exercises control, primarily technical, in the execution of the projects and maintenance of works. He submits budget proposals to the government in respect of all original and maintenance works in his jurisdiction and exercises control over the expenditure in collaboration with the Accountant General of the state or Controller and Auditor General in the case of centre. In the case of M.E.S. he controls accounts in collaboration with the Controller of Defence Accounts of the concerned command. Depending upon the progress of the works he initiates demand of additional funds or surrender of the existing funds. As administrative head, he controls employment, transfer, leave and discipline of the staff. He usually represents the department in the recruitment of gazetted semi-staff in the Selection Boards such as U.P.S.C's or State Service Commissions. In case of recruitment of subordinate staff he analyses their selection. As head of the organisation he enjoys the following financial and administrative powers/authority:

(*a*) **Financial**

(*i*) Administrative approval of works other than buildings upto ₹ 25,000, in respect of buildings and roads which do not fall under any other administrative control. This limit varies from state to state as well as from time to time.

(*ii*) **Acceptance of tenders for works by contract** —Full powers

(*iii*) **Sanction/Approval of estimates for repair** —Full powers

(*iv*) **Sanction Deposit Works** —Full Powers

(*v*) Purchase of livestock, repair of articles under the head 'T & P' excluding purchase of motor vehicle. — ₹ 30,000 at any one time.

(*b*) **Technical**

(*i*) To accord technical sanction for original work and repairs. — upto 5% in excess of the administratively approved amount.

2.4 FUNCTIONS OF SUPERINTENDING ENGINEER

He is responsible to the Chief Engineer for the following in respect of his circle:

(*a*) Administrative and technical control of the circle.

(*b*) Exercises financial control over execution of original and repair works.

(*c*) Carries out from time to time and as on required basis inspections of works in his jurisdiction.

(*d*) Arranges procurement of stores required and transfer/ disposal of surplus stores.

(*e*) Carries out inspection of offices of all divisions under him and checks for their proper working. A report of such inspections is submitted to the Chief Engineer.

(*f*) Exercises administrative control in respect of recruitment, transfer and discipline of all subordinate staff in his circle except Circle Office Superintendent, Head Draftsman and Accountants.

(*g*) Keeps himself informed about the progress of works in his circle and bottlenecks. For this purpose he holds monthly meeting with the divisional engineers and contractors. He exercises the following financial and administrative powers/authority:

(*a*) **Financial**

(*i*) Administrative approval of works other than residential accommodation upto ₹ 10,000.

(*ii*) Acceptance of tenders by contract upto ₹ 5 lacs.

(*iii*) Acceptance of purchase or manufacture material, tools and plant for use on works or for running and maintenance of machines and equipment within the sanctioned allotment. He holds full powers for that.

(*iv*) Sanction of deposit works upto ₹ 10,000.

(*b*) **Technical.** To accord technical sanction for original works upto ₹ 100,000 and for maintenance and repairs upto ₹ 400,000 at a time.

Note. In the Military Engineering Services the civilian cadre is designated as Superintending Engineer and the Army Cadre of the Service as Commander Works Engineer (CWE).

2.5 FUNCTIONS OF DIVISIONAL OFFICER/EXECUTIVE GARRISON ENGINEER

The Divisional Engineer/Executive Engineer is responsible to the Superintending Engineer for administrative and technical control of his division. In particular his main duties are:

(*i*) To see that no work is taken in hand without administrative approval, allotment of funds and technical sanction.

(*ii*) To exercise effective quality control and quantity control to see that the specifications laid down are strictly adhered to and that the progress is commensurate with the scheduled time.

(*iii*) To see that the contractors accounts are properly maintained and are regularly submitted to the Competent Financial Authority concerned. To carry out these duties the Divisional Accountant is attached to his division as financial advisor and representative of the Accountant General. In the case of M.E.S. the Unit Accountant does similar duties and is a representative of the CDA (Controller of Defence Accounts).

(*iv*) As drawing and disbursing officer of the division he draws money from the concerned treasury and makes payment to the contractor and labour and office establishment against funds placed by the Government in the concerned treasuries.

(*v*) Carries out inspection of the offices of AEE/AE/SDO atleast once a year and submits reports thereof to the Superintending Engineer.

(*vi*) Inspection of works in progress and site checking of measurements entered by the Junior Engineer in the Measurement Books (MBs).

(*vii*) Ensures that all tools, plant and machinery in the sub-divisions are properly maintained and utilised.

The Divisional Officer exercises the following financial and administrative powers/authority.

(*a*) **Financial**

(*i*) Acceptance of tender for work by contract upto ₹ 50,000.

(*ii*) Order piece works for works and repairs upto ₹ 10,000 at the current schedule of rates.

(*iii*) Sanctioning temporary increase in reserve limit of divisional stock upto 10% over the sanctioned scale laid down for the division.

(*b*) **Technical.** To accord technical sanction for original works and repair works upto ₹ 10,000 at a time.

2.6 FUNCTIONS OF AEE/AGE/AE/SDO

Assistant Executive Engineer (AEE) Assistant Garrison Engineer (AGE) Assistant Engineer (AE) Sub-divisional Officer (SDO) is responsible to the Executive Engineer for efficient management and execution of works in his sub-division. He is correctly designated as the engineer-in-charge of the works. He carries out the following duties:

(*i*) Arranges stock, execution, progress and completion of all original works and repairs in the sub division.

(*ii*) Carries out regular check of works in progress and ensures quality and quantity control over the works. Quality control is exercised by ensuring execution of works according to design plan and specification. Quantity control is exercised by checking the progress from time to time with respect to CPM/Bar Charts as the case may be.

(*iii*) Maintains construction accounts of works in his sub-division.

(*iv*) Carries out percentage checks of measurements recorded by the junior engineer in the MBs.

(*v*) Carries out physical verification of all the standard Measurement Books in the sub-division once a year.

(*vi*) Exercises proper care and control for safe custody of cash and stores.

(*vii*) Carries out physical verification of all stores including tools, plant, equipment and machinery at least once a year. A certificate to the effect that the verification has been done is entered on the body of the relevant ledgers and report of verification submitted to the Divisional Engineer.

(*viii*) Checks muster rolls in respect of daily engaged labour and casual rolls in respect of casual labour.

(*ix*) Maintains accounts of all the works in his charge and submits the same to the Divisional Engineer. Even when the disbursing officer is the Divisional Engineer he maintains close liaison with the Divisional Accountant/Unit Accountant for proper maintenance of the Construction Accounts.

(*x*) Maintains all buildings/Roads/Irrigation Works and other structures efficiently and keeps relevant documents up-to-date.

(*xi*) Reports to the Divisional Engineer any unusual occurrence or damage to Government assets in his charge.

(*xii*) Exercises administrative control of the office and field staff in the sub-division.

2.7 FUNCTIONS OF JUNIOR ENGINEER (JE)/ SECTIONAL OFFICER/OVERSEER

The Junior Engineer is responsible to the sub-Divisional Officer/ Engineer-in-Charge in respect to the works under his charge. In particular his duties consist of the following:

(*i*) Supervision of all works in his charge executed through contractor or departmentally.

(*ii*) Arranges labour for departmental works.

(*iii*) Maintains attendance of departmentally employed daily labour on muster roll and of casual labour on casual labour roll either directly or through the field staff consisting of sub-overseer or mate. Daily report is submitted to the SDO.

(*iv*) Takes measurements of all works in the Measurement Books.

(*v*) Exercises direct control in respect of specifications and progress of works under his charge.

(*vi*) Prepares running bills and final bills of all works in his charge. According to the contract agreement, the contractor is supposed to submit his bill but in actual practice the Divisional Officer waves this requirement for efficient running of the sub-division and hence the bills are prepared by the Junior Engineer.

(*vii*) Prepares pay bills of the work charged establishment of his section.

(*viii*) Carries out field survey of proposed projects and ground tracing (Dagbailing) of structures/constructions on the ground.

(*ix*) Prepares estimates for all types of works in the section.

(*x*) Reports any unusual/special event to the Engineer-in-charge.

(*xi*) Carries out check of tools, plants, furniture and fittings of inspections houses, rest houses and other departmental buildings and arranges collection of rents and revenue due to Government.

(*xii*) Carries out half yearly checks of all stores in his charge and submits reports thereof to the Sub-divisional Officer.

(*xiii*) Carries out annual inspection of all structures in his charge and submits report of such inspection to the Engineer-in-charge.

(*xiv*) Maintains accounts of his imprest and arranges its recoupment at fixed intervals.

(*xv*) Initiates disposal of unserviceable stock, tools and plants in the form of survey report.

2.8 DUTIES OF JUNIOR ENGINEER

(a) **Duties in Planning**

1. Preparation of Preliminary Estimate, and Detailed Estimate.
2. Preparation of N.I.T.
3. Checking of additional items, extra items, and variations in estimated quantities.
4. Test check of measurements.
5. Planning of works.
6. Preparations of Schedule of rates, specifications and analysis of rates.
7. Examination of amendments, deviations and special conditions of contracts.
8. Fixing and Revision of minimum fair wages.
9. Inspection of works and detailed examination of expenditure.
10. Preparation of simple designs and drawings.

(b) **Duties of Construction**

1. Land Acquisition.
2. Execution of works, according to drawings, design specifications and conditions of contract.
3. Checking Layout of works, and materials of site.
4. Issue of stores.
5. Labour welfare.
6. Keeping progress of works.
7. Measuring the works and preparation of contractor's bill.
8. Making Recovery statements.
9. Reporting of all accidents and thefts.
10. Keeping inspection book, order book.
11. Keeping Record of materials obtained from dismantling.
12. Giving completion Report.
13. Handling over of works for maintenance after completion.
14. Helping the department in arbitration.

(c) **Duties in Maintenance**

1. Taking over the charge of computed Buildings.
2. Maintenance of capital register.

3. Preparation of estimates (AR and MO ; work charged staff; material ; S R. works), and additions and alterations.

4. Allotment Register (Possession Report ; Vacation Report and inventory of houses).

5. Record of work charged staff ;

6. Maintenance of complaint book, suggestion book, daily task diary of workers and materials used.

7. Record of dismentled material (serviceable and unserviceable)

8. Furniture record (Receipt and Issue)

9. Material account (Receipt and Issue)

10. Tools and Plants.

11. Correspondences Record.

12. Periodical Returns

13. Inspection Record of Buildings.

14. Preparation of Standard Measurement Books.

15. Execution of works.

(*d*) **Handing over of charges.**

(*a*) **Planning.** Handing over of Estimates ; N.I.T; extra item statements, additional item statements, drawings, designs, specifications, schedule of Rates, Analysis of Rates, Reports about the works.

(*b*) **Construction.** Handing over of specifications, drawings, designs, contract documents, estimates; additional items ; variations record ; list of tools and plants ; list of stores ; recovery documents, MB's ; Road metal account ; surplus stores, unsettled claims of contractors/suppliers ; record of work charged establishments, List of level books, ident books, field books: progress reports ; account of advances paid ; Recovery statements ; imprest account, Labour reports, accident reports, record of materials obtained; inspection books, order book and other correspondences.

(*c*) **Maintenance.** Handing over of record of AR and M.O. works, S. R. works etc. Estimates, drawings designs, specifications, capital register ; allotment register ; inventories ; work charged record ; complaint books, suggestion books, inspection register ; dismentled material account, store account ; furniture account, tools and plants account, M B" S.M.B's and Transfer entry books, and other correspondences.

2.9 SET-UP OF DIVISIONAL OFFICE

See Art. 1.3.

2.10 ACCOUNTS BRANCH

The accounts branch is headed by the Divisional Accountant who is an adviser to the Divisional Engineer and represents the Accountant General. In the case of MES he is known as Unit Accountant (UA) and performs functions similar to that of the Divisional Accountant. He represents the CDA (Controller of Defence Account) of the command concerned.

The following duties are performed by the Accounts Branch :

1. Compilation of accounts of the division.

2. Advising the Divisional Engineers in matters concerning accounts, budget estimates and financial rules and regulation in day-to-day operation.

3. Keeps a watch on the financial transactions of the unit and carries out pre-audit of all payment vouchers in the Division. If he feels certain transactions are irregular he records his opinions for consideration of the Divisional Engineer. The Divisional Engineer can overrule such advise but in that situation he takes full responsibility for the transaction.

4. Carries out post audit of payments made by subordinate officer AEE/AGE/AE/SDO where such officers have been delegated the powers of drawing and disbursing.

5. Checks the payments with reference to the individual items of the administrative approval.

6. Scrutinises draft contract agreements in respect of financial propriety of the same.

7. The Divisional cashier, who does not belong to accounts department, works under the guidance and instructions of the Divisional Accountant. The cashier belongs to the regular establishment of the Division and maintains the following financial documents:

(*a*) Pass Books.

(*b*) Leave Accounts.

(*c*) Register of Receipts.

(*d*) Register of Unpaid Wages.

(*e*) Register of Security.

(*f*) Cheque Books and Cash Books.

8. Reviews MB's of the sub-division from time to time and brings irregularity if any, to the notice of the Divisional Engineer.

9. Prepares/Scrutinises and certifies the money expenditure return with respect to the cash book entries.

10. Prepares record for arbitration and legal cases of the division. In the case of MES this job is done by the contract/surveyor of works branch (E-8).

11. Checks TA bills and other account vouchers of the division before they are passed for payment.

12. Scrutinises the comparative statement before the same is placed before the Divisional Engineer.

13. The Divisional Accountant/Unit Accountant is in short the financial advisor of the Divisional Engineer although his advise may at times be ignored by the Divisional Engineer in which case he takes full responsibility for the transaction.

2.10.1 Sub-divisional Accounts

1. Funds. An SDO receives funds in one of the three ways:

(*a*) By fixed imprest of permanent advance given by Divisional Officer, which are recouped by the Divisional Officer when its balance diminishes after payments made by the SDO.

(*b*) By cash-transfer from the Division whenever money is needed.

(*c*) in some cases, by authorisation to draw cheques against the Divisional Officer's account with a treasury/bank.

S.D.O. generally, has a Cash Chest in which he places any departmental revenue received by him, and all sums drawn by him, which he is unable to disburse at once to the payees. He also keeps the unspent balance of Imprest or Advances (received from the Divisional Officer) in this cash chest. All payment are made by SDO on properly prepared and passed bills.

2. Sub Division's Account Record. Principal accounts records of a Sub-divisional office are:

Cash Book

Muster Rolls (*i.e.*, attendance register-cum-bill of labourers)

Work-charged establishments bills

Measurement Books

Works Abstracts, Stock account (*i.e.*, Bin Cards, Indents and Goods Received Sheets).

The following paragraphs explain their significance:

3. Cash Book. In the States, PWD Sub-Divisional Officers are authorised to issue cheques and to keep a Cash Book. This is the most important primary accounts-record. All receipts and payments, as they take place, are posted in it. Cash Book is regularly examined and balanced. At the end of the month, the Officer Incharge personally counts and certifies the cash balance in hand.

4. Muster Rolls. Muster Roll is a list of labourers employed daily on a work. It is a record of their daily attendance/amounts payable. There is a separate roll for each work. Payments on muster rolls are made and witnessed by the executive officer of the highest standing available on the spot. He actually counts the labourers, gets the payment made and attests the rolls.

5. Work-charged establishment bills. Work-charged establishment covers those members of staff, employed for supervision of the work, whose salary is chargeable to the work on which it is employed. Wages of members of such establishment are drawn on this bill. It is combined acquittance roll and Pay-bill form for the whole sub-division or a section of it.

6. Measurement Books. The measurement Book is an initial account record of the greatest importance in the Public Works Department. It is the basis of all accounts of work done and of materials received. Payments for work done/supplies received are made on the basis of the entries of quantity of work done recorded in the measurement book.

7. Works Abstracts. One works abstract is prepared each month for each work executed in a Sub-division. The Works Abstract records in detail, *i.e.*, voucher-wise and date-wise, all the expenses incurred on that work, no matter whether it is carried out departmentally or by Contractor. After all the expenses incurred in a month have been posted in it and totalled, it indicates the monthly expenditure on the work.

8. Stores Accounts. The Sub-divisional Officer keeps Bin Cards for each item of stock. These cards show the quantities of stock received, issued and balance on each day. The source of receipts and objects of issue are clearly recorded.

2.10.2 Divisional Accounts

1. Account Records. A Divisional Officer receives Revenue realised and makes payments for works and salaries. Salaries of all officers and staff are drawn by means of self-cheques (or cheques in favour of officers). Small amounts can be paid from cash-chest also. He has a Cash Chest and a Cash Book (and also Measurement Books, Muster Rolls & Works Abstracts for works which are directly under his charge). The main accounts which a Divisional Officer keeps, in addition to those kept by sub-divisions, are

(*i*) Contractors' Ledger,

(*ii*) Register of Works and

(*iii*) Transfer Entry Book.

2. Contractors' Ledger. This is a running account of each contractor working in the Division (including its Sub-divisions). A separate folio or set of folios is reserved for all the transactions of each contractor/supplier. The ledger shows in respect of each contractor - (1) the amounts due to him for work done by him, (2) amounts paid to him, and (3) The balance due to or by him. The Contractors's Ledger is closed and balanced every month.

No entry in the Ledger is to be made if the contractor/supplier is paid only on a first and final bill (*i.e.*, where no materials are issued from stock and no advance payments are made to them).

3. Register of Works. This register is kept for each work (except petty works) executed in the Division, and contains a record of total expenditure during the month and up-to-date expenditure on it. It shows the expenditure month by month compared to the estimates. The object of such a record is to show to the Divisional Officer the progress of the work along with its cost compared to its estimated cost. It is posted from Works Abstracts and agreed with the corresponding figure in the Monthly Account.

4. Transfer Entry Book. This book contains a record of all transfer entries included in the accounts of a Division like write back of erroneous debits or credits etc., or periodical adjustments.

5. Revenue Accounts. Two Registers are kept in the Division as accounts of revenue, namely (*i*) Register of Revenue Realised, and (*ii*) Register of Refunds of Revenue. Entries are made classified under each minor head and sub-head of account.

6. Monthly Divisional Account. The Cash and Stock accounts of the Divisional Office for a month are closed at the end of the month. The Transfer Entry Book is also closed as soon as possible after the expiry of the month. The transactions of Cash, Stock and Transfer Entries are consolidated together in the form of a monthly account to be submitted to the Accounts Officer between 7th and 10th of the month following that to which it relates.

2.11 DRAWING BRANCH

The branch is headed by the Head Draftsman (E-6 branch in the case of M.E.S.). This branch performs the following duties:

1. Maintains records and distribution of all drawing and mathematical instruments of the Division.

2. Maintains and keeps up-to-date all the road registers and road graphs and drawings of all constructed structures in the division. The final bill of any new construction is not passed till such time the relevant entry has been made in the connected register and verified by the Drawing Branch.

3. Prepares project drawings and detailed working drawings of all the works in the division.

4. Maintains departmental library.

2.12 CORRESPONDENCE BRANCH

The Office Superintendent/Divisional head clerk is responsible to the Executive Engineer in all matters concerning general correspondence, establishment and discipline. In the M.E.S. this is known as E-1 section.

The following functions are carried out by the section:

1. Receiving, opening, sorting and distribution of dak.

2. Deals with all confidential work such as confidential reports of the establishment, despatching cases and other confidential matter.

3. Handles all establishment matters such as

(*i*) Recruiting.

(*ii*) Promotions and transfer.

(*iii*) Salary bills.

(*iv*) T.A. Bills.

(*v*) Welfare.

4. To deal with cases involving Workmen Compensation Act.

5. Maintaining diary, indexing, filing, arrear statement, correction slip, reference books, typing and despatching.

6. Maintains confidential reports and Service Books. In addition to the above functions, which deal with establishment, the following additional duties in respect of works, cash and policy and contract are also performed in the Public Works Department. In M.E.S. organisation these functions are carried out by the following branches:

Works	E-2 Section
Cash	E-5 Section
Policy	E-7 Section
Contract	E-8 Section

Thus the additional duties in addition to the establishment section are:

1. Upkeep and handling of cash book and other financial documents dealt with under duties of Divisional Accountant in respect of the cashier. The Cashier is thus under the dual control of the Divisional Accountant and the Head Clerk.

2. Issue and receipt of money received on behalf of the Government.

3. Issue notes of tender, tender form and prepare tender agreement.

4. Reservation of rest houses and connected correspondence.

5. Compilation and submission of Reports and Return.

6. Deal with correspondence relating to estimate of works.

7. Procure stores for Divisional stock. (In the case of MES there is separate stores organisation under Barracks and Stores office).

2.13 REVENUE BRANCH

This branch is in Irrigation Department only. Deputy Revenue Officer/Deputy Collector/Senior Tahsildar is incharge of this branch which performs the following duties:

1. Collection of canal dues from users.

2. Demarcation of areas availing canal-irrigation facilities.

3. Maintenance of register of the cultivator/farmers along with the amounts to be paid by each.

2.14 P.W.D. ESTABLISHMENT

(See Art. 1.3 also)

In the M.E.S. two additional establishment exist. One of these is independent and works directly under the Chief Engineer of the command. Their usefulness has since been appreciated and they have been added to the C.P.W.D. establishment as well. These two establishments are S.W. (Surveyor of Works) and T.E. (Technical Examination).

2.15 REGULAR ESTABLISHMENT

(See Art. 1.3)

2.16 WORK CHARGED ESTABLISHMENT

It includes such establishment as is employed upon actual execution ; as distinct from the general supervision of a specific work or of sub works of a specific project or upon the sub-ordinate supervision of a specific work of sub-work of a specific project of the departmental labour, stores and machinery in connection with such work or sub-works.

The establishment provided for surveying, drawings, tracings etc., in estimates for preparation of project should be regarded as engaged on the execution of the works and should therefore be treated as work charged. The ministerial post such as Junior clerks; senior clerks; typist etc., are not sanctioned on work charged establishments. While appointing persons on work charge establishment officer concern should clearly mention the work; to which he is appointed, further persons appointed, should clearly be informed that his services are not likely to be continued.

The persons working on work charged establishment who have been recruited through employment exchange and who satisfy the recruitment rule criteria to a particular post on regular establishment, may be eligible for appointment on regular establishment subject to seniority and merits without reference to employment exchange provided that the person proposed to be taken upon regular establishment have been in continuous employment since their recruitment through the employment exchange on the work charge establishment and that they are otherwise qualified suitable to hold the regular establishment posts if vacant.

The cost of works establishment is clearly shown separately in the estimate at the prescribed percentage where applicable. The excess over such provision in the establishment need prior approval of Government.

A provision of 2 to 3 percent of estimated cost is made for work charge establishments and persons appointed are paid according to bills on prescribed proforma given below. Further these person appointed paid only on monthly basis for a period prescribed. Persons appointed on work charge establishment are also entitled for actual travelling allowance.

Pay bill of work charged establishment

No. of voucher Month of payment ....

Name of sub-division Name of section ....

Bill for the month .... 20 ....

Item No.	Name of person	Designation	Period	Rate	Amount due	Dated acknowledgement of payee	Dated initial of officer making payment

Certified that all the persons for whom wages have been drawn in this bill were on duty during the period shown against their names, each being employed on the work and on duties for which his appointment was sanctioned.

It is further certified that the wages of every person actually employed during the month have been claimed in this bill.

Pay ₹ .... (in words)

.... (in figures)

Checked and entered
S/d dated signature of
competent authority of
account sanction.

Sd. ....
dated signature of competent
authority

Remarks by Divisional (Higher) Officer if required any.

Sd. ....
Signature of higher competent authority
(if given some remark)

2.17 CONTINGENT ESTABLISHMENT

This term indicates the incidental expenses of a miscellaneous character which can not be appropriately be classified under any distinct sub-head or sub-work, yet pertains to the work as a whole. Provision of 3 percent to 5 percent of estimated cost of work is made to meet these expenses. Installation of watchmans temporary shed, purchase of electrical wire for power line at site, such expenditures can not be taken into detailed estimate and hence these expenses are met through contingencies.

2.18 PIECE WORK

In case of works having value less than ₹ 10,0000/- the petty contractors are invited to execute the job. Generally such works called petty works involved only a few items of identical nature. In this type of works only rates of items involved are fixed and contractor is asked to start the work. No written agreement bond is prepared and signed. No security money and penalty clauses are involved and no advance payment is made to the contractor. Such piece of works are generally carried out for urgent and small works. Here as there is no written agreement is signed the contract can be terminated at any time without giving any notice if contractor does not maintain the quality. The only drawback with this system is that good qualified and experienced contractors are not found to be interested and hence work is given to petty contractor having no experience or little experience and as such it becomes little difficult to execute works as per departmental procedure. The piece work agreement form used is as shown below:

Piece work agreement

Name of works .... Division ....

District .... Name of contractor ....

I hereby agree to execute the under-mentioned works by piece work and in accordance with the conditions noted below at a rate mentioned below in consideration of payment to be made by EE/SDO for the quantity of works executed actually.

Name of work	Number of item	Class and description of work to be executed	Unit of calculation	Rate of payment	Remark

Conditions:

1. ....
2. ....
3. ....

Date .... Signature of the contractor
Witness .... Name and Address
Accepted by me.
Date .... Signature of the EE/SDO
Division/Sub division

2.19 DAY WORKS

In civil engineering works; there are certain items and works; those are not included in schedule of rates; further these works can not be measured. Such works are executed by employing daily labour; generally skilled or semi-skilled on daily wages and payment is made on the basis of number of days worked. Such works are called *day works*. Under such conditions generally materials are supplied by the owner and labour employed to execute the work. The labour cost is usually very high to material cost. Following are the examples of such work:

1. Decorative works of all kinds.

2. Dressing of stones for this type of works now a days labours are not available hence are required to be brought from other places. These are paid very high rates.

3. Removal of tree roots during excavation.

The day work sheet is maintained as shown below. Labour employed and materials utilised are needed to be justified for out turns of works for that day.

Day work sheet

1. Name of the work ....
2. Name of owner/department ....
3. Name of engineer/Architect/departmental engineer (designation) ...
4. Particular of item for which day work is sanctioned ....
5. Date of sanction ....
6. Date of commencement of work ....

Materials consumed		Labour employed		Out-turn of work
Material	Quantity	Class	Number	

Date ....

Working time .... Signature of contractor

Person (competent) of work

This system of execution of work must be avoided as it is always expensive in nature. It needs close supervision.

2.20 DAILY LABOUR OR MUSTER ROLL SYSTEM

When the work is carried out by the department directly by employing the daily labour such as masons, builders, carpenters, coolies, blacksmiths, plumbers etc., it is known as *daily labour* or *muster roll system*. All the materials required for the construction are issued from stores or purchased directly chargeable to the concerned work.

Form part 1: Muster Roll of Daily Labour

Division .... District .... Name of work ....

Estimate to which chargeable .... Imprest holder's voucher No. ....

Gang Incharge ....

Part 1: Nominal Muster Roll

Sr. No.	Name of labour	Father's name	Designation	Days of month									Days worked	Rate of wages	Amount	Payees acknowledgment	To be filled in by the paying officer		
																	Actual paid	Dated initial	Amount unpaid
Daily total Daily initial Inspecting officer																			

Passed for ₹ .... (Rupees ....) Signature ...... Rank ....

Grand total of this muster roll ....

Deduct-Payments not made as per
details transferred to register arrears ....

Total amount paid in words Rupees ....

Date .... Signature .... Rank ....

The attendance of the labourers is maintained in a muster roll. The presence in muster roll of each labour should be marked by the proper officer at the starting hour of the day. Periodic inspections by higher authority are done to check the actual labourers working. On the basis of the muster roll the payment is made to the labourers, weekly, fortnightly, monthly or at the completion of work according to the requirement. The muster roll consists of two parts. In the first part names of workers, designation, date of attendance, rate of wages, total amount due to each worker, total amount of M.R., signature of persons taking the attendance, signature of the officer checking, making payment etc., are entered. In the second part details of quantities of work done and the progress of work are entered.

Part II: Details of measurements of work done by the labour employed as per this Nominal Muster Roll in cases in which the work is susceptible to measurements.

Description of work (Grouped sub-headwise)	Quantity	Deduct as shown on the last muster roll	Balance

Measurement taken on .... Date .... Signature .....
Measurement Book No. .... Page No. ..... Rank ....
Date ....

Details of measurements are taken and entered in the measurement book and abstract of quantities is prepared. M.B. page no. and reference is also shown on the M.R. where details of works are entered. The muster roll should never be made in duplicate and the entries are made in such a way that it is not possible to interpolate or alter them. Labourers may be paid after any period of interval but separate M.R. must be prepared for each period of payment.

When the muster roll is closed for payments the work done during the period are measured and entered in M.B. and it is completed by the J.E./S.O. showing the amount payable and the amount of work done. The completed muster roll is submitted to A.E./S.D.O./E.E. for payment. The amount of unpaid wages is usually drawn and paid on Hand Receipt when required. The maintenance and repair works of roads, canals, etc., are usally done by gangs on daily wages basis.

Muster Roll (M.R.) form as used in the department is given.

Daily Labour Report: When large work or group of works are done through daily labour, a consolidated daily labour report showing the number of labourers employed is prepared by Junior Engineer/Section officer from the M.R. in the following prescribed form, and is submitted daily to the A.E./S.D.O./E.E. for control and check. Duplicate copy of the D.L.R. is kept by the person who prepares it.

Daily Labour Report

Daily report of the day .... of ....

Name of work	Class of labour	No. of each class	Rate	Approx. quantity of work done	Remarks

Date ....

Signature ....

As soon as the muster roll is received in the A.E./S.D.O./E.E. office for payment, it is compared with the dialy labour report and if any discrepancies are found necessary actions are taken.

Example. What objection, if any, would you raise on the following Muster Roll?

Name of Work-Providing Office furniture.

Name	Father's name	Date (Month September)						Total days	Rate
		26	27	28	29	30	31		
1. Ramu	Nand	–	–	P	P	P	P	4	3
2. Shekhar	Ramu	–	P	P	P	P	P	5	3
3. Krishna	Raja	P	P	P	P	P	P	6	3
4. Harbans	Raja	P	P	P	P	P	P	6	3
5. Sohan	Mohan	–	–	P	P	P	P	4	4
6. Mohan	Ramlal	–	P	P	P	P	P	5	4
7. Shekhar	Ramu	–	P	P	P	P	P	5	3
8. Krishna	Raja	P	P	P	P	P	P	6	3

Passed for ₹ 192 only. Work not susceptible of measurement.

Sd/AB SDO

Following observations are made on this Muster Roll:

(*i*) The muster roll is not prepared from facts as a record of original entry. If it had been prepared from facts as and when they occurred, then the name of labourers should have appeared in the order of their employment. Persons at serials no. 3, 4 and 8 joined first, then came persons at serial no. 2, 6 and 7 and last of all came persons at serial no. 1 and 5. The muster roll is prepared from memory and is unreliable.

(*ii*) Total number of workers present on each day has not been worked out, leaving scope for subsequent insertion of names and any interpolations. Nor has any responsible Inspecting Officer checked the daily attendance. Even the signatures of the official marking their attendance are not there.

(*iii*) Column No. 6 for working out the amount is missing In fact the total works out to ₹ 132 (12 + 15 + 18 + 18 + 16 + 20 + 15 + 18) and not ₹ 192 for which it has been passed.

(*iv*) The work should have been measured and it should have been ensured that the value of work done is commensurate with the actual expenditure. It is wrong to say that the work of providing furniture is not susceptible of measurement.

(*v*) Shekhar, son of Ramu, and Krishan, son of Raja, have been taken on the roll twice. This would result in double payment. This would confirm the objection at serial no. (*i*) also.

(*vi*) September has only 30 days but attendance has been marked for the 31st. of September also. This clearly shows that the muster roll is not genuine.

Example. It is said that a Muster Roll represents the point of contract between the facts and accounts. Please illustrate.

Ans. A Muster Roll in the Public Work Department serves a dual purpose: namely, exhibiting facts and also financial transaction. It is a factual record of the employment of labourers on a work executed departmentally, their attendance and absence and fines, etc., inflicted on them. These facts are recorded in part 1 of the muster roll. The progress of work done by the labour (in all cases, where such work is susceptible of measurement is recorded in Part II thereof).

All these facts facilitate the correct calculation of the net wages of each person for the period of payment, and it is herein that a close contact between facts and accounts begins to develop. After the wages based on the above facts are calculated, the muster roll is passed for payment by the competent authority. Acknowledgement, duly stamped where necessary, is obtained from each payee on the muster roll itself. The Muster roll, after payment, constitutes an accounts document and is posted as paid voucher in the Cash Book, establishing thereby a close contact between facts and accounts.

Example. Will you pass the following Muster Roll? If not, what objections would you raise?

Muster Roll For February 2005

Name	Father's name	Date						Total days	Rate
		24	25	26	27	28	29		
1. Lala	Pyare	A	P	P	P	P	P	5	7
2. Prem	Ohri	P	P			P		6	7
			~~A~~	P	P	~~A~~	P	~~5~~	
3. Ganga	Ramu	P						5	7
		~~A~~	P	P	A	P	P	4	
4. Sohan	Ramdhar	A	P	P	P	P	P	5	6
5. Mohan	Shiama	P	P	P	P	P	P	6	7
Total		3	5			5			
		~~2~~	4	5	4	~~4~~	5		

Passed for ₹ 184 only. Work not susceptible of measurement. Sd/SDO

Ans. 9. The Muster Roll cannot be passed as it contains the following errors and omissions.

(*i*) Names of Prem and Ganga appear later than Lala, although they are shown to have been employed from 24th February that is earlier than Lala. Similarly Mohan who was employed earlier than Sohan has been entered in the Muster Roll later than Sohan. This confirms that attendance was marked at some rough sheets and the Muster Roll presented is not the original record.

(*ii*) Prem was marked absent on 25th and 28th and Ganga was marked absent on 24th. This absence has been changed into presence, obviously after the end of the entire week as the total number of days for which they worked has also been changed to 6 and 5 respectively. The daily total of attendance has also been tampered with, which is a fraud on the Government.

(*iii*) As February 2005 has only 28 days the entire Muster Roll seems to be bogus.

(*iv*) Initials of the persons who marked the attendance daily are missing. There is also no evidence that the Muster Roll was signed and checked daily by the Section Officer in Charge.

(*v*) The amount payable to each worker has not been shown in the Muster Roll.

(*vi*) The nature of work got done is not recorded and it is not possible to check whether the work is really not susceptible of measurement.

2.21 TERMS COMMONLY USED IN PWD

Introduction to special terminology. In each professional department, there are specific terms carrying a specific meaning in the context of that organisation. It would be worthwhile to be introduced to them at this stage itself.

I. TERMS IN RELATION TO CONTROL PROCEDURES

1. Estimate (of cost of Work). Estimate of cost of a work is prepared at two stages. One is for the purpose of obtaining approval from the authority administratively controlling the work. That is called preliminary estimate. The second one is detailed estimate and is prepared by PWD after obtaining administrative approval and after getting detailed designs from Architect.

2. Preliminary Estimate. Before taking up new construction work or repairs or additions and improvements of existing works, a preliminary estimate is prepared by PWD for consideration of the work requisitioning authority (*i.e.*, authority having administrative control of the work) before approval of the work is given by that administrative authority. Preliminary estimate is prepared on the basis of plinth area of the building or length of the road at the rate per unit adopted for rough and ready calculations to give an idea of the approximate cost involved in the proposal.

3. Administrative Approval. Administrative Approval is the formal acceptance by the Work-requisitioning Authority of the proposal contained in the preliminary estimate submitted by PWD. During execution of the work, material deviations from the original proposal should not be made by PWD without the sanction of the authority, which accorded the Administrative approval of the work (even if the cost of the deviations is covered by savings from other items of the work). The authorised PWD officers may allow excess upto 10% of the amount administratively approved. If the revised cost exceeds that amount, revised administrative approval is still not necessary if excess expenditure is covered by the expenditure sanction already given by that administrative department. If none of these conditions is met, a revised Administrative approval may be obtained from the administrative authority competent to approve the revised cost.

4. Detailed Estimate. Detailed Estimate of cost of a work is prepared by PWD on an assurance from the sponsoring department/authority that the site is available, and after receiving (*i*) The approval and expenditure sanction of the administrative department and (*ii*)detailed drawings of the work from the Architect. It consists of two parts, namely-

Part I. Report, and

Part II. Details of Measurements.

The Report part explains reasons leading up to the proposal, and its scope and purpose. It is prepared in simple and direct language understandable by non-technical officers of the administrative department concerned. Part II of the estimate contains calculations of the Quantities of each item of work based on the design. It indicates also the Rates per unit and Cost of each item of work. At the end, it lists various items of work in the form of an Abstract of Cost.

In the case of large projects consisting of several works, the Report can be a single document, but the cost component of the estimate can be separate for each sub-work of the project.

5. Expenditure Sanction. Besides an administrative approval, Administrative Department has also to issue Expenditure Sanction as usual. Expenditure sanction is a signal to PWD that funds for the project have been provided and that liability can be incurred. For minor works (*i.e.*, those costing less than ₹ one lakh), no expenditure sanction is needed as the order of appropriation and re-appropriation of funds itself operates as a sanction.

6. Technical Sanction. After receiving expenditure sanction and administrative approval, the PWD prepares detailed estimates of the work for obtaining Technical Sanction of authorised technical officer of PWD. It is an indication of the guarantee of PWD that the proposals are structurally sound, and that the estimates are accurately calculated and based on adequate data. The technical authority sanctioning the estimate has to ensure that the design and specifications are rich enough to provide the desired life to the work. *No work can be taken up by PWD unless the competent authority has given technical sanction for it.*

7. Works Contingencies. The estimate of cost of work based on schedule of quantities and Schedule of rates is comprehensive enough but still during execution of the work there may arise unforeseen items of work. To meet the cost of such unforeseen items of work, a lump sum provision at 3% to 5% of the total cost is made under the sub-head "Works Contingencies". Cost of workcharged establishment employed for the work is also to be met from this lump sum provision made under "*Works Contingencies*".

8. Contract. When two or more persons have common intention communicated to each other to create some obligation between them, there is said to be an agreement. An agreement, which is enforceable by law, is called a *Contract*. Under the Indian Contract Act, only those contracts are enforceable by law which:

(*i*) have not been *declared* by law *as void*,

(*ii*) are made by *free consent* of the *parties competent to contract*,

(*iii*) are made for a *lawful consideration* and a *lawful object*.

PWD, when it makes known its intention to get a work done through contractors, and floats tenders for it, Contractors offer their rates chargeable for it. It is for PWD to accept one of the offers and close the contract. *Communication of acceptance completes the contract*.

9. Notice Inviting Tender (NIT). Whenever a work is to be got done or supply obtained through contractor, the Department calls for tenders from the prospective contractors. For this purpose, a document known as N.I.T. is prepared. Some of the requirements to be included in the NIT are the following:

(1) Detailed Estimate of work.

(2) The Schedule of quantities of work.

(3) The set of Drawings referred to in the Schedule of Quantities of work.

(4) Specifications adopted for each item of work.

(5) Reasonable time in which the work is to be completed. (Remember "*Time is the essence of the contract*")

The NIT is prepared in standard approved form and it is serially numbered. Units used in NIT should be very specific; "*per hundred square metre*" should be preferred to "%Sq. Mt.".

The NIT and its documents as issued to each tenderer should be clear, legible and unambiguous as agreement with contractors is based on it. Each page of NIT should be serially numbered and all corrections made in it should be authenticated.

II. TERMS IN RELATION TO WORKS

1. Original Works. Original Works means new construction including additions and alterations to existing works. This terms also covers special repairs to newly acquired or previously abandoned works.

2. Repairs. The term Repair means operations undertaken to maintain buildings and works in proper condition. Repairs can be classified further as "*Annual Repair*" and "*Special Repair*".

Annual Repair covers those works, which are carried out *annually like white washing, colour washing, distempering.*

Special repair consist of works like plastering, replacement of doors and windows, flooring etc., which are not to be done yearly, but are required to be done as and when the necessity arises.

3. Petty Works. Works of minor additions and alterations to residential and non-residential buildings and to Roads etc., upto the limit prescribed in Financial Rules (say, ₹ 10,000) may be classified by the Superintending Engineer as "*Petty Works*" expenditure and debited to Repairs.

4. Major works. Major Work means a work the sanctioned cost of which is more than Rupees one lakh. The Estimate of cost of such a work is also called "*Major Estimate*".

5. Minor Works. Minor work is a work the sanctioned cost of which is Rupees one lakh or less. The estimate of cost of such a work is called "*Minor Estimate*".

6. Deposit Works. The term "*Deposit Works*" is applied to works of construction or repair, the cost of which is not met out of Government Funds. Works executed for Municipalities Port Trusts and other Public Bodies fall in this category. These bodies are required to deposit in advance the estimated cost of the work including Departmental Charges leviable by PWD. This deposit can be realized in instalments on fixed dates if Government is satisfied that money will be forthcoming when needed for expenditure. In the case of Municipalities or Public Bodies the cost of such works can be debited direct to their account in Treasuries.

7. Schedule of Rates. In each Division, a Schedule of Rates for each kind of work commonly executed is maintained up-to-date to facilitate the preparation of estimate and also as a guide to settle rates in connection with contract agreements. The Schedule of Rates is prepared on the basis of the rates prevailing in each Station. For this purpose, necessary analysis of the rates for each description of work and for the varying conditions thereof should also be recorded. These Rates are revised at least once in two years. The rates entered in the estimates should generally agree with the corresponding rate in the Division's Schedule of Rates. If any deviation is considered necessary, the reason therefore should be explained in the estimate.

8. Material Account. Materials are issued from the stores of a PWD Division *to contractors* or *to the work direct* as under:

(*i*) *To contractors* for use on the work, being done by them on basis of completed items of work, *i.e.*, for which they have quoted *at Finished Rates* (rates for labour including materials). In such a case the Division recovers the value of materials issued to contractors at rates fixed as per the provisions of the agreement with them. The Division can supply (against unstamped but dated acknowledgement of the contractor) only those materials, which it is required to supply as per the agreement with contractor. Any other material can be supplied, if available in the Division, only after approval of the Superintending Engineer who will also fix the rate at which it is to be issued.

(*ii*) *Direct to work* when the work is being done departmentally ; or by contractors whose agreements are for labour rates only.

Material at Site Account, in these cases, is a numerical account of the items of materials issued for use on a work, which is under departmental execution (or where the contractor is working at labour rates only). It supports the transactions taken under the head "*Materials*" in the Works Accounts. This account shows the progressive quantity of each item of materials brought at site for use on the Work. Hence it acts as a check on the total quantity of each material issued/obtained for the work, which ought to be restricted to the estimated requirements.

9. Dismantled Material Account. Materials obtained from dismantlement of a building or structure is recorded in the measurement Book for record purpose, *without value*. On the basis of these measurements, these are taken in the *Register of Dismantled Materials*. After making the entries in this Register, and their attestation by the Engineer in charge of the work, the measurement book entries are crossed by a diagonal red ink line with a suitable note that these materials have been entered in the Register.

10. Departmental Charges. Departmental Charges denote percentage charges levied on works undertaken by PWD on behalf of other Governments, Commercial Departments of the same Government, and local bodies and private parties. These are levied on a percentage basis and are intended to recover the cost incurred by PWD on Establishment (its salaries, pensions and Leave salaries etc.), on Tools and Plant, and on Audit and Accounts.

(However, from 27-9-2001, no departmental charges are levied on works undertaken by CPWD on behalf of autonomous bodies funded entirely by the Central Government.)

11. Percentage-Rate Tender. When tender is issued calling for rates for work to be done at a percentage higher or lower than the rates applied in the Estimate of work (*based on the prescribed rate in the Divisional Schedule of Rates or the District/State* PWD *Schedule of Rates*), then such a tender a called *Percentage Rate Tender*. This form of tender is used mainly for works of standard design such as Levelling and Development works including storm water drainage, sewer lines, and repetitive type of works like residential quarters of various types as per standard design/drawing.

12. Item-Rate Tender. When PWD floats Item Rate Tender, then the contractors are required to quote their rates for each item of work on the basis of schedule of quantities furnished by the department. This form ensures from the contractor a more detailed analysis of cost, as he works out the rate against each item himself.

13. Work Order. This is a kind of allotment of work to a contractor for execution instead of entering into an agreement with him. It is used for works costing ₹ six lakhs and below. There are two forms of Work Orders. One is that in which the work awarded may be stopped by the Engineer in-charge at any time, and conversely the contractor is also entitled to stop the work at any time. The second form binds the contractor in respect of quantity of work and time in which it is to be completed.

14. Lump-sum Contract. This form of contract is used for works in which the contractors are required to quote a lump-sum figure for completing the work in accordance with the given design, drawings and specifications and functional requirements. (Lump-sum contract may require the contractor to do design work and prepare structural drawings as well as subject to approval by the competent authority before hand. Essential characteristics of Lump-sum contract are as under:

(1) A Schedule of Rates should be specified to regulate the charges on account of additions and alterations not covered by the lump sum.

(2) Payments for work in progress are to be made to the contractor only on the certificates of the Officer in charge of the work that (*i*) value of the work done is not less than the amount being paid, (*ii*) work done is in conformity with the contract and (*iii*) it has been done in accordance with the designs and specifications. Such payments including payment for measured up Additions and Alterations are treated as Advance Payment.

(3) Final Payment is made only after Divisional Officer certifies completion of the work according to the prescribed specifications and Drawings.

15. Earnest Money Deposits (EMD) or Bid Security. Earnest Money is the amount of money that a tenderer deposits along with his tender to assure the Government that he is earnest in executing the work at the rates tendered. (*Financial Rules call it Bid Security*). This safeguards against withdrawal or alteration of his bid during bid validity period. In case he fails to commence the work awarded to him, the Earnest Money is absolutely forfeited to the President/Governor. If only a part of the work shown in the tender is awarded and the contractor does not commence the work, then the amount of Earnest Money to be forfeited to Government is worked out with reference to the estimated cost of the work awarded.

Earnest Money of all tenderers, except the lowest tenderer or the one whose tender is accepted, is refunded/returned.

16. Security Deposits. When work is allotted to a contractor, he is required to deposit 5% of the amount of the tendered value of the work as Performance Deposit/Security to ensure due performance of the contract. In addition to these two deposits, Security Deposits at the rate of 10% of the value of *work done and measured* is recoverable from each Running Account Bill of the contractor *till the amount so deducted along with the amount of Earnest Money Deposit already received with the tender/bid equals* 5% *of the Tendered Value of the work or a maximum of* ₹ 5 *lakhs*. This is a security for satisfactory completion of the work or supply as per agreement. This also safeguards that Government property handed over to contractor is received back on the completion of the work.

III. TERMS IN RELATION TO PAYMENT PROCEDURES

1. On Account Payment. A contractor is to be paid for work done after its verification and measurement. Any payment made to contractor *on the basis of work actually done and measured is called ON ACCOUNT PAYMENT*. Such a payment made at one stage only, after the work has been completed to the entire satisfaction of the Engineer-in-charge, is called ***FIRST AND FINAL PAYMENT.***

But if the work is large and takes a long time to finish, the contractor can be paid at regular intervals to make available to him funds to pay for his labour and to meet other liabilities. In that case, the work done by the contractor is measured at intermediate stages and payment is made for it on a running account basis. Such periodical payments are called ***RUNNING ACCOUNT PAYMENTS.*** A series of on account payments are also, thus, Running Account Payments, except the last one which is called ***LAST*** (*i.e.*, 8TH Or 9TH etc.) and ***FINAL PAYMENT.***

2. Advance Payment to Contractors. This advance is paid, in exceptional cases where it is absolutely essential to do so, with the sanction of the Superintending Engineer for the *work actually executed but not yet measured* on account of certain unavoidable reasons. The SDO in charge has to certify that work, not less than the quantity of work shown for Advance Payment, has actually been done. The amount paid as advance under this rule is recovered from the next "*On Account Bill*" in which payment is made in respect of the items of work for which 'advance payment' had been made. This Advance Payment is not treated as *final charge* in the account of the work *but only as a recoverable suspense transaction.* Grant of 2nd advance is not permitted before the 1st one has been recovered.

3. Secured Advances to Contractors. Secured Advance is an Advance given to a contractor on the security of materials brought by him to the site of work in cases where the contract is for Completed Items of Work (at Finished Rate, *i.e., tender is for labour and materials both*). The Divisional Officer can sanction secured Advance subject to the following conditions:

(1) The amount of advance does not exceed 75% of the value of materials brought to site by the contractor.

(2) The materials are of an imperishable nature and a formal agreement is drawn up with the contractor which gives Government a lien on the materials and safeguards its interest against losses or misuse.

(3) Expenses for the watch and ward of the materials shall be borne by the contractor.

(4) SDO in charge should certify that materials have actually been brought to site, that no secured advance had been paid on them previously, and that materials are required for use by the contractor on work being executed by him on finished rates.

Recoveries of this advance are made progressively from contractor's "*On Account Bill*" to the extent the materials are consumed on the work done and measured. Secured Advance paid is posted in the accounts as suspense transaction awaiting recovery.

4. Running Account Bill. In cases where a contractor is to be paid at periodic intervals for the part of the work done till then, as per specifications, the payments is called a *Running Payments*. The bills on which these payments are made are called *Running Account Bills*. Thus when (*i*) periodic On Account Payments, (*ii*) Advance Payments (*iii*) Secured Advances are paid to the contractor, it will be obvious that the system of Running Payments is in force and such payments will be made on Running Account Bills. In the System of making First and Final Payment, there is no scope for grant of Advance Payments or Secured Advances or Payment for a part of the work done (while the remaining work is still to be done).

5. Measurement Book. Measurement Book (in form 23) generally serves as a record of all payments for work done and all payments for materials obtained for works from the suppliers, other Divisions, or from other works etc. As the measurement Books constitutes the most important initial record of Works Accounts, all the Books relating to a Division are numbered serially and a control Register of them is kept in the Division (in Form 92). It is through this Register that the return of each Measurement Book to the Division, after it has been written up, is watched. There are two kinds of Measurement Books—namely, Detailed Measurement Books and Standard Measurement Books.

6. Standard Measurement Book. Standard Measurement Books are standard measurements (of already completed) Buildings and other such works, and can be used repeatedly for works relating to those Building such as for whitewashing, polishing or painting the doors and windows; as the area of walls, floors, doors and windows etc., doesn't change after the Building had been completed and entered in the Standard Measurement Book. A responsible Officer certifies the accuracy of Standard Measurement Books. These are used for preparing periodical repair estimates too. These books make the work of preparation of contractor's bill easier as the measurements are standard and there is no necessity to taking detailed measurements again and again.

7. Detailed Measurement Books. These Books constitute the most important and basic record of the Public Works Department. The initial accounts of all works executed by the contractors and of the materials obtained for works are kept in Detailed Measurement Books. All payments to the contractors or suppliers are made on the basis of entries in these Books. The importance of Detailed Measurement Book cannot be over-emphasised.

Precautions to be taken in writing Detailed Measurement Books

(1) All measurements should be taken neatly and directly on Measurement Books in Form 23 at the site of work (and not copied in them from some other record).

(2). Measurements are to be recorded by the authorised Officer in charge of the work to whom the Measurement Book has been supplied.

(3). Each set of measurements should start with entries stating (*i*) full name of the work as given in the estimate, (*ii*) situation of the work, (*iii*) name of the contractor, (*iv*) Number and date of the agreement, (*v*) date of written orders to commence work, (*vi*) due date of completion of work and (*vii*) date of actual commencement.

(4) For measurements relating to a running account, reference to the previous set of measurements is always to be recorded.

(5) All entries will be in ink only, never with pencil or linked over.

(6) No entry should be erased. If a mistake is made, it should be scored out and corrected by inserting entry in red ink.

(7) When a measurement is cancelled, the orders of the officer cancelling it should be recorded on it over dated initials of the Officer who had taken the measurements originally,

giving reason for cancellation. Better if the cancellation bears the initials of the Officer who ordered cancellation.

(8) Pages of MB should be Machine numbered. Entries should be made continuously, leaving no space or page blank. Diagonal lines bearing dated initials of the Officer taking the measurements should cancel a page left blank inadvertently.

8. Mobilisation Advance. In respect of certain specialised and capital-intensive works costing not less than ₹ 2 crores, Mobilisation Advance (as interest bearing loan) may be sanctioned to the contractors as per terms of his agreement. These loans are granted against a Bank Guarantee of a Scheduled Bank for the full amount of the advance. The advance is released in not less than two instalments.

9. Advance Payment for purchase of Stores. Officers of PWD are authorised to make advance payments up to 90% to the firms for the supply of stores on the following conditions:

(1) Sanctioning officer can exercise power only up to the limit of his power to accept tenders.

(2) Payments will be made only against Stores Despatch Documents after stores had been pre-inspected.

(3) Advance will be granted against a Bank Guarantee of an equivalent amount of a Scheduled Bank, that too only when the supplier pays transit insurance.

10. Bill Register. A consolidated record of all bills received from Sub-Divisional Officers to make payment (for work done or supplies received) is kept in a Bill Register in the Divisional Office. The bills are entered in it strictly in the order of their receipt. In no case should a bill received later be given priority over the one received earlier, except with the *written* orders of the Divisional Officer. The Divisional Accountant is responsible for maintaining this register properly and up-to-date. This register is put up to the Divisional Officer weekly to record where his instructions have not been followed.

2.22 LIST OF MAJOR & MINOR HEADS

1. Government Account. Government is not run for profit. Its object is to administer, to keep law and order and to render social and economic services. (This is, generally speaking, *service expenditure*). In the process of administration, it may acquire or construct assets of a lasting nature or permanent character (that is called *Capital Expenditure*). Some times Government has to obtain loans etc., (called *Public Debt*). It may also give loans for development of country's economy and social life (which is called *Loans and Advances*). These all are parts of Consolidated Fund.

Besides, other money may also come in the hands of the Government, which is to be paid back to the parties concerned in accordance with the rules (like earnest money, general provident fund, deposits etc. etc.). Reciprocally Government may also have to deposit money with other parties or Governments, which is to be received back on the satisfaction of certain terms. All these transactions are called **Public Account.**

2. Parts of Government Account. Government account is kept in three parts, namely, *Part I. Consolidated Fund; Part II. Contingency Fund; and Part III. Public account.*

3. Part I. Consolidated Fund. Expenditure from Consolidated Fund can be incurred only after vote of Legislature has been obtained either through annual Budget or through vote on account or supplementary grant. The Consolidated Fund comprises two divisions, namely, *Revenue Division* and *Capital Division.*

1. Revenue Division. For receipts and payments relating to Taxation, General services, Social services and Economic services.

2. Capital Divisions. Further comprising three distinct sections

(*i*) Capital Receipts and Capital Expenditure,

(*ii*) Public debt and

(*iii*) Loans and Advances.

4. Part II. Contingency Fund. This part has Revenue Division and Capital division just as under Consolidated Fund (Para 2 above). The only difference is that this Part II accommodates temporarily the payments made before Government is able to obtain vote of legislature for the same.

5. Part III. Public Account. This part of the Government account has the following further sub-divisions:

(*a*) *Debt (other than included in Part I),*

(*b*) *Deposits,*

(*c*) *Advances,*

(*d*) *Suspense, and*

(*e*) *Remittances.*

The Debt Division here covers money coming in the hands of Government from sources other than Internal debt or External debt. Examples are Provident Fund, Post Office Deposits and Savings Certificates etc. etc. In all these cases, Government has a liability to repay the moneys received, and has the claim to recover the amounts paid.

6. Sectors and Sub-sectors. Each division is again divided into sectors and sub-sectors like (1) A. General Services, (2) B. Social services, and (3) C. Economic Services etc.

7. Major heads and Minor heads. Under each sector Government has a Function to perform. Each of the prescribed major heads represents one such function. Minor heads under the Major heads identify the programmes taken up to achieve the objectives of the concerned Function (*i.e.*, Major head). Sub-heads below the minor heads represent the schemes or activities undertaken for the programme. A detailed head below the sub-head indicates the nature of inputs and is called the ***Object Classification.***

8. Nomenclature and Coding. This kind of classification is called ***"Functional Classification"***. The coding of the various heads of accounts is as under:

	Codes No.
Part I Consolidated Fund	
(*i*) *Revenue Division*	
Receipt heads (Revenue Account)	0001 to 1999
Expenditure heads (Revenue Account)	2000 to 3999
(*ii*) *Capital Division*	
Receipt heads (Capital Account)	4000
Expenditure heads (Capital Account)	4001 to 5999
(*iii*) *Public Debt, Loans and Advances*	6001 to 7999
Part II Contingency Fund	8000
Part III Public Account	8001 to 8999

(Paras 5.2.2 to 5.2.5 of C.P.W. Code)

9. Heads of accounts in P.W.D. In the P.W.D., the Major heads of account generally operated are the following:

Group I (for buildings)

0059 *Public Works*	(For revenue receipts)
2059 *Public Works*	(For revenue expenditure)
4059 *Capital Outlay on Public Works*	(For Capital expenditure)

Group II (for Roads)

1054 *Roads and Bridges* (For revenue receipts)

3054 *Roads and Bridges* (For revenue expenditure)

5054 *Capital Outlay on Roads and Bridges* (For Capital expenditure)

Group III (For Functional Buildings generally.) See para 2.10

All Major heads under Sector B. Social Services and C. Economic Services

Group IV (For Irrigation)

0701
2701
4701 — These three major heads are for Major and Minor Irrigation.

0702
2702
4702 — These three major heads are for Minor Irrigation

Group V (for Water Supply and Sanitation)

0215, 2215 and 4215 are Major heads for water supply and sanitation.

10. Classification of Expenditure on Buildings. You can justifiably ask what the difference is between the buildings of Group I and Group III in para 2.9 above. For this read Note 1 below the Major head 2059 Public Works in the List of Major and Minor Head of Accounts. This has been explained in paras 2.11 and 2.12 below but, before that, remember that Buildings can be *Residential* or *Non-residential*, and expenditure can be of the nature of *Construction* or *Maintenance*.

11. Residential Buildings

(1) *Construction.* If a residential building is part of a project, such as Hospital, College, Dam, etc., the cost of construction of such buildings will be treated as part of the cost of that Hospital, College, or Dam. Cost of construction of residential buildings for general allotment to Government staff is debitable to the Major Head "*4216 Capital Outlay as Housing*". (If it is a minor job of construction, it can be debited to "*2216 Housing*").

(2) *Repairs.* Cost of maintenance of the residential buildings forming part of a project is debited to the maintenance cost of the

project concerned. Cost of maintenance of other residential buildings is debited to *"2216 Housing"*.

12. Non-Residential Buildings. Non-Residential (N.R.) buildings again are of two kinds, namely *Functional* and *Non-Functional.*

Functional (N.R.) buildings are buildings like Schools, Colleges, Hospitals, Jails, Health Centres, High Courts, Rest Houses, Circuit Houses, Police Stations, Archives, Museums, Doordarshan Kendras. Their **Accounting Principle is that Construction** expenditure of functional (NR) buildings of *Sector* B Social Services and *Sector C* Economic Services would be debited to the major head of the department concerned. Construction expenditure of functional (NR) buildings of *Sector A* General Services would be debited *"2059/4059 Public Works"*.

Non-Functional Non-residential buildings are generally Office Buildings. Their **Accounting Principle** is as under:

Construction expenditure of all Non-functional Buildings would be debited *"2059/4059 Public Works"*.

Maintenance expenditure on all Non-residential buildings would be debited to *"2059 Public Works"* (See note 4 below this Major Head in the list of Major & Minor Heads of Accounts).

13. Summing Up

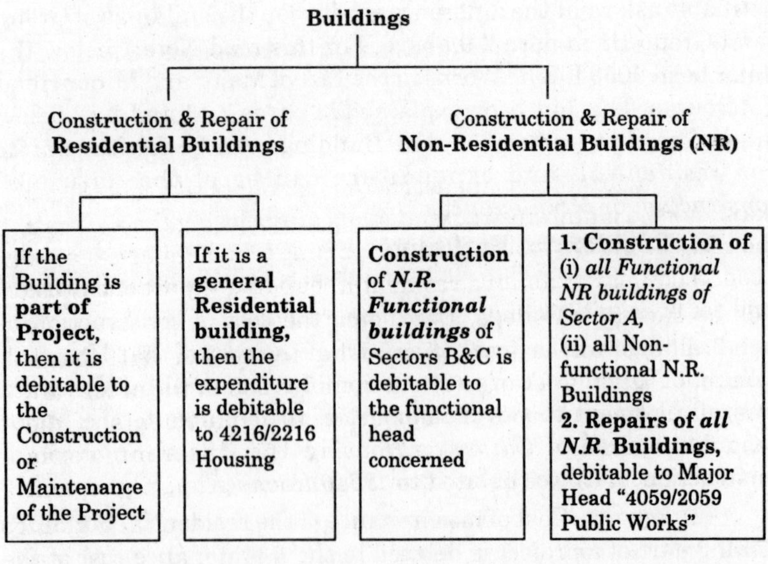

3

P.W.D. SYSTEM OF ACCOUNTS

3.1 SYSTEM OF ACCOUNTS

System of accounts is the procedure to be adopted by any organisation which receives and distributes money *i.e.*, is involved in cash transaction.

The essential requirements of the system are:

1. Day-to-Day transaction should be serially numbered and dated.

2. Each receipt of money should be recorded alongwith the source from which received.

3. Each payment should be supported by a payment voucher wherein the payment is authorised. It should be supported by the receipt of the payee.

4. Receipts and issues should not be mixed up but maintained separately.

5. Receipts and issues should have separates column for cash and cheque transactions.

6. To facilitate continuous check of accounts two sets of cash books should be maintained so that when after closing the accounts of the month, the cash book and supporting vouchers are sent to the concerned accounts authority for check and verification, the second set of cash book should be in operation.

7. The bank balance should be reconciled with bank statements. Although there is slight modification in the procedure or system of keeping accounts in different departments of the Government with slight variations in the different works department themselves the financial regulations primarily remain

the same. The main system of Accounting followed in the country are given below:

(*a*) **Civil Accounting System.** Under this system:—

(*i*) All receipts are deposited into the Treasury on which the station is based.

(*ii*) All money required for distribution/payment is drawn from the Treasury on presentation of bills.

(*iii*) Monthly return giving abstract of transaction is submitted to the Accountant General by the Treasury.

(*b*) **P.W.D. Accounting system.** Under this system the Government intimates the Accountant General the names of the drawing and disbursing officers and the head of the Department namely the Chief Engineer intimates the monthly limit of cash that can be placed at the disposal of the drawing and disbursing officers. The drawing and disbursing officer issues cheques for contractors payment or draws cash against the assignment. At the end of the month the drawing and disbursing officer submits the closed cash book alongwith all the connected vouchers to the Accountant General/Controller of Defence Accounts as the case may be.

The Accountant General carries a post audit of all such vouchers with respect to the entries and in the cash book and satisfies himself with respect to the following:

(*i*) Is the payment concerned against any administrative approval or other sanction.

(*ii*) Do funds exist for such a payment ?

(*iii*) In case of payment for works, has the work been technically sanctioned ?

(*iv*) Has there been an inordinate delay in the payment ?

It is very seldom that the Accountant General/CDA is satisfied in the first instance with such payments. The cash book and the vouchers are returned along with audit objections for reconciliation. This is the second check on the payments. The first check is the pre-audit carried out by the Divisional Accountant/ Unit Accountant prior to the payment.

The third check is carried out once a year. This is known as Test Audit. A team of auditors headed by the Accounts Officer visits the Division and carries out test audit of all the vouchers pertaining to any one month of the financial year for which test audit is being done. The test audit results in audit objections which have to be settled by the Government to the satisfaction of the AG/CDA. In the event of non-settlement of any audit objection at the level of the Head of the Department the matter is referred to the Public Accounts Committee of the Government and at the same time disciplinary/departmental action against defaulter is initiated.

(*c*) **Fresh Account System.** The system is similar to the P.W.D. system of accounting with slight variation to suit the departmental condition.

3.2 PWD SYSTEM OF ACCOUNTS

This has been briefly dealt within Art. 2.10 also.

3.3 CLASSIFICATIONS BASED ON CPWA CODE

System of accounts. PWD has a special system of accounts based on costing as explained below:

(*i*) The cost of each Work is worked out in the PWD account.

(*ii*) Each Division generally keeps a central Stores for issue of material for use on works as and when needed.

(*iii*) For materials purchased for Stores or Works, there is an inbuilt system in the PWD Accounts to watch payment of unpaid bills of suppliers.

(*iv*) Articles of Machinery and Equipment (called *Tools and Plant*) are kept in the Division for use on works as and when needed.

We shall discuss these specialities one by one and their effect on classification before listing out further items.

Central Stores (and suspense account). Each Major Head *i.e.*, 2059, 2701, 3054, and corresponding Capital Heads of accounts have minor head "*Suspense*" under various Sub-major heads. Each PWD Division is authorised to operate only one Suspense minor head on the basis of the nature of work allotted to it. (*If the Question indicates nothing, you may take that the minor head suspense under sub-major head* ***General*** *is to be operated*).

Sub-heads of Suspense. Suspense Minor Head is further divided into sub-heads like (*i*) Stock, (*ii*) Miscellaneous Works advances and (*iii*) Work-shop Suspense.

Suspense-Stock. The cost of all Materials purchased or received for general use of PWD Division is debited to this sub-head. When the materials are issued to Works (or other Divisions, Departments, accounts or parties), then their value is credited to this head. Net account balance under Suspense head '*Stock*', thus represents the value of materials in hand. If materials have been received from a supplier but his bill has not yet been paid, then that will cause difference in the balance appearing in the accounts and the value of the physical balance of stock in hand. To avoid this difference, an adjustment is made for all unpaid bills of suppliers for purchase of stores. Para 2.23 explains it.

Note 1. There is distinction between purchase of stores for (*i*) Works and (*ii*) for stock purposes. The cost of stores purchased for a Work is debited to the accounts of that Work, **and the cost of stores purchased for stock purposes is debited to the Suspense Head Stock.**

Note 2. All shortages (or surpluses) noticed on Physical verification of stores are also taken as stores issued (or fresh receipt of stores) pending investigation. (Paras 7.2.35 (*b*) and 7.2.36 of CPWA Code)

Note 3. If materials are to be issued at a rate different from the Cost Price, that will also cause a difference between the value of physical balance left in hand and value balance in the accounts. This variation is called *Profit or Loss due to revision of rates.* (Para 7.2.34 of CPWA Code)

Stock Suspense of Irrigation Projects. In the Sub Major heads of Irrigation, the Suspense head appears at two places both as *Minor head* and also as a *Sub-head under each Project*. If a Division handles only one Project, then it will operate the Sub-head Suspense under the project concerned. If on the other hand, it handles more than one project, then the Division will operate the minor head Suspense.

Suspense-Miscellaneous Works Advance. This subhead of Suspense is used to watch some special kinds of recoveries such as

(*i*) Recoveries for sale of stores on credit by PWD

(*ii*) Recoveries for expenditure on non-Government works in excess of the amount of deposits received in advance.

(*iii*) Storage or Losses of Cash or Stores etc.

(*iv*) Municipal taxes paid by PWD on behalf of tenants pending recovery.

Debits (on account of Cash-Payments and issues of Stores) which cannot be classified to the final head of account immediately for want of some information or details are also kept temporarily under this head pending their correct classification.

Tools and Plant. This term includes machinery and equipment. Tools and plants are of two categories:

(*i*) *Those required specifically for a sanctioned work.* Their cost is debited to the work concerned.

(*ii*) *Those required for general use in the division.* Their cost is debited to the minor head "*Machinery and Equipment*".

Please note that Machinery and Equipment is not a suspense head.

Recoveries for Tools and Plants (T&P). Necessity for recoveries for tools and plant arises when

(*i*) when T&P is sold.

(*ii*) when T&P is lost and recovery is made from a defaulter.

(*iii*) when departmental charges are levied on Works done in a division for other Governments, Local funds, and for Private Parties.

Amounts received from sale of T&P and on account of recoveries for loss of T&P are to be credited to the work concerned if the relevant T&P was purchased specially for a work. Similar recoveries for Tools and Plant acquired for general use in the Division are taken to Revenue under the head "*0059 Public Works; Genl; Other Receipts*" (if M&E was purchased from Revenue Account) or 4059 Capital Outlay on Public works; Genl; Receipts and Recoveries on capital account (if M&E was purchased from Capital account). Para 2.3 and 4.3 General Directions in the List of major and Minor heads of Account.

Departmental charges levied under item (*iii*) above are creditable to revenue. [Appendix 2-Statement E-Para 4(*ii*) to CPWA Code]

Purchases for work or Store, not paid for. Suspense head for such purchases is 8658 Suspense accounts; Material Purchase Settlement Suspense account. This head is credited and work concerned or "*Suspense Stock*" is debited. When?

(*i*) *Supplies for Works.* Immediately on the day of receipt of Materials, if they were not paid for on the day of purchase.

(*ii*) *Supplies for Stock.* At the time of closing the monthly account of stock if payment has not been made by then.

Example. Materials for a work valuing ₹ 5,000 and for stock valuing ₹ 6,000 were purchased on 21st April. Payment was made on the 22nd April. How will the transaction be classified, if the monthly accounts of stores are closed on 26th?

(*a*) *Materials for the work.* As payment was not made on 21st April (the date of purchase), an account of ₹ 5,000 will be debited by transfer entry to the account of the work concerned and credited to the suspense head 8658 Suspense Accounts ; Material Purchase Settlement Suspense Account. Rupees. 5,000 paid on 22nd April will be debited to this suspense head 8658 Suspense Account ; Material Purchase Settlement Suspense Account.

(*b*) *Material for Stock.* No action on 21st April. The payment made on 22nd. April (*i.e.*, before the stock account closes on the 26th of month) will be debited to Suspense Stock direct.

Recoveries of Expenditure. All recoveries of expenditure and Overpayments are taken in reduction of expenditure, under the head of account or of work under which these payments were classified.

However, there are some special instructions for Recoveries of Establishment Charges and Tools and Plant Charges on the cost of works undertaken for Other Governments and private parties on percentage basis. These recoveries are credited to revenue major head of the division. For example, in the CPWD this head is 0059 Public Works; General; Recovery of percentage charges. (Note below Para 14.2.5 and Para 4 (*i*) and (*ii*) of Statement E in Appendix 2)

Inter-Divisional Transfers in State PWD.

1. Recoveries on behalf of other divisions. Receipts appearing in the account of one public works division which cannot be adjusted to the credit of final head of receipts of the division and which have to be necessarily passed on to another division, are credited to the head "*8443 Civil Deposits; Public Works deposits; Miscellaneous Deposits*". The amount will then be paid by cheque if both the divisions are at the same station, or by bank draft if they are located at different stations. The payment so made is debited to the same head "*8443 Civil Deposits; Public Works deposits; Miscellaneous Deposits*".

2. Payment on behalf of other PWD divisions. In State PWD divisions, the payment will be classified under the head, "*8658 Suspense Accounts; Cash Settlement Suspense Account*". A claim will be sent to other divisions concerned and receipt of cheque or bank draft from that division will be watched. The amount of cheque or bank draft (when received) is credited to "*8658 Suspense Accounts; Cash Settlement Suspense Account*".

Inter-Divisional Transfers in CPWD. In the CPWD divisions, all receipts and payments on behalf of the Central government are accounted for under the final head of account in the account of the division. If the final head of account is not known, it will be kept under the minor head "*Receipts Awaiting Transfer (RAT) to other heads*" (if it is a receipt), or Expenditure Awaiting Transfer to other Heads/Departments (if it is a payment). The final head will be determined from the concerned Departments within the financial year.

Inter-Departmental transfers from CPWD divisions have been done away with and therefore the operation of the head Cash Settlement Suspense Account has been abolished from 1/4/1993. The Controller General of Accounts has prescribed that for Inter Divisional Adjustments like Supplies of Stores by one CPWD Division to another CPWD Division and Work done by one CPWD Division for another, the serving division must receive payments in advance from the indenting division before work is done or supplies are made. The accounting is done as under:

Indenting Division. Advance paid for work to be done is accounted for under the work concerned. Advance paid for supply of stores or other services is accounted for under "*2059 Public Works, Suspense, Stores/Services Advance.*"

On receipt of "*Invoice-cum-bill*" from the serving division, the head operated at the time or giving advance is cleared by minus debit; the corresponding debit is given to work or stock as may be.

Serving Division. The amounts received in advance will be minus debited to "*2059 Public Works, Suspense, Stores/Service rendered*". When the stores have been supplied or work completed, an "*Invoice-cum-Bill*" will be issued to the Indenting Division. The minus debit to Suspense head will be cleared by debiting to it the value of stores issued (or value of work done). The settlement of account of advance mentioned in this subpara would be made in the same financial year. (Authority: CGA's Office Memo No. 18(4)/92 T.A./237 dt. 16th March, 1993).

Example. A C.P.W.D. Division 'X' requests in July 2004 another C.P.W.D. Division Y to supply to it stores needed by X Division urgently and raise the debit through the accounts. Y Division issued the stores so indented valued at ₹ 50,000. Was it correct for Y Division to do so?

No, it was not correct on the part of Y Division to do so. In the C.P.W.D. inter-divisional adjustment is not permissible. One C.P.W.D. Division (X in this case) has to pay in advance the values of stores indented by it from another division of C.P.W.D. (Y in this case). X Division should have obtained payment in advance before issuing the stores indented by Y Division.

C.P.W.D Division '*P*' needs Stores valued at ₹ 25,000 from another C.P.W.D. Division '*Q*'. What procedure is to be followed if the stores are to be supplied by *Q* Division? The stores actually supplied valued ₹ 24,000.

P Division will obtain a proforma invoice from *Q* Division for supply of stores. After the receipt of invoice, the price of Stores as per proforma invoice (₹ 25,000) would be paid by *P* Division to *Q* Division.

Classification of advance in P Division. If the stores are indented for a work, the advance of ₹ 25,000 when paid would be debited to the account of the work concerned. If the stores are indented for general stock purposes, the amount paid (₹ 25,000) would be classified under the head "*2059 Public Works, Suspense, Stores/Service advance*".

Classification of receipt of ₹ 25,000 in Q Division. The receipt of advance of ₹ 25,0000 in *Q* Division would be classified under the head "*2059 Public Works, Suspense, Stores/Service rendered*". After the stores valuing ₹ 24,000 are issued by *Q* Division, it will debit the amount of ₹ 24,000 to the head "*2059 Public Works, Suspense, Stores / Service rendered*" by credit to its Stock a/c. *Q* Division will also issue an Invoice cum Bill for ₹ 24,000 to *P* Division. *Q* Division would return unspent balanced of ₹ 1000 to *P* Division. *Q* Division will also debit this repayment to the head "*2059 Public Works, Suspense, Stores / Service rendered*".

(*iii*) *On Receipt of Stores in P Division.* The value of stores as indicated in the Invoice cum Bill of *Q* Division, *i.e.*, ₹ 24,000 would be debited by it to the head of account of work concerned or stock (for which the stores were indented) by credit to the head of account from which the advance of ₹ 25,000 was paid vide para (*i*) above. The amount of ₹ 1000 received as un-spent balance, in *P* Division, would be credited in its cash book to the same head of a/c to which the advance of ₹ 25,000 was debited when it was paid.

3.3 CLASSIFICATION OF TRANSACTIONS

In order to have an effective control on the spending of the Government departments, all the transactions are divided into the following four divisions, namely:

1. Capital
2. Revenue
3. Remittance
4. Debit.

1. Capital. The capital expenditure is incurred for increasing assets of the government. The expenditure under this head is met from borrowed funds. Sometimes the recurring liabilities of the Government are reduced by paying off their surrender value. This surrender value is known as capitalised value.

2. Revenue. Proceeds from taxation, sale of deed or fallen trees, auction of demolition buildings and the expenditure which is met from these collection falls under this category.

For example, income from the royalty of a stone quarry and the expenditure incurred in watch and ward and keeping records of material quarried fall under this division. In the same way income from forest and expenditure on the establishment also fall under this category.

3. Remittance. This division covers cash remittances between treasuries. Such remittances, however, are merely '*adjustments*' and no physical transaction of money is involved. Similarly book adjustment between different accounting circles also come under this division.

4. Debts. Under this division all such receipts by the Government which has to be repaid at a later stage. Examples of such transactions are:

(*a*) **Provident Fund Contribution for Government Servants.** The sum has to be refunded at the time of retirement of the Government servant or when he leaves the service. The amount deposited is thus a debt of the Government Servant on the Government.

(*b*) **Public Debits.** Such debts form a part of Government receipts at the time of borrowing. The amount has, however, to be paid back with interest.

3.4 HEADS OF ACCOUNTS

All monetary transactions are primarily divided into two categories namely:

(*i*) Receipts, and

(*ii*) Expenditure

Separate heads of accounts therefore exist for these two categories.

From the year 1974-75 a scientific three digit classification has been introduced in accounting.

The important features of this classification are illustrated in Table 3.1.

Table 3.1. Three digits classification of Accounts

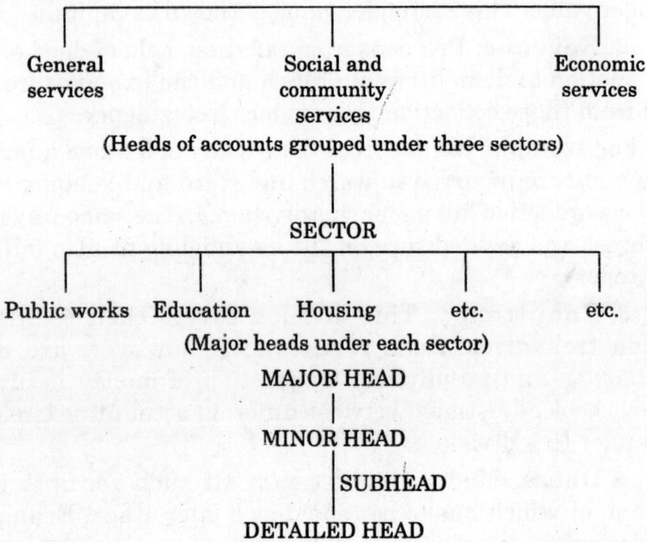

(Under each Major head are minor head, Sub-heads and detailed heads.)

All monetary transaction in Public Works Department can be classified as shown in Table 3.2.

For the Public Works, Major heads for Receipts Revenue is 059.

The minor heads are:

1. Non-residential buildings.
2. Rent.
3. Other Receipts.

Detailed heads for other receipts are:

(*i*) Sale proceeds of dead stock, waste papers or other items the cost of which is met from office expenses.

(*ii*) Other items.

Thus the rent realised for a non-residential building will be deposited into the treasury under the head 059—Public Works (2).

Table 3.2 Grouping of transactions in P.W.D.

		Major Head	*Block Allotted*	*Remarks*
		Receipt	020 to 199	1. There is a difference of 200 between the block numbers of revenue head and receipt head between capital outlay head and revenue head.
		Expenditure		
		Revenue Side	211 to 399	
		Capital Side	411 to 597	
		Public Debt		
		Loan Allowances	611 to 799	
		Public Account	801 to 899	
		Contingency Fund	800	

Table 3.3 gives further classification in respect of the receipt and expenditure heads.

Table 3.3. Receipt and Expenditure Heads

	Department	*Receipt Head*	*Expenditure Head*		*Remarks*
			Revenue	*Capital outlay*	
	Education	077	277	477	There is a change of 2 in the first digit, the second and third digits being the same.
	Housing	080	280	480	
	Roads and Bridges	137	337	537	

Similarly, money realised from the auction of unserviceable material will be deposited under the head 059—Public Works 3 (*i*).

Major Head expenditure revenue is 259 Public Works. There is no sub-major head and the minor heads are:

1. Construction of non-residential buildings.
2. Direction and administration.
3. Planning and Research.
4. Maintenance.
5. Furniture.

Thus ₹ 5000 spent on planning and research will be chargeable to the head 259—Public Works (3).

Table 3.4. Sectional Classification For Major Heads

Sl. No.	*Classification*	*Method of Denoting*
1.	Sectors	Denoted by Capital Letters in separate series. (*i*) REVENUE RECEIPT (*ii*) REVENUE EXPENDITURE (*iii*) CAPITAL OUTLAY
2.	Sub-Sectors	Denoted by small alphabets within brackets
3.	Major Head	Denoted by Code. No.
4.	Minor Head	Denoted by small alphabet within brackets
5.	Sub-Head	Denoted by Arabic numbers within brackets such as (1), (2) etc.
6.	Detail Heads	Standard objects of expenditure to indicate nature of expenditure. Table 3.5 gives the details of the items termed as SOE's.
7.	Plan Scheme	Denoted by Code Nos.

Table 3.5. List of Standard objects of Expenditure (SOE)

Sl. No.	*Particulars*	*Remarks*
1.	Salaries	
2.	Wages	
3.	Travel Expenditure	
4.	Office Expenditure	
5.	Payment for professional and special services	
6.	Rent, Taxes etc.	
7.	Publication	
8.	Advertising	
9.	Grants in Aid	
10.	Scholarship	
11.	Hospitability expenses	
12.	Secret Service	
13.	Major Works (over 1 lac)	
14.	Minor Works (below 1 lac)	
15.	Tools and equipment	
16.	Motor Vehicle	
17.	Maintenance	
18.	Investment	
19.	Material and Supplies	
20.	Interest	
21.	Pension/Gratuity	

(Contd.)...

Table 3.5. List of Standard objects of Expenditure (SOE) *(Contd.)*

Sl. No.	*Particulars*	*Remarks*
22.	Depreciation	
23.	Inter account transfers	
24.	Write off/losses	
25.	Suspense	
26.	Dietary charges	
27.	Medicines	
28.	Other charges	

Table 3.6. Statement of Earlier Major Heads and Minor Heads and the Revised Heads

Heads of Accounts prior to 1-4-74	*Heads of Accounts after 1-4-74*
V—Taxes on income other than corporate tax	021—Taxes on income other than corporate Tax
XXXVII—Public works	059—Public Works
Receipts for works Recoveries of Expenditure Miscellaneous	083—Housing 059—Public Work 083—Public Works 137—Roads and Bridges
XXXIV/XXX—V Irrigation, embankment and drainage works	133—Irrigation
XXXVI—Electricity schemes	131—Water and Power Development Scheme 134—Power Projects
XLIIA—viaition	136—Civil Aviation
45—Electricity scheme	334—Power Projects
50—Pubic Works	259—Public Works
52—Capital outlay on public works	Deleted.
71—Misc.	265—Other Administrative Services
Rent, Rates and Taxes	766—Loans to Govt. Servants
P—Loans and Advances	843—Civil Deposits
T—Deposits and Advances	805—State Provident Funds
State Provident Funds G.P. Fund	A — Civil Fund, G.P. Fund D — Other P. Funds WCP Funds

Details of other major heads can be had from booklets available in the Divisional offices.

As an additional example let us take Education.

Major head for Revenue Receipt is 077.

The sub-major heads are:

A. Primary

B. Secondary

C. Special

D. Pre-university

The minor heads are:

1. Tuition and Examination fee
2. Textbooks.

Thus money received for the sale of Secondary class books by the Government will be deposited into the Government treasury under the head 077-Education—B—(2).

Note. On the basis of the recommendations of the Second Report of the team of Reform in the structure of Account Heads, the Comptroller and Auditor General of India has prescribed the list of major and minor heads of accounts for classification of transaction of Union, States and Union Territories of Government. This has been done with the approval of the President of India and comes into effect from 1 April, 1974 *i.e.*, for the financial year for 1974-75. As a result of this the Major and Minor Head of classification given in Appendix 2 to PWD Accounts code has been modified. For ready reference some of the heads existing under the old system and the present are given in table 3.6.

3.5 MANUFACTURE ACCOUNT

3.5.1 Manufacture Defined

Manufacture is a Sub-head of Suspense head "*Stock*". Expenditure incurred on the manufacturing process is called "*Operation*" and the value of good manufactured is called "*Out-turn*". As the Register of Works is unsuitable for recording the progress of transactions of Manufacture, Form 42 of CPWA Code called the *Register Of Manufacture* is used instead. This Register has two sections, '*Operation' and* '*Out-turn*'.

The accounts of manufacture are closed as soon as the operations *i.e.*, processes of manufacture, are over. However, in the case of continuous manufacturing operations, accounts are closed periodically, at least once a year.

3.5.2 Operation

The debit to "*Operations*", *i.e.*, cost of manufacture, consists of

(*i*) Value of Raw Materials,

(*ii*) Cost of labour, and

(*iii*) Other incidental charges.

"*Incidental Charges*" are of two kinds, one whose benefit accrues to a single season of manufacture (such as Ordinary Repairs), and the other are those charges the benefit from whom extends to more than one season (for example, Special Repairs). Former is treated as operation charge of the year in which it is incurred. The latter, *i.e.*, Special Repairs, Renewals and other incidental charges whose benefit lasts over more than one season of manufacture, are treated as **Capital Charges** and are proportionally treated as operation charges for the remaining years of the working life of the assets so repaired.

3.5.3 Operation Charges include proportionate Share of Capital charges Also.

Cost of Land and Kiln, and Cost of Special Plants in respect of a manufacturing operation are called *Capital Charges*. The value of the Land taken on lease (of say ₹80000 for 2 years) would be zero after two years' operations. The Cost of Kilns and Special Plants would also be equal to their scrap value after their usual working life. It is, therefore, natural that their proportionate cost allocated to each year of manufacture is taken as cost of operations of that year.

3.5.4 Accounting of Capital Charges and Special Repairs

These charges are not initially debited to the Manufacture Account. These are kept under the Sub-head "*Land and Kilns*" of the Suspense Head "*Stock*". Their cost is recovered from operation charges of a manufacture account in suitable proportionate instalments. The following questions will clarify the matter.

Example 1. *Indicate how the following will be recorded in the "Manufacture Accounts" and what shall be the share of Capital Charges allocated to the "Operations" for the first year of operation, assuming that manufacture accounts are closed annually.*

(*i*) *₹20,000 being the Cost of special plants needed for 2 years only and to be scrapped thereafter at expected selling price of ₹5,000* (*ii*) *Second-hand Machinery having working life of five years costing ₹ 60,000. Its scrap value after five years is expected to be ₹ 10,000.*

(*iii*) *Special repairs to machinery in first year ₹ 55,000.*

(*iv*) *Ordinary repairs during each year ₹ 500.*

Ans. Amount debited to "*Land and Kiln*" Sub-head of Suspense head "*Stock*" is ₹ 20,000 + 60,000 + 55,000 = ₹ 1,35,000

Ordinary repairs will go to Operations direct.

Current year's share of Capital Charges to be borne by operations of the year is (20,000 – 5,000)/2 + ((60,000 – 10,000)/5 + (55,000)/5 = ₹ 7500 + 10000 + 11000 = ₹ 28,500.

Example 2. *In the next year special repairs to machinery for ₹ 42,000 were further undertaken. Calculate that year's share of Capital Charges to be borne by the operations of the year.*

Ans. The year's share is (20,000 – 5000)/2 + (60,000 – 10,000)/5 + (55,000)/5 + (42,000)/4 = ₹ 7500 + 10000 + 11000 + 10500 = ₹ 39,000.

Note that ₹ 42,000 are to be allocated to the remaining 4 years only.

Example 3. *From the data in the foregoing questions, calculate 3rd, 4th and 5th years' share of Capital Charges debitable to the Operation Charges of the Manufacture Account, presuming that ₹ 20,500 and 10250 were spent in the fourth and fifth year respectively on Special Repairs.*

Ans. Plant had life of two yeras. 3rd, 4th and 5th years are not to share its cost. Its balance is ₹ 5000 to be adjusted against selling price.

3rd year's share = (60,000 – 10,000)/5 + (55,000)/5 + (42,000)/4 = ₹ 10000 + 11000 + 10500 = ₹ 31,500

4th year's share = (60,000 – 10,000)/5 + (55,000)/5 + (42,000)/4 + (20,500)/2 = ₹ 10000 + 11000 + 10500 + 10250 = ₹ 41,750

5th year's share = (60,000 – 10,000)/5 + (55,000)/5 + (42,000)/4 + (20,500)/2 + 10,250/1 = ₹ 10000 + 11000 + 10500 + 10250 + 10250 = ₹ 52,000

Example 4. *On the basis of the foregoing questions, show the (i) Debit, (ii) Credit and Balances of each year of the head "Suspense-Land and Kilns".*

Ans.

(₹)

	1st. year	*2nd. Year*	*3rd. Year*	*4th. Year*	*5th. Year*
Opening Bal.	------	1,06,500	1,09,500	78,000	56,750
Debit	1,35,000	42,000	------	20,500	10,250
Credit	28,500	39,000	31,500	41,750	52,000
Closing Bal.	1,06,500	1,09,500	78,000	56,750	15,000

At the end of 5th year we have a closing balance of ₹ 15,000 which represents the scrap value of Plant (₹ 5000) and of Machinery (₹ 10,000). The amount realised by sale of these condemned assets would be credited to the sub-head "*Suspense-Land and Kilns*". Any difference left as a result of short/excess realisation would be adjusted under orders of authorised officer (competent authority).

3.5.5 Out-turn

Operation charges show the cost of manufacture. Out-turn is the value of goods produced. All the goods manufactured are valued and transferred to "*Stock*" at that value by credit to "*Out-turn*" account of Manufacture. Some times these goods produced or bye-products of manufacture or disposable waste or manufacturing process are sold out directly. These receipts are also Out-turn of the manufacture Account.

3.5.6 Register of Manufacture

In the Register of Manufacture, the transactions relating to the manufacturing process and value of out-turn are recorded as they occur. In this way figures of progressive expenditure and of progressive out-turn are worked out in this Register.

3.5.7 Closing of the Register of Manufacture

The register of Manufacture is closed at the end of each manufacturing season (or period) or at least once each year. At the time of closing the Register, all outstanding liabilities and assets (such as those listed below) are posted in the register so that the real gain or loss in the operations is determined.

Outstanding Liabilities

(*i*) Unpaid wages.

(*ii*) Outstanding expenses such as bills for consumption of electricity and water, value of stores used but not debited to operation charges etc.

Outstanding Assets

(*i*) Wages and expenses prepaid (*i.e.*, covering a period beyond the date up to which account are being closed).

(*ii*) Raw materials and consumable/non-consumable stores debited to Operation charges but lying unused.

(*iii*) Value of goods manufactured but not yet sold or transferred to Stock.

(*iv*) Recoveries due to be made for the accounting period.

Example 5. *Post and close the Register of Manufacture of lime for the year 2004-2005 from the data given below:*

Purchased quarry site (to last 5 years)	₹ 800
Cost of erection of kiln (to last 5 years)	₹ 2,500
Scrap value of Kiln	₹ 500
Special Tools and plants	₹ 1,000
Coal 100 tonnes at ₹ 20 per tonne	
Labour paid	₹ 2,400
Wages unpaid	₹ 50
Ordinary Repairs	₹ 400

Lime taken on Stock Account - 14,0000 Cu.M. @ 35 paise per Cu M.

Coal in hand - 25 tonnes.

Unburnt Limestone in hand - 250 Cu.M. @ 10 paise per Cu. M.

Scrap value of Tools and Plant after 5 years is Nil.

Ans. See table at page 199. There has been loss of ₹ 295 in the manufacture account.

Example 6. *Post the Register of Manufacture in manuscript Form CPWA 42 from the following transactions for the year 2004-2005 in respect of a Drag-line engaged in digging a canal. This is the fifth year of operation.*

(*i*) Cost of Drag-line. It is expected to run for 14,000 hours (2,000 hours per year). The residual value of equipment at the end of 14,000 hours is expected to be 1/7 th of its cost. ₹ 98,000 (*ii*) Expenditure on ordinary repairs and maintenance ₹ 8,400

(*iii*) Expenditure on extraordinary repairs ₹ 15,000

(*iv*) Expenditure on Work Charged Establishment excluding a sum of ₹ 2,500 accrued for payment on the 31st March, 2005 but not paid. ₹ 15,250

(*v*) Expenditure on Petrol and Lubricants. ₹ 76,652

(*vi*) A bill for ₹ 962 towards petrol and lubricants not adjusted till the end of March, 2005.

(*vii*) Value of earthwork done: 15 KM @ ₹ 10 per Metre.

(JAO 1994)

Ans.

Register of manufacturing-drag-line

Operation							Out-turn		Balance
Month etc.	Maintenance & Repair	POL	WC Estt.	Capital Exp.	Special Repairs	Total	Earth-work		Debit (+) Credit (–)
							Quantity	Amount	
₹	₹	₹	₹	₹	₹	₹		₹	₹
2004-2005	8400	76652	15250	-----	15000	115302	15 KM	150000	–34698
Adjustments	----	+ 962	+ 2500	12000	10000	5462		------	+5462
Total	8400	77614	17750	12000	5000	120764		150000	–29236

See also important Points at next page.

REGISTER OF MANUFACTURE — LIME

OPERATION							OUT-TURN					Balance
Month etc.	Coal		Wages	Repairs	Capital expenses	Total	Lime		Unburnt stone		Total	(Debit + Credit –)
	Qnty.	Amt.					Qnty.	Amt.	Qnty.	Amt.		
	Tonne	₹	₹	₹	₹	₹	Cu. M.	₹	Cu. M.	₹	₹	₹
2004-05	100	2000	2400	400	----	4800	14000	4900	----	----	4900	– 100
Adjustments	– 25	– 500	+50	----	+ 760	+ 310	----	----	250	25	25	295
Total	75	1500	2450	400	760	5110	14000	4900	250	25	4925	185

Total Capitalised charges under "*Lan-Ins*" of Stock suspense = 800 + 2500 + 1000 = ₹ 4300

Its share debited to Operations of Manufacture = 800/5 + (2500 – 500)/5 + 1000/5 = ₹ 760

Balance lying under Land and Kilns = ₹ 3540

Important Points relating to Ans. 6.

(1) Capital Expenditure chargeable to Manufacture Account is (98000 – 14000)/7 = 12000

(2) Special repairs are to be done by 5th., 6th. and 7th. year. Out of ₹ 15000, each year bears ₹ 5000. Share of 6th year and 7th year (₹ 10000) is carried over.

(3) There is a gain of ₹ 29236 in the Operations of the Dragline.

4

CASH

4.1 INTRODUCTION

All the financial transaction in the Division or Disbursing sub-division are entered in the cash book of the Division or sub-division as the case may be. An abstract of all such transaction is prepared at the close of the month in which all the entries of the cash book are shown. In some departments two cash books are maintained, when the cash book of the month is closed it is sent to the Divisional Office/Accountant General/CDA for post-audit and transactions pertaining to the succeeding months are entered in the second cash book.

A typical cash book from (PPWA Form 1) is given in Table 4.1.

The term cash inculdes the following:

(*i*) Legal tender coins

(*ii*) Currency notes

(*iii*) Deposits-at-call receipts of Government banks and demand drafts.

(*iv*) Accepted private cheques.

4.2 PRECAUTIONS IN KEEPING OF ACCOUNTS

The following precautions should be taken:

1. Whenever cash is received from private parties excluding proceeds on sale of blank tender form, a cash receipt in the prescribed form is invariably issued by the disbursing officer.

2. Instructions given on the flyleaf of the cash book (Form C.P.W.A. 1) should be strictly followed.

Table 4.1. Cash Book Form C.P.W.A. Form 1

Cash Book of Shri 'A' Executive Engineer ... Divn. for the month of 7/2009

	Receipts			*Payments*				
Date of Receipts July 2009	*From whom received*	*Amount*	*Classification of Receipt*	*Date of Payment*	*Voucher No.*	*To whom Paid*	*Bank or Treasury Cash No. of Amount/ Cheque*	*Classification of Charges*
Ist	Opening balance							
	Details of Balance: Cash Temporary Imprest to	Total	By Closing Balance ₹....					The balance at the closing of the Cash book at end of month should be the same in receipt and payment side.

Note:

1. Undisbursed pay of staff is kept in a subsidiary cash book and is not included in the opening cash balance.
2. Post-Office Savings Bank Pass Book balance and service postage stamps are not included in the opening cash balance.
3. Fine is credited to the same work.

3. The number of pages should be verified before operating the cash book.

4. Day-to-day entries should be made in the order in which transaction takes place. These entries should be completed the same day.

5. There should be no interpolations, erasers or overwriting in the entries. In case it becomes necessary to correct any figure of an entry, the wrong figure should be scored, initialled by the disbursing officer and correct figures entered.

6. In a Divisional Office, the cash book is closed at the end of the month. Cash books of disbursing sub-division are closed on the 25th of the month so that the closed cash book/copy of the closed cash book reaches the divisional office by the last day of the month.

In the M.E.S. the financial month starts on the 26th of the preceding month upto the 25th of the month under reference except for the month of March when the cash book is closed on the 31st of March.

7. The cash on the chest must be verified with respect to the cash book balances in the beginning of each month. It should also be checked occasionally during the month. In addition to this surprise check of cash book balances is arranged by the divisional officer without prior notice to cashier.

8. In the event of the transfer of the disbursing officer, the cash and cash documents are handed over to the relieving officer.

9. Sometimes the Divisional Officer holds assignment in more than one Treasury/Bank. In such cases separate cash books should be maintained in respect of each of the Treasuries/Banks.

10. Private money/collection should never be mixed up with the cash book.

11. The cash is kept in a strong treasure chest. The chest is operated by two keys. One key is kept by the disbursing officer and the other by the cashier. It is thus not possible for either the disbursing officer or the cashier alone to operate the treasure chest.

12. The opening balance and closing balance in the cash book comprises of the following:

(1) Cash in chest.

(2) Accepted cheque from outside party.

(3) Revenue stamp/money order forms etc.

(4) Outstanding balance of permanent imprest and temporary advances with subordinate officers.

The opening/closing balance should exclude the following:

(*i*) Govt. securities

(*ii*) Post office pass-books

(*iii*) Fixed deposit receipts.

13. **Cheques drawn at outstation.** Sometimes it becomes necessary for the disbursing officers to make at the spot payments by cheque for certain purchases. Such transaction should be recorded in the cash book on return to the headquarter. The dates of issue of cheque and recording of the entry should be made in the column for day.

14. **Renewal of cheque.** When a cheque becomes time barred and the party concerned requests for a new cheque in lieu of old one, and such a cheque is issued, entry is made on the payment side of the cash book in red ink without any entry in the bank column of the cash book. The fact that new cheque in lieu has been issued should be recorded in the counter foil of the original cheque.

15. **Cancellation of cheque.** Cheques are cancelled for one of the following reasons:

(*i*) Time-barred cheques.

(*ii*) Incorrectly drawn cheques.

(*iii*) Cash payment is desired by payee.

(*iv*) Amount of cheque needs to be altered.

Such cheques are called back from the concerned parties and cancelled.

The entry in respect of such cheques made at the time of issue is reversed by a minus entry under the cheque column on the payment side of the cash book.

16. **Cash found surplus or short.** During the surprise check carried out at least once a year or during office inspection of the divisional office carried out by the Superintending Engineer. Sometimes cash may be found surplus or short. In case of surplus, the amount by which the amount is surplus is taken in the cash book under the head '*Public Works Deposit*', '*Miscellaneous Deposit*'. In case of shortage an entry is made on the payment side under the head '*Miscellaneous Public Works Advances*'.

The matter in either case is investigated and responsibility for the lapse is fixed.

17. Each transaction should be classified as described in Art. 3.3.

4.3 TREASURY CHALLANS

When any money is deposited into government treasury or sub-treasury in Form No. 32-A shown in Table 4.2. The following particulars are given in the form.

(*i*) Nature of payment.

(*ii*) Person/Officer on whose account payment is made.

Table 4.2. Treasury Challan (Form No. 32-A)

Challan of cash paid with the State/Reserve Bank of India

By Whom Tendered	*To be filled in by the remitter*		*To be filled in by the Departmental Officer or the Treasury*		
	Name (or designation) and address of the person on whose behalf money to paid.	Full particulars of the remittance and of authority (if any)	Amount	Head of Account	Order to the Bank
					Dated: Signature and full designation of the officer ordering the money to be paid in.
Signature					(Sd)
Treasurer		Accountant			Treasury Officer/Agent

This challan is prepared in duplicate. One copy is retained in the treasury for record and the other is returned to the depositor duly signed.

4.4 IMPREST ACCOUNT

In order to carry out petty purchases for satisfactory execution of the work efficiently the disbursing officer sanctions a standing advance upto a maximum of ₹ 1000 at a time. Usually such advance is kept upto ₹ 250. The subordinate concerned submits details of expenditure by the 25th of every month in Form C.P.W.A.-2 along with supporting vouchers. The expenditure thus incurred during the month is recouped in the beginning of the month so that the amount of the permanent imprest is restricted in the beginning of the month.

4.5 TEMPORARY ADVANCE

In addition to the Imprest Account described above temporary advances are given by the Divisional Engineer to the Sub-divisional Officer against passed vouchers for making payment at site to muster roll labour or casual labour. The account of such advance is submitted to the Divisional Officer immediately after the disbursement is made.

4.6 CONSTRUCTION ACCOUNTS

Construction Account is maintained by the Divisional Engineer/ GE/AEE/AE/SDO to exercise financial control over the expenditure. It gives the financial position of this and gives at a glance the booked expenditure and expected liabilities. These accounts are compiled as below:

(*a*) **Expenditure.** The expenditure in respect of any job consists of the following:

(*i*) Paid bills.

(*ii*) Stores received for the work from the store.

(*iii*) Accepted book debits.

(*iv*) Any credits which may have been received.

(*b*) **Liabilities.** An order for execution of any work or for the provision of stores is a liability till the clearance of the bill. The following expected payments form the liabilities:

(*i*) Work order to the contract for the execution of the work. This order is initially a liability. As running payments are made the amount paid comes under the expenditure head and the liability is reduced by that amount.

(*ii*) Order for supply of stores.

(*iii*) Estimated cost of services ordered from other departments.

(*ix*) Wage bill of labour.

(*c*) **Credits.** The principles applicable to liability hold good for expected credits.

(*d*) **General.** Separate folios of construction accounts are operated for

(*i*) Each item of a major work.

(*ii*) Each item of a minor work.

(*iii*) Each minor head under sub-head.

These folios are grouped by budget heads and kept in the cover. If desired, separate covers may be used for major heads.

At the end of the month, each folio is closed. These accounts are sent to the accounts branch for scrutiny. The expenditure return is compiled after the abstract has been verified by the Accounts branch with respect to the cash book entries.

A typical form for construction accounts used in the Military Engineering service is given in Table 4.3.

4.7 SCHEDULE OF DEMANDS

Schedule of demands is an annual return submitted in the prescribed form asking for funds for both original work (in progress and expected to be taken in hand) and maintenance/repair.

In the case of original works (projects, major work) the demands for fund is based on the expected expenditure during the financial year under reference. In the case of minor works, however, back allotment is placed as lumpsum at the disposal of the departmental head and usually only such works are sanctioned as can be completed within the same financial year. However, if any minor works is not completed within the financial year, the additional minor works for the new year would include the balance of previous year's work.

Maintenance grant for building is given on the following consideration:

(*a*) Year of construction

(*b*) Nature of construction (permanent or temporary)

(*c*) Capital value of the building

The percentage varies from 2 to 5 per cent.

In the case of road (*i.e.*) concrete, black topped WBM, non-painted WBM, kankar road, earthen roads etc.,

Funds for new supplies and maintenance tools, plant, vehicles and machines are demanded separately.

Table 4.3. Form for Construction Accounts

Expenditure											
Item	*Date*	*Particulars*	*Voucher*		*Labour*	*Payments to Contractors*	*Materials*	*Transport*	*Other charges*	*Credits*	*Running Total*
			No.	*Date*							
(1)	(2)	(3)	(4)		(5)	(6)	(7)	(8)	(9)	(10)	(11)
		Grand Total									

Table 4.3 *(Contd.)*

Liabilities and Expected Credits					*Booked Expenditure*	*Contractors Accounts*			*Initial*	*Remarks*
Liability incurred or credits cancelled		*Liabilities cancelled or credits expected*		*Net liabilities out-standing Running Total*	*Liabilities Running Total*	*Charges against*	*Recoveries from*	*Running Total*		
Order No.	*Amount*	*Order No.*	*Amount*		*Col. 11+ Col. 16*					
(12)	(13)	(14)	(15)	(16)	(17)	(18)	(19)	(20)	(21)	(22)

Tables 4.4 and 4.5 show typical forms in respect of major works in progress and new major works.

Table 4.4. Schedule of Demand for Major Work-in-Progress

Sl. No.	*Minor head and detailed head*	*Name and locality of work*	*Amount of estimate as approved administratively*	*Anticipated expenditure in the Current year*	*Total anticipated expenditure to the end of current year*	*Amount required next year*	*No. and date of the authority for work*
(1)		(3)	(4)	(5)	(6)	(7)	(8)

Table 4.5. Schedule of Demands for New Major Work

New Major Work Administrative approval for which has been accorded Necessity accepted.

Sl. No.	*Minor and detailed heads*	*Order of priority*	*Locality and name of work*	*Anticipated expenditure in the Current year*	*Amount required next year*	*Remarks*
(1)	(2)	(3)	(4)	(5)	(6)	(7)

Normally the initial demand for funds for the coming financial year and the Ist change in grant in respect of the current year is initiated in the month of July of the current year. The second and third/final changes in the budget allotment for the current year are submitted in October and December along with the final forecast for the next year which is submitted in December.

4.8 CASH BOOK

Introduction

Initial Accounts. In this Chapter it is explained how to keep initial accounts of cash receipts and cash payments in the Cash Book in a Public Works Division.

Two modes of payment are adopted by the Public Works Divisional Officers for works and supplies made, namely.

(*i*) *By cash or cheque*—if the work is done or services are rendered by contractor or supplier or any other Central Public Works Division.

(*ii*) *By book transfer*—if the work is done by other Governments, departments as a standing arrangement.

Conditions attaching to each mode of payment are as below:

Cheques and cash—

For charges which are naturally to be a paid in cash, *e.g.*, the wages of labourers, of establishment charged directly to work and value payable postage, cash in chest is to be kept at minimum possible to meet the current requirements.

Payments to suppliers at outstations can be made by bank drafts. Petty payments can be made by postal money orders at public expense.

A cheque should not be drawn unless it is intended to be paid away. Cheques drawn in favour of the contractors and others should be made over to them by the Disburser direct or through cashier of the Department. Payments due to contractors can be made to their Bankers direct, if the contractor confers authority on the bank, through a legally valid document, to receive payment on his behalf.

Book Transfer—

Payment by Book Transfer relating to work done by another government department is to be made only when advice of debit is received. The advice of debit would contain a certificate of audit, certifying that payment-vouchers have been audited and passed in accordance with the rules (*Para 17.2.2 and 17.2.7 of C.P.W.A. Code*). All other procedures relating to recording of entries in Stores accounts and Measurement Books would be followed.

Cash. Payments and Receipts in cash are collected together in a Cash Book, maintained by every Disbursing Officer in Form 1. Cash collected on account of departmental receipts or drawn on cheques is entered on the Receipt Side of the Cash Book. Payments made out of that Cash are entered on the Payment Side of the Cash Book.

Definition of Cash. Cash has been defined in *Para 6.1.1 of CPWA Code*. It includes

(*i*) Legal tender Coins, Notes;

(*ii*) Cheques (in favour of the Executive Engineer or in-charge of the Cash Book);

(*iii*) Deposits-at-call Receipts of Scheduled Banks;

(*iv*) Bank Drafts payable on demand; and

(*v*) Revenue Stamps.

It does not include Debentures, Bonds, Government Securities, Fixed Deposit Receipts or any Deposit Receipts except Deposit at call Receipts. **Though** Deposit Receipts of Banks **are accepted as security, these will not be taken in the Cash Book till the Divisional Officer encashes them from the Bank.**

Cheques. Cheques are the usual means of payment. There are, however certain charges, which have necessarily to be paid in cash whatever the amount, such as petty purchases, wages of labourers, wages of work charged establishment, VPP Postage charges etc. For all such charges and petty payments, it is permissible to draw money in cash from the Bank to replenish the Cash Chest.

Currency of a Cheque. The Government cheque is valid for payment for a period of 3 months after the month of its issue.

Cash Book Entries. All Payments made and Receipts realised should at once be brought to account in the Cash Book.

Exceptions—

(*i*) *Earnest money received from tenderers* in legal tender Notes and Deposit at call Receipts received with the tenders, if refunded on the day on which the tenders were opened, need not be entered in the Cash Book.

(*ii*) In cases where the private cheques received are too many, a "*Register of Cheques Received and Adjusted*" in Form CPWA 1-A may be kept and only the daily totals of Cheques received and Cheques remitted to Bank/ Treasury may be entered in the Cash Book.

Use of Departmental Receipts for Departmental expenditure forbidden. Receipts realised by departmental officers should be paid as soon as possible in the treasury or bank for credit as miscellaneous receipts of the department.

If it is considered necessary by the Divisional Officer to make use of these receipts for current expenditure, he can do it. But, before the end of the month, he should send to the Treasury Office/ Bank a cheque for the amount thus utilised. Such a cheque should be in his own favour and endorsed with the words "Received Payment by transfer credit to the Public Works Department".

Imprest. Imprest is a standing advance of a fixed sum of money given to an individual to enable him to make certain classes of disbursement entrusted to his charge. The amount of an imprest is to be kept as low as possible and in no case should exceed ₹ 5,000 without the sanction of government. The Imprest-holder should submit the account of his imprest at the time of closure of monthly account by the Divisional Officer. The account of imprest may be closed earlier also if:

(*i*) the balance of imprest is small and needs recoupment; or

(*ii*) it is proposed to increase/decrease the amount of the imprest, or

(*iii*) the account of the imprest is to be closed altogether.

The amount spent by the imprest-holder out of his imprest is brought to account by the disbursing officer in his Cash Book. He generally pays back an equivalent amount to the imprest-holder so that the amount available with the imprest-holder is again equal to the amount of imprest originally granted.

Temporary Advance. When a Disbursing Officer makes a remittance to a subordinate officer to enable him to make specific petty *payments on vouchers, which have been already passed for payment*, the amount remitted is treated as a Temporary advance. After making payment, the subordinate submits an account of the advance along with the unspent balance, if any. Following are also treated as Temporary Advance:

(*i*) *Money taken out by the Disbursing Officer himself* for making disbursement at outstations when on tour.

(*ii*) *Advance on transfer to a government servant* pending drawal of the advance from the treasury/bank in the normal course.

WRITING A CASH BOOK

Columns of Cash Book—Receipt side. A Cash Book on the receipt side has the following columns:

Date	*From whom received*	*Amount* ₹	*Classification of Receipts*

Columns of Cash Book—Payment side. On the Payment side of the Cash Book, there are the following seven columns:

Date	*Vr No*	*To whom paid*	*Cash* ₹	*Bank or Treasury**		*Classification*
				Ch. no.	*Amount* ₹	

*Note carefully that *only cheques issued by the Drawing Officer on the treasury or bank are to be entered in these two columns.* If a person tenders a cheque in payment of the amount due from him, such a cheque is treated as cash receipt, and is entered on the Receipt Side of the Cash Book. When such a cheque is sent to treasury/bank for collection, it will be entered on the Payment Side of the Cash Book in the **Cash** column; **not in the Bank** column.

Opening Cash Balance. A Cash Book always starts with an opening Cash Balance. In determining the Opening Balance in a question on Cash Book, the following items should be included or excluded:

To be Included	To be Excluded
1. Legal tender coins, notes.	1. Counterfeit Coins, Private Cash.
2. Postal orders, Cheques, Demand Drafts in favour of the disbursing officer, Self-cheques.	2. Cheques, demand drafts in favour of contractors or other persons.
3. Revenue Stamps.	3. Service Postage Stamps, Air Letters for foreign countries, Service Books.
4. Imprests or Temporary advances issued to self or subordinates.	4. Cash forming part of the Sub-Cash Chest.
5. Undisbursed wages etc., of purely work charged staff. Also, unpaid salaries & Loans and Advances of regular staff received back from Sub-Cash Chest for deposit back in the Bank/Treasury.	5. Unpaid salaries of regular staff awaiting to be disbursed (usually these are kept in the Sub-Cash Chest).
6. Deposit-at-call Receipts of Banks. (See last sentence of para 3.2 above)	6. All other Deposit Receipts, Debentures, Bonds, any kind of interest bearing securities like Saving Bank Pass Books, Cash Certificates, National Savings Certificates etc.

Sub-Cash Chest. Undisbursed pay and allowances of staff and officers as well as festival advances and advances of travelling allowance etc., are kept in subsidiary Cash Book (generally by the Head Clerk). Therefore undisbursed cash on account of salaries non payments out of such undisbursed cash appears in the Cash Book. Only the drawal of salaries and advances appears in the Cash Book.

Illustrative examples. The various events and situations requiring the making of entries in the Cash Book are described in detail below. The Illustrations are exhaustive and thorough.

Payments made in Cash. All such payments are entered in the "*Cash*" column of the Cash Book on the payment side.

Payments made by Cheque. Amount paid by cheque is entered in the column headed "*Bank*" on the payment side of Cash Book; Cheque Number is entered in the immediately preceding column.

Example. *Enter in the Cash Book a cheque No. 385 for ₹5000 paid to A for repairs to a district road on 1st July on passed Vr. No. 5.*

Date	*Vr No*	*To whom paid*	*Cash*	*Bank or Treasury*		*Classification*
				Ch	*Amnt*	
1-7	5	By payment to Sh. A for repair to road		385	5000	3054 Roads and Bridges; District and Other Roads; Road works; Maintenance & Repairs

Cheque drawn while on Tour. All transactions should be entered in the Cash Book in chronological order as soon as they occur. If however, owing to the absence of the disbursing officer on tour, he issues a cheque while in camp, it should be entered in his Cash Book maintained at his headquarters as soon as he reaches there. The date on which it is entered in the Cash Book should be shown as numerator whereas the date on which the cheque was issued should be shown as denominator.

Example. *The Divisional Officer issued a cheque No. 879543 for ₹2000 to a contractor B for Work X while in camp on 16th March. He reached his headquarters on 20th March and entered it in the Cash Book as Vr. No. 7. The entries are made as shown below:*

Date	Vr.	To whom paid	Cash	Bank or Treasury		Classification
				Ch. no.	Amnt ₹	
20.3 / 16.3	7	By Payment to Contractor B for Work X		879543	2000	Work X

Receipt in Cash or by Cheque. All receipts collected, in cash or by cheque or by bank draft etc., should be entered on the receipt side of the Cash Book in the column headed "*Amount*".

Receipt by Cheque at Outstations. *Normally government offices should not accept out-station cheques in payment of amounts due to the government.* But banks are not allowed to charge any commission from government on outstation cheques. Hence the total amount of the cheque is treated as receipt.

Chalan submitted by Subordinate. If a government servant, who is not in charge of a Cash Book, receives money on behalf of government at exceptional times, he should remit it to the nearest officer having a Cash Book. In that case it is entered in the Cash Book in accordance with para 3.13.4 of this book. (Para 6.3.4)

Instead of remitting it to the officer having a Cash Book, he may also remit it direct into the bank or treasury. The acknowledgement of the bank or treasury on a chalan should be forwarded immediately to the next superior officer having a Cash Book to enable him to make the necessary entries therein. In this case cash has been received as well as paid into the bank/treasury. Thus there will be two entries in the Cash Book; one on the receipt side classifying it to the final receipt head of account, and the other on the payment side showing the amount as remittance into the bank/treasury.

Purchase and Sale of Revenue Stamps. Revenue stamps fall within the definition of the term "*Cash*". Hence sale or purchase of Revenue Stamps is nothing more than conversion of one form of cash into another. When revenue stamps are sold, no additional cash comes in; when they are purchased, cash does not go away. Hence no entry is to be made in the Cash Book if revenue stamps are sold or purchased.

Cancelled Cheque. The amount of cancelled cheque is written back by an entry in the Bank column on the Payment side of the Cash Book, exhibiting the amount as a minus figure. In actual practice, a note of cancellation of the cheque should also be kept against the original entry made in the Cash Book when the cheque was issued and also on the counterfoil of the cheque now cancelled. **Cancelling a Bank draft issued by the Division is different. It is entered on the Receipt side as reduction from payment head and on Payment side as remitted to Treasury/Bank.**

Renewal of cheque. If the currency of a cheque expires (Para 3.4 above), it can be revalidated. If it is more than a year old, a new cheque can be issued in its lieu. The amount of the new cheque is **not** entered in the Bank column of the Cash Book. Only a note that new cheque has been issued in lieu of the old one is kept in the column "*To whom paid*".

Cheque to replenish Cash Chest. When a Divisional Officer has to make payment in cash but has not enough money in his Cash Chest, he can replenish the chest by drawing money from the bank or treasury. This has no impact on the *income* or *expenditure* of the division; *cash previously in bank has now become cash in chest / hand.*

Example. *On 12th March cheque No. 456321 for ₹200 was issued to replenish cash chest. It was encashed from the bank on 15th March. Exhibit the transactions in the Cash Book.*

Receipt side of Cash book

Date	*From whom received*	*Amount*	*Classification of Receipts*
12-3	To cash drawn to replenish cash chest	200	Cash from Treasury or Bank

Payment side of Cash Book

Date	*Vr. no.*	*To whom paid*	*Cash*	*Bank or Treasury*		*Classification*
				Ch	*Amnt*	
12-3		By cash drawn for cash chest		456321	200	Cash from Treasury or Bank

*Entry is made on the day the cheque is issued.

Grant of temporary advance/Imprest. A Temporary advance or Imprest can be given to a subordinate (*i*) in cash, or (*ii*) by cheque.

If given in cash.

Only a note **in red ink** is kept in the column headed "To whom paid "*because the amount, though given to others officers, is still cash in hand*".

If given by cheque.

First make entries as if money has been drawn from bank to replenish cash chest as indicated in the preceding sub-para and thereafter, keep a note in red ink as if the imprest or advance is given in cash.

Example. *An advance of ₹ 500 in cash was made on 7th April to Mr. A for making payment of passed vouchers, and another advance of ₹ 800 was made on 15th April by means of cheque No. 765 to Mr. B for a similar purpose. Make necessary entries in the Cash Book.*

Receipt side of the Cash Book

Date	*From whom received*	*Amount*	*Classification of Receipts*
15-4	To Cash for chest	800	Cash from Treasury/Bank

Payment side of the Cash Book

Date	*Vr No.*	*To whom paid*	*Cash*	*Bank / Treasury*		*Classification*
				Ch	*Amt*	
7-4		Temporary advance granted in cash to A for petty payments. ₹ 500				
15-4		By cash for chest		765	800	Cash from Treasury/ Bank
		Temporary advance granted to Sh. B for making petty payments. ₹ 800				

Entries when account of temporary advance is rendered and the account of advance is closed. When the subordinates render account of temporary advance, the amount actually disbursed by them is shown as payment. At the same time, a note is kept on the receipt side in Red ink stating that the temporary advance has been adjusted and closed.

Remember that note in red ink is kept on the payment side when advance is given or its amount is increased. Conversely, a note is kept on the receipt side when the advance is closed or its amount is reduced.

Expenditure (from Imprest) recouped. On receipt of the account of the imprest, it is incorporated in the Cash Book, and an amount equal to the amount expended is paid to imprest holder in cash or by cheque to recoup his imprest. The following examples will make it clear.

Imprest recouped with increase or decrease in it. Different treatment is given according as the recoupment is made in cash or by cheque, as will be clear from the following examples.

Example. *A had an Imprest of ₹400 He submitted his account on 3rd July (Paid ₹350 for painting work Vr. 8). His Imprest was recouped and increased to ₹500 on the same day.*

B had an Imprest of ₹500. He submitted his account on 8th July (Paid ₹250 for a work). His account was passed on 9th July (Vr. 9) and imprest reduced to ₹300.

Indicate the entries in the Cash Book if recoupment was made

(*a*) in cash OR

(*b*) *by cheques No.569 and 571 respectively.*

Ans. (*a*) If recouped in cash

Payment side of Cash Book

Date	*Vr*	*To whom paid*	*Cash ₹*	*Bank or Treasury*	*Classification*
3 – 7	8	By Imprest of A recouped-charges for paint work Imprest of A raised ₹ 500 from ₹ 400 $	350		Work concerned
9 – 7	9	By Imprest of B recouped-Expr. on work	250		Work concerned

Receipt side of Cash Book

Date	From whom received	Amount	Classification of Receipts
9–7	Imprest account of B reduced from ₹ 500 to ₹ 300 $		

$ Obviously, to change their imprest amount, Sh. A was paid ₹ 450 in cash and Sh. B was paid ₹ 50 in cash. Note the entries.

(*b*) **If recouped by cheque**

Receipt side of Cash Book

Date	From whom received	Amount	Classification of Receipts
3–7	To cash from bank	450	Cash from Bank or Treasury
9–7	To cash from Bank Imprest account of B reduced from ₹ 500 to ₹ 300	50	—do—

Payment side of Cash Book

Date	Vr	To whom paid	Cash ₹	Bank or Treasury		Classification
3 –7		By cash for chest.		569	450	Cash from Bank Treasury
	8	By Imprest of A recouped—Charges for paint work Imprest of A raised to ₹ 500 from ₹ 400	350			Work concerned
9-7		By cash for chest		571	50	Cash from Bank Treasury
	9	By Imprest of B recouped-Work Expr.	250			Work concerned

Temporary advance/Imprest lost. Loss of any money is debited to "*Suspense; Miscellaneous Works Advances*" on the Payment side of the Cash Book. If the Divisional Officer does not recoup the loss by making available more money, then *a red ink* *note* has to be kept of the closure (or reduction) of the advance/ imprest on the receipt side. (If it is **recouped,** then *Red ink note* is not to be kept.) An example follows:

Example. *Sh. P *reported a loss of ₹200, which represented Temporary advance / Imprest granted to him. This report was treated as an account of the advance / imprest on 9th July and allotted Vr. No.9. Make entries in the Cash Book if it was decided (i) to close the account, or (ii) to recoup the loss in cash, or (iii) to recoup the loss by cheque No. 346.*

Ans. Payment side of the Cash Book

Date	*Vr*	*To whom paid*	*Cash* ₹	*Bank or Treasury*		*Clssification*
9–7	9	(*i*) **If Account closed** To Advance/Imprest of X adjusted; cash lost	200			Misc. works advances
9–7	9	(*ii*) **Recouped in Cash** To recoupment of Imprest/ advance of X; Cash lost	200			Misc. Works Advances
9–7	9	(*iii*) **Recouped by cheque** To recoupment of Imprest/advance of X; Cash lost		346	200	Misc. Works Advances

* Not to be taken in the Cash Book if it is only a report (*Unless it is treated as an account or till an account is rendered*).

Receipt side of the Cash Book

Date	*From whom received*	*Amount*	*Classification of Receipts*
9–7	(*i*) **Account closed** Imprest/temporary advance of X adjusted and closed Vr. 9 ₹ 200 Total ₹ 200		Receipts

Items in the Imprest account if objected to. The item objected to should nevertheless be recouped in full; and till the objection is settled it should be classified under the head "*Miscellaneous Works Advances*".

Amounts taken for Disbursement during Tour. If a Disbursing Officer takes cash from chest with him for disbursement during tour, it is treated as a temporary advance given to him.

Remittances into Bank or Treasury. All revenues collected by a Divisional Officer have to be remitted into Bank or Treasury as soon as possible. Cheques received from private parties are also treated as cash and entered in the Cash column on the Receipt side of the Cash Book when these were received. *When these cheques are remitted to the treasury, the entry of this outgo of cash is made in the Cash column on the Payment side of the Cash Book.* These remittance of cash to Bank etc., are classified as "*Public Works Remittances; Remittances into Bank / Treasuries.*"

Cheque remitted into Treasury/Bank; and Dishonoured. Cheque remitted to the treasuries/bank is entered on the payment side of the Cash Book as remittances into the Bank/ Treasuries *only after it has been delivered to Bank / Treasury for collection* (*classification being "Remittances into the treasury / bank"*). ***On the day its dishonour comes to notice****, two entries with minus sign should be made - one on the Receipt side* (*classifying it to the same head which was credited when the cheque was received*)*, and one on the Payment side* (*classifying it as "Remittances into the treasuries / bank*)".

If the bank does not accept any cheque for credit for any reason (such as over-writing not attested, amount in figures and words don'tally, or cheque is mutilated etc.) and the person sent to the bank to deposit it brings it back, this is technically called "*cheque dishonoured on the same day*". **In such a situation, that cheque will not be shown on the Payment side of the Cash Book as remitted into the Bank or Treasury** (*because Deposit slip is unacknowledged by the bank/treasury*). **We will also reverse the previous entry, made in the Cash Book, when the cheque was received, by making an entry** *now* **on the Receipt side with negative sign.**

Earnest Money Deposits. When received, these are classified on the Receipt side of the Cash Book under the head "*Public Works Deposits*". When refunded, similar entry is made on the Payment side. Earnest money received from tenderers, if refunded on the same day on which it was received, need not be entered in the Cash Book.

Sometimes tenderers deposit their earnest money into the Bank/Treasury on chalans endorsed by the Divisional Officer for credit to the account of the Division. The entries in the Cash Book are the same as in Question 6, classification on Receipt side is "*Public Works Deposits*".

Recoveries of overpayments of Pay, T.A., Advances of T.A. and Festival Advances. If these recoveries are made in cash, these are credited to "*Direction and Administration*" as reduction of expenditure. If these recoveries are made from their Pay Bills, then only net amount paid is taken in the Cash Book on the Payment side.

Classification of Recoveries from Pay Bills.

Income Tax	*0021 Taxes on Income*
CGHS Contribution	0210 Medical etc., Urban Health Schemes, Contribution to CGHS
GP Fund	8009 State Provident Funds, Civil, GP Fund
Loans & Advances	7610 Loans to Government Servants, House Building Advances/Advances for purchase of Motor Conveyances/Other Conveyances

Cash found excess or short on intermediate count. Cash found excess is credited to "*Public Works Deposits*" on the Receipt side; while cash found short is posted on the Payment side as "*Miscellaneous Works Advances*". Even if the person responsible makes the shortage good, two distinct entries are necessary-one on the Payment side showing shortage, the other on the Receipt side showing recovery-classification of both will be "*Miscellaneous Works Advances*".

Before the above-mentioned entries are made, **a note** indicating the result of intermediate counting of cash in chest (*i.e.*, excluding Temporary advances and Imprests etc.) should be recorded in the body of the Cash Book on Payment side (in the column "*To whom paid*"). (Para 6.6.3)

Recoveries creditable to other Works or Heads of Account. Sometimes details of Contractors bills or Pay Bills are given for entering into the Cash Book. In such cases, (*i*) the amount of the cheque should be entered on the payment side in the column for the amount of the cheque.

(*ii*) Recoveries/ Deductions creditable to a Work or Head of Account other than that to which the payment itself relates should be entered individually on the Receipt side duly classifying them.

(*iii*) Total of recoveries mentioned in item (*ii*) above should be posted in lumpsum on the Payment side in the "*Cash*" Column.

Deduction on account of Security. A distinction should be made between "*Security*" and "*Security Deposits*". If, in the question the word used is "*Security Deposits*", then the amount recovered is to be credited to "*Public Works Deposits*" (unless the context of the Question in the examination specifically requires a different treatment).

If the recovery is on account of "*Security*", then it is creditable to the work itself if the amount of security likely to be deducted for the work from the contractor during the year is less than ₹ 500. Otherwise, it is creditable to "*Public Works Deposits*". (Para 15.2.4 CPWA Code)

Fines. Fine for bad work is creditable to the work itself while fine for delay in completion or for other reasons, which do not affect the value/cost of the work are creditable to revenue as "*Other Receipts*".

Cheque in favour of self. A self-cheque is entered on the Receipt side of the Cash Book as soon as it is drawn vide para 3.13.10 above. When such a cheque is cashed at the Bank/Treasury on a subsequent date, no further entry need be made in the Cash Book. A cheque in favour of self is cash for all purposes and is counted as cash in hand of the Disbursing officer.

A cheque in favour of Contractor or an individual. This kind of cheque is also entered on the Payment side of the Cash Book as soon as it is drawn. If it is handed over to the person concerned after lapse of a few days, no entry at that time is to be made. A cheque in favour of a third party (contractors, employees, suppliers etc.), is not cash in hand of the Disbursing Officer, as he cannot draw cash from bank against such cheque.

Cheque/Demand Draft on account of recoveries made by one Division on behalf of another. Recoveries made by one

Division on behalf of another are classified by the recovering Division on the Receipt side of the Cash Book under the Head "*Public Works Deposits; Miscellaneous Deposits*". Simultaneously a cheque for that amount is issued in favour of the other Division, which is entered on the Payment side and classified to the same Deposit Head, thus clearing the earlier credit to it.

Closing Cash Balance. Closing Cash Balance should be detailed in the form of a note at the foot of the Cash Book as under:

Cash in chest	₹ 213
Revenue Stamps	₹ 20
Imprest with A	₹ 400
Temporary Advance with B	₹ 250
Total	₹ 883

Certified that cash has been counted this day, the ---- of --- 200-, together with balance of the Sub Cash Chest and found to be ₹ 233 *(Rupees two hundred thirty three only) which is correct.

Entries in Red Ink. While writing the Cash Book, the following entries and notes are to be written in red ink in the column headed **"From whom received"** or **"To whom paid etc."**.

Receipt side	***Payment side***
(*i*) When the existing entry is struck off and a new entry is made in between the lines.	(*i*) When an existing entry is struck off and a new one is made in between the lines.
(*ii*) When a temporary advance is closed.	(*ii*) When a temporary advance is made.
(*iii*) When an Imprest is decreased.	(*iii*) When Imprest is granted.
(*iv*) When an Imprest is altogether withdrawn.	(*iv*) When an Imprest is increased.
	(*v*) When a new cheque is issued in lieu of old.

These red ink entries are only notes and no amount on account of them can appear against them in the columns headed Cash, Amount etc.

*This should exclude the amounts, which are not actually in chest *e.g.*, Imprests & Temporary advances.

4.9 MONTHLY ACCOUNT

(Paras refferred to are from CPWA Code unless contrary is stated)

Introduction. The question on Monthly Account is usually set to test a candidate's overall and general understanding of the PWD Accounts, namely classifications, transfer entries, stock adjustments, balancing of Cash Book etc. etc. The technique of solving these questions is simple as explained in this chapter. In the Monthly Account, we are concerned with major heads only.

For the monthly account we must have or **must find out** the following:

(*i*) Opening and Closing Balances.

(*ii*) Amount of Cheques issued.

(*iii*) Amounts remitted to Treasuries or Bank.

(*iv*) Amount of Payment/Receipt of each head of Account.

Know the transactions. On examining the various kinds of transactions, you will conclude that basically they are of two kinds, (1) Cash and (2) Book Transfers & Stock.

Cash transactions will affect only one major head on the debit side (if it is payment) or on the credit side (if it is a receipt).

Book Transfer and Stock transactions will affect the account on both debit and credit sides, but the net debit and net credit due to these transactions shall always be equal or nil.

Working procedure. Against each Transaction write the major head of account affected by it.

(*i*) Naturally, against a Cash Transaction will be written only one Major Head to be debited or credited.

(*ii*) Against each Book Adjustment will be written the major heads to be debited as well as major heads to be credited along with the amounts to be so debited/credited.

(*iii*) No major head is to be written for Opening Cash Balance or Closing Cash Balance.

(*iv*) If the Opening Cash Balance is given but not the Closing Cash Balance, then find out the Closing Cash Balance by totalling the cash transactions and using the formula:

Opening Balance plus Cash Receipts
minus Cash Payments = Closing Balance.

OR

Closing Balance plus Cash Payments
minus Cash Receipts = Opening Balance.

(*v*) Transactions paid by Cheque affect two heads; one to be debited and the other is "*8782 Remittances, PW Remittances, PW Cheques*" which is to be credited (collectively for amount of all the cheques issued). If the total amount in respect of cheques issued is not given, find it out by adding the cheque transactions yourself.

Here is a small example to explain the various issues involved

Example. *Prepare the monthly account for October 2009 of a CPWD Division in charge of Building and Roads from the following particulars.*

	₹	notes
(*i*) *Opening Cash Balance*	1,540	
(*ii*) *Cash receipts during the month*		
(*a*) Rent of Residential Buildings	3,590	(0216) Cr.
(*b*) Rent Realised for Inspection Bungalow	215	(0059) Cr.
(*c*) Security Deposited by Contractors	3,000	(8443) Cr.
(*d*) Receipts on behalf of another Public Works Division	344	(8443) Cr.
(*e*) Deposits from District Panchayats for Works to be done	9,800	(8443) Cr.
(*f*) Miscellaneous Revenue Receipts of the Department	1,325	(0059) Cr.
(*g*) Sale proceeds of cement sold from Stock	1,870	(2059) Cr.
(*iii*) *Expenditure (All payments were made by cheque)*		
(*a*) Construction of School Building	25,010	(4202) Dr.
(*b*) Additions and alterations to the office of CPWD	7,550	(2059) Dr.
(*c*) Maintenance of Residential Buildings	78,770	(2216) Dr.
(*d*) Refund of Security Deposits	20,100.	(8443) Dr.
(*e*) Deposit Work carried out	8,000	(8443) Dr.
For which departmental charges are to be levied as under:	(8443)	Dr. 1460
* Establishment Charges 16 1/2 percent	(0059)	Cr. ₹ 1320
Tools & Plant Charges 3/4 percent	(0059)	Cr. ₹ 60
Audit and Account Charges 1 percent	(0071)	Cr. ₹ 80
(*f*) Purchase of Service Postage Stamps	300	(2059) Dr.
(*iv*) *Cash remitted into treasury (bank) during the month*	19,800	(8782) Dr.

* If rates are given as in this question, apply them without further check.

Ans. Collect the figures for each major head as under:

(1) 0059 = 215 + 1325 + 1320 + 60 = ₹ 2920

(2) 0216 = ₹ 3590

(3) 2059 = – 1870 + 7550 + 300 = ₹ 5980

(4) 2216 = ₹ 78770

(5) 4202 = ₹ 25010

(6) 8443 Dr. = 20100 + 8000 + 1460 = ₹ 29560

(7) 8443 Cr. = 9800 + 3000 + 344 = ₹ 13144

(8) 0071 = 80

(9) 8782 Dr. (Remittances to treasuries) = ₹ 19800

(10) 8782 Cr. (Cheques issued) = 25010 + 7550 + 78770 + 20100 + 8000 + 300 = ₹ 139730

(11) Closing Balance = 1540 + (3590 + 215 + 3000 + 344 + 9800 + 1325 + 1870) – 19800 = ₹ 1884

Ans.

Monthly Account for October 2004

Major Heads of Account	*Receipts* ₹	*Disbursements* ₹
0059 Public Works	2,920	
0216 Housing	3,590	
2059 Public Works		5,980
2216 Housing		78,770
4202 Education etc.		25,010
8443 Civil Deposits; PW Deposits	13,144	29,560
Miscellaneous heads of account *	80	
8782 Remittances; PW Remittances	1,39,730	19,800
Cash Balance increased		344
Opening Balance 1,540		
Closing Balance 1,884		
TOTAL	1,59,464	1,59,464

Important Point

1. Audit and Account Charges in CPWD divisions is creditable to "0071" which appears in the compiled account of a Division under the category of *"Misc. heads of Account"*. In the State PWD Divisions, this is creditable to the head *"Adjusting Account between Central and State governments"*.

Example. *Prepare the monthly account for May 2009 of a Central Public Works Division (B&R) from the following data:*

		₹	notes
(1) *Opening Balance*		740	
(2) *Cash Receipts during the month:*			
(*a*) Rent of Residential Buildings		632	(0216) Cr
(*b*) Rent from Inspection Bungalow		450	(0059) Cr
(*c*) Hire Charges of Tools and Plant		650	(0059) Cr
(*d*) Other Misc. receipts		370	(0059) Cr
Deposits for works to be done		6,500	(8443) Cr
Earnest money/Security deposit from Contractor		2,100	(8443) Cr
Receipts on behalf of other Divisions		500	(8443) Cr
Sale proceeds of dismantled material from work "*Construction of medical college*" (major work). The amount was realised on 31-5 and credited to the Bank next day.		350	(4210) Cr
(3) *Payments by cheques*			
(*a*) Construction of medical college building		5,620	(4210) Dr
(*b*) Additions and alterations to public library		3,480	(4202) Dr
(*c*) Maintenance of Central Government Residential Buildings		3,169	(2216) Dr
(*d*) Works outlay on a Minor deposit		<u>4,000</u>	(8443) Dr
works on which the departmental	23.25%	930	(0059) Cr
charges are to be levied.	0.25%	10	(0070) Cr
(in this case find out rates from Appendix 4 of CPWA code. Author)	0.25%	10	(0071) Cr
Total	23.75%	<u>950</u>	(8443) Dr
(*e*) Refund of Security Deposit		1,500	(8443) Dr
(*f*) Salary of Officers and Staff - Gross		9,650	(2059) Dr
Deductions: Income Tax		100	(0021) Cr
Licence Fee		300	(0216) Cr
CGHS Contribution		50	(0210) Cr
Advance to Govt Servants for purchase of conveyance		300	(7610) Cr
Postal Life Insurance premium		50	(8658) Cr
(*g*) Purchase of Service Postage Stamps		100	(2059) Dr
(*h*) Purchase-office Furniture and Equipment		3,400	(2059) Dr

(4) *Cash Payments*		
(*a*) Carriage charges of surplus materials transferred from work "*Construction of Staff Quarters*" to Stock.	50	(4216) Dr
(*b*) Petty Office Expenses	30	(2059) Dr
(5) *Misc. Cash Receipts remitted in the Bank*	11,202	(8782) Dr

Ans.

Monthly Account for May 2009

Major Heads of Account		*Receipts* ₹	*Disbursements* ₹
0059 Public works		2400	
0210 Medical		50	
0216 Housing		932	
2059 Public Works			13180
2216 Housing			3169
4202 Education etc.			3480
4210 C O on Medical etc.			5270
4216 C O on Housing			50
Miscellaneous heads of account			
0021	₹ 100		
0070	₹ 10		
0071	₹ 10	120	
7610 Loans to Government Servants		300	
8443 Civil Deposits; PW Deposits		9100	6450
8658 Suspense Accounts		50	
8782 Remittances		30119	11202
Cash Balance increased			
Closing Balance	₹ 1010		
Opening Balance	₹ 740		270
	TOTAL	43071	43071

After writing the classifications on each item as in the Notes in the example, collect the figures for each major head before drawing up the monthly account.

(1) 0059 = 450 + 650 + 370 + 930 = ₹ 2400

(2) 0210 = ₹ 50

(3) 0216 = 632 + 300 = ₹ 932

(4) 2059 = 9650 + 100 + 3400 + 30 = ₹ 13180

(5) 2216 = ₹ 3169

(6) 4202 = ₹ 3480

(7) 4210 = – 350 + 5620 = ₹ 5270

(8) 4216 = ₹ 50

(9) 0021 = ₹ 100 **(10) 0070** = ₹ 10

(11) 0071 = ₹ 10 **(12) 7610 Cr.** = ₹ 300

(13) 8443 Cr. = 6500 + 2100 + 500 = ₹ 9100

(14) 8782 Dr. = ₹ 11202

(15) 8443 Dr. = 4000 + 1500 + 950 = ₹ 6450

(16) 8658 Cr. = ₹ 50

(17) 8782 Cr. Cheque 5620 + 3480 + 3169 + 4000 + 1500 + (9650 – 100 – 300 – 50 – 300 – 50) + 100 + 3400 = ₹ 30119

(18) Closing Cash Balance = 740 + (632 + 450 + 650 + 370) + (6500 + 2100 + 500 + 350) – 50 – 30 – 11202 = ₹ 1010

Example. *Prepare the Monthly Account for September 2009 in form CPWD 80 of Central Public Works Division N. (Buildings) from the following particulars:*

		₹	notes
(*i*)	*Opening Balance*	2481	
(*ii*)	*Cash Receipts during the month*		
(*a*)	Deposits for works to be done	12,860	(8443) Cr.
(*b*)	Earnest Money from Contractors	7,500	(8443) Cr.
(*c*)	Rent of Residential Buildings	686	(0216) Cr.
(*d*)	Rent of Inspection Bungalow	380	(0059) Cr.
(*e*)	Other Miscellaneous Revenue of Deptt.	768	(0059) Cr.
(*f*)	Receipts on behalf of another PWD Division	878	(8443) Cr.
(*g*)	Hire charges of Tools and Plant	300	(0059) Cr.
(*h*)	Sale proceeds of Dismantled materials from the work "*Construction of Central Government Residential Quarters*" (major work). The amount was realised on 30 – 9 and credited into the bank on the following day.	1900	(4216) Cr.
(*iii*)	*Payments by cheque*		
(*a*)	Additions and Alterations to Income Tax building	28000	(4059) Dr.

(*b*)	Maintenance of Central Government Residential buildings	4600	(2216) Dr.
(*c*)	Construction of Central Government Residential Quarters	46500	(4216) Dr.
(*d*)	Refund of Security Deposit	1600	(8443) Dr.
(*e*)	Deposit work costing less than ₹ 1 lakh carried out for a local body (usual departmental charges as contemplated in Appendix 4 to CPWA Code are to be levied)	12000	(8443) Dr.
(*f*)	Purchase of Service Postage Stamps	800	(2059) Dr.
(*g*)	Purchase of Office Furniture	3600	(2059) Dr.
(*h*)	Salary of officers and Staff - Gross	16850	(2059) Dr.
	Deductions		
	(1) *Income Tax*	200	(0021) Cr.
	(2) *G P Fund*	1800	(8009) Cr.
	(3) *Licence Fee*	500	(0216) Cr.
	(4) *CGHS Contribution*	70	(0210) Cr.
	(5) *Advance to Govt. Servants for purchase of conveyances*	550	(7610) Cr.
	(6) *Central Govt. Employees Group Insurance Scheme*	180	(8011) Cr.
	(7) *Recovery of Leave Salary overpaid in June 2004 Pay Bill.*	60	(2059) Cr.
(*iv*)	*Cash Payments*		
(*a*)	Carriage charges for surplus material transferred from the work '*Construction of Central Govt. Residential quarters*' to Stock	160	(4216) Dr.
(*b*)	Petty Office expenses	150	(2059) Dr.
(*v*)	*Misc. cash receipts remitted into Bank*	23000	(8782) Dr.

Ans.

Monthly Account for May 2009

Major Heads of Account	*Receipts* ₹	*Disbursements* ₹
0059 Public works	4238	
0210 Medical	70	
0216 Housing	1186	
2059 Public Works		21340
2216 Housing		4600

4059 Public Works			28000
4216 Housing			44760
Miscellaneous heads of account			
0021	₹ 200		
0070	₹ 30		
0071	₹ 30	260	
7610 Loans to Government Servants		550	
8009 State Provident Funds		1800	
8011 Insurance and Pension Funds		180	
8443 Civil Deposits; PW Deposits		21238	16450
8782 Remittances		110590	23000
Cash Balance increased			
Closing Balance	₹ 4443		
Opening Balance	₹ 2481		1962
	Total	140112	140112

Important Points

(1) The following charges are to be levied on Deposit Works costing less than ₹ 1 Lakh in accordance with Appendix 4 of CPWA Code:

Dr. (23.75%) **₹ 2850** (8443); **Cr.** (23.25%) **₹ 2790** (0059)

Cr. (00.25%) ₹ **30** (0070)

Cr. (00.25%) ₹ **30** (0071)

(2) In this example, we have to work out the total amount of payments by cheque and Closing Balance of Cash.

Cheques = 28000 + 4600 + 46500 + 1600 + 12000 + 800 + 3600 + 16850 – (200 + 1800 + 500 + 70 + 550 + 180 + 60) = ₹ 110590

Closing balance = 2481 + (12860 + 7500 + 686 + 380 + 768 + 878 + 300 + 1900) – 160 – 150 – 23000 = ₹ 4443.

Other calculations are as under:

(1) 0059 = 380 + 768 + 2790 = 4238

(2) 0210 = 70

(3) 0216 = 686 + 500

(4) 2059 = 800 + 3600 + 16850 – 60 + 150 = 21340

(5) 2216 = 4600

(6) 4059 = 28000

(7) 4216 = – 1900 + 46500 + 160 = 44760
(8) 0021 = 200
(9) 0070 = 30
(10) 0071 = 30
(11) 7610 = 550
(12) 8009 Cr. = 1800
(13) 8011 Cr. = 180
(14) 8443 Cr. = 12860 + 7500 + 878 = 21238
(15) 8443 Dr. = 1600 + 12000 + 2850 = 16450
(16) 8782 Dr. = 23000.

4.10 TRANSFER ENTRY

(We have given brief narration in the answers. In actual practice give detailed and fully informative narration.)

Transfer entry is one of the important initial accounts records. All transfer entry orders are prepared in Form CAM 34 (or CPWA 53) :

(*i*) to set right any misclassification in accounts;

(*ii*) to clear suspense heads of accounts;

(*iii*) to carry out certain adjustments of miscellaneous character.

The two forms are given below.

CAM 34

<table>
<tr><td>₹</td><td>Dr. --
--</td><td>₹</td></tr>
<tr><td></td><td>To --
-- Cr.</td><td></td></tr>
<tr><td colspan="3">Narration (giving details and reasons in support of transfer entry)</td></tr>
</table>

CPWA Form 53

<table>
<tr><td rowspan="3">Particulars with reasons for adjustment</td><td colspan="2">DEBITS</td><td colspan="2">CREDITS</td></tr>
<tr><td>Name of work or head of account</td><td>₹</td><td>Name of work or head of account</td><td>₹</td></tr>
<tr><td></td><td></td><td></td><td></td></tr>
</table>

If no transfer entry is adjusted in accounts for a period of (say) six months, what will happen?

(1) All balances under suspense heads (Miscellaneous Works Advance, Material Purchase Settlement Suspense) shall remain uncleared.

(2) Materials issued to contractors and/or transferred to another will not appear in the accounts of those contractors/works.

(3) Accounts of works will not be closed where contractors delay to receive payment for more than one month after the final bill has been passed.

(4) Lapsed deposits, which are more than 3 years old will not be credited to revenue and cleared from Deposit Account.

(5) All errors and misclassifications will remain uncorrected.

(6) It will not be possible to levy percentage charges on deposit works and works undertaken on behalf of other governments etc.

(7) Amounts advised for adjustment by the Accountant General/P.A.O. representing payments made by the Director General Supply and Disposal will remain out of account.

(8) Balances under suspense head "*Contractor's Other Transactions*" will not be correct. It will not be advisable to settle contractors' accounts on the basis of Contractors' Ledger.

Broad Categories. Transfer entries fall in the following categories:

(1) Operating and clearing Suspense heads.

(2) Stores received from other works.

(3) Contractors delay to receive payments of final bill.

(4) Setting right errors.

(5) Purchases through DGS&D.

(6) Operating and clearing works' suspense.

(7) Departmental Charges and Miscellaneous.

1. OPERATING/CLEARING SUSPENSE HEADS

Scope. Operating the heads of account like "*Miscellaneous Works Advances*" and "*Material Purchase Settlement Suspense account*" and clearing the balances outstanding under them fall in this group.

Misc. Works Advances. *This head receives debit first. It is cleared by subsequent credit on Cash Recovery or by Adjustment.* Para 13.4 of CPWA Code explains the use of this head. There are 4 classes of transactions falling under this suspense head, namely:

(1) *Sales on Credit.* (for sale of stores on credit including supervision charges on such sales)

(2) *Expenditure on Deposit Works in excess of deposits received.*

(3) *Losses, retrenchments and errors.* Include

1. Deficiencies/losses of Stores and Cash,
2. Errors in accounts awaiting adjustments, and
3. Retrenchment and losses recoverable from employees.

(4) *Other items.* Include

1. Debits whose classification cannot be determined at once.
2. Recoverable debits (not relating to Works).
3. Recoverable debits of Works whose accounts are to be closed.

Material Purchase Settlement Suspense Account. This head receives Credit first which is cleared by subsequent **minus Credit** by Cash Payment or Adjustment. The scope of this head is explained in para 13.2 of CPWA Code.

This head is credited for the value of stores purchased for works but which have not been paid for immediately on purchase. This is done by debit to work concerned. Similarly, the value of stores purchased for stock but which have not been paid for by the time of monthly closing of Stock Account is also credited to this head. This is done by debit to Stock Account.

Note 1. If the actual value is not known, then adjustment is made for an estimated value. Any difference noticed, when price is known, is adjusted by plus or minus credit to this suspense head. (Para 13.2.3 of CPWA Code)

Note 2. Payment made for the purchases in the circumstances mentioned above is minus credited to "*Material Purchase Settlement Suspense*" which clears the earlier Credit to it. If the final payment is more than the amount already credited, the additional amount should be debited to Work or Stock, as the case may be, direct. (Note below para 13.2.4 of CPWA Code) (See also note 1 below head 8658 ordering clearance of debit by minus debit and credit by minus credit)

Example. *On counting the Cash Balance on 1st April 2009, the Divisional Officer found a sum of ₹ 50 short. On investigation, it was found, on 1st May 2004 that a sum of ₹ 40 received from a contractor for Tools hired by his men had been accounted for twice, and that a sum of ₹ 10 paid as cartage charges for office furniture had been left out of account. What account adjustments are necessary in the April and May accounts?*

Ans. On 1st. April 2004, ₹ 50 will be taken on the Payment side of the Cash Book and classified under the head "*Miscellaneous Works Advances*" (Para 6.6.7 & Para 13.4.4. of CPWA Code). The following transfer entry will be prepared for the account for May:

₹		₹
40	*Dr.* 0059 Public Works; General; Hire charges of Machinery and equipment	
10	*Dr.* 2059 Public Works, General, Direction and Administration; Office Expenses.	
	To 2059 Public Works, General, Suspense; Miscellaneous Works Advances *Cr.*	50
A sum of ₹ 50 found short in Cash, on 1st April, 2004, was kept under Advances. It was due to double credit of ₹ 40 received for hire of Tools and Plant; and payment of ₹ 10 (cartage of office furniture) left out of account (cash memo attached).		

Example. *Prepare transfer entries for adjustment of the following transactions of a B & R Division.*

(*i*) Wood received from Forest Department and issued direct to the work "*Constructing Residence for the Executive Engineer*" ₹ 5000.

(*ii*) Timber worth ₹ 2500 received from the Forest department and issued direct to the work "*Constructing Residence for Deputy Collector*".

(*iii*) Timber ₹ 7500 received from Forest Department and issued direct to work "*Construction of a Civil Court Building*".

(*iv*) Cost of 400 Cu. ft. of timber received in March 2004 from a Forest Division of the State. Debit is awaited but the invoice shows cost at ₹ 4 per cu. ft.

(*v*) Cement received from a firm for the work "*Construction of Government Primary School Building (Capital account)*" 5 tonnes at ₹ 3200 per tonne. Bill awaited from the firm.

(*vi*) Cost of materials received from the contractor for "Stock" not paid during the month of its receipt - ₹ 6500.

(*vii*) Cement received from a firm in June 2009 for carrying out some Minor Repair Work in an Urban Hospital-2 tonnes @ ₹ 2600 per tonne. Bill is awaited.

Ans. (*i*)

₹			₹
5000	*Dr.*	4216 Capital Outlay on Housing, Government Residential Buildings; Other Housing; Constructing Residence of Executive Engineer.	
	To	8658 Suspense Accounts, Material Purchase Settlement Suspense Account *Cr.*	5000
Timber received from Forest Department for ₹ 5000 for "Constructing Residence of Executive Engineer but debit is awaited. (Para 13.2.1 of CPWA Code)			

(*ii*) to (*vi*). Transfer entries would be the similar to the one in answer 2 (*i*) except that debit will be given to the following heads instead of 4216 etc.

(*ii*) Same as in Ans. 2 (*i*) above.

(*iii*) 4059 Capital Outlay on Public Works, Other Buildings, Construction.

(*iv*) Work concerned. (If this purchase was for stock would it be correct to debit its cost to 2059 Public Works, General, Stock? Answer it and then see Ans. 2 (*vi*) that follows.)

(*v*) 4202 Capital outlay on Education, General Education, Elementary Education Buildings. (₹ 16000)

(*vi*) No transfer entry is to be prepared. It will be adjusted through the Summary of Stock Indents automatically at the end of the month.

(*vii*) 2210 Medical and Public Health, Urban Health Services, Allopathy, Hospitals and Dispensaries.

Example. *Prepare transfer entries for the following transactions:*

(*i*) Two tonnes of steel materials (estimated cost ₹ 30000) were received from suppliers on 28-12-08 for the work of constructing of a technical college. The bill for the supply amounting to ₹ 29650 was received in January 2009 and paid in February 2009.

(*ii*) 8 Sleepers estimated to cost ₹ 6000 were received from a supplier A in January 2009 for the work of constructing an Assistant Engineer's Residence forming part of a major irrigation project. The bill for the supply amounting to ₹ 5500 was received and paid in March 2009.

Ans. (*i*) **On receipt of materials in 12/03**

₹ 30000	*Dr.* 4202 Education, Technical education, Engineering Colleges, Technical Colleges and Institutes	
	To 8658 Suspense Accounts, Material Purchase Settlement Suspense Account *Cr.*	₹ 30000
Estimated cost of steel materials supplied by – on 28 – 12 – 03 for the work Construction of a Technical College adjusted. (See M.B. no.--- page ---)		

On receipt of Bill in 2/04

₹ (–)350	*Dr.* 4202 Education, Technical education, Engineering Colleges	
	To 8658 Suspense Accounts, Material Purchase Settlement Suspense Account *Cr.*	₹ (–)350
Value of steel, adjusted ₹ 30000 vide TE no.--- in 12/03 for the work "*Constructing Technical College*", was actually ₹ 29650 (supplier's Bill no.---)		

Ans. (*ii*). The transfer Entry will be the similar to the one in Ans. 3 (*i*). The head of account to be debited is "*4701 Capital Outlay on Major and Minor Irrigation, Major Irrigation – Commercial, Name of the Project*".

2. STORES RECEIVED FROM OTHER WORKS

Adjusting Stores received from other Works. Read paras 10.3.6 (item 2), 10.3.11(item 2), and 10.3.13 (c) of CPWA Code. Sum and substance of it all is that the materials transferred are to be adjusted immediately and are to be priced within market rates in so far as that work is concerned from which these are transferred. (If the transfer was to another work, it will be valued at the same price. Of course, if these are issued to the contractor, the rate charged would be as per agreement, any gain or loss going to the head "*Additional Charges for Materials issued to the Contractor*".

Example. *Prepare transfer entries in the following cases:*

(*i*) Value of Cement transferred during October 2009 to work "*Construction of a bridge on a State Highway*" from the work "*Construction of Government High School Building*". ₹ 1500.

(*ii*) Cement transferred from "*Constructing Hospital*" to "*Constructing a Bridge*" 9 tonnes @ ₹ 1200 per tonne, EE's orders dt. 10–6.

(*iii*) Transfer of surplus material worth ₹ 5000 from the work of Constructing an allopathic Medical College building to that of construction of a tank for urban water supply.

(*iv*) Transfer of surplus material worth ₹ 4000 (market value ₹ 3500) from work "*constructing a medical college building back to stores.*"

(*v*) Surplus material worth ₹ 500 at the original issue rate (₹ 450 at current market rate) returned to stock from work "*Constructing a bridge*".

Ans. (*i*)

₹ 1500	*Dr.* 5054 Capital Outlay on Roads and Bridges, State Highways, Bridges.	
	To 4202 Capital Outlay on Education, General Education, Secondary Education, Buildings *Cr.*	₹ 1500
Value of cement transferred in October 2004 from the work of constructing a Govt. High School Building to the work of Constructing a Bridge.		

(*ii*) Debit as in 6 (*i*) above, Credit to "*4210 Capital Outlay on Medical and Public Health, Urban Health Services, Hospitals and Dispensaries*".

(*iii*) Debit "*4210 C. O. on Medical and Public Health; Medical Education, Training and Research; Allopathy*". Credit "*4215 Capital Outlay on Water Supply and Sanitation, Water Supply; Urban Water Supply*".

(*iv*) & (*v*). No transfer entry is needed. These will be adjusted through Goods Received Sheets & the Stock Account. [Para 7.2.4 (*d*) of CPWA Code]

BALANCES ON CONTRACTOR'S CLOSED ACCOUNT

Balance to go to Deposits or Advances. Para 10.5.19 of CPWA Code requires that the account of contractors should be closed as soon as the contract is completed. (If they refuse to receive the final payment for more than one month after the final bill has been passed, the amount payable to the contractor may be credited to *"8843 Civil Deposits; Public Works Deposits; Deposits of Contractors on closed accounts"* and the accounts of the work closed), On closing the account of the work if it is found from his personal account that something is recoverable from him, it may be debited to *"Suspense – Miscellaneous Work Advances"*.

Suspense Balances of Annual Maintenance Estimates. Accounts of annual maintenance are closed at the end of the last month of *working year* fixed for the purpose. If it is proposed to carry over the maintenance works to *next working year*, suspense balances in the accounts of such works are transferred to *"Deposits"* (if payable) or *"Misc. Works Advances"* (if recoverable). In the next working year they are transferred back to Suspense heads where they were outstanding. (Para 10.6.8 CPWA Code)

Example. *How will you adjust the following? Prepare necessary transfer entries.*

(*i*) Balance of ₹ 4750 remaining outstanding as due to contractor and a balance of ₹ 2105 remaining as unpaid wages of muster roll at the time of closing the accounts of a Major Work.

(*ii*) Adjustment of a sum of ₹ 700 representing amount due to a contractor as unsettled liability at the time of closing of accounts of a work *"Constructing Residence for a Superintendent of Police"*.

(*iii*) Adjustment of a sum of ₹ 437 being unsettled liabilities at the close of the year in the suspense account of Annual Repair Estimates.

Ans. (*i*)

₹ 4750	*Dr.* Work concerned, Contractor's Suspense A/cs.	
	To 8443 Civil Deposits; Public Works Deposits; Sums due to Contractors on closed accounts. *Cr.*	₹ 4750
Balance due to contractors of work ----adjusted (Para 10.5.19 CPWA Code)		

Wages of labourers unpaid are not to be adjusted (Para 10.5.18 CPWA Code)

(*ii*)

₹ 700	*Dr*. 4216 Capital Outlay on Housing; Government Residential Buildings; Police Housing.	
	To 8443 Civil Deposits; Public Works Deposits; Sums due to Contractors on closed accounts *Cr*.	₹ 700
Unsettled liabilities on closing account of work *"Constructing Residence for Superintendent of Police"* Adjusted under (Para 10.5.19 of CPWA Code).		

(*iii*)

₹ 437	*Dr*. Work Concerned; Contractor's Suspense A/cs.	₹
	To 8443 Civil Deposits; Public Works Deposits; Sums due to Contractors on closed accounts *Cr*.	437
Unsettled liability at the close of annual repair work of ---- adjusted under (Para 10.6.8 (2) of CPWA Code).		

4. SETTING RIGHT ERRORS

Rules for correcting errors. Rules for correcting errors are there in Paras 8.1.2; 8.1.3; and 8.1.4 of CPWA Code as under:

(1) *Transferring Debit (or Credit) from Debt, Deposit or Remittance heads to any other head.*

This correction must always be carried out. You Minus Debit (or Minus Credit) the Debt, Deposit or Remittance head and Debit the expenditure head (or Credit the Revenue head).

(2) *Transferring Debit from Expenditure head to Debt, Deposit or Remittance head.*

You Debit the correct Debt, Deposit or Remittance head and minus Debit the expenditure head *if correction is being carried out in the financial year in which the error occurred. If the correction is being carried out after the close of that financial year*, then, *instead of minus Debit to Expenditure head*, credit the amount to the relevant Receipt Head or 0075 Miscellaneous General services if there is no corresponding Receipt Head.

(**Note.** The idea is that previous years' errors should not affect the current year Budget. RECOVERIES OF OVERPAYMENTS ARE ALWAYS TAKEN IN REDUCTION OF EXPENDITURE IRRESPECTIVE OF THE YEAR OF RECOVERY).

(3) *Transferring Credit from Receipt head to Debt, Deposit or Remittance heads.*

You Credit the concerned Debt, Deposit or Remittance head and minus credit the revenue receipt sub-head if the accounts of the year are open. If the correction is being carried out in the next years' accounts, then minus credit the sub-head "*Refunds*".

(4) *Transfer from a Receipt/Expenditure head to another Receipt/Expenditure head.*

During the year, transfer is permissible from one such head to another such head. After the accounts for the year are closed, no transfer is permissible unless it affects the accounts of other governments or commercial departments. (Para 8.1.2 of CPWA Code)

Example. *Prepare transfer entries to set right the following errors in the accounts of the same year in which the error occurred:*

(*i*) Income tax received in July 2009 from a work-charged establishment employed on the maintenance of a Road of economic importance and erroneously credited to the work during the month.

(*ii*) Income tax recovered from work-charged establishment employed on maintenance of State Highway Road and erroneously credited to the work. ₹ 85.

(*iii*) A sum of ₹ 230 recovered from a mistri on account of licence fee has been wrongly credited to maintenance work of a Primary School.

(*iv*) Schedule of Public Works Receipts received from the Treasury for May 2009 includes ₹ 615 on account of the following items but no entry exists in the Cash Book.

Security Deposit of contractor	₹ 500
Remittance by SDO of another Division	₹ 100
Sale proceeds of grass of Office Compound	₹ 15

Ans. (*i*)

₹ 95	*Dr.* 3054 Roads and Bridges, Roads of inter-state or Economic Importance, Road works, Maintenance	
	To 0021 Taxes on Income, Income Tax on Union Emoluments including Pensions *Cr.*	₹ 95
Income tax recovered from work charged staff in July 2004 vide Vr. no. ...... was wrongly credited to work. The error is now corrected.		

(*ii*)

₹ 85	*Dr.* 3054 Roads & Bridges, State Highways, Maintenance	
	To 0021 Taxes on Income, Income Tax on Union Emoluments including Pensions *Cr.*	₹ 85
Income tax recovered from work charged staff vide Vr. no.---- was wrongly credited to work. The error is now corrected.		

(*iii*)

₹ 230	*Dr.* 2059 Public Works, Other Buildings, Maintenance	
	To 0216 Housing Government Residential Buildings, General Pool Accommodation, Licence Fee *Cr.*	₹ 230
Licence fee recovery from ... in Vr. no. ... was credited to work, now corrected.		

(*iv*)

₹ 615	*Dr.* 8782 Cash Remittances etc., PW Remittances, Remittances into Treasuries/Bank	
	To (*i*) 8443 Civil Deposits, PW Deposits, Cash Deposits of Contractors as Security *Cr.*	₹ 500
	(*ii*) 8443 Civ. Dep., PW Deposits, Misc. Deposits *Cr.*	₹ 100
	(*iii*) 0059 Public Works, General, Other Receipts, Other Items *Cr.*	₹ 15
Amounts deposited in the treasury/bank in May 2009, not appearing in the Cash Book, now adjusted. Details are as under: (details)		

Note 1. The last, item (*iv*) of the example can be corrected by making entries in the Cash Book of the day on which it is decided to correct the error.

Note 2. In State Division, Income Tax is creditable to 8658 Suspense, Tax Deducted at Source (TDS) Suspense instead of 0021 Taxes on Income.

5. PURCHASES THROUGH DGS&D

Procedure in the Central Government. The minor head "*Material Purchase Settlement Suspense Account*" has two sub-heads, namely,

(1) Purchases pending payment/Adjustment.

(Ii) Payment for purchases through DGS&D.

On receipt of stores. Their value will be debited to Work concerned (immediately) or to Suspense-Stock (at the time of monthly closing of Stock Accounts) by credit to "*8658 Suspense Account; Material Purchase Settlement Suspense Account; Purchases pending Payment / Adjustment*".

On receipt of PAO memo. When the PAO makes payment to DGS&D for these stores and informs the Division through PAO Memo the details of amount paid, the Division will carry out the following adjustment:

Deduct Credit *8658 Suspense Accounts; Material Purchase Settlement Suspense Account; Purchases pending payment / Adjustment*

To 8658 Suspense Accounts; Material Purchase Credit Settlement Suspense Account; Payment for Purchases through DGS&D.

Procedure in State Government Divisions. On receipt of stores, the amount is debited to work or Stock by credit to "*8658 Suspense Accounts; Material Purchase Settlement Account*". On receipt of AG Memo intimating payment by DGS&D (and consequent payment by AG to the DGS&D), The division will adjust it as under:

Deduct Credit 8658 Suspense Accounts;
Material Purchase Settlement Suspense Account.
To 8782 Cash Remittances and Adjustments *Cr.*
between Officers rendering Account to same AO
PW Remittances; III Other Remittances;
(*b*) Items adjustable by PWD

Example. Adjust the following:

(*i*) *Debit advised by PAO in the month of December 2009 of a payment of ₹ 1755 for stores purchased in B&R Division for constructing a bridge on a border road. The stores were received in February 2009.*

(*ii*) *Advice received from the PAO that ₹ 60,000 have been paid to the Cement Corporation of India through DGS&D for 25 tonnes of cement supplied to the Division earlier for the Stock.*

(*iii*) Advice from the AG for the cost of supply of 32 tonnes of cement - ₹ 64,000 plus 1% departmental charges. 16 tonne cement was required for work A, 8 tonnes for work B, and balance 8 tonnes for stock. A lump-sum of ₹ 40,000 had been credited to Suspense at the time of receipt of cement.

Ans. (*i*) **IN CPWD**

(*a*) *in February 2009*

₹		₹
1755	*Dr.* 5054 Capital Outlay on Roads and Bridges, Strategic and Border Roads, Bridges	
	To 8658 Suspense Accounts; Material Purchase Settlement Suspense; Purchase pending payment/adjustment *Cr.*	1755
On receipt of stores purchased through DGS&D.		

(*b*) *in December 2009*

₹		₹
1755	*Deduct Credit.* 8658 Suspense Accounts; Material Purchase Settlement Suspense; Purchases pending payment/adjustment	
	To 8658 Suspense Accounts; Material Purchase Settlement Suspense; Payment for purchases through DGS&D. *Cr.*	1755
On receipt of PAO memo for stores purchased through DGS&D.		

(*ii*) No TE on receipt of Stores. TE as at (*i*) above will be made on receiving PAO Memo.

(*iii*) **IN STATES** (₹ 40000 in ratio of 16:8:8 for work A, B, & Stores).

₹		₹
20000 10000	*Dr.* Work A Work B	
	To 8658 Suspense Accounts; Material Purchase Settlement Suspense. *Cr.*	30000
On receipt of Stores for Works purchased through DGS&D. (The remaining ₹ 10000 for stock will be adjusted through Goods Received Sheets)		

On receipt of AG Memo

₹		
12320	*Dr.* Work A	
6160	Work B	
	Deduct Credit. 8658 Suspense Accounts;	
40000	Material Purchase Settlement Suspense.	
	To 8782 Cash Remittances and Adjustments between Officers rendering Account to same AO; PW Remittances ; III Other Remittances; (*b*) Items adjustable by PWD *Cr.*	₹ 58480

On receipt of AG Memo for purchases through DGS&D (Para 13.2.4 & Note there under)

Name of Account	*Amount debitable*	*Amount debited*	*Now to be debited*
Work A	32,320	20,000	12,320
Work B	16,160	10,000	6,160
*Stock	16,160	10,000	6,160
Total	64,640	40,000	24,640

*Cement for Stock will be adjusted through Stock account.

6. OPERATING/CLEARING WORKS' SUSPENSE

Suspense accounts of Works. Following suspense accounts are operated within the accounts of works:

(1) **Contractor's**
- (*a*) Advance Payments.
- (*b*) Secured Advance.
- (*c*) Other Transactions.

(2) **Labourers.**

(3) **Materials.**

(4) **Land Acquisition.**

It has already been explained in Section 3 above how the balances under "*Contractor's Suspense*" are to be cleared on closing the accounts of the work and that the balance under "*Suspense Labourers*" are left uncleared.

Clearing "Suspense-Materials". Read para 10.3.18 of CPWA Code for the manner of clearing it. Para 10.5.7 ibid explains that this head is to be opened only (*i*) in cases where provision is made separately for "*Labour*" and "*Material*" and

(*ii*) the work is done departmentally or through Contractor at labour rates only.

Para 10.5.13 further explains that it is to be cleared in the Register of Works in the Division only on the closing of the account of the work. The process is simple:

(1) Materials required for use on other works may be transferred at lower of the issue rate or the market rate. (*By Transfer Entry*)

(2) Materials, which can be of use in a foreseeable period, may also be transferred to "*Stock*" at lower of the issue rate or market rate. (*No Transfer Entry will be needed, as transfer would be through stock account and Goods Received Sheets*)

Land Acquisition. Amount of money paid for land acquisition for a work is debited to this Suspense Head of the Work Abstract. In accordance with para 10.5.21 of CPWA Code, this Suspense head is cleared by the Divisional Officer by transfer from this sub-head to the sub-head of Final Charges "*Cost of Land Acquisition*" after receipt of account and Land Award Statement from the Land Acquisition Officer. If there is any delay in land acquisition proceedings or in final payment of compensation, this Suspense head may be left uncleared. Later the account of work may be re-opened if necessary.

Example. *Two girders costing ₹ 5895 were received for the work of constructing office of Director Public Health in July 2009. The work was allotted to contractor on labour rate only. The work on the building was stopped in August 2009. These girders were taken on Stock of the CPWD Division in September 2009. What account adjustments are necessary if market rate of girders was ₹ 2254.50P each?*

Ans. (*i*) **On receipt of Girders**

₹		
5895	*Dr.* 4059 Capital Outlay on P.W.; Office Buildings; Medical and Public Health; name of work; Materials.	
	To 8658 Suspense Accounts; Material Purchase Settlement A/c; Purchases pending Payment/ Adjustment *Cr.*	₹ 5895
Receipt of Girders in July 2009 for Office building of Director Public Health.		

(*ii*) **On their transfer to Stock in Sept. 2009.** (under Para 10.3.13 of CPWA Code). The account of the work will get credit through the Summary of Stock Receipts. No TE will be needed. The effect will be as below:

₹ 4509	*Dr.* 0059 Public Works ; Suspense; Stock	
	To 4059 Capital Outlay on P.W.; Office Buildings; Medical and Public Health, name of work; Materials *Cr.*	₹ 4509

The head Material Purchase Settlement Suspense will be cleared when payment is made.

7. DEPARTMENTAL CHARGES

Departmental Charges. Departmental charges leviable on works done by CPWD for P&T Department, Railways, Defence, State Governments, and Local Bodies are given in Appendix 4 of CPWA Code. The charges normally levied are the following:

(*i*) Establishment Charges.

(*ii*) Tools and Plant Charges.

(*iii*) Pensionary Charges

(*iv*) Audit and Account Charges.

Establishment Charges, Tools and Plant Charges and Pensionary Charges are levied on all works undertaken for:

(*a*) Other Governments and Defence Department.

(*b*) Govt. Autonomous Bodies and Non-Government Bodies.

(*c*) Commercial Departments of the same Government.

Audit & Account Charges are levied on works belonging to (*b*) and (*c*) above only.

Important.

(1) Pensionary Charges are always credited to Receipt head "0071" Receipt Head.

(2) Establishment; Tools and Plant; and Audit & Account charges charged:

(*a*) **from the departments of the same Government,** are taken in reduction of expenditure; (2059 Direction & Admn.; 2059 Machinery and Equipment; and 2016 Audit respectively)

(*b*) **from others,** are credited to Revenue (i.e. 0059, 0070 etc.).

(3) **Works done for non-Government Bodies entirely funded by Government are exempted from levy of these departmental charges from 27-9-2001.** Exempt them only if the question states that the Body is funded entirely by the Government.

Example 11. *Prepare transfer entry in respect of departmental charges levied on minor works expenditure of ₹40,000 in a CPWD Division incurred on behalf of Delhi Municipal Corporation.*

Ans.

₹		₹
9500	*Dr.* 8443 Civil Deposits; Public Works Deposits; Deposits for Works to be done	
	To 0059 Public Works; General; Recovery of percentage Charges (23.25% Estt and T&P Charges) *Cr.*	9300
	0070 Other Administrative Services; Fees for Government Audit. (0.25% Audit & Account Charges). *Cr.*	100
	0071 Contributions & Other Retirement Benefits; Civil; Subscriptions & Contributions (1/4% Pensionary) *Cr.*	100
Departmental charges levied on minor work ------ of Delhi Municipal Corp., expenditure during the month being ₹ 40,000 only		

Example 12. *Prepare a transfer entry levying departmental charges for a building worth ₹ 75 lakhs constructed on behalf of Posts and Telegraph Department by a CPWD Division.*

Ans.

₹		₹
9,00,000	*Dr.* 8658 Suspense Accounts; PAO Suspense, Transactions adjustable by PAO P&T	
	To 2059 Public Works; General	
	Direction & Admn. (10.75%) *Cr.*	8,06,250
	Machinery and Equipment (3/4%) *Cr.*	56,250
	2016 Audit; Deduct Establishment Charges recovered from other Government departments etc. (0.25%) *Cr.*	18,750
	0071 Pensions & Other Retirement Benefits; Civil Subscriptions & Contributions (0.25%) *Cr.*	18,750
Departmental charges levied on ₹ 75 lakh Building Work of P & T Deptt.		

5

STORES

5.1 INTRODUCTION

For the execution of any Civil Engineering project, the following resources apart from the manpower are required :

(1) Construction stores

(2) Tools and plant

(3) Vehicles

(4) Plant, machinery and equipment.

The success of any project thus depends on the proper procurement, utilisation, upkeep and transfer/disposal of resources not required for the project.

Proper maintenance of stores is as important as maintenance of cash. Proper maintenance of stores is, therefore, absolutely necessary.

5.2 SAFE CUSTODY OF STORES

The Divisional Engineer is ultimately, responsible for initial procurement, its safe custody, proper storage, distribution and disposal of surplus stores. In the Public Works Department the divisional stores is normally held by Junior Engineer. He is responsible to the Divisional Engineer for safe custody and proper distribution and accounting and submission of reports and returns.

Apart from the divisional store, every sub-division holds stores for its day-to-day work, usually drawn from the divisional stores. The sub-divisional officer usually makes one of the Junior Engineer or a sub-overseer as incharge for the sub-divisional stores.

5.3 CLASSIFICATION OF STORES

All stores can be classified under the following two categories namely :

(1) Stock

(2) Directly charged to works.

Stores procured for general use of construction work and maintenance work are initially kept under suspense head of the stock and issued to the required jobs on the basis of indents. Debit for such stores is raised against the job for which these stores have been issued and credit given to the suspense head of the stock. Further details of stock are given in Chapter 6.

In the case of projects, the requirement of stores is very large and a separate organisation is normally required to take charge of the stores transactions. Such stores, which are procured for specific projects are known as *Material-at-Site Stores*. Their cost is directly debited to the project. The difference in the cost of procurement and supply rate to the contractor is also directly adjusted in the project accounts. The term 'Material-at-Site' does not mean that such project material is necessarily stored at the project site.

5.4 THE ACCOUNTING AND CONTROL OF CONSTRUCTION STORES CAN BE DIVIDED INTO THE SAME TWO CATEGORIES UNDER WHICH STORES ARE CLASSIFIED (SEE ART 5.3), NAMELY :

(1) Stores for specific Works

(2) Stores for Divisional stock

The above two categories are dealt within in this article separately.

1. Stores for specific Works. As soon as procurement action for stores is initiated, it amounts to a financial commitment. It, therefore, follows that such action should be taken when the administrative approval for the work has been accorded and funds for the same have been allotted. However, as soon as the possibility of any project materialising is visualised planning has to be started. For example, exploring accurately of different categories of stores and collection of information in respect of their rates may be started in anticipation of the allotment of the funds.

On receipt of the stores, the officer in charge of stores (normally a Junior Engineer) prepares receipts voucher in triplicate. The allocation against the work is given in the vouchers. Two copies of the receipt voucher are sent to the Divisional Engineer. One copy is retained by the Divisional Engineer and the second copy is returned to the SDO/JE after recording therein the estimated cost of stores on the basis of which liability is booked in the construction accounts of the work concerned. On receipts of the bill, the same is processed in the normal manner. When the bill is paid the liability is cancelled and corresponding amount is added to the expenditure column. Thus the total of the expenditure plus liability remain unchanged. When stores are purchased from private agency, no separate receipt voucher is required. The entry of the stores is certified in the bill itself and amount paid debited to the work.

All stores received for a specific work are entered in the Material-at-Site register. One page is allotted for each article. The issue rate for such stores is fixed by the divisional engineer from actual procurement cost without percentage addition for overheads as is done for stock stores. When it is desired to book expenditure in respect of various items of the work on separate folio in the construction account, material account is opened. This account is maintained on the ordinary construction account form. The cost of bulk receipt is entered as debit and the value of issue is entered as credit. The account is closed on completion of the job.

In the case of important projects, all stores issued directly to the work and the amount such issue are kept for atleast two years, after the completion of the work. The account of such stores, showing the total quantity of stores received and incorporated in the work is subject to audit. At the close of the project the material account is cleared and statement of surplus stores is prepared. Such stores have to be cleared before the accounts of the project are finally settled and the project closed. The surplus stores are disposed off in one of the following ways :

(*a*) **By Transfer to the Divisional Stock.** In this case the cost of carriage and handling from site to divisional stock is debited to the project. Such a transfer is subject to the condition that the stores would be utilised within the next six months and that the holding limit of the stock would not be exceeded.

(*b*) By transfer to another project.

(*c*) By public auction.

Funds realised by disposal of surplus materials are credited to the work. The profit or loss consequent upon disposal of such surplus material is credited/debited to the work to balance the material account.

2. Stores for Divisional Stock. Direct financial control over the expenditure entailed in efficient handling, safe custody and proper maintenance of divisional stock is exercised by means of stores overheads estimates. Such estimates are sanctioned by the higher engineer and provide the basis for allowance for overheads to be made, when fixing stock book rates for stores held in divisional stocks.

The following accounts and records are maintained in connection with stock transaction :

(*a*) **Stock Register.** This shows daily receipts and issues of items and is closed annually. The register is kept by the store keeper.

(*b*) **Stock Purchase Register.** This register shows how stock book rate for each item is calculated. It is maintained by the Divisional Engineer.

(*c*) Stores-in-hand Ledger.

(*d*) Quarterly Stock Summary.

The estimate to cover the cash of operating the divisional stock is prepared annually by the Divisional Engineer/GE and sanctioned by SE/CWE. This estimate covers the following expenses :

(*i*) Wages of causual and muster roll labour, engaged in the maintenance of stores at site.

(*ii*) Cost of handling stores.

(*iii*) Cost of repairs and maintenance of divisional store building.

(*iv*) Cost of wastage of stores in stock.

(*v*) Cost of repairs and overhaul of stores in stock where applicable.

(*vi*) Cost of packing/unpacking of stores where necessary.

(*vii*) Other miscellaneous and minor expenditure.

6

Stock

6.1 INTRODUCTION

As already explained in Chapter 5 all stores in the civil engineering construction can be primarily be divided into stock and project stores. The term stock by usage does not only cover the stores held in the divisional store godown primarily for meeting day-to-day requirement of the division *i.e.*, for normal repairs/maintenance and such works but also includes the complete stores organisation. This organisation comprises of:

(*i*) Permanent, temporary personnel and casual and muster roll labour.

(*ii*) Building structure and storage arrangements for receipts holding and issue of stores from the divisional stock.

(*iii*) Watch and ward arrangements.

(*iv*) Fire fighting arrangements.

Stores are accounted for more or less on the same lines as cash though the system of accounting has to be different primarily on account of the fact that a number of varieties of items are involved.

6.2 ARTICLES IN STOCK/INVENTORY OF STORE

A number of articles are held in stock depending upon the average consumption in the previous year. The holding of construction and other consumable stores in the divisional store serves the following purposes:

(*a*) Articles of daily use, particularly for maintenance work and repair carried out departmentally, are readily available.

(*b*) Controlled construction stores such as steel, cement bricks etc., which the contractor may not be able to procure from the open trade source because of short supply, are readily available. The bid of the contractor for undertaking the work becomes lower.

(*c*) Before any material is accepted in the store, it is inspected from the point of view of its quality. The chances of inferior material being incorporated in the work are thereby considerably reduced.

In order that the accounting of stores may be done satisfactorily and articles may be readily identified and located, materials of similar nature are grouped under different sub-heads on the lines shown in Table 6.1.

Table 6.1. Grouping of Stores in the Divisional Stock

S. No.	*Sub-Head of Stock*	*Name of articles / materials*
1.	Building Materials	Cement, lime, brick, timber, M.S. bar, C.G.I. sheets, Asbestos sheets, etc.
2.	Painting Store	Turpentine oil, paints, etc.
3.	House Fittings/Sanitary Fittings	Watercloses, seats, Wash hand basin, Towel rail etc.
4.	Miscellaneous Stores	Baskets, tree guards, shuttering planks etc.
5.	Brick-kiln material	Sheets for chimneys, coal
6.	Fuel	Kerosene oil, woodfuel, charcoal etc.
7.	Small stores	Hinges, Handles, Nails, Rivets, Screws etc.

Under each of the above sub-heads, an inventory displaying the name of the articles held under the sub-head in the sub-stock is maintained. This list is termed as inventory of stores. Apart for such an inventory which gives the holdings in the sub-stock at a glance a tally card is placed where individual item is stored.

6.3 RESERVE STOCK LIMIT

The purpose of the divisional stock is to have a stock of such articles ready in hand which are required for day-to-day use. The articles to be stored and the, quantity of such articles are fixed on the basis of previous years consumption and on the expected store requirement for minor and major works. In the case of projects, the stores are procured and accounted for separately as project stores and their account maintained as Material-At-Site account.

The following factors determine the store-holding limit of a Divisional Stock.

(*a*) The procurement of stores from trade channels or Government deposits may take as much as six month. Hence a minimum of say 3 month requirement and a maximum of six months should be stocked.

(*b*) Huge quantity of articles if not consumed within a reasonable period of say 6 months are likely to deteriorate. The quantity of such stores should therefore be restricted to 3–6 months requirement.

(*c*) Stores held in stock is a blocked money and hence the value of such stock should be the minimum.

Table 6.2. Inventory of Stores under Sub-head Building Material

S. No.	*Name of Article*	*Upper Holding Limit*	*Min. Reserve Limit*	*Balance Held*	*Date*
1.	Cement				
2.	Lime				
3.	Bricks				
	(*i*) I class				
	(*ii*) II class				
4.	M.S. Bars				
	(*i*) 6 mm ϕ				
	(*ii*) 10 mm ϕ				
	(*iii*) 12 mm ϕ				
	(*iv*) 16 mm ϕ etc.				
5.	C.G.I. sheets				
	(*i*) Size				
	(*ii*) Size				
6.	Asbestos Sheets				
	(*i*) Size				
	(*ii*) Size				

Table 6.3. Tally Card

Upper Holding Limit ....

Reserve Limit ....

Date	*Quantity Received*	*Quantity issued*	*Balance*

(*d*) Large quantities of stores need larger accommodation, larger establishment to handle receipts, holding and issue of stores and larger expenditure in watch and ward and security arrangements.

Taking the above factors into consideration the Superintending Engineer, fixes the maximum limit of amount upto which materials can be kept in a division. The limit thus fixed is known as the **'RESERVE STOCK LIMIT'.** This limit for a division is fixed every year. Holding stores in excess of this reserve limit is a serious audit objection.

The Superintending Engineer may however increase such a limits in special cases when he feels that the work load of the Division has been increased by a number of minor and major works. This increased limit for a specified period is known as *Temporary Reserve Limit.*

Apart from and in addition to the Reserve stock limit in some of the Department effective measures are taken to ensure availability of stores in the Divisional stock. For this purpose a minimum and maximum holding limits of each article of day-to-day requirement is fixed. In fact the Reserve Stock limit itself represents the total value of the upper holding limit.

The purpose of the minimum holding limit is to ensure that before this limit is reached procurement action is initiated.

6.4 QUANTITY ACCOUNT OF STORES

The stores are as important as cash and hence by and large an effective check on the receipts, holding and issue of stores is necessary. All transaction pertaining to receipt and issue of stores is entered by the Junior Engineer incharge of stores daily in the same way as recording entries in the cash book. The register is closed monthly on a date fixed by the Divisional Engineer and forwarded to the divisional office more or less in the same manner as copy of the cash book. In the case of stores, however, only the abstract is forwarded.

The day-to-day transactions are maintained in the form as shown in Table 6.4.

6.5 BALANCE RETURN OF STOCK

In addition to the monthly abstract of receipt and issues, which the Engineer-in-charge sends every month to the Divisional Officer in the form shown in Table 6.5.

Table 6.4. Stock Register

Division ....
Sub-Division ....
Station ....

Month of ....

Date	*Reference to M.B. for receipts and indent for issue*	*Source of receipt or to whom issued*	*Head of Account*	*Name of Articles*					
				Cement	*Steel*	*Timber*	*Paint*	*etc.*	
(1)	(2)	(3)	(4)	(5)	(6)	(7)	(8)	(9)	
	Balance Brought Forward								
	Receipts during Month								
	Total Receipts								
	Grand Total								
	Issues								
	Total of issues								
	Balance C/O.								

The Divisional Engineer prepares a half yearly statement from the monthly record every month from the sub-division.

The purpose of monthly and half yearly returns is to provide an independent check on the transaction in the Divisional and Sub-divisional stores.

6.6 STOCK ACTION FOR VERIFICATION

The Superintending Engineer or other senior officer (Deputy Chief Engineer, Chief Engineer etc.), may carry out test check of the divisional stock at any time with a view of verify the physical holding with the book balance. Similarly, the Divisional Engineer may carry out a test verification of any item in the Divisional store or in the sub-divisional store.

Shortage or surplus during such checks are reconciled at the spot in the manner given below.

(*a*) **Articles found surplus.** The quantity by which the article is found surplus is taken on stock and credited to the head "*Reverse Receipt*". The reason for surplus has to be explained by the store holder.

(*b*) **Articles found short.** The quantity by which the article is found short is issued and cost thereof debited to the head '*Suspense head*' Miscellaneous Advances. The shortage is treated as loss and matter is investigated.

6.7 WRITING OFF LOSSES IN STOCK

If it is found that the loss has occurred inspite of taking all the precautions and that nobody is to be blamed, a loss statement is initiated of which the finding of the stock taking officer and the report of investigation is attached. The loss is finally written off under orders of the competent Authority. Various officers of the Department have the authority or writing off such losses. In case the loss is due to negligence, theft of fraud, the responsibility is fixed on the person responsible and disciplinary/departmental action including recovery of full/part value of the loss is made.

6.8 STOCK-TAKING OF STORES

To ensure proper utilisation of stores all the stores held in Divisional stock are verified once in a year. This verification is carried out in two ways. Firstly is the audit verification. This is carried out under

Table 6.5. Half Yearly Balance Return of Stock

Division........
Sub-Division........
Station........

Period........

S. No.	*Name of article*	*Units*	*Issue Rates*	*Balance Brought Forward*	*Receipts*	*Issues*	*Closing Balance*	*Divisional Store Holder Signature*	*Divisional Engineer Signature*
(1)	(2)	(3)	(4)	(5)	(6)	(7)	(8)	(9)	(10)

the control of the Accountant General/Controller of Defence Accounts as the case may be. This audit party carries out the following verification of the stocks.

(*a*) All the book balances at the end of previous audit are accounted for.

(*b*) All receipts are limited with the Measurement Book No. and page.

(*c*) All receipts and issue vouchers are entered in the same sequence in which the transactions take place.

(*d*) All stores issue to contractors, the cost of which is to be recovered from him are marked as such in the indent as well as in the stock book.

(*e*) Physical stock taking has been carried out and recorded on the relevant ledgers and that surpluses and discrepencies noted are adjusted according to the procedure laid down. Secondly the entries in stock of the Division is checked up once a year. The stock taking team records the physical ground balances irrespective of the book balance and discrepancies are reconciled as described in Art. 6.6.

In addition to the verification of the ground balance, this party may look into the following as well.

(*a*) Half yearly stock taking by the stock holder has been carried out and certificate to this effect given at the end of the ledger.

(*b*) Surprise checks of stores have also been carried on.

(*c*) The divisional and sub-divisional stores in respect of any article are checked in the divisional and sub-divisional stores at the same time.

(*d*) If certain categories of store have not been used in the preceding six months or are not likely to be used during the next six months, disposal action should be initiated.

6.9 TOOLS AND PLANT

Like stores, tools and plant are also classified under the following two categories, namely:

1. Tools and plant required for normal maintenance and minor or major works.

2. Tools and plant procured for a project work or for a specified purpose. The cost of such articles directly charged to the work concerned.

Expect in the M.E.S. where the construction equipment such as tools, plant, machinery vehicles are maintained by the E/M Section, scientific and engineering instruments by the E-6 section (Drawing branch) and furniture and general stores by the barracks and stores section, tools and plant includes plant, machinery, vehicles, tools, surveying instruments, engineering instrument, furniture and similar stock.

Tables 6.6 and 6.7 show typical forms for receipts and issue of tools and plant.

One receipt of an item of tools and plant it is entered in the form for receipt which is prepared in triplicate one copy is retained by the store keeper and the other two copies are sent to the Sub-divisional Officer for posting in the tools and plant register.

Table 6.6 Account of Receipt of Tools and Plant

Division.........

Sub-Division.........

Station.......... Month...........

Date	*Source of receipt with particulars*	*Names of articles with classification*						*To be filled in the Divisional office*
		Road Rollers	*Tar boilers*	*Sledge Hammers*	*and so on*			*Reference to voucher no. and date of adjustment of value*

(Sd.) Sub Divisional Officer

The Sub-divisional Officer carries out the posting in his ledger and gives reference of the page on which entered in both the copies and sends one copy to the divisional engineer. The suppliers 'bill is passed for payment on the basis of these entries in the relevant register.

Similarly, all issues are recorded in the tools and plant issue register. Tools and plant sent out from the sub-admission for repair or lent to other division is also treated as issue and entered in the form. The abstract of all issued is submitted to the Divisional Officer every month.

Table 6.8 shows tools and plant register in which a consolidated account of receipts issues and balance is maintained. The form is in three parts. First part shows article in hand, second part shows article temporarily let out or sent for repairs and the third part shows shortages awaiting adjustment.

Table 6.7. Account of Issues of Tools and Plant

Division.........
Sub Division.........
Station........

Date	*To whom issued with particulars*	*Name of article with classification*	*To be filled in Divisional office*
			Reference to recovery of Value

(Sd.) Sub Divisional Officer

Table 6.8. Head and Sub Head of Tools and Plant

S.No. (1)	*Head* (2)	*Sub-Head* (3)	*Example* (4)	*Remark* (5)
1.	Plant and Machinery	(*i*) Fixed	Stone, crusher shaper etc.	
		(*ii*) Move cable	Welding plant, compressor	
		(*iii*) Locomotives and rolling state	Wagon, trolley engine	
		(*iv*) Vehicle	Trucks, jeeps, car	
		(*v*) Boat bridge-ing and Navigation Equipment	boat, pontoons	
		(*vi*) Road making plant	Road roller Making plant	
2.	Tools	(*i*) Fixed	Sand	
		(*ii*) Movable	Vice, hammer	
		(*iii*) Hand tools	Pliers, tapes wrench	
3.	Scientific Apparatus	(*i*) Scientific apparatus	Thermometer	
		(*ii*) Mathematical drawing instruments	Pentagraph, drawing board	
		(*iii*) Surveying instruments	Theodolite, Compass, Level	
		(*iv*) Electrical instruments	Electrical motors	
		(*v*) Other energy instruments	Voltameter	
		(*vi*) Matrics	Water meter Electric meter	

(*Continued*)

S.No. (1)	Head (2)	Sub-Head (3)	Example (4)	Remark (5)
	Furniture			
		(*i*) Office (*ii*) Residential and Rest House (*iii*) Camp equipment	Chair, table, wash has basin, Cots, towel, stand folding chair, folding table, Camp cot	
	Hospital equipment			
		(*i*) Furniture	Dention chair operation table	
		(*ii*) Plant (Equipment)	Sterlising plant X-ray plant	
		(*iii*) Instruments	Forceps, Measure glass, Syranges	
	Live stocks		horses, camel donkey	

6.10 DISPOSAL OF UNSERVICEABLE ARTICLES OF T&P

When articles become unserviceable due to fair wear and tear it is not economical to hold them on the books. A survey report showing detailed reasons for the action is initialed by the holder of Y&P and submitted for sanction to the competent authority. Powers for sanctioning write-off in respect of such articles differ from department to department and from state to state. While accepting the write off the mode of final disposal of the articles is also indicated. For example, in the case of a car, the methods of disposal would be:

(*a*) Disposal by public auction

(*b*) Useful components be salvaged and the rest converted into scrap and auctioned as such

Note. In the M.E.S. such articles are sent to the Salvage Depots of the Defence establishment where the useful parts are used on repairs of other similar equipment and the rest auctioned as scrap or destroyed by burning.

6.11 PREPARATION OF SURVEY REPORT

Table 6.9. shows form for initiating survey report.

Table 6.9. Survey Report Form

Division.........

Sub-Division........

Location.........

Number or Quantity	*Description of article*	*Book Value*		*Date of Record*	*Remarks by the Officer in Chief*	*Remarks or orders of Divisional Officer*	*Order of S.E.*
		Rate	*Amount*				

Submits to the supervising Engineer

(Sd) Division Engineer

Returned to the Divisional officer to necessary action as per order above

In case the Divisional Officer is competent to sanction the survey report would be sanction it himself instead of sending to the J.E.

Just as accounting procedure for stores (stock) is as important as that of cash (Every store being equivalent to cash) the tools and plant are as important as stores or as cash. The points of differences between the accounting procedure of stock and tools and plants is given in Table 6.10.

Table 6.10. Difference between Account of Stock and Tools and Plant

Sl. No.	*Items of Comparison*	*Stock*	*Tools and Plant*
1	2	3	4
1.	Head of Accounts.	Suspense head 'stock' or directly changed to work.	Final head Machinery and equipment directly to work.

Sl. No.	*Item of Comparison*	*Stock*	*Tools and Plant*
1	2	3	4
2.	Mode of keeping Accounts	Both quality and value are kept.	Only quantity accounts are kept.
3.	Closing of register.	Closed half yearly	Closed yearly ending September
4.	Adjustment of loss, stock or short stores	Material founded short is charged off and deducted to Misc. P.W. Advances	Articles continue to be borne on account book of until written off
5.	Adjustment of surplus stores	Value of surplus stock is credited to revenue and articles taken in cheque as under receipt.	Articles found surplus are taken or is the basis of Supporting revenues without affecting the final value

6.12 ROAD METAL REGISTER

It is normal practice to stack road metal on the road side berm and issue from time to time to the road work on as required basis. The advantages of this system are:

(*i*) The material is supplied at the road side where it is actually required for road work and the delay is avoided thereby saving the cost of loading, unloading and transportation.

(*ii*) No separate watch and ward or storage space is required as the gang keeps a watch over the material along its beat.

The main disadvantage is that it is difficult to keep a continuous watch over the entire road length. This is taken care of by holding the gang-maters responsible for the safety of road side material and secondly making it obligatory in the form of submission of monthly road return showing the following information in respect of road metal:

1. Name of Road
2. K.M. No.
3. Nature of road metal, quantity carried over from last month receipts during the month issues during the month balance at the end of month.

The bill of labour (muster roll casual as well as regular labour) is not passed for payment unless it is supported by material statement.

The inspecting officer carries out surprised check of the material at site with the entry on the road metal register.

Table 6.11 shows the format which monthly road material return is submitted by the Junior Engineer incharge of the highway section.

Table 6.11. Statement of Receipts, Issues and Balance of Road Material

Division..........

Sub-Division........

Location......

Name of the Road....... Month of.......

No of Kilo-meter	*Name of Metal*	*Opening Balance C. M.*	*Receipts during the month*	*Total C.M.*	*Expen-diture during the month*	*Closing Balance*	*Actual checked by Mea-sure-ment*	*Remarks*

When fresh supply of material is received at site, the quantity received is entered on the MB and form the basis for payment of the supplies bill.

When material is found surplus it is taken as receipt. The quantity found short is shown in red under the remark column and is carried forward till the loss is recovered or it is written off with the approval of the competent authority.

Table 6.12 shows for indenting construction stores.

Table 6.12. Indent for Stores

Book No...... Indent No...... Date.......
Division......
Sub-Division........
Station.........
Name of the Work........
Name of the Contractor.........
No. of Construction Aspects or Works..........

Sl. No.	*Description of Material*	*Unit*	*Quantity*	*Remarks*

The material should be delivered.........

Sd/- AEETSDO

Note: The under has been complied as per quality show Receive the material and entire in (Sd). Supply Officer

M.B. No...... Pay...... Recery Officer.......

6.13 MATERIAL CHARGED DIRECTLY TO WORKS

Material used on works is obtained form the following two sources :

(*a*) From the Divisional stock on indents

(*b*) Directly from the trade.

(*a*) Material obtained from the divisional stock on indents.

The indent is prepared in triplicate.

The following points should be scrutinised by the officer preparing the ident.

1. Quantity of material is clearly specified.
2. Head of account is indicated.
3. Name of work as per administrative approval is correctly shown:

(*b*) Directly from the trades.

Stores purchased directly from the trade is debited directly to the work head concerned.

6.14 MATERIAL AT SITE ACCOUNT

It has already been stated in Article 6.3 that the stores in the divisional stock are primarily for the normal day to day running of the division. Evidently it does not cater for the requirement of major works and projects.

The accounts of such material issued to or received back from the work is kept under the suspense head 'material'. At the completion of the project/work a detailed statement showing the estimated quantity required for a work and actually incorporated in the work/issued to the contractor is prepared and cost debited directly to the work or deducted from the contractor's running/final bill as the case may be.

Excessive issue of controlled materials indicates possibility of pilferage or misuse. Less issue shows inferior construction.

Table 6.13 shows detailed statement of materials issued to work project compared with the estimated requirements.

6.15 DISPOSAL OF SURPLUS MATERIAL

MES store material becomes surplus under one of the following circumstances:

(*a*) On account of excess provisioning.

(*b*) Due to subsequent change in design and specification.

(*c*) Due to reduction in the scope of constructions.

Such material may be disposed off in are of the following ways:

(*a*) **Returning to the Divisional Stock.** The material is accepted by the Divisional stock if it is an item of normal usage in repairs, maintenance and minor works and the reserve limit would not burst and the materials is in usable conditions. The cartage of such material is debited to the project.

(*b*) **Transfer to another Project/Work.** Such a transfer would evidently take place when it can be utilised by the project to which it is transferred. The cartage it borne by either of the two projects.

(*c*) When the material is unserviceable or its cannot be disposed off in either of the two ways stated in (*a*) and (*b*) above it is disposed off by public auctions.

Table 6.13. Detailed statement of Materials issued to work project compared with the estimated requirement

Division.........

Sub-Division......

Name of work..........

Total Issue to the work.........

	Description of material	*Principal Item*					*Petty Item*	*Total*	*Dated, initial of SDO/ AE/AC*	*Dated, initial of Division Account*
	Unit									
Estimated requirement	*Quantity*									
	Value									
Balance B.F. from previous statement end of Dec.										
Total for the material Carried over										

7

WORKS

7.1 INTRODUCTION

The main purpose of having works and accounts procedure is to execute works which satisfy the following conditions:

(*a*) The structure should be technically sound. This is achieved by according technical sanction for each work or part thereof. At site quality of work is ensured by:

(*i*) Checking/inspecting the execution with respect to detailed specification in respect of material and workmanship.

(*ii*) Passing the work in stages.

(*iii*) Rectification of defective work.

(*b*) The work should be completed in specified period.

This is achieved by:

(*i*) Specifying period of completion and incorporation of penalty clause in the condition of contract for delay in the completion of project.

(*ii*) Having bar charts and CPM and PERT methods of work programming to ensure completion on time.

(*c*) Expenditure planned for the year should not be exceeded. This is achieved by fixing allotment for the financial year.

(*d*) The total expenditure on the completion of the work should not exceed the planned amount. This is achieved by according administrative approval in respect of each item of the work.

The various provisions of the works and accounting procedures have been developed primarily to satisfy the aforesaid requirements. The various agencies which undertake the execution of works have their own rules, prescribed forms of various reports and returns etc. As the present book has been written for general use of students the rules, regulations and form of reports and returns have been dealt in a general way instead of adhering to the central or state PWD forms.

7.2 CATEGORIES OF WORKS

The various categories of work are shown in Table 7.1.

Table 7.1

Categories of Works

- Original Works
  - New Works
  - Special Repair Works
  - Addition and/or Alteration to existing works (excluding minor works)
- Repair Works (Maintenance)
  - Normal Maintenance
  - Special Repairs
  - Addition and/or Alteration under minor works

Note: 1. The categorisation and scope of special repair varies from state to state and department to department. It also depends upon the nature of such repair. For example, special repair necessiated almost every year due to the damage caused by monsoon in the hilly region of the Himalayas (termed as **SRMD, SPECIAL REPAIR, MONSOON DAMAGES**) fall under the maintenance/repair of the road concerned. In the same department extensive repairs to a large structural complex would fall under the category of original works.

7.3 CLASSIFICATION OF WORKS

Table 7.2 gives normal classification of works based on the completion cost.

Table 7.2

Works

- Project (work exceeding ₹ 50,000)
- Major works (work exceedings ₹ 20,000 ₹ 50,000)
- Minor (work below ₹ 20,000/ ₹ 50,000)
- Petty (work costing below ₹ 2500)

Note. 1. It has already been brought out in Article 7.2 that the classification of normal work difference state to state and department to department. In view of the continuous increasing in the cost of living, proposals for increasing the present limit of ₹ 20,000 have already been initial for increasing ₹ 50,000.

2. The scope of minor works varies from department to department as well as from time to time. About 30 years back in MES for example, works below ₹ 5000 were termed as minor works. In course of time this limit was raised to ₹ 20,000 and would be in the near future go to ₹ 50,000.

7.4 CONDITIONS FOR TAKING WORK IN HAND

Before any work is taken in hand the following five requirements should be fulfilled:

(1) Administrative approval is obtained by the competent Administrative authority.

(2) Funds have been allotted by the competent Financial Authority.

(3) Technical sanction is accorded by the competent Engineering Authority.

(4) Land acquisition proceedings have been completed, compensation paid, and possession of land taken over.

(5) Work order has been placed by the competent Engineering Authority.

The above requirements are briefly explained below:

1. **Administrative approval.** This term denotes the formal acceptance by the administrative department concerned, of the proposals for incurring any expenditure by the department on an original work initiated by; or concerned with, the requirements of such administrative department. This formal acceptance by the competent authority is given after the scrutiny and examination of the details and financial implications involved therein; in consultation with the finance department whenever necessary, for the purpose of incurring expenditure thereon; as and when funds are provided by the authority competent to sanction funds. Thus it is in effect; an order to the P.W.D. department to execute certain specified work at a stated sum to meet the administrative needs of the department requiring the work. Every work except repairs needs administrative approval.

An approximate estimate the preliminary drawing if any necessary are submitted by engineering department to the administration to obtain approval to take up the work within sanctioned amount only. After administrative approval; detailed drawings; designs and estimates are prepared by engineering department and again submitted to administrative department for final sanction of detailed estimate. This is based on the estimate or work submitted by the engineering authority and is the primary authority for the project/work.

In the case of state P.W.D. the state government has full powers for according administrative approval works for while in the case for Central Government full powers are with the Central Government. In addition to this different heads of departments have various powers for according administrative approval.

2. **Allotment of Funds.** Within the overall budget allotment of works, funds of various works are allotted for each financial year in consultation with the representative of the finance attached to the Ministry concerned.

3. **Technical sanction.** No work should be taken in hand without a technical sanction. In urgent works, however, work may be taken in hand in anticipation of the administrative approval and allotment of funds. A work which has been taken in hand in anticipation of administrative approval and allotment of funds would be placed under audit objection till such time as these requirements are satisfied. In case of technical sanction however, any covering technical sanction would have no meaning once the same has been completed. Hence the importance of this requirement.

For every work proposed to be carried out; except annual repair works, costing not more than ₹ 5000/- for which lumpsum provisions have been made by competent authority, technical sanction is essentially required. This is an order to competent authority sanctioning a properly detailed estimate of the cost of work of construction or repair work costing more than ₹ 5000/- proposed to be carried out by the department. This sanction is accorded by the authorities of the department to whom the powers have been delegated. This further depends on the cost of the project work or repairs to be under taken. This gives guarantee that the work proposed is structurally sound and estimate is made accurately, based on all the data required for the estimate.

4. **Land Acquisition.** Starting any work without acquiring leads to serious legal complication and hence it should be ensured that not only land is acquired but physical possession is taken over through local civil authority.

5. The work order gives the legal authority for the start of the work. A work taken in hand in anticipation leads to a number of complications such as date of start, date of completion etc.

6. **Expenditure Sanction.** It implies concurrence of the Finance Department of the government for the expenditure proposed and allotment of funds to meet the expenditure thereof. Unless there is expenditure sanction; no amount can be spent on the proposed work.

7.5 METHODS OF CARRYING OUT WORKS

Works are carried out primarily by the following two methods:

(*a*) Through Contract Agency.

(*b*) Departmentally by employing D.E.L.

(*c*) Departmentally by engaging labour through contract agency.

The methods are briefly described below:

(*a*) **Through contract agency.** Work through contract agency is usually allotted on the basis of open tenders. The following information regarding the work is given in the notice calling for tenders:

(*i*) Name of the work.

(*ii*) Location of the work.

(*iii*) Estimated cost of the work.

(*iv*) Period of completion.

(*v*) Earnest money and security deposit required.

(*vi*) Cost of tender form.

(*vii*) Person from whom tender forms may be obtained along with time, day, date upto which the forms may be obtained.

(*viii*) Last day and time upto which tender forms can be submitted and method of submission.

(*ix*) Time, place and date of opening the tenders.

Normally lowest bid is accepted.

Another system of contract is the *Piece Work Agreement*. The work is given on the basis of quotation from approved contractors.

Sometimes the Executive/Assistant Engineer allots such work at the current schedule rates for works costing ₹ 10,000 on P.W.A. basis.

(*b*) **Departmentally by employing D.E.L.** For petty repairs and specialised jobs such as cement concreting work and construction work in the railway track and work in security installations, this method is adopted. In case of roads in the forward areas under Border Roads Organisation, extensive road building programmes have been carried out exclusively by this method.

(*c*) Sometimes a combination of (*a*) and (*b*) systems is adopted where in the contractor manages labour and is given a fixed prenegotiated percentage for arranging the labour. This is resorted to in situations suited for departmentally executed works but where it is difficult to get labour locally.

7.6 DIFFERENT TYPES OF CONTRACTORS

The different types of contracts are:

1. Item rate contract.
2. Lumpsum contract.
3. Scheduled contract.
4. Combination of lumpsum plus scheduled rate.
5. Percentage contract.

The above types are briefly described below:

1. **Item Rate Contract.** In this system of contract the schedule of quantity shown in Table 7.3 is the basis of allotting the work. The schedule is prepared from the estimate of the work in which the rate column is filled by the tenderer and normally the party whose quotation is the lowest is allotted the job.

Table 7.3 Schedule of Quantities (Schedule B)

Sl. No.	*Description of the Item*	*Quantity*	*Unit*	*Rate*	*Cost*
1.	Earthwork is excavated in hours etc.	—	—		
2.					
3.					
4.					
c					
			Total		

2. **Lumpsum contract.** Complete description of the work along with detailed specifications and details of working drawings and schedule of stores is supplied with the tender form and the contractor undertakes to complete the job for a specified sum. The advantage of this type of contract is that the payments are simplified. No measurement for running or final bills are necessary. However, the drawback in the system is that any modification or deviation has to be carried out by means of an amendment which may not be acceptable or agreed to, by the contractor.

3. **Scheduled Rate.** This is similar to item rate contract as the contractor undertakes the execution of work at approved schedule of rates plus a fixed percentage higher or lower as the case may be. Payment is made on the basis of actual quantity of each item or supplies made. The payment is made on the basis of through rates wherein the rate tendered includes cost of labour and material. Payment may be done on the basis of free supply of materials.

4. **Combination of lumpsum plus schedule rate.** Under this type of contract, a fixed sum is agreed to on the completion of a particular job and addition or alteration are carried out on the basis of current schedule of rates.

5. **Percentage Contract.** In this type of contract approximate value of work is indicated along with brief description and drawings (where applicable) and the tenderer bids his percentage above or below the current schedule of rates. No schedule of quantity is given. This type of contract is particularly suitable for *'Term contract'* where the works involved cannot be indicated or for periodical services (white washing, colour washing etc.). In the MES this is the only method of allotting work of repairs to defence buildings in cantonements.

7.7 ALLOTMENT OF WORK

Work is normally allotted to the contractor on the basis of properly advertised notice calling tenders for the work. The party which quotes the lowest is normally allotted the work. In case the work is allotted to other than the lowest party the officer who accepts such a tender has to record reasons for doing so. In case the reasons recorded by him are not convincing it would result in a serious audit objection by the Financial authority which may result in disciplinary/departmental action against the person concerned.

7.8 QUOTATION AND TENDER/PREPARATION, RECEIPT AND ACCEPTANCE

In order to select a suitable party for execution of any work, the Divisional Engineer invites quotations on plain paper to which non-judicial stamp may or may not be affixed. No contract agreement is executed wherever the department and the contractor and work is paid for the basis of actual measurement. No earnest money or security deposit is required. This type of contract is allotted for carrying out urgent works/petty works where the amount involved is below ₹ 10,000.

In all other cases, work is allotted on the basis of 'tenders' invited after giving reasonable publicity to the same.

The work involved in allotting the work by inviting tenders can be broadly divided into two types namely:

1. Pre-tender action, and
2. Post-Tender action.

The following pretender action involves the following:

(*a*) Preparation of contract documents.

(*b*) Issue of Notice inviting tenders.

2. Post tender action involves:

(*a*) Opening of Tenders.

(*b*) Acceptance of tenders.

1. Pre-tender action

(*a*) Preparation of contract document.

The following documents are prepared before tenders are invited:

(*i*) Layout plan of the area showing the location of the work.

(*ii*) Complete set of drawings including working drawings.

(*iii*) Schedule of stores specifying clearly the stores which would be issued, the place of issue and the issue rate.

(*iv*) Schedule of T & P along with the place of delivery and the condition of hire charges.

(*v*) General condition of contract.

(*vi*) General and particular specifications.

(*vii*) Mode of running payments and method of depositing security.

The above documents are scrutinised from the financial point of view by the Divisional Accountant/Unit Accountant by the works/ branch/contract branch/SW in respect of other details.

It is usual to indicate the competent authority for the acceptance of the tender. It should further be specified that the competent authority reserves the right to reject any or all the tenders without assigning any reason.

(*b*) Issue of notice inviting tenders when administrative approval has been accorded and funds for the work have been allotted notice of tender along with the information detailed in Articles 7.5 is invited. Wide publicity commensurate to the cost of the work as detailed in Table 7.4 is given.

2. Post Tender Action

(*a*) **Opening of tenders.** The day, date and time of opening of tenders along with the time upto which sealed tenders from parties may be accepted *i.e.,* specified in the notices of tenders. Normally the time fixed for opening is on the same day upto which tenders may be received. Allowance is made to the receipt by post and hence the time for opening is usually after normal postal delivery of the station. At any rate tenders received by post are considered as tenders in time if the party can establish beyond doubt the quotation have been posted before the same were opened. The Divisional Engineer nominates two officers of his district to open the tenders and all the contractors are invited to observe the opening.

(*b*) **Acceptance of tenders.**

Table 7.4 Publicity required for tender notice

Sl. No.	*Amount of work*	*Method Publicity*
1.	Above ₹ 50,000	(*a*) 3 Weeks notice through leading dailies. (*b*) Individually to registered contractors (*c*) Other Division of the Dept. and local office.
2.	Between ₹ 20,000 and ₹ 50,000	(*a*) 2 Weeks notice (*b*) As for (*b*) and (*c*).
3.	Between ₹ 10,000 and ₹ 20,000	(*a*) Ten days notice (*b*) As for 1 (*a*) (*c*)

7.9 CONTRACT AGREEMENT

The Contract Agreement is an undertaking by the President of India and the party whose tender has been accepted for fulfilment of the terms and conditions laid therein. In short the contractor gives an undertaking to execute the work according to drawing and specifications along with such other instructions as the Engineer-in-Charge or senior inspecting officer may issue from time to time. The party further agrees to complete the work within the period fixed in the notice of calling for tenders and in the event of delay the party is liable to be penalised upto 10% of the value of the contract or to the employment of debitable agency. The Executive Engineer who represents the President of India binds the government to pay the party for the work done according to the terms and conditions given in the Contract Agreement.

The following basic principles have to be strictly adhered to while preparing the Contract Agreement. Variation of these conditions particularly if the same are favourable to the contractor are liable to be challenged by other prospective parties who had submitted the tenders or by the department itself or by the Audit party.

1. There should be no modification in respect of design, drawing and specification form those given in the notice inviting tenders.

2. The scope of the work should not be changed.

3. Period of completion should not be changed.

While preparing the draft agreement the following precautions should be taken:

(*i*) There should be no ambiguity in the terms and conditions which may be taken advantage of by the contractor.

(*ii*) The date of starting should be clearly specified usually it is date on which work order is received by the contractor or his representative or the date on which possession of the site is given whichever is later.

(*iii*) No work should be allowed to be started till the Contract Agreement is signed by the contractor.

(*iv*) As far as possible there should be no correction, or other interpolation in the Contract Agreement. If it is unavoidable such corrections should be jointly attested by the Executive Engineer and the contractor.

(*v*) All relevant drawings, such as site plan, working drawings, and various schedules forming part of the contract agreement should be free from flaws so that the same may not be disputed in a Court of Law. In the case of large works it is usual to get the agreement scrutinised from the "*Legal Rememberencer*" so that the legal aspect of the agreement are taken care of.

(*vi*) Workmen Compensation Act, Minimum Wages Act should be referred to in the Contract Agreement so that the contractor is bound to act on the same.

Only printed form of contract deed should be used. It should not be necessary to add any typed material. In the event it becomes necessary, prior permission from the Superintending Engineer should be obtained.

When the tenders are accepted by the Executive Engineer, three copies of the agreement are prepared and distributed as below :

1. One copy along with attested copy is sent to the Superintending Engineer who scrutinises the agreement and returns the original to the Executive Engineer and retains the attested copy for his record.

2. One copy under lock and key is kept with Executive Engineer and is not taken out except when required in a court of law.

3. One copy to Accountant General/CDA.

In case the contractor asks for one set he is given the same on payment. When the tenders are accepted by the Superintending Engineer, four copies of agreement are prepared in the first instance.

Some of the important contract clauses of general application are given below:

1. Obligatory on the part of the contractor to get the sample of material approved and kept in the project museum for further reference.

2. Obligatory to get the work passed in stages.

3. Dismentling of defective work at contractor's risk and cost.

4. Imposition of a maximum of 10% of the cost of the work for delaying in the completion of work at the rate of 1% per week.

5. Incompleted work to be executed departmentally or through debitable agencies.

6. Change in the quantity of work under written orders of the Executive Engineer within the prescribed limits depending upon the type of the contract.

7. Extension time for completion of work to be applied with in a week of the cause of hinderance giving full reasons thereof. Extension of time is allowed by the authority who accepts the tender.

8. In case of any dispute, the case be referred to the Arbitrator appointed under the rules within 30 days of the preparations of the final bill.

7.10 WORK ORDERS

When order to start the work is given to the contractor on the basis of open tenders invited for the same, the contractor is intimated in writing by a registered letter that his tender has been accepted and he should attend the Divisional office to sign the contract agreement. After the contract agreement has been signed he is instructed to take over the possession of the site and take the work in hand. He is further informed that for purpose of completion of the work, the date of start shall be taken as the date of his receipt of the letter under reference or the date on which the side has been handed over irrespective of the actual date of starting the work. However, when the work is allotted on the basis of Piece Work System order to start the work is given in the form given in Table 7.5.

Terms and Condition of Work Order:

1. Work to executed according to instructions of Engineer-in-charge/as per PWD specifications.

2. The work may be terminated at any time by the Engineer-in-charge.

3. The contractor may withdraw his acceptance of the work.

4. The contractor should submit his bill for payment in respect of the work done during the preceding month.

5. Payment under Workmen's Compensation Act 1924, will be paid by the Government to the concerned party the cost of which may be recovered from the payments due to the contractor.

Order for work specified herein is given to Shri....... (contractor) to be executed on the condition given here as:

Table 7.5. Work Order Form

Division ....

Sub-division ......

HQ ....

Particular of Work	*Rate*	*Per*	*Remarks*
1. Extra work in excavation over areas including its disposal and dressing etc.			

Sd/- Sd/- Divisional Engg.

Contractor Sub-Divisional

6. No workman/labour below 12 years of age shall be employed.

7. The contractor shall be paid for the work actually executed irrespective of any payment made to the contracted.

7.11 DEPOSIT WORKS AND AGENCY WORKS

Non-government works fall under the following three categories, namely:

1. **Deposit Works.** Such works are taken in hand by the P.W.D. in the same way as other government works but the funds for the execution of works including departmental charges are deposited in government treasury in lumpsum on behalf of the Executive Engineer. Such funds may also be deposited by instalments on dates agreed to by the government before start of the work.

In addition to the departmental charges which are fixed from time to time by the concerned Central or State Government and may vary from 10% to 25%, provision for the following is also made in the estimate:

(*a*) Establishment Charge 2%

(*b*) Tools and Plants 1%

(*c*) Audit and Account 1%

Powers for accepting the execution of such works rests with the department (Chief Engineer). The Superintending Engineer and the Executive Engineer have also powers upto 1 lac and to ten thousand respectively for accepting such works.

The estimate of the work, including provision for departmental charges, is got countersigned by the depositing authority. Such a counter signature implies the implicit acceptance by the depositing authority in respect of the amount to be deposited.

An undertaking is also obtained from the depositing Authority regarding excess in the expenditure due to circumstances beyond the control of the department such as increase in procurement cost of controlled stores, higher bid of the contract etc.

Such deposit works may be carried out on behalf of:

(*a*) Municipalities.

(*b*) Other departments of the same of other State or Central government.

(*c*) Private parties.

2. **Takvi Works.** These works are executed by the Irrigation branch and consists of lining of water channels to minimise wastage of Canal water. The expenditure incurred is initially charged to *T*-Deposit and Advances. The expenditure incurred is recovered by the local civil authorities from the land owners concerned. The expenditure incurred however, is paid by the local civil authority and debited to *R*-Loan and Advance by central government or *Q* Loan and Advances by state government as the case may be and credit is offended to *T*-Deposit and Advances. The recovery is made from the landowner in the form of land revenues.

3. **Local Loan Works.** The expenditure incurred as such works is initially booked under the head *R*-Loan and Advances by the central government or *Q*-Loan and Advances by the state government as the case may be.

8

PAYMENT FOR WORKS

8.1 DAILY LABOUR/D.E.L.

When a work of short duration and of non-recurring nature involving engagement is skilled, semi-skilled or unskilled labour/ workers is to be executed daily or departmentally engaged labour is employed. The main features of this system are:

1. The attendance of such labour is marked on the muster roll form in which the name of the labour along with the father name and trade of labour is given. (See Table 8.1)

2. The Divisional Engineer normally exercises control over engagement of labour on muster roll by maintaining a register in the division, with the divisional accountant in which details are recorded as shown in Table 8.2.

3. The attendance of engaged labour is recorded daily and the person recording such attendance initials and totals of the person present daily. The inspecting officer EE/AE/SDO/JE checks the physical attendance without any prior notice.

4. No labour below 12 years of age is employed.

5. Muster roll are closed for payment every week, fortnight or latest every month.

6. Only one muster rolls is used for a specific work against all sanction (there may be any number of continuation sheets against such sanction).

7. The attendance is marked at work site where the muster roll is kept readily available. No duplicate record is maintained.

8. Payment is made by the AEE/AGE/SDO in the presence of the concerned subordinate.

Table 8.1 Muster Roll Form

Division..............
Sub-Division.......
Location.............
Name of work.....

Cash Book.......... Vr. No........... Dated..........

Sl. No.	*Name*	*Father's Name*	*Trade*	*Dates*	*Total*	*Rate*	*Amount*	*Dated initial and remarks of the officer making payment. Signature / LTI allotted is recorded.*
1. 2. 3. etc.								

Daily Total
Initial of Subordinate
Marking attendance
Initial of Inspection officer

Passed for ₹.............

Signature of (EE / AEE / SDO)

The amount paid and the amount remaining unpaid and transferred to the register of unpaid wages are both recorded (See Part II of Table 8.1). Part II may or may not be operated, however, separate register of unpaid wages is invariably kept.

Table 8.1 Part II

Register of Unpaid Work

Month and period to which arrear relates	*Sr. No. as per Muster Roll*	*Name*	*Father's Name*	*Amount Due*	*Amount paid*	*Dated initial of officer making payment*
Total						

Arrear as per this Muster Roll

Sl. No. as per muster roll	*Name*	*Father's Name*	*Amount Due*	*Amount paid*	*Dated initial of officer making payment*
Grand Total			₹		
Amount paid as arrear of previous Muster Roll. ₹ Balance carried to next Muster Roll.					

Table 8.1 Part III

Description of work	*Quantity*	*Deduct work already included in previous muster roll*	*Balance*	*Rate*

M.B. No............... Date of measurement

9. The work done is recorded in the Measurement Book as well as in Part III of the muster roll and rate of work arrived at. In case the work is not susceptible to measurement, remarks to indicate the same are recorded.

Table 8.2 Muster Roll Register

Sl. No.	*Date*	*Name of work*	*Period for which Sanctioned (Days)*	*Nos. Sanctioned (alongwith trade)*	*Remarks*

Note. *Maintenance of this register is not an audit requirement but it is usual practice to have one in the Divisional Office.*

8.2 CASUAL LABOUR

Sometimes it is not possible for the sub-ordinate at work site to get sanction for employment of labour on muster roll. Examples for such situations are:

(*a*) Road block due to slip in a hilly area.

(*b*) Breach in a canal.

The work has to be taken in hand immediately to avoid traffic jam and inconveniences to the passengers or to avoid loss of water and inconvenience to the public.

The attendance of the labour employed is recorded by the Junior Engineer in his diary and daily report is sent to the AEE/AGE/AE/SDO, on the completion of the job, payment bill is prepared in the form shown in Table 8.3.

In M.E.S. however, the term casual labour denotes such labour whose services are required for a comparatively longer duration (more than one month). The Garrison Engineer sanctions their employment and the pay bill is prepared as that of other works charged establishment.

Work done in any division by the casual labour is taken into consideration while recruiting labour for regular maintenance.

Table 8.3 Casual Labour Roll

Cash Book Vr. No.........

Dated.........

Division...............
Sub-Division.......
Location.............
Name of work.....
Period................

Numbers Employed	*Trade*	*Period (in days)*	*Rate*	*Amount*	*Dated initials and remarks of Paying officer.*	*Quantity of work done with reference to recorded measurement if any.*	*Work to which chargeable*

Total ₹...............
Deduct unpaid...............

Net Pay ₹...............
Total amount paid in ₹...............

Signature AEE/AGE/AE/SDO

8.3 PAYMENT OF WORK CHARGED ESTABLISHMENT

Sanction for work charged establishment is given in the same way as for regular temporary personnel but except for recruitment of a few skilled categories involving higher monthly rate of payment the Division/Garrison Engineer is usually the appointing authority subject to availability of the funds.

In the case of large projects, the entire establishment of the project is work charged and the power of appointing various categories rests with various authorities as in the case of regular/temporary establishment.

The bills are prepared in the form given in Table 8.4 on monthly basis.

When a number of person are appointed on work charged basis against different works, it is normal practice to prepare separate bills for each work.

8.4 LABOUR ENGAGED THROUGH CONTRACTOR

The working of the various works departments shows that as far as possible labour on muster roll needs to be discouraged and therefore every Divisional Engineer adopts his own method of discouraging such labour. As for muster rolls for normal maintenance work are concerned some of the Chief Engineers lay down the maximum amount which should not exceed on such labour.

Sometimes for work of comparatively short duration, local labour is not available or is only available through a contractor/agent. In such cases, payment is made directly to the contractor instead paying to the individual labour. The department is not bothered about the particular of individual labour but a report in respect of the type and number of daily labour employed and the quantity of work done is sent daily to the Engineer incharge. This compiled report from the basis of payment along with the measurements recorded in the M.B. (Both these evidently have to agree). To avoid disputes at a later date the daily report is got signed by the contractor as a token of his acceptance.

The payment is made to the contractor in one of the following ways:

(*a*) On the basis of work done at previously settled rates.

(*b*) On the basis of labourers actually employed. The profit of the contractor is either included in the rates of payment of the labour or in lump-sum or on percentage basis.

8.5 MEASUREMENT BOOK, INSPECTION, CHECKING AND MEASUREMENT

Measurement Book. Measurement book from the basis of all payments which can be measured. In other words it forms the original record of all works/supplies which are susceptible of measurement. The works/supplies include all contractors maintenance, repair done through departmental labour or through contractor. All supplies made by contractor are entered in the Measurement Book. The quantities thus entered are calculated and totalled and payments made.

The measurement book is an auditable document and deserves the same consideration in respect of its up keep as the cash book. To avoid duplication of payment or non-payment in respect of any work/supply, all payments made on the basis of these measurements are linked with the relevant cash voucher. The Cash Voucher, is actually the payment bill in the prescribed form giving abstract of work done and the payment due. It is scrutinised by the Divisional Unit Accountant and payments is issued by the District/Garrison Engineer or disbursing officer. Such cheque is issued for payment on entry is made in the cash book.

The number of the cash book entry and date is recorded on the voucher as well as the cheque no. .... through which payment is made. This serial number and date is recorded in red in the measurement book and the entries are scored in red ink thereby indicating that the payment has been made.

The measurement books are kept under lock and key by the cashier and all such books received in the division are recorded in the register of measurement books. Specified number of M.Bs are issued to the Junior Engineer, S.D.O's for use so that when some of them are under submission with the bills the entries in respect of other works/supplies may be entered in another book.

The following precautions should be taken in the upkeep of the measurement book.

1. The entries for any work done or supplies received should be made in the sequence shown in Table 8.4.

2. Each set of measurement should be closed with the dated signature of the person recording the measurements.

3. There should be no interpolation or overwriting in the entries. All corrections should be properly made and initialled.

Table 8.4 Paybill of Work Charged Establishment

Division.............. Month of Payments......... Cash Vr. No.........

Sub-Division.......

Location.............

Bill for the month of ....

S. No.	*Name of incumbent (Name to be written groupwise and sanction no. and date to be re-corded against each group in red ink)*	*Design-ation*	*Period*	*Rate*	*Amount due (In case more than one work is involved, the total of each work to be entered in red ink)*	*Amounts Paid*	*Dated acknowledg-ment Payee*	*Dated initials of the officer making payment*

Total amount paid in work..........

1. Certified that all persons for whom wages have been drawn in this bill have been actually employed during the month for the work shown and were employed on the work for which sanctioned.

Pay..........GE/EE (Sd)/- AEE/AGE/AE/SDO

Checked (Divisional/Unit Accountant)

4. There should be no blank page in measurement book. Any page left blank inadvertently should be crossed out by diagonal lines.

5. As far as possible all entries should be made in ink. If pencil entries are made they should not be inked/changed subsequently. Entries showing contents/arrears should invariably be in ink.

6. When measurement for a running bill are made, the date of previous measurement and measurement book no. and page no. should be linked. If the measurement are for first and final bill, the fact should be recorded in the measurement book.

Table 8.5 Recording of Measurement in the MBs

Recording of bills for work done	*Recording measurements for supply of materials*
(*i*) Name of the work as given in the AA	(*i*) Name of the supplies as given in W.O.
(*ii*) Location of the work	(*ii*) No. and date of agreement or W.O.
(*iii*) Name of the contract	(*iii*) Purpose of the supply *i.e.*, Stock/Direct issue to work (give name of work)/Direct issue etc.
(*iv*) No. and date of Contract Agreement	(*iv*) Date of supplies specified in S.O./W.O.
(*v*) Date of order to start work	(*v*) Date of completion of supply
(*vi*) Date of completion of the work (in case of running bill write work-in-progress)	(*vi*) Date of measurement
(*vii*) Date of measurement	

7. Entries in the Measurement Books should be continuous without leaving any blank space.

8. At the end of the measurements, the quantities are calculated and abstract of quantities is prepared. The rate and amount due are filled in the sub divisional office after verification of the calculation.

9. When the A.E.E./A.G.E./A.E./S.D.O. satisfies himself about the correctness of entries and after he has carried out percent site check of measurements, it not already done, the bill is prepared

and forwarded alongwith the Measurement Book to Divisional/Unit Accountant for pre-audit and payment.

10. Loss of measurement book should be immediately referred to the higher authorities alongwith a statement explaining the circumstances under which loss took place. Report of the loss should also be lodged to the nearest police station.

11. To avoid disputes in respect of the measurements it is desirable to intimate the contractor about the day, date and time of measurements and take his signatures at the bottom of the measurement as a taken of his acceptance.

12. Separate Measurement Books are usually kept for large work. In other cases as far as possible measurements pertaining to any work should be entered in the same Measurement Book.

13. An index of measurement showing the name of the contractor and page number where his work has been recorded shows immediately be made.

Table 8.6 shows a typical page of Measurement Book.

Table 8.6. Page of a MB

Date of Commencement.........

Date of Complete...................

Date of Measurement...........

S. No.	*Particular of Work No.*	*C*	*B*	*D*	*Contents*

Abstract of cost.

Date: (Sd) J.E.

In addition to the ordinary/common measurement book described above the following records are also entered in books known as measurement books. Such measurement books are:

1. Standard Measurement Book
2. Check Measurement Book.

1. Standard Measurement Books. Periodical services such as white-washing, colour washing, painting, distempering etc., of a building are carried out at regular intervals. If every time detailed measurements are made it would involves considerable time and energy. This difficulty has been won over by preparing standard measurement books in respect of all such buildings. The measurement pertaining to the normal periodical services are entered in the measurement book by a senior J.E./O.S. and accuracy of the measurements is certified by the A.E.E./A.G.E./A.E./S.D.O. concerned. The calculation of various periodical services are scrutinised and certified as correct by the Divisional/Unit Accountant. Subsequently only the quantity of work done as recorded in the bill of the contractor and certificate of the work having been carried out as per standard measurement book and according to the specification.

2. Check Measurement Book. Check Measurement Book is issued to the A.E.E./A.G.E./A.E./S.D.O. for the purpose of carrying out test check respect of measurement of a work carried out by the Junior Engineer/Overseer. At the end of the measurement the following certificate is given by the officer recording such measurement.

"Check measurement recorded by me in Check Measurement Book No. .... Page No. ...... The J.E. / S.D. concerned was / was not present when check measurements were made."

To eliminate chances of double payment, no payment is made on the basis of measurement recorded in the Check Measurement Book.

When the cost of work exceed ₹ 5000, the measurements are checked at site by the Divisional/Garrison Engineer and the A.E.E./A.G.E./A.E./S.D.O. The percentage of such checks depends upon the value of work and importance of the project and varies from 5% for E.E./G.E. to 25% for A.E.E./A.G.E.

In the M.E.S. and certain State P.W.D. the per cent check to be carried out by senior officer is specified and such checks are recorded on the main measurement book instead of keeping a separate Check Measurement Book.

The limit of variation between the original measurements and the test measurements usually permitted are:

1% in case of original work

5% in case of repair work

10% in case of earth work.

The measurements checked as above are corrected only in respect of checked measurement and the following noting recorded :

"Measurements corrected in accordance with check Measurement Book No............. pages no............ dated.......... When the difference between Check Measurement Book value and actually measured values exceeds the above limit, the entire work is measured again by the A.E.E. / A.G.E. / A.E. / S.D.O. and departmental action against the concerned J.E. / S.O. is initiated."

Although normally all payments are made on the basis of recorded measurements in the Measurement Books, in certain cases it is either not possible to record measurements or the same is not necessary. Such cases are given below.

(*a*) When the work is not susceptible to measurement such as snow clearance operation slip clearance etc.

(*b*) Services for which measurements duly verified already exist in the Standard Measurement Book (SMB).

(*c*) Advance payment on account of work done or supplies made. A certificate by the Engineer Incharge to the effect that the value of work done at site/supplies made exceeds the value of advance payment is adequate.

(*d*) **Lump-sum Contract.** No measurements are carried out in such cases. Running bill/Advance payments are made on the basis of certificate for the Engineer incharge certifying the percentage value of work done with respect to the total value of the work.

(*e*) **Secured Advance.** When the contract has physically delivered the supplies, payment may be made without recording measurement on the Measurement Book provided the Engineer incharge certifies that the value of materials supplied more than the amount being advanced.

Example. *A sub-divisional officer took the first set of running measurements of the work "Constructing a Library building" let out to Shri Lal Chand on regular contract at rates for finished items of work and recorded the following entries in the measurement Book:*

Name of work	*Construction of a Library Building*
Name of the contractor	Shri Lal Chand
Number and date of the agreement	8th of 2004-2005

Date of written order to start work	7-6-2004
Date of actual completion of measurement	5-6-2004
Items of work	*Content or Area*
(*i*) Excavation in foundations	3000 cft.
(*ii*) Filling in foundation	1000 cft.
(*iii*) Masonry in foundation	2000 cft.
(*iv*) Superstructure masonry up to height of 2 ft. from ground level as assessed by visual inspection.	750 cft.
(*v*) Hoisting and fixing in positions iron girders for roof	5 (numbers)
(*vi*) Brick collection at site of work on the security of which the contractor desires an advance	100000 (numbers)

Point out irregularities, if any.

Defects noticed in the measurements are:

(*i*) Written order to start work was given on 7-6-04. But work was executed earlier than the written order, because the date of measurement is recorded to be 5-6-04. On that day there was no order to commence the work. How future dates, *i.e.*, 7-6-04 could be filled in the M.B. on 5-6-04 needs clarification.

(*ii*) Superstructure masonry up to a height of 2 ft. from ground level has been assessed by visual inspection while rules require that measurements should be actual and not assessed. If this entry has been made to allow advance payment to the contractor, then this is specially to be so entered in the measurement book.

(*iii*) Bricks collected at the site of work for which secured advance is desired also do not require to be recorded in measurement book. There is a detailed procedure for recording and documentation of transactions of Secured Advance in Para 10.2. 20 & 22 of CPWA Code, which should have been followed.

(*iv*) Masonry has been done only in foundations. Superstructure Masonry is assessed to be 2 ft. high. It is not clear 5 girders for roof were hoisted and fixed on 2 ft. high walls.

8.6 PAYMENT TO CONTRACTORS AND SUPPLIERS

Payments to contractors and supplier may be classified as shown in Table 8.7.

Table 8.7

Bill for Payment to Contractors and Suppliers

- First and Final Bill (Table 10.5)
- Running Account Bill (Table 10.6)
- Account for Secured Advance (Table 10.7)
- Running Account Bill (Table 10.8)
- Final Bill (Table 10.9)

(See Tables 10.5 to 10.9)

8.7 CONTRACTORS' BILL

Introduction

General Rule. As a general rule every payment made in any accounts office must be supported by a voucher setting forth clear and full particulars of the claim and all information necessary for its proper classification. For this purpose the amounts due to Contractors for work done or supplies made are detailed in forms called "*Contractors' Bills*".

Nature of Contractors' Transaction

Transactions with Contractors for works undertaken by them. Transactions with contractors for works undertaken by them fall into four categories: (*i*) Payments for work done and measured. (*ii*) Payments for work done but not yet measured. (*iii*) Payments to Contractors for materials brought by them at the site of work for use by them on the work, (*iv*) Other Transactions. These are explained in the following paras.

Payments for Work done and measured (on account payment). After an item of work has been done/carried out/executed by the contractor as per the specifications, the department measures the quantity of work done and accepts its quality before making a payment for that item. A record of all work done and measured for its quantity and quality is kept in a register called the "*Measurement Book*".

Payments for Work done but not measured (advance payment). Necessity for this kind of payments arises when a contractor has done certain items of work according to the required specifications but the measurement of the quantity of work done is not taking place for some reason or the other. In such cases the contractor needs to be paid some money so that he is enabled to pay to his labourers and employees. This is Advance Payment against the value of work done but not measured. (See also Note 2 at page 11). **All intermediate payments made on a lumpsum contract, except the last one on its completion, are treated as advance payments** (Para 11.4.2. and 3 OF CPWA Code).

Payments for materials brought to site. Payment as secured advance can be made to the contractor only if his contract is for doing the work by using his own material, which he has brought to the site of the work. In other words, this is Advance paid to contractor on the security of **non-perishable** materials purchased by him and brought to **the site** of the work for use on the work. This advance is payable only if his contract is for completed items of work *i.e.*, for labour as well as materials. When the materials so collected are used up on an item of the work, then the contractor will be paid for that item at the contracted rates and the advance previously paid to him against the materials at site would be adjusted. (See also Note 3 at page 12).

Note. If his contract is only for the supply of material, then Secured Advance is not payable. In that case, he can be paid only under para 4.3, if the quantity has been measured or under para 4.4, if the quantity has not been measured.

Contractor's Other Transactions. In addition to the above-mentioned kinds of payments, a PWD Division has to issue materials to the contractor's from Government stores with a stipulation that its value will be recovered from his bills relating to the items of work on which the said material is used. Sometimes recoveries have to be made from him on account of fine for bad work. At times PWD may undertake to set right the incomplete or defective item or work at the risk and cost of the contractor. In some cases, some amounts may be withheld from the bill of the contractor till some deficiencies in the work are rectified. Amounts relating to such transactions are kept in the account of the work under the head "*Contractor's-Other Transactions*".

Types of Payments. It is clear that all payments for work done by a contractor fall into two specific categories, namely:

(*a*) **Final charges** (For work done and measured). These are called On account payments and relate to payment for work done and supplies made by him which have been duly measured. This can be in the form of First and Final Payment or on Running Account.

(*b*) **Suspense Payments**

(I) Advance Payments (For work done or supplies made but not measured)

(II) Secured Advances (For materials brought to site for work)

(III) Contractor's-Other Transactions (For amounts recoverable from or payable to contractor on satisfaction of conditions).

Question 1. Can a contractor ask for a secured advance in the following circumstances?

(1) He has brought glass panes at the site of the work for fixing on the windows.

(2) He has brought at the site 50 tonnes of steel issued to him free of cost by the Government for use on the work as per the agreement.

(3) He has 100000 bricks ready at the kiln site for use on the building work. He is in need or advance badly to get delivery of bricks from the kiln and to carry them to the site of the work.

(4) He has brought stones at the site of a work but it is meant for use on another work in the Division.

Ans. 1. Secured advances cannot be paid in any of these cases. In the 1st case, the material is perishable while in the 2nd case the material is of the Government (not of the contractor). In the 3rd case, the material is not at the site of the work whereas in the 4th case it is not required of that work.

First and Final Payment and Running Account Payment.

First and Final Payment against a contract is made only on its completion, and in full settlement. Bill for First and Final Payment is prepared in Form 24.

The term Running Account payment is applied to payments made to contractor at periodic intervals for work done by him till then. In the first and final payment, there is no question of payment of Secured Advances or Advance Payments (as these too are payments against a contract). Running Account Bill is prepared in Form 26. The form most in use is Form 26 Running Account Bill.

Substandard work. Contractors are required to execute all works satisfactorily and according to specifications. They can be asked to rectify the defect or even to dismantle the defective work and redo it. If a contractor does not rectify the defect, it can be rectified or redone departmentally by PWD at the contractor's cost.

Acceptance of sub-standard work at reduced rates can be resorted to in exceptional cases only for those items of work where it is structurally impossible to get the work redone. There are other conditions like prior approval of higher officers and monetary limits up to which it can be accepted.

Recoveries from Contractors

Nature of Recoveries from Contractor's Bills. Before we explain the form of the Contractor's Bill, it would be prudent to explain the nature of recoveries that are generally made from the bills of Contractors. Broadly, these recoveries are the following:

(1) Security Deposits.

(2) Income Tax (Tax deducted at source)

(3) Charges for materials issued to contractor from Govt.'s Stores.

(4) Hire Charges of Tools and Plant lent by Govt. for use.

(5) Fine for delay in completion of work.

(6) Fine for defective work.

(7) Recovery of cost of removing defects in contractor's work.

(8) Recovery of ordered by Court.

(9) Recovery of Mobilisation Advance.

Security Deposits. In CPWD, a contractor has to deposit Earnest Money along with the tender to show his earnestness in the offer to take up the work. When work is allotted to him, he is required to deposit 5% of the amount of the tendered value of the work as Performance Deposit. In addition to these two deposits, Security Deposits (usually given in the question itself) at the rate of 10% of the value of work done and measured is recoverable from each Running Account Bill of the contractor till the amount so deducted along with the amount of Earnest Money Deposit equals 5% of the Tendered Value of the work.

When Earnest Money taken from him is also given in the question, then Security deposit is recoverable in accordance with the formula that "*Earnest Money Deposit plus up-to-date Security*

Deposit does not exceed 5% of the tendered value of the work subject to a maximum of ₹ 5 lakhs".

Example 2. *Work out the Security Deposit recoverable from a contractor from his 2nd and 3rd bill from the particulars given below:*

Value of work at tendered rates. ₹ 5 lakhs.

Earnest Money Deposit, ₹ 10,000

Value of work done and measured in 1st Bill = ₹ 1 lakh

Value of work done and measured in 2nd Bill = ₹ 2 lakhs

Value of work done and measured in 3rd Bill = ₹ 3 lakhs

Ans. Limit on EMD + Security Deposit = 5% tendered value of the work = ₹ 25,000

Security Deposit in 1st Bill = 10% *i.e.*, ₹ 10000 (within limits)

Security Deposit in 2nd Bill = 10% (*i.e.*, ₹ 20000 due up to 2nd bill minus ₹ 10000 recovered in 1st bill) = ₹ 10000. This makes EMD ₹ 10,000 + SD ₹ 20000 on two bills exceed the limit of ₹ 25000. Therefore in second bill SD recoverable is ₹ 5000 so that 10000 + 10000 (1st bill) + 5000 (2nd bill) equals ₹ 25000.

No Security Deposit in 3rd bill (maximum Security Deposit already recovered)

Income Tax (Tax deducted at source).

(*i*) Under Section 194C of the Income Tax Act 1961, deduction of Income Tax is required to be made at source by Disbursing Officers. This recovery is made on Gross Amount of **On Account Payment paid* to the contractor (before making deductions for materials issued, penalties for delay etc., security deposit, and other deductions).

(*ii*) Recovery is to be effected at the time of credit of such sum to the account of a contractor, or when payment is made in cash or by cheque or draft or by any other mode **whichever is earlier.**

(*iii*) Under Section 194(4) ibid, it is open to the contractor to apply to the Income Tax Officer concerned to issue to him a certificate authorising the Disbursing Officer to make no deduction of Income Tax at source or to make it at lower rate during the validity period mentioned in that certificate.

Note.

(*i*) The rate of tax at present is 2%. In some years the Income Tax Act also levies surcharge and that too is to be recovered as Income Tax deduction at source in those years.

(*ii*) Under Section 1944C(3) of the Income Tax Act, income tax is not to be deducted at source if the consideration of the contract does not exceed ₹ 20000

(*iii*) Some Income Tax Officers are understood to have desired that TDS should be deducted on the sum of On Account Payment, Advance Payment, and Secured Advance. But Circular No. 681 dated 8-3-1994 issued by the Board of Central Revenue says as under:

"When advance payments are made during the execution of a contract, and such payments are to be adjusted at the time of final settlement of account, tax will have to be deducted at the time advance is paid."

Advance payments and Secured Advances do not fall in this category; they are adjusted in the next bill itself. The only advance payments covered by this circular are intermediate payments made in Lumpsum contracts. In actual practice follow the direction of your area's Income tax officer.

Materials issued to contractor from Govt.'s Stores.

(I) Cases in which no recovery is to be made. If the contract is for labour rate only, the cost of materials issued is not recoverable from the contractor.

(II) Cases in which recovery is to be made.

(*a*) When materials have been issued to the contractor in accordance with the terms of his contract, the recovery of its cost is to be at the rate specified in the contract. [Para 10.3.2(*b*) CPWA Code]

(*b*) Even if there is no provision in the contract for the supply of materials by the Department, these can still be issued to him for use on the work at his request after approval of Superintending Engineer.

The rate chargeable is the highest of the following:

(*i*) Issue rate including Storage charges.

(*ii*) Market Rate.

(*iii*) Rate used in preparing the Estimate of Cost of the work **Plus/Minus** the percentage at which the contract is allotted to him. (Para 10.33 CPWA Code)

(III) Mode of recovery for materials issued. The cost of materials issued to a contractor is ordinarily recoverable from the next bill of the contractor submitted by him after receipt of materials. If the Divisional Officer considers a lump-sum recovery undesirable (which is normally the case), it may be effected gradually. In that case recovery is made as and when the item of work, on which the materials are used, is billed for.

(Para 10.3.7 CPWA Code)

(IV) Materials issued in excess of requirements or lying unused with the contractor on completion of work. Normally, materials should not be issued from Divisional Stock arbitrarily or without keeping eye on requirements of the work. Contractor is not at liberty to remove or dispose of any such materials. If Divisional Officer orders then the contractor is bound to return it to the Government. The rate payable to him for such returned materials is Issue rate only (excluding storage charges). Failure to do so would invite recovery at penal rates mentioned in the contract beside action for breach of contract. ***(Practical Hint. If the rate for such recovery as per contract is not given in the examination question, then recover at market rate or issue rate plus storage charges whichever is higher)***

(V) Materials used in excess/short of requirements of work done. During the execution of work and on its completion, the quantity of materials issued, materials returned back and the materials required to be consumed theoretically on the quantities of work done (including permissible wastage and permissible +/– variation) would be calculated and reconciled. For any excess consumption or short consumption, recovery is to be made from the contractor at rates laid down in the contract.

Hire Charges of Tools and Plant lent by Govt. for use. Rates at which Division tools and plant like Road Rollers, Concrete Mixers, etc., would be issued to contractor for bonafide use on the work re given in the agreement. In exceptional cases where T&P articles are hired out to Contractor without being provided in the contract, full economic rate should be charged.

Fine for delay in completion of work. Fine for delay in completion of work is levied under the contract agreement and is creditable to Revenue Receipts of the Division. Its recovery is watched by keeping a note in the Register of Recoveries in Form 95 (see para 22.2.8 of CPWA Code)

Fine for defective work. Fine for defective work is creditable to work itself as it goes to reduce the cost of the work. As soon as fine for defective work is levied, the cost of work is reduced by debiting an equivalent amount to the account of the contractor to watch its recovery from his bill (see para 8.1.1 (*e*) (*ii*) of CPWA Code).

Recovery of cost of removing defects in contractor's work. Expenditure incurred by PWD to remove the defects in work, which a contractor fails to rectify, is debited to his personal account and not to the work concerned. Its recovery in the next bill of the contractor is watched through contractor's personal account.

Recovery ordered by Court. Courts' attachment orders are to carried out in some cases. The recovery is watched through the Register of Recoveries in Form 95. Recovery, when made from contractor's bill is credited to 'Public Works Deposits-Other Deposits' pending payment to the court.

Recovery of Mobilisation Advance. Mobilisation Advance is a loan on which interest is also recoverable. Its recovery is credited to the Loan head concerned. Interest is credited, when recovered, to the Interest Receipts head of account.

Contractors' Running A/C Bill Form

Specimen Form. First we print below a specimen of form of form of Contractor's Running Account Bill.

Specimen Form 26. Running Account Bill

1. Name of Contractor	: A
2. Name of Work	: Constructing 200 Type II Qrs. For Central Govt. Pool Residential Accommodation at Station D 98
3. Sr. No. of this Bill	: CCII & R
4. No. & Date of Previous Bill	: CCI & R Vr. No. 24 of 15-5-2004
5. Agreement No.	: 7/DCD/2004-2005 (2)
6. Date of Order to commence Work	: 17-2-2004
7. Due date of completion	: 16-2-2005

Filling up Form 26 (CPWA Code). This form consists of three parts so far as accounts are concerned. (The fourth part consists only of certificates to be given by the Engineering Officers in change of the work).

I. Account of work executed

Items of work	*Unit*	*Rate*	*Quantities upto date*	*Payments on the basis of actual measurements*	
				Upto date	*Since prev. bill*
		₹		₹	₹
1. Earthwork in foundation	Cu.m	20	248	4,960	2,420
2. Laying Cement concrete	-do-	360	180	64,800	32,400
3. RCC Work	-do-	565	40	22,600	10,400
4. Brick Work	-do-	80	154	12,320	8,160
5. Providing & fixing doors	Sq. m	432	20	8,640	5,320
Total value of work to date			(A)	1,13,320	
Deduct value of work shown on previous bill				54,620	
Net value of work since previous bill			(F)	58,700	58,700
Rupees fifty eight thousand seven hundred only					

Form 26 A-Account of Secured Advances

Quantity outstanding from previous bill	*Deduct quantity utilised since previous bill*	*Quantity outstanding*	*Full rate*	*Description of materials*	*Unit*	*Reduced rate*	*Upto date amt of adv.*
			₹			₹	₹
45	45	-----------	701	Shutters	m²	525	--------
1,50,0000	49,000	101000) + 80000)	1100	Bricks	0%	825	149325
Total amount outstanding as per this account					(C)		149325
Total amount outstanding as per this previous bill							147375
Net amount since previous bill					(E)		1950
Rupees One thousand nine hundred fifty only.							

III. MEMORANDUM OF PAYMENTS

Figures for Works Abstract	Particulars	₹		₹
	1. Total value of work actually measured		(A)	1,13,320
	2. Total up-to-date Advance Payments		(B)	-------
	(*a*) As per previous bill ₹ 14,750			
	(*b*) Since previous bill ₹(–) 14,750 (D)			
	3. Total up-to-date Secured Advances		(C)	1,49,325
	4. Total Items (1 + 2 + 3)			2,62,645
Figures for Works Abstract	5. Deduct amount with-held			---------
	(*a*) From previous bill	--------		
	(*b*) From this bill	--------		
	6. Balance		(K)	2,62,645
	7. Total amount of payments already made as per entry of last bill (54,620 + 1,47,375 + 14,750)		(K)	2,16,745
	8. Payments now to be made as below			
5,000	(*a*) By recoveries creditable to this work 2 Tonnes Cement @ ₹ 2500 per Tonne	5,000		
5,000	5(*b*) + 8(*a*) = *G*			
9,911	(*b*) By recovery of amounts creditable to other works or heads of account			45,900
	(*i*) 10% Security Deposits	5,870		
	(*ii*) Water charges	2,867		
	(*iii*) 2% Income Tax	1,174		
30,989	(*c*) By Cheque	30,989		
40,900	8(*b*) + 8(*c*) = *H*			

These three are:

I. Account of Work executed

II. Annexure-Form 26 A Account of Secured Advances

III. Memorandum of Payments.

Part I. Account of Work executed. How to fill it ?

(*i*) **Step 1.** Each item of work is written in column 1.

(*ii*) **Step 2.** The rate per unit is written in column 3. This rate is the rate applicable as per agreement. All Discounts or premium as per agreement will be applied while filling this column.

(*iii*) **Step 3.** Rate of work or supplies is always for each unit, namely per Cubic Metre, per Square Metre, per Piece, per Metre, or per Dozen. The unit of each item of work to which the rate applies is entered in column 2.

(*iv*) **Step 4.** The up-to-date quantities of work done (or supplies made) are entered in column 4.

(*v*) **Step 5.** Total amount due for payment on the up-to-date quantity of work done (*i.e.*, up-to-date quantity in column 4 multiplied by the Rate in column 3) is calculated and entered in column 5.

(*vi*) **Step 6.** The figures in column 6 are to be worked out by subtracting the figures of column 5 of the previous bill from the figures in column 5 of the current bill. (In other words, against each item we are to write the value-of up-to-date work done as per this bill minus the value of up-to-date value of work done as per last bill.)

(*vii*) **Step 7.** Total up columns 5.

(*viii*) **Step 8.** Then total of column 5 is rounded to the nearest rupee; fraction less than 50 paise being ignored, and fraction of 50 paise and more taken as one rupee.

(*ix*) **Step 9.** Work out the difference between the totals of column 5 and column 6 as they were before rounding. This difference should then be rounded and written in column 5 against the item "*Deduct value of work shown in previous bill*". (Why? Because this amount was rounded in the previous bill when step 8 above was taken while preparing the previous bill).

(*x*) **Step 10.** Net value of work since previous bill should then be worked out in Column 5. Simultaneously, the total of column 6 should be rounded making sure that it is equal to the Net value of work since previous bill as rounded and written in columns 5.)

Example-Account of work executed

Items of work	*Unit*	*Rate*	*Quantities upto date*	*Payments on the basis of actual measurements*	
				Upto date	*Since prev. bill*
		₹		₹	₹
1. Earthwork in foundation	Cu.m.			345.00	225.35
2. Laying cement concrete	-do-			200.00	103.65
3. RCC Work	-do-			500.50	456.40

4. Brick Work	-do-			950.75	760.00
5. Providing & fixing doors	Sq.m			620.25	405.70
Total value of work to date (A)				2,617	
Deduct value of work shown on previous bill (X)				665	
Net value of work since previous bill (E)				1952	1951.10
Rupees one thousand nine hundred fifty two only					*i.e.*, 1952

First (A), which is ₹ 2616.50, will be rounded to 2617 **(see step 8.)**.

Then (X), which is 2616.50 minus ₹ 1951.10 *i.e.*, ₹ 665.40 will be rounded to 665 **(see step 9.)**

From these two, the figure (F) works out to 2617-665 *i.e.*, 1952.

Hence figure (F) in column 5 will be 1952.

On the basis rounding of figure (F) in column 6, which is ₹ 1951.10, would be 1952 **(see step 10)**

Account of Secured Advances. It is kept in an Annexure to the Contractor's bill in Form 26-A and is filled up as stated below.

(i) Step 1. Description of materials, namely Bricks, Steel, Wood etc., are entered in column 5 of this form. In column 1 are entered the quantities on which secured advance stands granted as per the previous bill.

(ii) Step 2. In column 2 are entered quantities of these materials (on which secured advance was previously granted) as have been utilised on the work measured since previous bill (on which on account payment is being made now)

(iii) Step 3. Difference of figures in columns 1 and 2 is entered in column 3. (the figures in column 2 cannot be higher than those in column 1). Any further quantity of materials brought to site, on which secured advance is to be granted, are also entered in this column with a plus sign.

(iv) Step 4. For each material, full rate assessed by the Divisional Officer or its cost indicated in the tendered rate of the contractor (whichever is less) is entered in column 4.75% of this rate is entered in column 7 (in whole rupees ignoring paise).

(v) Step 5. In column 8 is entered the value of each material for the quantities noted in column 3 at the rates noted in column 7.

(vi) Step 6. Total up column 8. Below that total write the amount (of secured advance) outstanding as per entry (C) of the previous bill. (Yes, this is equal to quantity in column 1 multiplied by rate in column 7)

(vii) Step 7. The difference between these two figures (of step 6) is the net amount since previous bill.

Example 3. *Secured advance on 1,50,000 bricks @ ₹825 per 1000 bricks was outstanding in the previous bill out of which 49,000 bricks have been used on Brickwork for which on account payment is being made in the present bill. On 80,000 more bricks Secured Advance is to be given. How will Brick appear in the Annexure Account of Secured Advances? Will it make any difference if only Advance Payment was being made for the Brickwork instead of "On a/c Payment"?*

Ans. Secured Advance is adjusted only from bill for work done and measured in respect of items on which bricks were consumed.

Form 26A-Account of Secured Advances

Quantity outstanding from previous bill	*Deduct quantity utilised since previous bill*	*Quantity outstanding*	*Full rate* ₹	*Description of material*	*Unit*	*Reduced rate* ₹	*Upto date amt of adv.* ₹
150000	49,000	101000) + 80000)	1100	Bricks	0 %	825	1,49,325
Total amount outstanding as per this account						(C)	1,49,325
Total amount outstanding as per previous bill							1,23,750
Net amount since previous bill						(E)	25,575
Rupees twenty thousand five hundred seventy five only.							

If only Advance Payment is being made for the work, the figure in column 2 would be Zero (instead of 49000); consequential changes would follow.

How to fill in "Part III Memorandum of Payments".

(1) *1st 4 Lines.* The first 4 items of the memorandum of payment are self-explanatory. (We can also say that figure A of PART I of the Bill and Figure C of Annexure to the Bill are entered in line 1 and 3 respectively).

In the inner columns of line 2(*a*), we write the amount of advance payment made up to the previous bill. In line 2(*b*), is written the amount of further NET advance payment being made in this bill (*i.e., New advance payments made less previous advance payments recovered*) with plus sign (if net amount is payment) of minus sign (if net amount is deduction).

Please note that previous advance payment made against an item of work is recovered in full when any **"On Account payment" is made** against that item of work.

(2) *5th line.* Deduct amount with-held. This with-holding of payable amount may be for minor reasons like watering/curing of cement work not done yet, earth not removed from site, site not yet cleared etc. As soon as the minor deficiency is made good, the amount with-held is released in the next Bill. When amount is withheld, it is shown in line 5(*a*). When it is released, it is shown with minus sign in line 5(*b*). (Para10.5.12(4) & 15.2.4 CPWA Code)

Security Deposits are not to be shown as deducted in this line. The word *"Deposit"* decides once for all that it is not to be shown in this line. Of course, if the deduction is on account of Security without the word Deposit) and the amount of this deduction is likely to be less than ₹ 500, then it can be shown against line 5(*a*). But, as soon as the deduction of Security is likely to exceed ₹ 500, it should be shown as if the with-held amount has been repaid in line 5(*b*). Gross amount of Security recoverable should then be recovered in line 8(*b*) as explained in subsequent Steps.

(3) *6th line. Balance.* This is simple and easy to do.

(4) *7th Line.* Total amount of payment already made as per entry K of the previous bill. Start preparing the Memorandum of Payments of the previous bill and reach up to the entry 6 of that bill. That amount is to be filled in against line 7 of the current bill.

(5) *8th line (outer column).* Payments now to be made. This is equal to the difference between line 6 and line 7 of the bill in hand. Check this figure to be equal to the figure worked out as under. *"Sum up figures D, F and E of the bill in hand, and subtract therefrom the amount written against line 5(b)"*.

(6) *Line 8(a).* Recovery of amounts creditable to this work. The following are some of the recoveries to appear in this line:

1. Cost of materials supplied to contractor for this work.
2. Fine for bad work
3. Recoveries of expenses incurred on the work at contractor's risk and cost.

(7) *Line 8(b)*. Recoveries of amounts creditable to other works or heads of account. Following kinds of recoveries appear in this line:

(*a*) Security Deposits

(*b*) Income Tax

(*c*) Hire charges of Tools and Plant

(*d*) Supervision charges on issue of materials

(*e*) Court attachment

(*f*) Recovery for materials supplied to contractor for other works.

(*g*) Fines creditable to Revenue, for delay in completion of work.

(*h*) Recovery of Mobilisation advances and interest on them.

(*i*) Rebate as per agreement for prompt payment to contractor

(*j*) Additional charges levied for unused Government materials not returned by contractor.

(8) Pay order of the Disbursing Officer and Acknowledgment of the contractor. The Pay Order is for the amount of the cheque issued in favour of the contractor. Contractor's acknowledgment is for the gross amount *i.e.*, the figure against line 8. In the final bill, he should add the words "*in full and final settlement of all demands*".

Now we give three questions to make everything clear. [Learn what (A), (B), (C), (D), (E), (F), (G), (H), and (K) in the bill imply].

Example 4. *Prepare the 1st running A/c bill of contractor X from the following details for constructing school building on contract for finished items of work.*

Item of work	*Unit*	*Rate per unit* ₹	*Quantities*	
			up-to date	*in previous bill*
Earth work	Cu.M	500	5	---
Brick work in mud	Cu.M	70	20	----
Brick work in cement	Cu.M	1500	----	----
Reinforced cement concrete	Cu.M	4900	----	----
Wood work	Sq.M	350	----	----

Advance payment of ₹ 8000 was made in this bill for Brick work in cement. He had brought 100000 bricks and 500 bags of Material X at site for use on the work for which secured advance is to be paid to him taking the assessed rate of these articles as ₹ 800 per 1000 and ₹ 140 per bag respectively. In the analysis of rates of work as per rates tendered by the contractor, the material element of cost was ₹ 8.50 per 1000 bricks and ₹ 120 per bag for Material X.

An amount of ₹ 250 was to be withheld, as he had not yet removed the surplus earth from the site. 10% security was deducted and kept within the account of the work.

Cost of materials issued for this work (₹ 650) is also to be recovered. Recover Income Tax @ 2% of value of work done.

Ans.

I. Account of work executed

Items of work	*Unit*	*Rate*	*Quantities upto date*	*Payments on the basis of actual measurements — Upto date*	*Since prev. bill*
		₹		₹	₹
1. Earthwork	Cu.m	500	5	2,500	2,500
2. Brick work in mud	-do-	70	20	1,400	1,400
Total value of work to date			(A)	3,900	
Deduct value of work shown on previous bill				----	
Net value of work since previous bill			(F)	3,900	3,900
Rupees three thousand nine hundred only					

FORM 26 A-ACCOUNT OF SECURED ADVANCES

Quantity outstanding from previous bill	*Deduct quantity utilised since previous bill*	*Quantity outstanding*	*Full rate*	*Description of materials*	*Unit*	*Reduced rate*	*Upto date amt of adv.*
			₹			₹	₹
	---------	+ 500	120	Material X	per	90	45,000
	---------	+ 100,000	800	Bricks	0%	600	60,000
Total amount outstanding as per this account					(C)		1,05,000
Total amount outstanding as per this previous bill							--------
Net amount since previous bill					(E)		1,05,000
(Rupees One lakh five thousand only)							

III. MEMORANDUM OF PAYMENTS

Figures for Works Abstract		₹		₹
	1. Total value of work actually measured		(A)	3,900
	2. Total up-to-date Advance Payments		(B)	8,000
	(a) As per previous bill ₹ ---------			
	(b) Since previous bill ₹ 8,000 (D)			
	3. Total up-to-date Secured Advances		(C)	1,05,000
	4. Total Items (1 + 2 + 3)			1,16,900
				---------
	5. Deduct amount with-held			640
	(a) From previous bill	--------		
640	(b) From this bill (₹ 250 + Security 390)	640		
	6. Balance		(K)	1,16,260
	7. Total amount of payments already made as per entry of last bill		(K)	---------
	8. Payments now to be made as below			
	(a) By recoveries creditable to this work			
650	Cost of materials	650		
1,290	5(b) + 8(a) = G			
78	(b) By recovery of amounts creditable to other works or heads of account			
	(i) Income Tax	78		1,16,260
1,15,532	(c) By Cheque	1,15,532		
1,15,610	(H)			

Pay ₹ 115532 (Rupees one lakh fifteen thousand five hundred thirty two only by cheque. Sd./Disbursing Officer

Received ₹ 116260 (Rupees one lakh sixteen thousand two hundred sixty only) as per above Memorandum of Payments. Sd./Contractor

Important Points

(1) *Secured Advance.* The rates for grant of Secured Advance need clarification. Read Paragraph 10.2.22(*a*) of CPWA Code. The rate is 75% of the rate assessed by the Engineer in charge of 75% of the material element of cost in the tendered rate of finished item of work ---- whichever is lower.

(2) *Security.* It is stated that Security was kept in the account of the work. Read Paragraph 15.2.4 of CPWA Code. These recoveries are to be shown as deduction in line 5(*a*). In real life situation, all security deposits would be more than ₹ 500 and would be recovered in line 8 of the Memorandum of Payments.

(3) Checks to be made. Following 3 checks must be made:

(*I*) $H - F = D + E - G$ ($H - F = 115610 - 3900 = 111710$; $D + E - G = 8000 + 105000 - 1290 = 11710$ Agreed)

(*II*) Payments now to be made (Line 8) = $D + E + F$ – Figure in line 5(*b*). $D + E + F$ – Figure in line 5(*b*) = $8000 + 105000 + 3900 - 640 = 116260$. This agrees with the figure in line 8 of the answer.

(*III*) Figure *K* of previous bill = (*A* + *B* + *C* – Line 5) all of previous Bill

Example 5. *Prepare the 2nd Running A/c Bill of the contractor mentioned in question 3 from the further particulars given below.*

Item of work	*Unit*	*Rate per unit*	*Quantity up-to-date*	*Quantity in 1st bill*
Earth work	Cu.M	₹ 500	20	5
Brick work in mud	Cu.M	₹ 70	50	20
Brick work in cement	Cu.M	₹ 1500	50	---
Reinforced cement concrete	Cu. M	₹ 4900	10	---
Wood work	Sq. M	₹ 350	----	----

In this Bill advance payment of ₹ 5000 is to be made for wood Work. Out of the materials for which Secured Advance was given, 90000 bricks and entire quantity of Material X were utilised on the items of work for which on account payment is being made now. He had brought another 50000 bricks at site for which Secured Advance is to be paid.

He has not yet removed the surplus earth from the site. 10% security was deducted. The security deducted in the first bill is also to be credited to Deposits.

The following further recoveries are to be made from this Bill :

	₹
Cost of-	
Materials issued for this work	3000
Materials issued for another work (constructing Hospital)	800
Labour employed to rectify defective work done by contractor	150
Income Tax @ 2% of value of work done.	

Ans.

I. Account of work executed

Items of work	*Unit*	*Rate*	*Quantities upto date*	*Payments on the basis of actual measurements*	
				Upto date	*Since prev. bill*
		₹		₹	₹
1. Earthwork	Cu.m	500	20	10,000	7,500
2. Brick work in mud	-do-	70	50	3,500	2,100
3. Brick work in cement	-do-	1,500	50	75,000	75,000
4. Reinforced cement	-do-	4,900	10	49,000	49,000
Total value of work to date			(A)	1,37,500	
Deduct value of work shown on previous bill				3,900	
Net value of work since previous bill			(F)	1,33,600	1,33,600
Rupees one lakh thirty three thousand six hundred only					

FORM 26 A-ACCOUNT OF SECURED ADVANCES

Outstanding in previous bill	*Utilise since previous bill*	*Quantity outstanding*	*Full rate*	*Description of materials*	*Unit*	*Reduced rate*	*Upto date advance*
			₹			₹	₹
500	– 500	---------	120	Material X	per	90	---------
1,00,000	– 90,000	10,000 + 50,000	800	Bricks	0%	600	36,000
Total amount outstanding as per this account					(C)		36,000
Total amount outstanding as per this previous bill							1,05,000
Net amount since previous bill (Minus Rupees sixty nine thousand only)					(E)		– 69,000

III. MEMORANDUM OF PAYMENTS

Figures for Works Abstract		₹		₹
	1. Total value of work actually measured		(A)	1,37,500
	2. Total up-to-date Advance Payments		(B)	5,000
	(a) As per previous bill ₹ 8,000			
	(b) Since previous bill ₹ –3,000 (D)			
	3. Total up-to-date Secured Advances		(C)	36,000
	4. Total Items (1 + 2 + 3)			1,78,500
	5. Deduct amount with-held			250
	(a) From previous bill	640		
– 390	(b) From this bill	–390		
	(Security of previous bill)			
	6. Balance		(K)	1,78,250
	7. Total amount of payments already made as per entry of last bill		(K)	1,16,260
	8. Payments now to be made as below			
	(a) By recoveries creditable to this work			
	Value of materials issued	3,000		
3,150	Labour to set right the defects	150		
2,760	5(b) + 8(a) = G			
17,222	(b) By recovery of amounts creditable to other works or heads of account			61,990
	(i) Security Deposits	13,750		
	(ii) Income Tax	2,672		
	(iii) Material for other works	800		
41,618	(c) By Cheque	41,618		
58,840	(H)			

Pay ₹ 41618 (Rupees forty one thousand six hundred eighteen only) by cheque. Sd./Disbursing Officer

Received ₹ 61990 (Rupees sixty one thousand nine hundred ninety only) as per above Memorandum of Payments. Sd./ Contractor

Important Points. (1) Three checks.

(*i*) Line 8 = Payment now to be made $= D + E + F - 5(b)$

$= (-)\ 3000 + (-)\ 69000 + 133600 - (-)\ 390$

$= 61990$ Agreed

(*ii*) $H - F = 58840 - 133600 = (-)\ 74760$

$D + E - G = (-)\ 3000 + (-)\ 69000 - 2760 = (-)\ 74760$ Agreed.

(*iii*) In the Memorandum of Payments of this bill we are to fill in line 7, namely Amount of payment made as per entry (K) of the last bill. By seeing the last bill, we could fill it up easily. For examination purposes, we should learn to work out this figure from the bill under preparation. It is easy:

(A) of previous bill = 3900 as seen from PART I of this 2nd bill

(B) of previous bill = 8000 as seen from line 2 of this 2nd bill's Memorandum of Payments

(C) of previous bill = 105000 as seen from Annexure of Secured Advance prepared for this bill

Figure in line 5 of previous bill = 640 as seen from line 5(*a*) of this bill's Memorandum of Payments

Hence amount paid as per entry (K) of last bill is that bill's A + B + C – line 5 = 3900 + 8000 + 105000 – 640 = 116260.

Have patience. You will learn this by and by.

(2) *Security Deposits.* Normally the Security Deposits to be recovered are equal to 10% of up-to-date value done minus 10% of value of work done up to the previous bill. **But in this bill, Security Deposits would be 10% of up-to-date value of work done only** because the Security previously deducted (or with-held) has been released in this bill.

(3) *Amount withheld.* The manner in which withheld amount is released has been explained in this bill. But please note that the amount of ₹ 250 with-held in the 1st. Running Account Bill has not yet been released vide line 5(*b*).

(4) *Income Tax.* It is a general tendency to deduct 1/5th of Security Deposits as Income tax (the former is 10% while the latter is 2%). But this will not be a correct method. It is 2% of ₹ 137500 – 2% of ₹ 3900

Example 6. *Prepare the 3rd Running and Final Bill of the contractor mentioned in question 3 from the further particulars given below.*

Item of work	*Unit*	*Rate per unit*	*Quantity up-to-date*	*Quantity in Prev. bill*
Earth work	Cu.M	₹ 500	25	20
Brick work in mud	Cu.M	₹ 70	70	50
Brick work in cement	Cu.M	₹ 1500	80	50
Reinforced cement concrete	Cu.M	₹ 4900	30	10
Wood work	Sq.M	₹ 350	18	----

Adjust all advances Income Tax and Security Deposit to be recovered.

₹ 250 withheld in 1st bill to be released as the deficiency has been removed.

Ans.

I. Account of work executed

Items of work	*Unit*	*Rate*	*Quantities upto date*	*Payments on the basis of actual measurements*	
				Upto date	*Since prev. bill*
		₹		₹	₹
1. Earthwork	Cu.m	500	25	12,500	2,500
2. Brick work in mud	-do-	70	70	4,900	1,400
3. Brick work in cement	-do-	1,500	80	1,20,000	45,000
4. Reinforced cement concrete	-do-	4,900	30	1,47,000	98,000
5. Wood work	Sq.m	350	18	6,300	6,300
Total value of work to date			(A)	2,90,000	
Deduct value of work shown on previous bill				1,37,500	
Net value of work since previous bill (Rupees one lakh fifty three thousand two hundred only)			(F)	1,53,200	1,53,200

FORM 26 A-Account of Secured Advances

Outstanding from previous bill	*Utilised since previous bill*	*Quantity outstanding*	*Full rate*	*Description of materials*	*Unit*	*Reduced rate*	*Upto date adv.*
			₹			₹	₹
60,000	– 60,000	---------	800	Bricks	0%	600	---------
Total amount outstanding as per this account					(C)		---------
Total amount outstanding as per this previous bill							36,000
Net amount since previous bill (Minus Rupees thirty six thousand only)					(E)		(–)36,000

III. MEMORANDUM OF PAYMENTS

Figures for Works Abstract			₹		₹
	1. Total value of work actually measured			(A)	2,90,700
	2. Total up-to-date Advance Payments			(B)	---------
	(a) As per previous bill ₹ 5,000				
	(b) Since previous bill ₹ –5,000 (D)				
	3. Total up-to-date Secured Advances			(C)	---------
	4. Total Items (1 + 2 + 3)				2,90,700
	5. Deduct amount with-held				---------
	(a) From previous bill	250			
– 250	(b) From this bill	–250			
	6. Balance			(K)	2,90,700
	7. Total amount of payments already made as per entry of last bill			(K)	1,78,250
	8. Payments now to be made as below				
	(a) By recoveries creditable to this work				
(–) 250	5(b) + 8(a) = G				
18,384	(b) By recovery of amounts creditable to other works or heads of account				61,990
	(i) Income Tax		3,064		
	(ii) Security Deposits		15,320		
94,066	(c) By Cheque		94,066		
1,12,450	(H)				

Pay ₹ 94,066 (Rupees ninety four thousand sixty six only) by cheque.

Sd./Disbursing Officer

Received ₹ 112450 (Rupees one lakh twelve thousand four hundred fifty only) as per above Memorandum of Paytts in full and final settlement of all demands.

Sd./Contractor

Important points. Three checks.

(i) Amount of line 8

$= D + E + F - 5(b) = (-)\,5000 + (-)\,36000 + 153200 - (-)\,250$

$= -5000 - 36000 + 153200 + 250 = 112450$ Agreed

(ii) $H - F = 112450 - 153200 = (-)\,40750$

$D + E - G = (-)\,5000 + (-)\,36000 + (-)\,250$

$= (-)\,40750$ Agreed

(iii) Figures for line 7 = 137500 + 5000 + 36000 – 250 = 178250

Some More Hints. Here some more hints on the bills.

(1) Quantities. Unless contrary is stated in the question itself, the quantities given in a question generally indicated up-to-date work done.

(2) Working out gross amount paid where the amount of cheque is given. Sometimes the examiner does not give the data directly. He says, for example, that the contractor was paid ₹ 4400 in the previous bill after deduction of 10% security deposits and 2% Income Tax. You will have to work out the amount paid up to the previous bill. Proceed as under:

88% of the amount paid was = ₹ 4400

1% of the amount paid was = ₹ 4400/88

100% (*i.e.*, full) amount paid was = 4400 × 100/88 = ₹ 5000

(3) Full rate when reduced rate for Secured Advance is given. Some times it is given in the question that Secured Advance was given at the rate of ₹ 36 per unit. This means the reduced rate *i.e.*, 75% of Market Rate assessed or tendered rate was ₹ 36.

75% of Market Rate or tendered rate was = ₹ 36

1% of Market Rate or tendered rate was = ₹ 36/75

100% (Full) Market Rate etc., was

= ₹ 36 × 100/75 = ₹ 48 per Unit

(4) Payments in lump-sump contract. All payments for work done or measured up additions and alterations, in the case of Lump-sum contract, are treated as advance payments. **If security is withheld for the due fulfillment of the terms of contract,** the net amount left after deducting the security is treated as Advance Payment. (Para 11.4.3. & Note CPWA Code)

(5) Cases where Tendered value of work not given. When Earnest Money taken from contractor is also given in the question, then Security deposit is recoverable in accordance with the formula that *"Earnest Money Deposit plus 10% of up-to-date value of work done recoverable as Security Deposit does not exceed 5% of the tendered value of the work (Para 4.11 above). Then deduct 10% security deposit and write it is presumed that this 10% deduction + emd is within the limit of 5% of tendered value of work"*.

8.8 CONTRACTOR'S LEDGER

Contractors' Ledger. A Contractors' Ledger is kept in Form 43 in the Division. Only one account is kept in respect of one contractor irrespective of the number of contracts undertaken by him. A personal account must be opened in the ledger for a contractor unless the work or supply entrusted to him is un-important and no payment is made except on a First and Final Bill. Contractor's Ledger is intended to record and correlate:

(*i*) the amounts due to a contractor

(*a*) for work done and Measured or

(*b*) sum withheld from his bill; and

(*ii*) the amounts actually paid to them

(*a*) for work done, or

(*b*) as advance payment, or

(*c*) as secured advance or

(*d*) as value of materials issued to the contractor or

(*e*) as expenditure incurred at the risk and cost of contractor.

(Para 10.7.1&2 of CPWA Code)

Contractor's Ledger's Form. Its Form is CPWA 43.

@	*Net transactions detailed by Suspense Heads*			*Name of work or account*	*Gross transactions*		*Total value of work / supply*
	Advance Payment	Secured Advance	Other Transactions		Debit	Credit	
1, 2, 3	4 (D)	5 (E)	6 (G)	7	8 H	9 F	10 (A)
	₹	₹	₹		₹	₹	₹

@ Divided into 3 columns *i.e.*, 1. date; 2. no. & 3. Sr. No. of Running A/c Bill.

There is another column 11 with heading "*Remarks*". Columns 1, 2, 3, 7 and 11 are self-explanatory. Others are explained below.

Ledger Proper. Columns 8 and 9 constitute the Ledger account because it is here that the amounts paid to the contractor and amounts due to him are entered. *Debits i.e.*, (gross) payments made *are entered in column* 8 *and credits i.e.*, amounts due to the contractor *in consideration of work done* or *supplies made are entered in column* 9.

A general Rule is that figure (H) of the contractor's bill is debit to his account in column 8, *whereas figure (F) of the contractor's bill is credit to his account in column* 9. (Argue why it is so?) *Hint* : Recoveries made for other works or Heads of account is in fact amount paid to him and simultaneously recovered from him for other person and heads of accounts.

Difference between the amounts in Column 8 and Column 9. There shall be some difference between the amount credited (*column 9*) and (gross) amount paid (*column 8*). This difference due to items (D), (E), And (G) of the contractor's bill. (Argue why it is so?) (Hint: Do you remember the important check in Contractor's Bill H – F = D + E – G?)

Example. *Post the transactions of the bill in question 4 of chapter 4 at page 176 in the contractor's Ledger.*

Ans.

Net transactions detailed by Suspense Heads			*Name of work or account*	*Gross transactions*		*Total value of work or supplies*
Adv. Paytt	*Secured Advance*	*Other Transac-tions*		*Debit*	*Credit*	
4 (D)	5 (E)	6 (G)	7	8 (H)	9 (F)	10 (A)
₹	₹	₹		₹	₹	₹
8000	105000	+650 (–) 1290	Material issue 1st bill Constg. School bldg	650 115610	3900	3900

Important points.

(1) From the bill, we find that materials valuing ₹ 650 were issued to him before the bill was prepared. Hence ₹ 650 stood already paid (debit) to his account. As this amount will be recovered in Figure (G) of the bill, it has been shown as + entry in column 6 (G)

(2) *Figures (D), (E), and (G) will appear in Columns 4, 5 and 6 respectively. All payments as + (plus); and all recoveries as – (minus).*

(3) CHECK that Column 8 – Column 9 = Column 4 + Column 5 + Column 6

Example. *Post the transactions of the bill in question 5 of Chapter 5 at page 178 in the contractor's Ledger.*

Ans.

Net transactions detailed by Suspense Heads			*Name of work or account*	*Gross transactions*		*Total value of work or supplies*
Adv. Paytt	*Secured Advance*	*Other Transac-tions*		*Debit*	*Credit*	
4 (D)	5 (E)	6 (G)	7	8 (H)	9 (F)	10 (A)
₹	₹	₹		₹	₹	₹
		+ 3000	Material issued for school	3000		
		+800	-do- for Hospital	800		
		+150	Labour engaged	150		
–3000	–69000	–2760	2nd bill- Constg School bldg	58840	133600	137500
		–800	-do-Recovery for Hospital bldg		800	

Important points.

(1) From the bill, we find that materials valuing ₹ 3000 (and ₹ 800) were issued to him before the second bill was prepared. Hence ₹ 3000 (and ₹ 800) stood paid (debited) to his account, when materials were issued. As this amount will be recovered in Figure (G) of the bill, it has been shown as + entry in column 6 (G). (*Similar is the case with labour engaged to set right contractor's defects. Its entry in ledger will be made when that labour is paid.*)

(2) Figures (D), (E), and (G) will appear in Columns 4, 5 and 6 respectively. All payments in column 4, 5, 6 are shown + (plus) and all recoveries – (minus).

(3) CHECK that Column 8 – Column 9 = Column 4 + Column 5 + Column 6.

***MOST IMPORTANT.* REMEMBER THAT IN LEDGER, H – F = COL. 4 + 5 + 6**

(4) Recovery for another work. We find that recovery of ₹ 800 was made in the bill of the work *"construction of school Building"* on account of materials issued for another work (Construction of Hospital Building). For such recoveries appearing in a bill, we have to make additional entries in Column 6 (*Minus sign*) showing recovery of cost of materials, and in column 9, as done in the table above. [Para 10.7.5 (*c*) (*i*) CPWA Code]

Example. *Post the transactions of the bill in question 6 of Chapter 4 at page 180 in the contractor's Ledger.*

Ans.

Net transactions detailed by Suspense Heads			*Name of work or account*	*Gross transactions*		*Total value of work or supply*	*Remarks*
Adv. Paytt.	*Secured Advance*	*Other Transactions*		*Debit*	*Credit*		
4 (D)	5 (E)	6 (G)	7	8 (H)	9 (F)	10 (A)	11
₹	₹	₹		₹	₹	₹	
–5000	–36000	250	3rd bill-Constg School Bldg	112450	153200	290700	

Closing the Contractor's Ledger. Now contractor's ledger has been posted. All that is left is closing the ledger. It is a simple matter. Proceed as under:

(1) Total up columns 8 and 9 and write down the closing balance, *i.e.*, difference between these two columns.

(2) Total up columns 4, 5 and 6. These are the amounts still recoverable or still with-held. Check that the balance in these three columns totals upto the figure worked out in item 1 above.

Example 4. *Post the three bill of the Contractor given in Questions 3, 4 and 5 in the Contractor's Ledger, and close the ledger after posting of each bill.*

Ans. Please see the following three tables for Ledger of each bill.

Net transactions detailed by Suspense Heads			*Name of work or account*	*Gross transactions*		*Total value of work or supply*
Adv. Paytt	*Secured Advance*	*Other Transactions*		*Debit*	*Credit*	
4 (D)	5 (E)	6 (G)	7	8 (H)	9 (F)	10 (A)
₹	₹	₹		₹	₹	₹
		+650	Material issued	650		
8000	105000	(–)1290	1st bill-Constg School Bldg	115610	3900	3900
			Closing Balance		112360	
8000	105000	(–)640	TOTAL	116260	116260	

			Details of balance			
			(*i*) Constructing			
8000	105000	(–)640	School Building	112360		
8000	105000	(–)640	Opening balance	112360		
		+3000	Material issued for school	3000		
		+800	-do-for Hospital	800		
		+150	Labour engaged	150		
–3000	–69000	(–)2760	2nd bill-Constg School Bldg	58840	133600	137500
		(–)800	-do-Recovery for Hospital Bldg		800	
			Closing Balance		40750	
5000	36000	(–)250	TOTAL	175150	175150	
			Details of balance			
			(*i*) Constructing			
5000	36000	(–)250	School Bldg	40750		
5000	36000	(–)250	Opening Balance	40750		
			3rd bill-Constg School Bldg	112450	153200	290700
–5000	–36000	250	Closing Balance		NIL	
------	------	------	TOTAL	153200	153200	
			Details of balance			
			(i) Constructing			
------	------	------	School Bldg	NIL		

Contractor's delay in receiving Payment. If a contractor's bill has been prepared and passed for payment but has not yet been paid in cash or cheque not yet signed, no entry is to be made in the Ledger.

In case a contractor delays receiving the payment of his final bill for more than one month after the bill has been passed, the amount due to him may be credited to Public Works Deposits. If, however, it is seen that he has been overpaid, then the net amount recoverable may be debited to Miscellaneous Works Advances.

(Para 10.5.19 of CPWA Code)

Example. *A contractor's bill consisted of the following items:*

	₹
Value of work done since previous Bill	8600
Advance payment recovered since previous Bill	500
Secured Advance recovered since previous Bill	1800
Value of materials issued for same work recovered since previous Bill	600
Security Deposits recovered since previous Bill	800
Amount of cheque to be issued	4900

Indicate entries in the Ledger

(*a*) if only the bill has been prepared

(*b*) if it was final bill and credited to Deposits.

Ans. 5. (*a*) If only the bill has been prepared (and not paid), No entry is to be made in the ledger.

(*b*) Let us consider columns 8 and 9 first; then columns 4, 5, and 6.

Column 9 = Figure (F) = Value of work done = ₹ 8600

Column 8 = Figure (H) = Amount of cheque + Recoveries for other works/heads of Accounts = 4900 + 800 = 5700.

Always use the Formula H – F = Col 4 + 5 + 6

Remember for columns 4, 5 and 6: + *for payments;* – *for recoveries*

Column 4

= Figure (D) = Advance payment since previous bill = – 500

Column 5

= Figure (E) = Secured Advance since previous bill = – 1800

Column 6

= Figure (G) = Recoveries/Materials for the same work = – 600

Net transactions detailed by Suspense Heads			*Name of work or account*	*Gross transactions*		*Total value of work or supplies*
Adv. Paytt	*Secured Advance*	*Other Transactions*		*Debit*	*Credit*	
4 (D)	5 (E)	6 (G)	7	8 (H)	9 (F)	10 (A)
₹	₹	₹		₹	₹	₹
(–)500	(–)1800	(–)600	Final bill	5700	8600	

Important check: (H) – (F) = 5700 – 8600 = (–)2900 Agree

Lump-sum Contracts. As already stated in para 4.25(4) in Chapter 4 of this Book, all payments made (net payments as reduced by security) are treated as advance payments and entered in column 4 of the Ledger. Hence there is no entry in column 9 till the final bill is paid. Even payment for measured up additions and alterations is treated as Advance Payment.

(*Para* 11.5.2 *of CPWA Code*)

Example. *Enter the 1st bill of a contractor containing the following transactions in respect of a work on Lump-sum contract.*

	₹
Work done covered by lump-sum contract	16000
Additions and Alterations duly measured	1500
Secured Advance paid in this bill	2500
Cost of materials (issued to him for this work) recovered	3500

Security 10%

Ans. Column 4 = Advance payment

= 16000 + 1500 – Security 1750 = +15750 (+ for payment)

Column 5 = Secured Advance = 2500 (+ for payment)

Column 6 = Other Transactions = – 3500 (– for recovery)

Column 8 = Amount paid = (Cheque) + recoveries for other works or heads of account

= (16000 + 1500 + 2500 – 3500 – 10% of 17500) + 0 = 14750

Column 9 = Nil (All intermediate payments are Advance payments)

Net transactions detailed by Suspense Heads			*Name of work or account*	*Gross transactions*		*Total value of work / supplies*
Adv. Payment	*Secured Advance*	*Other Transactions*		*Debit*	*Credit*	
4 (D)	5 (E)	6 (G)	7	8 (H)	9 (F)	10 (A)
₹	₹	₹		₹	₹	₹
		3500	Opening balance	3500		
15750	2500	(–)3500	1st Bill (name of work)	14750	---	

Check 8 – 9 = (4 + 5 + 6) 8 – 9 = 14750;

4 + 5 + 6 = 15750 + 2500 + (–)3500 = 14750

There was opening balance of ₹ 3500 in column 6.

Important for Opening Balances. *Sum up the opening balances of column 4, 5 and 6. If it is positive, put it in column 8. If it is negative, put it in column 9*

Example. *The 2nd and final bill of the contractor of question 6 contained the following transactions. Post both of them in the ledger* :

	₹
Up-to-date Work done as per Lump-sum contract	55000
Up-to-date Measured up Additions and Alterations	2000
Recovery for materials issued for same work	5000

All advances adjusted. Security deposit recovered 10% of work done.

Ans. Let us analyse the 2nd and final Bill. In this Bill-

Column 4

= Advance Payment = (–)15,750 (+ for payment, – for recovery)

Column 5

= Secured Advance = (–)2,500 (+ for payment, – for recovery)

Column 6

= Other Transactions = (–)5,000 (+ for payment, – for recovery)

Cheque = (55,000 + 2,000 – 5,700 for security –15,7500 for Advance Payment – 2500 for secured Advance – 5,000 for materials) = 28,050

Recoveries creditable to other works or heads of account = ₹ 5,700

Column 8 = *Cheque* + Recoveries creditable to other works or heads of account = 28050 + 5700 = ₹ 33,750

(or use H – F = columns 4 + 5 + 6)

Column 9 = Work done = 57000 (because this is final bill)

CHECK: 8 – 9 = 33750 – 57000 = (–)23250;

4 + 5 + 6 = (–)15750 + (–)2500 + (–)5000 = 23250 Agreed

Net transactions detailed by Suspense Heads			Name of work or account	Gross transactions		Total value of work or supplies
Adv. Paytt	*Secured Advance*	*Other Transactions*		*Debit*	*Credit*	
4 (D)	5 (E)	6 (G)	7	8 (H)	9 (F)	10 (A)
₹	₹	₹		₹	₹	₹
		3500	Opening balance	3500		
15750	2500	(–) 3500	1st Bill Work A	14750		
		5000	Materials	5000		
–15750	–2500	–5000	2nd&Final Bill-Work A	33750	57000	57000
			Balance		Nil	
---	----	---	TOTAL	57000	57000	

Fines. There are some fines which are levied because they affect the quality of work and hence the value of the work, *e.g.*, fine for sub-standard work. *As soon as such fines are levied, they are posted as + entry in column 6 and column 8. Recovery, when made in the bill, is posted in the Ledger.* Recovery of all other fines is watched through *"Register of Recoveries in form 95 mentioned in Para 22.2.8 of CPWA Code. They do not find a place in the Contractor's Ledger."*

Example. *Post the following transactions and bills in the Ledger.*

		₹
(*i*)	Opening Balances-	
	Advance Payments outstanding (*Work X*)	1000
	Secured Advance recoverable (*Work X ₹ 6000; Work Y ₹ 1000*)	7000
	Value of materials issued still recoverable (*Work X ₹ 4000*)	5275
	(*Work Y ₹ 1275*)	
(*ii*)	Paid Bill for work *X*	
	Value of work done since previous bill	15000
	Advance payment recovered since previous bill	1000
	Secured Advance recovered	5000
	Recovery for stores issued for the same work	4000

	Fine for bad work recovered	500
	Cheque	4500
(*iii*)	Paid Bill for work *Y*	
	Value of work done since previous bill	4500
	Advance Payment made since previous bill	1500
	Secured Advance recovered since previous bill	1000
	Recovery for stores issued for the Work *Y*	800
	Recovery for stores issued for work *X*	475
	Security with-held in the account of work *Y*	225
	Cheque issued	3500

Ans.

Bill for work X.

Column 4 = (–) 1000 (+ for payment, – for recovery)

Column 5 = (–) 5000 (+ for payment, – for recovery)

Column 6 = [Materials issued, Recovery for Materials and amounts withheld] = (–) 4000 (–) 500 = (–) 4500 (+ for payments/ issues, – for recovery)

Column 8 = Cheque + Recoveries for other works or heads of account = 4500

Column 9 = Value of work done = 15000

CHECK: 8 – 9 = 4500 – 15000 = 10500; 4 + 5 + 6 (–) 1000 (–) 5000 (–) 4500 = 10500 OK

Bill for work Y

Column 4 = Advance Payment = 1500 (+ for payment, – for recovery)

Column 5 = Secured Advance = (–) 1000 (+ for payment, – for recovery)

Column 6 = Issue (+)/Recovery (–) of stores and amounts with-held (–) = (–) 800 (–) 225 = (–) 1025

Column 8 = Cheque + Recoveries for other works or Heads of account = 3500 + 475 = 3975

Column 9 = Value of work done = 4500

CHECK: 8 – 9 = 3975 – 4500 = 525; 4 + 5 + 6 = 1500 (–)1000 (–) 1025 = 525 Agreed.

Net transactions detailed by Suspense Heads			*Name of work or account*	*Gross transactions*		*Total value of work or supplies*
Adv. Paytt	*Secured Advance*	*Other Transactions*		*Debit*	*Credit*	
4 (D)	5 (E)	6 (G)	7	8 (H)	9 (F)	10 (A)
₹	₹	₹		₹	₹	₹
1000	7000	5275	Opening Balance	13275		
		500	Fine levied for bad work *X*	500		
– 1000	– 5000	– 4500	Bill for Work *X*	4500	15000	
1500	– 1000	– 1025	Bill for Work *Y*	3975	4500	
		– 475	-do-, Recovery for work *X*		475	
			Balance		2275	
1500	1000	– 225	TOTAL	22250	22250	
			Details of balance	2750		
----	1000	----	Work *X*			
1500	-----	– 225	Work *Y*			

IMPORTANT POINTS FOR WRITING CONTRACTOR'S LEDGER.

(1) *Remember to make additional entry* of recovery for other work in Columns 6 and 9 of the contractor's ledger. (*See Important Point 4 in Q. 2*).

(2) *Column 4 corresponds to figure (D) in the contractor's bill.* Net advance payment paid (+) or recovered in the voucher/bill (–) is posted.

(3) *Column 5 corresponds to Figure (E) in the contractor's bill.* Net secured advance paid (+) or recovered in the voucher/bill (–) is posted in this column.

(4) *Column 6 corresponds to Figure (G) in the contractor's bill.* In it is posted net result of Value of materials issued (+)/ recovered (–), Fines levied for bad work (+), and recovery of fines for bad work from the contractor's bill for the same work (–); amount withheld (–) and release of amounts withheld earlier (+).

(5) *Figures in columns 4, 5 and 6 are (+) if amounts are to be recovered; (–) if they are recoveries.*

(6) *Column 8-corresponds Figure (H) in the contractor's bill i.e.,* amount of cheque plus recoveries in line 8(*b*) for other works/ Heads of account.

(7) *Column 9-corresponds to Figure (F) in the contractor's bill.*

8.9 WORKS ABSTRACT

(*Paras referred to are from CPWA code unless contrary is stated*)

Definition. An account of all transactions relating to a work during a month is known as *Works Abstract*. It is prepared in Form 33. (*Para 10.50.1*)

Sub-head of a Works Abstract. In the Works Abstract a separate column is used for each sub-head. For opening these sub-heads, the abstract of estimate of work is taken as a guide.

Miscellaneous charges of general nature that do not pertain to any sub-head (such as, work charged establishment, Contingencies etc. etc.), should be treated as a separate sub-head. (*Para 10.5.3*)

Centage charges not to be posted in Works Abstract. Expenditure on Government establishment, their leave salaries and, pensions and expenditure on general Tools and Plant is recovered on a percentage basis on the cost of work undertaken on behalf of Commercial Government departments, local bodies or private individuals. Although these charges are included in the cost of works, these are not posted in the Works Abstract. (*Note below para 10.5.1*)

Two categories of sub-heads. Transactions during the month on a work may consist of (*i*) Payments for work done, and (*ii*) Receipts/Payments, which are adjustable by subsequent payment or recovery. Sub-heads of work can, thus, be divided into two broad categories, namely, (1) Final Charges, and (2) Suspense Accounts.

Final Charges. Final charges are divided into sub-heads such as "*Earth Work*", "*Brick Masonry*", "*RCC Work*", "*Doors and Windows*" etc. etc.

An Important sub-head of Final Charges. All the subheads under final charges are simple and require no special mention except the sub-head "*Additional Charges for materials issued to Contractors or direct to works*". The use of this sub-head is explained in the following sub-paras:

(1) Materials issued at stipulated rates (*not at Issue Rate*). In this case Stores Account would get credit for the value of material at the issue rate while the contractor's account (sub-head Contractor's Other Transactions or O.T., for short) would be debited at the stipulated rate. The difference between the two values is to be posted in this special sub-head as gain (*with minus sign*) if the Stipulated Rate is higher than the issue rate, or as a loss (with plus sign) if it is lower than the Issue Rate.

(2) Expenses incurred by Government on Materials issued. Some times Division has to incur expenses, in accordance with the agreement, on carriage of material to the promised place of delivery and other incidental charges. These charges are also posted in this Sub-head.

(3) Materials issued for Departmental Works or for Works on labour rate contract. The cost of all materials issued for works executed departmentally or for works on contract at labour rates is posted in the Works Abstract under Suspense head "*Materials*". A record of quantities is also kept in the "*Register of Material at site Account*". On completion of the work, the quantity of each material consumed on the quantity of work done is calculated theoretically with the help of engineering formula.

On these theoretical calculations, the value of materials estimated as used on the work, *at the standard issue rate prevailing at the time of completion of the work* is debited in the **"Register of Works"** to the final heads by minus entry under Suspense head "*Materials*". **Balance left in the suspense head "Materials" is transferred to** "*Additional charges for materials issued to contractors or direct to works*". (Para 10.5.10 of CPWA Code)

Suspense Accounts. As stated in para 6.4 above, a few suspense Accounts are also opened in the Works Abstract to record transactions of *temporary character which are either not adjustable as final charges in the account of the work concerned or the correct classification of which cannot be determined immediately*. These are:

(1) *Contractors-Advance Payments* (2) *Contractors-Secured Advances* (3) *Contractors-Other Transactions*	(Payments as plus; Recovery as minus)
(4) Labourers	(Payments as plus; unpaid wages as minus)

(5) Materials (Plus on receipt; Minus on adjustment on completion)

(6) Land Acquisition (Payment of advance as plus; on adjustment of account minus)

Contractors - Advance Payments/Secured Advances. These two sub-heads are self-explanatory and need no special mention.

Contractors - O.T. (*i.e.*, **Other Transactions).** The following transactions are classified under this suspense head of the work abstract.

(i) Value of stores material issued to a contractor, *for use on the work allotted to him,* which is recoverable from him is shown as plus entry in this sub-head. (Para 10.3.6).

(ii) Any payment made on behalf of the contractor, which is recoverable from him such as payment to his labourers, or to labour engaged to set right the defects in his work, is to be kept in this sub-head pending recovery.

(iii) Fine levied on a contractor for bad work too is posted in this sub-head to watch its recovery.

(iv) Advance paid to a contractor under *para 10.2.18 of* Old CPWA code (Para 31.1 of CPWD Works Manual 2003) *i.e.*, 75% *of the net amount payable on bill which is under check in the Divisional Office and which is likely to be delayed* is also kept under this sub-head as plus entry. Its adjustment when made is shown as minus entry. [*para 10.7.5(c)(iv) CPWA Code*]

(v) Amounts with-held from the contractor's bill in line 5(*a*) of its *Memorandum of Payments* either as security with-held or pending settlement or certain conditions of the contract are also kept in this sub-head as minus entries. Their repayment is posted as plus entries. (*para 10.5.16 CPWA Code*)

Labourers. "*Work charged establishment*" is different from Labourers. *The salary of Work Charged Staff* is drawn on Establishment Pay Bills. The amount of their pay is treated as "*final charges*" as and when paid. Unpaid salaries, if any, are also noted in the "*Register of unpaid wages*". Their subsequent payment is watched through this register (*Para 10.2.28*). *The emoluments of labourers* are drawn on Muster Rolls. The gross amount of the Muster Roll is entered in the accounts as *"Final charges"* but the unpaid amount is posted as minus entry under this Suspense head.

Subsequent payment of their unpaid balances is watched through this head.

Examples. There are some more items needing further explanation but before that, we would like you to grasp the points discussed so far with the help of some examples.

Example 1. *Post the following bill of contractor P for ₹2000 in the Works Abstract: - Vr. No. 56 of 12-5-2004; CC II&R; Name of work:*

Constructing a Hospital		₹
Payments	Brick work since previous bill	1,000
	Wood work since previous bill	800
	Advance Payment since previous bill	1,200
	Secured Advance since previous bill	(–) 500
	Total	2,500
Recoveries	Cost of materials issued for this work	400
	Security with-held	100

Example 2. Suppose in the Vr. above, recovery of ₹ 400 related to materials issued for another work and ₹ 100 were recovered on account of Security Deposit, how shall it be posted in the Works Abstract?

Ans. 1 & 2.

WORK ABSTRACT

Name of work *Constructing a Hospital* *Month May 2004*

Brief Particulars	*Vr. No.*	*Brick work*	*Wood work*	*Advance Payment*	*Secured Advance*	*O.T.*	*Total*
		₹	₹	₹	₹	₹	₹
Ans. 1 CCII & R of contractor P	56	1000	800	1200	–500	–500	2000
Ans. 2 -do-	56	1000	800	1200	–500	----	2500

Important Points.

(1) *Which figures of contractor's bill are to be posted?* Only figures since previous bill are to be posted.

(2) *Counter-check of the figure in column "Total".* This should be equal to figure (H) [*i.e.*, Amount of cheque + Recoveries in line 8(*b*) in the contractor's bill].

(3) *Name of contractor.* When posting the bill of a contractor, always record his name in the column for "*Brief Particulars*".

Example 3. *Post the following Vr. 4 of 8-4-2004 in Works Abstract of Work A (CCIII & R of Contractor R).*

	₹
Work done since previous bill	5,000
Advance Payment since previous bill	1,000
Secured Advance since previous bill	(–) 1,000
Total	5,000
Recovery of material issued for the same work	400
Recovery of material issued for another work	600
With-held pending clearance of site	1,000

Ans.

Name of work A *Month April 2004*

Brief Particulars	*Vr. No.*	*Final charges*		*Advance Payment*	*Secured Advance*	*O.T.*	*Total*
		₹		₹	₹	₹	₹
CCIII&R of contractor R	4	5000		1000	– 1000	– 1400	3600

Example 4. *Muster Roll of labourers for ₹ 1,500 (Vr no. 7 of 9-4-2004) was partly paid as ₹ 350 out of it remained undisbursed. ₹ 200 were paid on 13-4-2004 (Hand Receipt no. 12), and remaining ₹ 150 were not paid yet.*

Ans.

Name of work *Month April 2004*

Brief Particulars	*Vr. No*	*Final charges*	*Advance Payment*	*Secured Advance*	*O.T*	*Labourers*	*Total*
		₹	₹	₹	₹	₹	₹
M.Roll	7	1500				(–) 350	1150
Wages	12					200	200
Total April		1500				(–) 150	1350

Balance under "*Labourers*" indicates wages awaiting disbursement.

Example 5. *Post this 4th R.A Bill of contractor A in the Works Abstract.*

Brickwork since previous bill 10 Cu.M @ ₹ 500 per Cu.M.
Secured Advance since previous bill ₹ 500
Recovery of material for the same work ₹ 200
Hire charges of Tools and Plant ₹ 500

Issued cheque ₹ 4,800 (Vr. No.8). The work was undertaken for a local body and is to be charged 22.3/4% Departmental Charges on this bill.

Ans.

Name of work *Month*

Brief Particulars	*Vr. No*	*Final charges*	*Advance Payment*	*Secured Advance*	*O.T*		*Total*
		₹	₹	₹	₹		₹
4th bill of Contractor A	8	5000	------	500	(–) 200		5300

Important Points.

(1) Departmental Charges. Even though departmental charges go to increase the cost of the work, these are not entered in the Works Abstract.

(2) Check. "*Total*" = Cheque [4800] + Line 8 (*b*) [500]
= ₹ 5300

Example 6. *Post the following paid Vrs. in the Works Abstract of work M.*

(*i*) Vr. 23 of 25-6-2004 - Paid labourers on Muster roll for Brickwork ₹ 2500 ; ₹ 300 drawn on the Muster Roll remained unpaid.

(*ii*) Vr. 34 or 30-6-2004 - Drew salary of work charges establishment ₹ 2000; out of which ₹ 250 were left unpaid.

Ans.

Name of work M *Month June 2004*

Brief particulars	*Vr. No*	*Brick Work*	*Estt. Work charged*	*Labourers*			*Total*
		₹	₹	₹			₹
Muster roll	23	2800		(–) 300			2500
WCE Bill	34		1750	1750			

Important Point about Check on Column "*Total*"

(*a*) A contractors' bill, when posted in the Works Abstract, should add up to the figure (H) of its Memorandum of Payments.

(*b*) All Work-charged Establishment Bills when posted should total up to the amount disbursed. Subsequent payment of unpaid balances, made on Hand Receipt (a Voucher for the Cash Book), will be entered in Work Abstract at that time.

(Para 10.2.28(*b*) CPWA Code)

(*c*) All Muster Rolls, when posted in Works Abstract, should total up to the amount actually paid – Gross amount under "*Final Charges*"; unpaid amount goes as minus entry under Suspense head "*Labourers*".

Suspense-Land Acquisition Account. Advances paid by the Divisional Officers to the Land Acquisition Officer (L.A.O.) are posted as Plus entry under this Suspense Head. On receipt of detailed account like "*Land Award Statement*", "*Paid Vouchers*" from the L.A.O., a Minus entry (equal to the total of vouchers paid and sent by L.A.0.) is made in this Suspense head. A corresponding Plus entry is made in the Sub-Head **Land.** Any sum received back as unpaid is also posted as minus entry under this Suspense head.

(Para 10.5.21 of CPWA Code)

Materials. This sub-head is meant for recording the value of material issued for use on the Work *in the following circumstances only:*

(*i*) *when the work is being done departmentally OR by contractor on labour rates only, AND*

(*ii*) *in the estimate their is separate provision for labour and Materials.*

In the Works Abstract this is treated as a suspense head. The value of all materials purchased for the work direct and expenditure on their carriage etc., is posted as Plus entry on the basis of paid vouchers/Transfer entries etc. *The value of stores issued from Stock is posted as a single entry at the end of the month, on the basis of Stock Account.*

The value of any material returned or otherwise sold or disposed of is posted as Minus entry.

In the Works Abstract, this Suspense head is never cleared. The clearance of this suspense head is done only in the "*Register of Works*" kept in the Divisional Office.

Example. *Post the following in the Works Abstract of a Major Work.*

(*a*) Issue from divisional Stock of 1.2 Cu. M. of wood direct to Work, issue rate being ₹ 6000 per Cu.M., Storage charges ₹ 500 per Cu.M.

(*b*) *Vr.* 6 dated 5-7-2004. Paid ₹ 600 being the charges for the carriage of the above quantity of wood to the site of the work.

(*c*) *Transfer entry No. 9.* 0.2 Cu. M. of wood mentioned at (*a*) above having become surplus was transferred to another work in progress, the issue rate at that time being ₹ 5500 per Cu. M. and the market rate being ₹ 5000 per Cu. M.

Ans.

Description	*Vr / TE No.*	*Final charges*	*Materials*	*Total*
		₹	₹	₹
Carriage	Vr. 6		600	600
wood transferred	TE 9		(–) 1000	(–) 1000
Stock			7800	7800
Total			7400	7400

Important Points

(1) *Transfer of material to another work.* Please refer to *Para 10.3.13* of *CPWA Code* which, requires the materials returned to Stores or transferred to other works to be priced within Current Market Rates, the resultant loss being borne by the work.

(2) *Issue from Stock to work* is posted at the end of the month from Stock A/c. But *issue of materials to contractor* is adjusted at once by Transfer Entry.

(3) *Transfer to another Work.* As soon as the material is transferred, a transfer entry should be made to give the effect of the transfer *i.e.*, debit the work to which material is transferred and credit the work from which transfer takes place.

Example 8. *Post the following in the Works Abstract of a major work.*

(*i*) TE No.5. Supply of 5 bags of cement of contractor P at ₹ 160 per bag from the Divisional stock; issue rate being ₹ 120 per bag, storage charges ₹ 10 per bag.

(*ii*) TE No. 7. Issued 1 Cu. M. of wood to contractor P from Stores at a stipulated rate of ₹ 8000 per Cu. M.; issue rate + Storage charge being ₹ 6000 + ₹ 500 per Cu. M.

(*iii*) Vr. No. 5. Steel sheets for ₹ 8000 purchased and handed over to contractor P valued at ₹ 9500 at the rate stipulated in the agreement.

Ans. Read also para 6.6 of this Chapter.

Description	*Vr / TENo.*	*Additional charges for materials issued to contractor / direct to works*	*Contracts O.T*	*Total*
		₹	₹	₹
Steel sheets to P	Vr. 5	(–) 1500	9500	8000
Cement – Cont. P	TE 5	(–) 150	800	650
Wood to Cont. P	TE 7	(–) 1500	8000	6500
Total		(–) 3150	18300	15150

Example 9. *Exhibit it in the Register of works the following details of "Material-at-site" on the completion of the work,*

(*a*) Outstanding Balance under '*Suspense-Materials*' (at the issue rates prevailing from time to time at the time of their issue) ₹ 2,10,000.

(*b*) Value of materials used on the work (at the current issue rate):

Wood work	₹ 50,000
Brick work	₹ 1,00,000
Reinforced Concrete work	₹ 20,000
(*c*) Shortage attributed to Contractor	₹ 15,000
(*d*) Shortage recoverable from a workman	₹ 2,500
(*e*) Shortage for which no responsibility could be fixed	₹ 7,500
(*f*) Surplus unserviceable material still in hand	₹ 13,500
(*g*) Difference due to variation of issue rate	₹ 1,500

Adjusted by TE No. 5. Exhibit in the Register of Works.

Ans.

Descrip-tion	*Vr. / TE No.*	*Wood Work*	*Brick Work*	*RCC Work*	*Addl. charges*	*Mater-ials*	*Cont, O.T.*	*Total*
		₹	₹	₹	₹	₹	₹	₹
Materials	TE	50000	100000	20000	22500	– 210000	15000	– 2500

Important Points

(1) Shortage due to contractor. This will be taken to the sub-head *"Contractor's - Other transactions"* for effecting recovery.

(2) Additional Charges. The full nomenclature of this sub-head is *"Additional Charges for Materials Issued to contractors or Works direct"*. All outstanding balances under *"Materials"* left after carrying out necessary adjustments are kept under this sub-head. (See para 10.5.10 of CPWA Code). These leftover items would be

(*i*) Shortages for which no responsibility could be fixed,

(*ii*) Surplus materials not sold/transferred or disposed of, and

(*iii*) Differences due to variation of issue rates.

(3) Amounts recoverable from workman. (₹ 2500). This amount would be transferred to *"Miscellaneous Works Advances"* for recovery from him.

Other Topics

Carriage (& Incidental) Charges. We will deal it in two parts:

(A) Material issued to contractors. Carriage charges up to the promised place of delivery is the responsibility of the Division. These would be posted under *"Additional charges for materials issued to the contractor / works direct"*. Carriage charges beyond the promised place of delivery, if incurred by the Division, are posted under *"Contractor's O.T."*.

(B) Materials issued to works direct. Carriage charges from Store to work-site are treated as cost of materials and debited to the Suspense head *"Materials"* (if Rules require this sub-head to be opened) or *"Final Charges"*.

Carriage Charges of materials issued to work, which are surplus to requirements and are returned to Stores, are borne by the work concerned. However, if these are transferred to another work, the carriage charges are distributed to both the works as may be equitable. (Para 10.8.1 CPWA Code)

Closing Suspense Account. When the accounts of a work are to be closed, it should be seen that all out-standings under Suspense Accounts are cleared except (*i*) Labourers, (*ii*) Land acquisition and (*iii*) Materials vide para 10.5.18; 10.5.21 and 10.5.13 of CPWA Code.

If contractor delays to receive payment of his Final Bill. The accounts of a contractor should be closed as soon as the contract is completed. If he delays to receive the payment of his final bill for more than one month after it is passed, the passed bill should be taken in the Works Abstract by placing the balance due to him under "*Public Works Deposits*"

(Para 10.5.19 CPWA Code)

Details of Contractor's Suspense. A work may be under execution by more than one contractor. Therefore, a contractor-wise break-up should be recorded at the bottom of the Works Abstract, and reconciled with the work-wise break-up of balances worked out in the Contractor's Ledger.

Register of Works. Work Abstract is a consolidated record of transactions and expenditure of a work for one month. For next month there will be another Work Abstract.

A Register of Works intended to be record of progressive expenditure on a work from month to month. It has the same sub-heads, as the Works Abstract. The only difference is that there is one line entry for the expenditure of each month. Works Abstract supports that entry by providing voucher-wise break-up of the month-wise posting made in the Register of Works. The Suspense head "*Materials*" is cleared only in the Register of works. (Para 10.5.13. & 10.6.6 CPWA Code)

9

TRAVELLING ALLOWANCE

9.1 INTRODUCTION

When a journey is performed by any government servant in the interest of the public service the individual has to incur additional expenditure to cover which travelling allowance is granted. The allowance granted to officers for maintenance of conveyance also falls under this category. For different categories of officers Central and State Governments have prescribed scales of T.A. admissible to various categories of employees.

9.2 TYPE OF T.A.

The various travelling allowances admissible to Government servants are:

1. Permanent travelling allowance.
2. Conveyance or hour allowance.
3. Milage allowance.
4. Daily allowance.
5. The actual cost of travelling.

The above allowances are briefly described below:

1. **Permanent travelling allowance.** This allowance is drawn all the year round and covers T.A. for journeys with in the jurisdiction of the Government Servant. This allowance is not admissible for the following periods:

(*a*) During leave, temporary transfer or joining time.

(*b*) When an officer holds two or more posts for which separate permanent allowance is admissible, the competent authority may sanction necessary permanent T.A. subject to such allowance not exceeding the total of all the permanent T.A's.

(Based on SR's 21, 22, 23, 24.)

2. **Conveyance or house allowance.** This T.A. is drawn all the year round and no deduction is made for the period of absence from headquarters. Until the Permanent T.A. this allowance can be claimed in addition to other kinds of T.A. However, when the conveyance allowance is specifically sanctioned for the maintenance of a conveyance (motorcycle or motor car) no mileage allowance is admissible for the journey performed by the car or motor cycle to such an extent as prescribed by the sanctioning authority. The present rates of such allowances are given in Table 9.1.

Table 9.1. Transport Allowance

Grade Pay in ₹	*Rate of transport allowance per*	
	Month A-1/A class cities in ₹	*Other places in ₹*
5400 and above posts in the apex scale and cabinet secretary/ equivalent	₹ 3200 + D.A. thereon	₹ 1600 + D.A. thereon
4200 to 4800	₹ 1600 to D.A. thereon	₹ 800 + D.A. thereon
Below ₹ 4200	₹ 400 + D.A. thereon	₹ 300 + D.A. thereon

Note. (*a*) Journeys between residence and place of work are not considered for purpose of col. (1).

(*b*) If the mileage during the month as col. (1) is below 200 km. no allowance is admissible and conveyance allowance under col. (2) is admissible only to officers whose pay exceeds to ₹ 1000.00 p.m.

3. **Mileage allowance.** This allowance is given to meet the cost of a particular journey. Normally the allowance is given for the shortest route but the competent authority may permit mileage by any other route actually used, provided reasons are recorded. The entitlement of government employees in respect of various modes of travel are given in Tables 9.2 to 9.5.

Table 9.2. Class of accommodation according to grade pay by rail/road/air

Pay Range (grade pay)	*Travel entitled*
₹ 9000 and above	J class air/AC first class by train
6600 to 8400	Y class by air/AC first class by train
5400 to 6500	Y class by air/AC II tier by train
4200 to 4800	AC II class by train
less than ₹ 4200	First class/AC III tier by/AC chair car by train

Table 9.3. Class of accommodation according to grades by sea or river steamer

Grade of employee	*Class*
First	Higher class
Second	Upper class if only 2 classes, and II class if more than 2 classes
Third	Lower class if only two classes and II class if there are three classes and III class if there are four classes
Fourth	Lowest class

The above four grades are described below:
First grade Above ₹ 1100.00
Second grade Above ₹ 650 but below ₹ 1100.00
Third grade Above ₹ 330 but below ₹ 650.00 p.m.
Fourth grade below ₹ 330.00 p.m.

Table 9.4. Rates of road mileage

Grade of Govt. Servant	*Journey Performed by*			*Full Taxi / Own Car*
	Public Bus	*Bicycle / Foot*	*Motor Cycle* *Scooter, Auto Rickshaw Tonga / Cycle Rickshaw / Man driven Rickshaw*	
First and Second grade	Actual Fair	—	₹ 1.70 *p* per km	6.00 per km
Third and Fourth grade	do	—	do	Not entitled

Note. It is not necessary that the car/motor cycle should be registered in the name of Government servant claiming road mileage.

The permission of superior authority is not necessary to travel by full taxi/own car/scooter or motor cycle between places connected by public transport system. [Col. (1) S.R. 46]

If an officer of the fourth grade travels by road in a car or other means than by taking a single seat in a bus between places connected by rail, road mileage is restricted to:

(*a*) A Single first class fare if either first class or air-condition accommodation is available on the route, and

(*b*) A single rail fair of the higher class available on the line in all other cases.

A competent authority may however relax the above limitations under S.R. 31 read with G.I. order thereunder, if the road journey is preferred in the public interest.

4. **Daily allowance.** Daily allowance is admissible on the basis of the period of absence from the headquarters located beyond 8 km from the Headquarters. This allowance is meant to cover the additional expenditure incurred by a Government servant in performance of his duty or official work. In the case of transfer this allowance is admissible to the members of the family as well for the duration of the journey. (See. S.R. 49).

For the purpose of this allowance day means a full calendar day for 24 hours from midnight to midnight (from 0000 hrs. to 2400 hrs.)

Daily allowance for part of day is as per Table 9.6.

Table 9.5. Daily allowance admissible for part of day

Sl. No.	*Period of absence from H.Q.*	*% of normal D.A.*
1.	Below 6 hours	30%
2.	Between 6 and 12 hours	50%
3.	Exceeding 12 hours	Full

For purpose of this allowance the period of absence is reckoned with reference to the scheduled departure/arrival time of the train from the Railway Station. If the train is late by more than 15 minutes, actual time of arrival will be considered. When the total absence from the Headquarter is partly spent in journeys and partly in hotels under own arrangements in places where higher rates of D.A. are admissible, the D.A. admissible is calculated as below:

(*a*) Calculate the total number of daily allowances for absence from the Headquarter.

(*b*) Calculate the number of daily allowances for which higher rates of D.A. are admissible. This gives number of days at higher rates.

(*c*) From the total as per (*a*) above deduct the total as per (*b*) above. The balance gives the number of days for which D.A. is admissible at ordinary rates.

The rates of daily allowance admissible to a government servant are given in Tables 9.7 and 9.8.

Table 9.7. Rates of Daily Allowance when the Government Servant avails of Government or Public Sector guest house or makes his own arrangement.

Grade Pay	*Daily Allowance*
₹ 9000 and above	Reimbursement for Hotel accommodation of upto ₹ 5000 per day, reimbursement of taxi (AC) charges of upto 50 km for travel within city and reimbursement of food bills not exceeding ₹ 500 per day.
₹ 6600 to ₹ 8400	Reimbursement for Hotel accommodation of upto ₹ 3000 per day, reimbursement of taxi (non-AC) charges of upto 50 kms. per diem for travel within city and reimbursement of food bills not exceeding ₹ 300 per day.
₹ 5400 to 6500	Reimbursement for Hotel accommodation of upto ₹ 1500 per day, reimbursement of taxi charges of upto ₹150 per diem for travel within city and reimbursement of food bills not exceeding ₹ 200 per day.
₹ 4200 to 4800	Reimbursement for Hotel accommodation of upto ₹ 500 per day, reimbursement of travel charges of upto ₹ 100 per diem for travel within city and reimbursement of food bills not exceeding ₹ 150 per day.
Below ₹ 4200	Reimbursement for Hotel accommodation of upto ₹ 300 per day, reimbursement of travel charges of upto 50 per diem for travel within city and reimbursement of food bills not exceeding ₹ 100 per day.

Source: 6th Central Pay Commission report

"X" Cities: Hyderabad, Delhi, Bengaluru, Greater Mumbai, Chennai, Kolkata

"Y" Cities:

Andhra Pradesh: Vijaywada, Warrangal, Visakhapatnam, Guntur

Assam: Guhawati

Bihar: Patna

Chandigarh: Chandigarh

Chhatisgarh: Durg-Bhilai Nagar, Raipur,

Gujarat: Ahmedabad, Rajkot, Jamnagar, Bhavnagar, Vadodara, Surat

Haryana: Faridabad (Only for HRA purpose)

J & K: Srinagar & Jammu

Jharkhand: Jamshedpur, Dhanbad and Ranchi

Karnataka: Belgaum, Hubali-Dharwad, Mangalore, Mysore

Kerala: Kozhikode, Kochi, Thiruvanathapuram

Madhya Pradesh: Gwalior, Bhopal, Jabalpur, Indore

Maharashtra: Amravati, Aurangabad, Nasik, Pune, Nagpur, Bhiwandi, Sholapur, Kolhapur

Orissa: Cuttack, Bhubaneswar

Punjab: Amritsar, Jalandar, Ludhiana

Ponmdicherry: Pondicherry

Tamil Nadu: Salem, Tirruppur, Coimbatore, Tirucherapalli, Madurai

Rajasthan: Bikaner, Jodhpur, Kota Jaipur

Uttarakhand: Dehradun

Uttar Pradesh: Moradabad, Meerut, Aligarh, Agra, Bareilly, Lucknow, Kanpur, Allahabad, Gorakhpur, Kanpur, Ghaziabad (for HRA purpose only)

Note 2. The Scheduled Class III Staff. It consists of the following:

L and M Island

1. Head Constables

   N and N Islands

2. Head Warden
3. Lane Head Constables

   P and T Directorate

4. Village Postman
5. Postman
6. Wireman
7. Mali Guard
8. Lineman
9. Munshi Markers
10. Sub-Inspector
    Special Police Establishment
11. Head constables of states on deputation
    CRP/BSF/ITDP.
12. Naik
    Revenue Department.
13. Notice Servers
13. Laboratory Attendants.

5. **The actual cost of travelling.** No Government servant is entitled to be provided with means of conveyance by or at the cost of government or to draw as travelling allowance the actual cost or part of the actual cost of travelling (S.R. 53).

9.4 RAILWAY ACCOMMODATION

President, Prime Minister and Ministers are entitled to reserve railway accommodation for their exclusive use.

In addition to this, Secretaries, Joint Secretaries and other officers listed in S.R. 170 can also reserve an ordinary first class compartment when travelling by rail on duty. For this purpose first class compartment is defined as:

(*i*) A two berthed compartment.

(*ii*) An air-condition coupe where available.

(*iii*) A four berthed compartment if (*i*) or (*ii*) above are not available.

In such cases the entire cost or haulage is borne by the Government. The Government servants can claim actual travelling expenses upto the limit of daily allowances admissible to them for absence from the Headquarter. The officers may at their option take a single berth in air-conditioned coach and claim actual fare of the air conditioned class plus the admissible daily allowance to cover the way expenses.

9.5 HEADQUARTER

The Headquarter of a Government servant is the station of his posting fixed in his letter of appointment by the appointing authority.

When the stay of a Government servant at any station other than his Headquarter exceeds ten days, that station is considered as his temporary Headquarter and he is not entitled to any further daily allowance.

9.6 DEPENDANT

For purpose of travelling allowance dependents of a Government servant falling under the head family, consist of:

1. Wife/husband of the Government servant (only one wife).

2. Legitimate children, step children and children adopted under personal law applicable to Government servant. The adoption should however be legally recognised under the status of a natural child.

3. Widowed daughter.

4. Major children (sons and married daughter) provided they are dependent upon the Government servant.

9.7 T.A. ADMISSIBLE

(See Articles 9.2, 9.3 and 9.4)

9.8 RAILWAY FAIR PERMISSIBLE

(See Articles 9.4)

9.9 KILOMETRAGE ALLOWANCE PERMISSIBLE

(See Table 9.5).

9.10 ALLOWANCE FOR PERSONAL EFFECTS

Allowance for personal effects is applicable only in the case of transfers. No such allowance is admissible when the officer is on tour.

In the case of transfer T.A. allowance for personal effects consists of the cost of transport and conveyance by rail and road in accordance with the scale and subject to restriction laid down in S.R. 116.

Table 9.10 shows a comparative statement between tour and transfer, T.As by various modes of travel.

Table 9.10. Tour and transfer T.A. Comparison

No.	*Item of claim etc.*	*Tour*	*Transfer*
1.	By rail, self	Single far upto entitled class plus D.A. for absence from Head-quarter	Single fare to entitled class plus D.A. for period of journey.
2.	By rail, Family	Not admissible	Single fare for each adult and half fare per child accompanying, D.A. for the period of journey.
3.	Lump-sum Payment	Not admissible	Transfer grant according to pay range.
4.	By road, self	One road mileage.	One road mileage
5.	By road, Family	Not admissible	One road mileage of two members; two road mileages if more than two members accompany.
6.	Personal Effects	Not admissible	Actual cost of transport and conveyance by rail and road in accordance with scale and subject to restriction laid down in S.R. 116.
7.	Daily Allowance	Admissible for the period of absence from headquarters. Different rates exist for ordinary, especially expensive localities stay in hotels	Not admissible.
8.	Travel by ACC.	Officers drawing pay above ₹ 2250	Not admissible
9.	Road mileage rates	Different rates exist for the following 1. Full taxi/own car 2. Scooter/motor cycle 3. Bicycle/Foot 4. Public Buses Grade III and IV not eligible for full taxi/own car. However, when travelled, actual charges limited to the amount at 20 *p.* per km will be admissible.	

Note. In the case of T.A. claim (tour) the controlling officer should check the purpose of the journey besides the actual checks. In the case of transfer TA's he should satisfy that the claim for personal effects is reasonable and certify accordingly besides other checks.

9.11 PREPARATION OF T.A. BILLS

In the Works departments and other establishments where tour transfer TA's are a normal feature, standard forms are available.

The amounts of TA admissible/claimable by Government Servants in respect of some of the cases are given below as illustrations. Relevant entries can be made in the form applicable to the department.

Example 1. *Work out the detail of TA claim due to an officer stationed at New Delhi drawing a pay of ₹ 1900.00 in the scale 1800-100-2000-125-2250 for the month of January 1978 from the following data.*

Station H.Q.	*Departure*		*Stn.*	*Arrival*		*Remark*
	Date	*Hours*		*Date*	*Hours*	
A	16—1	22 Attends	B Office	17—1 5 km	0700	480 km by rail
B	18—1	1500 Office	C to	18—1 Rly. Stn. 19 to 21	1800 4 km halt at C	270 km by rail
C	22—1	0800	D	22—1 23 Halt	1600 at D	150 km by rail
D	24—1	2000	A H.Q.	24—1	2200	7 km by road

Note. Stations B, C, D are ordinary localities. Railway fares are given below. Road journeys were performed in full taxi.

Distance	*First Class Fare* ₹	*Second Class Fare* ₹
480 km	56.00	17.00
270 km	34.00	10.00
150 km	21.00	6.00

Ans. (Only example quoted, refer actual fare as per ticket.)
Grade I
Class by rail I
Rate of DA ₹ 18.50

		₹ P.
16—1	*A* to *B* rail fare I class	56.00
17—1	Road mileage at *B* 4 km × 60 p	2.40
18—1	*B* to *C* rail fare I class	34.00
	Road mileage at *B* and *C* (4 + 4) = 8 km × 60	4.80
22—1	*C* to *D* rail fare I class	21.00
	Road mileage at *C* 4 km × 60 p	2.40
24—1	Road mileage *D* to *A* 7 km × 60 p	4.20

Daily Allowance

Period of absence from Headquarter	
20-00 hr. on 16-1 to 1600 hrs on 22-1,	0.3 DA
16-1 30% of DA = 17-1 to 22-1 Full	6DA
Total 6.3 D.A's × 18.50	₹ 116.55
Total	241.35

On 22-1 the officer reaches a station *D* which is within 8 km from the Headquarter 'A' and no DA is admissible for his stay at *D*.

Example 11.2. *Calculate T.A. admissible to an officer drawing a pay of ₹ 1500 during August 1977 from the details given in table*

Ans.

Grade I

Rail Class	First
Rate of DA	
	Ordinary ₹ 16.25
	Calcutta ₹ 26.00

(Ex. quoted Refer actual fare)

The officer has used staff car for all his road journeys and duty pass for journey by rail. He is therefore not entitled to any railway fare or road mileage.

He is entitled to claim the following daily allowance.

Total duration of absence from 3-8 to 10-8	8 days.
Less C.L. on 6th	1 days.
Balance	7 days.

Deduct No. of DA's admissible at special rate (Calcutta rate) *i.e.*, from 0.900 4/8 to 1830, 9/8 less CL — 5 days

Remaining number of DA's admissible at ordinary rate — 2 days

5 DA's at ₹ 26.00	₹ 130.00
2 DA's at ₹ 16.25	₹ 32.50
	Total ₹ 162.50

(Refer D.A. rules example quoted)

Departure			*Arrival*			*Remarks*
Station	*Date*	*Hour*	*Station*	*Date*	*Hour*	
Delhi Residence	3/8	0630	Delhi	3/8	0715	Distance from Station to resistance 15 km.
Delhi Rly. Station	3/8	0800	Howarh	4/8	0815	From Station to Office 8 km.
I class Duty Pass						
Howarh Rly. Station	4/8	0830	Inspection Bangalow	4/8	0900	By Staff Car distance 5 km.
Halt at Calcutta 4th to 8th Availed casual leave on 6th						
Calcutta 1.B.	9/8	0630	Howrah Rly. Station	9/8	1900	By Staff Car. distance 5 km.
Howrah Rly. Station	9/8	1940	Delhi Rly. Station	10/8	1950	By I Class. Availed Duty Pass
Delhi Rly. Station	10/8	2000	Residence	10/8	2100	Used Staff Car

Note. Distance from Delhi Railway Station to Howrah Railway Station = 1337 km.

I Class Fare ₹ 162.00

10

SERVICE RULES

10.1 SCALE OF PAY

Before the implementation of the Third Pay Commission w.e.f., 1 April, 1973, there used to be number of scales. These scales have now been considerably rationalised and the various categories may be summarised as below:

Table 10.1 Scale of Pay

Scale in ₹	*Category*	*Grade Pay in ₹*
4860 – 20200	PB1	1800 to 2800
8700 – 34800	PB2	4200 to 5400
15600 – 39100	PB3	5400 to 8400
39000 – 67000	PB4	9000 to 13000
80000 (fixed)	Apex	Nil
90000 (fixed)	"	Nil

Grade pay varies according to basic in the same scale. D.A. is given as per Index. Other allowances given are

1. Dearness allowance
2. City Compensatory allowance
3. Transport allowance
4. House Rent allowance and
5. Other Compensatory allowance and services, leaves etc., as given here onward.

10.2 LEAVE RULES

Each organisation allows certain amount of leave to its establishment. The various circumstances under which leave is granted are

(*i*) Recreation (*ii*) Private affairs

(*iii*) Medical grounds.

Leave is, however, not a right. It is a concession granted at the discretion of the government subject to the exigencies of the service. The sanctioning authority has to take the following into consideration before leave is granted:

(*i*) Duty strength is adequate to carryout the work.

(*ii*) Leave is not granted beyond the date of relevance.

(*iii*) Maximum continuance absence from duty does not exceed 5 years in the case of permanent employee (C.S.R. 30).

Some of the important factors in connection with grant of leave are given in Table 10.1.

Table 10.2. Important factors regarding grant of leave

S.No.	*Item*	*Entitlement / Particulars*
1.	Commencement and end	(*i*) Within 35 days of sanction in case of ordered leave. *(C.S.R. 840)* (*ii*) Leave begins on the day on which transfer of charge is effected.
2.	Medical Leave	(*i*) In the case of Government servant whose leave on medical certificate terminates on a Saturday or a day followed by a holiday, and he returns to duty with a certificate of fitness on a Monday or working day immediately following a holiday, his leave terminates on the day preceding that on which he is actually certified as medically fit to resume duty. (*ii*) Medical certificates of fitness is necessary when an officer returns from leave on medical grounds. *(C.S.R. 225)*

Leave admissible to government servants of various categories is given in Table 10.2.

Table 10.3. Kind of Leave Admissible to Government Servant

S.No.	Whether Permanent or Temporary Employees	Kind of Leave	Class of Service	Admissibility	Max. Accumulation Allowed	Leave Salary	Remarks
(1)	(2)	(3)	(4)	(5)	(6)	(7)	(8)
1.	Permanent	Earned	I, II, III and IV	1/1th of the period spent on duty	180 days limited to 120 days at a time.	Greater of the two (*a*) Substantive pay on the day before leave commences. Or (*b*) For first 60 days E.L. the average monthly pay earned during the 12 complete months preceding the month in which leave commences and thereafter average monthly pay earned during 36 complete months preceding the month in which leave commences.	
2.	Temporary	Earned	I, II, III and IV	1/22 of duty during the first year and 1/11 of duty thereafter.	120 days	Same as for 1 (*b*) above	
3.	Permanent and temporary	Half pay	I, II, III and IV	20 days for each complete year of service.	No restriction	Half of 1 (*a*) 1 (*b*) above	

(Continued)

4.	Permanent and temporary	Commuted	I, II, III and IV	Half pay leave can be allowed with half the amount of full pay leave but on M.C.	240 days in the entire service.	Some as for 3.	
5.	Permanent	Not due	I, II, III and IV	Granted in advance of earning	360 days in the entire service 90 days at a time, 180 days in all not on medical certificate	Same as for half pay leave	
6.	Permanent	Extra-ordinary	I, II, III and IV	No limit to frequency	Total continuous absence not to exceed 5 years	Without pay	
7.	Temporary	Extra-ordinary	I, II, III and IV	No limit to frequency	3 months on one occasion	Without pay	
8.	Temporary	Special Tuberculosis	I, II, III and IV	As recommended by medical officer	18 months including 3 months extra-ordinary leave	Without pay	
9.	Permanent	Quarantine	I, II, III and IV	21 days in normal cases but upto 30 days in special cases on the recommendation of medical officer.	Any number of times in the service in consequence of an infectious disease in the family.	Full Pay	No substitute is appointed and officer is treated on duty

10.3 SALARY BILLS

There are different methods of preparation of pay bills of various establishment and payment of wages. Every organisation lays down procedures for preparation of such bills.

The preparation of pay bills may broadly be classified as under:

(*a*) Officer's (Gazetted Staff)

(*b*) Subordinates (Non-Gazetted) Permanent and Temporary

(*c*) Casual

(*a*) **Officers.** Officers are themselves responsible for preparation of their pay bills. These pay bills are stamped and prereceipted. They should by presented to the concerned treasury by the 20th of the month for which pay is claimed. The treasury officer audits the bill and issues cheques (Not payable till Ist of the next month) according to instruction enclosed in the bills.

Note. The centre has decentralised the working of the AGCR as a result of which Accounts officer have been attached to the various ministries. The concerned officers now prepare consolidated bills separately for the Gazetted and non-Gazetted staff.

(*b*) **Subordinate Staff (Permanent and Temporary).** One bill in duplicate is prepared for the entire staff category-wise separately for the permanent and temporary staff. The bills are submitted to the treasury by 20th of the month for which the claim pertains.

The following points should be considered:

(*i*) Arrears of pay should not be claimed with the mothly pay bill.

(*ii*) Nominal periodical increments are claimed in the monthly bills duly supported by increment certificate (in case of subordinate).

(*iii*) In case of transfer the LPC (last pay certificate) from the previous organisation should be attached with the first pay bill.

(*iv*) Regular monthly deduction should be made in respect of deductions such as House rent, GPF, Insurance, I. T. etc.

(*v*) Persons who are absent on long leave should not be included in the normal pay bill.

(*vi*) In case of death pay and allowance are claimed upto the day of death in irrespective of the time of death.

(*vii*) On appointment to a permanent post medical certificate of fitness should accompy the first pay bill.

(*c*) **Casual Personnel.** Casual labour on daily rates of pay are paid on muster roll. In the military Engineering Service Casual personnel are employed for a period not exceeding 90 days at a time and their pay bills are prepared separately as for permanent and temporary establishment.

10.4. CIVIL SERVICE RULES

Civil Service form the network of the administration of the country. It is therefore necessary that the general principles and policies of employment of personnel in the various departments/organisation of the Central and State Governments are well defined. For the guidance of the various controlling offices of the Government and for the information of the employees the book entitle '*Civil Service Regulations*' has been published by the government. The regulations are generally applicable to all the government employees except such personnel as are under the Army Act. The Central Service Regulations are however by and large applicable to civilian in Defence Services as well. They however continue to be under the Army Act and corresponding Acts of the Air Force or Navy by virtue of which they are subjected to additional restraints. The following subjects are dealt with in the CSR.

(*a*) Age limit of appointment

(*b*) Scales of pay

(*c*) Leave—civilians

(*d*) Record of service

(*e*) Beginning of qualifying service

(*f*) `Pensions and gratuities

(*g*) Joining time

(*h*) Posting and transfer

(*b*) and (*c*) have been dealt with in Sections 10.1 and 10.2 respectively, where (*f*) is dealt within the following Article 10.5.

Some of the important rules are given below:

1. **Duty Allowance.** It is the special allowance granted to an employee in addition to the normal pay and salary applicable to the individual in consideration of arduous nature of duties or increased work or responsibility.

2. **Pay and Salary.**

(***a***) 'Pay' is defined as the monthly substantive pay and includes "*overseas allowance*" as well where applicable.

(*b*) 'Salary' is defined as the sum of pay and acting allowance, or charge allowance. It does not include local allowance, deputation allowance, house rent, cartage or travelling daily allowance.

(*c*) For purpose of calculating pensions and leave allowance, duty allowance and deputation allowance are included in the term emoluments.

3. **Date of reckoning allowance.** The salary of an employee begins when he takes over charge of the appointment. If the charge is transferred afternoon, the transfer does not affect allowances until the next day.

4. **Charge of office.** The charge of an office must be made over at its Headquarters in the presence of both relieving and relieved officer.

5. **Promotion during leave.** An employee on leave has no claim to substantive promotion during leave other than privilage or earned leave when not combined with any other kind of leave.

6. **Deputation.** An employee is said to be on deputation when he is detatched on special temporary duty for the performance of which there is no permanently or temporarily sanction appointment. An allowance not exceeding 20 per cent of salary already drawn or ₹ 10 per day whichever is less is granted to an officer deputed on special duty.

7. **Officiating Service.** An officiating service in any stage of time scale, whether continuous or not, counts towards increment in the stage.

8. Counting of time spent or leave and under suspension towards increment.

(*a*) Time spent on leave with allowance counts towards increment.

(*b*) Time passed under suspension does not count towards increment as suspension is penalty for misconduct.

9. **Charge allowance.** Allowance granted to an officer appointed to be incharge of the current duties of an office in addition to his own duties is termed as charge allowance. This entails a substantial increase of responsibility.

10. **Dismissal.**

(*a*) Date of cessation of salary.

An officer who is dismissed ceases to draw his salary from the date of his dismissal. No allowance is granted for any period occupied in the prosecution of appeals against the order of dismissal.

11. **Salary on honourable acquital.** If an officer is honourably acquited of a charge he may be granted full salary which he was in receipt of before his suspension, and the period of his absence from duty may be treated as a period spent on duty.

12. **Leave while under suspension.** Leave of absence for a definite period is not admissible to an officer suspended from duty.

10.5 PENSION AND GRATUITIES

An employee is allowed pension/gratuity for the qualifying service on retrenchment/discharge.

Pension is defined as a payment made to an individual on retrenchment/discharge in consideration of his past service. Pension is granted under the following conditions:

(*a*) Implied future good conduct.

(*b*) Service must be Government. (*C.S.R. 351 and 361*)

(*c*) Employment should be substantive.

(*d*) The service should be paid by Government.

(*CSR 351 and 361*)

The government reserve the right of withholding or withdrawing a pension or any part of it if the pensioner is convicted of serious crime or is found guilty of grave misconduct. (*CSR 351*)

The resignation of a public servant entails forfeiture of the past service. (*CSR 418*)

Service rendered before attaining the age of twenty years is not a qualifying service except for compensation gratuity. The average emoluments means the average of pay and allowances drawn by an employee during the last ten months of his service.

The following allowances are included under the term emoluments:

(*i*) Pay

(*ii*) Personal pay

(*iii*) Duty allowance

(*iv*) Deputation allowance

(*v*) Dearness pay.

The following five kinds of pension are admissible:

(*a*) Retiring Pension,

(*b*) Superannuation Pension,

(*c*) Compensation Pension,

(*d*) Invalid Pension,

(*e*) Extraordinary Pension.

The formula for calculating pension is as under:

$$\text{Pension} = \frac{\text{Length of qualifying service in complete years} \times \text{Average emolument}}{80}$$

Subject to maximum length fixed from time to time.

Note. 1. Fraction of a year is not taken into account for the purpose of calculating pensions.

2. Pensions are calculated to the nearest anna.

Family Pension. A family pension may be granted to the family of an employee who dies while still in service or after retirement after completion of not less than 20 years of qualifying service for a period of ten years provided that the period of payment of family pension will in no case extend beyond a period of 5 years from the date on which the deceased officer retired or on which he would have retired on a superannuation pension in the normal course, according as the death takes place after retirement or while the officer is in service.

The amount of family pension will be:

(*a*) In the event of death while in service, one half of the superannuation pension which would be admissible to the person had he retired on the date following the date of his death and

(*b*) In the event of death after retirement, half the pension sanctioned for him at the time of retirement subject to a maximum of ₹ 150 p.m. and a minimum of ₹ 30 p.m.

Table 10.3 gives at a glance the pension rules (Liberalised Pension Rule) in respect of pension and gratuity.

Table 10.4 Pension and Gratuity at a glance

No.	*Type of benefit*	*Amount*
1.	Retiring Max pension.	30/70.
2.	Invalid and superannuation.	Based on actual length of service.
3.	Gratuity for qualifying service.	One month emoluments for each completed year of service upto 4 years and

(Continued)

		thereafter at 3/4 of monthly emoluments for each completed upto 9 years. Total gratuity for 9 years service 7 3/4 months emoluments.
4.	Gratuity on death of an officer in service.	Death-cum retirement gratuity.
5.	Family Pension.	Admissible under certain conditions.
6.	Death-cum-retirement gratuity is admissible to pension or gratuity.	
7.	Commutation limit.	1/3 of pension.

10.6 ROUTINE INSPECTION OF OFFICE

In any project/works organisation, a properly run/managed/ establishment is an essential requirement. To ensure this the Senior Executive/Administrative officers arrange routine inspection of the offices once a year. The points which are looked into by the inspecting officer are known beforehand to the Executive whose office is to be inspected as well as to the inspecting officer. Proper upkeep of the records and documents is thereby ensured. The main objects of such an inspection are:

(*a*) To see that the officers work efficiently in accordance with the rules and instructions.

(*b*) To streamline the offices where work is not being carried out in a satisfactory manner.

(*c*) To examine the difficulties faced by the executive in complying with orders and instructions.

Some of the important points which should be borne in mind by the inspecting officer as well as by the executive whose establishment is being inspected are given below:

1. General

(*a*) Do satisfactory arrangements for the security of documents exist?

(*b*) Are discrepencies brought to the notice of immediate superior officer?

(*c*) Have the observations made during the previous annual inspection been progressed and

(*d*) Is system of filing, recording, submission of reports/return efficient?

(*e*) Do separate files exist for policy and other important rulings?

(*f*) Are books of regulations and periodicals available and upto date?

(*g*) Do adequate fire precautions exist and are surprise practices carried out?

(*h*) Do the executive staff inspect works on progress regularly?

2. Establisment Branch

(*a*) Is office accommodation adequate and suitable?

(*b*) Is the authorised establishment held and surplus/ deficiencies regularised.

(*c*) Is central registry maintained and works efficiently?

(*d*) Are class IV employees supplied liveries as per authorisation?

(*e*) Are service records properly maintained?

(*f*) Are pay accounts of personnel settled in time?

(g) Are securities furnished by subordinates entrusted with custody of cash or store?

(*h*) Do suitable welfare arrangements exist?

(*i*) Are disciplinary cases progressed properly?

(*j*) Are old records destroyed regularly?

3. Works Branch

(*a*) Are the following registers maintained:

(*i*) Register of works showing progress of each work?

(*ii*) Register of Administrative approval of work?

(*iii*) Road Register.

(*iv*) Road Metal Register.

(*v*) PSMBS.

(*vi*) Register of Buildings.

(*vii*) Register of Contractors.

(*viii*) Bill Register.

(*ix*) Register of Security Deposits.

(*x*) Demolition Register.

(*b*) Have any works been started without approval?

(*c*) Are completion reports (Part A and B) sent on due dates?

(*d*) Is list of sanctioned special repairs maintained?

(*e*) Is there adequate policy and programme for renewals and periodic repair?

(*f*) Is road renewal programme maintained?

(*g*) Are road graphs properly maintained?

(*h*) Are works diaries maintained for each work?

(*i*) Are CPM/Bar charts prepared and maintained?

(*j*) Are stores properly preserved?

(*k*) Is action taken for clearence of unwanted structures?

(*l*) Is photographic record of major works maintained.

4. Stores Branch

(*a*) Are arrangements for storage of stores satisfactory?

(*b*) Are articles preserved satisfactorily?

(*c*) Is the authorised numerical account of stores maintained?

(*d*) Are up-to-date tally cards maintained for all articles?

(*e*) Are proper receipts obtained from contractors and others for stores issued?

(*f*) Are surplus stores properly disposed off according to rules?

(*g*) Is security from theft ensured?

(*h*) Is the stocking of stores according to approved manner?

5. Cash Section

(*a*) Are the following register maintained up-to-date?

(*i*) Register of securities.

(*ii*) Register of unpaid wages.

(*iii*) Register of appropriation.

(*b*) Are schedule of demands submitted in time?

(*c*) Are construction accounts properly maintained?

(*d*) Are monthly expenditure returns submitted in time?

(*e*) Are expenditure charts kept up-to-date?

(*f*) Is cash book maintained properly and checked regularly by Divisional Unit Accountant.

(*g*) Are audit objections settled expeditiously?

(*h*) Are muster rolls compiled correctly and supported with details of stores issued and work done.

6. Drawing Branch

(*a*) Are the following register/ documents maintained up-to-date?

(*i*) Record Drawings.

(*ii*) Type Plans.

(*iii*) Register of Plans.

(*iv*) Register of permanent and temporary buildings.

(*v*) Register of books and periodicals.

(*vi*) Road Graphs.

(*vii*) Is the system of keeping drawings satisfactory?

7. **Accounts Branch**

(*a*) Are the books and accounts of Divisional/Unit Accountant kept satisfactorily and the returns rendered on due dates?

(*b*) Has the Accounts branch any difficulty on having access to executive accounts for purpose of reconciliation?

(*c*) Is the register of sanction complete and up-to-date?

(*d*) Has the register of measurement books properly maintained?

(*e*) Are the completed Measurement Books returned for record to the Accounts Branch?

10.7 FINANCE AND BUDGET

Budget estimates are prepared annually for expenses of different departments of the government to ensure proper planning for expenditure. It must be borne in mind by all executives that any waste/abuse of public funds results in depriving the country of the money meant for the welfare and development of the nation.

The following financial cannons should be observed by all offices exercising financial powers:

(*a*) Government money should be spent with the same vigilence as one would do in respect of his own money.

(*b*) No officer can sanction expenditure which would benefit him directly or indirectly.

(*c*) Travelling and other allowances granted to meet expenditure of particular type should not be on the whole be a source of profit.

The following guidelines should be observed in respect of any work/project:

(*a*) The following three requirements should be satisfied before a work is taken in hand.

(*i*) Administrative approval from C.C.A. (Competent Administrative Authority).

(*ii*) Allotment of funds for C.F.A. (Competent Financial Authority).

(*iii*) Technical sanction from C.E.A. (Competent Engineer Authority).

(*b*) The budget allotment for the year should not exceed in any financial year under any sub or minor head, except in so far as one may within ones power of transfer of funds, be able to meet excess expenditure on one items by equivalent saving in another.

Control over the execution of any work/project in the department is exercised in the following way:

(*a*) **Administrative Control.** This is exercised by the competent administrative authority.

(*b*) **Financial Control.** Once the allotment for the work for a year is received, expenditure is controlled in the following manner:

(*i*) Economical expenditure of funds.

(*ii*) Evenly spreading of expenditures.

(*iii*) Timely surrender/demand to adjust expected excess/ savings.

(*c*) **Technical Control.** This is exercised by according technical sanction by competent engineer authority.

Proposals for surrender in excess demand are submitted in the changes in grants statement. The first change in grant is initiated in the month of July, second in the October and the third and final in July.

The utilisation of savings in the budget provision under one sub/minor head to meet excess expenditure under another with the approval of the competent financial authority is called *reappropriation of funds*.

The Chief Engineer and Superintending Engineer/C.W.E. are authorised full power of reappropriation, within the funds placed under their disposal between the minor heads under sub-head ordinary repair.

Credits arising from the disposal of surplus stores against Major Work/Minor Work/special repairs are adjusted by minor allotment.

The expenditure for the year against allotment is reviewed every month by bringing the expenditure chart upto date. A typical expenditure chart is shown in Fig. 10.1.

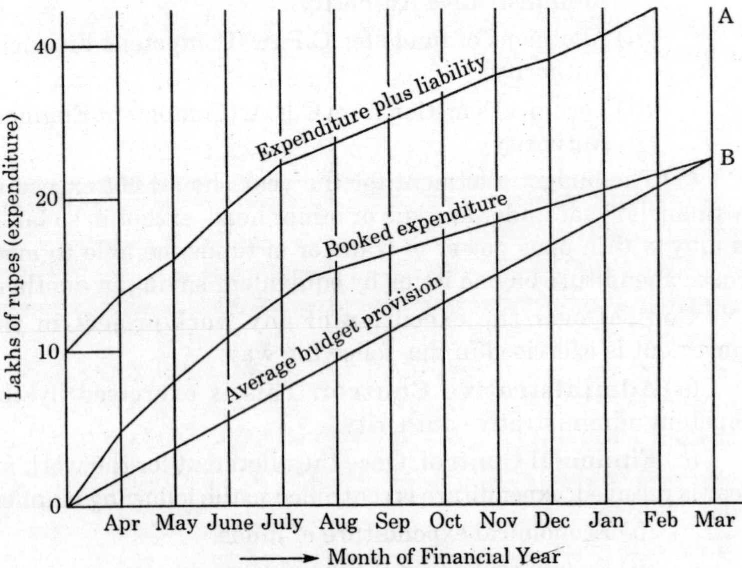

Fig. 10.1 Typical expenditure chart.

Note. A = Total liability incurred during the last quarter of the previous final year (not paid but committed payment).

B = Liabilities incurred in the last quarter of the current final year.

The following points should be taken care of in connection with financial column (see Fig.10.1).

1. Keep expenditure well above the average budget provision and equal to approxing 1/3rd of the budget provision in the first quarter.

2. The Budget provision should equal expenditure plus liability by the end of December.

3. Arrange uniform expenditure all round the year.

4. Expenditure should not be slack during the first quarter of the year.

5. Don't rush expenditure at the close of the year.

6. Don't surrender funds at the close of the year.

10.8 CASH ASSIGNMENT

All persons holding public funds should be conversant with the mode of obtaining these funds and should ensure proper utilization. The person thus holding public money is personally responsible for any losses of public money through fraud or neglect on ones part.

The following precautions should therefore be taken when conducting transctions with treasure/bank:

(*a*) Provision of suitable escort in transit.

(*b*) Withdrawal exceeding ₹ 1000 should be made by an officer specially deputed for the purpose.

To meet the requirement of funds if a disbursing officer cash assignment is made available by the Accountant General concerned or by the Controller of Defence Accounts in the treasury or bank in favour of the officer. The Administrative head of the department (Chief Engineer) makes such a request against budget allotment of the department to the Accountant General/CDA.

The Accountant General/CDA supplies separate cheque books for each treasury/bank. These are kept under lock and key in the personal custody of the drawing officer. When the officer is transferred, a receipt is obtained from the relieving officer in respect of numbers of blank cheques handed over and the specimen signatures of the Relieving Officer are forwarded to the Treasury Officer, Bank and Accountant General/CDA as the case may be.

Cheques issued on 31st March but not cashed during that financial year are still accounted for in that year in the year of issue. Any unspent amount lapses after the last day of the financial year.

All assignment holder maintain a passbook which is sent monthly to the treasury officer bank to be completed from the register of paid cheques. On return of the passbook reconciliation statement is prepared.

Table 10.5. First and Final Bill (CPWD Form 2)

Division----- Sub-Division------

(To be used when a single payment is made for a job or contract, *i.e.*, only on its completion)

Name of the work----- Cash Book Voucher No----- Date-----

Name of contractor or suppliers	*Items of work*	*Reference to recorded measurement and date*	*Date of*		*Quantity*	*Unit*	*Rate*	*Amount*	*Total Amount payable*		*Payees dated signature*	*Dated signature of witness*	*Dated certificate of Disbursement*	
			Orders to Commence work	*Completion of work*					*In figures*	*In words*			*Mode of payment*	*Paid by me*
(1)	(2)	(3)	(4)	(5)	(6)	(7)	(8)	(9)	(10)	(11)	(12)	(13)	(14)	(15)

M.B.No------- Pay------ Date---- Signature / Rank } Officer preparing the bill

Pay ₹------ (Rupees----) Signature / Rank } Officer authorising payment

For use in AG's Office

Reviewed

(Accounts Clerk) Divisional Accountant Audited Supdt. Gazetted Officer

Table 10.6 Running Account Bill (CPWD Form 26)

(Final payments must invariably be made in form printed on yellow paper which should not be used for intermediated payment).

Division------ **Sub-Division-----**

Cash Book Voucher No----- **Date------**

Name of contractor-------

Name of work------

Serial No. of this bill-------

No. and date of previous bill for this work------

Reference to Agreement No------

Date of written order to commence work

Date of actual completion of work-----

I— ACCOUNTS OF WORK EXECUTED

Item of work	*Unit*	*Rate*	*Quantity executed up-to-date as per M.B.----*	*Payment on the basis of actual measurement*		*Remarks*
				Up to date	*Since previous bill*	
(1)	(2)	(3)	(4)	(5)	(6)	(7)

II— CERTIFICATES AND SIGNATURES

1. The measurements on which entries in columns 1 to 6 of Account of I are based, were made by-----on-----, and are recorded at page-----of Measurement Book No-----

2. Certificate regarding actual execution of work.

Dated signature of officer preparing the bill--------

Dated signature of officer authorising payment-----

Dated signature of contractor------

III— MEMORANDUM OF PAYMENTS

1. **Total value of the work actually measured.**
2. **Total upto date advance payments for works not yet measured.**
3. **Total upto date secured advances.**

(Table 10.6 contd.)

4. Total of items (1 + 2 + 3).
5. Deduct: Amount withheld
   (*a*) From previous bill as per Running Account Bill.
   (*b*) From this bill.
6. Balance (Item 4-5).
7. Total amount of payment already made.
8. Payments now to be made, as detailed below:
   (*a*) By recovery of amounts creditable to this work.
   Total 5 (*b*) + 8 (*a*)
   (*b*) By recovery of amounts creditable to work.
   (*c*) By cheque.
   Total of 8 (*b*) + (*c*).

Pay ₹------ (by cheque)

Dated initials of disbursing officer------

Received ₹-----(Rupees------) as above memorandum on account of this work.

Stamp

Signature of contractor-----------------

Paid by me *vide* Cheque No------ Date-----

Dated initials of person actually making the payment-----

IV—REMARKS

For use in Divisional Officer

Checked

Accounts Clerk Divisional Accountant

For Use in A G's Office

Audited Reviewed

Auditor Superintendent Gazetted Officer

Other Compensatory allowances

- The Commission has suggested changes in the rates of Special Compensatory (Hill Area/Remote Locality), Tribal Area Allowance, Project Allowance and Bad Climate Allowance were revised as follows:
- Project Allowance: ₹ 1500 p.m. For posts in the grade pay of ₹ 5400 and above; ₹ 1000 p.m. for posts in the grade pay of less than ₹ 5400.

Table 10.7. Account of Security (CPWD Form 26-A)

Division-----

Sub-Division-----

Name of contractor------

Name of work-----

Serial No. of the Bill to which the account pertains---- Cash Voucher No----- Date------

Reference to Agreement-----

Account of secured advances allowed on the security of materials brought to site.

Quantity outstanding from previous bill	*Deduct— Quantity utilised in work measured since previous bill*	*Quantity outstanding including brought to site since previous bill*	*Full rate as assessed by the Divisional Office*	*Description of materials*	*Unit*	*Reduced rate at which advance is made*	*Up-to-date amount of advance*	*Reference to Divisional Officer's written orders authorising the Adv.*	*Reasons for non-clearance of advance when outstanding for more than 3 months*
(1)	(2)	(3)	(4)	(5)	(6)	(7)	(8)	(9)	(10)

Total amount outstanding as per the accounts-----(C)

Deduct: Amount outstanding as per entry----(C)----of the Annexure to the previous bill.

Net amount since previous bill (in words) Rupees----

Dated signatures of officer preparing the bill-------

Dated signatures of officer authorising payment-----

Table 10.8 (CPWD Form 27-A)

RUNNING ACCOUNT

Cash Book Vr. No------ Name of Contractor-------
Name of work------ Serial No. of Bill-------
No. and date of previous bill------ Reference to Agreement-----
Date of written order to commence work------

I—ACCOUNT OF WORK

1. Approximate value of work upto date
2. Value of measured work
3. Deduct amount to a work held
4. Balance upto date (1 + 2 –3)
5. Deduct intermediate payment
6. Intermediate payment now to be made (4-5)
7. Amount of secured advance
8. Total payment now to be made
   (*a*) By recovery of amount creditable to this work
   (*b*) By recovery of amounts creditable to other work
   (*c*) By cheque

II ACCOUNT OF SECURED ADVANCE ALLOWED OR SCRUTINY OF MATERIALS BROUGHT TO SITE

Quantity outstanding from previous bill	*Deduct utilised in work*	*Quantity outstanding*	*Full rate as assessed by the Divisional Officer*	*Description of materials*	*Unit*	*Reduced rate at which advance is made*	*Up-to-date amount of advance*	*Reference to Divisional Officer's written order*	*Reasons for non-clearance of advance when out-standing for more than three months*
(1)	(2)	(3)	(4)	(5)	(6)	(7)	(8)	(9)	(10)

Total outstanding as per the accounts
Amount outstanding as per previous bill
Net amount since previuos bill (in words) Rupees-----

Table 10.8 (CPWD Form 27-A) (*contd*)

III—CERTIFICATE AND SIGNATURE

I have certified myself that

1. Value of work done up-to-date is not less than-----
2. Detailed measurement was made by me ₹-----on at page No-----M.B.
3. Quantity of material have actually been brought at site-----signature of contractor

   Signature of officer preparing the bill pay (₹------)

Dated signature of the officer authorising the payment------

IV ACQUITTANCE

Received (₹------) as an intermediate payment in connection with the contract to above.

Stamp

Witness

Full Signature of Contractor-------

Paid by me $\frac{\text{Cash}}{\text{Cheque}}$

Dated initials of the person actually making the payment-------

V—REMARKS

For use in Divisional Office

Checked
A/C Clerk

Divisional Accountant

For use in AG's Office

Audited
Auditor

Supdt.

Reviewed
Gazetted Officer

Table 10.9 (CPWD Form 27-B)

FINAL BILI

(To be used for "Final payment" to contractors on lump sum contracts)

Dated------
Name of work-----
No. and date of previous bill for this work
Date of written order to commence work------

Cash Book Vr------No-----
Name of Contractor-----
Serial No. of this Bill-----
Reference to Agreement------
Date of actual completion of work--------

I—ACCOUNT OF WORK EXECUTED

Sub-work	*Rate*	*Unit (lump sum for each)*	*Up-to-date*		*Remark*
			Quantity	*Amount*	

II and III as for Form 27-A, Table 10.8

IV—ACQUITTANCE

Received Rupees------as above in full settlement of all demands on account of the contract.

Stamp

Full Signature

Paid by me $\frac{\text{Cash}}{\text{Cheque}}$

Dated initials of person actually making payment

Rank

V—REMARKS

For use in Divisional Office
For use in AG's Office

Divisional Account

Checked
A/C Clerk
Audited
Auditor

Supdt

Gazetted Officer

- The Commission recommended automatic revision of rates of all the above allowances by 25% whenever the Dearness Allowance payable on the revised pay bands goes up by 50%.
- In Commission's opinion, there was no logical ground to continue Special Compensatory Allowance for Gandhinagar and Special Compensatory (Border Area) Allowance and hence recommended this to Abolish.
- However, Special (Duty) Allowance for postings to North East Regions at the existing rates was recommended to all Central Government employees on their posting on transfer to any North East Region.
- The Special (Duty) Allowance as well as other concessions allowed to the Government employees in North East Region were extended to the Government employees posted in Ladakh.
- Island Special (Duty) allowance: This allowance was also recommended to made available to all Central Government employees on their posting on transfer to any place in these islands without insisting on an all India transfer liability.
- Recommendation was made to pay Hard Area Allowance to the employees posted in the Nicobar group of Islands separately along with Island Special (Duty) Allowance and broadened to the Lakshadweep group of islands.

Project Allowance

Project Allowance

Category	*Project allowance*
For posts in the grade pay of ₹ 5400 and above	₹ 1500 p.m.
For posts in the grade pay of less than ₹ 5400	₹ 1000 p.m.

Bad Climate & Special (Hill Area) Allowance

Special Compensatory (Remote Locality) Allowance

Category	*Part A (₹/PM)*	*Part B (₹/PM)*	*Part C (₹/PM)*	*Part D (₹/PM)*
For posts in the grade pay of ₹ 5400 and above	2600	2100	1500	400

(*Continued*)

For posts in the grade pay of less than ₹ 5400	2000	1600	1200	320

Special compensatory (Hill Area) Allowance/Bad climate Allowance/Tribal Area Allowance

Category	*Bad Climate / Tribal Area Allowance*	*Special Compensatory (Hill Area) Allowance*
For posts in the grade pay of ₹ 5400 and above	₹ 400 p.m.	₹ 600 p.m.
For other posts	₹ 240 p.m.	₹ 480 p.m.

Source: 6th Central Pay Commission report

The Commission recommended that the existing amount of following interest free advances should be doubled:

- Festival Advance
- Advance in the event of natural calamity like flood, drought, cyclone, etc.
- Advance for training in Hindi through Correspondence Course.

The rates of these allowances shall be increased by 25% every time dearness allowance on revised pay bands increases by 50%. All other existing conditions in respect of various interest free advances shall be maintained without any change.

Interest Bearing Advances

- No interest should be charged on advances for purchase of warm clothing and bicycle. Like in the case of other interest free advances, the existing rates of advances for purchase of warm clothing and bicycle should also be doubled.
- The Commission was of the view that in order to spread the benefit in a more equitable manner, it was desirable to provide only for the element of interest subsidy and make available various interest bearing advances to government employees through arrangements with public sector banks.

- The Government will give an interest subsidy equal to 2 percentage points in rate of interest being charged by the bank to the employee.
- The interest subsidy for employees with disabilities will be equal to four percentage points in the rate of interest being charged by the bank.
- Simultaneously, the existing limit of various interest bearing advances should also be doubled for the purpose of getting the subsidy. This limits should automatically be increased by 25% every time the dearness allowance payable on revised pay bands goes up by 50%.
- The eligibility for taking the advances should also be removed because the repaying capacity would, in any case, be considered by the concerned bank at the time of processing the loan application.

Non-Practicing Allowance (NPA)

Accordingly, the Commissions recommends that Doctors should continue to be paid NPA at the existing rate of 25% of the aggregate of the band pay and grade pay subject to the condition that the Basic Pay + NPA does not exceed ₹ 85,000.

Risk Allowance

- Risk Allowance is withdrawn.
- Employees be provided with free medical and life insurance of ₹ 5 lakhs for employees in PB-1 pay band; ₹ 7 lakhs for employees in PB-2 pay band; ₹ 10 lakhs for employees in PB-3 pay band/higher pay bands/scales.
- The amount of the insurance should automatically be increased by 50% every time the DA payable on the revised pay goes up by 50%. The entire expenditure on paying premium for this insurance will be borne by the government.
- The amount insured will be paid in case of any serous injury/ death sustained in the course of employment and will be over and above the other benefits available to all categories of government employees.
- These employees should also be provided with additional health benefits with mandatory health check-ups every quarter and enhanced leave, wherever the same is necessary for proper recuperation.

Uniform related Allowances:

- The Commission recommends the following rates of Uniform Allowance for different categories of such personnel:

CPMFs/CPOs/RPF/IPS

Initial grant ₹ 14000; Renewal grant ₹ 3000; payable after every three years.

Uniform allowance for Coast Guard officers

Initial grant ₹ 16000; Renewal grant ₹ 5000; payable after every three years.

- Existing rates of Kit Maintenance Allowance be doubled for all categories of employees presently in receipt of this allowance. Uniform Allowance for nurses should also be increased to ₹ 500 per month.

  The rates of Uniform Allowance and Kit Maintenance
- Allowance for all the above categories shall be increased by 25% every time the Dearness Allowance on revised pay bands goes up by 50%.

T.A. on Transfer

Deputation (Duty) Allowance

- The rates of Deputation (Duty) Allowance and Central (Deputation on Tenure) Allowance may continue to be paid at the rate of 5%, 10% and 15% of the aggregate of pay in the pay band and grade pay without any pecuniary limit. This will, however, be subject to the limit that the aggregate of pay in the pay band and Deputation (Duty) Allowance/Central (Deputation on Tenure) Allowance does not exceed ₹ 39,200 being the minimum pay in the pay band PB-4.

Miscellaneous Allowances

- The Commission recommended doubling of the extant rates of Cycle Allowance, Washing Allowance, Cash Handling Allowance, Special Allowance, Night Duty Allowance and Split Duty Allowance.
- The rates of these allowances will be increased by 25% every time the Dearness Allowance payable on revised pay scales goes up by 50%.
- Machine Allowance withdrawn.

Over Time Allowance

- Abolition of compensation in the form of Over Time Allowance or any other similar allowance to any of the Central Government employees except those belonging to the categories of operational staff and industrial employees governed by statute.

Advances

Interest Free Advances

Holidays:

- The government offices will remain closed only on the 3 National holidays.
- No other closed holidays be allowed.
- Restricted Holidays available to an employee shall be increased to 8 with the list of Restricted Holidays being suitably enlarged to include all the erstwhile Gazetted Holidays therein:
- Every Head of Department (HoD) should be allowed the option of declaring the office closed for a maximum of two Restricted Holidays in a year based on local considerations.
- The number of Casual Leave, Half Pay Leave and Earned Leave available to Government employees shall remain unchanged.
- The number of casual leave for physically disabled employees will stand increased to 12 days. From 1/9/1981, Teachers, Principals and Head Masters working in schools and from 28/7/1984, Librarians, Laboratory Assistants and Watermen working in schools have not been allowed the facility of half pay leave. This facility needs to be restored for these categories as the present rules place them in difficulties in times of sickness, etc.

These categories should be made eligible for half pay leave on par with other Central Government employees.

11

Administrative Orders Issued by the Govt. of India and State Governments

11.1 FUNDAMENTAL AND SUPPLEMENTARY RULES—SERVICE RULES PARA 5 (*B*) (1)

"If the government servant sub-lets or shares a part of his accommodation with one or more adults, not belonging to his family, whether Government Servant(s) or not, a reduction of 40 per cent of the actual rent charged by him from the subtenant/co-sharer, whichever is higher, shall be made from the rent actually paid by him to the landlord for the purpose of compating the amount of house rent allowance admissible to him. A reduction of 40 per cent shall also be made where a part of the accommodation hired by the Government Servant for which he claims house rent allowance is used for other than bonafide residential purpose.

[Govt. of India Ministry of Finance (Department of Expenditure Office Memorandum No. 11013/4/EII (B)/76, dated 22-9-1977 and C & AG's Endt. No. 843-Audit/2-77 (39), dt. 15-10- 1977].

11.2 CASH PAYMENT IN LIEU OF UNUTILISED EARNED LEAVE ON THE DATE OF RETIREMENT

Government servants may be paid cash equivalent of leave salary in respect of the period of earned leave at their credit at the time of retirement on superannuation.

This decision will be applicable to Central Government Servants retiring on superannuation on or after 30-9-1977.

This concession will be subject to the following conditions:

(*a*) The payment of cash equivalent of leave salary will be limited to a maximum of 180 days earned leave.

(*b*) The cash equivalent of leave salary thus admissible will become payable on retirement and will be paid in one lump sum as a one time settlement.

(*c*) Cash payment under this order will, subject to (*d*) below, be equal to leave salary as admissible for earned leave and dearness allowance admissible on that leave salary at the rates in force on the date of retirement. No city compensatory allowance and/or house rent allowance shall be payable.

(*d*) From the cash amount worked are in accordance with (*c*) above will be deducted the pension and pensionary equivalent of other retirement benefits for the period for which cash equivalent is payable.

(*e*) The authority competent to grant leave shall *suo-motu*, issue order granting cash equivalent of earned leave at credit on the date of retirement.

These orders shall not apply to cases of premature/voluntary retirement.

A Government servant already on leave preparatory to retirement who has been allowed to return to duty shall also be entitled to benefit under this decision on the date of retirement. Consequent on issue of this order, refusal of earned leave preparatory to retirement, will no larger be necessary.

[Govt. of India, Ministry of Finance (DE) Office Memorandum No. P 14028/1/77 E IV (A), dt. 29-10-1977 and C & AG's Endt. No. 946, Audit/2-77 (48), dt. 24-11-1977].

11.3 PAYMENT OF ADDITIONAL DEARNESS ALLOWANCE TO CENTRAL GOVERNMENT EMPLOYEES

It has been decided that the rates of additional DA sanctioned to Central Government employees therein shall be revised as follows with effect from 1st Sept, 1977.

Pay range	*Rate of additional DA*
Upto ₹ 300	17.5% of pay subject of a minimum of ₹ 35 and a maximum of ₹ 50
₹ 300–1600	12.5% of pay minimum ₹ 50, maximum ₹ 100

₹ 1600–1640	Amount by which pay falls short of ₹ 1700.
₹ 1640–2250	₹ 60 subject to marginal adjustment such that pay plus total DA does not exceed ₹ 2400.

[Govt. of India, Ministry of Finance (DE) Office Memorandum No. 13017/3E II (B) 77, dated 19-11-1977 and C & AG's Endt. No. 910, Audit 2-77 (42), dated 26-11-77].

11.4 PENSION RULES

11.4.1 C.C.S. (Pension) Rules, 1972 Amendment of:

The following rules may be called the Civil Central Service (Pension) (Eighth Amendment) Rules 1977. In C.C.S. (Pension) Rules, 1972, in Rule 51, after sub-rule (6), the following explanation shall be inserted.

11.4.2

Only that disability which manifests itself before the retirement or death of the Government Servant while in service shall be taken into account for the purpose of family pension under this sub-rule.

11.4.3

A daughter shall become ineligible for family pension under this sub-rule from the date she gets married.

11.4.4

The family pension payable to such a son or daughter shall be stopped if he or she starts earning his/her livelihood.

The pension authorised under these rules shall not be reduced although proof of the service having been not satisfactory may come to the notice of the appointing authority subsequent to the authorisation of pension.

[Govt. of India, Ministry of Finance (DT), Notified No. F. 11 (6)—EV/76 dated 27-9-1977 and C and AG's Endt. No. 857—Audit/2-77 (40) dated 24-14-1977.]

11.4.5

Revision of the rate of widow pension to motherless children admissible under CCS (EOP) rules consequent to the revisiion of the rates of contributory family pension on the recommendation of the third pay commission.

(*c*) ₹ 12,000 and above	20% of pay subject to a maximum of ₹ 460.00 and minimum of ₹ 270.00.

[Govt. of India, Ministry of Finance (Department of Expenditure) Office Memorandum No. F. 23(37) E V (A)/E dt. 26-10-79 and C & AG's Endt. No. 916 audit/2-77/43, dt. 24-11-1977].

11.5 GRANT OF EXTENSION/RE-EMPLOYMENT TO CENTRAL GOVERNMENT EMPLOYEES BEYOND THE AGE OF SUPERANNUATION ISSUE OF CONSOLIDATED INSTRUCTION REGARDING

Vide Notification No. 7 (7) – EVA/74, dt, 7-2-75 of the Ministry of Finance (Department of Expenditure) age of retirement has been laid down in the Fundamental rule (Amendment) salient features of these rules are:

(*i*) In attaining the age indicated in the above rules, retirement is automatic and in the absence of specific orders to the contrary by the competent authority, a government servant must retire on the due date. It is the responsibility of the administrative authority concerned to ensure that the government servant under their control so retire.

(*ii*) No proposal for extension of service re-employment beyond the age of superannuation should ordinarily be considered.

(*iii*) In exceptional cases 60 years of age should be dead line for non-scientific non-technical posts and 62 years in the case of scientific/technical personnel, over-riding consideration for such cases are:

(*a*) Other officers are not ripe enough to take over the job; or

(*b*) The retiring officer is of outstanding merit

11.6 EXTRACTS TAKEN FROM NOTIFICATION NO. 7(7) EV (A)/74, DATED 7th FEBRUARY, 1975 FROM THE MINISTRY OF FINANCE (DEPARTMENT OF EXPENDITURE)

11.6.1

Except as otherwise provided in this rule, every Government servant shall retire from service on the afternoon of the last day of the month in which he attains the age of fifty-eight years.

11.6.2

A workman who is governed by these rules shall retire from service on the afternoon of the last day of the month in which he attains the age of sixty years.

Note. In this clause a workman means a highly skilled, skilled, semi-skilled or unskilled artisan employed on a monthly rate of pay in an industrial or work-charged establishment.

11.6.3

A Government servant whose date of birth is the first of a month shall retire from service on the afternoon of the last day of the preceding month on attaining the age of fifty-eight or sixty-years, as the case may be.

11.7 PROFORMA FOR SENDING PROPOSALS FOR APPROVAL OF MINISTRY OF HOME AFFAIRS OR FOR INTERNAL USE IN A MINISTRY DEPARTMENT FOR GRANT OF EXTENSION/RE-EMPLOYMENT TO GOVERNMENT SERVANTS BEYOND THE AGE OF SUPERANNUATION

1. Designation of the post.
2. Duration of the post.
3. Scale and terms of the post and prequisites attached if any.
4. Whether financial sanction for the creation of the post/ continuance of the post for the duration shown at (2) has been obtained.
5. Method of recruitment.
6. Name and date of appointment of the outgoing incumbment of the post.
7. Name of the officer proposed for appointment and the service to which he belongs.
8. Full service particular of the officer with date of birth and pay drawn.
9. Names of other officers considered.
10. If promotion post, whether copies of proceedings of a D.P.C. are being enclosed, if not why not?
11. If the proposal involves extension/re-employment please indicate:

(*i*) (*a*) Whether the post is scientific/technical or non-scientific/non-technical.

(*b*) Whether the officer is to be granted extension of service or re-employment.

(*c*) Periods of extension/re-employment granted earlier to the officer, if any.

(*d*) Date from which extention/re-employment is to be granted.

(*e*) Period of extension of service/re-employment:

(*ii*) Justification for the grant of extension re-employment if the post is scientific/technical.

(*iii*) Justification for the grant of extension re-employment if the post is non-technical/non-scientific.

(*iv*) (*a*) The date from which it was known that the vacancy would occur.

(*b*) Action taken to select a successor which chronological details.

(*c*) If selection is being made, reasons why this could not be finalised in good time.

(*d*) If proposal involves extension/re-employment, can some officiating or *ad-hoc* arrangements be made, pending fresh appointment by proper selection, if not, why not?

(*v*) If the case is referable to A.C.C., whether the case has been discussed with cabinet secretary? If so, his reaction to the proposal.

(*vi*) Whether orders of the Minister-in-charge have been obtained.

13. Whether the prescribed integrity certified from the appropriate authority, is enclosed.

11.8 SCHEME OF VOLUNTARY RETIREMENT FOR CENTRAL GOVERNMENT EMPLOYEES

[Govt. of India, Ministry of Home Affairs (Department of Personnel and Administrative Reform), Office Memorandum No. 25013/7-77-Estt (A) dt. 26 August 77, and C & AG's. No. 701-A/2-77 (33), dt. 8 September 1977 read with the Govt. of India M.H.A. (Dept. of P & AR), Office Memorandum of even number dated 23rd November, 1977 and C & AG's Endt. No. 1016, Audit/2-77/48, dt. 2 Dec., 1977].

Scheme of Voluntary Retirement of Central Government Employees

The following instructions will regulate the voluntary retirement of Central Government servants in pursuance of the Government's decisions.

(*i*) Government servants also have put in not less than 20 years qualifying service may, be giving notice of three months in writing to the appointing authority, retire from service voluntarily. The Government does not have the reciprocal right to retire Government servants or its own, under the scheme.

(*ii*) The benefits of '*retiring pension*' will be admissible to Govt. servants retiring under this scheme.

(*iii*) A notice of voluntary retirement may be withdrawn subsequently only with the approval of the appointing authority provided the request for such a withdrawal is made before the expiry of the notice.

(*iv*) While granting proportional pension to a Govt. servant retiring voluntarily under this scheme, weightage upto five years would be given as an addition to the qualifying service actually rendered by him. The grant of weightage of upto five years will, however, be subjected to the following conditions:

(*a*) The total qualifying service after allowing the weightage should not be in any even exceed 30 years qualifying service; and

(*b*) The total qualifying service after giving the weightage should not exceed the qualifying service which he would have had, if he had retired voluntarily at the lower age/minimum service limits applicable to him to voluntary retirement prescribed under FR 56 (K) or Article 459 (*i*) of the CSRs or Rule 48 of the CCS (Pension) Rule or any other similar rule appplicable to him.

Illustrations

(*a*) If a government servant seeks voluntary retirement under this scheme, after he has attained the age of 47 years and has rendered 22 years of service, the weightage in pension would be limited only upto three years.

(*b*) If a government servant who could be prematurely retired seeks voluntary retirement under this scheme after he has attained the age of 51 years and has rendered 24 years of service, the weightage in pension could be admissible upto four years.

(*c*) If a government servant belonging to group 'C' seeks voluntary retirement under this scheme after he has rendered 25 years of service and has attained the age of 48 years, the weightage in pension would be admissible upto five years.

11.9 PAYMENT OF PENSION THROUGH BANKS TO THE STATE GOVERNMENT PENSIONERS

The pensioners who opt for the scheme need not present every month a bill to the disbursing office as at present. He has only to open an account in a Bank or a Branch of a Bank which adopts this scheme and intimate the Treasury Office Sub-treasury Officer/ Pension Payment Officer about his intention to draw his pension through that account, furnish the necessary letter of authority and surrender half of pension payment order at the Treasury/Sub-treasury. Thereafter the treasury concerned will arrange for remittance of the pension amount of the Bank concerned every month.

This scheme has been implemented w.e.f., January 1978 *i.e.*, the pension for January 1978 payable on the last date of January 1978.

[G.O. Ms. No. 422 Finance and Planning, dt. 3 Dec., 1977].

11.10 ADDITIONAL BENEFITS TO GOVT. EMPLOYEES

The Govt. of India has improved the service conditions of the employees considerably. Some of the benefits are given below.

11.10.1 Dearness Allowance

Dearness allowance which goes a long way in reducing the hardships caused by the rise in prices has been increased three times. Two additional instalments, the sixth and the seventh, were given from January 1978 and December 1978 respectively.

The rate of dearness allowance for the instalment has been raised. For the sixth instalment, those drawing a pay up to ₹ 300 got four per cent of their pay instead of 3.5 per cent per instalment and others with pay over ₹ 300 got three per cent instead of 2.5 per cent. For the seventh instalment dearness allowance at the rate of four per cent of the pay was allowed to those whose pay was below ₹ 400.

As from Jan. 14, 1977, the dearness allowance was make permissible during study leave on the leave salary sanctioned during such leave.

In the case of the terminal leave, dearness allowance has been made admissible during the first 180 days of such leave. This concession became effective from February 24, 1979.

11.10.2 House Rent Allowance

House rent allowance is now granted within the area of the urban limits of a city.

11.10.3 Conveyance Allowance

Blind and orthopaedically handicapped Government employees with disability of upper and lower extermities have been granted conveyance allowance at 10 per cent of pay subject to maximum of ₹ 50 per month with effect from August 1, 1978.

11.10.4 Project Allowance

The Central Government employees working in the project areas but not connected with the project work have been allowed project allowance from July 1978 at 50 per cent of rates admissible for the project staff.

11.10.5 Advances

The rates of various advances paid to Government employees for the purchase of motor car, scooter motor cycle or cycle have been increased. Non gazetted employees can be sanctioned a non-interest bearing advance of ₹ 500 or three months' pay, whichever is less, if their property has been damaged by a natural calamity in the area declared as such. The amount of advance for house-building has been raised to 75 months' pay.

11.10.6 Leave

A Central Government servant can now obtain a lump sum cash payment for leave at his credit at the time of retirement. It is equivalent to the leave salary payable for the unutilised earned leave upto 180 days.

Terminal leave on full pay can now be availed of up to 180 days in preparation for retirement.

A non-permanent Government servant who quits his post is also entitled to terminal leave upto 90 days, instead of 60 days allowed under the earlier rule.

Non-gazetted personnel can submit medical certificates issued by any registered medical practitioner in support of their leave requests.

Women employees are eligible to combine maternity leave with any other kind of leave. There is now no need to produce a medical certificate for such leave.

11.10.7 Leave Travel Concession

The Government has dispensed with the condition that the employee should bear the fare for himself and his family members for the first 400 kms of the journey to any place in India while availing leave travelling concession. This has given rise to greater enthusiasm among the employees and afford an attractive incentive for holidaying.

Provident Fund. Interest rates payable on Provident Fund accumulations have been raised. The balances at the credit of the employee in the General Provident Fund and other similar funds carry from April 1977 an interest of eight per cent a year for the first ₹ 25,000. Amounts in excess of this sum will fetch 7.5 per cent.

11.10.8 Deposit-linked Insurance

In the case of death of subscriber occurring before January 31, 1978, the requirement of a minimum balance under the 1975 rule for paying the government's amount under the deposit-linked insurance scheme will not be insisted upon. The government will pay an amount equal to the average monthly balance during the 36 months before his/her death without insisting on any minimum balance.

11.10.9 Retirement Benefits

(*a*) **Gratuity.** From September 1977, the government have done away with the rule requiring the employees to contribute two months' pay out of the gratuity amount due to him/her towards the family pension scheme.

This action was taken, as the government considered that the family pension scheme being a social security measure, it was not proper to ask the employees to contribute to it. The employees are, therefore, permitted to enjoy full retirement gratuity.

(*b*) **Family Pension.** Every government servant, whatever be the length of service is now covered by the family pension scheme, provided he/she is medically examined and found fit for appointment. Earlier, only families of those who put in a continuous service of one year benefited from the scheme.

Unmarried daughters of the employees are now eligible to get family pension till they attain the age of 24 years. Under the earlier rules they were entitled to the family pension up to the age of 21 years. Sons are eligible to get family pension up to the age of 21 years as against the previous limit of 18 years.

The procedure for authorising family pension and death gratuity of government servants who die while in service has been further simplified to expedite payment so that the families are not put to hardship. Qualifying service and qualifying emoluments shall have to be determined within one month. The head of office is given power to draw provisional family pension and death gratuity up to hundred per cent pending authorisation by the Accounts Officer.

(*c*) **Pension.** Government took a number of steps to streamline. For commutation of pension if he/she applies for it within one year of retirement medical examination is not required. Earlier, the Government servant was subjected to medical examination and the commuted value was determined on the basis of the medical report on the condition of health.

The quantum of pension which a retired government servant gets has been substantially increased with effect from March 31, 1979.

Under the new rates, low-paid employees who form the bulk of the Central Government servant will be entitled on retirement after 33 years of service to a pension of 50 per cent of their average emoluments.

According to the new scheme, the amount of pension for 33 years qualifying service will be 50 per cent of the first ₹ 1,000 of the pay, 45 per cent of the next ₹ 500 and 40 per cent of the rest. The maximum amount pension has also been raised from ₹ 1,000 to ₹ 1,500.

Emoluments for the purpose of pension calculation will now be reckoned by merging dearness allowance with pay at the twelve monthly average of the consumer price index level of 272. The minimum and maximum amount of dearness allowance to be so merged with pay are ₹ 70.60 and ₹ 243 respectively. This measure has also resulted in enhancing the pension and gratuity to employees retiring on or after September 30, 1977.

11.10 RELIEF TO PENSIONERS

(*a*) Three instalments of graded relief had been allowed to pensioners and family pensioners. Each instalments is equal to five per cent of the pension subject to a minimum of ₹ 5 and a maximum of ₹ 25. The last instalment was given from December 1978.

From April 25, 1977, employees on retirement can get retirement travelling allowance in full to the place where they are to settle down permanently even though such a place may be farther than the home town. They are also entitled to the allowance within one year of retirement as against six months earlier, permissible earlier.

(*b*) **Compassionate Appointments.** The scheme for compassionate appointments in respect of a Government servant who dies in harness has been liberalised. Restriction on the number of such appointments have been abolished.

(*c*) **Career Development and Training.** A large number of training progrmmes have been organised with a view to helping the employees in their career advancement.

(*d*) **Foreign Assignments.** During 1977 and 1978 a large number of Government employees under the Central and State Governments with requisite expertise were selected to assignments in developing countries, under bilateral agreements.

12

WORKMEN COMPENSATION ACT, 1923

12.1 INTRODUCTION

The aim of the Act is to provide for payment by certain classes of employers to their workmen of compensation for injury by accident.

Some of the important features of the Act such as Schedule of compensation in case of death and permanent and temporary disablement, injuries deemed to result in permanent partial disablement and list of injuries deemed to result in permanent total disablement have been briefly described in Article 5.7. However, in view of growing complexity of industry in this country, with the increasing, use of mechanical equipment and consequent danger of workman it is in the fitness of things that those executing big projects be familiar with comparatives more detailed information about this important Act.

12.2 DEFINITIONS

1. **"Commissioner"** means a Commissioner for Workmen's Compensation appointed under Section 20;
2. **"Compensation"** means compensation as provided for by this Act;
3. **"Dependent"** means any of the following relatives of a deceased workman, namely: (*i*) a widow, a minor legitimate or adopted son, and unmarried legitimate or adopted daughter, or a widowed mother; (*ii*) if wholly dependent on the earnings of the workman at the time of his death, a son or a daughter who has attained the age of 18 years and who

is infirm; and (*iii*) if wholly or in part dependent on the earnings of the workman at the time of his death,

(*a*) a widower,

(*b*) a parent other than a widowed mother,

(*c*) a minor illegitimate son, an unmarried illegitimate daughter or a daughter legitimate or illegitimate or adopted if married and a minor or if widowed and a minor,

(*d*) a minor brother or an unmarried sister or a widowed sister if a minor,

(*e*) a widowed daughter-in-law,

(*f*) a minor child of a pre-deceased son,

(*g*) a minor child of a pre-deceased daughter where no parent of the child is alive, or

(*h*) a parental grandparent if no parent of the workman is alive.

Explanation: For the purposes of sub-clauses (*ii*) and items (*f*) and (*g*) of sub-clause (*iii*), references to a son, daughter or child include an adopted son, daughter or child respectively;

5. **"Employer"** includes any body of persons whether incorporated or not and any managing agent of an employer and the legal representative of a deceased employer, and, when the services of a workman are temporarily rent or let on hire to another person by the person with whom the workman has entered into a contract of service or apprenticeship, means such other person while the workman is working for him;

6. **"Managing agent"** means any person appointed or acting as the representative of another person for the purpose of carrying on such other person's trade or business, but does not include an individual manager subordinate to an employer;

7. **"Minor"** means a person who has not attained the age of [illegible] years;

8. **"Partial disablement"** means, where the disablement is of a temporary nature, such disablement as reduces the earning capacity of a workman in any employment in which he was engaged at the time of the accident resulting in the disablement, and, where the disablement is of a permanent nature, such disablement as reduces his earning capacity in every employment which he was capable of undertaking at

that time, Provided that every injury specified in Part II of Schedule I shall be deemed to result in permanent partial disablement;

9. **"Prescribed"** means prescribed by rules made under this Act;

10. **"Qualified medical practitioner"** means any person registered under any Central Act, Provincial Act, or an Act of the Legislature of a State providing for the maintenance of a register of medical practitioners, or, in any area where no such last-mentioned Act is in force, any person declared by the State Government, by notification in the Official Gazette, to be a qualified medical practitioner for the purposes of this Act;

11. **"Seaman"** means any person forming part of the crew of any ship, but does not include the master of the ship;

12. **"Total disablement"** means such disablement, whether of a temporary or permanent nature, as incapacitates a workman for all work which he was capable of performing at the time of the accident resulting in such disablement:

    Provided that permanent total disablement shall be deemed to result from every injury specified in Part I of Schedule I or from any combination of injuries specified in Part II thereof where the aggregate percentage of the loss of earning capacity, as specified in the said Part II against those injuries, amounts to one hundred per cent or more;

13. **"Wages"** includes any privilege or benefit which is capable of being estimated in money, other than a travelling allowance or the value of any travelling concession or a contribution paid by the employer a workman towards any pension or provident fund or a sum paid to a workman to cover any special expenses entailed on him by the nature of his employment;

14. **"Workman"** means any person (other than a person whose employment is of a casual nature and who is employed otherwise than for the purposes of the employer's trade or business) who is – (*i*) a railway servant as defined in clause (34) of Section 2 of the Railways Act, 1989 (24 of 1989), not permanently employed in any administrative, district or sub-divisional office of a railway and not employed in any such capacity as is specified in Schedule II, or (*ia*) (*a*) a master, seaman or other member of the crew of a ship,

(*b*) a captain or other member of the crew of an aircraft,

(*c*) a person recruited as driver, helper, mechanic, cleaner or in any other capacity in connection with a motor vehicle,

(*d*) a person recruited for work abroad by a company, and who is employed outside India in any such capacity as is specified in Schedule II and the ship, aircraft or motor vehicle, or company, as the case may be, is registered in India, or

(*ii*) employed in any such capacity as is specified in Schedule II, whether the contract of employment was made before or after the passing of this Act and whether such contract is expressed or implied, oral or in writing; but does not include any person working in the capacity of a member of the Armed Forces of the Union; and any reference to a workman who has been injured shall, where the workman is dead, include a reference to his dependants or any of them.

12.3 EMPLOYER'S LIABILITY FOR COMPENSATION

1. If personal injury is caused to a workman by accident arising out of and in the course of his employment, his employer shall be liable to pay compensation in accordance with the provisions of this Chapter:

   Provided that the employer shall not be so liable—

   (*a*) in respect of any injury which does not result in the total or partial disablement of the workman for a period exceeding three days;

   (*b*) in respect of any injury, not resulting in death or permanent total disablement, caused by an accident which is directly attributable to–

   (*i*) the workman having been at the time thereof under the influence of drink or drugs, or

   (*ii*) the willful disobedience of the workman to an order expressly given, or to a rule expressly framed, for the purpose of securing the safety of workmen, or

   (*iii*) the willful removal or disregard by the workman of any safety guard or other device which he knew to have been provided for the purpose of securing the safety of workmen,

2. If a workman employed in any employment specified in Part A of Schedule III contracts any disease specified therein as

an occupational disease peculiar to that employment, or if a workman, whilst in the service of an employer in whose service he has been employed for a continuous period of not less than six months (which period shall not include a period of service under any other employer in the same kind of employment) in any employment specified in Part B of Schedule III, contracts any disease specified therein as an occupational disease peculiar to that employment, or if a workman whilst in the service of one or more employers in any employment specified in Part C of Schedule III, for such continuous period as the Central Government may specify in respect of each such employment, contracts any disease specified therein as an occupational disease peculiar to that employment, the contracting of the disease shall be deemed to be an injury by accident within the meaning of this section and, unless the contrary is proved, the accident shall be deemed to have arisen out of, and in the course of, the employment:

Provided that if it is proved,

(*a*) that a workman whilst in the service of one or more employers in any employment specified in Part C of Schedule III has contracted a disease specified therein as an occupational disease peculiar to that employment during a continuous period which is less than the period specified under this sub-section for that employment, and

(*b*) that the disease has arisen out of and in the course of the employment; the contracting of such disease shall be deemed to be an injury by accident within the meaning of this section:

Provided further that if it is proved that a workman who having served under any employer in any employment specified in Part B of Schedule III or who having served under one or more employers in any employment specified in Part C of that Schedule, for a continuous period specified under this sub-section for that employment and he has after the cessation of such service contracted any disease specified in the said Part B or the said Part C, as the case may be, as an occupational disease peculiar to the employment and that such disease arose out of the employment, the contracting of the disease shall be deemed to be an injury by accident within the meaning of this section.

2A. If a workman employed in any employment specified in Part C of Schedule III contracts any occupational disease peculiar to that employment, the contracting whereof is deemed to be an injury be accident within the meaning of this section, and such employment was under more than one employer, all such employers shall be liable for the payment of the compensation in such proportion as the Commissioner may, in the circumstances, deem just.

3. The Central Government or the State Government, after giving, by notification in the Official Gazette, not less than three months' notice of its intention so to do, may, by a like notification, add any description of employment to the employments specified in Schedule III, and shall specify in the case of employments so added the diseases which shall be deemed for the purposes of this section to be occupational diseases peculiar to those employments respectively, and thereupon the provisions of sub-section (2) shall apply in the case of a notification by the Central Government, within the territories to which this Act extends or, in case of a notification by the State Government, within the State as if such diseases had been declared by this Act to be occupational diseases peculiar to those employments.

4. Save as provided by Sub-sections (2), (2A) and (3), no compensation shall be payable to a workman in respect of any disease unless the disease is directly attributable to a specific injury by accident arising out of and in the course of his employment.

5. Nothing herein contained shall be deemed to confer any right to compensation on a workman in respect of any injury if he has instituted in a Civil Court a suit for damages in respect of the injury against the employer or any other person; and no suit for damages shall be maintainable by a workman in any Court of Law in respect of any injury—

(*a*) if he has instituted a claim to compensation in respect of the injury before a Commissioner; or

(*b*) if an agreement has been come in between the workman and his employer providing for the payment of compensation in respect of the injury in accordance with the provisions of this Act.

12.4 AMOUNT OF COMPENSATION

1. Subject to the provisions of this Act, the amount of compensation shall be as follows, namely:
   (*a*) where death results an amount equal to fifty from the injury per cent of the monthly wages of the deceased workman multiplied by the relevant factor; or an amount of fifty thousand rupees, whichever is more;
   (*b*) where permanent total an amount equal to disablement results from sixty the injury per cent of the monthly wages of the injured workman multiplied by the relevant factor, or an amount of sixty thousand rupees, whichever is more.

   Explanation I: For the purposes of clause (*a*) and clause (*b*), "*relevant factor*", in relation to a workman means the factor specified in the second column of Schedule IV against the entry in the first column of that Schedule specifying the number of years which are the same as the completed years of the age of the workman on his last birthday immediately preceding the date on which the compensation fell due;

   Explanation II: Where the monthly wages of a workman exceed two thousand rupees, his monthly wages for the purposes of clause (*a*) and clause (*b*) shall be deemed to be two thousand rupees only;

   (*c*) where permanent partial disablement results from the injury
      (*i*) in the case of an injury specified in Part II of Schedule I, such percentage of the compensation which would have been payable in the case of permanent total disablement as is specified therein as being the percentage of the loss of earning capacity caused by that injury, and
      (*ii*) in the case of an injury not specified in Schedule I, such percentage of the compensation payable in the case of permanent total disablement as is proportionate to the loss of earning capacity (as assessed by the qualified medical practitioner) permanently caused by the injury;

   Explanation I: Where more injuries than one are caused by the same accident, the amount of compensation payable under this head shall be aggregated but not so in any case as to exceed the amount which would have been payable if permanent total disablement had resulted from the injuries;

Explanation II: In Assessing the loss of earning capacity for the purposes of sub-clause (*ii*) the qualified medical practitioner shall have due regard to the percentages of loss of earning capacity in relation to different injuries specified in Schedule I;

(*d*) Where temporary a half monthly payment of the sum disablement, whether equivalent to twenty-five per cent of total or partial, results monthly wages of the workman, to from the injury be paid in accordance with the provisions of sub-section (2).

1A. Notwithstanding anything contained in sub-section (1), while fixing the amount of compensation payable to a workman in respect of an acident occurred outside India, the Commissioner shall take into account the amount of compensation, if any, awarded to such workman in accordance with the law of the country in which the accident occurred and shall reduce the amount fixed by him by the amount of compensation awarded to the workman in accordance with the law of that country.

2. The half-monthly payment referred to in clause (*d*) of sub-section (1) shall be payable on the sixteenth day-

(*i*) from the date of disablement where such disablement lasts for a period of twenty-eight days or more; or

(*ii*) after the expiry of a waiting period of three days from the date of disablement where such disablement lasts for a period of less than twenty-eight days; and thereafter half-monthly during the disablement or during a period of five years, whichever period is shorter:

Provided that–

(*a*) there shall be deducted from any lump sum or half-monthly payments to which the workman is entitled the amount of any payment or allowance which the workman has received from the employer by way of compensation during the period of disablement prior to the receipt of such lump sum or of the first half-monthly payment, as the case may be; and (*b*) no half-monthly payment shall exceed the amount in any case, if any, by which half the amount of the monthly wages of the workman before the accident exceeds half the amount of such wages which he is earning after the accident.

Explanation: Any payment or allowance which the workman has received from the employer towards his medical treatment shall not be deemed to be a payment or allowance received by him by way of compensation within the meaning of clause (*a*) of the provison.

3. On the ceasing of the disablement before the date on which any half-monthly payment falls due, there shall be payable in respect of that half-month a sum proportionate to the duration of the disablement in that half-month.
4. If the injury of the workman results in his death, the employer shall, in addition to the compensation under sub-section (1), deposit with the Commissioner a sum of one thousand rupees for payment of the same to the eldest surviving dependent of the workman towards the expenditure of the funeral of such workman or where the workman did not have a dependent or was not living with his dependent at the time of his death to the person who actually incurred such expenditure.

12.4.1 Compensation to be Paid When Due and Penalty for Default

1. Compensation under section 4 shall be paid as soon as it falls due.
2. In cases where the employer does not accept the liability for compensation to the extent claimed, he shall be bound to make provisional payment based on the extent of liability which he accepts, and such payment shall be deposited with the Commissioner or made to the workman, as the case may be, without prejudice to the right of the workman to make any further claim.
3. Where any employer is in default in paying the compensation due under this Act within one month from the date it fell due, the Commissioner shall–

(*a*) direct that the employer shall, in addition to the amount of the arrears, pay simple interest thereon at the rate of twelve per cent per annum or at such higher rate not exceeding the maximum of the lending rates of any scheduled bank as may be specified by the Central Government, by notification in the Official Gazette, on the amount due; and

(*b*) if, in his position, there is no justification for the delay, direct that the employer shall, in addition to the amount of the arrears and interest thereon, pay a further sum not exceeding fifty per cent of such amount by way of penalty:

Provided that an order for the payment of penalty shall not be passed under clause (*b*) without giving a reasonable opportunity to the employer to show cause why it should not be passed.

Explanation: For the purpose of sub-section, "*scheduled bank*" means a bank for the time being included in the Second Schedule to the Reserve Bank of India Act, 1934 (2 of 1934).

3A. The interest payable under sub-section (3) shall be paid to the workman or his dependant, as the case may be, and the penalty shall be credited to the State Government.

12.5 METHOD OF CALCULATING WAGES

In this Act and for the purposes thereof the expression "*monthly wages*" means the amount of wages deemed to be payable for a month's service (whether the wages are payable by the month or by whatever other period or at piece rates), and calculated as follows, namely: —

(*a*) where the workman has, during a continuous period of not less than twelve months immediately preceding the accident, been in the service of the employer who is liable to pay compensation, the monthly wages of the workman shall be one-twelfth of the total wages which have fallen due for payment to him by the employer in the last twelve months of that period;

(*b*) where the whole of the continuous period of service immediately preceding the accident during which the workman was in the service of the employer who is liable to pay the compensation was less than one month, the monthly wages of the workman shall be the average monthly amount which, during the twelve months immediately preceding the accident, was being earned by a workman employed on the same work by the same employer, or, if there was no workman so employed, by a workman employed on similar work in the same locality;

(*c*) in other cases [including cases in which it is not possible for want of necessary information to calculate the monthly wages under clause (*b*), the monthly wages shall be thirty times the total wages earned in respect of the last continuous period of service immediately preceding the accident from the employer who is liable to pay compensation, divided by the number of days comprising such period.

Explanation: A period of service shall, for the purposes of this section be deemed to be continuous which has not been interrupted by a period of absence from work exceeding fourteen days.

6. **Review.** (1) Any half-monthly payment payable under this Act, either under an agreement between the parties or under the order of a Commissioner, may be reviewed by the Commissioner, on the application either of the employer or of the workman accompanied by the certificate of a qualified medical practitioner that there has been a change in the condition of the workman, or, subject to rules made under this Act, on application made without such certificate.

   (2) Any half-monthly payment may, on review under this section, subject to the provisions of this Act, be continued, increased, decreased or ended, or if the accident is found to have resulted in permanent disablement, be converted to the lump sum to which the workman is entitled less any amount which he has already received by way of half-monthly payments.

7. **Commutation of Half-Monthly Payments.** Any right to receive half-monthly payments may, by agreement between the parties or, if the parties cannot agree and the payments have been continued for not less than six months, on the application of either party to the Commissioner be redeemed by the payment of a lump sum of such amount as may be agreed to by the parties or determined by the Commissioner, as the case may be.

12.6 DISTRIBUTION OF COMPENSATION

(1) No payment of compensation in respect of a workman whose injury has resulted in death, and no payment of a lump sum

as compensation to a woman or a person under a legal disability, shall be made otherwise than by deposit with the Commissioner, and no such payment made directly by an employer shall be deemed to be a payment of compensation:

Provided that, in the case of a deceased workman, an employer may make to any dependent advances on account of compensation of an amount equal to three months' wages of such workman and so much of such amount as does not exceed the compensation payable to that dependent shall be deducted by the Commissioner from such compensation and repaid to the employer.

(2) Any other sum amounting to not less than ten rupees which is payable as compensation may be deposited with the Commissioner on behalf of the person entitled thereto.

(3) The receipt of the Commissioner shall be a sufficient discharge in respect of any compensation deposited with him.

(4) On the deposit of any money under sub-section (1), as compensation in respect of a deceased workman the Commissioner shall, if he thinks necessary, cause notice to be published or to be served on each dependent in such manner as he thinks fit, calling upon the dependents to appear before him on such date as he may fix for determining the distribution of the compensation.

If the Commissioner is satisfied after any inquiry which he may deem necessary, that no dependent exists, he shall repay the balance of the money to the employer by whom it was paid.

The Commissioner shall, on application by the employer, furnish a statement showing in detail all disbursements made.

(5) Compensation deposited in respect of a deceased workman shall, subject to any deduction made under sub-section (4), be apportioned among the dependents of the deceased workman or any of them in such proportion as the Commissioner thinks fit, or may, in the discretion of the Commissioner, be allotted to any one dependent.

(6) Where any compensation deposited with the Commissioner is payable to any person, the Commissioner shall, if the person to whom the compensation is payable is not a woman or a person under a legal disability, and may, in other cases, pay the money to the person entitled thereto.

(7) Where any lump sum deposited with the Commissioner is payable to a woman or a person under a legal disability, such sum may be invested, applied or otherwise dealt with for the benefit of the woman, or of such person during his disability, in such manner as the Commissioner may direct; and where a half-monthly payment is payable to any person under a legal disability, the Commissioner may, of his own motion or on an application made to him in this behalf, order that the payment be made during the disability to any dependent of the workman or to any other person, whom the Commissioner thinks best fitted to provide for the welfare of the workman.

(8) Where, on application made to him in this behalf or otherwise, the Commissioner is satisfied that, on account of neglect of children on the part of a parent or on account of the variation of the circumstances of any dependent or for any other sufficient cause, an order of the Commissioner as to the distribution of any sum paid as compensation or as to the manner in which any sum payable to any such dependent is to be invested, applied or otherwise dealt with, ought to be varied, the Commissioner may make such orders for the variation of the former order as he thinks just in the circumstances of the case:

Provided that no such order prejudicial to any person shall be made unless such person has been given an opportunity of showing cause why the order should not be made, or shall be made in any case in which it would involve the repayment by a dependent of any sum already paid to him.

(9) Where the Commissioner varies any order under sub-section (8) by reason of the fact that payment of compensation to any person has been obtained by fraud, impersonation or other improper means, any amount so paid to or on behalf of such person may be recovered in the manner hereinafter provided in Section 31.

12.7 COMPENSATION NOT TO BE ASSIGNED, ATTACHED OR CHARGED

Save as provided by this Act, no lump sum or half-monthly payment payable under this Act shall in-any way be capable of being assigned or charged or be liable to attachment or pass to any person other than the workman by operation of law, nor shall any claim be set off against the same.

12.8 NOTICE AND CLAIM

(1) No claim for compensation shall be entertained by a Commissioner unless notice of the accident has been given in the manner hereinafter provided as soon as practicable after the happening thereof and unless the claim is preferred before him within two years of the occurrence of the accident or, in case of death, within two years from the date of death:

Provided that, where the accident is the contracting of a disease in respect of which the provisions of sub-section (2) of Section 3 are applicable, the accident shall be deemed to have occurred on the first of the days during which the workman was continuously absent from work in consequence of the disablement caused by the disease:

Provided further that in case of partial disablement due to the contracting of any such disease and which does not force the workman to absent himself from work, the period of two years shall be counted from the day the workman gives notice of the disablement to his employer:

Provided further that if a workman who, having been employed in an employment for a continuous period, specified under sub-section (2) of Section 3 in respect of that employment, ceases to be so employed and develops symptoms of an occupational disease peculiar to that employment within two years of the cessation of employment, the accident shall be deemed to have occurred on the day on which the symptoms were first detected.

Provided further that the want of or any defect or irregularity in a notice shall not be a bar to the entertainment of a claim– (*a*) if the claim is preferred in respect of the death of a workman resulting from an accident which occurred on the premises of the employer, or at any place where the workman at the time of the accident was working under the control of the employer or of any person employed by him, and the workman died on such premises or at such place, or on any premises belonging to the employer, or died without having left the vicinity of the premises or place where the accident occurred, or (*b*) if the employer or any one of several employers or any person responsible to the employer for the management of any branch of the trade or business in which the injured workman was employed had knowledge of the accident from any other source at or about the time when it occurred:

Provided further that the Commissioner may entertain and decide any claim to compensation in any case notwithstanding that the notice has not been given, or the claim has not been preferred in due time as provided in this sub-section, if he is satisfied that the failure so to give the notice or prefer the claim, as the case may be, was due to sufficient cause.

(2) Every such notice shall give the name and address of the person injured and shall state in ordinary language the cause of the injury and the date on which the accident happened, and shall be served on the employer or upon any one of several employers, or upon any person responsible to the employer for the management of any branch of the trade or business in which the injured workman was employed.

(3) The State Government may require that any prescribed class of employers shall maintain at their premises at which workmen are employed a notice-book, in the prescribed form, which shall be readily accessible at all reasonable times to any injured workman employed on the premises and to any person acting bonafide on his behalf.

(4) A notice under this section may be served by delivering it at, or sending it by registered post addressed to, the residence or any office or place of business of the person on whom it is to be served, or, where a notice-book is maintained, by entry in the notice book.

12.8.1 Power to Require From Employers Statements Regarding Fatal Accidents

(1) Where a Commissioner receives information from any source that a workman has died as a result of an accident arising out of and in the course of his employment, he may send by registered post a notice to the workman's employer requiring him to submit within thirty days of the service of the notice, a statement, in the prescribed form, giving the circumstances attending the death of the workman, and indicating whether, in the opinion of the employer, he is or is not liable to deposit compensation on account of the death.

(2) If the employer is of opinion that he is liable to deposit compensation, he shall make the deposit within thirty days of the service of the notice.

(3) If the employer is of opinion that he is not liable to deposit compensation, he shall be in his statement indicate the grounds on which he disclaims liability.

(4) Where the employer has so disclaimed liability, the Commissioner, after such enquiry as he may think fit, may inform any of the dependents of the deceased workman that it is open to the dependents to prefer a claim for compensation, and may give them such other further information as he may think fit.

12.8.2 Reports of Fatal Accidents and Serious Bodily Injuries

(1) Where, by any law for the time being in force, notice is required to be given to any authority, by or on behalf of an employer, of any accident occurring on his premises which results in death, or serious bodily injury, the person required to give the notice shall, within seven days of the death or serious bodily injury, send a report to the Commissioner giving the circumstances attending the death or serious bodily injury:

Provided that where the State Government has so prescribed the person required to give the notice may instead of sending such report to the Commissioner send it to the authority to whom he is required to give the notice.

Explanation: "*Serious bodily injury*" means an injury which involves, or in all probability will involve, the permanent loss of the use of, or permanent injury to, any limb, or the permanent loss of or injury to the sight or hearing, or the fracture of any limb, or the enforced absence of the injured person from work for a period exceeding twenty days.

(2) The State Government may, by notification in the Official Gazette, extend the provisions of sub-section (1) to any class of premises other than those coming within the scope of that sub-section, and may, by such notification, specify the persons who shall send the report to the Commissioner.

(3) Nothing in this section shall apply to factories to which the Employees' State Insurance Act, 1948 (34 of 1948), applies.

12.9 MEDICAL EXAMINATION

(1) Where a workman has given notice of an accident, he shall, if the employer, before the expiry of three days from the time at which service of the notice has been effected, offers to

have him examined free of charge by a qualified medical practitioner, submit himself for such examination, and any workman who is in receipt of a half-monthly payment under this Act shall be, if so required, submit himself for such examination from time to time:

Provided that a workman shall not be required to submit himself for examination by a medical practitioner otherwise than in accordance with rules made under this Act, or at more frequent intervals than may be prescribed.

(2) If a workman, on being required to do so by the employer under sub-section (1) or by the Commissioner at any time, refuses to submit himself for examination by a qualified medical practitioner or in any way obstructs the same, his right to compensation shall be suspended during the continuance of such refusal or obstruction unless, in the case of refusal, he was prevented by any sufficient cause from so submitting himself.

(3) If a workman, before the expiry of the period within which he is liable under sub-section (1) to be required to submit himself for medical examination, voluntarily leaves without having been so examined the vicinity of the place in which he was employed, his right to compensation shall be suspended until he returns and offers himself for such examination.

(4) Where a workman, whose right to compensation has been suspended under sub-section (2) or sub-section (3), dies without having submitted himself for medical examination as required by either of those sub-sections, the Commissioner may, if he thinks fit, direct the payment of compensation to the dependents of the deceased workman.

(5) Where under sub-section (2) or sub-section (3) a right to compensation is suspended, no compensation shall be payable in respect of the period of suspension, and, if the period of suspension commences before the expiry of the waiting period referred to in clause (d) of sub-section (1) of Section 4, the waiting period shall be increased by the period during which the suspension continues.

(6) Where an injured workman has refused to be attended by a qualified medical practitioner whose services have been offered to him by the employer free of charge or having accepted such offer has deliberately disregarded the

instructions of such medical practitioner, then if it is proved that the workman has not thereafter been regularly attended by a qualified medical practitioner or having been so attended has deliberately failed to follow his instructions and that such refusal, disregard or failure was unreasonable in the circumstances of the case and that the injury has been aggravated thereby, the injury and resulting disablement shall be deemed to be of the same nature and duration as they might reasonably have been expected to be if the workman had been regularly attended by a qualified medical practitioner, whose instructions he had followed, and compensation, if any, shall be payable accordingly.

12.10 CONTRACTING

(1) Where any person (hereinafter in this section referred to as the principal) in the course of or for the purposes of his trade or business contracts with any other person (hereinafter in this section referred to as the contractor) for the execution by or under the contractor of the whole or any part of any work which is ordinarily part of the trade or business of the principal, the principal shall be liable to pay to any workman employed in the execution of the work any compensation which he would have been liable to pay if that workman had been immediately employed by him; and where compensation is claimed from the principal, this Act shall apply as if references to the principal were substituted for references to the employer except that the amount of compensation shall be calculated with reference to the wages of the workman under the employer by whom he is immediately employed.

(2) Where the principal is liable to pay compensation under this section, he shall be entitled to be indemnified by the contractor, or any other person from whom the workman could have recovered compensation and where a contractor who is himself a principal is liable to pay compensation or to indemnify a principal under this section he shall be entitled to be indemnified by any person standing to him in the relation of a contractor from whom the workman could have recovered compensation, and all questions as to the right to and the amount of any such indemnity shall, in default of agreement, be settled by the Commissioner.

(3) Nothing in this section shall be construed as preventing a workman from recovering compensation from the contractor instead of the principal.

(4) This section shall not apply in any case where the accident occurred elsewhere than on, in or about the premises on which the principal has undertaken or usually undertakes, as the case may be, to execute the work or which are otherwise under his control or management.

12.11 REMEDIES OF EMPLOYER AGAINST STRANGER

Where a workman has recovered compensation in respect of any injury caused under circumstances creating a legal liability of some person other than the person by whom the compensation was paid to pay damages in respect thereof, the person by whom the compensation was paid and any person who has been called on to pay an indemnity under Section 12 shall be entitled to be indemnified by the person so liable to pay damages as aforesaid.

12.12 INSOLVENCY OF EMPLOYER

(1) Where any employer has entered into a contract with any insurers in respect of any liability under this Act to any workman, then in the event of the employer becoming insolvent or making a composition or scheme of arrangement with his creditors or, if the employer is a company, in the event of the company having commenced to be wound up, the rights of the employer against the insurers as respects that liability shall, notwithstanding anything in any law for the time being in force relating to insolvency or the winding up of companies, be transferred to and vest in the workman, and upon any such transfer the insurers shall have the same rights and remedies and be subject to the same liabilities as if they were the employer, so, however, that the insurers shall not be under any greater liability to the workman than they would have been under to the employer.

(2) If the liability of the insurers to the workman is less than the liability of the employer to the workman, the workman may prove for the balance in the insolvency proceedings or liquidation.

(3) Where in any case such as is referred to in sub-section (1) the contract of the employer with the insurers is void or

voidable by reason of non-compliance on the part of the employer with any terms or conditions of the contract (other than a stipulation for the payment of premia), the provisions of that sub-section shall apply as if the contract were not void or voidable, and the insurers shall be entitled to prove in the insolvency proceedings or liquidation for the amount paid to the workman:

Provided that the provisions of this sub-section shall not apply in any case in which the workman fails to give notice to the insurers of the happening of the accident and of any resulting disablement as soon as practicable after he becomes aware of the institution of the insolvency or liquidation proceedings.

(4) There shall be deemed to be included among the debts which under Section 49 of the Presidency-towns Insolvency Act, 1909 (3 of 1909), or under Section 61 of the Provincial Insolvency Act, 1920 (5 of 1920), or under Section 530 of the Companies Act, 1956 (1 of 1956), are in the distribution of the property of an insolvent or in the distribution of the assets of a company being wound up to be paid in priority to all other debts, the amount due in respect of any compensation the liability wherefore accrued before the date of the order of adjudication of the insolvent or the date of the commencement of the winding up, as the case may be, and those Acts shall have effect accordingly.

(5) Where the compensation is a half-monthly payment, the amount due in respect thereof shall, for the purposes of this section, be taken to be the amount of the lump sum for which the half-monthly payment could, if redeemable, be redeemed if application were made for that purpose under Section 7, and a certificate of the Commissioner as to the amount of such sum shall be conclusive proof thereof.

(6) The provisions of sub-section (4) shall apply in the case of any amount for which an insurer is entitled to prove under sub-section (3), but otherwise those provisions shall not apply where the insolvent or the company being wound up has entered into such a contract with insurers as is referred to in sub-section (1).

(7) This section shall not apply where a company is wound up voluntarily merely for to purposes of reconstruction or of amalgamation with another company.

12.13 RETURNS AS TO COMPENSATION

The State Government may, by notification in the Official Gazette, direct that every person employing workmen, or that any specified class of such persons, shall send at such time and in such form and to such authority, as may be specified in the notification, a correct return specifying the number of injuries in respect of which compensation has been paid by the employer during the previous year and the amount of such compensation together with such other particulars as to the compensation as the State Government may direct.

12.14 CONTRACTING OUT

Any contractor agreement whether made before or after the commencement of this Act, whereby a workman relinquishes any right of compensation from the employer for personal injury arising out of or in the course of the employment, shall be null and void in so far as it purports to remove or reduce the liability of any person to pay compensation under this Act.

12.15 PENALTIES

(1) Whoever -

(*a*) fails to maintain a notice-book which he is required to maintain under sub-section (3) of Section 10, or

(*b*) fails to send to the Commissioner a statement which he is required to send under sub-section (1) of Section 10A, or

(*c*) fails to send a report which he is required to send under Section 10B, or

(*d*) fails to make a return which he is required to make under Section 16, shall be punishable with fine which may extend to five thousand rupees.

(2) No prosecution under this Section shall be instituted except by or with the previous sanction of a Commissioner, and no Court shall take cognizance of any offence under this section, unless complaint thereof is made within six months of the date on which the alleged commission of the offence came to the knowledge of the Commissioner.

12.16 REFERENCE TO COMMISSIONERS

(1) If any question arises in any proceedings under this Act as to the liability of any person to pay compensation (including any question as to whether a person injured is or is not a workman) or as to the amount or duration of compensation (including any question as to the nature or extent of disablement), the question shall, in default of agreement, be settled by a Commissioner.

(2) No Civil Court shall have jurisdiction to settle, decide or deal with any question which is by or under this Act required to be settled, decided or dealt with by a Commissioner or to enforce any liability incurred under this Act.

12.17 APPOINTMENT OF COMMISSIONER

(1) The State Government may be, by notification in the Official Gazette, appoint any person to be a Commissioner for Workmen's Compensation for such area as may be specified in the notification.

(2) Where more than one Commissioner has been appointed for any area, the State Government may be, by general or special order, regulate the distribution of business between them.

(3) Any Commissioner may be, for the purpose of deciding any matter referred to him for decision under this Act, choose one or more persons possessing special knowledge of any matter relevant to the matter under inquiry to assist him in holding the inquiry.

(4) Every Commissioner shall be deemed to be a public servant within the meaning of the Indian Penal Code (45 of 1860).

12.18 VENUE OF PROCEEDINGS AND TRANSFER

(1) Where any matter under this Act is to be done by or before a Commissioner, the same shall, subject to the provisions of this Act and to any rules made hereunder, be done by or before the Commissioner for the area in which—

(*a*) the accident took place which resulted in the injury; or

(*b*) the workman or in case of his death, the dependent claiming the compensation ordinarily resides; or

(*c*) the employer has his registered office provided that no matter shall be processed before or by a Commissioner, other than the Commissioner having jurisdiction over the area in which the accident took place, without his giving notice in the manner prescribed by the Central Government to the Commissioner having jurisdiction over the area and the State Government concerned:

Provided further that, where the workman, being the master of a ship or a seaman or the captain or a member of the crew of an aircraft or a workman in a motor vehicle or a company, meets with the accident outside India any such matter may be done by or before a Commissioner for the area in which the owner or agent of the ship, aircraft or motor vehicle resides or carries on business or the registered office of the company is situate, as the case may be.

(1A) If a Commissioner, other than the Commissioner with whom any money has been deposited under Section 8, proceeds with a matter under this Act, the former may for the proper disposal of the matter call for transfer of any records or money remaining with the latter and on receipt of such a request, he shall comply with the same.

(2) If a Commissioner is satisfied that any matter arising out of any proceedings pending before him can be more conveniently dealt with by any other Commissioner, whether in the same State or not, he may, subject to rules made under this Act, order such matter to be transferred to such other Commissioner either for report or for disposal, and, if he does so, shall forthwith transmit to such other Commissioner all documents relevant for the decision of such matter and, where the matter is transferred for disposal, shall also transmit in the prescribed manner any money remaining in his hands or invested by him for the benefit of any party to the proceedings:

Provided that the Commissioner shall not, where any party to the proceedings has appeared before him, make any order of transfer relating to the distribution among dependents of a lump sum without giving such party an opportunity of being heard.

(3) The Commissioner to whom any matter is so transferred shall, subject to rules made under this Act, inquire there into and, if the matter was transferred for report, return his report thereon or, if the matter was transferred for disposal,

continue the proceedings as if they had originally commenced before him.

(4) On receipt of a report from a Commissioner to whom any matter has been transferred for report under sub-section (2), the Commissioner by whom it was referred shall decide the matter referred in conformity with such report.

(5) The State Government may transfer any matter from any Commissioner appointed by it to any other Commissioner appointed by it.

12.19 FORM OF APPLICATION

(1) Where an accident occurs in respect of which liability to pay compensation under this Act arises, a claim for such compensation may, subject to the provisions of this Act, be made before the Commissioner.

(1A) Subject to the provisions of sub-section (1), no application for the settlement of any matter by a Commissioner, other than an application by a dependent or dependents for compensation shall be made unless and until some question has arisen between the parties in connection therewith which they have been unable to settle by agreement.

(2) An application to a Commissioner may be made in such form and shall be accompanied by such fee, if any, as may be prescribed, and shall contain, in addition to any particulars which may be prescribed, the following particulars, namely:

(*a*) a concise statement of the circumstances in which the application is made and the relief or order which the applicant claims;

(*b*) in the case of a claim for compensation against an employer, the date of service of notice of the accident on the employer and, if such notice has not been served or has not been served in due time, the reason for such omission;

(*c*) the names and addresses of the parties; and

(*d*) except in the case of an application by dependents for compensation a concise statement of the matters on which agreement has and of those on which agreement has not been come to.

(3) If the applicant is illiterate or for any other reason is unable to furnish the required information in writing; the application shall, if the applicant so desires, be prepared under the direction of the Commissioner.

12.19.1 Power of Commissioner to Require Further Deposit in Cases of Fatal Accident

(1) Where any sum has been deposited by an employer as compensation payable in respect of a workman whose injury has resulted in death, and in the opinion of the Commissioner such sum is insufficient, the Commissioner may, by notice in writing stating his reasons, call upon the employer to show cause why he should not make a further deposit within such time as may be stated in the notice.

(2) If the employer fails to show cause to the satisfaction of the Commissioner, the Commissioner may make an award determining the total amount payable, and requiring the employer, to deposit the deficiency.

12.20 POWERS AND PROCEDURE OF COMMISSIONERS

The Commissioner shall have all the powers of a Civil Court under the Code of Civil Procedure, 1908 (5 of 1908) for the purpose of taking evidence on oath (which such Commissioner is hereby empowered to impose) and of enforcing the attendance of witnesses and compelling the production of documents and material objects and the Commissioner shall be deemed to be a Civil Court for all the purposes of Section 195 and of Chapter XXVI of the Code of Criminal Procedure, 1973 (2 of 1974).

12.21 APPEARANCE OF PARTIES

Any appearance, application or act, required to be made or done by any person before or to a Commissioner (other than an appearance of a party which is required for the purpose of his examination as a witness) may be made or done on behalf of such person by a legal practitioner or by an official of an Insurance Company or registered trade union or by an Inspector appointed under sub-section (1) of Section 8 of the Factories Act, 1948 (63 of 1948), or under sub-section (1) of Section 5 of the Mines Act, 1952, (35 of 1952), or by any other officer specified by the State Government in this behalf, authorised in writing by such person, or, with the permission of the Commissioner, by any other person so authorised.

12.22 METHOD OF RECORDING EVIDENCE

The Commissioner shall make a brief memorandum of the substance of the evidence of every witness as the examination of the witness proceeds, and such memorandum shall be written and signed by the Commissioner with his own hand and shall form part of the record:

Provided that, if the Commissioner is prevented from making such memorandum, he shall record the reason of his inability to do so and shall cause such memorandum to be made in writing from his dictation and shall sign the same, and such memorandum shall form a part of the record: Provided further that the evidence of any medical witness shall be taken down as nearby as may be word for word.

12.23 REGISTRATION OF AGREEMENTS

(1) Where the amount of any lump sum payable as compensation has been settled by agreement, whether by way of redemption of a half-monthly payment or otherwise, or where any compensation has been so settled as being payable to a woman or a person under a legal disability a memorandum thereof shall be sent by the employer to the Commissioner, who shall, on being satisfied as to its genuineness, record the memorandum in a register in the prescribed manner:

Provided that—

(*a*) no such memorandum shall be recorded before seven days after communication by the Commissioner of notice to the parties concerned;

(*b*) Omitted;

(*c*) the Commissioner may at any time rectify the register;

(*d*) where it appears to the Commissioner that an agreement as to the payment of a lump sum whether by way of redemption of a half-monthly payment or otherwise, or an agreement as to the amount of compensation payable to a woman or a person under a legal disability ought not to be registered by reason of the inadequacy of the sum or amount, or by reason of the agreement having been obtained by fraud or undue influence or other improper means, he may refuse to record the memorandum of the agreement and may make such other including an order as to any sum already paid under the agreement, as he thinks just in the circumstances.

(2) An agreement for the payment of compensation which has been registered under subsection (1) shall be enforceable under this Act notwithstanding anything contained in the Indian Contract Act, 1872 (9 of 1872), or in any other law for the time being in force.

12.24 EFFECT OF FAILURE TO REGISTER AGREEMENT

Where a memorandum of any agreement, the registration of which is required by Section 28, is not sent to the Commissioner as required by that Section, the employer shall be liable to pay the full amount of compensation which he is liable to pay under the provisions of this Act, and notwithstanding anything contained in the provison to sub-section (1) of, Section 4, shall not, unless the Commissioner otherwise directs, be entitled to deduct more than half of any amount paid to the workmen by way of compensation whether under the agreement or otherwise.

12.25 APPEALS

(1) An appeal shall lie to the High Court from the following orders of a Commissioner, namely:

(*a*) an order awarding as compensation a lump sum whether by way of redemption of a half-monthly payment or otherwise or disallowing a claim in full or in part for a lump sum;

(*aa*) an order awarding interest or penalty under Section 4A;

(*b*) an order refusing to allow redemption of a half-monthly payment;

(*c*) an order providing for the distribution of compensation among the dependents of a deceased workman, or disallowing any claim of a person alleging himself to be such dependant;

(*d*) an order allowing or disallowing any claim for the amount of an indemnity under the provisions of sub-section (2) of Section 12; or

(*e*) an order refusing to register a memorandum of agreement or registering the same or providing for the registration of the same subject to conditions:

Provided that no appeal shall lie against any order unless a substantial question of law is involved in the appeal and, in the case of an order other than an order such as is referred to in clause (*b*) unless the amount in dispute in the appeal is not less than three hundred rupees:

Provided further that no appeal shall lie in any case in which the parties have agreed to abide by the decision of the Commissioner, or in which the order of the Commissioner gives effect to an agreement come to by the parties.

Provided further that no appeal by an employer under clause (*a*) shall lie unless the memorandum of appeal is accompanied by a certificate by the Commissioner to the effect that the appellant has deposited with him the amount payable under the order appealed against.

(2) The period of limitation for an appeal under this Section shall be sixty days.

(3) The provision of Section 5 of the Limitation Act, 1963 (36 of 1963) shall be applicable to appeals under, this Section.

12.26 POWER OF THE STATE GOVERNMENT TO MAKE RULES

(1) The State Government may make rules to carry out the purposes of this Act.

(2) In particular and without prejudice to the generality of the foregoing power, such rules may provide for all or any of the following matters, namely:

(*a*) for prescribing the intervals at which and the conditions subject to which an application for review may be made under Section 6 when not accompanied by a medical certificate;

(*b*) for prescribing the intervals at which and the conditions subject to which a workman may be required to submit himself for medical examination under sub-section (1) of Section 11;

(*c*) for prescribing the procedure to be followed by Commissioners in the disposal of cases under this Act and by the parties in such cases;

(*d*) for regulating the transfer of matters and cases from one Commissioner to another and the transfer of money in such cases;

(*e*) for prescribing the manner in which money in the hands of a Commissioner may be invested for the benefit of dependents of a deceased workman and for the transfer of money so invested from one Commissioner to another;

(*f*) for the representation in proceedings before Commissioners of parties who are minors or are unable to make an appearance;

(*g*) for prescribing the form and manner in which memorandum of agreements shall be presented and registered;

(*h*) for the withholding by Commissioners, whether in whole or in part of half-monthly payments pending decision on applications for review of the same;

(*i*) for regulating the scales of costs which may be allowed in proceedings under this Act;

(*j*) for prescribing and determining the amount of the fees payable in respect of any proceedings before a Commissioner under this Act;

(*k*) for the maintenance by Commissioners of registers and records of proceedings before them;

(*l*) for prescribing the classes of employers who shall maintain notice-books under sub-section (3) of Section 10, and the form of such notice-books;

(*m*) for prescribing the form of statement to be submitted by employers under Section 10A;

(*n*) for prescribing the cases in which the report referred to in Section 10B may be sent to an authority other than the Commissioner;

(*o*) for prescribing abstracts of this Act and requiring the employers to display notices containing such abstracts;

(*p*) for prescribing the manner in which diseases specified as occupational diseases may be diagnosed;

(*q*) for prescribing the manner in which diseases may be certified for any of the purposes of this Act;

(*r*) for prescribing the manner in which, and the standards by which, incapacity may be assessed.

(3) Every rule made under this section shall be laid, as soon as may be after it is made.

12.27 LIST OF PERSONS WHO SUBJECT TO THE PROVISIONS OF SECTION 2(1)(n), ARE INCLUDED IN THE DEFINITION OF WORKMEN

The following persons are workmen within the meaning of Section 2(1)(n) and subject to the provisions of that Section, that is to say, any person who is—

(*i*) employed, otherwise than in a clerical capacity or on a railway, in connection with the operation, repair or maintenance of a lift or a vehicle propelled by steam or other mechanical power or by electricity or in connection with the loading or unloading of any such vehicle; or

(*ii*) employed, otherwise than in a clerical capacity, in any premises wherein or within the precincts whereof a manufacturing process as defined in clause (*k*) of Section 2 of the Factories Act, 1948 (63 of 1948), is being carried on, or in any kind of work whatsoever incidental to or connected with any such manufacturing process or with the Article made, whether or not employment in any such work is within such premises or precincts and steam, water or other mechanical power or electrical power is used; or

(*iii*) employed for the purpose of making, altering, repairing, ornamenting, finishing or otherwise adapting for use, transport or sale of any article or part of an article in any premises wherein or within the precincts whereof twenty or more persons are so employed.

Explanation: For the purposes of this clause, persons employed outside such premises or precincts but in any work incidental to, or connected with, the work relating to making, altering, repairing, ornamenting, finishing or otherwise adapting for use, transport or sale of any articles or part of an article shall be deemed to be employed within such premises or precincts; or

(*iv*) employed in the manufacture or handling of explosives in connection with the employer's trade or business; or

(*v*) employed, in any mine as defined in clause (*j*) of Section 2 of the Mines Act, 1952 (35 of 1952), in any minor operation or in any kind of work, other than clerical work incidental to or connected with any mining operation or with the mineral obtained, or in any kind of work whatsoever below ground; or lwa-173

(*vi*) employed as the master or as a seaman of–

(*a*) any ship which is propelled wholly or in part by steam or other mechanical power or by electricity or which is towed or intended to be towed by a ship so propelled; or

(*b*) any ship not included in sub-clause (*a*), of twenty-five tons net tonnage or over; or

(*c*) any sea-going ship not included in sub-clause (*a*) or sub-clause (*b*) provided with sufficient area for navigation under sails alone; or

(*vii*) employed for the purpose of—

(*a*) loading, unloading, fuelling, constructing, repairing, demolishing, cleaning or painting any ship of which he is not the master or a member of the crew, or handling or transport within the limits of any port subject to the Ports Act, 1908 (15 of 1908), or the Major Port Trusts Act, 1963 (38 of 1963), of goods which have been discharged from or are to be loaded into any vessel; or

(*b*) warping a ship through the dock; or

(*c*) mooring and unmooring ships at harbor wall berths or in pier; or

(*d*) removing or replacing dry dock caissons when vessels are entering or leaving dry docks; or

(*e*) the docking or undocking or any vessel during an emergency; or

(*f*) preparing splicing coir springs and check wires, painting depth marks on Dock-sides, removing or replacing fenders whenever necessary, landing of gangways, maintaining life-boats up to standard or any other maintenance work of a like nature; or

(*g*) any work on jolly-boats for bringing a ship's line to the wharf; or

(*viii*) employed in the construction, maintenance, repair or demolition of—

(*a*) any building which is designed to be or is or has been more than one story in height above the ground or, twelve feet or more from the ground level to the apex of the roof; or

(*b*) any dam or embankment which is twelve feet or more in height from its lowest to its highest point; or

(*c*) any road, bridge, tunnel or canal; or

(*d*) any wharf, quay, sea-wall or other marine work including any moorings of ships; or

(*ix*) employed in setting up, maintaining, repairing or taking down any telegraph or telephone line or post or any overhead electric line or cable or post or standard or fittings and fixtures for the same; or

(*x*) employed, otherwise than in a clerical capacity, in the construction, working, repair or demolition of any aerial ropeway, canal, pipeline, or sewer; or

(*xi*) employed in the service of any fire brigade; or

(*xii*) employed upon a railway as defined in Clause (31) of Section 2 and sub-section (1) of Section 197 of the Railways Act, 1989 (24 of 1989), either directly or through a subcontractor, by a person fulfilling a contract with the railway administration; or Iwa-175

(*xiii*) employed as an inspector, mail guard, sorter or van peon in the Railway Mail Service, or as a telegraphist or as a postal or railway signaller or employed in any occupation ordinarily involving outdoor work in the Indian Posts and Telegraphs Department; or

(*xiv*) employed, otherwise than in a clerical capacity, in connection with operations for winning natural petroleum or natural gas; or

(*xv*) employed in any occupation involving blasting operations; or

(*xvi*) employed in the making of any excavation in which on any one day of the preceding twelve months more than twenty-five persons have been employed or explosives have been used, or whose depth from its highest to its lowest point exceeds twelve feet; or

(*xvii*) employed in the operation of any ferry board capable of carrying more than ten persons; or

(*xviii*) employed, otherwise than in a clerical capacity, on any estate which is maintained for the purpose of growing cardamom cinchona, coffee, rubber or tea, and on which on any one day in the preceding twelve months twenty-five or more persons have been so employed; or

(*xix*) employed, otherwise than in a clerical capacity, in the generating, transforming, transmitting or distribution of electrical energy or in generation or supply of gas; or

(*xx*) employed in a lighthouse as defined in Clause (*d*) of Section 2 of the Indian Lighthouse Act, 1927 (17 of 1927); or

(*xxi*) employed in producing cinematograph pictures intended for public exhibition or in exhibiting such pictures; or

(*xxii*) employed in the training, keeping or working of elephants or wild animals; or

(*xxiii*) employed in the tapping of palm-trees or the felling or logging of trees, or the transport of timber by inland waters, or the control or extinguishing of forest fires; or

(*xxiv*) employed in operations for the catching or hunting of elephants or other wild animals; or

(*xxv*) employed as a driver; or

(*xxvi*) employed in the handling or transport of goods in, or within the precincts of,—

(*a*) any warehouse or other place in which goods are stored, and in which on any one day of the preceding twelve months ten or more persons have been so employed, or

(*b*) any market in which on any one day of the preceding twelve months fifty or more persons have been so employed; or

(*xxvii*) employed in any occupation involving the handling and manipulation of radium or X-rays apparatus, or contact with radioactive substances; or

(*xxviii*) employed in or in connection with the construction, erection, dismantling, operation or maintenance of an aircraft as defined in Section 2 of the Indian Aircraft Act, 1934 (22 or 1934); or

(*xxix*) employed in horticultural operations, forestry, bee-keeping or farming by tractors or other contrivances driven by steam or other mechanical power or by electricity; or (*xxx*) employed, otherwise than in a clerical capacity, in the construction, working, repair or maintenance of a tube-well; or

(*xxxi*) employed in the maintenance, repair or renewal of electric fittings in any building; or Iwa-191

(*xxxii*) employed in a circus;

(*xxxiii*) employed as watchman in any factory or establishment; or

(*xxxiv*) employed in any operation in the sea for catching fish; or

(*xxxv*) employed in any employment which requires handling of snakes for the purpose of extraction of venom or for the purpose of looking after snakes or handling any other poisonous animal or insect; or

(*xxxvi*) employed in handling animals like horses, mules and bulls; or

(*xxxvii*) employed for the purpose of loading or unloading any mechanically propelled vehicle or in the handling or transport of goods which have been loaded in such vehicles; or

(*xxxviii*) employed in cleaning of sewer lines or septic tanks within the limits of a local authority; or

(*xxxix*) employed on surveys and investigation, exploration or gauge or discharge observation of rivers including drilling operations, hydrological observations and flood forecasting activities ground, water surveys and exploration; or

(*xl*) employed in cleaning of jungles or reclaiming land or ponds in which on any one day of the preceding twelve months more than twenty-five persons have been employed; or

(*xli*) employed in cultivation of land or rearing and maintenance of live-stock or forest operations or fishing in which on any one day of the preceding twelve months more than twenty-five persons have been employed; or

(*xlii*) employed in installation, maintenance or repair of pumping equipment used for lifting of water from wells, tube wells, ponds, lakes, streams and the like; or

(*xliii*) employed in the construction, boring or deepening of an open well or dug well, bore well, bore-cum-dug well, filter-point and the like; or (xliv) employed in spraying and dusting of insecticides or pesticides in agricultural operations or plantations; or

(xlv) employed in mechanised harvesting threshing operations; or

(xlvi) employed in working or repair or maintenance of bulldozers, tractors, power tillers and the like; or

(xlvii) employed as artist for drawing pictures on advertisement boards at a height of 3.66 meters or more from the ground level; or

(xlviii) employed in any newspaper establishment as defined in the Working Journalists and Other Newspaper Employees (Conditions of Service) and Miscellaneous Provisions Act, 1955 (45 of 1955) and engaged in outdoor work, employed as divers for work under water.

Explanation: In this Schedule, "*the preceding twelve months*", relates in any particular case to the twelve months ending with the day on which the accident in such case occurred.

12.28 FACTORS FOR WORKING OUT LUMP SUM EQUIVALENT OF COMPENSATION AMOUNT IN CASE OF PERMANENT DISABLEMENT AND DEATH

Completed years of age on the last birthday of the workman immediately preceding the date on which the compensation fell due		*Factors*
	1	ds 2
Not more than	16	228.54
	17	227.49
	18	226.38
	19	225.22
	20	224.00
	21	222.71
	22	221.37
	23	219.95
	24	218.47
	25	216.91
	26	215.28
	27	213.57

28	211.79
29	209.92
30	207.98
31	205.95
32	203.85
33	201.66
34	199.40
35	197.06
36	194.64
37	192.14
38	189.56
39	186.90
40	184.17
41	181.37
42	178.49
43	175.54
44	172.52
45	169.44
46	166.29
47	163.07
48	159.80
49	156.47
50	153.09
51	149.67
52	146.20
53	142.68
54	139.13
55	135.56
56	131.95
57	128.33
58	124.70
59	121.05
60	117.41
61	113.77
62	110.14
63	106.52
64	102.93
65 or more	99.37

13

T.A. Rules and Pension Rules

PART I: T.A. AND LTC RULES

INTRODUCTION

TA rules undergo change with the revision of pay structure under the various pay commissions. As a result of the acceptance of the recommendations of the fourth pay commission, drastic changes have taken place and the contents of the different aspects of travelling allowance given in Chapter 9 have undergone major changes and hence the need of this chapter which supercedes some of the information given in Chapter 9.

13.1 TA ON TOUR

TA on tour is from duty point/residence/headquarters to the duty point at the destination and vice-versa. It comprises:

- Fare for journey by rail, road, air and steamer
- Road mileage for journey otherwise than by public transport and
- DA for the entire period of absence from HQ including the journey period.

The eligibility for travelling by specific class of accommodation and the rate of daily allowance is decided with reference to the pay of the employee. The grading of employees for journey is according to the pay as follows:

1. Entitlements for Journeys on Tour

Travel Entitlements within the Country

Grade Pay	*Travel Entitlements*
Officers drawing grade pay of ₹ 16,400.00 and above and those in pay scale of HAG + and above	Business/Club Class by air/AC First Class by train
Officers drawing grade pay of ₹ 8000.00 to ₹ 16,400.00	Economy Class by air/AC First Class by train
Officers drawing grade pay of ₹ 6500.00 to ₹ 8000.00	Economy Class by air/AC II Tier Class by train
Officers drawing grade pay of ₹ 6500.00	AC II Tier Class by train
Officers drawing grade pay below ₹ 4100	First Class/AC III Tier/AC Chair Car by train

The Travel entitlements are subject to following:

(*i*) In case of places not connected by rail, travel by AC bus for all those entitled to travel by AC II Tier and above by train and by Deluxe/ordinary bus for others is allowed.

(*ii*) In case of road travel between places connected by rail, travel by any means of public transport is allowed provided the total fare does not exceed the train fare by the entitled class.

(*iii*) Henceforth, all mileage points earned by employees on tickets purchased for official travel shall be utilized by the concerned department for other official travel by their officers. Any usage of these mileage points for purposes of private travel by an officer will attract departmental action.

2. International Travel Entitlement

(*i*) Cabinet Secretary/Secretary to G.O.I. and Equivalent – First Class

(*ii*) Officers drawing grade pay of ₹ 16,400 and above and those in pay scale of HAG + – Business/Club Class

(*iii*) Others – Economy Class

Entitlements for Travel by Rail

Pay Range (Basic pay + NPA + Stagnation increment)	*Shatabdi Express*	*Rajdhani Express*	*Other Trains*
₹ 16,400 and above	Executive Class	AC First Class	AC First Class
₹ 8000 to ₹ 16,399	AC Chair Car	AC 2-tier	AC 2-tier
₹ 6500 to ₹ 7999	-do-	AC chair Car*	First Class/AC 3-tier/AC Chair Car
₹ 4100 to ₹ 6499	-do-	-do-*	-do-
Below ₹ 4100	-do-	-do-*	Sleeper Class

3. Travel by Rajdhani Express

Pay Range	*Entitlements*
₹ 16,400 and above	AC First Class
₹ 8000 and above, but less than ₹ 16,400	IIAC-2 Tier Sleeper
All others drawing pay below ₹ 8000*	AC Chair Car**

Trave by AC III Tier Sleeper will be permissible in trains in which AC Chair Car accommodation is not provided.

Travel by Shatabdi

Pay Range	*Entitlements*
₹ 16,400 and above	Executive Class
All others drawing pay below ₹ 16,400*	AC Chair Car

Those entitled to travel by First Class/AC 3-tier/ AC Chair Car may travel on tour/transfer by AC 2-tier, if any of the trains connecting the originating and destination stations by the direct shortest route do not provide for any of the three classes.

When journey is performed by longer route by rail, partly by lower class and partly by the entitled class, the claim is to be regulated on proportionate basis, by calculating mileage allowance for different modes/classes by the shortest route in the ratio of the distance covered by such modes by the longer actually used.

Mileage Allowance for Journeys by Road

Grade Pay	*Entitlement*
(*i*) Officers drawing grade pay of ₹ 18,400 and above and those in pay scales of HAG + and above	Actual fare by any type of public bus including air-conditioned bus *Or* At prescribed rates of AC Taxi when the journey is actually performed by AC Taxi *Or* At prescribed rates for auto rickshaw for journeys by autorickshaw, own scooter motor cycle, moped etc.
(*ii*) Officers drawing grade pay of ₹ 8000.00 to ₹ 18,400.00	Same as at (*i*) above with the exception that journeys by AC taxi will not be permissible
(*iii*) Officers drawing grade pay of ₹ 6500.00 to ₹ 8000.00	Same as at (*ii*) above
(*iv*) Officers drawing grade pay of ₹ 4100.00 and above but less than ₹ 6500.00	Actual fare by any type of public bus other than air-conditioned bus *Or* At prescribed rates for autorickshaw for journeys by autorickshaw/own scooter/motorcycle/moped etc.
(*v*) Officers drawing grade pay below ₹ 4100.00	Actual fare by ordinary public bus only *Or* At prescribed rates for autorickshaw/ own scooter/motorcycle/moped etc.

(*b*) Mileage allowance for road journeys shall be regulated at the following rates in places where no specific rates have been prescribed either by the Director of Transport of the concerned State or of the neighbouring States:

(*i*) For journeys performed in own car/taxi : ₹ 16 per km

(*ii*) For journeys performed by auto rickshaw own scooter, etc. : ₹ 8 per km

It is not necessary that the Car/Scooter/Moped should have been registered in the name of the staff member. The claim for taxi/auto rickshaw shall be regulated in accordance with the rates fixed by the State Transport Department.

4. Entitlement for journey by Air

All those who are in receipt of basic pay of ₹ 16,400 and above are entitled to travel by Air.

Those drawing basic pay of ₹ 12,300 and above may also travel by air if the distance involved is more than 500 km and the journey cannot be performed overnight (ordinarily covered between 6 p.m. and 8 a.m.) by direct train/direct slip coach service with approval of the authority competent to authorise the tour.

In all other cases specific approval of the Executive Director shall be required with justifications.

The entitled class of accommodation for travel by air is Economy/Standard Class.

5. Entitlement for journeys by Sea or by River Steamer

Grade Pay	*Entitlement*
Officers drawing grade pay of ₹ 8000.00 and above and those in pay scale of HAG + and above	Highest Class
Officers drawing grade pay of ₹ 6500.00 and above but less than ₹ 8000.00	If there be two classes only on the steamer, the lower class.
Officers drawing grade pay of ₹ 4100.00 to ₹ 6500.00	If there be two classes only on the steamer, the lower class If there be three classes, the middle or the second class If there be four classes, the third class
Officers drawing grade pay less than ₹ 4100.00	The lowest class

(*ii*) Accommodation entitlements for travel between the mainland and the A&N Group of Islands and Lakshadweep Group of Island by ships operated by the Shipping Corporation of India Limited will be as follows:

Grade Pay	*Entitlement*
Officers drawing grade pay of ₹ 8000.00 and above and those in pay scales of HAG + and above	Deluxe Class
Officers drawing grade pay of ₹ 6500.00 but less than ₹ 8000.00	First/'A' Cabin Class
Officers drawing grade pay of ₹ 4100.00 to ₹ 6500.00	Second/'B' Cabin Class
Officers drawing grade pay less than ₹ 4100.00	Bunk Class

6. Transportation of personal effects by Road

Pay Range	*A-I / A / B-I Class Cities*	*Other Cities*
	₹ per km	*₹ per km*
₹ 8000/- and above.	30.00	18.00
₹ 6500/- and above, but less than ₹ 8000/-	15.00	9.00
₹ 3350/- and above, but less than ₹ 6500/-	7.60	4.60
Below ₹ 3350/-	6.00	4.00

Note 1 : The allowance at hour rate mentioned in Col. (2) will be admissible, as at present, only for carriage of personal effects from one place to another within the limits of A-1/A/B-1 class cities.

Note 2 : Such of those employees as are in receipt of revised pay of ₹ 3,350 p.m. and above will, however, be entitled to the rates of allowance prescribed for the employees in the next higher pay range of ₹ 1,100 as above but less than 6,500. The higher rate mentioned in column (2) will be admissible in their cases as well only for carriage of personal effects from one place to another within the limits of A-1/A/B-1 Class cities.

In case of carriage of personal effects by road between places connected by rail, a Govt. servant can draw the actual expenditure on transportation of personal effects by road or the amount admissible on transportation of the maximum admissible quantity by rail and an additional amount of not more than 25 per cent thereof, whichever is less.

7. Mileage Allowance for journeys on foot or bicycle

The rate of Mileage Allowance for journeys on bicycle, on tour and transfer, is revised from 60 paise to ₹ 1.20 per kilometer.

13.2 DAILY ALLOWANCE ON TOUR

Grade Pay	*Daily Allowance*
Officers drawing grade pay of ₹ 16,400.00 and above and those in pay scales of HAG + and above	Reimbursement for Hotel accommodation/guest house of upto ₹ 5000 per day ; reimbursement of AC taxi charges of upto 50 kms. for travel within the city and reimbursement of food bills not exceeding ₹ 500 per day.
Officers drawing grade pay of ₹ 8000.00 to ₹ 16,400.00	Reimbursement for Hotel accommodation of upto ₹ 3000 per day ; reimbursement of AC taxi charges of upto 50 kms. per diem for travel within the city and reimbursement of food bills not exceeding ₹ 300 per day.
Officers drawing grade pay of ₹ 6500.00 to ₹ 8000.00	Reimbursement for Hotel accommodation of upto ₹ 1500 per day ; reimbursement of taxi charges of upto 150 per diem for travel within the city and reimbursement of food bills not exceeding ₹ 200 per day.
Officers drawing grade pay of ₹ 4100.00 to ₹ 6500.00	Reimbursement for Hotel accommodation of upto ₹ 500 per day ; reimbursement of travel charges of upto 100 per diem for travel within the city and reimbursement of food bills not exceeding ₹ 150 per day.
Officers drawing grade pay of below ₹ 4100.00	Reimbursement for Hotel accommodation of upto ₹ 300 per day ; reimbursement of travel charges of upto 50 per diem for travel within the city and reimbursement of food bills not exceeding ₹ 100 per day.

In case of stay/journey on Government ships, boats etc., or journey to remote places on foot/mules etc., for scientific/data collection purposes in organization like FSI, Survey of India, GSI etc., daily allowance will be paid at rate equivalent to that provided for reimbursement of food bill. However, in this case, the amount will be sanctioned irrespective of the actual expenditure incurred on this account with the approval of the Head of Department/ controlling officer. For journeys on foot, an allowance of ₹ 5 per kilometer travelled on foot shall be payable additionally.

(a) When a Council Servant stays in Govt / Public Sector Guest House or makes his own arrangements:

Pay range	*Localities other than those mentioned in col. (3), (4) & (5)*	*B-1 Class cities and expensive localities*	*A Class cities and specially expensive localities*	*A-1 Cities*
(1) ₹ 16400/- & above	135	170	210	260
(2) ₹ 8000/- & above, but less than 16400/-	120	150	185	230
(3) ₹ 6500/- & above, but less than 8000/-	105	130	160	200
(4) ₹ 4100/- & above, but less than 6500/-	90	110	135	170
(5) Below ₹ 4100/-	55	70	85	105

(b) ***When the Council servant stays in a hotel or other establishment providing boarding and/or lodging at Scheduled Tariffs***

Pay range	*Localities other than those mentioned in col. (3), (4) & (5)*	*B-1 Class cities and expensive localities**	*A Class cities and specially expensive localities**	*A-1 Cities*
₹ 16400/- & above	335	425	525	650
₹ 8000/- & above, but less than 16400/-	225	330	405	505
₹ 6500/- & above, but less than 8000/-	200	250	305	380
₹ 4100/- & above, but less than 6500/-	130	160	195	245
Below ₹ 4100/-	65	85	100	125

* as notified by the Govt. of India from time to time

13.3 DAILY ALLOWANCE

Absence from headquarters will be calculated on calendar day basis *i.e.,* from mid-night to mid-night and DA for each day will be as follows:

Absence not exceeding six hours	Nil
Absence exceeding six hours but not exceeding 12 hours	70%
Absence exceeding 12 hours	100%

If free Boarding and/or lodging are provided, the entitlement to DA will be as follows:

Free Boarding and lodging	... 25% of DA
Free boarding alone	... 50% of DA
Free lodging alone	... 75% of DA

DA for journey period will be at the ordinary rate.

All members are expected to stay in C-MET's guesthouse where this facility exists. If the employee makes alternate arrangements even when accommodation was available in the Guest House, the lodging charges shall be limited to one third of limits prescribed above.

Expenditure on Local Journey while on Tour. Expenditure on local journeys at the station of halt shall be reimbursed if it exceeds 10% of ordinary DA applicable to the place of halt limited to two DA per day of halt.

Procedure. The tour approval obtained from the competent authority contains sanction of TA advance also. Based on this sanction Finance will pay advance to the Official proceeding on tour. The Officer on completion of journey will prefer a final TA claim enclosing the air ticket in respect of the journey, hotel bills where claimed, used rail tickets, etc., based on which the claim will be finally admitted by Finance.

In case of officers not eligible to travel by air, prior approval of the competent authority should be obtained.

13.4 T.A. FOR LOCAL JOURNEYS

Local Journeys mean journeys on duty on any day beyond 8 km from the duty point at Headquarters and within the limits of suburban or other Municipalities, Notified Areas or Cantonments contiguous to the Municipality/ Corporation of the Town or City in which the duty point is located. Journeys performed within the limits of an Urban Agglomeration within which the employee's headquarter is located will also be treated as *'local journeys'*.

T.A. for local journeys : Mileage allowance for the journeys performed on all the days spent on temporary duty and in addition 50% of the admissible D.A. Option is available either to claim reimbursement of conveyance hire charges under Delegation of Financial Powers Rules or to claim normal T.A. as above.

T.A. for a local journey is admissible if the temporary place of duty is beyond 8 km from the normal place of duty, irrespective of whether the journey is performed from residence or from the normal place of duty.

Local journeys should normally be performed in the same way as journey to duty point, *i.e.,* by bus, local trains or own conveyance. Where travel by special means like taxi, scooter, etc., is considered necessary, prior permission of superior authority is necessary. If more than one official is deputed for duty at the same point, they should, as far as possible, travel together by sharing the hire charges of the taxi or scooter or other conveyance, if necessary, by assembling at the normal duty point.

For journeys to temporary duty point within a distance of eight kilometers from the residence, if performed by public conveyances, such as bus, local trains, trams and ferries, fares paid will be reimbursed. In case of travel by 'White line buses' plying in Delhi/New Delhi, reimbursement will be made on production of tickets. If such journeys are performed by taxi/auto rickshaw/own car/scooter, no mileage allowance is admissible.

The bus/rail fare/mileage allowance for local journeys should be based on the actual distance traveled or the distance between the normal duty point and temporary duty point, whichever is less.

If provided with conveyance free of charge, D.A. only will be admissible.

D.A. for *'local journeys'* will be admissible only at the ordinary rates. The special rates of D.A. prescribed in respect of certain expensive cities are not applicable to officers having headquarters in those cities and performing local journeys.

180 days limit: An official required to perform duty at a temporary duty point, will be paid D.A. for the first 180 days only. Beyond 180 days, no D.A. will be admissible.

13.4.1 TA When Deputed For Training

An employee deputed to undergo a course of training in India (refresher/in-service/pre-promotional) is entitled to draw T.A. and D.A. as on tour as follows:

When boarding and lodging not provided-

First 180 day: Full D.A.

Beyond 180 days: Nil

Training Institutes where boarding and lodging facilities exist (including mess run on co-operative basis at the training center)-

First 30 days: Full D.A.

Next 150 days: Half D.A.

Beyond 180 days: Nil

If the training exceeds 180 days, option to draw either T.A. as on transfer or tour T.A. plus D.A. for the first 180 days is available.

If theoretical training and practical training are given in two different stations, D.A. in the second station will commence afresh irrespective of whether D.A. was drawn for 180 days or less in the first station. If both theoretical and practical trainings are at the same station, D.A. will be admissible for the first 180 days only.

An employee on training at a particular station going on tour to another station will be entitled to draw D.A. at full rate for stay in the touring station, but this period will also be taken into account for computing 180 days of halt at the training station.

No T.A./D.A. is admissible for training at the headquarters irrespective of the distance between normal duty point and the training centre.

An employee drawing D.A. during training will be entitled to draw HRA and CCA only at the rates admissible at his headquarters from where he has been deputed to the training. Even beyond 180 days when no D.A. is admissible, the HRA and CCA will be admissible only at the rates admissible at his headquarters.

13.4.2 T.A. On Temporary Transfer

In all cases of transfers for short periods not exceeding 180 days, the journeys from headquarters to the station of deputation and back will be treated as on tour and D.A. granted for the first 180 days only.

Joining time is not admissible. Only actual transit time as for tour allowed.

No advance of pay is admissible.

If a transfer originally made for a period more than 180 days is reduced to 180 days or less later, the T.A. claim originally allowed should not be changed to the disadvantage of the official.

If a temporary transfer originally made for a period of 180 days or less is later extended beyond 180 days, the T.A. already drawn shall be adjusted in the transfer T.A. claim ; but D.A. is admissible up to the date of issue of the revised orders.

13.4.3 T.A. On Transfer

Transfer means the movement of an employee from headquarter/one station in which he is employed to another such station, either to take up the duties of a new post, or in consequence of a change of his headquarters.

Admissibility. Admissible only if the transfer is in the interest of C-MET and not at one's own request.

1. **Transfer T.A. entitlement.** Transfer T.A. comprises of the following elements:

(*i*) a composite transfer grant equal to one month's basic pay ;

(*ii*) actual fares for self and family for journey by rail/steamer/air ;

(*iii*) road mileage for journey by road between places not connected by rail ;

(*iv*) cost of transportation of personal effects from residence to residence ; and

(*v*) cost of transportation of conveyance possessed by the employee.

While the grade of the employee is determined with reference to the facts on the date of his transfer, the number of fares admissible is to be determined with reference to the facts on the date of journey. No travelling allowance is admissible for any member added to the family after the date of transfer.

In addition to the above, the employee will be entitled for an additional fare by the entitled class for self for both onward and return journeys, if he has to leave his family behind due to non-availability of Government accommodation at the new place of posting.

An employee whose family does not accompany him to the new station while joining on transfer, has an option to claim for him

either for the first journey undertaken to join the new post

or for the journey subsequently undertaken alongwith family members.

2. **At the Same Station.** No T.A. if no change of residence is involved.

If there is compulsory change of residence solely due to the transfer-

(*a*) Actual cost of conveyance for self and family limited to the road mileage and actual cost of transportation of personal effects admissible subject to the prescribed limits and

(*b*) Composite Transfer Grant equal to one-third of basic pay.

3. **Between two stations within a short distance not more than 20 km:**

No T.A. if no change of residence is involved. If change of residence is involved-

(*a*) Full transfer T.A. will be allowed and

(*b*) Composite transfer grant equal to one-third of basic pay.

4. **Definition of family:** Family includes, Spouse residing with the employee. (Need not be dependent). Only one wife is included in the term '*family*'.

Legitimate children and stepchildren, residing with and wholly dependent. Children include major sons, legally adopted children and widowed daughters, residing with and wholly dependent. Restricted to two children with effect from 1st January 1999. However, this restriction does not apply to existing employees with more than two children including those born up to 31-12-1998. Does not apply also to employees with no/one child on 31-12-1998 but next confinement resulting in multiple births thereby increasing the number to more than two.

Married daughter, if divorced, abandoned or separated from her husband and residing with the financially dependent on the parent.

Parents, stepmother, unmarried sisters and minor brothers residing with and wholly dependent. (Major brothers are not included).

Widowed sisters residing with and wholly dependent (provided their father is either not alive or is himself wholly dependent on the employee).

EXPLANATION

In the case of wife/husband, the necessary condition is—'*reading with*'. Other members of the family should satisfy both conditions—'*residing with*' and '*wholly dependent*'.

Children studying in educational institutions away from their parents at the time of transfer but joining their parents at the time of vacation are treated as members of family subject to other conditions for drawal of T.A.

Wards. Children taken as wards by the employee under the **"Guardians and Wards Act, 1890"** will be as treated as employee's children if the employee treats the ward as member of the family and through a special will gives the ward the same status as that of natural children.

Definition of dependent: Any family member whose income from all sources, including pension (inclusive of pension equivalent of DCRG, but excluding Dearness Relief) does not exceed ₹ 1,500 p.m., is deemed to be wholly dependent on the employee. Children getting stipend, scholarship, etc., in excess of ₹ 1,500 p.m. are not considered as dependents.

5. **For journeys by Rail/Road/Air/Steamer** entitlement will be as for journeys on tour.
6. **By road between places not connected by rail:** For journey by public bus, actual bus fare for self and each member of family is admissible and if the journey is performed otherwise than by public bus, mileage allowance at the appropriate rate will be admissible as follows:

   One mileage for self/self and one additional member;

   Two mileages if two members of family accompany;

   Three mileages if more than two members of family accompany.
7. **By road between places connected by rail:** Road mileage limited to rail mileage by the entitled class.

   Option to family -The family may travel-

   (*i*) from the old headquarters to the new headquarters; or

   (*ii*) from any other station to the new headquarters; or

   (*iii*) from the old headquarters to any other station.

   But the claim will be restricted to that admissible from the old to the new headquarters
8. **Time Limit:** The members of the family should perform the journey not earlier than one month prior to the date of relief at the old station or within six months of his taking over charge at the new station. This time limit can be extended in deserving cases by Head of Department.

Personal effects should be transported by goods train between places connected by rail. If transported by road, the actual expenditure or $1\frac{1}{4}$ times of the amount admissible for transport by goods train for the maximum admissible quantity, whichever is less, will be admissible.

9. Entitlements at a glance

Basic pay + NPA + Stagnation Increment	*Composite Transfer Grant*	*Personal effects*		
		By train / steamer	*Rate per km for transport by road*	
		Maximum	*'A-1', 'A' and 'B-1' cities*	*Other places*
₹ 16,400 & above	Equal to one Month's basic Pay + NPA + SI	Full four-wheeler wagon, or 6,000 kg by goods train, or one Double container	₹ 30.00	₹ 18.00
₹ 8,000 to 16,399	Equal to one month's basic pay + NPA + SI	Full four-wheeler Wagon, or 6000 kg by goods train, or one Single Container	₹ 30.00	₹ 18.00
₹ 6,500 to 7,999	-do-	3,000 kg	15.00	9.00
₹ 4,100 to 6,499	-do-	1,500 kg	7.60	4.60
₹ 3,350 to 4,099	-do-	1,500 kg	7.60	4.60
Below ₹ 3,350	-do-	1,000 kg	6.00	4.00

The higher rate of road mileage is admissible for transport of personal effects between one place and another within the limits of 'A -1', 'A' or 'B-1', Class cities.

The lower rate of road mileage is admissible for transport of personal effects between stations not connected by rail.

With a view to encouraging the adoption of small family norms by Central Govt. employees, it has also been decided that Travelling allowance on transfer will be restricted to only two depending children of an employee prior to issue of these orders. Further children of employees born up to 31.12.1998 will also be entitled for such benefits as are admissible under the Travelling allowance rules to employees and their families on transfer irrespective of the number of children that they may already have. The restriction shall also not be applicable in respect of those employees who are at present issue-less or have only one child and the subsequent pregnancy results in multiple births as a consequence of which the number of children exceeds two.

13.4.4 Transportation of Conveyance

Grade Pay	*Scale*
Officers drawing grade pay of ₹ 6500.00 and above and those in pay scales of HAG + and above	One motor car etc. or one motor cycle/scooter, or one horse
Officers drawing grade pay less than ₹ 6500.00	One motorcycle/scooter/ Moped, or one bicycle.

13.4.5 Transport by Rail

By Passenger: Actual freight charged by the Railway.

By Goods: Cost of packing, cost of transporting the packed car, motor cycle to and from the goods-shed, cost of crating the car, loading and unloading charges, cost of ropes, etc., are all reimbursable. Claim to be limited to the amount under para above.

One Second Class fare by the shortest route between the stations from and to which the car is actually transported by rail can be drawn for a Chauffeur or Cleaner.

13.4.6 Transport by Road

Car/scooter or motor cycle/moped

Mode of transportation	*Between places connected by rail*	*Between places not connected by rail*
When the conveyance is sent loaded on a truck	Actual expenses/amount at the prescribed rate */ cost of transportation by passenger train, whichever is the least.	Actual expenses are limited to the amount at the prescribed rate*.
When the conveyance is sent under its own propulsion.	Amount at the prescribed rate* limited to cost of transportation by passenger train.	Amount at the prescribed rate*.
* *Prescribed rate:* The rate prescribed for journey by taxi/auto rickshaw, as the case may be, by the Director of Transport at the starting point		

Note. When the conveyance is sent under its own propulsion, the employee /members of family traveling in the car will not be entitled to separate fare by air/rail/road mileage. Separate air/rail/road mileage will be admissible for the employee and/or members of family if they travel otherwise than by the conveyance being transported under its own propulsion.

Bicycle: Between the places connected by rail, actual cost of transportation limited to the freight charges by passenger train; between places not connected by rail, mileage at the rate of 60 P. per km.

13.5 LUMPSUM TRANSFER GRANT AND PACKING ALLOWANCE

(*i*) The composite transfer grant equal to a month's pay last drawn as defined in para 3 of this O.M., may be granted in the case of those employees who, on retirement, settle down at places other than the last station(s) of their duty located at a distance of or more than 20 kms. The transfer incidentals and road mileage for journeys between the residence and the railway station/bus stand, etc., at the old and new station, presently admissible are subsumed in the composite transfer grant and will not be separately admissible.

(*ii*) As in the case of serving employees, government servants who, on retirement, settle at the last station of duty itself or within a distance of less than 20 kms may be paid one third of the composite transfer grant subject to the condition that a change of residence is actually involved.

The TA/DA rates mentioned in para 2 D(b) and (c) (mileage for road journey by taxi/ own car/ autorickshaw/ own scooter/ bicycle etc.), para (3) (all components of daily allowance on tour including rate of DA for journey on foot) and para 4(c) (rates of transportation of personal effects) of this Annexure, shall automatically increase by 25% whenever Dearness Allowance payable on the revised pay structure goes up by 50%.

13.6 T.A. ON RETIREMENT

13.6.1 Entitlements

When the retired employee settles down in a station other than the last station of duty: - Same as on transfer including lumpsum Composite Transfer Grant. Travel by air is also admissible.

The retired employee and family may travel from the last headquarters to the declared Hometown, or to any other selected place of residence where he wishes to settle.

When the person settles down in the last station of duty but with change of residence or at a place not exceeding 20 km:

Self and family	Actual cost of conveyance not exceeding the road mileage allowance admissible for transfer.
Personal effects	Actual cost of transportation not exceeding the amount admissible for transfer.
Transportation of Conveyance	An allowance at the rates prescribed by the Director of Transport for journey by taxi/ auto rickshaw, as the case may be. Where the above allowance is claimed, no mileage will be admissible for self. If the family also travels by the same conveyance, they will also not be entitled to mileage allowance.
Composite Transfer Grant	Amount equal to one-third of his Basic pay.

Note: The last station of duty means and includes the areas falling within the Urban Agglomeration of such station.

T.A. not admissible on Resignation, Dismissal, etc. The concession is admissible only to persons who retire on retiring pension or on superannuation, invalid or compensation pension. It is not admissible to employees who quit service by resignation or who may be dismissed or removed from service. The concession is also not admissible to persons who are compulsorily retired as a measure of punishment.

Time Limit: The concession should be availed by the employee during leave preparatory to retirement or within one year of the date of his retirement.

Advances: Advances may be sanctioned only when the journey is performed during leave preparatory to retirement. Advance will be limited to the amount to which the employee may be entitled under the rules, and will be adjusted in full on submission of the T.A. Bill. No advance is admissible when the journey is performed after retirement.

13.7 T.A. TO THE FAMILY OF A DECEASED EMPLOYEE

1. **Entitlements:** Same as for retirement.

The family of an employee who dies in service may travel from the last headquarters of the employee to the Hometown, or to any other selected place of residence where the family wishes to settle down.

If at the time of the death of the employee any member of his family happens to be at a station other than his headquarters, such member may travel from that station to the Hometown or selected place of residence. But the claim will be restricted to what is admissible from the last headquarters to the Hometown or selected place of residence, as the case may be.

If any member of the employee's family proceeds from the last headquarters to a place other than the selected place of residence, the claim will be restricted to what is admissible from the last headquarters to the selected place of residence.

The journey should be completed within one year after the date of death.

The concession is not admissible to families of (*a*) Employees who die while on leave preparatory to retirement; and Retired employees who are re-employed.

2. **Advance of T.A:** (*a*) Amount - Limited to three-fourths of the probable amount of traveling expenses admissible under the rules.
3. **Conditions:** (1) Only one member of the family can receive on behalf of all. (2) Only one advance is admissible. (3) Surety of a permanent employee of comparable or higher status is necessary. (4) An undertaking from the person receiving the advance to abide by the conditions for recovery is also necessary.
4. **Recovery:** - (1) Account should be rendered within one month of the completion of the journey if the family travels in one batch. (2) If the family travels in more than one batch, account to be rendered within one month of completion of the journey by the last batch. (3) In any case, the journeys should be completed within one year and account rendered within one month thereof. Otherwise, the amount should be refunded.

13.8 ADVANCE OF T.A. ON TOUR

1. **Amount:** (1) An amount sufficient to cover the official's personal traveling expenses for a month, viz., daily allowance, road/rail/air fares, for journeys both ways. (2) In the case of prolonged tour in the interior, to places difficult of access, an amount sufficient to cover daily allowance, road/rail/air fares and contingent charges such as for the hire of conveyance, conveyance of records, tents, etc., for six weeks.
2. **Eligibility:** All cases where T.A. is admissible as for a journey on tour.
3. **Conditions:** The advance should be adjusted within fifteen days of completion of the tour/rejoining duty if gone on leave immediately on completion of tour. A second advance cannot be sanctioned until an account has been given of the first except when a second journey is required to be undertaken soon after the completion of the first leaving no time for the employee to prefer his T.A. Bill in respect of the first advance.
4. **Recovery:** By adjustment from the T.A. Bill submitted after completion of the journey.

13.9 ADVANCE OF PAY AND T.A. ON TRANSFER

1. **Amount.** One month's pay in cases of normal transfer.

Two months' pay if the transfer is due to shift of headquarters as a result of policy decision.

Advance of pay can be taken at the new station, if so desired.

In addition, advance of T.A. as admissible under the rules, for self and family. This can be drawn either in one installment or separately for self and family in two installments.

2. **Eligibility.** Employees under orders of transfer, including those on leave.

Employees proceeding on Foreign Service in India or on reversion from such service.

Not admissible when the transfer is at official's request and not in public interest.

Not admissible when the transfer is within the same station.

3. **Recovery.** Advance of pay of one-month—In not more than 3 installments.

Advance of pay of two months—In 24 installments.

Monthly rate of recovery should be in whole rupees, the balance being recovered in the last installment.

Should commence from the month in which the official draws a full month's pay and/or leave salary after joining new appointment.

Advance of T.A. should be recovered in full from the T.A. Bill.

13.10 TOURS ABROAD

Cases of Foreign tours/visits in regard of Executive Director/ Director/Head of Laboratory in the grade ₹ 18,400-450-22,400 and above will require the approval of Chairman, Governing Council and such visits by other officers including Head of the Laboratories will require the approval of the Executive Committee.

TA/DA on foreign visit shall be applicable as per Government orders. However, hotel charges will be paid on actual basis or as per the entitlement as fixed by Indian Embassies in the respective countries for equivalent grade officers in government, since such facility may not be available to them from concerned embassies of the government. To avoid inconvenience to ascertain entitlement as fixed by Indian Embassies. Hotel charges shall be same as the rate of daily allowance for the respective countries. The rates of Daily Allowance are the same throughout a country.

Full Daily Allowance shall be applicable up to 14 days, 75% of Full Daily Allowance for the next 14 days, and 60% of full Daily Allowance thereafter in case of long tours/Temporary duties including long term training, deputation etc.

The rates of Daily Allowance fixed for various grades of officers do not include any element towards cost of transport for official journeys. Accordingly, the actual cost of taxi or conveyance hired for trips on duty, which is considered necessary and reasonable to the controlling authority, will be reimbursed to the officers subject to specific provision of funds in the sanction order sanctioning the deputation/delegation.

Where the officer makes his own arrangements for accommodation or where accommodation alone is provided free, he shall be granted Daily Allowance only at the rate prescribed for his Grade.

Hotel entitlement of officers going abroad or non-representational visits such as training courses on seminars shall be equal to half DA under normal entitlement.

Where an officer is treated as State Guest and is provided all meals free of cost, only 25% of the daily allowance rates shall be admissible. Where the hotel charges include breakfast charges, the Daily Allowance shall be reduced by 10%.

In the case of countries, where local currencies are freely convertible, the equivalent amount of prescribed Daily Allowance in US Dollars for the country concerned may be paid in the local currency. The local currency equivalent may be arrived at via Rupee, by using the official rates of exchange fixed by the Ministry from time to time. In the case of Missions where local currencies are not freely convertible, the prescribed Daily Allowance for the country concerned may be paid in US Dollars.

Visa Fees will be reimbursed and if there is any sponsoring agency then the sponsoring agency has to reimburse the cost of Visa Fees.

Travel Class. Members shall travel by Economy Class. Members shall be allowed to make intercity travel abroad by appropriate train/bus service as admissible. The foreign currency requirement admissible against D.A. Accommodation, Intercity travel, etc., will be collected by the member prior to his/her departure.

Medical Insurance. All the members undertaking foreign tour will be entitled to reimbursement against medical insurance. Members will be able to claim this amount at the time of settling their foreign tour claim.

D.A. and Accommodation charges will be calculated for the number of nights spent in the foreign country. One additional DA (excluding hotel charges) shall be allowed towards to and fro journey time.

Table 13.10. Tour TA when Certain Facilities are Provided

Facility	*TA admissible*	*Remarks*
1. Two or more officers travelling in conveyance belonging to one of them	Owner gets full TA, Others get only DA	See SR-6
2. Free railway pass is provided.	Rail fare is deducted	SR-176
3. Two or more officers share hire of a taxi	Each may draw the actual share of the hire paid limited to half the entitled rate in addition to DA	SR-46

(cont.)

4. Free airlift	Only DA is admissible	SR-181-A
5. Free road transport and combined with rail journey	Actual rail fare plus DA	SR-182
6. Free transport	Only DA admissible	SR-182
7. Treated as state guest	1/4 DA if both boarding and lodging is provided If only free board is provided 1/2 DA If only free lodging is provided 3/4 DA	SR-51
8. For stay in office premises	Three-fourth DA	SR-51
9. Free stay in Circuit House/Inspection bunglow/Rest house	Full DA if electric charges are paid, otherwise 3/4 DA	SR-51
10. Journey by friend's scooter sharing cost of proportion	Mileage allowance as for sharing automobile	SR-46

13.11 LEAVE TRAVEL CONCESSION

1. **Eligibility.** Any employee with one year of continuous service on the date of journey performed by him/his family is eligible.

Example: An official appointed on 31-12-2002 will be eligible for the two-year block 2002-03, but those appointed on or after 1-1-2003, will not be eligible for that block.

Employees whose spouses are working in Indian Railways/ National Airlines are not eligible for LTC.

Period of unauthorized absence, declared so under rules, will be treated as break in service for calculating the continuous period of service, unless the break is condoned by the Competent Authority.

If an official is under suspension, the concession is admissible only to his family members.

When both the husband and wife are Employees either of them is a Central Government employee, they can declare separate Home towns independently; they can claim LTC for their respective families, viz., while the husband can claim for his parents/minor brothers/sisters, the wife can avail for her parents/minor brothers/ sisters; either of the parents can claim the concession for the children in a particular block; the husband/wife who avails LTC as a member of the family of the spouse, cannot claim independently for SELF.

2. **'Family' means**–The wife or husband and two surviving unmarried children or stepchildren wholly dependent on the Employee irrespective of whether they are residing with the Employee or not; married daughters divorced, abandoned or separated from their husbands and widowed daughters and are residing with the Employee of and wholly dependent on the Employee.

Parents and/or stepmother residing with and wholly dependent on the Employee ;

Unmarried minor brothers as well as unmarried, divorced, abandoned, separated from their husbands or widowed sisters residing with and wholly dependent on the Employee, provided their parents are either not alive or are themselves wholly dependent on the Employee.

3. **Explanations.** The restriction of the concession to only two surviving children or stepchildren shall not be applicable in respect of (*i*) those employees who already have more than two children prior to 20-10-1998; (*ii*) where the number of children exceeds two as a result of second child birth resulting in multiple births.

Only one wife is included in the term "*Family*" for LTC Rules. However, if an Employee has two legally wedded wives and the second marriage is with the specific permission of the Government, the second wife shall also be included in the definition of "*Family*".

It is not necessary for the spouse and children to reside with the Employee so as to be eligible for the concession. The concession in their cases shall, however, be restricted to the actual distance traveled or the distance between the headquarters of the Employee and the Home town/place of visit, whichever is less.

Children of divorced, abandoned, separated from their husbands or widowed sisters are not included in the term "*Family*".

A member of the family whose income from all sources, including stipend, or pension, temporary increase in pension but excluding Dearness Relief does not exceed ₹ 1,500 p.m. is deemed to be wholly dependent on the Employee. As and when Government of India issues any changes in this income limit it will be applicable mutatis mutadis.

Husband and wife is one unit for purpose of LTC and hence the condition of dependency is not applicable.

4. Salient Points

Concession can be availed of for self and family separately on different occasions, even in different calendar years of the same block.

Family can travel in one or more group ; but each group should complete its return journey within six months from the date of its outward journey.

Circular tour tickets can be availed of in conjunction with the concession.

Can be availed of during any leave including study leave, casual leave and special casual leave.

While on study leave, the entitlement will be as under:

Family staying with Employee, from place of study to Hometown limited to admissibility from headquarters to Hometown.

Normal Hometown entitlement and can be combined with transfer/tour.

Cannot be availed of during closed holidays only, without taking any leave.

Carry forward. Concession for one block can be carried forward to the first year of the next block, *i.e.*, the outward journey for 2009-2010 block can be performed up to 31-12-2011. Employees entitled to LTC to Hometown for self-alone every year cannot carry forward the concession.

Hometown concession by some members of the family and "*any where in India*" by others in the same two-year block permissible–Some members of family may avail the concession to Hometown while others may avail the same for "*anywhere in India*" in the same two-year block.

5. Entitlements:

(*a*) **Journey by Air/Rail:** Pay Ranges ₹ 18,400 and above: Air Economy (Y) Class by National Carrier.

Pay Range	*Shatabdi Express*	*Rajdhani Express*	*Other Trains*
₹ 16,400 and above	Executive Class	AC First Class	AC First Class
₹ 8,000 to ₹ 16,399	AC Chair Car	AC 2-tier	AC 2-tier
₹ 4,100 to ₹ 7,999	-do-	AC 3-tier	*First Class/ AC 3-tier/AC Chair Car
Below ₹ 4,100	Not Entitled	Not Entitled	Sleeper Class

*All Employee who are entitled to travel on LTC at their discretion by First Class/AC 3-tier/AC Chair Car may, travel by AC 2-tier, in cases where any of the trains connecting the originating and destination stations by the direct shortest route do not provide these three classes of accommodation.

Notes:

Entitlement by Rajdhani Express/Shatabdi Trains up to an *en route* railway station by direct shortest route and thereafter the journey is completed in a train other than Rajdhani/Shatabdi Trains, fare for both the types of trains by the entitled class will be admissible for the respective portion of journey.

If the journey is performed partly by Rajdhani/Shatabdi Trains and partly by other trains/modes of transport, the claim shall be reimbursable subject to the condition that the shortest route performs the journey.

The journey can be performed by Rajdhani/Shatabdi Trains up to the nearest en *route* station which should not be beyond the destination, *i.e.*, Hometown or declared place of visit.

(*b*) **Journey by Sea or by River Steamer:**

Pay Range Officers drawing pay	*A & N Islands and Lakshadweep Islands (Shipping Corp. of India)*	*Others*
₹ 8,000 and above	Deluxe Class	Highest Class
₹ 6,500 to ₹ 7,999	First/"A" Cabin Class	If there be two classes only on the steamer, the lower class
₹ 4,100 to ₹ 6,499	"Second/B" Cabin Class	If there be three classes, the middle or second class. If there be four classes, the third class
Below ₹ 4,100	Bunk Class	The lowest class

(*c*) **Journey by Road:**

	Pay Range	*Entitlement*
1	₹ 8,000 and above	Actual fare by any type of public bus, including Air-Conditioned bus
2	₹ 4,100 and above but less than ₹ 7,999	Same as at (*i*) above with exception that journeys by Air-Conditioned bus will not be permissible
3	Below ₹ 4,100	Bus fare by ordinary bus

Restrictions in respect of road journeys

Admissible for journeys performed in vehicles operated by Tourist Development Corporations in Public Sector, State Transport Corporation and Transport services run by other Government or local bodies, *i.e.*, the receipt for the journey should be from the Government Body concerned for eligibility of LTC.

Admissible for travel by private buses operating as regular service from point to point at regular intervals on fixed fare rates with the approval of Regional Transport Authority /State Government Concerned.

No reimbursement permissible for journeys undertaken (*a*) in a private car (owned, hired or borrowed), chartered railway coach, or chartered bus, van or other vehicle owned/chartered by private operators; (*b*) in vehicles even if owned by Government Bodies but chartered/run by private operators.

Journeys by taxi, auto rickshaw, etc., are permissible only between places not connected by rail. Journey by these modes on LTC between places connected by rail is not permissible.

Between places not connected by rail, if more than one State Roadways Corporation operates on the route, the lowest fare applicable on the route is reimbursable.

6. Reimbursement

Fares for journeys between duty station and Hometown, both ways, will be reimbursed in full. If the employee and family reside away from the duty station, fares for journeys between place of residence and Hometown, both ways, restricted to that from duty station to Hometown and back will be reimbursed in full. Reservation charges are reimbursable; but telegram charges for reservation of onward/return journeys, etc., are not reimbursable.

7. Advance

Up to 90% of the fare can be taken. Advance admissible for both outward and return journeys if the leave taken by the official or the anticipated absence of members of family does not exceed 90 days. Otherwise, advance may be drawn for the outward journey only.

The official should furnish Railway ticket numbers, PNR No., etc., to the Competent Authority within ten days of drawal of the advance. Advance can be drawn separately for self and family.

Claim. When advance is taken; the claim should be submitted within one month from the date of return journey. If not, outstanding advance will be recovered in one lumpsum and the claim will be treated as one where no advance is sanctioned. Further, penal interest at 2% over CPF interest on the entire advance from the date of drawal to the date of recovery will be charged.

When claim submitted within stipulated time but unutilized portion of advance not refunded, interest is chargeable on that amount from the date of drawal to the date of recovery.

When a part of the advance becomes excess drawal due to genuine reasons beyond the control of the Employee of C-MET, the Administrative Authority may, if satisfied, exempt charging of interest.

When no advance is taken, claim should be submitted within three months from the completion of return journey. Otherwise, the claim will be forfeited.

13.11.1 LTC to Home Town

Admissible to all employees irrespective of the distance involved.

Hometown once declared is treated as final. In exceptional circumstances, the Head of the Department may authorize a change, only once during entire service.

Admissible once in a block of two calendar years. The blocks are 2007-08, 2009-10 and so on.

An employee (including unmarried) having his family at his Hometown can avail of this concession for himself alone every year instead of having it for both self and family once in two years.

13.11.2 LTC to Any Place in India

This concession is admissible in lieu of one of the two journeys to Home Town in a block of four years. The current block is 2007-08. The last date for commencement of the outward journey is 31-12-2009 (including the grace period of one year).

Available for travel to any place in India-mainland or overseas-including employee's Hometown.

Officials availing LTC to Hometown for self-alone once every year, are not entitled to LTC to anywhere in India.

Spouse/dependent children residing away from Employee's headquarters: Claim will be limited to the amount admissible from the employee's headquarters to the declared place of visit.

Different places: Members of family can visit either the same place as that visited by the Employee or different places.

Different batches: Members of family can travel in one or more batches, as the case may be. Each batch should complete the return journey within six months of its outward journey.

Different calendar years: Members of family can travel either in the same calendar year or in different years in respect of the same block.

Intended place of visit to be declared: The intended place of visit should be declared by the official to the Controlling Authority in advance.

Change in the declared place of visit: Any change in the declared place of visit should be intimated to the Controlling Authority before commencement of the outward journey. If, however, it is established that the request could not be made before commencement of the outward journey for reasons beyond the control of the official, change of destination can be admitted by the Head of Administration.

Carry forward: Concession not availed in a block of four years can be carried forward to the first year of the next four-year block. In respect of the officials entitled to Hometown LTC, the concession can be carried forward to the first year of the next block only if the official is entitled to a carried forward LTC to Hometown for that year.

Example. Suppose an official is entitled to two concessions during the two blocks of 2007-08 and 2009-10.

(*i*) In respect of 2007-08 the can avail the concession to Hometown before the grace period, *i.e.*, by 31-12-2009. Then he is entitled to carry forward his LTC to anywhere in India to be availed before the grace period, *i.e.*, by 31-12-2011.

(*ii*) In the above case, suppose the official avails of LTC to Hometown after 31-12-2009. This will be debited against the block 2009-10 and hence he will not be entitled to "*anywhere in India LTC*". In this case, he will lose his entitlement for 2007-08 by not availing it before the grace period.

13.11.3 LTC for Escort

Escort to single handicapped employee : LTC is admissible to an escort accompanying handicapped employee proceeding on LTC journey provided that—

(*i*) The nature of physical disability is such as to necessitate an escort.

(*ii*) The physically handicapped employee does not have an adult family member.

(*iii*) Any other employee entitled to LTC does not accompany the physically handicapped employee on the journey.

(*iv*) Prior approval of the Head of Department is obtained on each occasion.

(v) Concessions, if any, allowed by the Railways/Bus services should be availed.

13.11.4 Encashment of EL during LTC

Encashment of earned leave while availing LTC: Will be admissible subject to the following condition:

(*i*) Limited to 10 days of earned leave on one occasion and 60 days in the entire career.

(*ii*) Will be taken into account while computing the maximum admissible for encashment at the time of quitting service.

(*iii*) At least equal number of days of earned leave should be availed along with encashment.

(*iv*) The balance at credit should be not less than 30 days after deducting the total of leave availed plus leave for which encashment was availed.

The misuse of LTC shall be dealt with as per provisions contained under CCS(LTC) Rules.

13.12 PENSION

Pension is a periodic payment made to public servants who have completed their service. The pension rules provide for various kinds of pension based on the nature of retirement, duration of service, and mode of retirement under statutory rules.

Future good conduct is an implied condition for the grant of pension or its continuance. Pension could be withheld or withdrawn for conviction or serious crime or grave misconduct of the pensioner after following certain formalities. Pensioners are prohibited to be member or associated with communal organisations as decided by Government and the pension could be withheld or withdrawn. Such reduction in pension shall not ordinarily be made at a rate exceeding one third of the pension subject to entitlement of minimum pension.

1. **Superannuation Pension**

A Government employee is retired on superannuation on the afternoon of the last day of the month in which he or she attained the age of 58 years in case of superior service and 60 years in case of basic service, and the pension sanctioned is called *superannuation pension*. Based on the duration of service or qualifying service and average emoluments the pension is paid. Previously it was 33 years of qualifying service to get 50% of average emoluments as pension. From 1.4.2003, maximum qualifying service has been enhanced to 33 years from 30 years to become eligible for full pension and the pension is determined based on the average emoluments drawn during the last 10 months of service rendered.

2. Retiring Pension or Pension on Voluntary Retirement

A Government employee is permitted to retire voluntarily, if he has completed 20 years of qualifying service or 50 years of age. He should give 3 months notice and there is no provision for waiver of the notice period. He should join duty if he has gone on leave and then retire. If a bond was executed to serve the Government till a particular date, then he could not be allowed to go on voluntary retirement. Voluntary retirement notice can be withdrawn before the expiry of notice period with the approval of the appointing authority. In cases of voluntary retirement, the employee is given additional weightage of service in addition to the actual service, which will add to the qualifying service for pension.

Actual Qualifying Service	*Weightage in Years*	*Age at date of Voluntary Retirement*		*Weightage in years*
		Superior Service	*Basic Service*	
25 yrs and below	5	53 yrs & below	55 yrs & below	5
26 years	4	54 years	56 years	4
27 years	3	55 years	57 years	3
28 years	2	56 years	58 years	2
29 years	1	57 years	59 years	1
29 years	Nil	58 years	60 years	Nil

The other conditions for calculation of pension are the same as for Superannuation Pension.

3. Pension on Absorption in or under a Corporation or Government or Body

When a Government employee is permitted to be absorbed in a Corporation or company owned or controlled by Government or autonomous body a Pro rata Pension shall be calculated with reference to his service under Government at the time of absorption. But the actual payment of pension will be made from the date of his actual retirement from the institution in which he was absorbed. In such cases there is no liability of Government to pay family pension in case of his death. In a few cases, Government allowed lump sum payment in lieu of monthly pension even prior to the date of retirement like TANSI CASE in 1970's.

4. Invalid Pension

If a Government employee has become permanently incapacitated for further service and declared so by an appropriate authority, he will be granted an invalid pension. Once invalidation is accepted, he cannot seek employment even if he produces a certificate of fitness at a later date. If he is on unearned leave on medical certificate and he is invalidated, then he need not join duty as per leave rule 15A. In addition to his pension and other benefits admissible under rules, one of his dependents may get appointment on compassionate grounds if the invalidated employee has not completed 53 years of age on the date.

5. Compensation Pension

If a Government employee is selected for discharge for owing to abolition of his permanent post, he has option either to accept another post offered to him or taking compensation pension to which he may be entitled for the service he has rendered.

6. Compulsory Retirement Pension

A Government employee can be compulsorily retired by the competent authority in public interest, after giving him notice of not less than 3 months or 3 months salary in lieu of such notice after he has attained the age of 50 years (55 years in case of basic servants) or after he has completed 30 years of qualifying service. Further, Rule provide for imposing a punishment of compulsory retirement as a result of disciplinary action. He will be entitled to the normal pension under rules, if he is compulsorily retired under FR 56(2). If he is retired as a result of disciplinary action as a penalty, an appropriate authority may impose such penalty on Pension or Gratuity or both and allow Pension and Gratuity not less than two thirds and not more than full compensation entitlements. This will not be less than the minimum pension admissible.

7. Compassionate Allowance

In case of Government employees dismissed, or removed from service, normally no pension or gratuity is payable. But the competent authority may in deserving case sanction Compassionate allowance not more than two third of pension or gratuity or both which would have been admissible, if he had retired on medical certificate subject to the minimum pension. Such allowance is not admissible in case of dismissal or removal under Provision (c) to clause 2 of Article 311 of the Constitution of India for anti-national activities.

8. Qualifying Service

To obtain pension, the employee must have qualifying service of prescribed duration. All regular pensionable service, temporary service excluding break, half of contingent service, work charged service, Central Government service before joining state service, Military service, Service in local body excluding break, service in State Government before absorption in undertakings, Extraordinary leave to go for higher studies, service prior to resignation to take up another appointment in State Government shall be treated as qualifying service.

Apprentice service, Extraordinary leave without medical certificate, suspension as penalty, boy service, over stayal of joining time, unauthorised absence, interruption in service, service in non pensionable post do not count for qualifying service (Pension rules 11 to 25) Resignation from service or post entails forfeiture of past service. For purpose of pension, the minimum qualifying service is 10 years (20 half years) and maximum 33 years (66 half years). The fraction of three months and more shall be taken as one half year and less than three months ignored.

To get full pension, the qualifying service required at various points of time were:

	Prior to 1960	*30 years*
From 01.06.1960	30 years	G.O. 710 Fin 10.07.1960*
From 02.10.1970	25 years	228 Fin 08.02.1971*
From 01.01.1973	30 years	601 Fin 27.04.1974
From 01.10.1979	33 years	57 Fin 02.02.1980*
From 01.07.1996	30 years	461 Fin 31.07.1996
From 01.04.2003	33 years	71 Fin 19.03.2003

* From 1.06.1960 the pension was admissible at 30/80 of average emoluments at the retirement age of 55 years.

\# In case of 30 years of qualifying service addition of 3 years allowed G.O. 397 Fin 14.06.1984 from 01.10.1984.

9. Average Emoluments

The quantum of pension is based on the percentage of average emoluments drawn by the employee during the 36 months prior to date of retirement upto 31.05.1960, @ 50% ; 30/80 upto 25.02.1970 ; 12 months @ 30/80 upto 31.12.1973 ; 10 months @ 30/80 upto 30.09.1979 @ graded percentage of 50%, 45%, 40% from 01.10.1979 to 13.12.1987 and @ 50% of average emoluments of 10 months from 14.12.1987 to 30.06.1996 and @ 50% of average emoluments of 10 months or pay last drawn on the date of retirement whichever is advantageous from 01.07.1996. From 01.04.2003 onwards, the quantum of pension is based on the average emoluments drawn during the last 10 months of service. Till 30.09.1984 there was a ceiling on maximum pension and from 01.10.1984 the ceiling was removed.

Example:

Date of Birth	*20.09.1942*
Date of Commencement of Service	*10.04.1965*
Date of retirement	*30.09.2000*
Qualifying Service	*30.09.2000 – 10.04.1965*
	= 35 years 5 months 20 days.

Non qualifying Service Nil.

Emoluments from 1st July 1999, Pay ₹5875 + Special Pay ₹50 + Personal Pay ₹50. From 1st July 2000, Pay ₹6000 + Special Pay ₹50 + Personal Pay ₹50 in the Scale of ₹4500-125-7000. Pay last drawn ₹6100/-.

Total pay for 7 months	:	*5975 × 7*	=	*₹ 41,825*
Total pay for 3 months	:	*6100 × 3*	=	*₹ 18,300*
Total pay for 10 months	:			*₹ 60,125*

Average emoluments is ₹ **6012.50/-.**

10. Provisional Pension

The retired employee to whom the Accountant General's authorisation is not received in time due to administrative reason, shall be sanctioned provisional pension and gratuity. This can be allowed in the following cases also:

(*i*) In respect of officers who are permitted to retire without prejudice to the pending disciplinary proceedings.

(*ii*) Cases where pension could not be assessed for want of details of qualifying services and other particulars.

100% of pension admissible will normally be allowed as provisional pension. It can be sanctioned by Government in respect of head of department, by Head of department in respect of self drawing officers and by heads of offices in respect of other employees. In addition to the Provisional pension, D.A., Medical allowance shall also be paid to the retired official. The head of office shall draw provisional pension for a period of 12 months in the first instance and thereafter as extended by the Accountant General. In respect of self drawing Gazetted Officers, the A.G. shall authorise anticipatory pension pending finalisation of pension proposals.

11. Revision of Pension

The Pension schemes were modified from time to time and in particular with every Pay Commission/recommendation and various important changes are listed below:

(*i*) Till 31.05.1960 when the age of retirement was 55 years, the Pension was regulated at 50 % of average emoluments based on 36 months pay. There was no gratuity scheme.

(*ii*) With the Liberalised Pension Scheme introduced in 1960, pension was allowed for 10 years of service upto 30 years from 01.06.1960 @ 10/80 to 30/80 of average emoluments. Gratuity upto maximum of 15 months pay was allowed.

(*iii*) From 02.10.1970 it was revised to have full pension for 25 years of service @ 15/80 for 10 years for qualifying service and 30/80 for 25 years of qualifying service.

(*iv*) The duration for calculating average emoluments was reduced from 36 months to 12 months from 26.02.1970 and it was ordered to include D.A. as on 31.12.1966 for purpose of arriving average emoluments. Based on the court decision, the concession of adding D.A. for average emoluments was extended to those who retired prior to 26.02.1970 also.

(*v*) For those retired from 01.02.1975 to 31.03.1978, the D.A. of ₹ 55 up to the average emoluments of ₹ 299 and ₹ 70 for the emoluments of ₹ 300 and above was treated as dearness pay and counted for average emoluments.

(*vi*) From 01.04.1978, the pension was revised based on the third pay commission as follows:

Pension as on 31.03.1978.

Add DA and Ad hoc increase upto 31.03.1978. 5 % on pension subject to minimum of ₹ 10 and maximum of ₹ 25.

(*vii*) From 01.10.1979, the quantum of pension was regulated in slab system as 50% on the first ₹ 1000 of average emoluments, 45% on the next ₹ 500 and 40% on the balance of average emoluments. To obtain full pension, the qualifying service was fixed at 33 years. The slab system was modified with uniform rate of 50% of average emoluments from 14.12.1987. The existing pensioners with the pension fixed under the slab system were entitled for the benefits and the Accountant General was required to revise pension without any application from the pensioners.

(*viii*) The liberalised pension formula adopted was given effect to those retired on or after 30.09.1979. Based on court decision, Government have extended the benefit of the formula to all the pensioners and the existing pension of all those retired prior to 30.09.1979 were revised with the monetary effect from 01.10.1979. With 4 Groups of ready reckoner:

Pensioner	retired prior to	01.07.1960
Pensioner	retired between	01.07.1960 to 25.02.1970
Pensioner	retired between	26.02.1970 to 31.03.1978
Pensioner	retired between	01.04.1978 to 30.09.1979.

Based on further representation it was modified in G.O. 742 Fin 25.10.1988.

(*ix*) Based on the fourth pay commission report, the pension was revised as follows:

Pension

Add Adhoc increase ₹ 20

Percentage increase:

30% for those retired prior to 01.06.1960

15%/ 30% # from 01.06.1962 to 01.10.1970

10% from 02.10.1970 to 31.03.1978

7% from 01.04.1978

D.A. at 528 points as on 01.05.1984.

This was given effect from 01.10.1984.

(*x*) Based on the Fifth Pay Commission report, the pension was revised as follows from 01.06.1988:

Pension. Add D.A. at 608 points as on 01.05.1986 as per:

Period	*Percentage of Increase*	
	Pension of ₹ 500	*Above ₹ 500*
Retired prior to 01.06.1960	60%	50% Min. ₹ 300
Retired From 01.06.1960 to 01.10.1970	50%	40 % Min. ₹ 250
Retired From 02.10.1970 to 31.03.1978	40%	30% Min. ₹ 200
Retired From 01.04.1978 to 30.09.1984	35%	25 % Min. ₹ 175
Retired From 01.10.1984 to 30.09.1987	20%	15% Min. ₹ 100

In respect of those who retired after 01.06.1988, the following increases were allowed for purposes of reckoning Average Emoluments:

Pay	*Increase*
Upto ₹ 3500	13% of pay
More than ₹ 3500 and upto ₹ 6000	9% of Pay Min ₹ 455
More than ₹ 6000	8% of Pay Min ₹ 540.

(*xi*) Dearness Allowance has to be reckoned for purpose of Pension and Gratuity.

(*xii*) From 01.01.1996 the pension was revised as follows:

Pension

Add D.A. as on 01.01.1996

Interim relief I & II

40% of Basic pension.

(*xiii*) The revised pension as on 01.01.1996 should not be less than 50% of the minimum of the revised scale of pay applicable to the post last held by the pensioner subject to the condition that he had put in 33 years of qualifying service. If the service is less than 33 years then it should be fixed on pro rata basis or the actual fixation under (*xii*) above which ever is higher, with monetary effect from 01.04.1999.

(*xiv*) In respect of those retired from 02.10.1970 to 31.01.1975 and from 01.04.1979 to 30.06.1988, the court ordered to treat the

D.A. actually drawn by them for calculation of average emoluments and Government issued ordered incorporating a ready reckoner. The pensioners or the legal heir of the pensioners are eligible for arrears of the pension and gratuity consequent on such revision. The authority which forwarded the pension proposals is the authority to revise the pension and gratuity and intimate the pension disbursing officers.

(*xv*) Minimum and maximum pension:

Date	*Minimum* ₹	*Maximum* ₹
Upto 31.03.1982	100	1500
01.04.1982	125	1500
01.10.1984	235	no ceiling
01.04.1988	245	no ceiling
01.06.1988	375	no ceiling
01.01.1996	1275	50% of highest pay scale

(*xvi*) Under Section 11 of the Pension Act 1971 the Pension cannot be attached by any Civil Court order at the instance of a creditor for any demand against the pensioner.

PART II: PENSION RULES

13.13 CHANGES AFTER THE FOURTH PAY COMMISSION

1. **Change after Fourth Pay Commission Recommendations.** The liberalised pensions are applicable in case of Central Government servants who retire from service/die within service on or after 1st January, 1986.
2. **Average Emoluments.** Emoluments drawn by the Government servant during the last 10 months of his service.
3. **Service Gratuity.** Service gratuity for qualifying service of less than 10 years shall be calculated at a uniform rate of half month's emoluments for every completed six months of service.
4. **Pension.** Pension for a qualifying service of 10 years or more shall be calculated at 50% of average emoluments in all cases and will be subject to a minimum of ₹ 375 and a maximum of ₹ 4500.

5. **Retirement Gratuity.** Admissible on retirement of government servant after completion of five years qualifying service and will be equal to one fourth of his monthly emoluments for each completed six months period of qualifying service subject to a minimum of $16\frac{1}{2}$ times the emoluments and Maximum of ₹ 1 Lac.
6. **Death Gratuity.** Admissible in the event of death of a person while in service and will be equal to 12 times of the emoluments if he had completed the qualifying service of 5 years or more but less than 20 years. If he had completed qualifying service of 20 years or more, the death gratuity will be equal to half month emoluments for every completed six months period of qualifying service subject to a maximum of 33 times the emoluments and to a maximum of ₹ one lakh.
7. **Family Pension.** The minimum family pension of ₹ 60 per month has been increased to ₹ 375/-.
8. **Dearness Relief to Pensioners.** The rate of neutralisation of price rise will be 100% to those in receipt of pension upto ₹ 1750, 75% to those in receipt of ₹ 1751 to ₹ 3000 and 65% to those in receipt of pension above ₹ 3000.
9. **Commercial Employment after Retirement.** If a pensioner, who immediately before retirement was a member of Central Service Group 'A' wishes to accept any commercial employment before expiry of two years from the date of his retirement, shall obtain previous sanction of the Government to such acceptance. [Rule 10 of GIOD (6) there under].
10. **Employment after Retirement under Government Outside India.** If a pensioner, who immediately after, was a member of Central Service Group 'A', wishes to accept any employment under any Government outside India, he shall obtain the previous permission of the Central Government for such acceptance and no pension shall be payable to such pensioner who accepts such an employment without prior permission in respect of any period for which he is so employed or such larger period as the government may direct.
11. **Interruption which Entail Forfeiture of Past Service.** The following interruptions entail forfeiture of past service of a Government servant:

    (*a*) Dismissal from service.

    (*b*) Removal from service.

(*c*) Resignation from a service except resignation for the purpose of taking another appointment with proper permission.

12. Interruption not Entailing Forfeiture of Past Service

(*a*) Authorised leave of absence.

(*b*) Unauthorised absence in continuation of authorised absence so long as the post of absentee is not filled substantially.

(*c*) Suspension when it is immediately followed by reinstatement in the same or different post.

(*d*) Transfer to non-qualifying service in an establishment under the Central Government.

(*e*) Joining time while on transfer from one post to another.

(*f*) Abolution of the office.

13.14 FAMILY PENSION

13.14.1 Admissibility

The Family pension 1964, is admissible to the family of a deceased government servant, when he dies (*a*) after completion of not less than one year's continuous service or before completion of one year's of continuous service if the deceased government servant immediately prior to his appointment was examined by the appropriate medical authority and declared fit.

13.14.2 Benefits to Family Members after the death of a Government Employee

1. Death While in Service

When a Government employee dies while in service, the members of his family are eligible to get the following benefits. Encashment of leave, Special Provident Fund-cum Gratuity, G.P.F. balance, T.A. to go to native place, Advance to meet funeral expenses, transport expenses, to take dead body of the official to native place, lump sum payment under Employees Family Security Fund, Relief under house building advance, Educational Allowance to children, Compassionate Ground appointments to dependents. DCR Gratuity, Family Pension, Dearness Allowance, Medical Allowance, etc. The various aspects of Life Time Arrears and Family Pension are indicated below:

2. Life Time Arrears

(*i*) On the death of Government employee, the members of the family or legal Heirs are eligible to claim the duty pay and allowances due to the employee or the leave salary upto the date of death if he had been on earned leave. They are also eligible for any arrears due to him consequent on sanction of increments or fixation of pay.

(*ii*) The following authorities have full powers to sanction the lifetime arrears of salary due to the family of the deceased government servants.

Sl. No.	*Sanctioning authority*	*To Whom sanction to be Accorded*
1.	Head of Office	Subordinates to the Head of Office
2.	Head of Department/ Secretary to Government	Subordinates working in the office of the Head of Department/ Secretary to the Government and Heads of Offices
3.	Government	All Heads of Departments

3. Family pension

(*i*) The system of Family Pension was given effect to from 01.04.1964, in a very restricted way. As per pension rule 49(2) (*a*) if the employee dies after completion of not less than one year continuous service at any time during his service, the family of the deceased was entitled to a family pension as follows with effect from 1.04.1979

At least one year service 30% of pay min ₹ 100 Max. ₹ 500

In such cases D.A. was not allowed (G.O. 748 Fin 26.05.1979)

In respect of the persons who died prior to 01.04.1964 the family pension to the surviving members of the family was allowed from 01.04.1979.

(*ii*) In the event of death of a Government employee, while in service after having put in not less than 7 years of continuous service, the rate of family pension shall be equal to 50% of the pay last drawn or twice the family pension admissable @30% of pay last drawn or ₹ 500 which ever is less from the date following the date of death of employee, for a period 7 years or for a period upto the date on which the deceased employee would have attained the age of 65 years had he survived which ever is less.

(*iii*) Family Pension is not admissible in cases of family of an employee whose services were regularised and any one of the family was appointed under Compassionate grounds if he died before completion of one year of service.

(*iv*) In case of Unmarried Government Employee, Family Pension is payable to Father, failing which to the mother who were dependent on the deceased employee for support.

(*v*) If an employee dies after having put in service of one year but less than 7 years, and is not survived by a widow or widower but is survived by child or children, such child or children are eligible for family pension if it is higher than that sanction under Extraordinary Pension Rules, if any.

(*vi*) If the Husband has another wife living at the time of death of the female employee, it is the same as remarriage and the husband is not entitled for family pension. If the minor child is alive, the family pension could be paid through the father as guardians of the child subject to the recognition of his legal guardianship.

(*vii*) Provisional Family Pension: In the case of death of a Government official while in service, the Head of Office shall sanction provisional family pension to the eligible member of family without insisting legal heirship certificate to whom the lump sum amount of ₹ 5000/- was paid for funeral expenses. It is adjustable against the regular family pension payable.

4. On the death of pensioners

(a) Life Time Arrears. The legal heir or nominee of the pensioner who is dead, is eligible to claim life time arrears of pension. Under T.R. 16 S.R. 88, the pension is payable upto the day of death of the pensioner irrespective of the hour of death. The pensioner has to file a nomination with the pension disbursing Officer in favour of is family member in form A.

If there is nomination, legal heirship certificate and No Objection Certificate from family members are not necessary and the production of death certificate is adequate for the payment of life time arrears. However nomination for L.T.A. of Family Pension is not necessary as the right to receive L.T.A. of family pension pass on to the next eligible member.

(b) Enhanced Family Pension. In the event of death of a pensioner, the provision of payment of enhanced family pension indicated as in para (*ii*) above, shall apply and such payment shall be made for a period of seven years or for a period upto the date on which the deceased pensioner would have attained the age of 65 years had he survived whichever is less.

5. Family Pension on the death of a Pensioner

(*i*) If a pensioner dies, his family is entitled to family pension as follows:

Pay *Maximum*	%		*Minimum*
Prior to 1.04.1979		₹	₹
Below 200	30	50	—
₹ 200 and above But below ₹ 800	15	60	—
Above ₹ 800	12	150	300
From 1.04.1979	30	100	500
From 01.04.1982		125	500
From 01.10.1987		235	800
From 14.12.1987		235	1000
From 01.04.1988		245	1000
From 1.06.1988	30	375	1250
From 01.01.1996		1275	30% of Maximum pay of the highest scale of Pay

The family pension was raised to the level of 30% of the minimum of the revised the scale of the pay applicable to the post held at the time of retirement/death of the employee or 30% of the pay last drawn which ever is higher from 01.01.1996. (Minimum Family Pension ₹ 1275 and Maximum: 30% of Maximum pay of the Highest scale of pay).

Family Pension is admissible in respect of all the pensioners—superannuation, compensation, invalid, retiring, compulsory pensioners. When a person dies in harness while in service, family pension is admissible as follows:

Has put in at least one year of service 30% of pay with minimum ₹ 100 and Maximum ₹ 500. Retirement after one year of service but not adequate service for pension minimum ₹ 100 and maximum ₹ 580. No family pension if he has not put in one year service.

(*ii*) If the pensioner dies after retirement, the family pension is payable to the widow/widower upto the date of his/her death or remarriage whichever is earlier. In respect of son and unmarried daughter upto the age of 25 years or until the daughter gets married whichever is earlier.

(*iii*) If the son/daughter of the pensioner is suffering from any disorder or disability of mind or is physically crippled or disabled, and unable to earn livelihood, a family pension shall be paid to him or her for life after exhausting the priority like widow and widower or son first, second or unmarried daughter until the last person attains the age of 25 years. (rule 49(6) proviso) Such family pension shall be paid through the guardian as if he or she was minor or mentally retarded son or daughter. To support such a claim, a certificate to the effect of the disability from a civil surgeon has to be produced to the sanctioning authority every 3 years. Necessary certificate on the disability or unmarried status has to be furnished by the guardian every month to the treasury or bank.

(*iv*) If a widow is not survived by any child, the family pension shall cease to be payable.

(*v*) **Legally wedded wives.** The second wife gets the status of legal wife in two cases : Second marriage solemnised before coming into force of the Hindu Marriages Act as per the customary law among the community; and the second marriage solemnised as per legal requirements in the case of persons governed by Mohemmaden law where bigamy is permissible. In these cases, second wife is eligible to have the family pension. The child born to the wife other than those covered by the above two cases is treated as illegitimate and not eligible for family pension.

(*vi*) Twin children born at a single birth shall be treated as of the same age and made eligible for family pension in equal shares. In case of twin children the family pension shall be paid in equal shares irrespective of the sex rule.

(*vii*) A Judicially separated wife/husband does not lose her or his legal status of wife or husband of the employee and is eligible for family pension. The Competent Authority to sanction a family pension for recorded reason may pay the family pension to minor children in preference to the judicially separated person.

(*viii*) Family Pension be granted to children of female government employee born through second husband and it shall be divisible @50% to the first husband of deceased female Government employee and 50% to the children born through the second husband.

(*ix*) Family Pension is admissible to the post retiral spouse from the date of death of pensioner irrespective of the date of retirement.

(*x*) Posthumous children are eligible for family pension.

(*xi*) In case of unmarried Government Servant, father, mother, step mother, are entitled for family pension.

(*xii*) Family for purposes of family pension will mean: wife or husband/sons and unmarried daughters in the order of birth, and in case of unmarried pensioner, father or mother.

(*xiii*) In cases of both mother and unmarried children or father and unmarried children are government employees and are governed by the pension rules, and one of them dies while in service or after retirement, family pension in respect of the deceased shall be payable to the surviving father or mother and in the event of death of father or mother, the surviving mother or father in respect of the deceased father or mother and unmarried children shall be granted two family pensions and the quantum of pension shall be regulated as:

(*a*) If both family pensions are payable at the enhanced rate, the quantum of two family pensions shall be limited to ₹ 2500.

(*b*) If one of the two family pensions is payable at the enhanced rate, and another at the ordinary rate, the quantum of the pension shall be restricted to ₹ 2500.

(*c*) If both the family pensions are payable at the ordinary rate, the quantum of family pensions shall be limited to ₹ 1250.

(*xiv*) Where the Government employee's widow or widower to whom the family pension is granted dies or remarries or when there is no widow or widower, the family pension shall be paid to the minor sons or unmarried minor daughters if any, on the date of death or remarriage till such minors attained the age of 25 years whichever is earlier. In the absence of natural guardian payment will be made through the de facto guardian who shall be required to file an affidavit that he is in-charge of the property of the minors and is looking after it. If minors have no properties other than family pension he has to declare that the minors or in his custody and care and furnish an indemnity bond which suitable sureties. In disputed cases, payment shall be made through the legal guardian.

(*xv*) If a person who is entitled to family pensions on the death of a pensioner is charged with the offence of murdering the pensioner or for abetting the offence, his claim will remain suspended pending disposal of the criminal case. If he is acquitted, he will be permitted to draw pension from the date of entitlement and if he is convicted of the offence, he will be debarred from drawing family pension.

(*xvi*) A military pensioner who was re-employed in civil service on his superannuation may opt either for family pension rules under military pension or family pension under State Government.

(*xvii*) Person who is already in receipt of family pension shall not be permitted to draw family pension under rule 49, unless he forgoes family pension under other rules.

(*xviii*) Any person absconding for more than 7 years is deemed to have been dead for all practical purposes. Hence the claims of the Government employee absconding and whose whereabouts are not known for more than 7 years can be claimed along with family pension and paid to the members of his family.

Further

(*a*) when the employee disappears, the family can be paid in the first instance the amount of salary, leave encashment due and the General Provident Fund amount having regard to the nomination made by the employee;

(*b*) After lapse of two years from the date of filing FIR with the Police, the Family Pension, and D.C.R. Gratuity at normal rate be sanctioned at Government level but the Family Benefit Fund and difference in D.C.R. Gratuity shall be paid after lapse of seven years.

(*xix*) Adoption of a person after retirement will not entitle for family pension.

(*xx*) Sub Treasury Officer/Assistant Treasury Officers are authorised to pay family pension.

(*xxi*) Pension Pay Officer/Sub Treasury Officer/Assistant Treasury Officer are authorised to sanction life time arrears.

(*xxii*) When the joint photo was recorded, there is no need to obtain the photo of the spouse again while applying for family pension on the death of the pensioner. In such cases, there is no need for heirship certificate.

(*a*) If the family pension is paid to the wives equally and one of them dies without issue, such share shall be payable to the other widows.

(*b*) If the family pension or share of the family pension to the spouse or children is stopped due to the ineligibility on reasons like remarriage, death, attaining age of 25 years etc., the family pension shall not lapse but will pass on to the other eligible heirs.

(*xxiii*) **Revision of Family Pension :** From 01.01.1996 the existing family pension was revised as family pension plus D.A. as on 01.01.1996 plus interim relief I & II plus 40% of family pension.

6. Festival Advance

Family pensioners are not eligible for festival advance.

7. Medical Facilities

The family pensioners are entitled for medical allowance per month from 01.12.1995. In case of family pensioners of the

Government employees who died while in service, they can opt for either medical reimbursement or medical allowance till the date of retirement had he been alive. In respect of hospitalisation, the family pensioners are entitled to the facilities at Government Hospitals.

13.15 COMMUTATION OF PENSION

A government servant is entitled to commute from a lump sum payment a fraction not exceeding one third of his pension.

1. **Calculation of Dearness Relief Payable to Pensioners.** Dearness relief admissible to pensioners will be calculated on the original amount of pension even after computation of a portion of the pension.
2. **Commuted Amount is not Taxable Under IT Act.**

PART–III

CONSTRUCTION EQUIPMENT

1. Construction Equipment
2. Planning and Works Management

1

CONSTRUCTION EQUIPMENT

1.1 INTRODUCTION

In order to have proper quality construction projects the use of mechanical equipment has become an important and essential feature. It is only on account of mechanised construction that within two working seasons in the Ladakh sector of J & K (Project Beacon) with which the author was associated in October, 1962, Shaktiman could be taken right upto Chisul border by the Army.

1.2 COMMON CONSTRUCTION EQUIPMENT

(*i*) Equipment for excavation and transportation of earth.
(*ii*) Soil stabilisation and compaction equipment.
(*iii*) Hauling equipment.
(*iv*) Hoisting equipment.
(*v*) Rock drilling equipment.
(*vi*) Pneumatic equipment.
(*vii*) Pumping dewatering equipment.
(*viii*) Rock blasting equipment.
(*ix*) Pile foundation and pile driving equipment.
(*x*) Stone crushers.
(*xi*) Concrete mixing plant.
(*xii*) Grouting and guniting equipment.
(*xiii*) Bitumen mixing plant.
(*xiv*) Welding equipment.
(*xv*) Shield tunneling.

The above equipment are briefly described in the following articles.

1.3 EQUIPMENT FOR EXCAVATION AND TRANSPORTATION OF EARTH

1.3.1 Introduction

Almost every Civil Engineering project, starts with earthwork. Whether earthwork involves excavation, or filling or both, excavation has necessarily to be carried out as even though the formation may involve earthwork in filling, yet this earth for filling would have to be procured by excavating earth from some other location. In the case of dams, highways and airports the first phase of the construction is earthwork of comparatively large magnitude. There are a number of variables in the earth work which affect the output of earth moving equipment. Before describing the equipment, therefore, these factors are discussed in the following articles.

1.3.2 Rolling Resistance

The resistance which a vehicle encounters while moving over a road surface is known as rolling resistance. The condition of the surface and its type have great influence on the rolling resistance offered by the surface. If the earth is hard the rolling resistance as compared to soft earth will be less and comparatively less effort will be required by the vehicle. If the vehicle has pneumatic tyres, the rolling resistance depends upon the size, pressure and the design of the tread of the tyres. In the case of vehicle moving on crawler tracks, the rolling resistance depends directly on the surface of the road. A narrow-tread tyre under comparatively high pressure suffers less rolling resistance on hard surface as compared to a broad-tread low pressure tyre. The reason for this is that the area of contact between the road surface and the tyre is smaller. On the other hand, ground is soft, the broad-tread low pressure tyre has less rolling resistance. This is because the narrow tyre under high pressure penetrates into the soft soil and has to climb up and extra effort has to be applied in doing so.

Moisture content is another factor which has great influence on the hauling of earth. Under suitable conditions namely highly compacted well maintained soil under optimum moisture content the rolling resistance of the surface would be as small as that of asphalt or cement concrete road surface. For a major earth project, therefore, it is advisable to maintain the low rolling resistance of

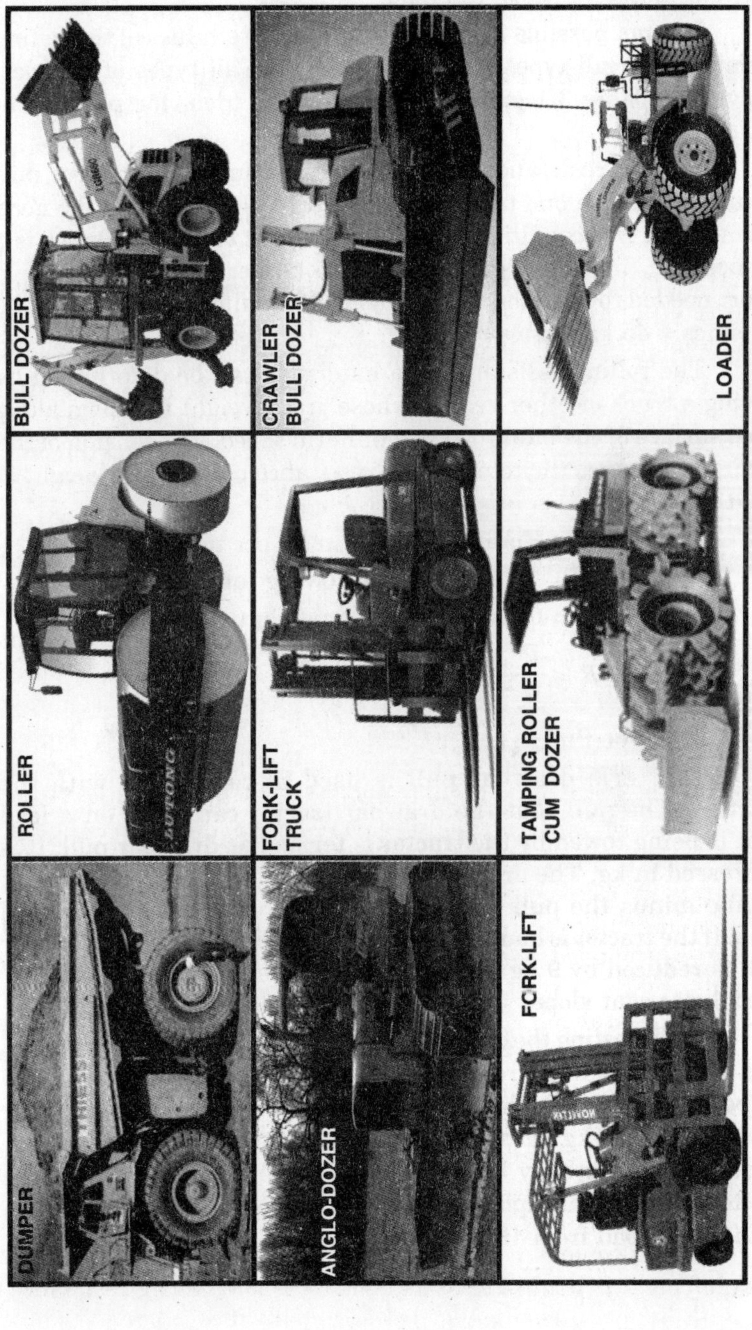

Fig. 1.1 Common construction equipment.

the earth by having a patrol grader, sprinkler trucks and rollers for efficient maintenance of the road.

It is not possible to provide very accurate values of the rolling resistance for all types of haul of roads and all types of vehicles. However, Table 3.1 gives an approximate idea, for purpose of estimating.

Rolling resistance can be expressed in kg of tractive pull required to move one tonne load over a level surface for the good surface and tyre condition. If the gross weight of a loaded truck is 1 tonnes and the rolling resistance is 45 kg per tonne, the tractive effort needed to keep the truck moving at a uniform speed would be 1 tonnes × 45 kg/tonnes = 450 kg.

The rolling resistance of a haul road can be determined by towing a truck or other vehicle whose gross weight is known along level surface of the haul road at a uniform speed. The tension of the towing rope gives the total rolling resistance of the gross weight of the truck.

Thus if R = Total resistance in kg per tonne

P = Total tension in towing cable kg

W = Gross weight of truck in tonnes

$$R = \frac{P}{W}.$$

1.3.3 Drawbar Pull

The term drawbar pull is used in connection with the tractors. The pull that the drawbar tractor can exert on a load that is being towed by the tractor is termed as drawbar pull. It is expressed in kg. The drawbar pull is the total pulling effort of an engine minus the pull required to move the tractor over a level road. If the tractor is hauling the load along an upgrade, the drawbar pull is reduced by 9 kg for each tonne of weight of the tractor for each 1 per cent slope.

While testing the drawbar pull at the various available speeds, it is assumed that the road surface has a rolling resistance of 49.5 kg per tonne. If the rolling resistance of the level road is higher or lower than 49.5 kg per tonne, the drawbar pull will be reduced or increased respectively by an amount equal to the weight of the tractor in tonnes multiplied by the difference of the rolling resistance of the haul road from 49.5 kg per tonne.

Example 1.1 *The weight of a tractor is 15 tonnes. It has a drawbar pull of 2.600 t, while operating on a level road in the sixth gear. The rolling resistance of the road is 495 N/tonne. Determine the drawbar pull of the tractor when it is operating on a level surface having a rolling resistance of 805 N/tonnes.*

Solution. Reduction in drawbar pull

$$= 15 \times (805 - 495)$$

$$= 15 \times 310 \text{ N} = 4650 \text{ N}$$

The effective drawbar pull

$$= (2.60 - 0.465) \text{ t} = 2.135 \text{ t}.$$

The drawbar pull of a tractor varies inversely with the speed of each gear. In the first-gear, when the speed is minimum, the drawbar pull is the highest while at the top gear when the speed is highest, the drawbar pull is the least. The variation of drawbar pull is shown in Table 1.1.

Table 1.1 Drawbar Pull at Different Gear Speeds

Gear	*Speed kmph*	*Drawbar pull t*
1st	2.7	15.5
2nd	3.5	12.0
3rd	4.4	7.7
4th	5.6	6.2
5th	7.1	4.5
6th	11.2	2.5

1.3.4 Rimpull

Rimpull denotes the tractive force between the rubber tyres of the driving wheel and the surface on which the tyres operate. If the co-efficient of traction is such that slippage is eliminated, the maximum rimpull depends upon the power of the engine and the gear ratio between the engine and the driving wheels. In case the driving wheels slip on the surface, the maximum rimpull is equal to the total pressure between the tyres and the surface multiplied by the co-efficient of traction: Rimpull, is expressed in N or t. As in the case of drawbar pull, the rimpull is also highest at the lowest speed (1st gear) and lowest at maximum speed. Table 1.2 illustrates the variation of rimpull for different gear/speed of the tractor.

Table 1.2 Rimpull at Different Gear/Speeds

Gear	*Speed kmph*	*Rimpull t*
1st	5.1	6.3
2nd	11.0	2.64
3rd	20.0	1.60
4th	34.0	0.9
5th	54.0	0.59

While calculating the rimpull which can be exerted by a tractor while towing a load, the tractive force required to over come the rolling resistance plus grade resistance should be deducted from the rimpull of the tractor. For example, in Table 1.2, the maximum rimpull in the first gear is 6.3 t. If the tractor weighs 12.5 tonnes and is operating along a 2 per cent upgrade and the rolling resistance is 450 N/tonne, the pull available for towing a load will be determined in the following way:

Maximum rimpull = 6.3 t

Pull required to overcome grade

$$12.5 \times 90 \times 2 = 2250 \text{ N}$$

Pull required to overcome rolling resistance

$$12.5 \times 450 = 5600 \text{ N}$$

Total pull to be deducted

$$= 7850 \text{ N}$$

Pull available for towing the load

$$= 63000 - 7850$$

$$= 55150 \text{ N } (5.5 \text{ t}).$$

1.3.5 Dragline

(*a*) *General.* A dragline is a useful equipment for removing earth from ditch, canal or pit containing water. It is generally possible to have a dragline with a fairly long boom. The increased length of the boom enables the disposal of earth in one operation thereby saving the cost and time required for employing a hauling unit. As compared to a power shovel the output of the dragline in terms of excavation of the earth is about 80 per cent, the size of the buckets being the same in both the cases.

(*b*) *Type.* Draglines are of three types as given below:

(*i*) Crawler mounted

Fig. 1.2 Dragline.

(*ii*) Wheel mounted (self-propelled)

(*iii*) Truck mounted.

(*i*) *Crawler mounted.* This type of dragline is used in comparatively soft surfaces where the wheel mounted or track mounted equipment cannot be used. This type of equipment can be used for local area of isolated works where mobility is not required. Its speed is as low as 2 kmph.

(*ii*) and (*iii*) The wheel and truck mounted units have the advantage of mobility. They can travel at as high as 50 kmph speeds.

Figure 1.3 shows a typical diagram of a dragline.

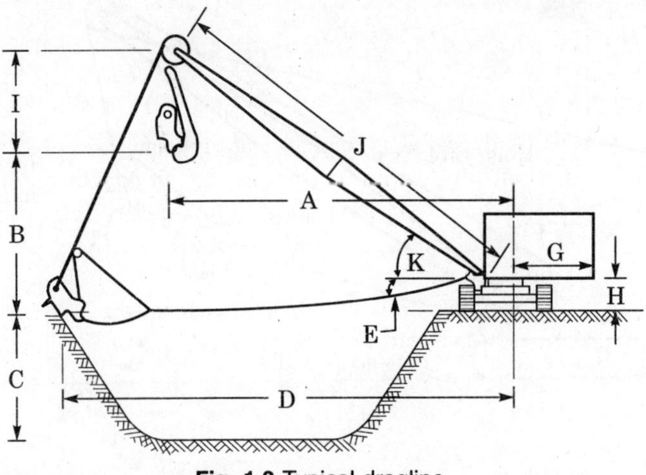

Fig. 1.3 Typical dragline.

(c) *Size.* The range of the various components, illustrated in the above diagram is given below to give the idea of the range of the size. See Table 1.3.

Table 1.3 Typical Ranges for a Dragline

Sl. No.	*Particulars of the components with reference to Fig. 1.3*		*Range*	*Remarks*
1.	Boom length	(J)	15 m to 24 m	Combined weight of bucket and material should not exceed the capacity.
2.	Capacity t		2.7 to 5.4	
3.	Boom angle deg	K	20 to 45	
4.	Dumping radius-metre	A	12 to 26	
5.	Dumping Height-metres	B	3 to 13	
6.	Max digging depth metres		12 to 6	

The size of the buckets from the standard size may be increased or decreased but the length of the boom should also be changed accordingly as the maximum tilting capacity of a dragline is limited by the force which will cause tilting of the machine.

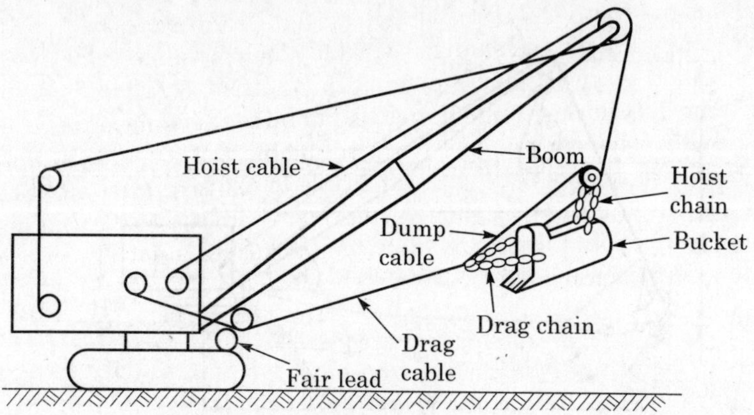

Fig. 1.4

(*d*) Basic parts and operation of a dragline. Figure 1.2 shows the basic parts of a dragline.

The various stages of operations are given below:

(*i*) Swing the empty bucket to the digging position and simultaneously release the drag and hoist cable.

(*ii*) Pull the buckets towards the machine for excavation.

(*iii*) Take in the hoist line and pay out the drag cable.

(*iv*) Hoist, swing and dump the loaded bucket.

Repeat the cycle.

Note. The bucket is so constructed that unless desired by the operator, it will not dump its contents.

(*e*) *Optimum depth of cut.* The optimum depth is defined as the depth at which, rest of the conditions being the same, the output, in terms of quantity of earth excavated and dumped would be maximum. In other words, it is the depth at which the working of the equipment is most efficient and economical.

The facts which affect the optimum depth are the types of the soil and size of the bucket.

(*f*) The effect of the size of the bucket and the length of the boom on the output of dragline.

In order to obtain best results the capacity, and the type of the buckets and the dragline should be chosen after studying the corelation of these components. Normally three standard sizes of the bucket namely light duty, medium duty, and heavy duty are available. Where the material is soft, light duty bucket is useful, for example digging in sandy clay, sandy loam or sand. For general excavation services such as digging clay, soft shale or loose gravel, medium duty bucket would be useful. For mine stripping, excavating highly abrasive materials or for handling blasted rock, heavy duty buckets are useful. While it is advisable to use largest size bucket for increased output, it should be properly investigated that the combined weight of the load and the bucket does not exceed the safe load recommended for the dragline.

1.3.6 Hydraulically Powered Excavators

The conventional shovel excavators are being improved upon to provide all hydraulic operation. This type of excavator has the following advantages over the conventional shovel excavator:

(*i*) The power for excavation is derived from the thrust of double acting hydraulic rams. The dead weight of the bucket or the boom do not come into play. As a result of this, the weight of the machine is reduced thereby increasing the power/weight rate.

(*ii*) Because of better power/weight ratio the machine can operate on surface like rock, frozen clay, soft or boggy soil.

The bucket can exert a force upto 18 t.

(*iii*) The system provides a shock free operation.

(*iv*) Efficient and easy controls are provided.

(*v*) Reduction in service cost and operational cost.

1.3.7 Cable Excavator

When building materials or minerals have to be recovered from under-water areas or when dredging has to be carried out in rivers, lakes, or harbours, the excavated material has to be conveyed to very long distances. The conventional excavators such as shovel excavators or dragline cannot do this type of work. In such situations cable excavators are used. A 2.5 cu. m working over a distance of 160 metres can deliver 85 cu. m of excavated sand and gravel material per hour. These cable excavators have been successfully used for haulage of excavated material upto 33 metre distances. They can deposit the excavated material upto 330 metre heights above the level of the cut. Cable track is stretched between two towers known as the head tower which is fixed and the tail tower, which is movable. The track cable runs between the two towers and hangs loosely so that after emptying at the tail end the bucket returns for further filling to the excavation

Fig. 1.5 Cable excavator.

site by force of gravity. The digging is carried out by operating the drag cable. The track cable is lowered to enable the bucket to do the excavation and it is then used and conveyed at high speed to the dumping point. The equipment is illustrated in Fig. 1.6.

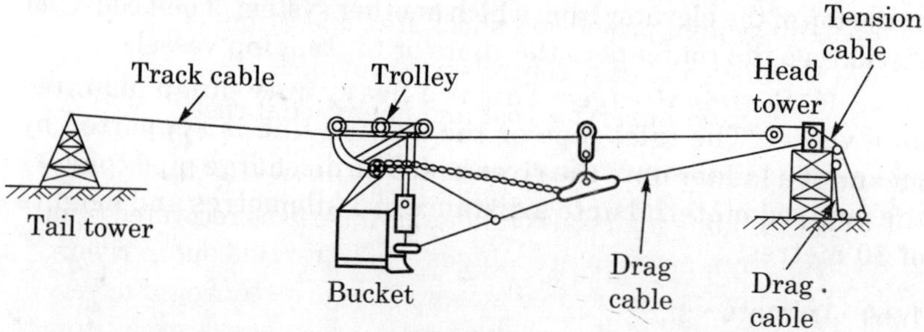

Fig. 1.6

1.3.8 Dredgers

The excavation of the bed of a river, lake or sea for the purpose of depending is known as 'dredging'. It is a very important and continuous operation in harbours and navigation canals. The equipment used for this sub-aqueous excavation is known as *dredger*.

Fig. 1.7

Dredgers are of three types as given below:

(*a*) Dipper dredger

(*b*) Ladder dredger

(*c*) Suction dredger.

(*a*) *Dipper dredger*. A dipper dredger is an underwater shovel which excavates all types of soil and discharges the loaded bucket either on the bank or on a floating vessel. These dredgers can operate upto 20 metre depth and has a range upto 35 metres. The buckets are available upto 12.25 cu. m in size and output of 50 cu.m/hour can be achieved.

(*b*) The ladder dredger has a bucket elevator mounted on the vessel. The bucket dips into the soil and is lifted because of the belting. As the bucket moves up it discharges into the hopper located at the top of the elevator from which another system of belt conveyor discharges the contents to the shore or to standing vessel.

(*c*) *Suction dredger.* This is a heavy duty pump mounted on a vessel. The inlet pipe or the suction line is supported by means of a ladder upto the river bed. The discharge pipe conveys the pumped material upto a distance of 3 kilometres and heights of 30 metres.

1.3.9 Tractors

(*a*) *General.* The primary purpose of tractors is to pull or push the loads. However by various modifications and attachments to the basic unit, they can be used for variety of purposes.

Fig. 1.8 A Tractor.

(*b*) *Types.* Tractors are of two main types:

(*i*) Crawler.

(*ii*) Wheel or mounted, the tractor may be two wheeled or four wheeled.

(*i*) *Crawler tractors.* These tractors are designated by their size, weight or power. The maximum tractive effort that can be provided by a unit is restricted to the product of the weight and the coefficient of traction irrespective of the power supplied by the engine. The performance data of light duty, medium duty and heavy duty crawler tractors are given in Table 1.4.

Table 1.4 Performance Data of Crawler Tractors

Gear	*Approximate operating weight*					
	8.2 t		*14.5 t*		*2.1 t*	
	Speed kmph	*Drawbar pull t*	*Speed kmph*	*Drawbar pull t*	*Speed kmph*	*Drawbar pull t*
Forward						
1st	2.7	7.7	2.4	15	2.4	20.0
3rd	6	3.2	5.0	6.8	4.3	11.2
5th	8.2	1.4	9.5	2.7	5.4	6.0
Reverse						
1st	3.4	6.1	2.9	12.0	2.4	20.0
3rd	7.5	2.4	6.0	5.4	4.3	10.5
4th	10	1.7	8.7	3.4	5.8	7.7

(*ii*) *Wheel tractors.* Wheel tractors are two wheel type and four wheel type.

The two wheel type has the following advantages:

1. Increased maneuverability.
2. Increased traction.
3. Decreased rolling resistance because of the absence of extra axles.
4. Fewer tyres of provide and maintain.

The advantages of the Four-wheel type are given below:

1. Better steering properties. This gives better confidence to the operator of the machine.
2. More stable on rough roads.
3. Greater speed specially on rough roads because of factors (1) and (2) above.
4. When separated from the trailing unit, it can operate as an independent unit.

(*c*) **Gradability of Tractors.** It is the minimum slope, expressed as percentage, upto which a machine may move at a uniform speed. Separate gradability is determined for an empty and a loaded vehicle. Gradability, for different gears is different. The forward motion of a prime mover is governed by the following factors:

(*i*) Power developed by the engine and available as drawbar pull or rimpull.

(*ii*) Rolling resistance of haul road.

(*iii*) Gross weight of the prime mover and its load.

(*iv*) The grade to be negotiated.

From the available drawbar pull, the pull required to overcome the rolling resistance in the unit and the load on the unit that is to be pulled is deducted. The balance pull is available to negotiate a gradient. In order to have a reasonable safety factor, only 85 per cent of the rated draw barpull is used for determining the gradability of the equipment.

1.3.10 Bulldozers

(*a*) *General.* Bulldozer are very popular earth moving equipment which can be used for the following jobs:

(*i*) Site clearance.

(*ii*) Cutting in mountaneous and rocky terrain.

(*iii*) Moving earth for haulages upto 100 metres.

(*iv*) Loading tractor pulled scrapers.

(*v*) Spreading earth fill.

(*vi*) Back filling trenches.

(*vii*) Earth road maintenance.

The blades of the bulldozers are at right angles to the direction of the travel. The same basic equipment may be converted into an angle dozer by mounting separate cutting blades set at an angle with the direction of travel. The size of the bulldozer is indicated by the length and height of the blade.

Fig. 1.9 A Bulldozer.

(*b*) *Cable Control Versus Hydraulic Control.* The cable controlled operation has the following advantages.

(*i*) Simple to operate.

(*ii*) Easier repairs.

(*iii*) Less danger of damage to the machine.

The hydraulic controlled operation has the following advantages:

(*i*) Ability to provide high down pressure on the blades.

(*ii*) More precise setting can be maintained.

(*c*) Crawler-mounted *versus* wheel mounted bulldozers.

The crawler mounted dozer has the following advantages:

(*i*) Higher tractive effort.

(*ii*) Can operate in rough and muddy surface.

(*iii*) Can work in rocky area.

(*iv*) Can travel over rough surface.

The wheel mounted dozers have the following advantages:

(*i*) High travel speed.

(*ii*) No hauling equipment is required for transporting the dozer from one job to the other.

(*iii*) Greater output.

(*iv*) Less operator fatigue.

(*v*) Ability travel over paved highway without damaging the surface.

(*d*) *Moving Earth with Bulldozers.* In general, when the haulage is within 100 metres, crawler mounted or wheel-mounted tractor may be used depending upon whether the ground is soft or hard. When the haulage is comparatively longer and the surface is firm, it is advantageous to use wheel mounted dozer.

(*e*) *Output.* The dozer output depends upon the operating conditions. Sometimes the output can be increased by as much as 50 per cent if two dozers work side by sides with adjacent blades in contact. In case the earth can be pushed downhill, the output can be substantially increased.

If the capacity of the blade is known, the approximate output of the machine can be evaluated from the number of passes it will make in one hour.

Example 1.2 *Determine the output of a bulldozer from the following operating conditions.*

(*i*) Material—Sandy loam top soil.

(*ii*) Swell 25%.

(*iii*) Haul distance 30 metres.

(*iv*) Mold board size 2.9 m long, 9.90 m high.

(*v*) Rated mold board capacity = 3 cu. m loose volume.

(*vi*) Operating factor 50 min/hour.

(*vii*) Probable round trip time.

Pushing 30 metre @ 2.5 kmph	= 0.72 minutes
Returning 30 metre @ 5.6 kmph	= 0.32 minutes
Loading, shifting gear	= 0.30 minutes
	1.34 minutes

Calculation. Net mold board capacity

$$= \frac{3}{1.25} = 2.4 \text{ cubic metres.}$$

Time per haul = 1.34 minutes.

Trips per hour $= \dfrac{50}{1.34} = 37.3$

Output per hour = 37.3 × 2.4 cubic metres.

= 89.5 cu. m.

(*e*) *Clearing land.* The following land clearing operations can be performed by the bulldozer.

(*i*) Complete removal of trees and stumps including roots.

(*ii*) Removal of vegetations.

Types of equipment used. The following equipments are used for land clearing operations.

(*i*) Tractor mounted bulldozers.

(*ii*) Tractor mounted special blades.

(*iii*) Tractor mounted rakes.

(*iv*) Tractor-pulled chain and steel cables.

(*v*) Special machine with pusher bars equipped with special blades to chop the vegetation.

(*i*) *Tractor mounted bulldozers.* These machines are not suitable for clearance job. There are two disadvantage in using bulldozers for this job. Firstly, the bulldozers have to excavate earth round the trees and cut the main roots leaving holes in the ground secondly, while stacking the felled trees the machine transports considerable earth along with the tree.

(*ii*) *Tractor mounted special blades.* Two types of blades are mounted on the front end of the tracted for felling the trees.

In one type a single angle blade with a projecting stringer on the lead side extend ahead of the blade. This blades into and through a tree to split and weaken it.

In the second type a special V-blade having a protruding stringer is used. This blade is so designed that it is able to slide along the surface of the ground. Any projecting material above the ground surface is cut. It can also be lowered below the surface to remove the stumps.

(iii) Tractor mounted rakes. The rake mounting is used to grub and pile trees, boulders and similar materials without transporting soil. Granular material such as sand and gravel falls from the openings between the rakes.

(iv) Tractor-pulled Chains and Steel Cables. A heavy chain is pulled by two tractors. The chain is kept slightly above the ground by attaching one or more heavy balls which may be a few metres diameter. The chain may be replaced by a wire rope.

(v) Special machines. The tractors are mounted with special auxiliary equipment which can fell trees and other vegetation. The material can also be chopped or shred in such a way that it may be disposed off by stock pilling and burning.

1.3.11 Ditcher or Trencher

These machines are used for digging trench for mains, gas lines oil pipe lines, telephone cables, drainage ditches, sewers etc. They provide fast digging operation with positive control for depth and width. In order to increase their stability and for distribution of weight over greater area they are usually crawler mounted. They are of two types namely the wheel type and the ladder type.

Wheel Type Trencher

Figure 1.10 shows a wheel type Ditcher or Trencher.

Fig. 1.10 Ditcher.

The trench width that can be dug by this type of machine varies from 30 cm to 1.50 metre depending upon the size of the cutting wheel. They are capable of digging upto 2.5 metres of even more. The maximum depth and width vary with the weight of the requirement.

1.3.12 Scraper

(*a*) *General*. The scraper is a self operating equipment which combines the operations normally carried out by various machines. The scraper can load itself, carry the material and discharge at the other end. The self loading scrapers are available upto 40 cu. m capacities. If any operative part of the machine stops functioning due to a breakdown the other part can still be operative. Since this machine combines in it the operation of loading and hauling it is not expected to give the performance of shovel, dragline, belt loaders etc., which carry cut the operation of loading only. In the same way as a hauling unit the performance of trucks will be better specially over fairly good roads. Inspite of these disadvantages, the combined operation of loading and hauling carried out by the same equipment makes the equipment very useful.

Fig. 1.11 Scrapper.

The machine deposits the load in uniform thick layers and succeeding layers can be easily laid.

(*b*) *Sizes.* Size of scraper is designated by the struck or heaped capacity of the bowl. In cubic metres. In the case of heaped capacity the slope of heap measured horizontally to vertically has also to be specified. The SAE (Society of Automobile Engineers USA) specifies this slope as 2 : 1.

The loose volume which can be held by the scraper is multiplied by the swell factor to get the rated capacity of the scraper.

The swell factor depends on the type soil and the moisture content and degree of compactness. This factor is from 0.63 for well blasted rock to 0.89 for dry gravel.

(*c*) *Type.* Scraper are of two types, namely crawler tractor pulled and wheel-tractor pulled. The wheel tractor pulled are further divided into the following categories:

(*i*) Single-engine.

(*ii*) Twin-engine.

(*iii*) Two-bowl tandem.

(*iv*) Multi bowl, multi-engine all-wheel electric drive.

(*v*) Elevating scraper.

The Crawler Tractor. The equipment consists of crawler tractor pulling a pneumatic self-loading scraper. Even on rough and poor roads because of the high drawbar pull of the tractor and superior traction, it gives good performance. If the haulage distance is long it is better to use the wheel tractor pulled scraper.

Wheel-tractor scraper. When the haul distance is long, this type of tractor is better suited for the job. A job analysis would therefore have to be carried out to determine the haulage distance up to which the crawler type scraper would be more economical.

(*d*) **Operations**

(*i*) *Loading.* The front of the bowl is lowered till the cutting edge reaches the ground. Simultaneously the front apron is raised and an open slot is provided. The earth flows into the bowl through this slot. The pull is the forward direction makes the flow into the bowl. The operation is continued till bowl is filled.

(*ii*) *Dumping.* The cutting edge is lowered to the required height above the fill. The apron is raised. The earth is forced out between the blade and the apron by a movable ejector. The movable ejecter is mounted at the rear of the bowl.

The elevating scraper contains two horizontal slats. These slats are operated by two endless chains. The ends of the endless chains are connected to the ends of slats. With the forward movement of the scraper, the cutting edge digs into the earth and loosens it. The loosened earth is racked by the slats into the bowl. The energy required in filling the bowl in this case is less as the earth has not been pushed into the filled bowl. The output of these scrapers is therefore greater.

1.3.13 Motor Grader

(*a*) *General*. The motor grader is primarily an equipment for levelling and finishing earthwork. It is particularly suited for maintenance of earthen roads.

(*b*) *Types*. Motor graders are of two types namely towed and motorised. The towed grader is comparatively a smaller unit. The controls are operated manually sometimes however a small petrol engine is mounted for the operation of the controls.

The motorised unit is a very popular equipment. The front of the frame rests on a pair of front wheelsy. The rear wheels, which are the drive wheels are heavy tandem wheels support the rear. The blade can be turned through 360°.

Fig. 1.12 Motor Grader.

(*c*) *Attachments*. The various attachments of grader are given below:

(*i*) *The blade*. It is curved like the door blade and is fitted with replaceable edges on the sides and at the bottom. It can swivel through complete horizontal circle and be tilted vertically to the desired inclination. By fixing extension pieces to the sides, its operating width can be increased.

(*ii*) *The Sacrifier*. It is a tool for loosening hard soil. It can be attached in the front or in the rear of the machine. The number of teeth are replaceable depending upon the nature of the soil. The number of cutting teeth is inversely proportional to the hardness of the soil.

(*iii*) *Bulldozer and Snow plough.* These are front end attachments to the grader for pushing loads for clearing snow.

(*iv*) *The elevator attachment.* This helps the grader to pick up the cut material. This picked up material is dropped over an inclined belt conveyor. The conveyor transmits the material into carrier units or throws it out through the window.

(*v*) *Rollers.* These are attached to the rear of the grader to consolidate the graded surface. Articulated models of motor grader have been introduced which have better maneuverability and hence better utility. The other improvements in this model are:

1. Hydraulic blade controls.

2. Arrangement for lifting the rear wheels so as to keep them out of the ditch bottom for better traction and efficiency of the blade operation.

(*d*) *Motor Grader Operation.* For grading, the machine moves forward and the steering is controlled by the Steering wheel.

To suit the type of work the blade can be moved in any desired position. By lifting or tilting the blade the depth of the cut can be varied. For dressing of the banks the blade can be held in a vertical position. The entire length of the road surface being graded is traversed before the blade is reversed for the second cut. The machine can also be returned in high gear and the second cut in the forward direction can be started.

The following operations can be performed by the grader:

(*i*) Grading

(*ii*) Spreading

(*iii*) Side cutting

(*iv*) Road crowning

(*v*) Bank dressing

(*vi*) Mixing materials.

The grader is moved in top gear 40 kmph on no load condition that is when it is not giving output in respect of any of the above operations. The lowest gear is used for abnormally heavy works such as moving on steep grades (upto 3 kmph). For normal loading the speed of the grader varies from 10 to 15 kmph depending upon the type of work.

1.4 SOIL STABILISATION AND COMPACTION EQUIPMENT

1.4.1 Introduction

The alteration of the property of the soil so as to improve its load bearing or load transferring property is termed as soil stabilisation. The purpose of the soil stabilisation is given below:

(*a*) To increases the bearing capacity of the soil.

(*b*) To reduce the sensitivity of bearing capacity to environment changes, particularly to changes in moisture content.

(*c*) To reduce compressibility.

Figure 1.13 shows how the soil compaction is carried out with various tools. Here complete process is illustrated.

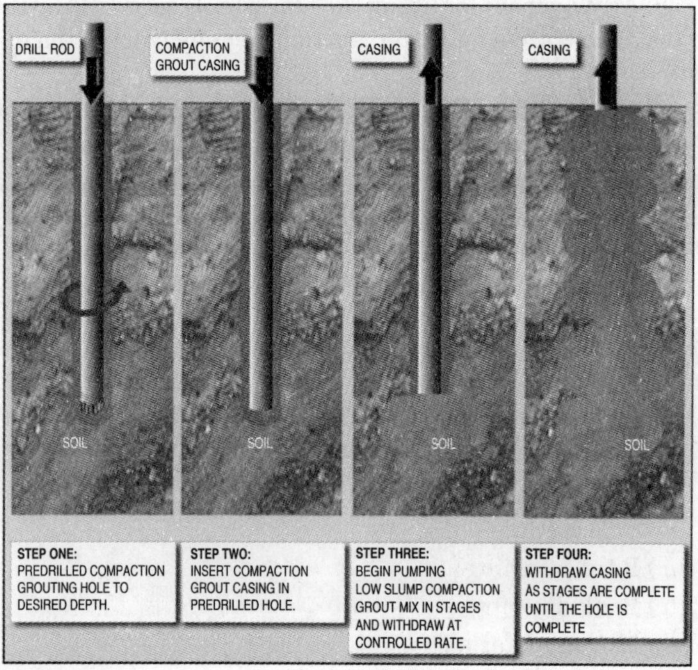

Fig. 1.13

Soil stabilisation is particularly useful in strengthening the formation of highways, airports and railways.

1.4.2 Types of Compacting Equipment

Compaction of soil is carried out by one of the following methods:

(*a*) Kneading.

(*b*) Static weight.

(*c*) Vibration.

(*d*) Impact.

Various equipments used for compaction are described below:

1. Tamping Rollers. This is the sheep foot type of roller and is illustrated in Fig. 1.14(*b*). The roller consists of a hollow steel drum. A number of projecting steel feet (sheep foot formation) are welded on the body of the hollow drum. One or more such rollers constitutes a unit. In case there are more than one units, all of them are mounted on a horizontal axis and may be towed by a tractor or the system may be self propelled. Pressure upto 50 kg/cm^2 may be produced under each foot by filling the hollow drum of water or sand. The feet of the roller penetrate soil and compact of soil from top to bottom by kneading it. The rolling is continued over the surface (passes) till the feet do not penetrate the soil. Although this type of roller is very good for compacting clayey soil or soil containing mixture of sand clay, granular soils such as sand gravel cannot be compacted by this roller.

Fig. 1.14(a)

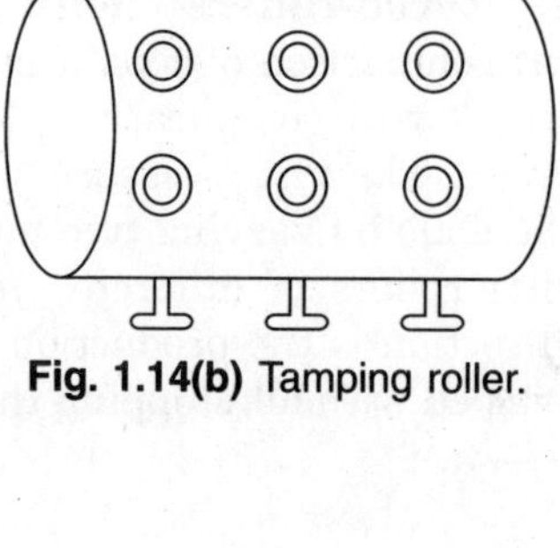

Fig. 1.14(b) Tamping roller.

Recent modification to these rollers is the replacement of the welded feet by segments or pads. In another modification grids have been used instead of the feet. This modified form can be used satisfactorily for compacting material as well.

2. Smooth wheel rollers. These rollers are designated by weight. It may be a two wheel or a three wheel one. In the case of three wheel roller, the front wheel is for steering and the rear wheels are for driving. The three-wheel unit gives better performance than the two wheel unit because of concentration of pressure on the middle wheel when the roller passes over high spots in the surface that is being compacted.

A roller designated as 14–20 tonnes indicates that the minimum weight of the roller is only 14 tonnes but it can be ballasted to give a maximum weight of 20 tonnes. These rollers are not very effective for compaction of cohesive soils as they tend to form a (crust) over the surface which prevents adequate compaction of the lower strata. They are however very well suited for compacting granular material.

3. Pneumatic-tyred Rollers. The compaction is effected by the kneading action of the pneumatic tyres. The rollers vary in size from 1 to 15 tonnes (small size) and 15 tonnes weight to 200 tonnes weight (large size). The smaller units may be self propelled or towed but the large units are generally self propelled.

The small tyred units have two tandem axles with four to nine tyres on each axle. Gaps in the front wheels are covered by rear wheels thereby providing complete coverage.

The large units are used for compaction of subgrades and bases on airfields and earthfill dams. The compacting ability of these rollers is indicated by one of the following methods:

(*a*) By indicating air pressure in the tyres.

(*b*) By indicating weight per cm width of tyre.

(*c*) Gross weight of the unit.

(*d*) Gross weight per wheel.

4. Pneumatic tyred-rollers with variable tyre pressure. For efficient compaction of soils it is desirable that the initial pass should be made with comparatively low tyre pressure to increase ground coverage. The tyre pressure should be gradually increased. This may be done by varying tyre pressure, by varying the ballast or by using rollers of different weights. The recent development in this direction is the production of rollers in which tyre pressure can be varied without stopping the machine.

5. Vibrating Compactors. Soils, sand gravel or stones get well compacted by a combination of pressure and vibration. On being vibrated the smaller particles get into the voids of larger particles and form a dense mass. For this purpose separate engines are mounted on the rollers to produce vibrations from 1000 to 5000 per minute. For maximum effectiveness the actual number of vibration should correspond to the natural resonant frequency of the soil.

1.5 HAULING EQUIPMENT (LOADERS AND WAGONS)

1.5.1 Introduction

Steam, diesel and electrically operated locomotives constitute the equipment for rail transport. The term haulage equipment is however by usage reserved most exclusively for haulage by road by equipment such as trucks, dumpers and trailers. Some important projects have however employed steam or diesel locomotive for transportation of excavated earth.

Road haulage may be carried out by trucks, rubber tyred tractor with wagons or crawler tractors with wagons. The advantages of these modes of transportation are given below:

Fig. 1.15 Hauling loader.

Trucks

(*a*) High mobility.

(*b*) Good speed.

(*c*) Adaptability of various categories of hauling demand.

(*d*) Good maneuverability.

Disadvantages

The performance is adversely affected on rough roads and bad weather.

Rubber Tyred Tractors with Wagons

(*a*) Good mobility.

(*b*) Good haulage speed.

(*c*) Capable of carrying heavier loads as compared to trucks.

(*d*) Rough roads and bad weather do not adversely affect performance to the same extent as it affects truck operation.

Crawler-tractors with Wagons

(*i*) Can move on very rough roads (sometimes even if there are no roads).

(*ii*) The performance is not affected by weather conditions.

Disadvantages

Very slow speed.

Locomotive with wagons moving on rail—

Advantages

(*i*) High speed.

(*ii*) Very well suited for long distance haulage over fixed routes.

(*iii*) Very low operational cost.

(*iv*) Not effected by limitation on weather.

Disadvantages

(*i*) On account of the initial high cost of the track and the equipment the method is economical where large scale haulage between two fixed points is involved.

(*ii*) Quite unsuitable where steep grades are involved.

The road transportation of goods is further divided into two types namely road hauls and construction hauls. The road haul involving long distance transportation is commonly done by light or heavy duty tracks while the construction hauls are carried out by special dumpers which may be pneumatic wheel type or crawler type pulling heavy trailers. These extra heavy dump trucks have pay load capacity varying from 10 to 50 tonnes.

1.5.2 Trucks

Trucks are essential equipment on any construction project. They are available in various sizes and types with capacities from 0.4 cu. m to 20 cu. m. The average speed of the truck varies from 10 to 50 kmph and top speed from 30 to 100 kmph. Depending upon their carrying capacity they are classified into light (½ to 1 tonne), medium (1.5 to 3 tonne) and total number of wheels and the number of wheel drives. For ordinary condition of road a 4 × 2 truck having four wheels, two of them only being driving wheels is quite popular. Where heavy load is to be carried over comparatively poorly maintained roads or roads with steeper gradients a 6 × 6 or 4 × 4 truck would be required.

1.5.3 Dump Trucks

The experience of various construction projects shows that the performance of a hauling equipment for short distance haulage is considerably improved if the period spent in loading and unloading is reduced. Take the example of 3 tonne truck carrying construction material such as bricks, aggregates, steel, cement etc., from the godown to the work site. Assuming an average of 10 km trip (both ways) the total period spent in transit would be approximately 15 minutes (assuming average speed of 40 kmph). If conventional method of loading and unloading manually is done, as much as 30 minutes would be spent in loading and about 20 minutes in unloading. The truck would thus be usefully employed for less than 25 per cent of the working time say one trip per hour. If, however, both loading and unloading periods are reduced to 5 minutes each, the time spent per trip would be reduced to 25 minutes per trip from 65 minutes, thereby improving the performance of the vehicle or the output by more than 100 per cent. Trucks fitted with automatic unloading devices are known as Dump Trucks. The loading is normally done by loading shovels or loaders.

So for these dump trucks were available in carrying capacities of upto 50 tonnes. The Hindustan Motors, license of General Motors Corporation, who claim as the manufacturers of the largest construction equipment with the latest technology have come forward with dump trucks with pay loads of 317.5 tonnes, the largest in the world. This TEREX 317.5 tonnes dump truck has the following features (as claimed by the manufacturers).

(*i*) An output equal to 35 average highway trucks or 18 times the load capacity of an average 18 tonnes railway wagon.

(*ii*) Gross H.P. = 33000.

(*iii*) Weight 231.105 t kg. (equivalent to 6 hectares of earth, 25.4 mm deep).

(*iv*) Its body hydraulic pump can fill swimming pool of 113.27 cu. m. in 85 minutes.

(*v*) Tyres are over 3.35 m higher than a basket ball goal.

(*vi*) Weight of each tyre = 3.18 tonne.

(*vii*) Operator's compartment is 4.42 m above the ground. (like being on Ist floor of a building).

(*viii*) The only truck that moves such heavy loads without roads.

(*ix*) Moderate fuel consumption.

(*x*) Simple maintenance.

(*xi*) Adequate supply of spare parts.

(*xii*) GMMCOS' net work of trained experts available for servicing and repairs (Based on advertisement of General Marketing and Manufacturing Co. Ltd., 9/1, R.N. Mukherjee Road, Calcutta – 700001. Hindustan Times, dated 18.6.76).

1.5.4 Rear Dump Trucks

The following are the special features of this type of dumper:

1. Heavy duty truck having a strongly built body.
2. Hinged at the back.
3. Fitted with hydraulic ram on the under side for lifting the front of the body and tilt it backward while unloading or dumping.
4. Tapered sides for forming a chute to facilitate dumping.
5. Body frame consists of channel section rigidly braced.
6. Tandem or single rear axle.
7. Hoisting valve is actuated by a lever near operator's seat.

Fig. 1.16 Rear Dump Truck.

1.5.5 Bottom Dump Truck

The important features of these trucks are:

1. Front of the trucks is supported on the rear of the hauling tractor.

2. The rear rests on own wheels.

3. The bottom is fitted with two longitudinal gates made of thick steel plate. These gates are reinforced with channel sections swinging on steel hinges.

4. The gates, which are hinged to the sides of the truck body, are actuated from driver's cabin by single control lever.

1.5.6 Side Dump Trucks

These are very popular dumpers specially when material is required to be dumped along narrow length on one or both the sides of the road. Heavy large size material such as boulders coarse aggregate and bricks can be discharged conveniently. The two sides are hinged to the body and kept in position by means of latches. The material can be discharged on any side by lifting the rams.

1.5.7 Dampers

Trucks with special pneumatic wheels and capable of moving at high speeds having short chasis and strong dumping bodies are known as dumpers. The material can be dumped in front, or at the back. While dumping the body takes up upright vertical position. The machine is particularly useful for short distance haulage and on rough roads. The loading transporting and dumping can be done in quick succession. The engine of the dumper may be diesel operated or petrol operated. They are available in capacities upto 4.5 cu. m. Situation where these dumpers are very handy is hauling of muck during excavation of tunnel.

1.5.8 Trailers

Trailer are carriages hauled by power units. The power units may be tractors or trucks. Trailers are of two types, namely full trailer or wagons and semi-trailers. The full trailers are self supported. They are connected to the power unit with swivelling axle and drawbar. The semi-trailers are supported in the front by the power unit and at the rear on their own wheels. These trailers can be operated in a smaller space than that required for a full trailer but better driving skill is required.

Fig. 1.17 Trailer.

The braking system of both types of trailers is hydraulically operated. Some braking systems are operated by vaccum or air pressure. In some trailers the braking is synchronised with the braking system of power unit. In some types separate controls operated from the power units are available. Similarly the lighting system of the trailers is operated from the main unit.

1.6 HOISTING EQUIPMENT

1.6.1 Introduction

Hoisting is the operation of lifting the loads, holding them in suspension during transfer from one location to the other and placing them at the desired location. The modern construction requires lifting of material from its location and depositing it to the place where it is required for incorporation in the work. It would either not be possible or much more time consuming and far more costly if such work is done manually. The various equipments used for hoisting are:

(*i*) Pulleys

(*ii*) Chain hoists

(*iii*) Jacks

(*iv*) Winches and cranes.

Among the available hoisting equipments crane is the most popular machine which provides all the possible movements required for load transfer.

These machines are described in the following articles:

1.6.2 Pulley and Sheave Block

Pulley and sheaves are suitable for lifting rough surfaced and heavy objects. Both chains and wire ropes are used for this purpose. Alloy chains are best suited for hoisting operation. The weakest component of this system is the load hook. The hook fails by straightening. Once the hook gets elongated or straightened, it should be replaced.

A typical sheave and pulley block is shown in Fig. 1.18.

Fig. 1.18

1.6.3 Chain Hoists

Chain hoists are popular mechanism for lifting loads upto 50 tonnes. The system consists of two sets of chains namely the hand chain and the load chain. The hand chain hoists are particularly useful for use in isolated locations where electric power or other types of mechanical equipment are not available. These hoists are available in capacities of ½ tonne to 50 tonnes. The pull applied through the hand chain is transmitted to the load chain with a multiplication factor or over 20. The load to be lifted is held by a hook while another hook at the top supports the mechanism. The two hooks, however, should not be interchanged as the support hook is made much stronger than the load hook. Four types of hand operated chain hoists are in use. They are (1) Differential (2) Screw geared (3) Spur geared and (4) Pull lift.

1. Differential Chain Hoists. This is the simplest type of hoist consisting of a set of different diameter sheaves. An endless chain is wound over these sheaves. If the pendent loop is pulled in one direction the load is lifted, when pulled in the other direction it is lowered. It is used for handling small item weighing below one tonne.

2. Screw Geared Hoist. It consists of a worm-wheel arrangement with a set of chains namely hand chain, and load chain when the hand chain is pulled the worm mounted on the shaft of the chain moves. The rotation of the worm is conveyed to the load sheaves through the wheel and the load is raised or lowered depending upon the direction of the pull of the hand chain. These hoists are capable of handling load upto 3 tonnes.

3. Spur Gear Hoist. The main components of this hoist are the hand chain, the load chain and a series of planetary gears assembled in a case. Hand operated hoists of this type are available upto lifting capacities of 10 tonnes using single gear trains. Multiple gear trains have capacities upto 50 tonnes. A typical spur gear hoist is illustrated in Fig. 1.19.

4. Pull Lift. This machine is primarily used for pulling in horizontal direction. The hoisting operation is carried out by means of a lever. The chain used is roller type instead of the link type chain used in other hoists. The load chain can be replaced by a load cable. The equipment is illustrated in Fig. 1.20.

Fig. 1.19

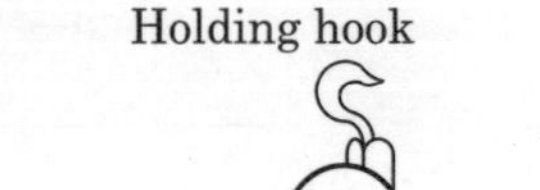

Fig. 1.20. Pull lift.

1.6.4 Jacks

Jacks of various types and various capacities. The smallest jack may have 5 tonnes capacity used for lifting an automobile wheel, while the bigger variety may be of 100 tonnes capacity or more. They are primarily of two types namely (*a*) Mechanical and (*b*) Hydraulic.

(a) Mechanical Jack (b) Hydraulic Jack

Fig. 1.21 Jacks.

The mechanical jacks are further classified into ratchet type and screw type. The ratchet type contains a long bar having ratchet teeth cut on a side. An operating level is used for moving the teeth.

In an screw jack arrangement, the lift lug is mounted on a threaded spindle. When the spindle is rotated, the lug moves over it. Another modification of this jack is the geared type screw jack. A steel screw moves in a gear of large size. A ratchet attachment is provided for operating the lever.

The principle of working of the hydraulic jack is that the pressure exerted by a liquid on a surface is proportional to the area of the surface. These jacks are available from 10 tonnes to 200 tonnes capacities.

1.6.5 Hoist Winch

A winch is a combination of gears, clutches and brakes. The operation is controlled through a series of levers. Power operated winches have their own prime movers, which may be diesel engine or

Fig. 1.22 Hoist winch.

an electric motor mounted on a frame. In the case of winches operated by hand the handle for operating the winch extends out from the frame. Some of the earth moving machines and cranes have winches fitted to them which are operated from the power from the main unit.

1.6.6 Fork Trucks

These are self propelled or manually operated mobile units. For easy mobility they have short wheel base. It is a very handy machine for handling loads upto 6 tonnes. The hand operated variety is cheap and useful for lifting loads upto 100 kg. The electrically operated trucks are suitable for short hauls and medium loads upto 3 tonnes. For longer haulage the gasoline truck is more suitable. Fig. 1.1 illustrates a typical fork lift truck available upto 6 tonnes capacities.

1.6.7 Cranes

Cranes are most widely used equipment as an independent unit in combination with other machines. Their lifting capacities vary from ½ tonne to 500 tonnes. They are of two types namely: (1) stationary known as derrick ; and (2) mobile. The whirler crane is a combination of stationary and mobile cranes. In addition to the conventional mobile crane, a nomenclature which by usage denotes comparably small capacity cranes mounted on mobile unit, tower cranes, hydraulic cranes and gantry cranes though basically mobile form a category of cranes in themselves.

Fig. 1.23 Truck mounted crane.

In the recent years very massive cranes upto 1900 tonnes capacities have been developed. Boom length up to 57 metres and boom heights upto 118 m have also been manufactured in U.S.A. To increase precision and safety some computer controlled machines have also been constructed.

For working in steel works, dock yards and railways rail mounted cranes are used. These cranes are low carriage units moving on rail track and are driven by steam, or diesel engines. Another special type of cranes are those used for track laying and bridge repairing. They are known as permanent way cranes. These cranes are specially designed to conform to railway gauge clearances.

Important types of cranes are described in the following articles.

1.6.8 Derrick Cranes

Derrick cranes are of two types namely : (1) Guy derrick and (2) Stiff leg derrick. The guy derrick consists of a mast. This mast is supported by a number of guys and can revolve through 360°. While revolving the radius of revolution should be such that the revolving structure is not obstructed by the guys. The power is supplied by a diesel engine or by an electric motor. A typical derrick crane is illustrated in Fig. 1.24. These derricks can be constructed upto 200 tonnes capacity.

Fig. 1.24 Derrick crane.

In the stiff leg type derrick the guy wires as replaced by trussed structure. This type of derrick is suitable for loads from 10 to 50 tonnes.

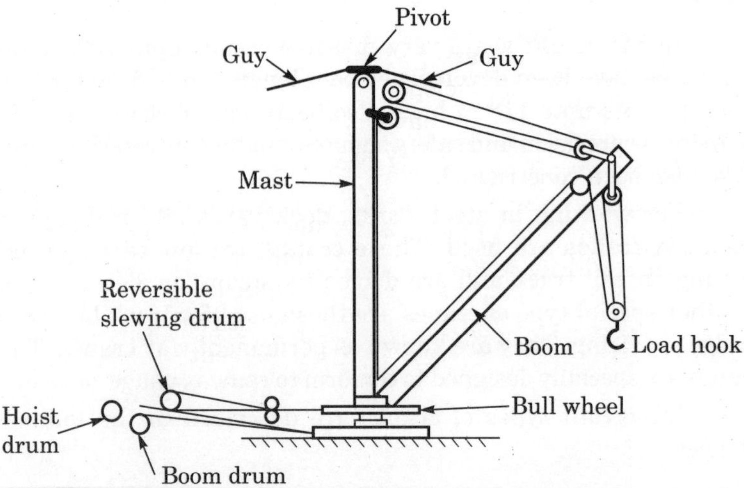

Fig. 1.25 Schematic diagram of Derrick crane.

1.6.9 Mobile Cranes

Cranes mounted on pneumatic tyred truck on crawler tractor chassis are termed as mobile cranes. The crawler mounted trucks are suitable for rough terrain where pneumatic tyres would not be able to travel. They are used for operation with a small area. When they are to be transported over long distances the machine is stripped and reassembled in the new location. Where electricity is available electric drive is preferred to diesel operated units. Crawlers however have diesel drives.

Fig. 1.26 Mobile Crane.

1.6.10 Whirler Cranes

The cranes combine the advantage of long boom of derrick crane and mobility of the mobile crane. The rotating structure has an outer framework. To the front of this framework is attached the boom. At the rear it has the counterweight. The movement of the central shaft is obtained by means of separate motors which are mounted on two diagonally opposite corners of the base. Fig. 1.27 illustrates a whirler crane.

Fig. 1.27 Whirler Crane.

Cranes

Soilmec has developed a full range of multipurpose foundation cranes ranging from 20 to 120 ton capacity.

The base carrier is designed with built-in facilities for foundation technologies such as:

- — hydromill
- — CT-Jet
- — hydraulic vibrohammer
- — casing oscillator
- — hammer grab
- — hydraulic rotary

Model	*max load capacity* ton	*nominal line pull* kN	*engine power* kW	*weight* ton	*max boom length* m
SC-20	21,5 @ 3 m	84	119 @ 2200 rpm	26	21
SC-40	40 @ 3,5 m	160	220 @ 2000 rpm	43	30
SC-60	60 @ 3,5 m	240	350 @ 1900 rpm	60	36
SC-70	70 @ 3,5 m	240	330 @ 1900 rpm	71	36
SC-80	80 @ 3,5 m	240	400 @ 1900 rpm	81	42
SC-90	90 @ 4,5 m	305	480 @ 1900 rpm	108	42
SC-120	120 @ 4 m	400	522 @ 1800 rpm	133	54

Hydraulic Rotary Rigs mounted on crawler unit

Model	*max diameter* mm	*max depth* m	*max torque* kNm (35 MPa)	*engine power* kW	*weight tot* total
SR-20	1200	40	96	127	27
SR-30	1500	48	121	205	36
SR-40	1500	55	161	224	49
SR-50	1500	61	173	224	54
SR-60	1800	66	201	358	63
R-625	2000/2500*	77	237	360	72
SR-70	2000/2500*	77	271	360	79
SR-80	2000/2500*	77	292	360	88
SR-80C	2000	77	292	388	85
SR-90	2500	77	333	500	113
SR-100	3000	92	452	500	140

*Removing the bottom section of the max

Truck Mounted Hydraulic Rotary Rigs

Model	*max diameter* mm	*max depth* m	*max torque* kNm	*engine power* kW	*weight total* t
STM-20	1100	30	96	127	19*
STM-30	1500	50	113	205	29*

* w/o truck

Crane Attachment Rigs

Equipment for execution of bored piles up to diameter 2500 mm (3000 mm using underreamer) and 102 m max excavation depth. Both rigs can be used together with casing oscillator. SA-25 can drive casing directly with the rotary. This equipment can be mounted on any type of crane with min 40/50 ton capacity giving high performance and great reliability.

Model	*max diameter* mm	*max depth* m	*max torque* kNm	*min crane capacity* t
RT3-ST mechanical drive	2500	80	206	40
SA-25 full hydraulic drive	2500	102	240	60

1.7 ROCK DRILLING EQUIPMENT

1.7.1 Introduction

Before rock is excavated, it is necessary to loosen it. In the case of hard rocks this loosening is done by drilling the holes, filling these with explosives and discharging the explosives.

The particular type of drilling equipment depends upon the nature of the terrain, type of rock and the size of the broken pieces required.

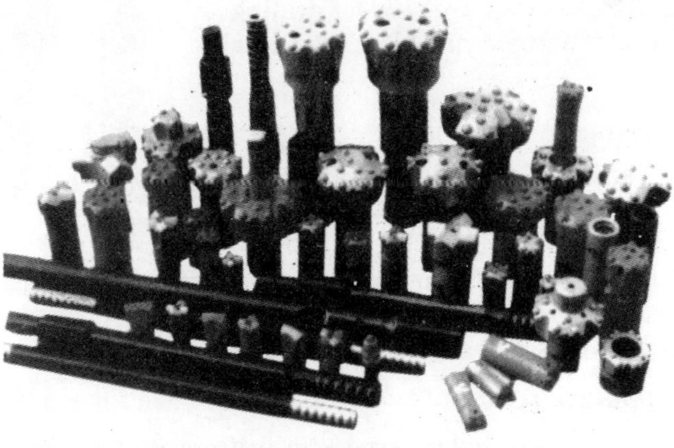

Fig. 1.28 Rock drilling equipments.

1.7.2 Bits

The part which directly engages the rock for its disintegration is known as the '*drill bit*'. Till recently the ends of the drilling rods were forged on the drilling end. The present practice is to screw detachable bits to the drilling rods. These bits are available in different sizes. They can be sharpened as well as replaced and are relatively inexpensive. These bits can be used for boring holes for 1 metre to 12 metres in depth depending upon the type of the rock.

In case of vary hard variety of rocks the steel drill bits have to be replaced after only a few centimetres of drilling. In such cases carbide-insert bits are used. The drilling points consists of a very hard metal tungsten carbide, which is embedded in the steel. These bits are costly but considering the rate of drilling and the depth of borings per bit, these bits afford an overall economy.

1.7.3 Jack Hammers

These are hand held air operated percussion type drills. These hammers are held in position by drillers and weigh form 20 to 25 kg. They are used for drilling holes upto 3 metres though they can drill upto 6 metres. The hammering effect is caused by the compressed air flowing through the hammer. This air reciprocates the piston at a speed of about 2000 blows per minute. The steel rod transmits the energy to the drill bits. Because they are used for drilling holes, these hammers are also known as 'Sinkers'.

Fig. 1.29 Jack hammer.

1.7.4 Drifters

These are similar in operations to jack hammers. They are used for deeper holes and weigh from 35 kg to 120 kg. Because of higher weight they are mounted for horizontal, down or up drilling. The cuttings from bore holes are removed by jetting air or water.

1.7.5 Wagon Drills

For very deep holes large size drifters are required. The drifters are mounted on masts. These masts are in turn mounted on wheels which provide mobility to the equipment. The name *'wagon drill'* is primarily due to these wheels which convert the drifter into wagon drill. Fig. 1.30 illustrates a typical wagon drill.

Fig. 1.30 Wagon Drills.

1.7.6 Track Mounted Drill

Track mounted drill is an improvement over the wagon drill which it is replacing fast. Because of the track mounting the equipment can be shifted from one working location to the other comparatively easily. Another advantage due to track mounting is that it can operate almost at any angle along the sides, vertically up or vertically down. All the operations are powered by compressed air. Holes upto 15 cm in diameter and 15 metres deep can be drilled by the machine.

1.7.7 Rotary percussion Drilling

By combining the hard-hitting reciprocal action of percussion drill with the turning under pressure action of rotary drill, the equipment is able to drill at a much faster rate than the normal percussion drill. Special carbide bits with inserts set at angles different from those used with normal carbide bits are used. The drilling rate varies from 1.5 to 3 metres per minute depending upon the hardness of the rock.

Vibrators

Hydraulically powered units for driving and extracting casings and sheet piles.

Model	*eccentricity mon.* kgm	*frequency* cycles/m	*centrifugal force* t	*max extraction force* t	*engine* kW
VTH-1	685	1600	19 600	9.5	—
VS-4	15.2	1800	55 078	20	135
VS-8	30.4	1800	110 156	40	277

Drilling Tools

- Buckets
- Augers
- Rock augers
- Underreamers
- Chisels
- Core barrels

1.7.8 Piston Drills

This is a self-propelled machine mounted on crawler tracks. The drilling equipment is of percussion type and a hollow drill tube is attached to the piston. The machine is worked with carbide insert bits of upto 15 cm diameter and can drill holes upto 20 metre depth.

1.7.9 Blast Hole Drills

For very deep borings in soft and medium rocks such as dolomite and limestone this equipment can drill holes upto 90 metre depths. This self-propelled drill is mounted on a track or on crawler tracks. A tri-cone roller type bit is attached to the lower end of the drill pipe. A continuous blast of compressed air is forced down the pipe and actuates the bit to do the rock cutting. The drilling speed varies from 0.5 m per hour to 15 metre per hour.

Fig. 1.31 illustrates the working of this type of drill.

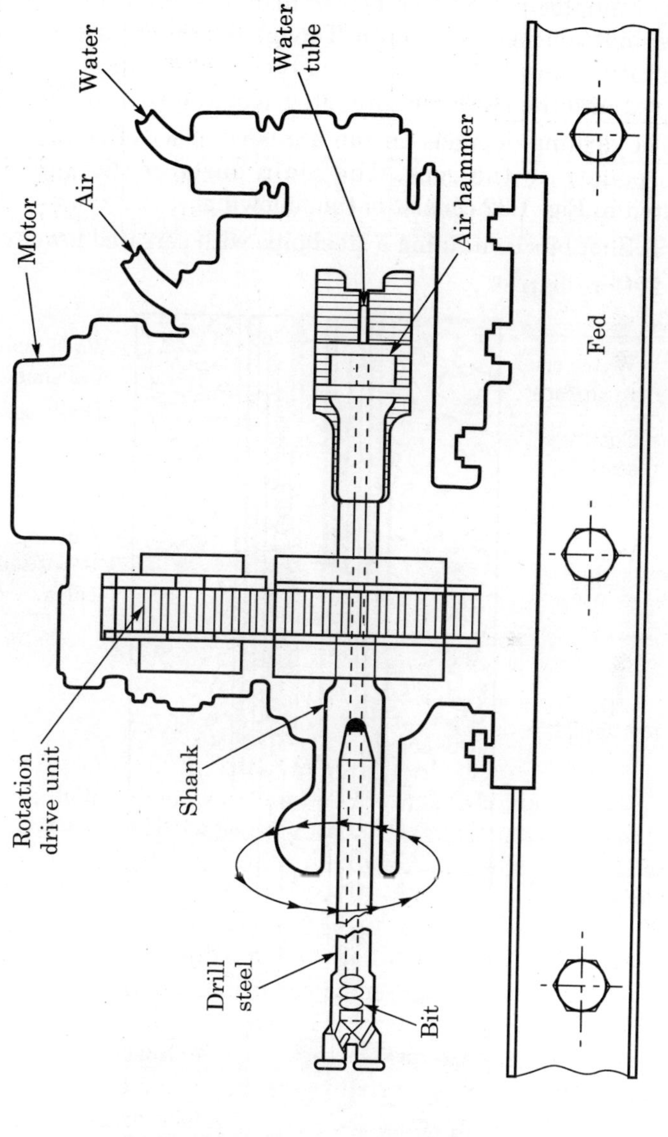

Fig. 1.31

1.7.10 Short Drills

For boring holes of very great depth over any type of rocks standard short drills capable of drilling holes from 6.5 cm to 50 cm in diameter and in depths upto 200 metres are used. With special auxiliary equipment the machine can drill holes upto 1.8 metre in diameter and 300 metres in depth. Though the rate of drilling large holes is rather slow (0.3 metre/hour), these holes permit a man to be lowered into the holes for through geological examination.

The drilling depends on the abrasive effect of chilled steel shot to penetrate the rock. The main parts of the machine, illustrated in Fig. 1.32 consist of the following:

1. Shot bits containing a steel pipe with serrated lower end.
2. Core barrel.

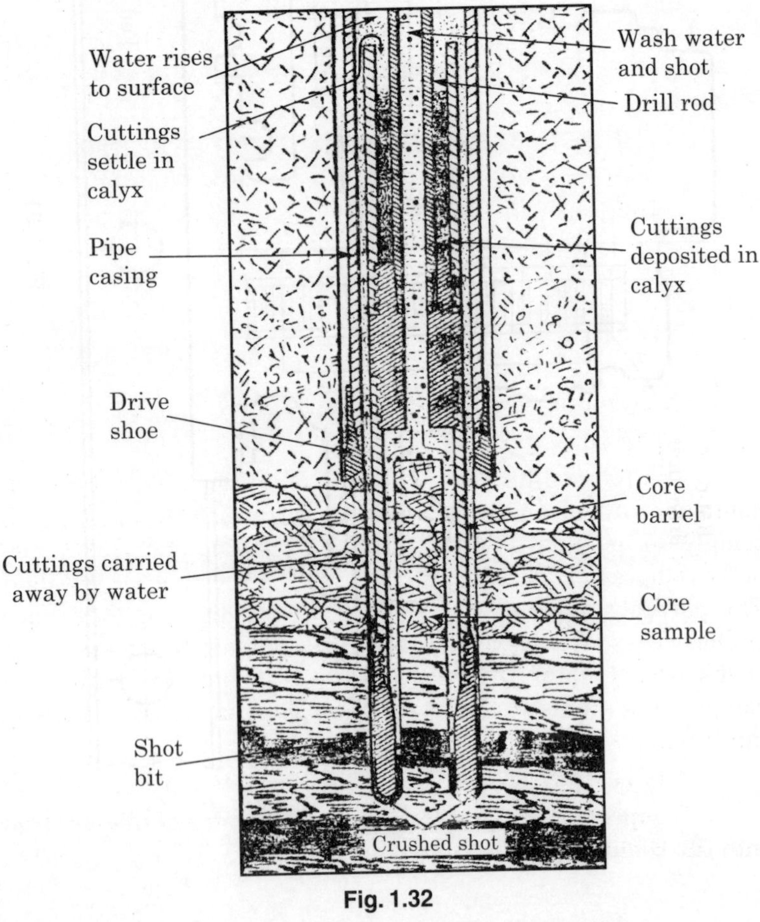

Fig. 1.32

3. Drill rod.
4. Water pump.
5. Rotation unit (Power driven).

Simultaneously with the rotation of the bit, snots are fed to the lower end through the drill rod. The eroding of the rock is done by the shots under pressure.

Water is supplied through the drill rod. This water forces the cuttings up around the outside of the drill. The sludge thus formed is removed when the unit is pulled from the hole.

1.8 PNEUMATIC EQUIPMENT

1.8.1

Compressed air is a very useful medium of power and has the following advantages:

1. Safe to work and easier to transmit from one point to another.
2. The working tools are light, rugged and durable.
3. The tools are lower in initial cost and maintenance.

Compressed air is used for the following operations:

1. Rock excavation.
2. Paving breakers.
3. With Wagon drills and drifters.
4. Sand blasting and jetting.
5. Running hoist, sump pumps, and
6. Pile driving.

Compressed air for pneumatic operations delivered to the equipment from compressors through airlines. The receiver of the compressor may have two to six lines depending upon the capacity of the compressor. These compressors may be portable or stationary. The portable types are mounted on two wheels or four wheels trollies. These trollies are towed from one place to another with a truck or a tractor. For construction projects portable type compressors are used. The stationary type compressors are heavy duty compressors with permanent foundation.

A typical compressor system is illustrated in Fig. 1.33.

Compressors are designated by the volume of free air drawn into the compressor per minute.

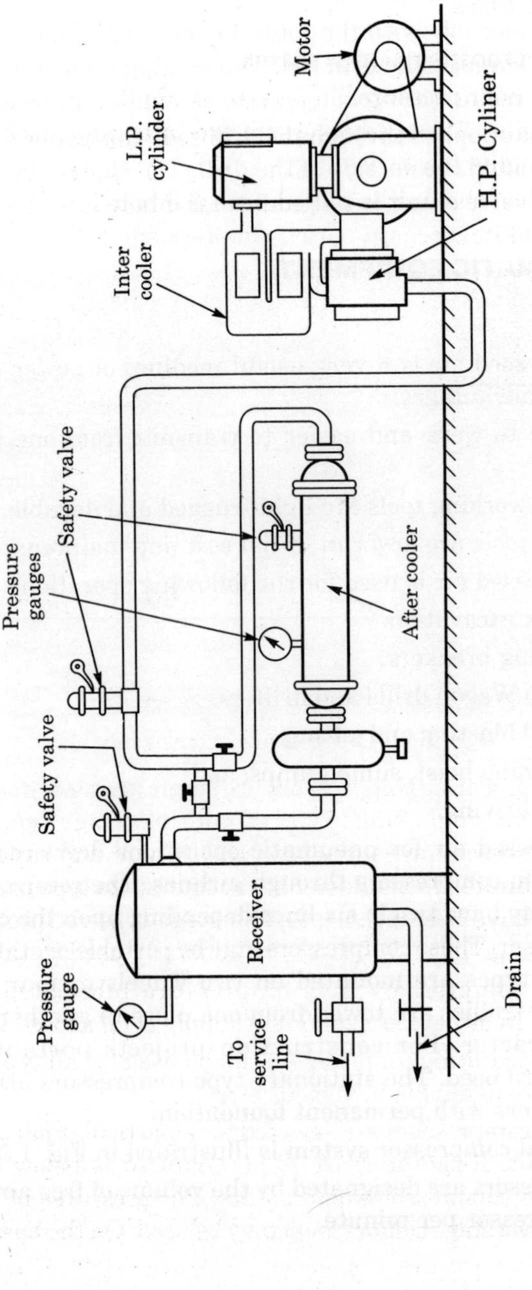

Fig. 1.33 Typical compressed air system.

The compressors may be positive displacement type (Reciprocating or Rotary) or non positive displacement type (Centrifugal and Axial Flow type). These types are described in the following articles.

1.8.2 Reciprocating Compressors

The reciprocating compressor is similar in construction to an I.C. engine. These compressors are integrally combined into a common engine block.

The valve operation regulates air intake into the compressor cylinder and its discharge after compression.

Fig. 1.34 A reciprocating compressor unit.

Reciprocating compressors are single acting or double acting. They may be single stage type of multiple stage type. In single stage compressors pressures upto 1.05 N/mm^2 and capacities upto 5.7 cu. m/minute are available. In the four stage type pressure upto 35 N/mm^2 have been achieved. Two stage type reciprocatory type compressors giving 3.5 N/mm^2 are generally used in the industry.

The compressors may be pressure lubricated or splash lubricated. In either case adequate supply of oil should be ensured.

Reciprocating compressors can be used for all types of works and they are available in various sizes.

The compressors are selected for a particular job on the basis of its output. If the pressure of air required is below 0.7 N/mm^2 single stage compressor would suffice. For pressures of 0.7 N/mm^2 and above two stage compression may be used. On the basis of output in cu. meter/minute single stage compressors may be employed upto 8.4 cu. m/min. The compressor installed should be reliable and capable of continuous operation and have adequate capacity.

1.8.3 Rotary Compressors

These are smaller machines than the reciprocating type. These compressors are available in three types namely:

1. Two impeller-positive displacement type.
2. Sliding vane type.
3. Liquid Piston type.

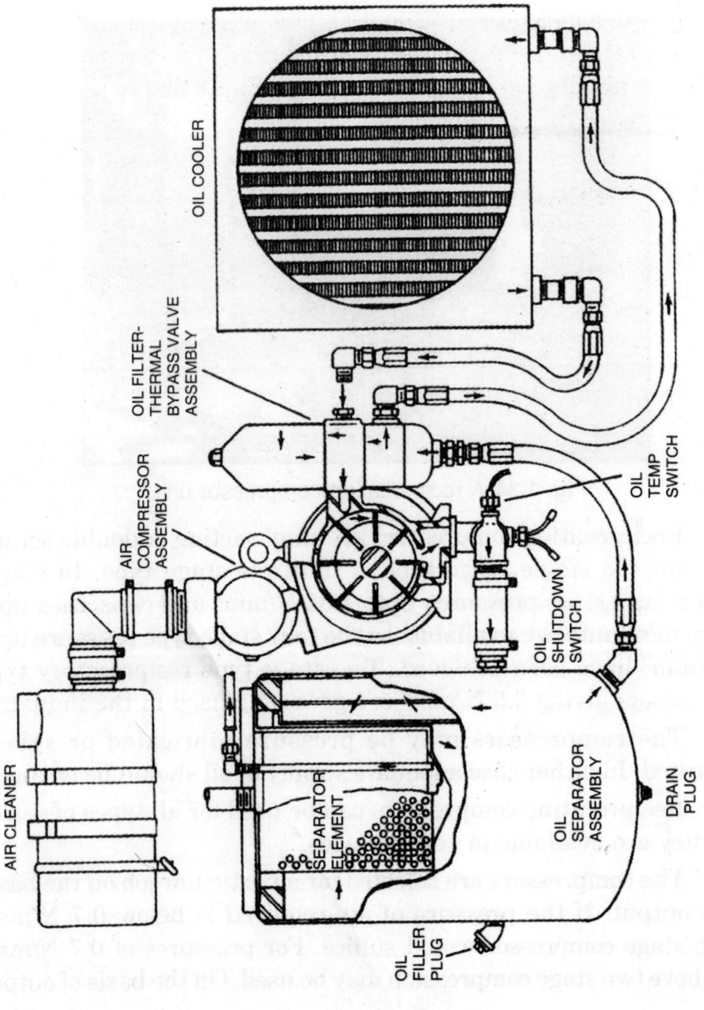

Fig. 1.35 A Rotary compressor unit.

The two impeller positive displacement type is used for delivering large volumes of air at low pressures (1 to 0.35 N/mm^2). The other types of compressors are used for delivering small volumes at low pressure as vacuum pumps. Rotary compressors are also used for scavanging operations in two stroke engine.

Oil is used for internal cooling and sealing the casing of rotary compressors. A typical oil cooling and sealing system of rotary compressors is illustrated in Fig. 1.35.

1.8.4 Centrifugal Compressors

The compressor consists of an impeller or rotor having vanes and moving in a casing. To minimise entry losses, the inlet section at the hub of the impeller on one side is curved and contains vanes to direct the air to the eye as illustrated in Fig. 1.36(*b*).

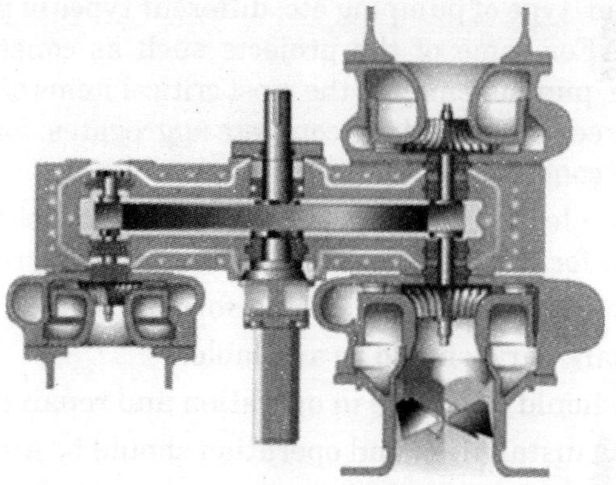

Fig. 1.36(a) Three stage centrifugal compressor.

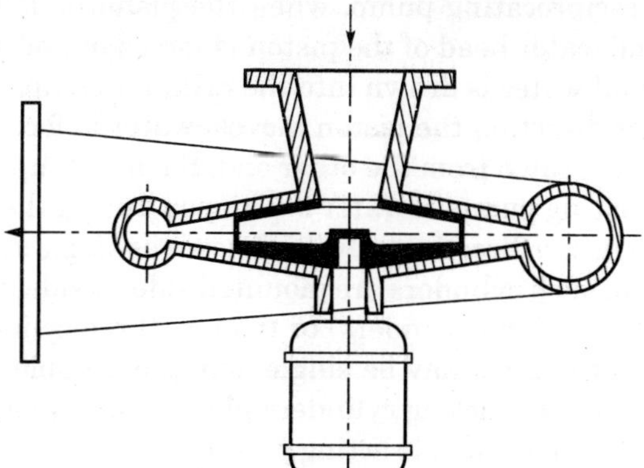

Fig. 1.36(b)

In the multiple stage compressors two or more impellers operate in series on a single shaft. These impellers are provided in the single casting.

The purpose of having multistage is to increase the pressure of air. The air compressed in one stage is fed into the next stage for further increase in compression.

Steam, gas turbines or electric drives are preferable as prime movers for centrifugal pumps.

1.9 PUMPING AND DEWATERING EQUIPMENT

1.9.1 Introduction

At various stages during the execution of projects pumping has to be resorted to. Depending upon the job requirements that is pumping head, type of pumping etc. different types of pumps would be required. For some of the projects such as construction of a concrete dam, pumping may be the most critical items of construction as it is required to wash all the concrete aggregates, for mixing and for curing of concrete.

While selecting a pump for any special purpose, apart from its suitability for the job it should meet the following requirements:

1. Should be dependable in performance.
2. Spare parts should be available.
3. It should be simple in operation and repairs.
4. The installation and operation should be economical.

1.9.2 Reciprocating Pumps

In a reciprocating pump, when the piston is moved in one direction, the water head of the piston is forced out of the cylinder and additional water is drawn into the cylinder behind the piston. In whichever direction the piston moves, water is forced out from one end and is drawn from the other end. Such a pump is designed as a double acting pump. If water is pumped during the movement of the piston in one direction only it is known as *single acting pump*. If a number of such cylinders are mounted side by side, the pump is known as duplex (two cylinders) or triplex (three cylinder) pump. These types of pumps may be single acting or double acting. For example, two double acting cylinders placed side by side would be designated as duplex double acting pump.

The volume of water pumped in one stroke is equal to the area of the cylinder times the length of the strokes less 3 to 5 per cent slippage allowance.

Let Q be the capacity of the pump in liters per minute.

c = 1 — slip allowance varies for (0.95 to 0.97)

d = Diameter of cylinder in cm

l = Length of strokes in cm

n = Number of strokes per minute (the movement of the piston in either direction equals one stroke).

The volume pumped in litres per minute by simplex double acting pump is given by

$$Q = \frac{c\pi d^2}{4} \times \frac{1 \times n}{1000} \text{ (1000 cc = 1 litre)}$$

$$Q = \frac{Nc.\pi d^2 l n}{4 \times 1000} \text{ (}N\text{ = number of cylinders in pump)}$$

If W = energy-metre-kg per minute

w = weight of 1 litre of water = 1 kg (10 N)

H = total pumping head, in metre.

e = efficiency of the pump.

$$W = \frac{wQH}{e}.$$

High Pressure Pumps

High pressure triplex pumps are designed to perform mono, bi or triple fluids jet grouting technology.

Linear size in	*Stroke* in	*Max Output Press* bar	*Max Delivery* lt/min	*Nominal Power* kW	*Mass (approx.)* kg
$3\text{-}3_{1/2}\text{-}4$	5	900	442	298	12500
$3\text{-}3_{1/2}\text{-}4$	7	900	600	379	13400
$3_{1/2}\text{-}4\text{-}4_{1/2}$	7	800	760	423	14000
$3_{1/2}\text{-}4_{1/2}\text{-}4_{3/4}$	7	750	614	597	23000

Grouting Equipment

Full range of accessories such as grouting units, mixers and stirrers of grouting jobs.

Model			
Containerized grouting unit	Output	m^3/h	22
Skid mounted Grouting unit	(GT-30; GA 45; GP-12)	m^3/h	5-7
Grouting Pump	Max delivery	l/min	0-120
	Max pressure	bar	200
Grout mixer	Output	m^3/h	5
	Output	m^3/h	3
Stirrer	Tank capacity	lt	900
	Tank capacity	lt	450

Concrete Pumps

Self-propelled and crawler mounted pumping units engineered to work next to the hydraulic rotary rigs, CFA version.

These pumps are fitted with a water tank and a built-in air compressor to clean the concrete pipe after piling execution.

Volumetric Output m^3/h	*Gate Pressure* bar	*Weight* kg
51	50	6900
64	50	7500
80	50	8300
90	50	8500
110	50	10000
120	50	9000

Bentonite Mud Equipment

Bentonite mud equipment are available to meet job site requirements.

Model			
Desander Unit	Feeding capacity	m^3/h	50
	Feeding capacity	m^3/h	70
	Feeding capacity	m^3/h	100
	Feeding capacity	m^3/h	140
	Feeding capacity	m^3/h	180

(Contd.)

	Feeding capacity	m^3/h	200
Bentonite mixer	Bentonite production	m^3/h	12-10
Automatic Mixing Unit	Output	m^3/h	24
Containerized	Feeding capacity	m^3/h	50
Bentonite plant	Bentonite production	m^3/h	12

1.9.3 Centrifugal Pumps

The principle of centrifugal pump can be illustrated by considering a drop of water at rest at a height of 'h' above a surface. If the drop falls freely it would strike the surface with a velocity $V = \sqrt{2gh}$, where V = Velocity in m/s, g is the acceleration of gravity and h = height of fall in metres. If on the other hand this drop of water is forced up with a velocity of $\sqrt{2gh}$ it would reach a height of h metres before coming to rest assuming that there are no frictional losses.

The centrifugal pump contains rotating element called *an impeller*. This impeller imparts to water passing through the pump a velocity sufficiently great to cause it to flow from the pump even against atmospheric pressure.

A centrifugal pump may have an open or enclosed impeller. Though the enclosed impeller has higher efficiency it does not handle water containing trash as efficiently as the open type impeller.

Energy required to operate the pump is as given by formula in Article 1.9.2.

1.9.4 Multiple Rotor Pump

If a few individual pumps are grouped together by connecting them externally or by combining the individual rotors in series in a single casing so as to form one compact unit, high liquid pressure can be built up. Such combination of rotors in series is known as multiple rotor pumping and the integrated equipment is known as multiple rotor pump.

1.9.5 Multiple-stage Pump

Multi-stage pumps are particularly suitable for pumping against high head of pressures. In this system water discharged from one impeller of centrifugal pump flows into the section of another. This type of pumps are very useful for supplying water for jetting where water is required under very high pressure.

1.9.6 Self Priming Pump

The operation of a self priming pump is illustrated in Fig. 1.37.

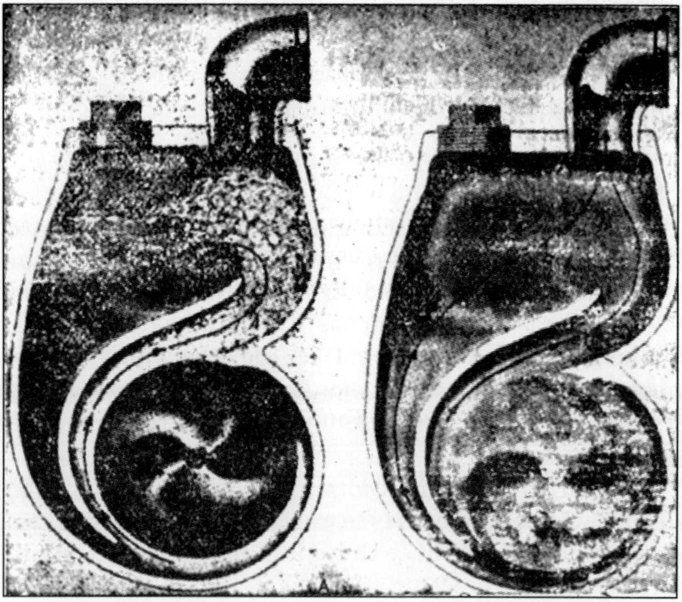

Fig. 1.37

The suction side of the pump is fitted with a check valve which permits the chamber to be filled with water before starting the pump. When the pump is started the water in the chamber forms a seal. This seal enables the pump to draw air from the suction pipe. The air and water get into position marked A. The air escapes through the discharge and water flows from chamber B to the impeller. The process continues till the air from suction pipe is exhausted and water enters the pump. On stopping the pump, the priming water is retained in the pump.

1.10 ROCK BLASTING

1.10.1 Introduction

Rock blasting is resorted when rock has to be loosened so that the entire rock or part of the rock may be removed. The geological formation influences the type of equipment and the drilling pattern. If the rock is of a comparatively soft variety it can be removed by angle dozers or rippers can be used for its removal. In the case of hard variety of rocks holes are drilled usually by pneumatic drilling machine using compressed air as energy for driving the holes. The holes are packed with explosives. On being fired the gases under very high pressure are formed. In the process of trying to escape these gases fracture the surrounding rock. This operation of removing rock is known as rock blasting.

1.10.2 Drilling Equipment

The main factor which determines the particular type of drilling equipment is the greatest overall economy for the particular project. In other words the equipment which would give maximum output per unit of cost would be the best. There are however various other factors which have to be considered before selecting. Some of these factors are given below:

1. Geological formation. If the strata to be bored is rough, jack-hammer is more suitable than any other type.
2. Depth of the bore hole.
3. Toughness and hardness of the rock.
4. Condition of the strata whether formation is broken, fractured or sound.
5. The purpose for which rock blasting is required.
6. Purpose for which drilling of holes is required *i.e.*, for injection, exploration or for blasting.
7. Size of cores. Large cores would require shot drills while small cores would need the use of diamond drills.
8. In case bores are for blasting, the purpose for which blasting is required *i.e.*, for crushing into road metal or for use as block masonry or boulders.
9. Availability of water. Dry drilling would be suitable where water is not available.

Fig. 1.38 Rock blasting in operation.

The other factors which govern the choice of equipment are:

1. When small-diameter holes on rough surfaces are required, Jack hammers are used even if the cost and speed of drilling would be uneconomical.

2. Track mounted, rotary percussion, or piston drills are suitable for blast holes upto 15 cm in diameters and 15 metres in depth.

3. Blast hole or rotary drill is most suitable for holes between 15 cm to 30 cm diameter and 15 to 90 metres in depth.

4. Diamond drilling gives satisfactory results when the size of the bore is less than 7.5 cm.

5. For intermediate size holes (between 7.5 cm and 20 cm) either diamond drill or shot drill can be employed. While shot drill is employed in vertical or nearly vertical holes, diamond drills, can be used to bore holes in any direction. The diamond drill is also faster in operation as compared to shot drill.

Casing Oscillators

Hydraulic equipment for casing driving and extraction:

— VRM Hydraulic casing oscillator

— VRM/KL Compact type

Model	*diameter* mm	*max extraction force* kW	*max closing force* kN	*max torque* kNm
VRM/KL	1000	770	500	630
VRM/KL	1300	1790	1560	1700
VRM/KL	1500	1790	1560	1950
VRM/KL	2000	1790	1560	2430
VRM	2000	265	190	3180
VRM	2500	515	217	7070
VRM	3000	725	478	8350

Extractors

Heavy duty equipment of simple design for extraction of diaphragm wall stop-end pipes ranging in diameter 400 to 1200 mm. These are used for pipes and sheet piles.

1.10.3 Dynamic Explosives Types and Uses

This explosive is largely used for small size bore holes. The explosive is available in cartridge varying from 2.5 cm to 20 cm in diameter and 20 cm to 60 cm in length. The strength of the cartridge is specified as percentage indicating the weight of nitroglycerin to the total weight of the cartridge. The charge is fired with the help of a Primacord fuse or by means of a blasting cap. In the case of blasting cap, it is placed in a hole made in one of the cartridges. This cap serves as a primer. The caps have two terminals of lengths varying from 0.6 metre to 30 metre. These wires are connected in series or in parallel to wires from other holes to form a closed electric circuit. In the case of primacord fuse, the fuse wire is connected along with similar fuse wires from other holes to the main fuse.

1.10.4 Blasting Operation

The operation of blasting, after the hole has been drilled to the desired depth, consists of filling with explosives, along with primer and detonator, stemming and firing.

The quantity of explosive to be used in each hole depends upon the following parameters:

- Depth of the hole
- Spacing of the hole
- Size of the bore
- Type of the rock.
- Based on the working experience however for average conditions, data have been compiled for sizes of the hole and use of explosive per linear metre of the hole. Table 1.1 can be used as a guide for average conditions.

Table 1.1 Explosive Data

Diameter of hole	*Surface area per sq. metre of hole*	*N of explosive per linear metre of hole*	*Remark*
4 cm	2.5	40	These data are
5 cm	5.0	5	based on
10 cm	10	35	dynamite
15 cm	40	70	weighing
22.5 cm	90	15	1.35 t/m^3

Primers. The primer is supplied with the explosive and is attached to the explosive. It is denoted by Primacord, which is a high explosive fuse.

In case several holes are fired at a time, fuse from each hole is tied securely to a common fuse.

In case of electric firing, which is most popular method of exploding the explosive, the primer is detonated by means of a detonator. The detonator itself is exploded by passing an electric current through a wire bridge inside the cap.

Stemming. After the hole is filled with the desired explosive to the required depth, the remaining portion of the hole is filled with rock cuttings or other inert material to confine the energy released due to explosive and thereby to increase the effectiveness of the blast.

The process of packing the inert material is known as *stemming*.

Figure 1.39 illustrates the method of loading blast holes with explosive.

Firing Charge. It is common practice to fire several holes using parallel circuit, series circuit or combined parallel and series circuit as illustrated in Fig. 1.40 (*a*), (*b*) and (*c*).

1.10.5 Precautions in the Use of Explosives

Transportation and handling of explosives are hazardous operations and hence great care should be taken.

Following precautions should be taken for transportation of explosives:

1. Vehicles carrying explosives should be marked "Explosives" in 10 cm height letters on all the four sides.

2. Blasting caps or detonators should not be carried along with explosives.

3. Vehicle carrying explosive should not be overloaded.

4. The vehicle should not be used for carrying passengers.

The following precautions should be taken for handling the explosives:

1. Cases of explosives should not be dropped.

2. Containers of explosives should not be opened within 15 metres of magazines.

3. Wooden tools only should be used in opening containers.

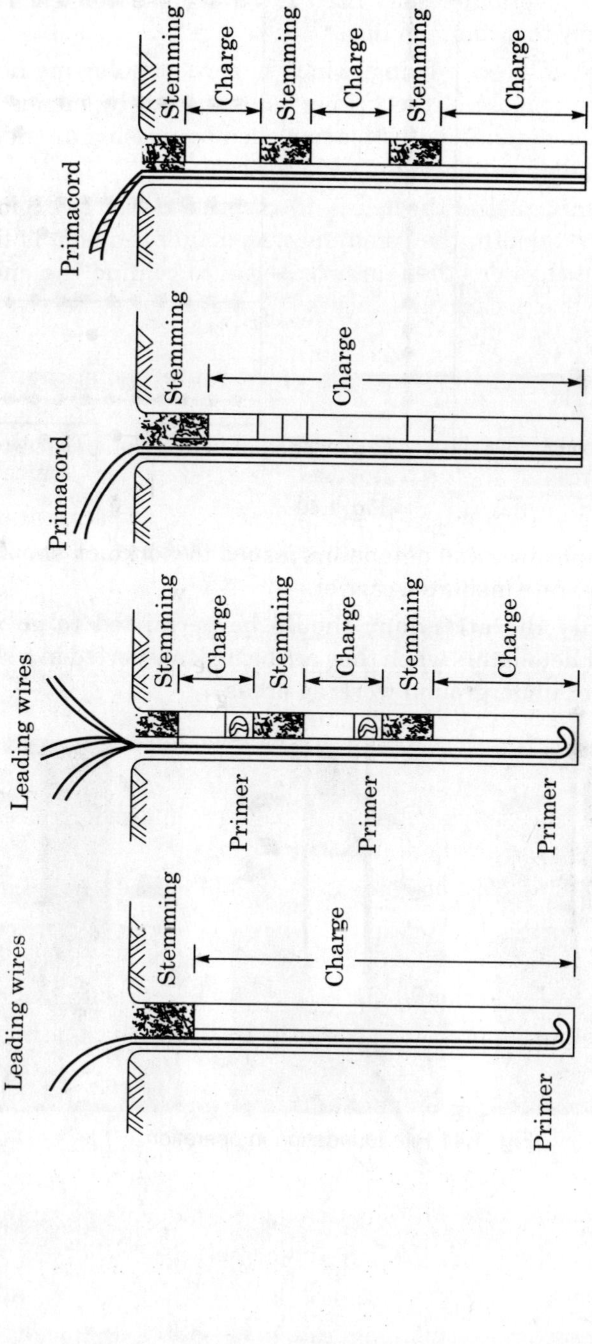

Leading wires
Stemming
Charge
Primer
Leading wires
Stemming
Charge
Stemming
Charge
Stemming
Charge
Primer
Primer
Primer
Primacord
Stemming
Charge
Primacord
Stemming
Charge
Stemming
Charge
Stemming
Charge

Fig. 1.39

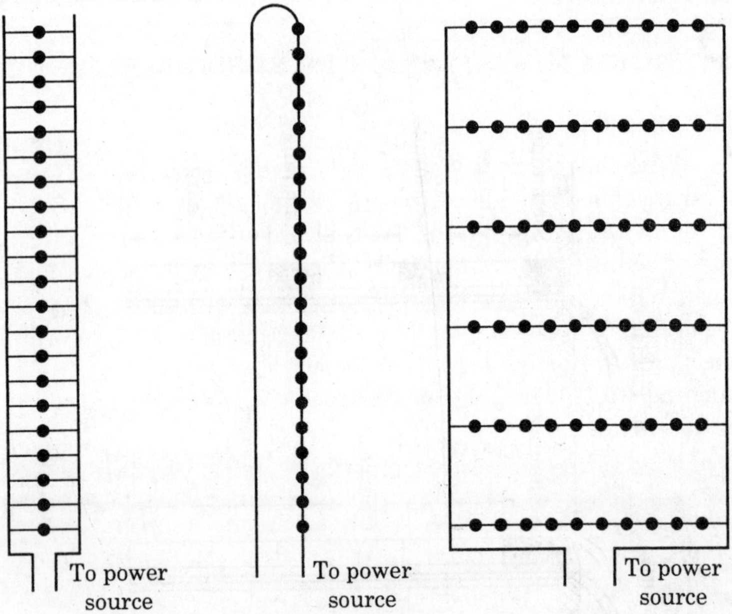

Fig. 1.40

4. Explosives and detonators issued to workmen should be placed in separate insulated carriers.

5. Only the attendant should be permitted to go with explosives or detonators when they are being transported in a shaft, ramp or other underground working areas.

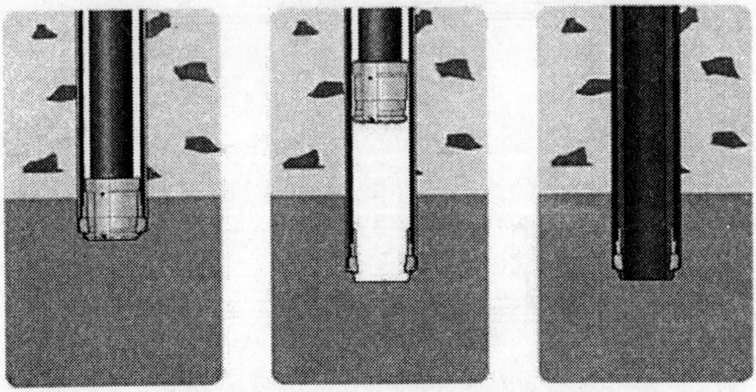

Fig. 1.41 Pile foundation in operation.

1.11 PILED FOUNDATION AND PILE DRIVING EQUIPMENT

1.11.1 Piled Foundations

When heavy concentrated loads have to be carried out through soil strata of low bearing capacity to deeper soil or rock having high bearing capacity, the load is transmitted through piles. Piles are also particularly useful when foundation is over water such as jetties or bridge piers. An entirely different family of piles are the sheet piles used for supporting members to earth or water in cofferdams. Sheet piles are also used in foundation excavation as well as for returning walls. The present discussion is however restricted to foundation piles.

Foundation piles can be broadly classified into two categories *i.e.*, (*a*) End bearing pile.

(*b*) Friction pile.

These piles are illustrated in Fig. 1.42 (*a*) and (*b*).

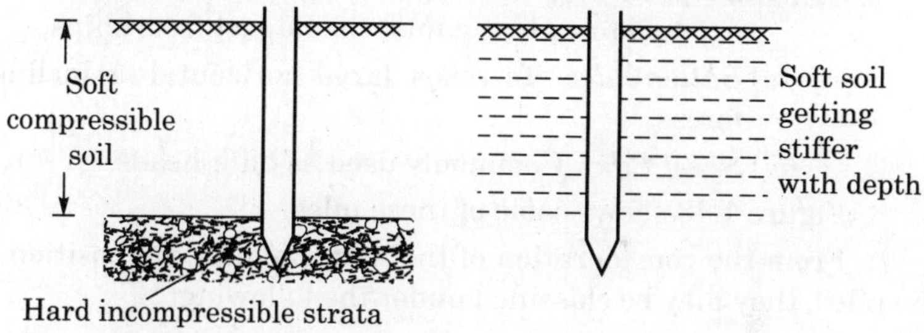

(*a*) End bearing pile (*b*) Friction pile

Fig. 1.42

From the point of view of driving, piles are classified into:

(*a*) Displacement piles.

(*b*) Non-displacement piles.

(*c*) Composite piles.

(*d*) Miscellaneous.

(*a*) Displacement Piles. They are further divided into:

(*i*) *Driven piles.* These are piles driven into the soil by blows of hammer.

(*ii*) *Driven and-cast-in-place-piles.* Tube with a closed end is driven into the soil. This tube is filled with concrete. At the end of the operation the tube may be withdrawn or allowed in position.

(*iii*) *Screw Piles.* These may be steel or concrete piles. They are screwed into soil.

(*b*) Non-displacement Piles

(*i*) *Board and-cast-in-place Piles.* A hole is bored into the soil and the filled with concrete.

(*c*) Composite piles. These piles may form combination of the above piles or different materials may be used in the same type of pile.

(*d*) Miscellaneous

(*i*) *Compact Piles.* These are used to compact loose granular soil; thereby increasing its bearing capacity.

(*ii*) *Tension or Uplift Piles.* Used for holding down structures subjected to uplift due to overtuning moment or due to hydrostatic pressure.

(*iii*) *Anchor Piles.* For providing anchorage against horizontal piles.

(*iv*) *Dolphin or Fender Piles.* To protect the surface exposed to water against the impact from ships.

(*v*) *Batter Piles.* To resist large horizontal or inclined forces.

(*vi*) *Sheet Piles.* Commonly used as bulk heads.

Figure 1.43 shows some of these piles.

From the consideration of the material and composition of the piles, they may be classified under the following:

(*a*) Concrete Piles.

(*b*) Timber Piles.

(*c*) Steel Piles.

(*d*) Composite Piles.

(*a*) *Concrete Piles.* These can further be divided into:

(*i*) Pre-cast.

(*ii*) Cast-in-situ.

(*i*) *Pre-cast concrete Piles.* They are used for a maximum design load of 80 tonnes. They have to be designed to withstand additional stresses caused by handling.

(*ii*) *Cast-in-situ.* They are installed at worksite by pre-excavation. This helps in eliminating stress due to vibration during driving and handling. A number of cast-in-situ piles are in use, each being patented by the manufacturer. Some of the common types are:

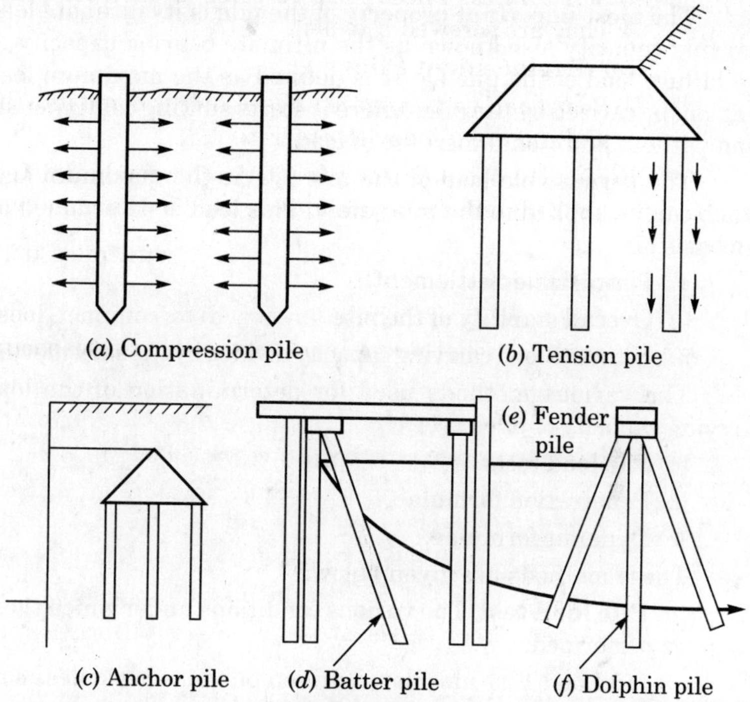

Fig. 1. 43

1. Franki Standard Pile.
2. Western Buttar Bottom Piles.
3. MacArthur Cased Piles.
4. MacArthur Compressed Uncased Pile.
5. Union Metal Pile or Monotube.
6. Raymond Step Taper Pile.
7. Raymond Standard Pile.

(*b*) *Timber Piles.* They have small bearing capacity and are not durable unless suitable treated.

(*c*) *Steel Piles.* These may be H-pile, Pipe-pile or sheet pile. The H-piles are suitable where long piles are required to reach the hard strata. They are however comparatively very costly and rarely used.

(*d*) *Composite Piles.* The usual materials used in combination are:

(*i*) Concrete and Timber.

(*ii*) Concrete and Steel.

The most important property of the pile is its ultimate load carrying capacity also known as the ultimate bearing capacity or the failure load of the pile Q_f. It is defined as the maximum load that can be carried by the pile, before it starts sinking continuously even without additional increase of load.

The permissible load of the pile (Q_a) is the maximum load which can be applied to the pile safely. This load is determined on the basis of:

(*i*) Permissible Settlement.

(*ii*) Overall stability of the pile.

(*iii*) Ultimate load carrying capacity divided by the safety factor.

The various methods used for determination of the load carrying capacity of piles are:

(*a*) Pile load tests.

(*b*) Penetration formulae.

(*c*) Dynamic formulae.

These methods are given below:

(*a*) **Pile load test.** The various conditions under which these tests are performed:

(*i*) Load Test in isolated driven pile in cohesionless soil.

(*ii*) Ultimate load determination on driven and cast-in-place piles in cohesionless soil.

(*iii*) Ultimate loads on bored and cast in place piles in cohesionless soil.

(*iv*) Ultimate load on piles driven in cohesive soils.

(*v*) Driven and cast-in-place piles on cohesive soil.

(*vi*) Bored and cast-in-place piles in cohesive soil.

(*vii*) Driven piles founded on rock.

(*viii*) Bored piles founded on rock.

(*i*) *Load tests on isolated driven pile in cohesionless soils.* If the soil is loose it gets compacted by the pile and there is practically no heave of the ground. If the soil is very loose the pile driving causes compaction and results in formation of depression around the pile. In case of dense soils however, no further compaction is possible and pile driving results in heaving of the ground. Because of the high resistance heavy driving is required to achieve penetration of the piles. Heavy driving, however, lowers the shearing resistance of the soil beneath the foot of the pile due to displacement of angular soil particles. No advantage is therefore gained by over driving pile in such cases. On the other hand over-driving may damage the pile itself.

The frictional resistance of piles in cohesionless soils is small as compared to the end resistance. This is probably on account of the formation of a shell of compacted soil around the pile shaft.

It is difficult to get undisturbed soil samples in cohesionless soils and hence the load carrying capacity is estimated from the insitu tests.

(*ii*) *Ultimate load determination on driven and cast-in-place piles in cohesionless soil.*

This type of piles is constructed by driving a tube into the ground. When the tube reaches the level of the foundation, the tube is filled with concrete. In some cases as concreting is done, tube is simultaneously withdrawn and a bulb gets formed at the base. In other cases, where the steel tube is left in position, the shaft friction load can be readily calculated from the area of external face of the piles in contact with the soil. In case the end of the tube is closed, the end resistance is calculated on the bases area at the pile tip.

In cases where the driving tube is withdrawn, the nature of the soil in contact with the shaft cannot be properly assessed. The degree of compaction given to the concrete and the efficiency of withdrawing of the tube produce considerable changes in the denseness of the soil.

(*iii*) *Ultimate loads on bored and cast-in-place piles in cohesionless soil.* Bored piles are made by drilling with rigs. The drilled holes are filled with concrete and casing is withdrawn after or simultaneously with pouring of concrete. Sometimes the casing is left in position.

Even if the soil is initially dense or medium-dense, it becomes loose as a result of the boring. This leads to the conclusion that the ultimate load carrying capacity of bored pile in cohesionless soil will be much lower than that of a pile drawn under similar conditions.

Where both driven and cast-in-place type can be provided with an enlarged base, the base of the bored piles cannot be enlarged without adopting costly ground consolidation techniques such as freezing or chemical injection.

(*iv*) *Ultimate load of piles driven in cohesive soils.* The carrying capacity of the pile in cohesive clays is the sum of skin friction between the pile surface and the soil and the end resistance. The skin friction depends upon the properties of the soil and the type

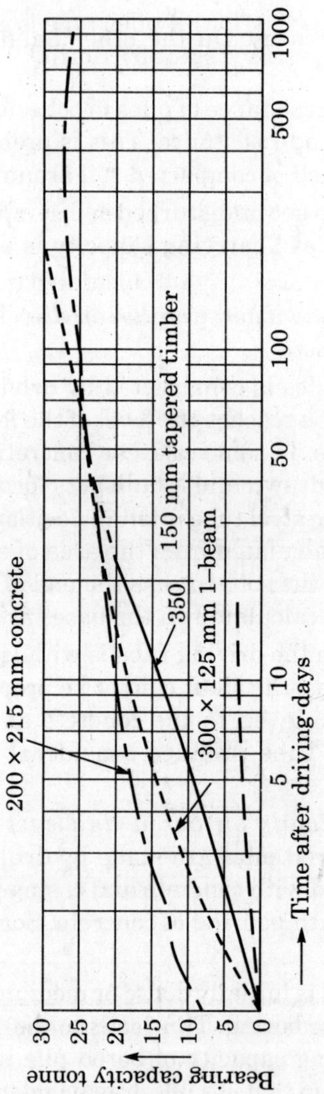

Fig. 1.44

and shape of the pile. The physical characteristics of the pile undergo a change due to the driving of the pile. Consolidation of the soil is relatively slow and heave of the ground surface at early stages after driving takes place. Fig. 1.44 shows the gain or carrying capacity of piles driven into soft clay with time.

Gain of carrying capacity of piles. 75% ultimate capacity is achieved within 30 days of driving. Such piles should therefore not be loaded for at least 30 days.

The working load Q_a for all piles type is equal to the sum of the base resistance Q_b and the shaft friction (Q_s') divided by suitable safety factor say 2.5.

$$\text{Allowable load } Q_a = \frac{Q_b + Q_s''}{2.5}$$

$$Q_a \text{ should also be} < \frac{Q_b}{3} + \frac{Q_s'}{1.5}.$$

Where Q_s'' is the skin friction calculated from adhesion factor in Fig. 1.45. Here safety factor for skin friction is taken as 1.5.

(*v*) *Driven and cast-in-place piles on cohesive soil.* Piles where the steel tubing or precast concrete shell remain in the ground, develop skin friction given by the equation.

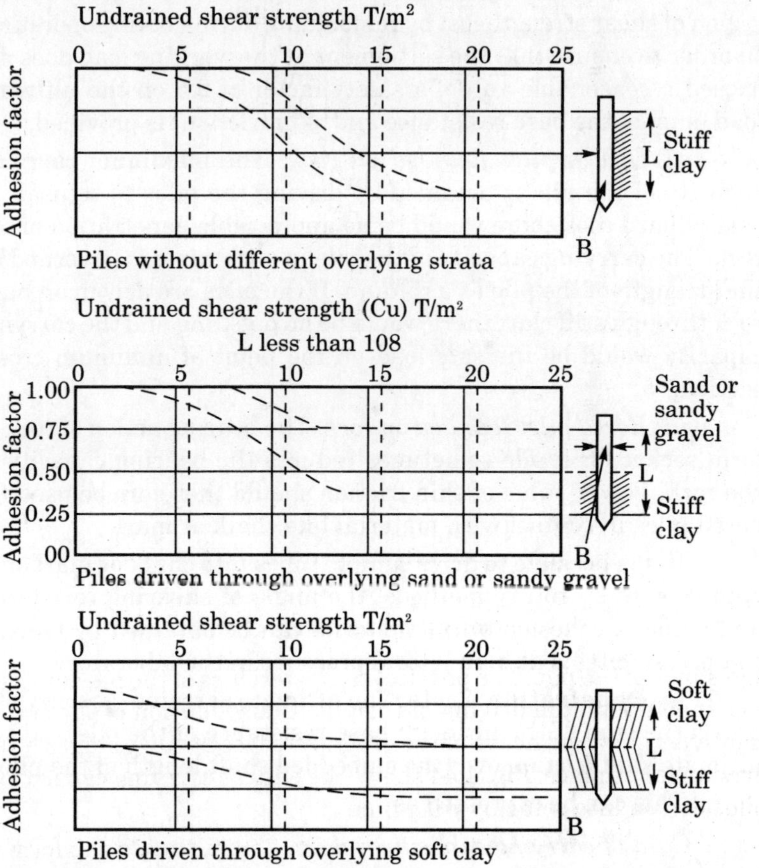

Fig. 1.45

$$Q_s = \alpha \times \overline{c}_d \times A_s$$

Where α = adhesion factor. (See Fig. 1.45)

$\overline{c}_d$ = average undisturbed shear strength of clay adjacent to the shaft.

A_s = Surface area of the shaft.

Because of the frequently low skin friction values associated with piles driven into stiff clays, proprietary piles which have enlarged bases have come into use. These piles have notable advantages over straight sided piles.

(*vi*) *Bored and cast-in-place piles in cohesive soils.* It can be presumed that full shear strength of vary soft to soft clay can be mobilised to develop skin friction if adequate time is given for the region of shear strength lost by remoulding during boring operation. In order to ensure that the settlement at the working load does not exceed a reasonable value, a safety factor of 2.5 on the ultimate load (sum of the base resistance and skin friction) is provided.

(*vii*) *Driven piles founded on rock.* The maximum carrying capacity of the pile is obtained by driving the piles to refusal. In case of hard rock there would be no appreciable penetration of the rock. The carrying capacity of the pile in such cases is governed by the strength of the pile as a column. If the piles are driven on hard rock through stiff clay, there would be no buckling and the carrying capacity would be the safe load on the point of minimum cross-section.

(*viii*) *Bored piles founded on rock.* The bearing action of rock to form socket for a pile sometimes reduces the bearing capacity of the rock. Lower value of skin friction should therefore be used for bored piles in contact with material like chalk or marl.

If it is possible to drive sample tubes into chalk or marl or to obtain cores by rotary methods, the angle of shearing resistance and value of cohesion of the material can be obtained by triaxial compression tests at high lateral pressure in the laboratory.

(*b*) **Penetration Tests.** The ultimate carrying capacity of a pile is the sum of the ultimate base resistance of the pile and the ultimate skin friction over the embedded shaft length of the pile.

This can be expressed as

$$Q_u = Q_b + Q_s$$

where Q_u is the ultimate load carrying capacity of the pile.

Q_b = Base resistance of the pile

Rotary-rigs Augor boring

Fig. 1.46 Pile-boring.

Q_s = Frictional resistance offered to the shaft.

The penetration is plotted in the form of a load settlement curve. The ultimate load is indicated in the load settlement curve as the load at the point where the curve approaches the vertical. The settlements/penetration are recorded with the help of dial gauges of sensitivity of 0.02 mm. Each load is kept for sufficient time till the rate of settlement becomes less than 0.02 mm per hour. Test piles are baded till ultimate load is reached.

Normally the test load is increased to 2½ times the estimated allowable load or to a load which causes a penetration/ settlement equal to one-tenth of the pile diameter whichever takes place earlier.

The cone penetration (Dutch) has been extensively used in Holland and Belgium. It is recognised as a standard test procedure (the Dutch Cone Test) in a number of countries. The cone is illustrated in Fig. 1.47.

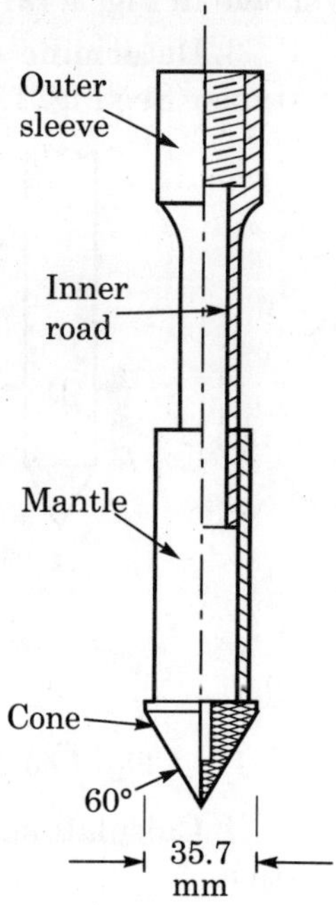

Fig. 1.47 Dutch cone.

The cone has the following vital measurements:

- Apex angle 60°
- Overall diameter 35.7 mm.
- End Area 1000 mm^2.
- The results of the test are correlated directly with the bearing capacity and settlement of shallow foundation and piles.

The ultimate bearing resistance of the pile is taken as being equal to the resistance of the cone.

The steps involved using static cone test are:

1. Select a provisional depth for pile tip level. This will as far as possible utilise the maximum permissible shear on the material of the pile shaft. The cone resistance depth diagram is studied before arriving at the depth.

2. Determine average cone resistance over the range of depth as shown in Fig. 1.48.

3. Determine end resistance of pile from average cone resistance (See Fig. 1.48).

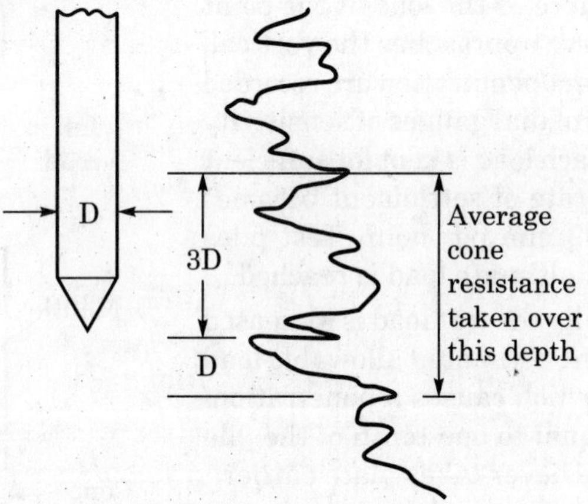

Fig. 1.48 Calculation of end resistance of pile.

4. Calculate skin friction from average cone resistance using equation.

$$\text{Ultimate unit skin friction} = \frac{\overline{q}_c}{20} \text{ tonne/m}^2 \text{ (Displacement piles)}$$

$$= \frac{\overline{q}_c}{40} \text{ tonne/m}^2 \text{ (For H-beam piles)}$$

Here $\bar{q}_c$ = Average cone resistance (kg/cm^2) over the length of the pile shaft under consideration.

5. Determine the total ultimate pile resistance from the sum of end resistance and skin friction divided by a safety factor of 2.5.

(*c*) **Dynamic formulae.** The commonly used dynamic formulae are:

(*i*) Engineering News formula and (*ii*) Hiley's formula.

These formulae are best suited for coarse grained soils for which the shear strength does not depend upon the rate of loading. It may be borne in mind that whereas the load carrying capacity is based on dynamic loading, in actual practice the piles are subjected to static loading test. The adverse effect of impact of driving would cause liquifaction of the soil thereby reducing the resistance of the soil.

These formulae are based on the assumption that the total driving energy is equal to the weight of the hammer times the height of the drop or stroke. In the case of steam hammers, some energy is also imparted by the steam pressure during the return stroke.

The total downward energy is consumed by the work done in penetrating the pile.

(*i*) *Engineering News Formula.* The formula was proposed by A.M. Willington (1818) and is given by

$$Q_a = \frac{WH}{F(S+C)}$$

Here Q_a = Permissible load, W = Hammer weight

H = Fall of hammer, F = Safety factor 6

S = Final penetration per blow

It is taken as average penetration or set per blow for the last 5 blows of a drop hammer or 20 blows of a steam hammer

C = empirical constant

If W is in kg, H in cm, S in cm

C = 2.5 cm for drop hammer and 0.25 cm for double acting

$$\text{Permissible load } Q_a = \frac{WH}{(S+2.5)} \text{ drop hammer}$$

$$= \frac{WH}{6(S+0.25)} \text{ single acting steam hammer}$$

$$= \frac{W(a\ p.)\ H}{6(s + 0.25)} \text{ double acting steam hammer}$$

Here a = Effective area of piston (cm^2)

p = Mean effective steam pressure (kg/cm^2)

(ii) Hiley's Formula. I.S. 2911 (Part I) 1964 gives the following formula which is based on the original formula given by **Hiley**.

$$Q_f = \frac{\eta_h W H \eta_b}{S + \frac{C}{2}}$$

Here Q_f = Ultimate load on the pile

W = Weight of the hammer in kg

H = Height of drop hammer in cm

S = Penetration or set in cm per blow

C = Total elastic compression, $C_1 + C_2 + C_3$

C_1, C_2, C_3 = Temporary elastic compression of dolly and packing, pile and soil respectively

η_h = Efficiency of hammer

= 65% for double acting steam hammer 100% drop hammer released by trigger

η_b = Efficiency of hammer blow

$$= \frac{W + e^2 P}{W + P} \ (W > ep)$$

$$= \frac{W + e^2 P}{W + P} \left\{ \frac{W - eP}{W + P} \right\}^2 \ W(< eP)$$

P = Weight of pile, anvil, helmet follower.

e = Coefficient of restitution (This varies from zero for a timber pile with poor condition of head to 0.5 for double acting hammer driven steel piles without driving cap).

The allowable load is obtained by using a factor of 2 or 2.5.

1.12 STONE CRUSHERS

1.12.1 Introduction

The various stages involved in the production of crushed aggregates are drilling, blasting, loading, transporting, crushing, screening, handling and storing. The operations of drilling, blasting loading and transporting have been described in the preceding chapters. The remaining operations are described in the following articles. The operations preceding crushing should be so arranged that only such stones are fed to the crushers as can pass through the opening of the crushers.

Fig. 1.49 Stone crusher in operation.

1.12.2 Types of Crushers

One of the methods of classifying crushers is according to the stage of crushing such as primary, secondary, tertiary etc. On this basis crushers are divided into the following categories.

1. Jaw crushers
2. Gyratory crushers
3. Hammer Mill crushers

} Suitable for primary crushing

4. Cone crushers
5. Roll crushers
6. Hammer Mill crushers

} Suitable for secondary crushing

7. Roll crushers
8. Rod Mill crushers
9. Ball Mill crushers

} Suitable for tertiary crushing

1.12.3 Jaw Crushers

This machine is particularly useful for primary crushing as the width of the feed opening varies from 25 cm to 140 cm and the size of the discharged (primary crushed material) varies from 2.5 cm to 22.5 cm. In other words, large size crusher can take up directly blasted rocks and convert them into boulder sizes after which it can be subsequently crushed in other types of crushers or in jaw crusher of smaller capacities. The smallest size crusher (25 cm) produces 20 tonnes of 5 cm size stone or 11 tonnes of 2.5 cm size stone whereas the largest variety (1.4 m) produces about 300 tonnes of 100 mm size stone or 650 tonnes of 225 mm size stone.

The stone is fed between the jaws. One of the jaws is fixed while the other is movable. The stone travels downward under its own weight. The opening between the two jaws reduces from top to bottom. By the time the stone reaches the lower portion the movable jaw has exercised sufficient pressure to crush the hardest rock.

Figure 1.50 illustrates a typical jaw crusher.

Fig. 1.50

1.12.4 Gyratory Crushers

The upper part of the unit contains a coneshaped crushing chamber. This chamber is lined with hard steel or manganese, steel plates known as *concaves*. The crushing is done by a hard-steel crushing head. This crushing head is mounted on a vertical steel shaft. As the shaft rotates, the eccentric support at the bottom gyrates. This gyrating motion causes variation in the width of opening between the concaves and the head. As the rock fed from the top, moves down, it gets reduced in size and finally passes out through the opening at the bottom.

The size of gyratory crusher is the width of the receiving opening measured between the concaves and the crusher head. The width of the bottom opening is known as *setting*. When setting is specified, it should also be mentioned whether it is open or closed setting.

Gyratory crushers are available in sizes varying from 200 mm to 2000 mm. 40 mm is the smallest size crushed stone and depending upon the size the production capacity varies from 30 tonnes to 80 tonnes per hour. The size of the largest crushed stone may be 160 mm and the rate of production may be upto 70% tonnes per hour.

1.12.5 Cone Crusher

A cone crusher differs from the gyratory crusher in the following aspects:

1. Smaller inlet and outlet openings.
2. The maximum size of crushed stone is less than the smallest broken piece that comes out from the gyratory crusher.

Figure 1.51 shows a standard cone crusher.

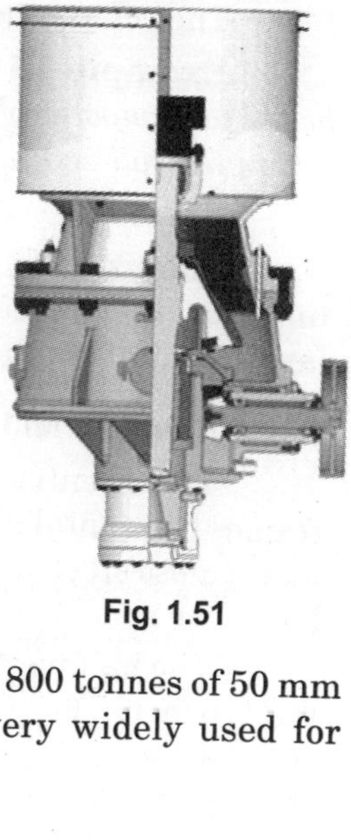

Fig. 1.51

The conical head of the crusher is made of manganese steel. It is mounted on the vertical shaft and forms one of the crushing surface. The concave attached to the other part of the crusher frame is the other crushing surface. The size, designated by the size of the feed opening or inlet varies for 50 mm to 280 mm and the crushed aggregate is from 6 mm to 5 cm sizes depending upon the capacity of the crusher. The output per hour of the smallest crusher is 15 tonnes per hour of 6 mm size aggregates while the largest size can produce 800 tonnes of 50 mm size aggregate. This crusher is therefore very widely used for secondary crushing.

1.12.6 Roll Crusher

A roll crusher consists of a heavy cast iron frame. The frame is equipped with two hard steel rolls. Each roll is mounted on a separate horizontal shaft. Each roll can be driven independently. The adjustment in the width of the discharge opening between the rolls is effected by mounting one of the rolls on a sliding frame.

In case a non-crushable material passes through the machine, safety of the machine is ensured by making the movable roll spring-loaded.

The maximum-size particles that can be crushed is given by the formula

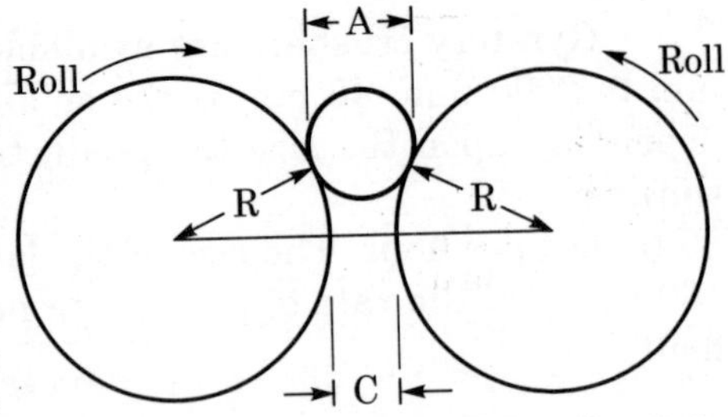

Fig. 1.52 Crushing rock between two rolls.

$$A = 0.085\,R + C$$

where A = maximum size feed

R = radius of rolls

C = roll setting (size of finished product)

The roller crushing action is illustrated in Fig. 1.52.

Example 1.1 *Determine the maximum size s one that may be fed to a smooth roll crusher where rolls are 1000 mm in diameter where the roll setting is 2.5 mm*

Solution. $A = 0.085 \times 500 + 25 = 42.5 + 25 = 67.5$ mm

The size of feed varies from 40 mm to 120 mm. The smallest unit can produce 15 tonnes of 6 mm size aggregate whereas the largest unit can produce 240 tonnes of 70 mm size aggregate.

1.12.7 Hammer Mill

The essential components of the hammer mill are the housing frame, horizontal shaft carrying a number of arms, one or more manganese steel or hard steel breaker plates and a series of grating bars. The spacing of the grating bars is adjustable.

The hammers travelling at high speed crush the stone fed on the crusher. These crushed stones are further reduced to smaller sizes by the breaker plates. The output of the crusher depends upon the type of stone, the size of the feed and speed of the shaft. A 73 mm feed size stone in the small capacity crusher can be crushed to 3 mm size stones at the rate of 2.5 tonnes/hour while 150 mm feed size stone in the larger capacity crusher can be crushed to 4 cm size stone at the rate of 140 tonnes/hour.

1.12.8 Rod and Ball Mills

A rod mill contains a circular steel shell. The interior of the shell is lined on the inside with a hard mineral wearing surface.

The shell contains a number of steel rods. The length of these rods is slightly less than the length of the shell. Crushed stone is fed through the inlet and fine aggregate of the size of sand is discharged at the other end. The mill may operate dry or wet. The size of the crusher is specified by the size (diameter and length) of the shell such as 2.5 × 3.6 m. Figure 1.53 shows a section through a rod mill.

If the rods are replaced by steel balls to provide the impact required to grind the stones, the crusher is known as a *ball mill crusher*. Figure 1.54 shows a section through a ball mill.

Fig. 1.53

Fig. 1.54

1.13 CONCRETE MIXING PLANTS

1.13.1 Introduction

Basically concrete consists of the binding medium (cement), aggregates (coarse and fine) mixed with water and allowed to solidify and harden. To improve the performance or to have specific results admixtures are also used. Figure 1.55 shows the flow diagram showing the operations involved in the production of concrete.

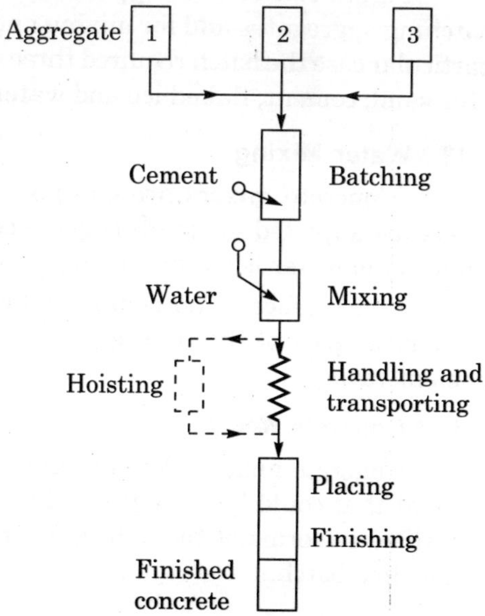

Fig. 1.55

1.13.2 Batching

For specific job requirements the ingredients of concrete vary even for getting the same strength of the concrete. The size and quality of stone, the quality of sand and the climatic conditions along with the water cement ratio and methods employed for mixing and placing are some of variables which influence the proportioning of the ingredients. The proportioning of the different components of concrete is known as *batching*. The batching methods vary from mixing with the help of measuring boxes to the use of sophisticated batching equipment of capacities of batching bins upto 50 tonnes of aggregates.

For small size projects wheel barrow scales are satisfactory. The net weight of each wheel barrow of material is set on an appropriate weight beam. Each beam is operated independently.

For larger projects elevated storage bins are fitted with weighing batchers. Aggregates from stock pile to the bin are conveyed by means of a tractor mounted scoop or a loading shovel. When required quantities of materials have been discharged from bins into the weighing hopper, they are discharged into the skip of the concrete mixer. In the case of very large projects multiple-compartment overhead bins are used. The bin is fitted with a beam type weighing batcher. The capacity of such bins is taken as the combined capacity of all the bins.

Figure 1.56 shows a typical layout for storing, handling and batching aggregates and for mixing and handling concrete. In this particular case the batch required three different sizes of aggregates, plus sand, cement, flaked ice and water.

1.13.3 Water Mixing

Concrete mixers are equipped with water mixing tanks. These are adjusted so that during the period of mixing the required quantity of water is fed to the mixer.

Free surface water contained by the aggregate is taken into account as part of the total quantity of water required for water cement ratio.

1.13.4 Concrete Mixers

Concrete mixers were designated by the number of bags of cement that could be mixed at a time in the mixer. They are now classified in terms of the cubical contents of the mix that can be mixed in a batch.

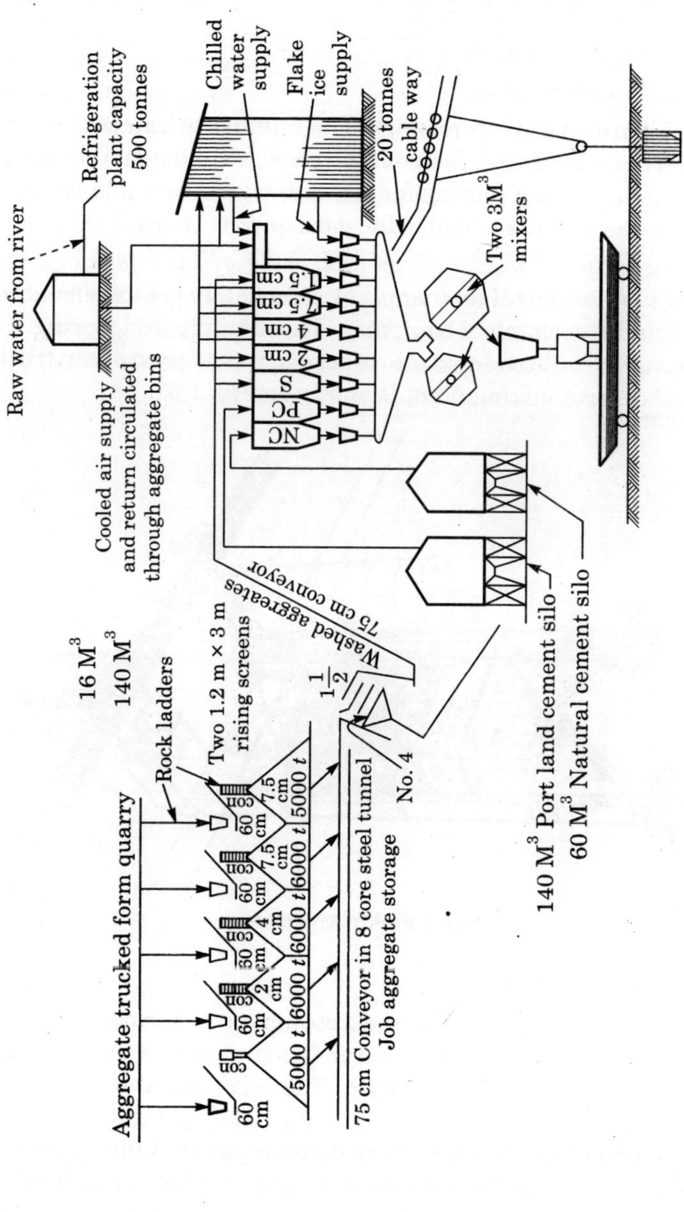
Raw water from river
Refrigeration plant capacity 500 tonnes
Cooled air supply and return circulated through aggregate bins
Chilled water supply
Flake ice supply
20 tonnes cable way
Two 3M^3 mixers
NC
PC
S
2 cm
4 cm
7.5 cm
1.5 cm
Aggregate trucked form quarry
Rock ladders
16 M^3
140 M^3
Two 1.2 m × 3 m rising screens
60 cm
30 cm
2 cm
4 cm
7.5 cm
con
5000 t
6000 t
75 cm Conveyor in 8 core steel tunnel
Job aggregate storage
No. 4
$1\frac{1}{2}$
Washed aggregates
75 cm conveyor
140 M^3 Port land cement silo
60 M^3 Natural cement silo

Fig. 1.56

Concrete mixers may be classified into the following three categories:

1. Construction mixers.
2. Transit mixers.
3. Paving mixers.

1. Construction mixers. The number of batches that can be mixed per hour depends upon the average time per cycle. ASTM specifies one minute mixing for one cubic yard and additional 15 seconds for every additional cubic yard or part thereof.

For large projects such as multi-storeyed complex or a dam construction, a central mixing plant is normally established. Such plant include mechanical equipment for handling and storing. The mixed concrete is discharged into brackets, trucks or on dump trucks. A typical central mixing plant is shown in Fig. 1.57.

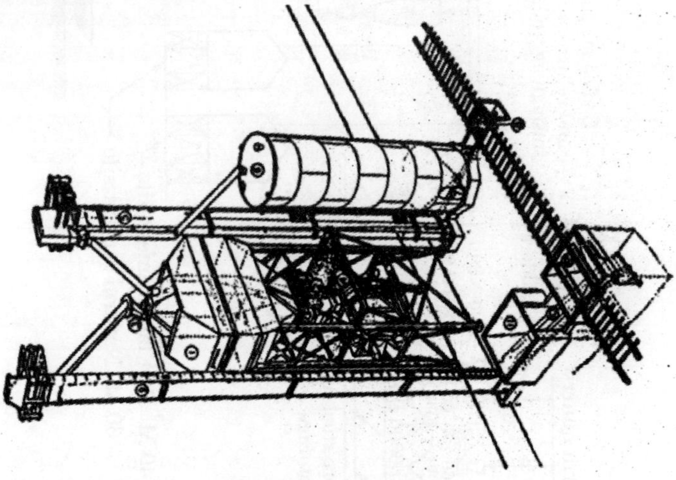

Fig. 1.57 A mixing plant.

1.13.5 Transit Mixers

A truck fitted with a concrete mixer is termed as transit mixer or agitator truck. The mixer is fed at the central batching plant and mixing is done enroute. The term agitator is meant to denote a unit hauling ready made mix. The agitation enroute is done to prevent the mix from getting segregated. A unit used as an agitator has a comparatively greater capacity than when used as a transit mixer because in the former case concrete is pre-mixed and hence occupies less volume.

1.14 GROUTING AND GUNITING EQUIPMENT

1.14.1 Introduction

Fissures cavities slips, faults or cracks sometimes develop in various structures such as dams, reservoirs, buildings bridge piers, locks, tunnels etc. The most satisfactory corrective measure for the rectification of defects in the structure on account of the above is by grouting under pressure. The best way to find out whether a structure needs grouting is to obtain samples from different positions of the structures. For smaller size structures bores may be obtained by using diamond drills. In the case of massive structures such as foundations of dams, it may be necessary to have several shotdrilled holes of 75 cm diameter or even larger so that it may be possible to carry out the examination of the fissures by visual examination of the strata. The number of holes to be made would depend upon the nature of the fault and importance of the structure. A few borings would however decide if borings on a large scale are called for. The result of such borings may sometimes establish the desirability of abandoning the structure instead of carrying out large scale repairing by pressure grouting.

The various materials used for grouting are cement, clay, asphalt and chemicals.

Before grouting is done the following operations have to be carried out:

1. Drilling of holes for injecting grout.
2. Washing of seams.
3. Determination of grouting pressure.

1.14.2 Cement Grouting

The equipment for cement grouting consists of the following:

1. Air compressors.
2. Grout mixers.
3. Agitator type reservoir tank.
4. Grout pump.
5. Grout discharge pipe.

The grout mixer is motor operated. The grout is mixed and fed into the tank. The tank has an agitator to prevent the separation of solids from the water.

Figure 1.58 illustrates a typical grouting unit. For important works a unit of two grouting pumps is employed so thus in the event of failure of a pump, the standby unit may be commissioned.

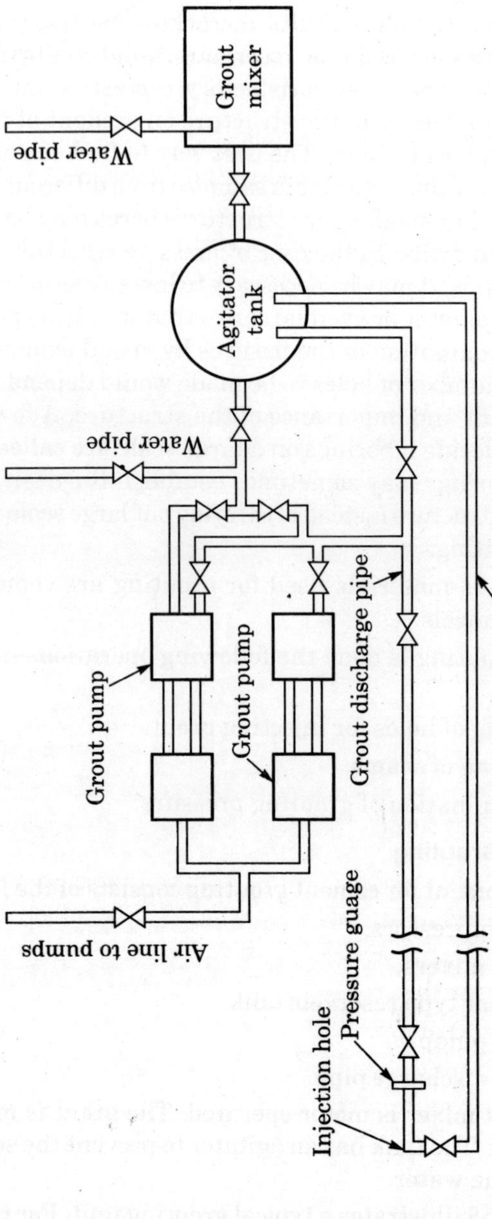

Fig. 1.58 A grouting unit.

For best results thickest grout that can be used without plugging the holes should be injected. Initially a comparatively lean mix may be used and in the succeeding groutings water cement ratio may be gradually reduced until the maximum possible thick grout is injected. The grouting pressure is reduced as the depth of grouting becomes less.

1.14.3 Pressure Grouting with Asphalt

In situations where water flows through the fissures, initially it is not possible to treat with cement grout. The use of asphalt grout in such cases has proved very useful to seal the leakage. In the second stage the final rectification is carried out by means of cement grouting.

Fig. 1.59 Photoview of grouting process.

Perforated pipes are used to inject the heated asphalt. In order to maintain the temperature of asphalt a steam line runs through this pipe. Alternatively the pipe is kept heated by installing an electric wire inside the pipe. As the grout solidifies under pressure, it takes up the shape of the fissure and seals it against the flow of water. The following equipment is used for asphalt grouting:

1. Heating kettle.
2. Piston-type pump.
3. Air Compressor or electric supply to operate the pump.
4. Auxiliary equipment such as hose pipe, values and pressure gauges.

1.14.4 Clay Grouting

Large seams and cavities having low hydrostatic head have been successfully grouted by mixture of clay and water or clay, cement and water. Clay has been successfully injected upto pressure of 0.7 N/mm^2. The chief advantage of the use of clay grout is its cheapness.

1.14.5 Chemical Grouting

As compared to the other method of grouting, chemical grouting has the following advantages:

1. Being in the liquid form it can be injected into openings in which it is not possible to inject other types of grouts.

2. The flow of water is checked by chemical grouting. The liquid grout forms a gel. The period of formation of the gel varies from a few seconds (say 5 seconds) to a few hours.

3. Because of the free flowing property of the grout fewer holes are required.

4. The time required for injecting the material is less.

1.14.6 Guniting

Guniting is useful for building up shapes without a form or on one side. Compressed and dry mix are fed to the guniting gun. The material is jetted out through a nozzle equipped with a perforated manifold. Water flowing through the perforation is mixed with the dry mix before it is ejected. The principal equipment for direct application into form by an air jet consists of the following:

1. Gunite gun or mechanical feeders.
2. Mixer.
3. Compressor.

1.15 BITUMEN MIXING PLANT

1.15.1 Introduction

Bitumen mixes have become very popular on account of the fact that it provides a comparatively cheap, durable and water proof surfacing. In road construction bitumen is used for surface painting over water bound macadam surfaces, and for various types of pavments such as penetration macadam and, bituminous concrete. It is also used as sheet asphalt for providing a smoother riding surface particularly for city streets. It consists of a mixture of sand and asphalt with a proportion of filler, usually finely ground lime stone or portland cement. The sand is graded to the required specifications and optimum proportion of cement and bitumen is determined by determining the stability of trial mixes so as to produce a most economical sheeting consistent with the desired stability. In the case of isolated jobs the aggregate filler and binder are heated together after being mixed dry in the required proportions and the binder of the specified grade is heated to the required temperature and mixing is done on specially devised mixing platform at a central location from which the mix is carried to the location of placement by means of wheel barrows. In case of large projects the mixing for sheet asphalt is done centrally in stationary plant mixers and the material carried to the site of placement in trucks or dumpers. These dumpers discharge into paving machines. The bituminous concrete is also mixed in stationary or portable plant depending upon the magnitude of the project. The initial high cost of the stationary plant can be justified if the project involves provision of bituminous concrete over a few hundred kilometers of highway or for providing premix over a series of airfields. In such cases the saving in terms of man power and other auxiliary mixing equipment more than pays back the initial high cost of procurement. The additional advantage of such a plant is the very high output (about 1.5 km length of 3.75 m wide pavement can be provided 100 mm thick concrete consolidated to 81 mm. For smaller works such as normal maintenance works in the highway department, the portable type mixers are more useful and are vary commonly used. For minor works such as patch repairs or provision of premix carpet to the approach of an inspection house, the mixing and laying is best carried out manually. The aggregates and bitumen are heated separately and mixing is done over platform prepared out of old bitumen drums.

Fig. 1.60 A typical bitumen mixing plant.

1.15.2 Bitumen Heaters

Bitumen heater is essential equipment for portable mixing plant as well for hand mixing. It is also required for surface painting, primary coats, tack coats and for penetration macadam. Bitumen heaters are available in various sizes. They are heated either by steam coal or by kerosene oil. Bitumen at elevated temperature is taken out into pouring cans and spread over the surface at predetermined rate of application. The improved types of bitumen heaters are provided with mechanical pressure distributors. The rate of application is calibrated and hot bitumen is sprayed over a given area so as to give the required coverage. Application by pressure distributors gives a better surface as the binder is spread over the surface more uniformly than by pouring cans. In the case of mixing plant the aggregates are heated separately and the two are mixed together in the specified proportion to produce at batch. In continuous type continuous spray of hot bitumen and feed to aggregates get mix at the mixer and the mix is discharged in the standing truck. For isolated and petty works bitumen is heated directly in the drums or containers of 200 liters capacity.

1.15.3 Bitumen Mixers

A number of mixing plants are available in the country. One such popular plant is manufactured by Barber and Green Co. of U.S.A. and is known as Barber and Green Plant. The various components of this plant are given below:

1. Bins for storage of various size aggregates.
2. Aggregate drier.
3. Aggregate heating arrangement.
4. Bitumen storage tank.
5. Bitumen heater.
6. Weighing machine.
7. Mechanical mixer.

Automatic feed consisting of coarse aggregates of various sizes is fed to the drier through cold elevator. These aggregates are heated and then fed into bins in case of batch type mixing plant or to the set of screen in case continuous type mixing plant. The hot aggregate from the bins is fed into the hopper which discharges them into the pug mixer. At the same time weighed quantity of hot bitumen is fed into the mixer and the timing is so arranged that by the time the mill discharges the mixed aggregate into the truck or dumper, the second instalment of the feed form the hopper is ready and the process of feeding, mixing and discharging into the truck goes on. In the case of continuous type mixer the screened aggregates at high temperature and the heated bitumen are continuously fed into the mixer at predetermined rates of feed and a continuous discharge comes out at the exit end. The discharged mix is received by the dumper directly or is otherwise collected in a hopper which is kept heated. The hopper discharges into the truck or dumper at predetermined interval so that by the time the hopper is filled up equivalent to the capacity of a truck or a dumper a carrier unit is ready to receive the discharge of the hopper.

For efficient working of a bitumen mixing plant the following points should be taken into the consideration:

1. In the case of very large plants such as the Japanese **NIGATTA** plant having a capacity of 40 tonnes of mix per hour adequate supply of all the materials should be ensured before work on the mixing plant is started.

2. Satisfactory transportation arrangements for carriage of discharged material are made so that the output of the plant is taken care of by the carriers which transport the mix from plant site to the work site. For example, assuming the rated capacity of the plant as 40 tonnes per hour and carrying capacity of dumper as 5 tonnes, one dumper load would be available after every 7.5 minutes. If the maximum distance of the worksite is taken 20 km, at least 8 dumpers would be required to maintain the continuity of the work.

3. The dumpers should be covered with trapaulins to maintain the temperature of the mix and secondly to prevent the roadside dust getting deposited on the mix.

Fig. 1.61 Truck mixer.

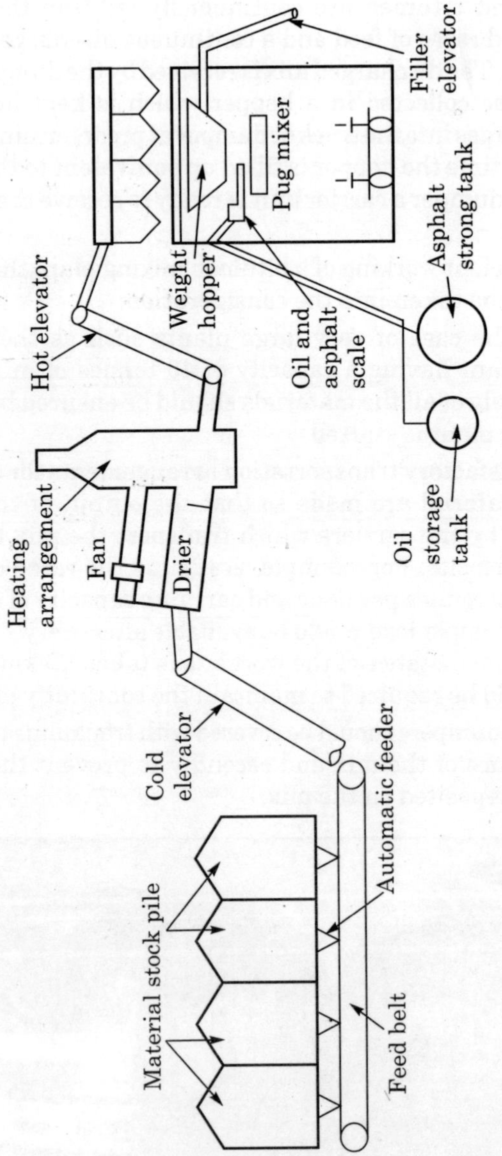

Fig. 1.62(a) Line Diagram of a Batch Type Mixing Plant.

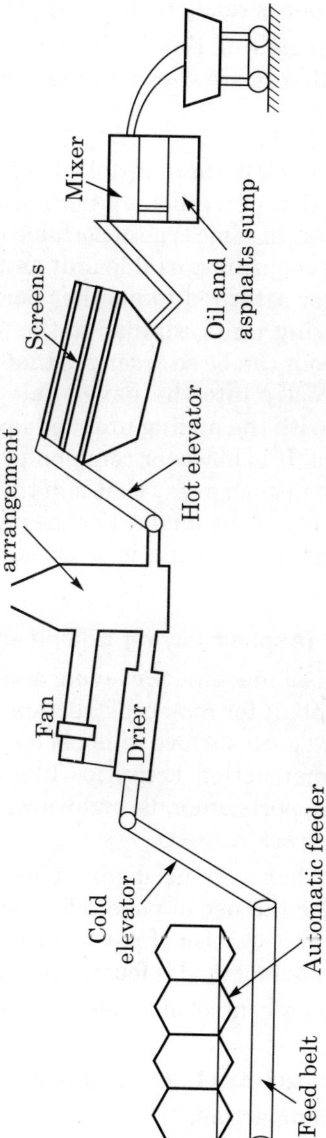

Fig. 1.62(b) Line Diagram of a Continuous Type Mixing Plant.

4. At the worksite suitable number of pavers and road rollers should be deployed on the work so that the pavers receive the mix immediately from the dumpers and laying on the surface is so arranged that by the time the paver has emptied its contents the next installment of dumper is ready to discharge its content.

Typical line diagrams of Batch Type Plant Mixers and continuous Type Plant Mixers are shown in Fig. 1.62 (*a*) and (*b*).

1.15.4 Bitumen Truck Mixers

Bitumen mixing units have been installed in trucks or tractors to facilitate the preparation of a quick and efficient mix. Various types of units are available. In some type of portable unit the heating of aggregate is done in a separate portable unit and the bitumen is heated in bitumen heater attached to another portable unit. The mixing is done in revolving units, similar to the mixers used for mixing concrete. The layout can be so arranged that the bituminous concrete discharges directly into the paver unit and the entire construction unit along with the mixing unit and laying unit moves forward at the same rate. It is however common practice to install the mixer in one location in such a way that half the day's work can be covered from one setting of the mixer. For the next day's setting of the portable mixer the next setting is so chosen that the day's work is controlled from it.

1.15.5 Pavers Finishers (Asphalt Laying Equipments)

A Paver finisher is a machine for laying and spreading sub-base, base courses or asphalt for road construction to give accurate depth, even levelling and good surface finish before rolling. Pavers are used in various construction activities like construction of footpaths, parking areas, sports grounds, highways, airport runways and railways (for laying track ballast).

Earlier paver finisher were used only in asphalt works, but during last three decades the use of pavers for sub-base and base courses had gained popularity. Use of paver finisher, compared to the traditional Motor-Grader method is found more suitable, because,

(*a*) Better and easier control of levels, both longitudinal and transverse.

(*b*) Improved homogenity of the plant prepared mix.

(*c*) Uniform pre-compaction.

(*d*) Complete elimination of final levelling, reduces the efforts and thus costs.

(*e*) Improved adherence of asphaltic courses.

The pavers can easily handle asphalt and all asphalt mixes, coated and uncoated materials, crushed stones and dry clean concrete, in fact all road making materials other than wet concrete.

A paver finisher, during constructing bituminous pavements, is fed by the mix transporting vehicle into the hoppers at the front. Two conveyor belts take up the mix which has been fed into the hopper,

Fig. 1.63

to an auger which distributes it in the prescribed thickness over the operating width. The mix is then laid in required width and depth and levelled and compacted partially by the screed. The screed is heated either by propane gas burners or electrically heated rods, evenly distributed over the entire operating width. Although the degree of compaction achieved by the screed has, in course of time, been steadily increased, final compaction by rollers is still necessary.

Compactability of a bituminous mix is considerably reduced as the mix cools and then requires more compacting energy to achieve a certain degree of compaction at a lower temperature.

To enable paver to deal with changes in road width, without interrupting operations, hydraulically extendible screeds for both sides of the finishers were developed during last few years.With such units it is possible to infinitely vary the basic operating width of the paver finishers. For pavers with rigid extensions widths upto 12.0 m can be reached. Single layer upto 30 cm thickness can be placed. The operating speeds which depends upon the size of the object and the type of work ranges from 1 to 60 m/min and can be infinitely selected. Maximum extendable width of the screed, may be hydraulically or mechanically, determines the size of the paver.

The screeds used in pavers are of three types:

(*i*) having only tamping,

(*ii*) having only vibrating,and

(*iii*) having a combined tamping and vibrating.

The pavers are either mounted on tyres or on crawler tracks. The power is provided by a suitable diesel engine.

1.16. CONCRETE COMPACTION (CONCRETE VIBRATORS)

For compacting the concrete after its placement, concrete vibrators are used. With the help of these vibrators it has become possible to place large volume of concrete quickly and easily particularly in intricate positions. The vibrators help in producing concrete of higher density by reducing air voids in the concrete. The concrete thus produced has better resistance to the seepage and gives better strength.

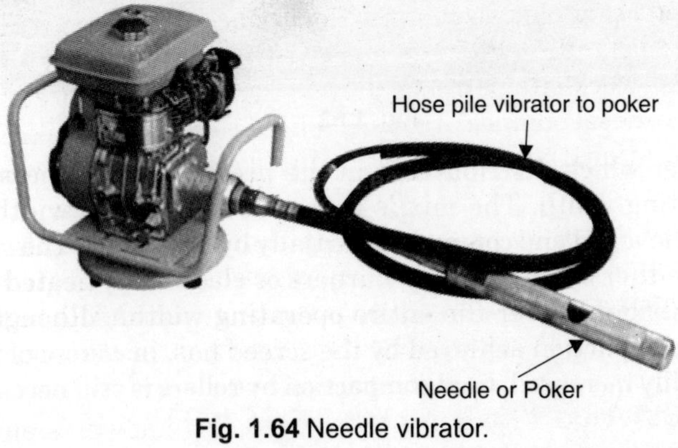

Fig. 1.64 Needle vibrator.

Concrete vibrators of following two types are generally used for construction purposes:

(*i*) **Internal Vibrators.** These are also known as immersion, needle or poker vibrators. These are immersed in the freshly placed concrete. This type of vibrator is very effective for mass concreting as it vibrates the concrete while in immersed position. Generally vibrators with 10,000 to 15,000 vibrations per min. at amplitudes between 0.8 mm to 1.6 mm are available for providing rapid and reliable compaction. The pokers of size 25 mm to 60 mm in dia are commonly used. These vibrators can be lifted and can be placed near the work place manually by a single man.

Fig. 1.64 Surface vibrator.

The vibrators are driven by petrol engine, diesel engine, compressed air or electric motors. Pneumatic vibrators are lighter and easy to handle, when compressed air or electricity is not available at work site petrol or diesel engine driven vibrators are used. Since diesel engines are more reliable and gives less troubles during operation, the vibrators with diesel engines are now-a-days preferred.

These vibrators have a flexible shaft, which gets its drive from the engine, and is enclosed in a hose. The shaft produces vibrations in the needle through an eccentric. Care should be taken that while using it, avoid bending of the flexible hose through small radii.

(*ii*) **External Vibrators.** These are also known as surface or *platform vibrators*. External vibrators are placed on the surface of the concrete through which vibrations are conveyed to the interior. These are generally used in construction of pavements, canal linings and various types of precast work where use of internal vibrator is not convenient, for example, long post, concrete products with mesh type reinforcement etc., where lack of space restricts the use of internal vibrators.

The surface vibrators consist of a rectangular pan, which is placed on the surface of concrete to be compacted. The driving unit which may be either an engine or an electric motor, is mounted above the vibrator and is carried on anti-vibration springs. The power is supplied to the vibrator, securely fixed to the pan. The effective depth of compaction by these vibrators vary from 20 cm to 30 cm.

1.17 SCRAPERS

Scrapers are the devices to scarape the ground and load it simultaneously, and transport it over the required distance, dump at desired place and then spread the dumped matreial over the required area in required thickness level, and return to the pit for the next cycle. Thus the scrapers are designed to dig, load, haul, dump and spread.

Fig. 1.65 Photo view of Scraper.

The scrapers are mainly of two types: (*a*) self propelled or motorised or conventional type, and (*b*) self loading or elevating scraper. Self-propelled or motorised scrapers are most popular. These are generally manufactured in ranges from 10 to 25 cubic metres. It needs push loading by a crawler mounted or wheeled tractor. Wheeled scrapers have more hauling speed and hence are suitable for long distance hauling while crawler-towed scrapers travel at slower speed and can be used for short hauls only. Its efficiency increases the production cost. The cycle time for a pusher includes the time required to load one scraper plus the time needed to move into position to load another scraper. It depends on the conditions in the loading pit, sizes of the pusher and scarpers and loading method.

Following formula should be used to determine the number of scrapers that a push dozer can serve:

$$\text{Number of scrapers served} = \frac{\text{Cycle time for Scraper}}{\text{Cycle time for Pushdozer}}.$$

1.17.1 Elevating Scraper

Scrapers described earlier depends upon a pusher tractor for loading, the elevating scraper is self loading one in addition to self propelled capabilities. It is similar to a conventional scraper except that its apron has been replaced by an 'elevator', also known as 'ladder'. This ladder is made up of chains with buckets bolted to it. The chain is rotated by power independent of the travel of the scraper. It has a variable speed and also reversing of the chain and buckets is possible. Loading of this scraper is done by forcing incoming earth over the cutting edge and subsequently ladder will carry it up into the bowl. They are capable of loading most materials except rock and boulders which are too large to pass between the cutting edge and the elevator buckets, and cohesive material with high moisture content.

By using elevating scraper, cost of a pusher and its operator is eleiminated. Elevating scrapers also have very good finishing ability, and hence very useful in preparing final layer of earth work in road or airfield construction work.

The operating cost and maintenance cost of the elevating scraper is higher by nearly 30% as compared to that of conventional scrapers. Due to dead weight of the loading mechanism, its transportation efficiency is reduced.

Operation. Operation of an elevating scraper is described hereunder. The working cycle is similar to that of conventional scraper.

(*i*) **Loading.** For making a cut, the bowl is first lowered to a depth which can permit the elevator and tractor to operate at a high and constant engine speed. The cut will force material towards the bowl and elevator buckets will sweep the material into the bowl. Soft surfaces like, sand, silt and top soil are dug and loaded at high speeds. Low speeds are used for loading tough materials like, hard clay. When the bowl is fully loaded, stop the elevator to avoid sweeping of the material from the face of the face of the load and also to avoid spilling over to sides of the bowl.

Fig. 1.66 Elevating scraper.

(*ii*) **Transporting.** When the scraper is loaded, the elevator should be stopped and bowl is raised until it clears the ground, move the scraper and raise the bowl further during travelling.

(*iii*) **Unloading.** The bowl is lowered at the place of dumping. With the machine in motion, the ejector floor is opened, thus allowing the bowl to unload itself and the loading edge of the ejector floor will strike off the unloaded material in the bowl, in a smooth and even layer. When unloading is complete, the bowl can be raised, ejected floor is closed and the scraper is returned for the next cycle.

10.18 LOADERS

A bucket is attached to the arms in the front and capable of being raised, lowered and dumped through mechanical or hydraulic controls. The loaders are versatile, self propelled equipment mounted either on crawler or wheel type running gear. The buckets are operated through rams, with which they dig, scoop, lift, transport, carry, dump or load into hauling units, bins, hoppers, converyors and stockpiles. With the help of additional front and rear mounted attachements these can doze, scrap, gurb, forklift, trench, grade, raking, snow clearing ditch ripping applications of a loader vary from handling coal, sand, stone aggregate etc to earth moving and digging work in quarries.

Loaders are of two types, namely (*a*) Crawler loaders; and (*b*) wheel loaders.

1.18.1 Crawler Loaders

Crawler truck type loaders are generally preferred for digging and loading jobs where ground conditions are poor and low pressure characteristics are required and are also preferable for applications involving rock and sharp stony ground. These need to be transported from one site to another after loading on the trailers.

1.18.2 Wheeled Loaders

As a result of the development of more capable power trains (axles and tires), there was a steady trend towards wheel loaders at the expense of crawlers. Protective chains for tires, that considerably increase tire operating life, even in quarry applications, additionally favoured the wheel loader against the rather more difficult to manoeuvre crawler.

Wheeled loaders are generally four wheel drive. However, for handling light jobs on good ground conditions two-wheel drive varients are also used. Four wheel drive loaders are generally used for construction jobs, whereas, two wheel drive loaders are used for bulk handling of coal, cement, fertilizer etc., to feed into hoppers and trucks.

Fig. 1.67

1.19 TUNNEL BORING MACHINES

Tunnel Boring Machines (TBMs) also known as Moles are the recent developments in the tunnel driving technique. The function of T.B.M. is to loosen the earth or break the rock continuously in the entire section of the tunnel, into cuttings and convey to the rear of the machine, where it can be loaded into much cars or dumpers or on to conveyor belts for the transportation to the ultimate disposal site. The Moles are transported to the site of work in parts and then assembled at the project site either outside the tunnel portal, if space for assembly is available, or inside the tunnel by driving the tunnel sufficient in length for enabling its assembly using conventional method. For proper operation of the

Moles, auxiliary services like workshop facilities, electric power, lighting ventilation, drainage, compressed air and water supply etc., be provided.

1.19.1 Working Principle and Constructional Features of TBM

These machines perform the boring operation through rotation of the front head against the rock face. The mole has circular cutter head in the front provided with fixed cutters of desired shape. The cutterhead while rotating is pressed against the rock to cut or pulverize it. The cuttings while falling down is collected in the buckets provided around the cutter-head periphery. These buckets discharge the muck into a hopper to feed it into the belt conveyor leading to the rear of the machine. This conveyor then discharges the muck either into the mine car or to another belt conveyor leading to the portal of the tunnel. The mine cars are hauled by using the loco. The muck of cuttings can also be disposed off by using the slurry pipelines after mixing the fine much into water to form slurry.

Fig. 1.68 (*a*) Photo view of Tunnel boring machine

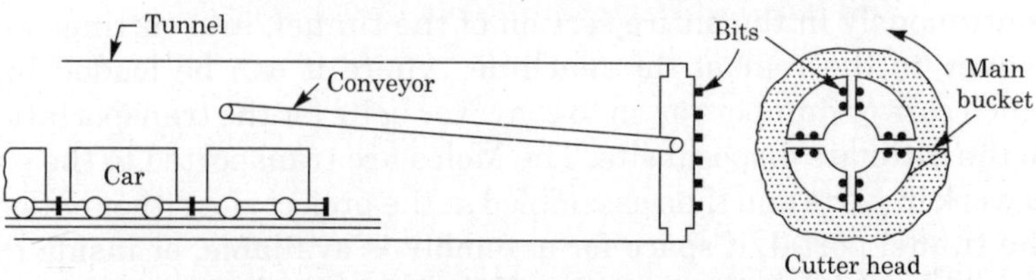

Fig. 1.68 (*b*) Outline diagram of Tunnel boring machine

For driving through full-face on full-face TBMs number of cutter heads are mounted on a drum. The drum when rotates in one direction, the individually driven cutterheads having projected Tungston carbide tipped tools can be rotated in another direction and the drum advances into the tunnel face, by providing a thrust with the help of hydraulic system. The tips of the tools when worn out can be easily replaced. The tips are kept cooled by spraying a mixture of water and compressed air into the cutting area. This also suppress the dust formed during cutting.

1.19.2 Advantages of Tunnel Boring Machines

(*i*) There is very less danger of fall outs in machines bored tunnels, since adjacent or surrounding rocks are undisturbed as no blasting is done.

(*ii*) Mucking is also safe and convenient, since muck is conveyed from the face to the rear of the machine and is loaded automatically by means of belt conveyors.

(*iii*) Higher speed of excavation.

(*iv*) Reduction in the tunnel supports requirement.

(*v*) Less manpower requirement.

(*vi*) Produces smooth and round opening which is supposed to be strongest available geometrical configuration.

(*vii*) Overbreak is generally within 5% as compared to 25% obtained by conventional method. Thus requirement of cement concrete is also reduced.

(*viii*) Muck removal is continuous and fast.

Major disadvantages from TBMs are high investment costs, long delivery periods in purchase and importation, manufacturing of the machine is required to be done for the exact diameter of the tunnel, repair of the mole is cumbersome and time consuming.

1.19.3 Application

Full face TBM is not suitable in weak rock strata conditions, as immediate support at the face cannot be erected. TBM may also not be suitable where there is continuous ingress of water, chimney formation due to continuous flowing of the rock-mass and presence of river borne material as these zones may cave in and thereby jam the entire cutter head of the TBM. These are also not useful where there is continuous squeering pressure from all sides of the tunnel, presence of shear zones or fault zones with highly plastic seams.

TBMs are available for boring tunnels of 2.1 m to 11.5 m in dia. They are also provided with a cutter head for a pilot hole of lesser dia and enlarging cutter to bore tunnels upto 15 m diameter.

T.B.Ms. are available either for single stage machine *i.e.,* for face tunnel boring, or multistage tunnel boring. In first case cutter head is of a single full diameter, while in later case it is for a pilot of lesser diameter and enlarging cutter to bore tunnels of bigger diameter.

1.19.4 Type of Tunneling Machines

Mechanical modes though can be classified in many ways, namely; according to the type of material to be mined, or cutting principle employed, or cutter head movement, but mainly fall under following two categories based on the action of their cutter-heads:

(1) Rotary type and (2) Oscillating type.

Rotary type moles consist of a wheel fitted with either teeth or disc cutters or roller bits which revolves in either direction around the central shaft. These are primarily used in firm underground formations including hard rock applications.

Oscillating type of mechanical moles are generally used for soft or semistable formations *i.e.*, in clays, sands and gravels. These machines are used in changeable ground conditions or where underground formations vary.

2

Planning and Works Management

2.1 MANAGEMENT OF CONSTRUCTION INDUSTRY

2.1.1 Introduction

In any construction project whether it is executed by Government, Public or Private Undertakings the main purpose of management and planning is to combine structural stability along with being the most economical. In the case of private firms and organizations the object is to combine profit with high degree of business ethics.

Past experience shows that where as the private firms and organizations have far better performance in terms of cost and quality than government controlled projects, the profit earned by these firms goes to big industrialists whereas the expenditure incurred by government in the execution of the project partly goes to the common worker in pay and allowances and other state undertakings which produce plant machines and equipment for the project. However one of the most important reasons for increased cost and inferior quality of products produced by government undertakings is the inadequate project management.

While the efficiency of the project depends directly upon the site organization and supervisory staff, the overall responsibility rests with the project management and hence the need for providing proper personnel for project management and planning. Various aspects which influence the performance of the project are:

(*i*) Organization and planning

(*ii*) Delegation of responsibility

(*iii*) Managerial ability
(*iv*) Understanding money
(*v*) Public interest
(*vi*) Human relations
(*vii*) Congenial environment
(*viii*) Career prospects
(*ix*) Modern technique of Management.

MASONS TOOL

Trowel

Chiesels

Curved end edger

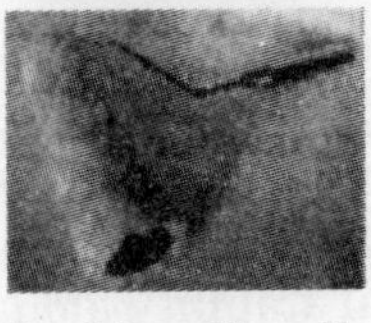
Metal handle roller (811502)

Plastering trowel (163824)

Wooden handle brush

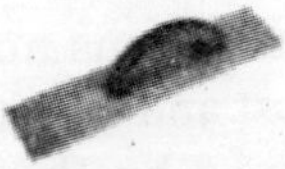
Wood float

Bevel float

Masonry float

Brick and block jointer

Laminated Hardwood

Highest quality laminated African walnut levels. Two level bubble vials. Extremely accurate and durable. All with green vials, 42" and 48" available with strike plate.

No.	Description	Wt (lbs)
TBL L12W	12"	1
TBL L18W	18"	1.3
TBL L24W	24"	1.8
TBL L30W	30"	2.6
TBL L36W	36"	2.9
TBL L42W	42"	3
TBL L42WS	42" with Strike Plate	3
TBL L48W	48"	3.4

TBL L48WS	48" with Strike Plate	3.4
TBL L72W	72"	6
TBL LWL	Clear Lense	0.1

Clear vials special order

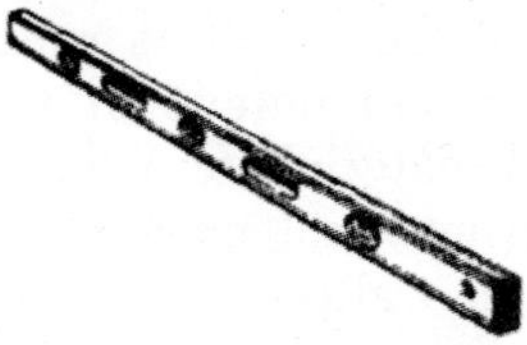

Levels

Aluminium

Designed to be hit with the trowel. One third lighter than laminated wood levels. Centered hand holes optimize balance. Top reading horizontal vial. Stands up to thousands of drops, will not wrap or twist. Vials never to fog, leak or require adjustable. Water and brush cleanup.

No.	Description	Wt (lbs)
TBL L12A	12"	0.5
TBL L24A	24"	0.7
TBL L36A	36"	1.5
TBL L48A	48"	1.15

Line

Made of hexagon aluminium tubing, furnished with two strongly built line dips. This level can be used on the line or as a surface level.

The above aspects if not taken into consideration can have very adverse effects on the overall performance of the project and have therefore been dealt with separately in the following articles.

2.1.2 Organization and Planning

The MATRIX system at head office level and 'Team System' headed by an effective Project Manager has been found to be most satisfactory. The manager should be vested with adequate power delegation at the project site. A sound management system ensures loyalty and job satisfaction from its workers. The routine 'Line and Functional Organization' system has its own shortcomings since the decision making is delayed.

At the top level, the working of the project has to be properly planned into various phases such as procurement of project machinery at the commencement of the relevant phase, procurement of men and material etc. Very often lack of planning and procurement of men, material, machine and other resources, if not done properly, adversely affects the performance of the project with respect to its *time* and *progress* schedule for which executives at the lower level are blamed although responsibility rests with the lower people.

The assets, resources and goals of the organization should be discussed with the experts and executives, who can, if needed suggest available alternatives.

Departments such as Accounts, Finance, Administrative personnel and planning are generally vested with powers by virtue of which they create bottlenecks at every stage instead of helping effective and economical execution of the project. This system needs to be drastically changed so that for these lapses the field workers are not penalized.

2.1.3 Delegation and Responsibility

Decentralization is the only responsible way of running a business satisfactorily. Senior executives normally reject delegation of power on the grounds that there is no one to whom the power may be delegated. Such persons can never develop staff to whom he can delegate powers. Even if the same executive delegates power to his junior, he is seldom trusted and vested with adequate authority. It is therefore main responsibility of the senior executive to ensure that the chosen junior be provided with adequate authority and should be trusted unless proved otherwise.

In the early stage of delegation of power, some failures should be taken for granted and the juniors should be given adequate time to improve. Occasional failures due to delegation should not result in the abolishment of the system but the solution is to change the person and not the system.

Simply by delegating power to the junior, the senior executive is not freed from his responsibility for failure and success even though the person to whom power has been delegated is held directly responsible for the failure. Half hearted delegation results in poor performance of the organization.

2.1.4 Managerial Ability

The success of any company depends upon the following:

(*i*) Head office (Administration)

(*ii*) Plant and equipment

(*iii*) Promises

(*iv*) Site construction organization.

Choitic working conditions result due to inefficient management. The success of the organization depends upon optimum utilization of its assets (men, material equipment and other resources).

2.1.5 Understanding Money

The principal unit responsible for successful implementation of the project is the Engineer-in-charge. Whereas proper execution of the project leads to improvement in the finances of the financier, his inefficiency leads to his bank bankruptcy.

2.1.6 Public Interest

The construction companies have not only to secure reasonable profit on the investment but have also to keep in view the service which they have the good fortune of rendering to the public, community and the society.

To encourage investment of extra earnings towards welfare of the society such as construction of hospitals, education institutions, dharmshalas etc. the government exempts from income tax the amount spent in such activities.

2.1.7 Human Relations

Persuasive management and enlightened leadership are qualities much more necessary than ever. The top executive should show justice, equality, tolerance and freedom. On the other hand the employees must conform to the decisions and procedures laid down by the top executives. In dealing with inability and indiscipline, ruthlessness is necessary. However if such ruthlessness disregards human emotions, injures pride and self respect of the employee and ruffles tempers, the very purpose of ruthlessness is defeated. Injustice done to the employee rankles more in the mind of the employee than injustice under other circumstances. Even good workers will leave the organization and distrust will prevail in the setup. Such a situation should never be allowed to develop.

2.1.8 General Environment

People of various abilities and thinking will act harmoniously if the top management makes it understood to its employees the formation of the objective and creation of facilities and environment. Success of any undertaking depends upon its execution to be carried out as one unity. It is the responsibility of the top management to maintain that unity.

2.1.9 Career Prospects

Employees should be given a feeling that promotion to higher levels depends upon the improvement in his/her performance and that the vacancies at the top are not based on personal choice of the top executive.

2.1.10. Modern Technique of Management

Due to hurdles like centralisation of decision making, lack of short term controls, lack of supporting policy measures, inadequacies in coordination and follow up action, lack of co-operation and lack of trained personnel, the Indian construction industry has not been able to take full advantage of modern technique.

2.2 CONSTRUCTION COMPANY ORGANIZATION

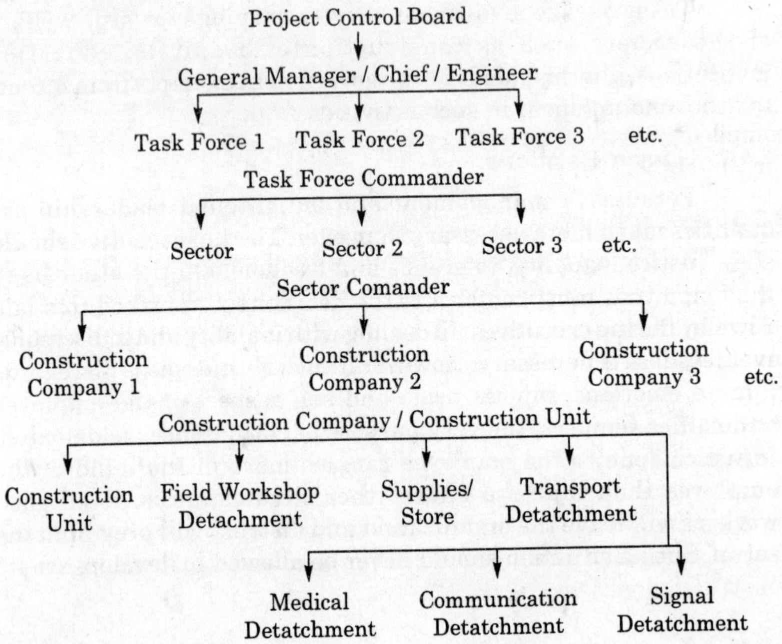

2.3 CONSTRUCTION PLANNING AND SCHEDULING

2.3.1 Collection of Data from Site Investigation and from Available Record

Before designing any structure it is necessary to find out all particulars in respect of the place where the structure is to be constructed. Site investigation normally is carried out to determine the bearing capacity of the soil so as to design safe depth of foundation and the area at the foundation level to take up the loading.

Data to be collected from available records normally refers to the highest flood levels in the vicinity of the bridge site to determine the area under the bridge required to discharge the peak flow.

2.3.2 Compilation of Data

The site investigations in respect of the structure extends to over a period of number of years. The authors have seen site investigations team working in connection with Marora Dam for a period of nearly eight years sending about 80 million rupees. The project had ultimately to be abandoned as the sub-structure below was not considered safe. Even though 80 million rupees were spent on the proposed 8000 million project the result of the investigations, which were necessary save the failure of the dam. Tehri Dam and Narmada Sarovar Dams are other examples.

In the same way, investigation for selection of bridge site is not only confined to the site but also 500 metres upstream and down stream of the proposed structure.

The information/data collected from site investigations is compiled to arrive at satisfactory depth of foundation, fixing waterway for the highest floods etc.

2.3.3 Preparation of Project Report

The project report consists of the following:

1. **Introduction.** A summary from initiation of the proposal to its finalisation including brief description of various surveys, investigations and data collection carried out.

2. **Design parameters and standards adopted, codes followed etc.** For example if it is a report on highways the geometric standards followed, design speed, type and width of pavement shoulder, grade, curvatures and sight distances adopted are included. In the same way if the report is a proposed dam construction, the type of dam, structural features, area to be submerged, phases of construction and time schedule is to be indicated.

3. **Salient features of the project.** In the case of a highway project, details of alignment starting from point of commencement to its termination, reasons for adopting the final alignment and other features such as grades, curves and obligatory points are briefly described.

4. Foundation conditions including soil classification and various strata as well as particulars of soil samples and marshy areas are indicated.

5. **Weather conditions prevailing.** For example, in the forward areas working period starts in the beginning of June and ends with the end of October. Arrangements for induction and deinduction as well as utilization of resources has to be brought out.

6. **Availability of resources.** Phasewise requirement of men, material, machinery and equipment has to be given so that in the case of acceptance of the project procurement action for procurement of the resources required may be initiated. In case of machinery available in the country be obtained.

7. **Details of land to be acquired along with towns and villages affected.** For example, in the case of a dam the towns and villages to be shifted and compensation to be paid has to be spelt out in detail along with the environmental effect of the project. Pollution control or environmental effect has now acquired priority over other considerations. The progress of Tehri Dam has been considerably retarded for environmental considerations. Similar is the case with Narmada Sarovar Dam.

8. **Specifications of the project.** Under this heading may be included all such information from the point of view of the project which are important but may not have been included under any of the headings indicated earlier.

9. **Annexures to the Project Report.** The following annexures are normally supplied with the project report:

1. Index plan.
2. Site plan.
3. Longitudinal and cross-sections along with estimated quantities of earthwork.
4. Details of protective works.
5. Drainage details along with details of bridges, culverts etc.
6. Available construction material with details of resources available within the country and those to be imported.

7. Design details of structures.
8. Land acquisition and land compensation schedule.
9. Estimated cost of the project.
10. **Conclusions.** Under this the total estimated cost of the project specifying separately the amount earmarked for compensation of the property of various types to be acquired and contingencies is specified. A request for according administrative approval of the project along with specified demand for yearwise allotment of funds from the proposed date of starting of the construction is made.

The breakdown details and basis for arriving at the cost of the project is also specified. At the end the officer initiating the project signs the report giving his/her designation and date of signing.

2.3.4 Manpower Requirement

Workers, material, Executive, supervisors, skilled and unskilled labour and watch and ward personnel (security staff) together form the manpower requirement of the project. Once Administrative Approval of the project is accorded by the Competent Administrative Authority (CAA) procurement action for manpower is started. For example, the Border Roads Organization which was conceived in 1959 had the Prime Minister as the Chairman of the Border Roads Organization with the Defence Minister as one of its members and Secretary Ministry of Transport as its member Secretary, although the project on the ground started in early 1960, recruitment of workers (Pioneers), Procurement of machinery and equipment (Under Capital Outlay) and recruitment of Executives (Deputionists from Defence Services, Army, Navy and Air Force), through UPSC had started much earlier. In a particular project under Project Beacon in Ladakh sector, recoinnance, preliminary survey as well as work on obligatory points had started along with the finalisation of the First meeting of the Board. The regular work under this project started in 1961 and during the two working seasons (July to October 1961 and 1962) the project achieved the distinction of opening the road for Shaktiman from Sonamarg to Chisul.

2.3.5 Local Advantage of Manpower and Materials

In order that the project be economical, maximum advantage should be taken from local manpower and materials. For example, in the Ladakh region, the workers (Pioneers) were recruited at

Bengal Engineer Group Roorkee for a period of two months, were subjected to high altitude effect at Srinagar for 2-4 months and then transported to the work site. They were provided necessary accommodation, transport, medical facilities and leave. As compared to this the overall expenditure on local labour was only 10% of the expenditure incurred on imported labour. On the other hand the output of local labour was about 50% more than that of imported labour. This explains the importance of utilising local labour to the maximum. The same applies to maximum utilization of local material. For example, if coarse aggregate has to be imported by transportation over long distances, the cost of transportation alone would exceed the total cost of material available locally.

2.3.6 Benefits of the Project

While giving Administrative Approval for any project the competent Administrative Authority (CAA) in collaboration with Competent Financial Authority (CFA) and Competent Engineer Authority (CEA) has to evaluate the expenditure to be incurred in the Project with the return. The only exceptions are:

1. Construction of Works in the Forward areas by Defence or Paramilitary Authorities (Such as Boarder Roads Organization) or other Central or State organizations for strategic reasons and for works taken in hand to provide jobs in famine struck areas of that the affected people earn for themselves to pay for procuring essential items for their livelihood.

2. Projects for Medical services, Educational facilities etc., where the return from the project cannot be equated with the earning from the project.

With the exception of above mentioned cases, the return from the project has to be evaluated in term of the interest on the Capital invested.

2.4 DRAWING AND SPECIFICATIONS

2.4.1 ISI Standard Codes (Now Standard Bureau Codes)

Before independence British Standard Specifications (BSS) were followed all over the country. However, with the country getting freedom Indian Standard Institution was established to provide Code of Practice for all items of work. These standards are framed with the help of special committees formed from outstanding persons in the particular field. These committees frame *'Draft'* recommendations for various items of work. These draft specifications are circulated to various departments as well as to private enterprises and are finalised taking into consideration the comments received from various departments, industries and enterprises. The Indian Standard Institution has now been renamed as Bureau Indian Standards.

2.4.2 Madras Detailed Specification

Various Public Works Departments have laid down detailed specifications for various items of work as well as schedules of rates. Although the standard specifications seldom undergo any changes, the standard schedule of rates go on changing from time to time depending upon the variation in the procurement cost of materials, transportation charges and labour rates. Moreover, labour, material and transportation charges not only changes from time to time but also vary from place to place. For example, the work of CPWD extends over the entire country and hence these rates also vary for different zones. In the same way Military Engineering Service has different schedules of rates for different areas.

The specifications for different items of work for various zones and states do not undergo any changes from time to time except when new techniques are developed. It has been noticed that inspite of different State/Pradesh, Public Works Department have their own specifications, but they are all based on standard specification laid down by Government of India Ministry of Works and Housing, National Building Organization and UN Regional Housing Centre ESCAP, Nirman Bhawan, New Delhi.

The reproduction of these specification is beyond the scope of the present book (as in itself will be a complete book). These specifications are however available from the Publication Division of Government of India and hence they have been briefly dealt with separately in Article 11.4.5.

2.4.3 General and Special Conditions

In the construction works executed through contractors, the work is allotted by calling for tenders. Depending upon the nature of work the various forms of contract are:

(*i*) Item rate contract.

(*ii*) Percentage above or below standard schedule of rates (A very generalised form of item rate contract).

(*iii*) Lumpsum contract.

(*iv*) Piece-work contract.

While submitting the rates in case of item rate contract and amount in the case of Lumpsum and negotiated contracts, the contractor has not only to carry out work as per specifications but the agreed Time and Progress Chart, Passing the work in stages and completion of the work in specified time has to be considered. In addition to removal of defective work, penalty for not completing the work in specified time, employment of debitable agency in case the department feels the progress of the work is slow, adherence to minimum wages act, provision of amenities for the labour, provision of accommodation and sanitary arrangements for the labour working at the site of the project has to be specified and agreed to by the contractor. This forms the basis of the general conditions of contract. These conditions are specified in the tender form along with the set of drawings. Along with the tender form brief description of the work involved are also given separately with the tender document.

In the case of certain specialised works, details of which have not been provided in the standard specifications and the requirements to be fulfilled by the contractor have not been incorporated in the general conditions of contract. Special conditions of contract are added as annexure to the general conditions of contract. Sometimes the general conditions given in the contract agreement need modification. Such modifications which form the special condition of contract have precedence over the general conditions of contract.

2.4.4 National Building Code

Specifications for various items of work given in the Standard specifications issued by National Building Organization and UN housing Centre (ESCAP) do not cover such items of work as are of special interest for building industry. This has resulted in the formation of National building code. This Code not only specifies the salient features of specifications particular to the item of work but lays down special emphasis on the design details of various components of the buildings. These design details are not covered in the Standard Specifications. The various structural details specified in the National Building Code are:

1. General building requirements including size of drawing sheets
2. Civil Aviation requirements
3. Fire protection
4. Building material

5. Structural design
   (*i*) Loads
   (*ii*) Foundations
   (*iii*) Wood
   (*iv*) Masonry
   (*v*) Concreting
      A—Plain and reinforced
      B—Prestressed
6. A—Structural design-steel
   B—Prefabrication and system building
7. Constructional Practice on safety
8. (*i*) Building service
   (*ii*) Electrical installation
   (*iii*) Air conditioning and heating
   (*iv*) Acoustics, Sound installation and noise control
   (*v*) Installation of Lifts and Escalator.
9. Plumbing Services.

2.5 CONTRACT DATA FROM REMOTEST ANTIQUITY

The contract system of construction in civil engineering field is very old. In Ancient Greek; when structures were built, Greek law laid down certain relationships between the construction agency *i.e.,* contractor and the owner. They had framed certain rules; regulations by laws and conditions. Those rules; regulations and other conditions of contract laid down by them are still prevailing today with certain modifications and changes as per changed conditions. At that period also contractors were required to hire sufficient skilled; unskilled persons and qualified workmen. They were required to give the guarantee of the quality of materials and workmanship and work. Penalties were prescribed for failure or delay of the works. Payments were made in instalments as per the progress of work. Advances were paid if required by the contractor. Owner had binding to make the payments as per approved bills. All these conditions are existing today also.

The recognised system for carrying out works otherwise then by the employment of daily labour are *'Piece Work'* rate list and *'Contract Works'*. 'Piece Work' is that for which only a rate is agreed upon by a piece worker without reference to the quantity of works to be done or the time within which it is to be completed. In the rate list system petty works can be carried out by a number of piece workers on schedules of costs known as rate lists without references to quantity and time.

All other works done or supply made under agreement is termed as contract work. This agreement should be in writing; clearly specifying quantity and time within which it is to be completed besides other conditions for penalties and labilities.

2.5.1 Contract and Contractor

As per Indian Contract ACT of 1872 '*Contract*' is an agreement between competent parties. enforceable at law whereby each acquires a right to what is promised by the other. Two persons can have any sort of agreement; they can promise to each other for certain job, but unless such promises are enforceable at law; the work is legal; they form no contract. Hence it should be noted that every contract is an agreement enforceable at law but every agreement is not necessarily a contract.

As per P.W.D.; the term contract means any kind of undertaking; written or verbal; expressed or implied; by a person not being a government servant, or by a syndicate or firm, for the construction; maintenance or repairs of one or more works; for the supply of materials, or for the performance of any service in connection with the execution of works or the supply of the materials.

The term 'contractor' means a person; syndicate or firm that has made such an undertaking; but often its use is restricted to contractor for the execution or for services in connection thereon.

2.5.2 Essentlals of Contract

Following are the essential requirements for formation of a contract. These have been recognised universally:

1. Legally competent parties
2. A lawful subject matter
3. Proper and valid considerations
4. Genuine agreement signed by both the parties

Engineering contract is a contract concerning to engineering projects. It is a type of business agreement. As per Indian contract Act; parties involved into a contract must be legally competent. Infants; lunatics; drunken people are not competent. There is no hard and fast rule that two persons doing engineering contract with each other should not have any close relations or blood relations, but still as far as possible it is avoided. In many departments; persons having blood relations are not permitted to get themselves involved in any contract agreement. In certain states a husband and wife having no blood relations; equally competent parties cannot contract to each other. The contract should be on a lawful subject matter which is enforceable at law. Further these contracts must not violate state or union territory *i.e.,* if a contract has been made in one state it will be invalid for other state. Another important condition for a contract to be legal and enforceable at law is that it should have been made by free consent of both parties involved *i.e.,* contractor and owner. A work for which a contract is made should not have been expressly declared to be void by any statute; otherwise it does not remain legal and lawful subject matter.

There should be proper and valid considerations between a contractor and owner whether Government organization or private party. In absence of these considerations; it becomes difficult to execute the work properly. In Engineering contracts; there are mutual promises. The contractor promises to execute the work properly as per drawings and specifications; maintaining the quality performance faithfully similarly owner promises to make the payments when due. It is only possible when the work is a lawful subject matter and there are proper and valid considerations in the form of under standing between the parties involved in contract. Further a contract must be genuine. Subject matter and work should be clear. There should not be any misrepresentations or fraud. The contract documents further must be made on the stamp paper of the value as prescribed by the Indian stamp Act 1899 duly signed by both the parties involved with due witnesses. The contract agreement in the absence of a signature of any of the party no longer remains valid.

For a contract to be valid; there must be an offer from owner (Government or Private body) to set some definite work executed and similarly there must be an acceptance from the contractor to execute the defined work as per laid terms and conditions. Both the offer and acceptance must be definite and legal.

2.5.3 Free Consent

Free consent is the consent which has been obtained by the free will of the parties involved in contract, out of their own accord. A consent is said to be free when it is not carried out by any of the following:

1. ***Coercion:*** It is utterness of threat to commit an act forbidden by the Indian Penal Code to induce someone to enter into a contract.

2. ***Duress:*** It is the fear caused by the threat of a bodily harm.

3. ***Undue influence:*** It is an influence which compels a person to do something which he would not have done if he had been a free agent. The relation between the parties is such that one of the parties having taken an unfair advantage is in a position to dominate the will of the other.

4. ***Fraud:*** Related to an absence of a honest belief and a wicked mind. It also includes false statement made by parties.

5. ***Mis representation:*** That is, incorrect statement unknown to all the parties involved in contract that materially affects the contract. For example, though water is supplied to the contractor but it is mentioned in document that contractor will have to make his own arrangement of water for construction work. It is mis representation. Another example time period given for work is too less and then time granted is extended with escalation.

6. ***Mistakes:*** It is an error made in contact document that may lead to mis representation or may affect contract. The mistake can be either by one party of contract or by both the parties. This mistake is called *bilateral*.

2.5.4 Type of Contacts

There are many ways of getting a work executed in contract system; the work is got executed through an agency called contractor, who arranges all materials, labour, equipments etc., for the completion of the work in time. The main idea behind any contract system is:

(*i*) To get lowest total cost of construction.

(*ii*) To achieve greatest speed of construction to have minimum indirect expenditure.

(*iii*) To have best workmanship and

(*iv*) To have future business between owner and contractor based upon previous experiences.

These different system of contracts are listed below.

Each method has its own merits and demerits.

(1) Lump-sum contract.

(2) Cost plus a fixed percentage contract.

(3) Cost plus a fixed fee contract.

(4) Target contact.

(5) Item rate contract (B 2-system)
(6) Percentage rage contract (B 1-system).
(7) Labour contract.
(8) Joint venture contract.
(9) Turn-key projects.

1. ***Lump-sum contract:*** This is an offer by a contractor, that he undertakes the execution of a specific work for a definite lump-sum amount and to complete the same within specified time period. The detailed drawings and detailed specifications are supplied to the contractor by the owner *i.e.,* department or private agency having capital to get the work executed. It is duty of contractor to complete the work as per drawings and specifications supplied and as per terms and conditions agreed upon. On the completion of the work; the work is checked as per drawings and specifications and if approved; the amount is paid to the contractor. Hence quantities of various items are not measured. The difficulty arises when engineer-in-charge or owner makes certain changes in the drawings and specifications. Further some contractors also have tendency to use cheap materials of construction to reduce the cost of that work so as to earn maximum profit. In this type of system, contractor takes the risk of unfavourable circumstances, he therefore quotes a good percentage so that he may be sure of his profit whatever may happen. Hence cost of work becomes very high. Therefore this type of system of contract have become obsolete where it is possible to measure the quantities. In civil engineering works this system has totally become obsolete except for a few works where work can not be measured; for example, construction of some decorative piece; or construction of some sculpture etc., where labour cost involved is very high and quantity measurement has no relation with its work this lump-sum system of contract is used.

2. ***Cost Plus fixed percentage contract:*** Under this type of system of contract, contractor furnishes all labour and material necessary to complete the work for actual cost of work plus an agreed percentage of the said cost as the profit of the contractor. This percentage profit is fixed. Hence due to this fixed percentage of profit of actual work; contractor always tries to increase the cost of project. No doubt the speed and quality of work is maintained but there is always tremendous wastage of various materials used in construction. This consequently increases the cost of project and hence the profit of contractor making project more costly. This type of system of contract has become obsolete now a days and used only in case of emergency works.

3. ***Cost plus a fixed fee:*** This was implemented to modify the above method; to control the tendency of contractor to increase the cost of project unnecessarily. This is similar to cost plus fixed percentage of actual cost except this fixed percentage is converted to fixed fee irrespective of the actual cost. In this system contractor gets a fixed amount in the form of profit, what so ever may be the cost of work. Due to fix amount of profit contractor always tries to complete the job earliest possible so that he can get himself involved in other contract. Here work progress is maintained properly quality of materials used also maintained but workmanship quality is not, as contractor is always in hurry to complete work early. Smaller the completion time; more will be profit as contractor can execute more jobs in lesser period of time. However this system of contract is still better than cost plus fixed percentage, still this method could not become very popular and hence not used in general.

4. ***Target system of contract:*** This is a slight modification over cost plus fixed fee contract system. Under this system, the contractor is paid a fixed fee on a prime cost bases for the work performed under the contract and in addition he receives a percentage on saving affected against either a prior agreed estimated total cost on a target value arrived; without changing the specification. It was presumed that contractor due to proper management of work and labour can reduce the cost of work consequently earning more profit and making structure economical. The desire for extra gain encourages the contractor to use his skill and experience in keeping the cost as low as possible.

But due to continuous increase in the prices of materials and labour and due to other reasons; it is rather very difficult to save the amount from earlier estimated cost. Rather it has been experienced that the cost of work is always more than the estimated cost and hence no extra earning is possible what so ever may be used. Due to this reason; this method of contract system is not getting popularity.

5. ***Item-Rate contract (B 2-system):*** In item rate contract the contractor undertakes the execution or construction of a work on the item basis. The amount the contractor receives depends upon quantities of various items of works executed. In this system; bill of quantities is prepared mentioning various items of construction and their quantities; contractors bidding contract are required to quote the rates of various items mentioned in bill or quantity with the stipulation that work will be subjected to measurement and payments are made at the unit price quoted. This particular system is called

item rate contract. The difficulty with this system is; it is rather difficult to scrutinize the tenders submitted by various bidders; hence modified. In modified system of item rate contract; the department generally quotes various items of construction along with their quantities and rates. The bidders *i.e.,* contractors are required to quote various percentages at which he wants to execute that item. As such for each item a separate percentage is quoted. This system of contract is called as '*percent item rate contract*' system. This system was very popular in P.W.D. and still used many times. This system is also called B 2-system of contract in P.W.D.

Schedule B

Memorandum showing items of work to be carried out

Item No.	Quantities estimated but may be more or less	Item of work	Estimated Rates		Unit	Total amount according to estimated quantities
			In figures ₹ P.	In words		
As Per Separate Sheet Attached						

Department Hand book

Note 1: All work shall be carried out as per other specifications of the Division or as directed.

Note 2: Rates quoted include clearance of site (Prior to commencement of work and at its close) in all respects and hold good for work under all conditions, site moisture, weather etc.

Signature of contractor Signature of $\frac{\text{Executive Engineer}}{\text{Assistant Engineer}}$

***Note:** To be continued on additional sheets if found necessary.*

When the quantities of various items are not available; then there was practice to adopt item rate contract system. The drawback in this system, as the quantities of various items are not known. The contractor always gives higher rates for those item quantities which are likely to increase and low rates for those likely to be decreased. The same is found in percentage item rate contract. The contractor quotes higher percentage for items likely to increase and lower percentage for items likely to be decreased. This results in unbalanced contract. Therefore this type of contract system should be avoided as far as possible. Unless until detailed estimate is made; quantities of different items are evaluated correctly and got ascertained that there will not be more than five percent variation in each quantity maintaining the overall cost variation less than 5 percent only; this contract system should not be used.

6. ***Percentage rate contract (B 1-system):*** This system of contract is very popular and common now a days. Most of the works either in P.W.D. or private organization are undertaken with this system only. In this system detailed estimate is prepared and contractors are required to quote single percentage either higher or lower at which he wants to execute this job. As such all item rates are changed with the same percentage; hence tender generally does remains balanced and scrutinity becomes comparatively very easy. Now a days materials like cement and steel are supplied by the department hence chances of manipulation becomes still less. Most of the engineering contracts are performed with this method only. The rate of recovery of matrial is given in schedule A. It helps the contractor to decide his rates to be quoted for item involved with use of these materials.

Schedule A

Schedule showing (approximately) the materials to be supplied from the Departmental stores for work contracted to be executed and preliminary and ancillary works and the rates at which they are to be charged for the construction of ....(work)

Particulars	Quantity	Rates at which the material will be charged to the contractor			Place of delivery
		Unit	In figure	In words	
1. Cement in plastic bags	76.75 MT 1527 bags	Per one MT	1800.00	Rupee one thousand eight hundred only	at departmental store
2. 120 mm dia hume pipes NP-2 class-20 running meters *i.e.*, 8 numbers of 2.5 m each	20 running meter *i.e.*, 8 nos of 2.5 m each	Per one metre running	1400.00	Rupee one thousand four hundred only	at departmental store

Note 1: The person of firm submitting the tender should see that the rate in the above schedule are filled up by the Executive Engineer-in-charge on issue of the form prior to the submission of the tender.

Note 2: The contractor should furnish the account of all materials before placing demand for further material and furnish full account of all Department. If any material remained unused with the contractor, he should return the same to the Department. In the event of non return of such matrial recovery at penal rate of twice the issued rate with S.T. and G.T. will have to be effected from the contractor.

Note 3: Wastage of steel to be borne entirely by the contractor.

Signature of contractor Signature of $\frac{\text{Executive Engineer}}{\text{Assistant Engineer}}$

7. ***Labour contract:*** This is the most common system of construction for private individual buildings; particularly in small cities and big towns. Under this system of contract; the contractor arranges all necessary labour; tools and plants and equipments required for. The construction and all the materials required are supplied by the owner. This type of system of contract is also particularly suitable for those cases where the owner or Government departments is in a privileged position to buy large quantities of materials at cheap rates. This system is very common for small and private works. Most of the private dwellings are given on a labour contract only and the owner arranges all the materials required for construction. Generally owner also appoints some engineer to supervise the work to maintain the quality and to economise the cost of construction at a fixed fee or percentage of actual cost of construction as supervision charges.

8. ***Joint venture contract:*** This system of contracting has developed due to tremendous increase in the size of work or due to development of specialised persons for certain specialised job. In case of important and big projects, it is rather difficult to individual contractor to complete the work in specified period of construction. Further different specialist firms have developed who can undertake such work at a reasonable rate with less time for its construction. Hence it was thought and then decided to divide the whole work into different parts either on the basis of amount of work involved or on the basis of special type of work with which a specific firm may be familiar. Hence the work was divided into different contractors and hence joint venture system of contract developed. The first joint venture system involved six competing construction

firms headed into line under one management at the construction of Hoover Dam. The system has become very popular and common now. In a building itself different works are given to different specialists firms under a main contractor and work is got done efficiently and early. Wiremen; plumber etc., are specialist persons for these jobs. Similarly gangs for concreting work are very popular in India. Their jobs is only to do concreting of various elements or reinforced concrete work.

9. ***Turn key-projects:*** Now a days in civil engineering construction for certain type of works; turn-key system of contract/ project has become very common. This system was used during the construction of apartments and flats. The person who wants a flat; is required to complete the paper work and transaction work and then enter into his own house simply by turning the key *i.e.,* opening the door.

In this system; the contractor is required to prepare the project including its planning designing; estimation and execution. Once the project is complete the whole project work is handed over to the owner. Most of the elevated storage reservoirs (ESR) are constructed by Turn-key-project system only.

10. A new method of contract has developed in India now a days. This is an indirect type of lump sum contract. In this system a rate of construction per square meter of plinth area is decided jointly by owner and contractor or builder. The specifications are generally fixed or decided jointly and based on these specifications a rate per sq. meter plinth are excluding land cost is decided. This rate includes the contractors profit. Once this agreement is made contractor or builder develops or constructs a bungalow on owners land and payments are made by owner to the contractor or builder at a regular interval at various stages of construction. Many times even the drawings; specifications and rates are fixed by builder, owner asks builder/contractor to construct/develop the plot.

This system is becoming very popular in India. In big cities or towns; most of the bungalows are constructed with this type of system of contract. Here the owner fully gets relived of all problems come across during construction.

11. ***BOT i.e., Built operate and transfer:*** This is a new system in which land is acquired by govt. and contractor is asked to built the civil works, operate it by collecting some fee from its users

to collect the cost of construction and once the cost is collected, to transfer it to the owner *i.e.,* Government. No investment is made by government under this system. Drawings, estmates are prepared by Government and contractor is required to execute the work as per designs and specifications given by Engineer. No payment is made to the contractor. All expenditures incurred are to be made by contractor. In return he is authorised to collect some charges as specified by government from the users of that civil work and once the cost is recovered by contractor, the site is transferred from contractor to department *i.e.,* department takes possession of that site. The security however is provided to the contractor by Government regarding law and order problems, if any.

Mostly Bridges and Roads are constructed and developed by this particular system of contract.

These are the various systems of getting a work constructed and executed. Each method has its speciality in itself and can be used effectively as per the prevailing conditions.

2.5.5 Labour Co-operative Society

In most of the states; labour co-operative societies have been formed; and generally it is a practice to award contract for an amount less than ₹ 1.00 lakh to these labour co-operative societies without calling the tenders and at the estimated rates based on divisional schedule of rates, brought upto date. While awarding the works; class of society is taken into consideration and these classes are formed based on capacity of that society to undertake the work. Based on their financial status. Managerial and technical capacity and staff; these labour co-operative societies in general are classified as.

Class A : Maximum eligibility upto ₹ 1,00,000.00

Class B : Maximum eligibility upto ₹ 50,000.00

Class C : Maximum eligibility upto ₹ 20,000.00

These labour co-operative societies are generally exempted from the production of solvency certificate for getting registered but are required to produce a certificate from the District Deputy Register/ District federation regarding its capacity and financial resources. Chairman of that labour co-operative society is generally consulted for dealing with. The number of works allotted to one society is generally restricted to three only.

2.5.6 Registration of Contractor

Each contractor is required to get himself registered to various departments where he is interested to work. In case of Government contract these contractors get themselves registered to Government and hence called as Government contractor; however one should not get confused by the meaning Government contractor. These contractors are not serving the Government as an employee but are entitled to do Government jobs, if awarded.

To get a contractor to be registered under certain class, he has to apply to the competent authority. He is further required to submit following documents along with the application:

1. Solvency certificate for an appropriate amount.
2. Attested copy of deed of partnership and power of attorny on stamp paper.
3. Current Income tax clearance certificate.
4. Works certificate for all works performed during last three year and for works in progress.
5. Undertaking (for class I and class II) for employment of the staff.
6. Application in duplicate with all documents.
7. Attested photo of all partners, if any.

Latest revision has been made in this regard and some new rules have been implemented. The Engineer contractors now a days have been permitted for registration for class VI *i.e.*, for works cost upto ₹ 5 lakhs without producing solvency certificate.

2.5.7 Prescribed Application Form for Registration as Contractor

1. Name of applicant with full postal address.
2. Detail of firm *i.e.*, whether partnership deed, Hindu undivided family, individual etc.
3. Name of person holding power of attorney.
4. Name of sole proprietors / partners with particulars.
5. Name of Bankers with full address.
6. Place of Business.
7. Class in which registration sought.
8. Whether contractor desires to deposit lump-sum money for securing exemptions from EMD or will pay EMD with each tender.

9. List of works executed during last three years (contractor is required to furnish all dteails like works, its location, cost, stage of construction etc.)

10. List of Tools and Plants possessed by him.

11. Technical qualification of contractor, his partner and employees working under him.

12. Has the applicant or his partner black listed by the govt. in the past.

13. Whether registered with other department, state, organization (if yes, give list).

14. Upto date income tax clearance certificate enclosed or not.

15. Amount of solvency certificate enclosed.

I/we certify that I/we have not been and will not get myself/ ourselves registered as contractor in the department under more than one name.

Date: Signature of applicants with address

Pre-qualification of Contractor: Sometimes jobs are awarded on the basis of the quotations received from *'selected tenderer'*, which means tenders are invited from a group of known reputed contractors who are considered suitable for that job. This method is known as *'Pre-qualification'* and saves a lot of time on the part of the employer, consultant and contractor. Sometimes, for special type of jobs, it is mentioned in the advertisement that specialist contractors having considerable experience alone apply. In order to judge the capability of contractor for that job employer asks contractor to furnish relavent date and it is obligatory on the part of the contractor to supply all such informations required to the employer and oblique. Sometimes department or consultants or owner have their own list of empanelled contractors. Those have already worked with them. The distribution of tender papers is then restricted to these contractors only. This, no doubt saves a considerable time but at the same time reprive other good contractors to tender the works, and show their capabilities. Sometimes for a very specialised job only one specialised firm is consulted and job is awarded by due negotiations. This is of course common in private works, however objectionable in government jobs. The possibility of malpractice can not be totally avoided in prequalification.

2.5.8 Conditions Of Contract

While preparing a contract agreement or agreement deed; certain conditions are laid down which are binding to the contractor as well as owner; it is mainly to avoid dispute during the progress of work, if any. These conditions of contract though remain same for all works in general, but then changes in certain cases from person to person and also depends on type of work and amount of work to be executed. The certain basic principles have to be strictly adhered to while preparing the contract agreement. Variation in these conditions are liable to be challenged by either of the parties. If there are minor variations, they are generally accepted by both but for major decisions; the matter is solved jointly. If there is a wide variation in the cost; The matter is referred to higher authorities for approval.

There are two types of conditions that are generally made in tender document:

(1) General conditions of contract.

(2) Special conditions of contract. (Particular).

The general conditions are those which do not affect the work. These are obligatory bindings on the contractor whilst special conditions are bared on type of work and the conditions very from work to work.

A few general condition of contract are as tested below:

(1) Work should be executed as per the drawings and specifications mentioned in agreement bond.

There should be no modification in design; drawing etc., from those given in notice inviting tender.

(2) Period allotted for that should not change. Only when it may become essential to change the period due to unavoidable reasons or natural calamities; it may be changed but only with due permission from higher authorities.

(3) It is obligatory that it is the responsibility of contractor to clear the site, to give medical aid to labour if required and to give free access to departmental engineers at site.

(4) Contractor is bound to pay minimum wages to the labour as per Workmens Compensation Act.

(5) There should be no flaw in agreement deed. It is usual practice in case of large works to get agreement scrutinised from law department so that legal aspect of the agreement are taken care of.

(6) Contractor can not assign or sublet the work to other contractor. Only for special type of works this can be done but only with due permission of engineer in charge.

(7) It is responsibility of engineer incharge to see that proper payments as per progress of works are made to contractor. He is also required to see that work progress is maintained by the contractor maintaining the quality as per specifications.

(8) Dismantling of works not approved by the engineer, if any and construction of new one, dismantling defective work in contractor's job. No extra payment is made for dismantling and reconstruction of dismantled work to the contractor.

(9) It is responsibility of contractor to provide potable water to the labours employed by him.

(10) The contractor is required to make his own arrangement for electric power at his own cost and no claim can be made in this behalf. The layout and method of laying lines and wiring and the nature of connected leads must be approved by engineer incharge.

(11) In case of errors, omissions and discrepancies; and doubts the matter should be referred to competent authorities and the decision of competent authorities shall be final and binding on the contractor.

(12) All the materials excavated is of the government or of owner and should be disposed of as directed by the competent authorities as Deputy Engineer or Executive Engineer as the case may be.

All these conditions are binding on the parties involved in agreement deed. Along with these some other special condition can be laid down which are binding on both the parties. These special conditions depend on type of work and amount and quality of work. A few examples of these special condition are:

(1) The concrete used is of grade M 30 and contractor is required to get a mix designed from an approved laboratory before concreting is made.

(2) Concrete should be compacted only by 60 mm diameter and 600 mm long needle vibrator giving 5000–6000 vibration per minute.

(3) Through stone of size as mentioned in drawings should only be used at a spacing shown in drawings.

2.5.9 Contract Documents

The contract documents in general consist of following items:

(1) Title page giving the detailed location of site; division/circle issuing tender, type of tender and type of work to be performed.

(2) Index-page giving content of contract documents.

(3) Tender notice.

(4) Special conditions of contract including schedule A and B.

Schedule A – is bill of quantities specifying the quantity of various items involved in that work and rates in case of B 1 tender.

Schedule B – is list of materials to be supplied by the department and their recovery rate.

(5) Detailed specification all items of works.

(6) Detailed Drawings.

(7) Deed of pledge.

This contract documents called agreement deed is always in written/typed on required stamp paper duly signed by the owner as well as contractor. Each page of this deed is to be signed by both the parties. Generally three to four copies of the agreements are prepared and distributed as below:

1. One copy along with attested copy to higher authority. Higher authorities sometimes the agreement and returns original copy to engineer in charge and retain one attested copy for record.

2. One copy is kept in locker and is taken out only in case of dispute if required by a court of law.

3. One copy is issued to accountant general.

4. One copy is given to the contractor duplicate copies of contract documents can be held, if required.

2.5.10 Performance of Contract

Performance of contract means to deposit a sum equal to security deposit with the department and to sign performance bond for a value mentioned in tender notice. It is on a form approved by engineer, architect viz. government bond. Government security. It remains in the custody of architector department till the defect liability period is over.

2.5.11 Breach of Contract

In every contract system; generally two parties are involved. These parties in civil engineering are contractor and owner when each acquires a right what is promised by other. If one of party fails to perform or fulfil his obligations, under the contract; it results into breach of contract which may lead to determination or termination of contract. It causes a loss to one party that gives an immediate cause of action and a right to damages as compensation for loss occurring from the breach.

As far as determination of contract by owner or employer; this can be done under following conditions:

(1) Default on behalf of contractor like

a: Contractor loses the job for any reason known to him only.

b: If contractor suspends the work and does not start again even after receiving notice.

c: Does not maintain the progress and quality inspite of several notices.

d: Does not dismantle and reconstruct the faulty work pointed out by department.

e: Sublets part of the work to other contractor without prior permission.

(2) Bankruptcy: If contractor becomes bankrupt, Under such condition; owner takes the work in possession like materials and machineries laying at site. The owner however is required to make payment of materials and equipment at site. No payment however is made to contractor in any form.

Sometimes there is breach of contract from owner also. It is fundamental right of contractor also to recover the damages that have caused him due to breach of contract, not because of his fault. He will have to be put in the same position; where he could have been if had completed the work as per contract deed. Contractor is therefore entitle to cover the loss of profit on full job. He is also entitled to get interest on his capital invested for period of determination of the profit amount depending upon whether the breach is their before starting of work or part work has been executed.

In case contractor commits breach of contract; the employer is also entitled completing or correcting the contractors balance work.

Finally; it is to be noted that aggrieved party will have to prove that he has suffered loss on account of wrong action of other party.

2.5.12 Qualification of Contractor

Qualifications of contractors has been laid down by different Works Departments according to the technical and financial capabilities of the contractor. Some departments categories them as class 1, 2, 3 and 4 contractors while others classify them as Class A, B, C and D contractor.

The general requirements of these contracts are given below:

Class A Contractor. Contractors who have executed important works in one or more works departments such as CPWD, MES, Railways and various State/Pradesh works departments come under this category. They are required to maintain qualified engineering staff and standing security deposit of Rupees one lac. There is no limit of the work for which they may quote. Examples of such contractors are:

1. Hindustan Construction Company Ltd.
2. German's Limited (Specialisation in RCC and Prestressed Concrete Structure)
3. M/s. Duggal & Co. Ltd.
4. M/s. Som Nath Builders Ltd.
5. M/s. Tirath Ram Ahuja Ltd.
6. National Building Construction Corporation.
7. Various State/Pradesh Construction Corporations for Buildings, Roads and Bridges.

Class B Contractor. The financial and technical capabilities of this type of contractor are similar to class A type. However various limits are tender. The standing security deposit is also less (say ₹ 50,000/-). If after being listed as class B contractor with any of the recognised works departments, the category may be upgraded to class A if the contractor has executed important works to the satisfaction of the department concerned. He has then to deposit additional security deposit. These contractors are required to have trained and qualified technical staff and financial soundness guarantee from the bankers.

Class C Contractor. This type of contractor does not have any standing security deposit with the works department. They are however given contract documents for comparatively smaller (Say costing upto ₹ 5 lacs). They may be upgraded to type B if their work over a period of time justifies their technical and financial capability. They have to deposit aditional security deposit.

Class D Contractor. These contractors are known as petty contractors. They are borne on the list of approved contractors and are allowed to tender for comparatively smaller works such as piece work contract for which no earnest money or security deposit is required and are given petty works (Say consting upto ₹ 50,000.00). This category of contractors are though local in nature form a very important class for the Zone or Division concerned. They are given contract on prevailing/sanctioned schedule of rates and the contract may be terminated any time if the standard of work and period of completion are not satisfactory. Examples of works for which such contractors are employed are:

1. Slip clearance in hilly regions (In most cases the contract agreement is executed when the work has been completed since delay in the execution may break the road communication system).
2. Improving bends and corners in hilly regions.
3. Repairing patries.
4. Petty silt clearance.
5. Transport of materials from railway siding to departmental store or to siding.

In a number of cases Class A contractors have started with the category of contractors.

2.5.13 Contract Documents

Contract documents normally contains the following documents:

1. Brief description of Work/Project.
2. Estimated cost of the project.
3. Security deposit and earnest money required (The earnest money is required to be deposited along with the tender, 1.5 to 2.5% of the estimated cost of the project/work).

Security deposit is made up from running payments (Normally 10% of the estimated cost of the project/work).

4. **Tender form.** This depends upon the type of the contract. For example, in the case of item rate contract all the items of work along with approximate quantities are given and the contractor is required to fill in his rates for all the items, and at the end endorsed total cost as per the quoted rates.

In case of lumpsum contract the total cost of completing the work as per drawing and specifications is quoted by the contractor.

In case of percentage tender, only percentage above or below the SSR rates is quoted. The period of completion on the basis of which the tender is to quote his rates is also specified.

In case certain stores such as cement, steel, bricks etc., are to be provided by the department, the issue rates and the place of delivery are specified.

Hire charges of plant and machinery provided departmentally are also specified.

5. **General conditions of contract.** This is the main contract document which binds the contractor to deliver and carryout work as per specifications, to get it approved at various stages, to rectify or demolish defective work, to bear penalty for not showing progress as per Time and Progress schedule agreed between the department and the contractor (The penalty is 1% of the amount of delayed work per week to a maximum of 10% of the total cost of contract, to provide site accommodation for labour, to provide canteen and recreational facilities for the labour along with sanitary facilities, to display strength of workers (Skilled and Unskilled) as well as the rates of payment. These rates of payment shall not be less than the minimum wages fixed by the competent authority as per minimum wages act.

6. Brief specifications of the items of work involved.
(General as well as special)

7. All connected drawings consisting of:
   1. Site plan (layout plan)
   2. Plan, sections and elevations of all connected-structures.

2.5.14 Earnest Money

Every contractor while submitting documents has to deposit 1.5 to 2.5 percent of the estimated value of the works as earnest money. This is required to restrict submission of tender by contractors to ensure that they do not withdraw from the contracting case of allotment of work on the basis of lowest quotation or for other reasons which need not to be explained by the department. In case the contractor fails to start work allotted to him after work order has been given, not only his earnest money is forfeited but the contractor is liable to be blacklisted.

2.5.15 Security Deposit

Normally about 10% of the estimated cost of the contract or cost as per tender is retained as security deposit. It serves the following purposes:

1. Sometimes the advance payment made to the contractor on account of work done or material supplied at the worksite exceeds the value of the work done or material supplied. To ensure that such overpayments are recoverable from the contractor. For other running payments also 10 per cent deductions are made till the amount of security deposit sums up to 10 per cent of the tendered cost of the work/project.

2. Getting the part of work done through debitable agency in case the progress of the contractor is slow or some item of the work is found defective and order of the department for demolition is not carried out by the contractor. In such part of the work is executed departmentally or through another agencies. The agency which executes the work is paid as per rates with the agency and the excess payment is divided to the payments due to the contractor. In case the extra payment is not recoverable from the payments due to the contractor the excess amount is adjusted again security deposit.

3. **To cover period of maintenance.** As per conditions of contract the contractor is required to rectify the defects noticed during warranty period which is generally one year from the date of completion of the work or project. In case the contractor fails to rectify such defects, the work is carried out departmentally by engaging debitable agency and the cost of such rectification is adjusted against security deposit.

2.6 MATERIAL HANDING

2.6.1 Transportation of Material

Very often the cost of transportation of materials exceeds the cost of procurement at site. This is particularly so in the case of natural resources such as coarse and fine aggregates, timber etc. In the case of manufactured articles such as cement, steel etc., the cost of transportation is comparatively less as the material reaches the nearest rail head directly from the factories. However the distance from the train head affects the cost at site.

It has been established that the time taken in loading and unloading the vehicle used for transportation far exceeds the time taken for actual transportation particularly if the distance is not very long. In the case of large projects this problem is solved partly by using loaders and lifters at the loading site and tippers for transportation and unloading. The problem of transportation in some cases is overcome by the use of belt conveyors which pick up the material at the quarry and deliver the same at the destination.

2.6.2 Breach of Contract and Handling of Material

In the case of large projects, it is convenient, if not economical to have separate organization for transporting materials. This, however, requires separate setup for vehicles against Capital outlay. The project is debited usage rates on the basis of the period during which the vehicle remains in the project. If however, the off road period exceeds a fortnight, the cost of the monthly usage rate is not debited to the project for the duration for which it remained idle.

Sometimes in the case of smaller projects it is convenient as well as economical to employ contract agency for loading, unloading and transporting the materials from say rail yard to the work site for carriage of materials brought to the nearest rail head by railway wagons and arranging contract agency for taking delivery of the materials from the railway siding and transporting it to the worksite. The contract is treated as contract for supply of stores and the conditions of the contract usually specify 1% of the estimated payment for normal delivery of materials as penalty for delay. However such penalty is restricted to 10%.

2.6.3 Handling of Materials

Materials brought to worksite or required for project work has to be handled properly so that:

1. From the moment it is delivered at the work site to its incorporation in the work, it is not misappropriated or stolen.

2. If the material is of explosive nature it has to be stored in specially constructed magazines and is to be handled according to the safety instructions issued by the manufactures/Excise department of the State or Central government.

3. The inspected material is stacked in such a way that the quantity of material delivered may be readily verified. For example, if the contracting agency delivers stone metal for road construction the same shall be stacked along the sides and the section of the stacked material is checked with the help of special templates. A typical template for road side stacks is illustrated in Fig. 2.6.1.

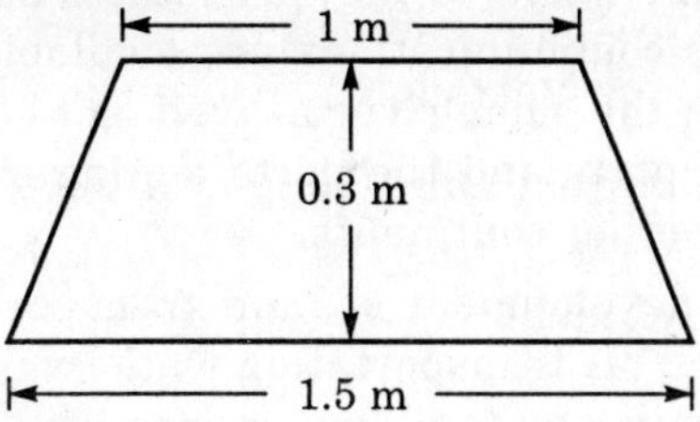

Fig. 2.6.1 Standard template for stacking stone metal on the road side.

In the case of railway ballast, the material is transported by railway wagons and depth of the metal in the wagon itself gives indication of the quantity delivered at site. For this reason the contract for supply of such material incorporates the condition of supply (For quarry site or FOR railway siding). In the case of fine material such as sand for concreting work in the roads, pits of standard size are kept ready before the material is brought to site.

Types of Materials

The various types of construction materials are:

1. Road metal (Boulders, natural aggregates)
2. Tar and bitumen products
3. Timber and its products including plywood
4. Coal
5. Bricks
6. Cement
7. Steel (Brass, rods, sheets, plates and girders)
8. AC sheets
9. Paints and varnishes
10. Explosives.

2.6.4 Hauling Equipment

1. Road transport
2. Rail transport
3. Belt conveyors
4. Cable ways
5. Fork lift.

6. **Waterways.** Waterways, where transportation facilities available are the most economical made of transportation. It is for this reason that almost all important cities the world over are located along the sea shore from where communications from sea are

available all over the world, or they are located on the banks of the rivers from where communications are available to other towns along the banks of the same river as well as to overseas through rivers joining the ports and the ports joining other ports in the same continent or other continents.

In spite of development of land transportation (Rail-road transportation) and air transportation water ways transportation has not lost its significance and importance. The only difference is that whereas in the past both passengers as well cargo transportation from one country to another was exclusively along the sea (waterways) bulk of cargo transportation only is now done with the help of steamers and most of passenger transportation is done by airways. Except very light articles and personal luggage of the passengers, all the heavier goods are transported by sea. With the increase in sea borne traffic container service on streamer transporters is becoming more popular. The reasons for increase in container transportation services are:

1. Comparatively pilferage free service. Whereas smaller articles and packed cases can be misplaced or pilferred there is no such likelihood in the case of transportation through containers. For this reason even the railways have started container service in which containers are transported through goods wagons and delivered at the doors of the customer through railway container service.

2. Easier and efficient handling (loading and unloading). Instead of handling individual packages container loads are crane lifted and unloaded in the ships.

In some cases waterways provide cheap transportation on the one hand and improve quality of the material transported. For example, logs felled on hilly regions are allowed to be carried down along the hill slope and collected on the river bank where they are converted into sleepers. These sleepers are transported down the yards and godowns upto the railhead and transported to the place where they are required either by rail, road or waterways. It takes a few weeks or even months for the timber sleepers to cover distance of hundreds of kilometers from the place of origin to the railhead destination. During the period of transportation the sap wood from the timber is removed and the moisture content is reduced to the optimum contents of the reason.

2.6.5 Selecting Type of Transportation

Selection of the type of transportation depends upon the following factors:

1. Mode of transportation available.

2. Comparative cost of handling the goods (loading, unloading and safe transit) and ultimate cost of transportation at the delivery end.

3. Period taken in transit.

4. Stages involved in the process of transportation from the place of supply to the worksite or delivery end.

5. Security arrangements and watch and ward required during transit and comparative cost.

The above aspects are briefly described below:

1. **Mode of transportation available.** Selection of mode of transport arises when more than one mode of transport is available and it is left to the individual to make use of one which would be most economical not only from the point of view of total expenses per unit of the goods transported but also speed, safety and sound delivery (without involving any breakages in transit and involving least breakage). For example, if timber sleeper is to be transported from remote areas in the hills (inaccessible to railroad transportation) the only available mode of transportation of goods is to employ local labour or load pack animals. In such cases it is normal practice to employ local labour or pack animals through incharge or mate.

For safety purposes it is sometimes better to get such labour or animals through local contractors. The local contractor will charge his own profit in the bargain but it is advisable to engage him since he knows the people who would be delivering the goods and would be personally responsible for safe delivery and loss of goods during transit would be recoverable from the contractor.

Sometimes there is only one mode of transportation such as transportation of timber through river to the final destination at the rail head.

To ensure safety of the sleepers along the free transit from the place of origin to the railhead, the contractor employs his own labour which follows the course of the floating sleepers. In the process sometimes sleepers belongings to one agency get mixed up with those of the other agency. This type of confusion is avoided by having special markings on the sleepers.

The party which is deputed by the contractor to provide watch and ward enroute follows the path of sleepers enroute. The task of the party is:

(*a*) To check the total number of sleepers floated from the point of origin.

(*b*) To check enroute and clear such sleepers which get stuck to the banks during the transit.

(*c*) To check at the destination the number of sleepers collected at the end.

2. Comparative cost of handling the goods and ultimate cost of transportation at the delivery end. The comparative cost of transportation has great influence on the mode of transportation selected where more than one mode is available. For example, from the railhead at which timber sleepers have been collected, it is upto the individual to transport the material through rail road or through navigation channels.

3. Period taken in transit. In some cases the period taken transit does not affect the selection of the mode while in other case the ultimate cost of transportation takes a back seat if the delivery is quick.

For example, if the sleepers are transported along the river the time taken in transit may be much longer as compared to their transportation by rail or road. If the sleepers are to be stacked in the godown where they may remain for a period of one or two years to get air-seasoned, it would be advantageous to get the sleepers transported by waterway. If however, the sleepers are required for use in a building complex, the sleepers would require kiln seasoning and early use. The extra cost of transportation from the place of supply would be justified.

4. Stages involved in the process of transportation from the place of supply to the worksite or delivery end. From practical considerations even if the cost of transportation may be greater, for certain type of articles, transportation in containers through railway roadway or steamer would be considered as the best mode of transportation. The container service is not only limited to railway containers which collect the goods at the doors of the customer and deliver at the delivery end.

5. Security arrangements. This factor over-rides all other considerations and is self explanatory.

2.6.6 Fixed and Recurring Cost of Material Handling

The various agencies involved in material handling (excluding the cost of transportation) are:

(*i*) Loading/unloading using manual labour.

(*ii*) Mechanical loading/unloading (using loaders for loading and tippers for unloading).

(*iii*) **Cableways.** The above modes of handling are briefly described below:

1. Loading/unloading using manual labour. In case local labour is available no fixed cost is involved since the mate-in charge or the labour itself makes own arrangements. However if the labour has to be brought from outside, they have to be provided temporary accommodation, sanitary arrangements, medical, canteen and recreation facilities. The recurring cost consists in payment of wages.

2. Mechanical loading/unloading. The fixed cost is the procurement cost directly divided to the project or the usage rates of payment if the initial procurement is against capital outlay. The recurring cost is the cost of POL and wages of the operator and attendant and proportion of establishment/administration charges.

3. Cableways. The fixed cost is the cost of installation while the recurring cost is the cost of operation.

2.7 INDUSTRIAL RELATIONS

2.7.1 Psychological Attitude to Work and Working Conditions

It is very necessary that the workers on the one hand gets job satisfaction and is happy with his output on the other hand he should feel assured that he would be given leave and transit facilities to visit members of his family. This is particularly applicable to workers employed in far off areas such as ONGC personnel working in remote areas in the Eastern sector or personnel employed in the Border Roads Organization or civilians in the Military Engineering Service. To achieve these measures the following measures are taken:

Suitable initial training of the recruits. During the period of training on the one hand the worker gets confidence in his capability to undertake the work he is expected to perform and on the other hand the employer is able to judge the capability of the worker so that if necessary he may be discharged. The feeling of satisfaction of his ability to perform the work he is expected to undertake and getting acquainted with the living conditions under which one would be required to work in places under hazardous conditions such as snow bound areas, hilly regions, desert regions etc. Such a training improves psychologically the attitude of the worker towards his work and installs confidence to the worker to face the working conditions of the work site.

2.7.2 Fatigue

Experimentally it has been established that reversal of stresses in any metal reduces the ultimate stress bearing of the material and it breaks at a lower stress than it would if it were subjected to unidirectional stress or stress of the same type either tensile or compressive. In the case of metals it is experimentally determined by subjecting the metal specimen to reversal of stresses *i.e.,* compressive stress followed by tensile stress alternately. The failure stress of a piece of metallic specimen subjected to alternating stresses may be as low as 75% of the stress at which the same metallic piece subjected to unidirectional stress would fail. This again depends upon the number of reversal of stresses undergone by the specimen.

In the case of manual labour the effect of fatigue may be determined from the per hour of per day of say 8 hours work/output of the worker. If the working conditions of the worker are frequently changed from working in higher altitudes and snow bound areas to plains or desert areas, the performance in both these areas would be less/reduced as compared to the output he would if he were to work under only one condition. The output under the above two conditions (High altitude and snow bound areas and plains or desert areas) would in any case would be less if the worker is subjected to changing conditions frequently.

2.7.3 Communications in Industry

For satisfactory working of any industry it is necessary that the Apex body is kept informed about the daily progress, successes, failures or bottlenecks at every stage. Wireless and telephonic communications are provided for the purpose.

The Apex body communicated with the Directors and General Managers while the Directors and General Managers are in communication with the executives and the field staff. The office establishment is invariably linked with the head of the organization as well as with each other by intercom communication.

2.7.4 Cause And Effect of Industrial Dispute

Industrial disputes arise primarily due to dissatisfaction of the workers in respect of pay and allowances and other facilities which they feel is their right and denial to them by the management gives rise to industrial disputes.

Some of the common grievances of the workers which give rise to industrial disputes are:

(*a*) Interference with, restraint or coersing or workmen in the exercise of their rights to organise, follow, join or assist a trade union.

(*b*) Interference with the formation or administration or any trade union or to contribute any financial or other support to it.

(*c*) To discharge or otherwise discriminate against any officer of a recognised trade union because of his being such an officer.

(*d*) To discharge or otherwise discriminate against any workman because he has made allegations or given evidence in an enquiry or proceedings relating to any matter.

Industrial disputes between the workers and the management gives rise to decrease in the output which results in reduction in the profit of the industry/factory or organization. Non-settlement of the dispute ultimately results in resorting to strike by the workmen. On the one hand the management suffers great loss because of the loss of earning capacity due to non-production while on the other hand the workers and their families undergo hardships due to non-payment of their wages during the period of strike.

2.7.5 Method of Settlement of Disputes

Article 9.4 gives the reasons which lead to disputes between the workers and the management. Normally the settlement has to be done between the trade union leaders and the employer. A rigid attitude of the employer only results in further complicating the matter. In all important organizations where number of workers exceeds 100, Government appoints a Welfare officer to see that the workers are not victimised and are provided all amenities and other facilities required under the various industrial laws in the various acts passed by it.

This officer is the most important link between employer, workers and the government and is normally responsible for getting the dispute sorted out.

The industrial disputes Act 1947 [Amended in 1956 and Industrial Disputes (Central) rules 1957] is applicable to both the employer and the workers. The welfare officer attached to the organization holds meetings with the trade union-leaders as well as the workers and in these exercises some of the demands of the workers and the union which are considered unreasonable are partly removed and partly amended. The remaining demands are discussed firstly with the welfare officer and the employer followed by a joint meeting between the employer, welfare officer, trade union leaders and the workers.

In the opinion of the welfare officer, if the attitude of the employer is not co-operative in settling reasonable demands of the workers within the framework of the Acts passed by the Government from time to time the labour Ministry ensures that reasonable demands of the workers are accepted by the employer.

The employer has to provide facilities to the industrial workers under the following Acts passed by the Government as amended from time to time:

(*i*) Factories Act 1947
(*ii*) Workmen Compensation Act 1923
(*iii*) Employees State Insurance Act 1948
(*iv*) Employees Standing Orders Act 1948
(*v*) Payment of Minimum Wages Act 1948

Other Acts passed by the Government from time to time to protect legitimate dues to the workers and to prevent his exploitation are:

(*i*) Industrial disputes Act, 1947
(*ii*) Payment of Wages Act, 1956
(*iii*) Employees provident Fund Act, 1952
(*iv*) Maternity Benefit Act, 1961
(*v*) Contract Labour Act, 1961
(*vi*) Equal Remuneration Act, 1976
(*viii*) Bonded Labour Act, 1976

In addition to welfare officer, Inspector of Factories under Ministry of Labour have been appointed by the Government to inspect working conditions of the factory/industry. They are provided full facilities to go round and inspect machines and other aspects of the factory.

In the case of civilian employees in defence installations two institutions for prevention and settlement of industrial disputes are:

(*i*) Works committees consisting or representative of employers and workers.

(*ii*) Negotiating machinery set up at various levels.

The object of the Act is to regulate the settlement of industrial disputes.

2.7.5.1 Definitions

(*a*) **Industrial dispute.** It means any dispute or difference between employees and employer or between workmen and workmen which is connected with employment or non-employment or the terms of employment or with the condition of labour or any person.

(*b*) **Strike.** It means a cessation of work by a body of persons employed in any industry acting in combination or a concerted refusal under a common understanding of any number of persons who are or have been so employed.

(*c*) **Illegal Strike.** It means a strike by virtue of which any lay for the time being in force is illegal.

(*d*) **Irregular Strike.** It means a irregular strike or a strike declared by Trade Union in contravention of its rules referred clause (*d*) para 7, *i.e.*, rules provided for the procedure for declaring a strike.

(*e*) **Workmen.** It means any person (Including and apprentice) employed in any industry to do any skilled or unskilled, manual supervisory or other work who does not exercise functions mainly of managerial or administrative nature.

2.7.5.2 Works Committees

In the case of any industrial establishment in which one hundred or more persons are employed on any day preceding 12 months, a Works Committee consisting of representatives of employers and workmen employed in the establishment shall be constituted.

Duties or Works Committee. It shall be the duty of the Works Committee to promote measures for security and preserving amity and good relations between employers and workmen and to that end to comment upon matters of common interest or concern and endeavour to compose any material difference of opinion in respect of such matters.

2.7.5.3 Members

The number of members constituting the committee shall be fixed so as to afford representation to the various categories groups and classes of workmen engaged in the establishment.

Provided that the total number do not exceed twenty and also the number of representatives of workmen is not less than the number of representatives of employer.

Representatives of employer. The representatives of employer shall be nominated by the employer and shall be in touch towards the working of the establishment.

2.7.5.4 Consultation with Trade Unions

Where any workers of the establishment are members of the registered union, the election will be made in consultation with the trade union.

2.7.5.5 Negotiating Machinery

Members of Defence have set up permanent negotiating machinery for settlement of disputes between civilians employed in Defence Installations and the Government.

Subjects for discussion:

(*a*) *Lower level.* All local matters regarding welfare and allied questions.

(*b*) Cases of individual employees.

(*c*) Matters of general nature

Middle level:

(*a*) Matters where no settlement could be reached.

(*b*) Consideration of general grievances.

(*c*) Piece work rates, wage structure, conditions of service security of service etc.

Top-Level:

(*a*) Matters on which no settlement could be reached. In case of points which can not be resolved by negotiating machinery, the matter may be referred to an Adhoc tribunal.

2.7.6 Collective Bargaining

Collective bargaining is normally carried out by the workmen through their unions. The activities of the union are covered under the Trade Union Act (1967) amended in 1956 Industrial Act (amendment 1947).

Note. The above Acts extend to whole of India except the states of Jammu & Kashmir. It came into force in 1927. The object of the Act is to regulate conduct of trade unions.

Definition:

(*a*) **Employer.** The prescribed authority under any central or state department of the Head of the Department.

(*b*) **Trade Union.** It means any combination temporary or permanent formed for the purpose of regulating between the workers and the employer.

(*c*) **Recognised Trade Union.** It means the body (Trade Union) recognised under the law.

(*d*) **Executive.** It means the body to which the affairs of the Trade Union are entrusted.

(*e*) **Officer.** In the case of Trade Union includes any member of the Executive thereof, but does not include an auditor.

2.7.6.1 Registration of Trade Union

A Trade Union making the necessary application to the Registrar of trade union, will on compliance of specified condition designated to ensure that the Union is a bonafide Trade Union, be entitled for registration. The registrar on being satisfied that all the requirements of the Act, registers the union and issues a certificate of registration.

Recognition by Employers

On an application being made by the Registrar of Trade Unions the employer agrees to recognise it and a memorandum of understanding is signed by the employer and the trade union for recognition of the trade union.

For recognition of the trade union the following conditions are required to be fulfilled:

(*a*) All the ordinary members are employed workers of the industry/organization.

(*b*) It is the representative of all the workers employed in the organization.

(*c*) No member is excluded from the membership.

(*d*) Its rules provide fordeclaring a strike.

(*e*) That it is a registered trade union.

2.7.6.2 Rights of Recognised Trade Union

The executive of a recognised trade union shall be entitled to negotiate with the employer in respect of matters connected with the employment or condition of the labour of all or any of its members, and the employer shall receive and send reply to letters sent by the executive, and grant interviews to that body regarding such matters. The executive of the recognised trade union shall be entitled to display notices of the trade union in any premises where its members are employed and the employers shall afford the executive reasonable facilities for this purpose.

2.7.6.3 Withdrawal of Recognition

Recognition of trade union may be withdrawn on any of the following grounds:

(*a*) That the trade union has ceased to be representative of the workers.

(*b*) That the majority of the members take part in an irregular strike.

(*c*) That the executive of the trade union advises or actively supports or investigates an irregular strike.

(*d*) That the trade union has failed to submit any return required to be submitted to the Registrar of the trade union.

2.7.7 Conciliation

In the case of civilian employees in Defence employment installations the Works Committee described in Article 2.7.5.2 tries to reconcile the grievances of the workers with the competent authority.

In other cases the Welfare Officer serves a link between the state or Central Government, the employers and the employees tries their reconciliation.

2.7.8 Arbitration, Adjurisdiction

2.7.8.1 Arbitration

Arbitration means settlement of dispute between two parties involved; generally contractor and owner. This settlement is generally done not by court of law but by a few persons having complete knowledge of that work and deputed by parties involved. These person or persons appointed to settle the dispute are called '*Arbitrator*' and process of setting dispute is called '*Arbitration*'. Arbitrator gives decision on the basis of evidences available; inquiries made and his own skill and knowledge. His decision is generally accepted by both the parties and also incorporated into the decree of the court if required *i.e.,* if earlier decision is not accepted by either of the parties and if matter is referred to court of law. Arbitrator has to take such decision which must be correct and acceptable by both the parties.

The essential requirement for a person to work as an arbitrator is that:

(1) He is in a quasi judicial position, therefore, the first essential requisite in persons occupying that post is judicial impartiality and freedom from partiality and freedom from bias.

(2) He should be honest; impartial and disinterested in any of the parties involved.

(3) He must be qualified person having thorough knowledge of that subject matter under dispute.

(4) He must be a person of high integrity and unshakable faith in justice.

Arbitration Act: It is an act to consolidate and amend the law relating to Arbitration. This act called as Arbitration Act 1940 extends to whole India except Jammu & Kashmir. According to this act amended upto date; an arbitrator has following five powers:

(1) To administer Oath to the parties and witnesses appearing.

(2) To state a special case for the opinion of the court or any question of law involved, or state the award wholly or in part, in the form of a special case of such question for the opinion of the court.

(3) To make the award conditional or in the alternative.

(4) To correct in an award any clerical mistake or error arising from the accidental slip or omission.

(5) To administer to any party to the arbitration interrogatories as may be in the opinion of the arbitrator, if necessary.

According to Arbitration Act, 1940; various kinds of arbitrator are:

(1) Arbitration with no intervention of court of law.

(2) Arbitration with intervention of court of law but with no suit under pending.

(3) Arbitration in suits.

According the Arbitration Act. 1940, Clause 25; the procedure adopted for settlement of dispute in civil engineering contract consist of followings steps:

(1) Appointment of arbitrator by higher competent authority within 30 days after receiving complete detailed grivences and claim from contractor. Contractor is required to '*Submit his statement of facts*' within 90 days *i.e.,* period of limitation.

(2) Preparation and submission of case for Arbitration. All documents are required to be submitted to Arbitrator. These documents consist of agreement deed; drawings; specifications; conditions of contract and the grievances and claims in the form of 'statement of facts' and the bills; vouchers corresponding to dispute.

(3) Hearing of the case by arbitrator as per provisions in the Act. Both parties are permitted to plead their case with due arguments by other. Arbitrator requires to hear both the sides pleading and then to scrutinise and examine all documents. The direction for this hearing should be completed within four months.

(4) Issue of Award: Arbitrator later on; going through all details give the decision. The award should be obtained by parties on non-judicial stamp paper. Once the award is issued by Arbitrator his duty and authority ceases. He can not make any second award.

(5) Finally is the filling of award *i.e.,* if the decision is acceptable by both the parties; the award is written on stamp-paper and then duly signed by Arbitrator; both the parties involved and witnesses. This if required can be filed in court of law to its validity.

If the decision in not acceptable by either party; then the party has right to file a suit in court of law for further necessary action and then matter is resolved in court of law only by the regular judicially procedure.

As such Arbitration is an expensive way of settling the dispute between owner and contractor. As far as possible matter is solved at very first or second level only. In extreme cases matter is referred to court. The Judiciary procedure and law takes very long time hence people to avoid it.

2.7.8.2 Adjudication

When other methods of reconciliation of disputes fail to resolve the differences, a third party, acceptable to both the employers and the employee, who is a person of judicial background, say a retired judge of a High Court or Supreme Court, is requested to settle the dispute. Such a reconciliation of the dispute is termed as Adjudication.

2.7.9 Code of Discipline and Grievances

2.7.9.1 Procedure

Code of discipline has been the basic and main purpose of directing grievances of the workers through the manner prescribed by the Registrar of societies. The procedure prescribed by Government for settlement of grievances of workers is

(*i*) In case the workers have a Trade Union registered with the Registrar of grievances have to be discussed firstly in a general meeting followed by discussions between the executives.

(*ii*) The grievances are discussed with the Welfare Officer appointed by the Government to ensure that legimate grievances are removed by the employees.

(*iii*) The Welfare officer may take up to matter of settlement of grievances with the State or Central Government directly or through Inspector of factories.

(*iv*) The Union may also directly take up the matter with the Registrar of Societies.

2.7.9.2 Recognition of Union: See Article 9.6.1

2.7.9.3 Unfair Labour Practice

The following practices which are considered unfair should be avoided by the employers:

(*a*) To interfare with, restraint or coerse his workmen in the exercise of their right to organise form or join or assist a Trade Union.

(*b*) To interfare with the formation or administration of a Trade Union or to contribute any financial support to it.

(*c*) To discharge or otherwise to discriminate against any officer of a Trade Union because of his being such an officer.

(*d*) To discharge or discriminate against in any worker because he has made allegations or given evidence in any enquiry relating to any matter.

Note. The refusal of any employer to permit his workmen to engage in Trade Union Activities during the hours of work shall not be deemed to be an unfair practice.

2.7.9.4 Trade Union Rivalries

There are well over 3000 trade unions in India. A number of these unions have political background and it very often happens that the workers having attachment to one of the political parties would like to form their own unions and try to get 50% of the workers of the factory industry to become members of the proposed union. The political parties also try to persuade the active members to form a union by becoming members of the proposed union. The political parties also try to persuade the active members to form a union in which they have their influence. This leads to trade union rivalries.

Some of the Important All India Trade Unions are:

1. All India Trade Union Congress. (Under Communist Party of India) AITUC.
2. Indian National Trade Union Congress (Under Congress Party of India) INTUC.
3. Hind Mazdoor Sabha (Set up by PSP) HMS.
4. United Trade Union Congress (Leftist Oriented) UTUC.
5. Bhartiya Mazdoor Sangh (BMS).

2.7.10 Minimum Wages Act

(Refer Article 5.5).

2.7.11 Wages and Productivity

(Refer Article 5.1).

2.7.12 Workers Participation in Management

So long as the worker is engaged in any industry as a link for producing goods and manufactured articles for the employer, he is not bothered about putting in his best to increase productivity. However if he knows that the profit gained by the industry would be passed on to him as a shareholder of the industry, his attitude towards work undergoes great change. Hence need for workers participation in the industry including its management. Even today some of the modern progressive industries have reserved some percentage of shares thrown to general public for the workers in the industry.

The Government of the country is committed to workers participation in the industry including by providing reservation of shares in public and private sectors for the workers. There is already a section of parliamentarians who are thinking to handover complete management of some of the industries (Particularly those who are not showing porfit) to the workers in the hope that the top heavy administration would be eliminated and not only workers would give betters performance but the nation would benefit from this. At the first instance a few would be tried on an experimental basis.

2.7.13 Labour Welfare and Security

2.7.13.1 Labour Welfare

See Article 5.3.

2.7.13.2 Security

Security to the workers is provided under the following:

(*i*) Recognition of the Trade Union.

(*ii*) Payment of Wages Act (Refer Article 5.4)

(*iii*) Minimum Wages Act (See Article 9.10)

(*iv*) Workmen Compensation Act (Refer Article 5.6)

(*v*) Contract Labour Act (Refer Article 5.7)

2.7.14 Regulation of Working Condition and Hours of Work

2.7.14.1 Regulation of Working Condition

See Article 2.7.1.

2.7.14.2 Hours of Work

Working hours are as under:

Timings are fixed by the employer.

(*a*) Adults : Weekly 48 hours.
Daily 9 hours.

(*b*) Children : Daily 4½ hours.

Note:

(1) No period of work shall exceed 5 hours and no worker shall work for more than 5 hours before he has had interval for rest.

(2) No woman is employed except between hours of 6 AM and 7 PM.

(3) No child is employed,

(*i*) For more than 4½ hours on any day.

(*ii*) Between the hours of 7 PM and 6 AM.

Weekly Holidays. No worker shall be required or allowed to work in a factory on the first day of the week unless he has or will have a holiday for the whole day on one of the three days immediately before or after the said day.

Employment of Young persons. No child who has not completed his 14th year shall be required or allowed to work in a factory.

Over time. Where a worker in a factory works for more than 9 hours in a day or for more than 48 hours in a week, he shall in respect of overtime work entitled to wages at the rate of twice his ordinary rate of payment.

Prior permission of the Chief Inspector of factories of the area concerned is obtained by telegram to work over time in emergency.

2.7.15 Industrial Safety and Welfare Provision

2.7.15.1 Industrial Safety

Factories Act 1948 caters for industrial safety of the worker. Main features of the Act are:

1. Before starting any industry written permission of the Government is required along with relevant particulars of the industry. At least 15 days notice is required.

2. Industrial safety. Complete security arrangements shall be made. Children shall not be employed in big or dangerous machines.

2.7.15.2 Welfare Provision

The following welfare provisions shall be provided:

1. The provision of light, fresh air, and cleanliness shall be made and suitable space shall be provided to workers.

2. Weekly hours of work shall be restricted to 48 hours.

3. Leave, weekly holidays and other obligatory holidays shall be provided.

4. Half hour interval between working hours shall be provided.

5. Half hour difference between day and night shifts shall be provided.

6. Children below 14 years of age shall not be employed.

7. Any worker who has put in 240 days of work is entitled to annual leave.

8. **Other facilities.** Canteen, recreation, toilet and First Aid shall be provided. In case of female worker creshes shall be provided.

2.7.16 Role of State in Welfare Provisions

Welfare of workers is the primary responsibility of the Government. The factory or industry produces goods and manufactured articles which are required by the country for domestic use as well as for export purposes. Only a satisfied and properly looked after group of workers can give maximum output.

The various welfare measures adopted by the state have been given in article.

Some of the important ones are:

1. Factories Act 1948 (See Article 9.11)
2. Trade Union Act (Refer Article 5.2)
3. Payment of Wages Act (See Articles 5.4)
4. Minimum Wages Act (See Article 5.5)
5. Workmen Compensation Act (See Article 5.6)
6. Contract Labour Act (See Article 5.7)

2.7.17 Role of Labour Welfare Office

(See Article 5.3).

2.7.18 Social Security, Principles and Practice

(Refer Article 9.15).

2.7.19. Social Problem of Industrial Relations

The various agencies which are watch dogs for the purpose of implementing social security and industrial relations provided by the state under the various acts passed by the state as detailed in Article 9.5 are:

1. The Trade Union
2. Labour welfare officer
3. Inspector of factories
4. Registar of societies

2.7.20 Cost of living and other economical indices in relation of wages, contract labour, and safety requirements

2.7.20.1 Economic Indices in Relation to Wages

Under the Minimum Wages Act, the District Magistrate has the overall responsibility to see that the minimum wages for various categories of labour and revised from time to time (normally every six months) taking into consideration the changes in the level of various commodities. The factory/industry management is bound to pay the workers as specified from time to time under the "*Minimum wages Act*".

The employer is required to display the rates of payment to the employees as well as the date of payment. The visiting/inspecting officers, the Trade Union members and the workers cross check the payment made to them.

3

CONSTRUCTIONAL PRACTICES

3.1 PLANNING MANAGEMENT

Construction planning aspects aim to identify and develop various stages of project execution on site which should be consistent with the management considerations. Planning aspects evolve out of the objectives of project and requirements of the final completed constructed facility. These objectives could relate to the final constraints, cost considerations, quality standards, safety standards, environmental considerations and health considerations. Construction practices would, then have to satisfy these objectives during construction phase of the project.

Having established objectives of the construction phase, planning determines processes, resources (including materials, equipments, human and environmental) and monitoring system to ensure that the practices are appropriately aligned. Adequate knowledge about pre-construction phase evolution of project, especially related to customer's requirements, is as essential prerequisite for construction planning.

3.1.1 Preconstruction Phase

Besides the design aspects, preconstruction phase should also address all the issues related to the implementation of the design at the site through suitable construction strategy. During the design stage, the site conditions should be fully understood with anticipated difficulties and avoid the risk of subsequent delays and changes after the construction has started. The selection of construction methods, building systems and materials, components, manpower and equipments and techniques are best done in the preconstruction phase. Such selection is influenced by the local conditions like terrain, climate, vulnerability for disasters, etc.

Construction in busy localities of cities needs special considerations and meticulous planning due to restricted space, adjoining structures, underground utilities, traffic restrictions, noise and other environmental pollution and other specific site constraints. The constructability aspects of the proposed construction methods needs to be carefully evaluated at the planning stage to ensure ease of construction besides optimizing the construction schedule and achieving quality, reliability and maintainability of the constructed facilities. Constructional practices in hilly regions needs to take into considerations the problem of landslides, slope stability, drainage, etc., besides ensuring no adverse impact on the fragile environmental conditions.

Durability of constructions in corrosive atmospheric conditions like coastal regions and aggressive ground situations with high chlorides and sulphates should also be taken care of with appropriate constructional practices. Constructional practices in disaster prone areas need specific planning. The type of construction, use of materials, construction techniques require special considerations in such areas. Adverse weather conditions have strong bearing on construction phase. Situations wherein constructions are to be carried out in adverse weather conditions, such as heavy and continuous rainfall, extreme hot or cold weather, dust storms, etc., the practices have to address the relevant aspects. Accordingly, suitable design and field operations should be adapted or redefined in anticipation of these aspects. Some of these aspects are:

(*a*) Site layout which enables accessibility in adverse weather.

(*b*) Adequate protected storage for weather sensitive materials/equipments.

(*c*) Protections to personnel from extreme hot/control conditions.

(*d*) Scheduling to allow maximization of outdoor activities during fair weather conditions.

(*e*) Special design and construction provisions for activities in extreme temperature conditions like hot or cold weather concreting, staple of false work in extreme wind conditions (gusts).

(*f*) Adequate lighting for shorter days in winter/night work.

(*g*) Design for early enclosure.

3.1.2 Resource Planning

Resource planning aims to identify requirement, availability and regulatory/control processes related to resources. Resource planning is a generic expression but the actual process of planning is specific to the resources considered.

In construction phases, the resources can be categorized as materials, manufactured products, equipments for construction, installation and fabrication, human resources as a part of overall organization, information resources, such as, reference standards and other practice documents, environmental conditions for work on site and infrastructure facilities. Therefore, the resource planning encompasses identification, estimation, scheduling and allocation of resources. Resource planning needs to establish a control system for controlling consumption monitoring, corrective action and resource reappropriation in the event of favourable deviation. Organizational capability, commitment to the project requirements and other constraints such as time and cost, need to be considered as inputs while planning resources. Techniques of management and planning, such as, Programme Evaluation and Review Technique (PERT) and Critical Path Method (CPM) should be used.

Non-availability of basic building materials within reasonable lead would influence the constructional practice by alternative materials. The constructional practices should be decided by the local skills of the manpower for constructional activities. The equipment selection should be governed by the site constraints. Therefore, as, the resource planning is critical to the project viability itself, the inputs to the resource planning need to be validated appropriately and established for such management. Resource planning should establish a proper system of data collection so as to facilitate effective resources control mechanism. Resource planning responsibility has to be specifically defined in the overall organizational setup.

3.1.3 Construction Phase

The site management should be carried out through suitable site organization structure with roles and responsibilities assigned to the construction personnel for various construction related functions. Safety management is one of the important components of site management.

Site layout

The layout of the construction site should be carefully planned keeping in view the various requirements to construction activities and the specific constraints in terms of its size, shape, topography, traffic and other restrictions, in public interest. A well planned site layout will enable safe smooth and efficient construction operations. The site layout should take into considerations the following factors:

(*a*) Easy access and exit, with proper parking of vehicle and equipments during construction.

(*b*) Properly located material stores for easy handling and storage.

(*c*) Adequate stack areas for bulk construction materials.

(*d*) Optimum location of plants and equipments.

(*e*) Layout of temporary services like (water, power, power suppression unit, hoists, cranes, elevators, etc.)

(*f*) Adequate yard lighting and lighting for night shifts.

(*g*) Temporary buildings; site office and shelter for workforce with use of non-combustible materials as far as possible including emergency medical aids.

(*h*) Roads for vehicular movement with effective drainage plan.

(*j*) Construction safety with emergency access and evacuations and security measures.

(*k*) Fabrication yards for reinforcement assembly, concrete precasting and shuttering materials.

(*m*) Fencing, barricades and sign boards.

Access for fire fighting equipment should be provided to the construction site at the start of construction and maintained until all construction work is completed. Free access from the street to fire hydrants/static water tanks, where available, should be provided and maintained at all times. No materials for construction be placed within 3 m of hydrants/static water tanks. During building operations, free access to permanent, temporary or portable first-aid fire fighting equipment be maintained at all times.

Access to the upper floors during construction

In all buildings over two storeys high, at least one stairway be provided in usable condition at all times. This stairway be extended upward as each floor is completed. There must be a handrail on the staircase.

Construction strategy and construction sequence

Construction strategy and construction methods are to be evolved at the planning and design stage specific to the conditions and constraints of the project site and implemented by the site management personnel to ensure ease of construction and smooth flow of construction activities. Sites of high water table conditions with aggressive chemical contents of subsoil needs special design considerations. Buildings with basement in sites of high water table should be planned with dewatering scheme with appropriate construction sequence. Duration of dewatering should continue till sufficient dead loads are achieved to stabilize the buoyancy loads with adequate factor of safety. The construction sequence should be planned taking into consideration the following aspects:

(*a*) Availability of resources (men, material and equipment);

(*b*) Construction methods employed including prefabrication;

(*c*) Planned construction time;

(*d*) Design requirements and load transfer mechanism;

(*e*) Stability of ground like in hilly terrain;

(*f*) Ensuring slope stability with retaining structure before the main construction;

(*g*) Installation and movement of heavy equipments like cranes and piling equipments;

(*h*) Effect of weather; and

(*j*) Minimum time to be spent below ground level working.

Construction management efforts should ensure that the project features and functions that characterise the project scope remain as established during the design finalization stage. Accordingly, construction phase practices need to be oriented to manage the project. As a part of overall project management functions, the processes of planning, and verification are associated with the preconstruction phase of the project. The monitoring and the change control are critical to the construction phase leading to serious implications on the time and cost aspects.

Construction phase of the project transfers the project conceived on paper in the form of plans and designs, into reality by use of resources like materials, machines and men through one or more construction agencies. To fulfil the construction scope with quality, in time and under safe conditions within a reasonable cost, it is desired that the project is planned for managing construction for amalgamation of above resources for their optimum use and its continuous monitoring. Agencies managing the supervision and/or construction are desired to plan and document a management system with clear cut responsibilities and for managing various parameters like scope, time, quality, health, safety and environment and cost for implementation, monitoring and control for their effectiveness. This may be preferably inline with proven National/ International documentation system covering all aspects of monitoring and controls. Various parameters to be managed during construction are as below.

3.2 TIME MANAGEMENT

Considering the importance of time in a project, it is desirable that project is completed in the defined time schedule to get its fruitful benefits. The system planned should cover total schedule of completion with one or more construction agencies, number of vendors, identification of total resources, timely availability of all inputs, including critical ones, its processing during construction of a project. The system should include a periodic review of a project with all parameters as well as catch up plans in case of delay identified for controls and reporting from time to time. The system planned should preferably by computer friendly and simple to follow for implementation, monitoring and controls and for reporting from time-to-time.

3.3 QUALITY MANAGEMENT

Quality of a project should be planned for all activities from inception to completion. It is desirable that the system planned gives adequate assurance and controls that it meets projects quality objectives. The system should cover review of existing requirements, subcontracting, materials, processes and controls during process, auditing, training of personnel, final inspection and acceptance. All activities should be planned and controlled. Quality systems approach should be referred for planning, suitable to a particular project for implementation.

3.4 HEALTH SAFETY AND ENVIRONMENT MANAGEMENT

Each project affects the safety and health of the workmen and surroundings during construction. Various activities having impact on health, safety and environment need to be identified with their likely effect and proposed preventive corrective actions, together with the concerned statutory obligations. The system planned for health, safety and environment should address and cover the above including use of personnel protective equipments by all concerned, and reporting on their monitoring and controls during project implementation.

3.5 COST MANAGEMENT

To keep the project under viable proposition, it is desired that cost of the project during construction are monitored and controlled through a documentation system. The various parameters which may affect the basic cost, escalations, cost due to variation in scope and quantities, etc., need to be monitored at a defined frequency. The system planned may be in line with a proven cost control method or similar in nature and cost incurred vis-a-vis cost sanctioned and cost anticipated to be reported and controlled from time to time.

3.6 MATERIAL STORAGE MANAGEMENT

For any site, there should be proper planning of the layout for stacking and storage of different materials, components and equipments with proper access and proper manoeuvrability of the vehicles carrying the material. While planning the layout, the requirements of various materials, components and equipments at different stages of construction should be considered.

Materials should be segregated as to kind, size and length and placed in neat, orderly piles that are safe against falling. If piles are high they should be stepped back at suitable intervals in height. Piles of materials be arranged so as to allow a passageway of not less than 1 m width in between the piles or stacks for inspection or removal. All passageways be kept clear or dry vegetation.

Materials be stored, stacked and handled in such a manner as to prevent deterioration or intrusion of foreign matter and to ensure the preservation of their quality and fitness for the work.

Materials should be stacked on well drained, firm and unyielding surface. Materials should not be stacked so as to impose any undue stresses on walls or other structures.

Materials should be stacked in such a manner as not to constitute a hazard to passerby. At such places the stacks must have suitable warning signs in day time and red lights on and around them at night.

Stairways, passageway and gangways should not become obstructed by storage of building materials, tools or accumulated rubbish.

Materials stored at site, depending upon the individual characteristics, be protected from atmospheric actions, such as rain, sun, winds and moisture, to avoid deterioration.

When heavy materials have to be handled manually each workman be instructed for the proper method of handling such materials. Each workman be provided with suitable equipment for his personal safety as necessary. Supervisors should also take care to assign enough men to each such job depending on the weight and the distance involved.

3.6.1 Protection Against Fire and Other Hazards

Materials, like timber, bamboo, coal, paints, etc., should be stored in such a way that there may not be any possibility of fire hazards. Inflammable materials like kerosene and petrol, be stored in accordance with the relevant rules and regulations so as to ensure the desired safety during storage. Stacks should not be piled so high as to make them unstable under fire fighting conditions and in general they must not be more than 4.5 m in height. Explosives like detonators should be stored in accordance with the existing regulations of *Indian Explosives Act*.

Materials which are likely to be affected by subsidence of soil like precast beams, slabs and timber of sizes be stored by adopting suitable measures to ensure unyielding supports.

Materials liable to be affected by floods, tides, etc., be suitably stored to prevent their being washed away or damaged due to floods, tides, etc.

3.7 SAFETY MANAGEMENT

The safety of personnel engaged in building construction should be ensured through a well planned and well organized mechanism.

For this, depending on the size and complexity of building construction project, safety committee shall be constituted to efficiently manage all safety related affairs. The site in-charge or his nominee of a senior rank shall head the committee and a safety officer shall act as member secretary. The meetings of the safety committee shall be organized regularly say fortnightly or monthly depending on the nature of the project, however, emergency meetings shall be called as and when required. The safety committees shall deal with all the safety related issues through well structured agenda, in the meetings and all safety related measures installed at the site and implementation thereof shall be periodically reviewed.

Notwithstanding the guidelines given above all provisions given in relevant Act/Rules/Regulations as amended from time to time should be followed; in this regard, reference be made to the *Building and Other Construction Workers Act,* 1996 and the Rules/ Regulations framed thereunder.

3.8 SITE PREPARATION

While preparing the site for construction, bush and other wood, debris, etc., be removed and promptly disposed of so as to minimize the attendant hazards.

Temporary buildings for construction offices and storage be so located as to cause the minimum fire hazards and shall be constructed from non-combustible materials as far as possible.

3.9 GARRAGE AND FLEET MANAGEMENT

For contractors having a few machineries and vehicles, it is economical to send them for repairs and maintenance to workshop. But for a big concern, having large number of equipments, machineries and vehicles, it is always profitable to have own workshop for repair and maintenance of equipments, machineries and vehicles. However it has to be assured in advance before a workshop is set up that all types of repair and maintenance works can be completed therein and good mechanics and technicians are available having good knowledge of various parts of machineries and know hawz to repair and maintain available equipments and machineries. Moreover the equipments like lathe, milling, turning etc., required to maintain and repairs should be available in workshop without which the workshop may have no meaning. Moreover these service facilities should be available and located in the company garrage or vehicle service department near worksite so as to avoid unnecessary time lost in sending and bringing vehicle from site to workshop.

Generally these vehicles or equipment and machineries are operated by drivers or operators and repaired and maintained in condition by mechanics or technicians. Therefore it is essential to these two persons to have cordial relations with each other else each will throw responsibility on other for non-working of equipment and machinery. It is the duty of the mechanic to satisfy the driver/ operator of the machinery by rectifying the faults indicated promptly and satisfactorily so that he could win the goodwill of the operator/driver. At the same time it is responsibility of the operator to keep the machinery upto date condition at any time and should use it properly. It is also duty of operator to inform mechanic about any fault if suspected at any time, immediately.

Equipment for Tunnel Consolidation

The demand for safer and faster execution of tunnel excavation has led SOILMEC engineers to design tunnelling equipment with a longer rotary stroke capable of installing reinforcing elements over 50 m long, with a minimum idling time.

The range includes single or double boom rigs, all fitted with a sliding turntable that can be set at different heights to centre the tunnel axis.

Rigs such as ST-30 are easily configured for vertical drilling.

Model	*Engine power* kW	*Working radius at 0°* mm	H_{max} *from ground level at 0°* mm	*Weight* t
ST-15	103 (or 75)*	1880 ÷ 2550	4570	12,5
ST-20	127 + (90)*	1700 ÷ 4696	6196	21
ST-30	155 + (90)*	1528 ÷ 5037	6787	33
PST-60	155 + (118)*	3700 ÷ 6500	10700	60
ST-120	205 + (2 × 90)*	3600 ÷ 6600	10100	119

*electric motor for boom

Some of the tools used in construction are illustrated below:

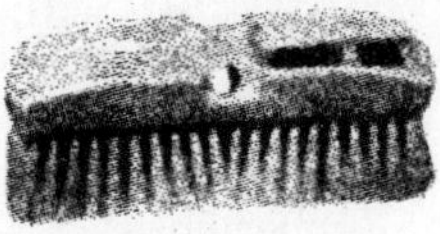
Acid wash brush

Adjustable line strenchers

Arm acid brush

Barbell jointer

Brick brush

Brick hammer

Brick jointer

Brick splitter

Cement coater

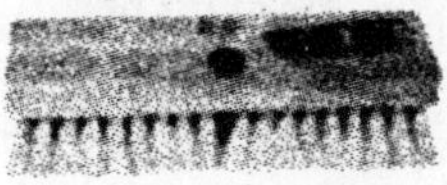
Heavy duty acid brush

Masonry hammer

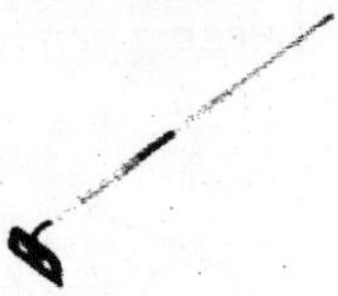
Mortar hoe

Mortar hole

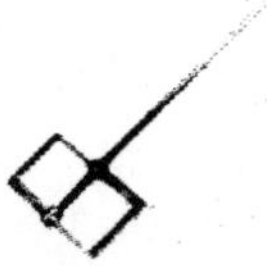
Mud mixer

Sled runner

Mold rubber float

Wide float

Sponge rubber float

Molded rubber float

Bevel float

Rubber float

Magnes float

Redwood float

Morter making machine

Concrete saw

Wrecking bar

Brick bolster

Masonry peg

Brick trowel

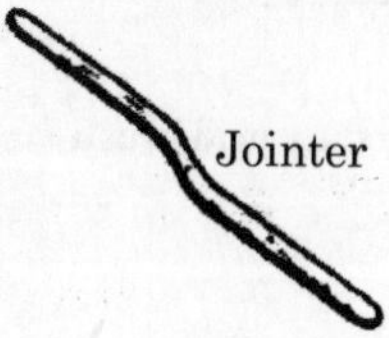
Jointer

Buttering trowel

Pointing trowel

Hammer

Chisel or bolster

Masons tool

Brass plumb bobs

Plum bobs

Levels and plumb

Plumb bob

PB2
Laser plumb

The plumb
bob plumb

Solid brass
plumb

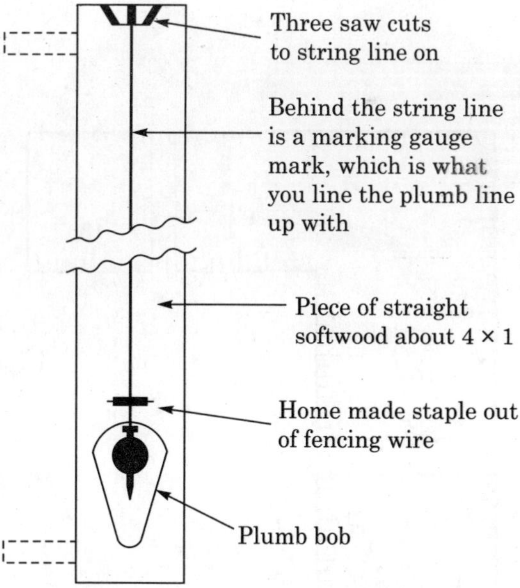

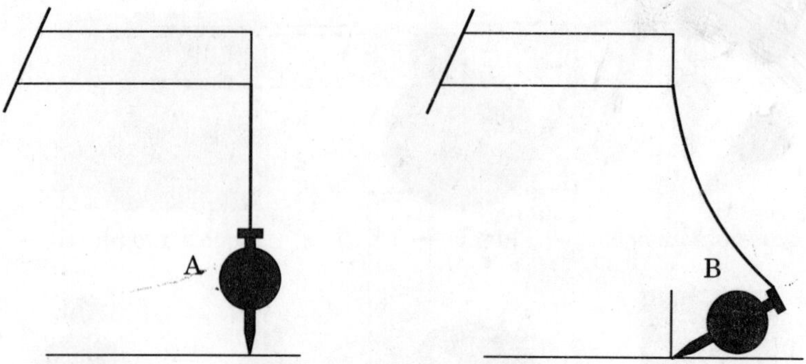

Side view
Transferring-point to ground

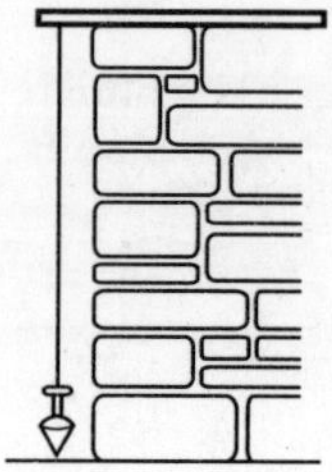

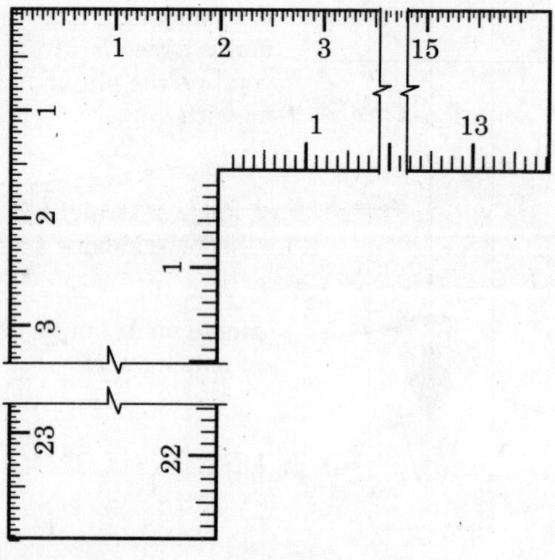

1. Square

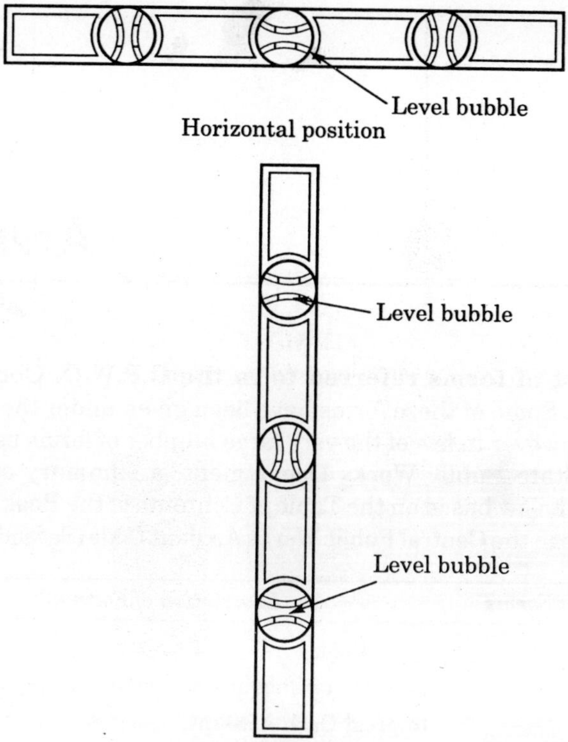

2. Mason's level

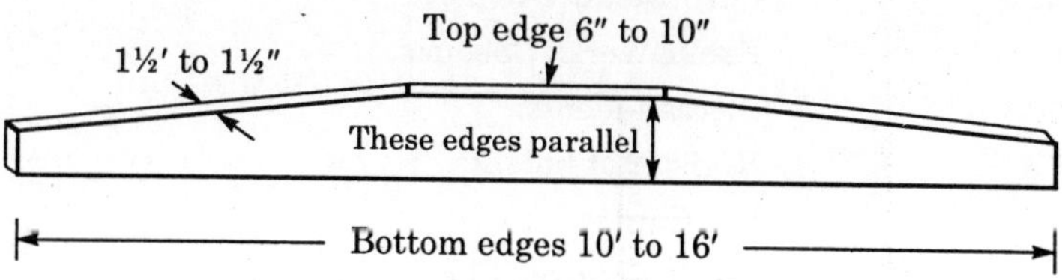

3. Straightedge

APPENDIX

List of forms referred to in the C.P.W.D. Codes (2nd Edition). Some of these forms have been given under the relevant article. However in few of the very large number of forms used in the Central/State Public Works Department, a summary of form is produced below based on the Table of Contents of the Book of Forms referred to in the Central Public Works Account Code (Second Edition).

Sl. No. of Forms	*Description of Forms*
1.	Cash Book.
1A.	Register of Cheques Received and Adjusted.
2.	Imprest Cash Account.
3.	Receipt for Payments to Government.
3A.	Cash Memos for Goods sold by Government.
4.	Treasury Remittance Book.
5.	Cash Balance Report.
6.	Public Works Cheques.
7.	Stores Indents.
7A.	Register of Indents.
8.	Bin Card.
8A.	Goods Received Sheet.
9.	Summary of Stock Receipts.
10.	Summary of Indents.
11.	Deleted.
12.	Priced Stores Ledger.
12A.	Register of Goods Received Sheets.

Sl. No. of Forms	Description of Forms
12B.	Register of Bin Cards.
13.	Tools and Plant Received Sheet.
14.	Tools and Plant Indent.
15.	Tools and Plant Ledger.
	Part I. Articles in hand.
	Part II. Articles temporarily lent or sent out.
	Part III. Stores awaiting adjustment.
16.	Statement of Receipts, Issues and Balances of Road Metal.
17.	Road Metal Rate Book.
18.	Survey Report of Stores.
19.	Sale Accounts.
20.	Deleted.
21.	Muster Roll.
21A.	Register of Unpaid Wages.
22.	Casual Labour Roll.
23.	Measurement Book.
23A.	Standard Measurement.
24.	First and Final Bill.
25.	Deleted.
26.	Running Account Bill.
27.	Deleted.
28.	Hand Receipts.
29.	Pay Bill of Work Charged Establishment.
30.	Deleted.
31.	Indenture for Secured Advances.
32.	Petty Works Requisition and Accounts.
33.	Works Abstracts—A for Major Works.
34.	Works Abstract—B for Minor Works.
35.	Register of Material-at-Site Accounts.
35A.	Account of Material Issued to Contractors.
35B, C, D	Deleted.
36.	Out-turn Statement of Manufacture.
37.	Deleted.

Sl. No. of Forms	Description of Forms
38.	Register showing the Clearance of the Suspense Head "Materials".
39.	Work Slip.
40.	Register of Works—A—for Major Work.
41.	Register of Works—B—for Minor Works.
42.	Register of Manufacture.
43.	Contractors' Ledger.
44.	Detailed Completion Report.
45.	Completion Statement of Works and Repair.
46.	(1) Register of Revenue Realised (2) Register of Refund of Revenue (3) Register of Receipt and Recoveries on Captial Account
46A.	Schedules of: (1) Revenue Realised (2) Refund of Revenue (3) Receipts and Recoveries on Captial Account
47.	Deleted.
48.	Statement of Rent Recoverable in Cash or by deduction from Pay Bill.
49.	Register of Rents Buildings and Loans.
50.	Consolidated Treasury Receipts.
51.	Schedule of Monthly Settlement with Treasuries
52.	Register of Cheques/Receipts/Cash Memo Books.
53.	Transfer Entry Order.
53A.	Omnibus Transfer Entry of Stores Received.
54.	Trans Entry Book.
55, 56.	Deleted.
57.	Register of Transfers Awaited.
58.	Register of Sanctions of Fixed Charges.
59.	Register of Miscellaneous sanctions.
60.	Register of Divisional Account Objections.
61.	Scheduled Docket.
62.	Scheduled Docket of Percentage Recoveries.

Sl. No. of Forms	Description of Forms
63.	Deleted.
64.	Schedule of Works Expenditure.
65.	Schedule of Deposit Works.
66.	Schedule of Takvi Works.
67.	Suspense/Deposit Register.
68.	Deleted.
69.	Abstract Account of Credits, Debits and Balances of the Purchases Account.
70.	Schedule of Misc. P.W. Advances.
71.	Deleted.
72.	Schedule of Debits to Stock.
73.	Stock Account.
74.	Classified Abstract of Expenditure.
75, 75A.	Deleted.
75 B.	Certificate Regarding Correction of Form 49 and Revision of Rent.
76.	Schedule of Debits/Credits of Miscellaneous Heads of Accounts.
76A.	Schedule of Transactions adjusted under the head "Cash Settlement Suspense Account".
77.	Schedule of Credits/Debits of Remittance.
77A.	Schedule of Debits/Credits to adjust Account between Central and State Governments/Adjusting Account with Railways/Adjusting Account with P&T/Adjusting Account with Defence.
78.	Deleted.
79.	Schedule of Deposits.
80.	Monthly Account.
81.	Abstract Book.
82.	Deleted.
83.	List of Account Submitted to Accountant General.
84.	Divisional Officer's Report of Scrutiny of Accounts.
85.	Register of Interest Bearing Securities.
86.	Account of Interest Bearing Securities.
87, 88, 89, 90.	Deleted.
91.	Annual Certificate of Balances.

Sl. No. of Forms	*Description of Forms*
92.	Register of Measurement Books.
93.	List of Monthly Sub Divisional Accounts.
94.	Detailed List of Works Abstract.
	A—For Minor Work
	B—For Minor Work.
	Petty Work
	Requisition and Accounts.
95.	Register of Miscellaneous Recoveries.
96.	Memo of Review of Register.
97.	Register of Destructions of Record.
98.	Deleted.

APPENDIX–B

RAILWORKS

1. DEALINGS WITH RAILWAYS

The Works Department is very often required to deal with the Railways primarily in connection with the receipt of goods despatched from other departments or by the trade. Similarly the department is sometimes required to book consignments to other departments or from rail head to various stations in the Division. For example the crushed stone is very often passed measured and taken over at the quarry site and subsequently despatched to the destination under departmental arrangements. The officers and subordinates of the Division should therefore be conversant with consigning and receiving goods through the Railways.

Some of the terms peculiar to the Railways are given below:

1. **Consignee.** The person to whom the goods (material) are consigned from one station to the other.

2. **Consignor.** The person who despatches goods (material) by rail at the despatching station.

3. **Merchandise.** Goods (material) despatched or received.

4. **R.R.** Railway Receipt. This is the receipt by the goods section on the basis of which goods are delivered at the destination station.

5. **Credit note.** These are adjustment vouchers the payment of which is adjusted between the concerned department and the Railway Department. This system of payment of transit charges by Railway is applicable only in case of Government departments.

The normal procedure for booking of goods and taking delivery of the same is explained below. The various steps involved in the booking of a consignment and taking delivery of the goods from the Railway are.

2. BOOKING OF CONSIGNMENT

At the Booking end. Goods may be booked either in complete wagon loads or in packages. In the case of complete wagon load, a demand for wagon is placed with the station master along with security deposit. When the wagon has been alloted, it has to be loaded within the specified time and at the same time a "Forwarding Note" in the prescribed form is handed over to the station master duly signed by the consignor. These forwarding notes are one of the following three types :

(*a*) **Yellow form.** Used for general merchandise when the value of the goods consigned is below ₹ 500.00.

(*b*) **White form.** Used when the goods are insured such as precious goods, livestock.

(*c*) **Pink form.** When the goods are of strategic importance or when they are explosives.

Since the wagon has been loaded, it is verified for its contents in respect of material specified and its weight after which the booking clerk issues a receipt known as Railway Receipt (RR). Booking may be freight paid or freight to pay. It may be consigned to 'self' or to the party concerned. The R.R. contains the following information:

1. Name of the consigner
2. Name of the consignee
3. Description of the goods consigned
4. Station of booking
5. Station to which booked
6. Weight of consignment
7. Amount of freight paid/To pay.

The R.R. is sent to the party concerned by registered post or taken to the destination station by special messenger.

3. TAKING DELIVERY

The RR is presented to the station master of the destination station. The payment in respect of freight charges is made by a 'Credit Note'. A credit note is given on a printed form which is machine numbered. The amount is adjusted as credit to the Railways and debit to the working department concerned.

In case the goods are not received the booking clerk puts his dated initials which implies that the goods have not been received and no demurrage or wharfage would be charged.

Sometimes the goods are received but the R.R. is delayed in transaction or is lost. "To avoid demurrage and wharfage delivery of the goods is taken forthwith after filling an undertaking to the effect that the goods belong to the party taking the delivery. Typical form of such an undertaking known as *Indemnity Bond* is shown below :

INDEMNITY BOND

I hereby acknowledge to have received from the .... Railway Wagon valued at ₹ .... which was despatched to my address from the .... Station of the .... Railway the R.R. for which has been lost. I for myself, my heirs, executors and administrators undertake in consideration of such delivery as aforesaid, to hold President of India, his agents and servents, Railway Administration, its agents and servants harmless and indemnified in respect of all claims to the said goods.

And I, the undersigned, signing below the consignee of these goods certify that the first signatory is the bonafide owner of the goods, and that I undertake the whole of the said liability equally with the consignees and for this I affix my signature hereto.

Sinature of witness	Signature of consignee
Father's name	Father's name
Caste Age	Caste Age
Profession	Profession
Residence	Residence
Witness	Surety
Father's name	Father's name
Profession	Profession
Caste Age	Caste Age
Residence	Residence
Date :	
Executed in my presence	Station Master

When the consignee feels that the goods have been tampered with damaged or short, a not to this effect should be recorded in the Delivery Book with the station master. The note should be recorded before taking physical possession/delivery of the goods.

On the basis of the noting in the delivery book claims are sub-mitted to the Chief Commercial Superintendent of the Railways concerned within six months from the date of booking.

The consignee should ensure the following:

4. DEMURRAGE CHARGES

The wagon should be unloaded at the earliest. If the wagon is not unloaded within specified time, the period being counted from the time the wagon is placed on the siding, penalty is imposed on the consignee. The amount of such a penalty is charged on the number of hours of detention per quintal of goods. The weight is based on carrying capacity of the wagon recorded therein. Such a penality is known as *Demurrage.*

5. WHARFAGE CHARGES

The goods unloaded on the siding should be removed within twenty-four hours, so that Railway premises are not kept occupied. For the first 24 hours period, delivery of goods can be had between 6 a.m. to 8 p.m. The penality imposed for not clearing the siding is known as *Wharfage.*

6. CLAIMS

In the event of goods not being taken delivery of by the consignee, the railway intimates the consignee by registered letter and in case the delivery is not taken within the specified period, the goods are auctioned.

7. DUTIES OF JUNIOR ENGINEER S.O., O.S.

The Junior Engineer (also known as section officer, or overseer is the back bone of the works department as he is the main departmental officer who is directly responsible for supervision of the original or maintenance work, handling of stores, maintenance of the accounts handled by him. His duties may thus be defined under the following heads:

(*a*) **The original works:**

(*i*) Handing over possession of the site.

(*ii*) Demarcating of plan of the structure on the ground in case of buildings and marking' on the ground the elements of road, canal, railways etc.

(*iii*) Inspection of all material brought to site by the contractor.

(*iv*) Passing of works in stages.

(*v*) Preparation of running and other bills for the work done or for supplies of stores.

(*vi*) Keep a watch on the progress of the work with respect to CMP/bar charts.

(*vii*) To see that no work is taken in hand without technical sanction. It is normally for the Engineer Officer according T.S. to see that Administrative Approval and funds exist for the work.

(*viii*) Recording of measurements in the M.B.

(*ix*) Maintenance of works Diary and the Order Book.

(*x*) Maintain muster rolls and send daily progress report of such works as are executed departmentally directly for original work or for debitable agency.

(*xi*) Preparation of estimate of work.

(*b*) **Maintenance:**

(*i*) Preparation of maintenance estimates and the annual maintenance plan on which maintenance estimate is based.

(*ii*) Execution of maintenance work through permanent temporary, casual and muster roll labour.

(*iii*) Keeping record of work done by maintenance gang departmental labour.

(*iv*) Maintenance of building, roads, canals railway track etc. (which ever is applicable) in good condition.

(*v*) Preparation periodical series plan. (White-washing/colour washing/distempering) in case of building repainting plan in case of roads, track renewal in the case of railways etc.

(*vi*) Supervising the execution of maintenance work/works carried out through contractor as for original works.

(*vii*) Recording measurement of work done in measurement book.

(*viii*) Carrying out annual inspection of buildings, bridges and culverts.

(*ix*) Maintain muster rolls and send daily progress report of such works as are executed departmentally directly for original work or for debitable agency.

(*x*) Preparation of estimate of works.

(*c*) **Stores:**

(*i*) Submission of indent on the Divisional stock in time so that no work in his section is held up for want of stores.

(*ii*) Maintaining of record of all stores received and consumed on works.

(*iii*) Arranging safe custody of stores to avoid theft, fire or deteioration.

(*iv*) Issing stores to contractor against signed indents indicating the name of work against which issued.

(*v*) Maintening accounts of receipt/ issues of stores, tools and plant, materials at site and road metal and submission of monthly account by due dates.

(*vi*) Arranging stock taking of tools and plant and stores every six months and submitting report of his physical verification to his immediate office (AEE/AGE/AE/SDO).

(*vii*) Initiation of survey report in respect of all tools and plant and other materials rendered unserviceable due to fair wear and tear.

(*viii*) Initiation of any unusual occurrence such as theft of stores road/canal breach etc. In the case of theft of any Government property in his charge in addition to informing the immediate officer, report to the nearest Police Station is also required to be lodged.

(*d*) **Accounts:**

(*i*) Submission of monthly accounts of stores, T & P. Materials. At Site, and Road Metal.

(*ii*) Preparation of pay bills of work charged establishment and supporting details of work done.

(*iii*) Submission of account of Imprest alongwith supporting vouchers by due date to the Sub-Divisional Offices so that the accounts may be incorporated in the cash book for the month.

(*iv*) Submission of account of temporary advance (such as wages of work charged/muster roll/casual labour) alongwith unpaid wages to the subdivisional office by due dates.

(*v*) Submission of return showing work done by vehicles, machines etc. allocating the head to which the expenditure is to be debited.

(*vi*) Depositing with treasury the amount received from rent of Rest Houses alongwith copies of the challans.

8. INSTRUCTIONS ON TRANSFER OF CHARGE

The most important transfer of charge amongst Engineer Officers to the Works Department is that of the Junior Engineer who is responsible for duties handling all stores. T & P, material-at-site, Accounts, etc. In the case of the Chief Engineer, for example, his handing ever charge is quite simple as he is primary the Administrative Head of the Department and except relinquishing the office and certain secret documents there is no physical transaction involved. Similarly the Suprintending Engineer, C.W.E. etc., is the administrative Head for all non-Gazatted staff in his circle and has his staff officers to take care^of the various branches, stores, documents. His responsibilities are thus 50% Executive and 50% Administrative. The duties of the Executive Engineer/G.E. are 25% Administrative and 75% Executive. He too however does not hold any charge except the cash in hand and the cashbooks which he is required to hand over personally to the successor through in practice it amounts to physical verification of all accounts documents held by the cashier. The same more or less applies in the case of a disbursing sub-division. In other cases the Engineer-in charge (AEE/AGE/AE/SDO) hands over the various sections and the relieving officer has to satisfy himself about the correctness. As however the physcial custodian of the stores/T&P/MAS does not change very often only the balance held at site are verified with the balances in the ledgers and charge transferred on paper. In the case of Junior Engineer however a detailed handing/taking over memo has to be prepared for this reason maximum time for handing/taking over charge is allowed in the case of the Section officer/Junior Engineer.

The handing/taking over is carried out as below:

1. The section officer under orders of transfer should not leave his Headquarter till he has handed over the charge to his successor.

In case it becomes necessary to do so on medical grounds he should obtain written permission from his immediate officer to do so. The charge should be handed over to the successor immediately on the arrival of the relief within the period prescribed for such a handing/taking over.

2. The Junior Engineer being relieved should prepare all the charge papers and keep them ready with the balance struck in the ledgers ready for esay checking/verification. The imprest account, if any should be closed and submitted to the Divisional officer through the subdivision along with the supplementary vouchers and cash in

hand. Separate sanction for operating permanent imprest is accorded by the Divisional Engineer and fresh imprest is placed at the disposal of the relieving officer. In some of the departments the closed imprest is handed over to the relieving officer. The balance (cash in hand) is signed by both the officers in token of the transfer of such accounts.

3. All stores borne on the ledgers, T and P, Material at Site Account and Road metal register are posted uptodate. The lists of such stores are prepared in triplicate under the following heads. One copy each is retained by the relieved and relieving officer and one copy is forwarded along with other handing over memos to the sub-divisional officer :

(*a*) List of materials with balances in hand and their distribution supported by proper receipts.

(*b*) List of articles of T and P in hand along with their distribution supported by receipts.

(*c*) List of material at site account of works.

(*d*) Road metal return.

Stores as above are physically checked by the relieving officer who is personally responsible for the accuracy of the balances. The relieved officer enters the remark 'handed over' under his dated signature and the relieving officer renters the remark 'Taken over as per remarks given against each item. The remarks against these items are recorded only in case of discrepencies. If there are no remarks by the relieving officer it is presumed that the balances held at site agree with the balances shown in the ledger.

4. All work done by departmental labour or through contractors is entered in the MB's and in the case of contractor's work running bills/final bills as the case may be are finalised. This is necessary to fix responsibility for the work in the case of defective workmanship or other discrepencies.

5. A memorandum of all work in hand along with the position of work, date of completion etc., along with work for which estimates have been submitted is prepared by the relieved officer. The relieving/relieved JE's both inspect all such works in progress. It is the responsibility of the relieving JE to verify the accuracy of the various memos. Discrepencies subsequently brought to notice have an adverse effect on the relieving section officer/JE.

6. The following documents lists are also prepared in triplicate and distributed per serial 3 above.

(*a*) List of contractors along with particulars of works being exeuted by them.

(*b*) Register of buildings.

(*c*) No claim certificate from contractor.

(*d*) Pending claim of contractor.

(*e*) List of work charged establishment along with the sanction against which each individual is appointed and the work to which charged.

(*f*) List of the following:

(*i*) MB's

(*ii*) Level books

(*iii*) Field Books

(*iv*) Indent books

(*v*) Sanctioned estimates

(*vi*) Other important documents.

The charge memo-proforma is filled and this memo along with the supporting documents stated above is prepared in triplicate. All the copies are signed by both the relieved and relieving officer. Cutting/overwriting etc., should be avoided. In case some correction becomes necessary the entry should be recorded and signed by both the relieving/relieved officer.

The charge papers are examined initially in the sub-divisional office and finally in the divisional office where they are filed for record and reference.

9. ISSUE OF MATERIALS TO THE CONTRACTORS

Constructions stores are issued to the contractors for the following reasons:

(*a*) To ensure quality material to be incorporated in the work.

(*b*) To ensure that proper quantity of material is incorporated in the work.

(*c*) To ensure that the work progresses as scheduled and not held up for want of stores. It is comparatively easy for the department to procure controlled material in time. Secondly the department can initiate procurement of the construction stores required for any work from the time the acceptance of the necessity of the work in principle is obtained whereas the contractor cannot do so till his tender has been accepted, he has signed the contact agreements and received the order to start the work.

The contractor's rates for undertaking any work are a directly dependent on the stores to be issued for work and the place of issue and the issue rate. These decisions should therefore be clearly specified in the notice of calling for tender and incorparted in the contract agreement. The issue rate specified in the notice of tender may be any thing from free of cost to market or blackmarket price. The difference in cost of stores is credited/debited to the project as the case may be. In the case of scarcity available controlled stores, the black market price of stores issued by the department is restored to in extreme cases where it is felt that the contractor is likely to use less than specified quantity of such stores and dispose off the rest in the black market. If he is charged higher issue rates he would not be tempted to dispose off the stores. He would quote comparatively higher rates but at the same time the difference between the procurement price and issue price would afford credit to the work and hence the higher rates would be compensated. In the same way stores issued free of cost would bring down the tendered rate but the cost of the stores would be added to the work.

The issue of stores described above is sometimes classified as NIT stores (notified in tender). Sometimes the stock holds such stock as is not likely to be used. During the next six months or longer, storage may be cause the stores to deteriorate. Such stores may be issued to the contractor at market rate or the issue rate which ever is higher. The issue rate is the rate per unit fixed in respect of articles for purpose of issue on bonafied works. This rate is arrived at by dividing the total cost involved in procurement from the source upto the godown (including transportation and handling charges) along with the expenditure incurred in its upkeep, maintenance (*i.e.*, storage and supervision charges). This type of issue of stores to the contractors however amounts to giving financial aid to the contractor and hence no such material is issued to the contractor. However the Engineer in-charge under special circumstances may issue such stores upto Rs. 50 for any one contact in any month.

10. MAINTENANCE OF LOG BOOK

Log books are essential documents in respect of static plant and machinery as well as in the case of runway vehicles to enable the Engineer-in-charge and other inspecting/supervising authorities effective control over the operation.

A typical log book in case of static plant and machine is given in table 1.

Table 1. Typical log book for static machine

Log Book No. ....
Particulars of the Machine ....

Name of the work ....
Month of ....

Date	*Working hour*				*Hours worked*	*Work done*		*POL issued*	*Spares issued / repair carried out*	*Name and signature of operator*	*Signature of incharge*	*Remarks by inspecting officer*
	Starting time		*Closing time*			*Quantity*	*Name of work*					
	hrs.	*mts.*	*hrs.*	*mts.*								

In case of the static equipment Hour Meters are fitted and in such case the hour reading at the beginning and end of the work are entered and hours worked arrived at.

Table 2. Shows typical log ledger page in respect of vehicles

Log book No. ....

Particular of Machine/Plant/Equipment .... Month of .. ..

Date	*Form*	*To*	*Time of departure*	*Time of arrival*	*Meter Reading*		*Purpose of journey*	*Name of work*	*POL issued*	*Spares repair*	*Signature of the officer authorising move*	*Remarks of inspecting officer*
					From	*To*						

As would be seen from the above tables the log books for static machines provide the following data:

(*i*) Daily hours worked by the machine.

(*ii*) Idle hours

(*iii*) POL (petrol oil lubricant)

(*iv*) Repairs done and spare issued

(*v*) Name of the work.

The above information is adequate for exercising effective working control as well as for compiling cost control data.

In the case of running vehicles the data from table 2 provides the following:

(*i*) Daily distance travelled

(*ii*) Particulars of the various journeys

(*iii*) POL consumed

(*iv*) Repair done/spares fitted

(*v*) Name of the work to which cost is chargeable.

In both the cases the first page of the log book contains the following information.

(1) Division/subdivision where plant/vehicle is working

(2) Serial no. of the log book

(3) Particulars of the machine

(*i*) Registration number.

(*ii*) Enquiry number.

(*iii*) Chasis number.

(*iv*) Sanction scales of POL.

Before the log books is issued the engineer-in-charge certifies the entries after proper verification.

In some departments two log book are maintained so that when one is sent for post audit the other is used. In other department monthly abstract is prepared and the statement submitted to the Engineer-in-charge.

APPENDIX—C
MANAGEMENT AND ARBITRATION IN CIVIL PROJECTS

1. BASED ON ISSN 0020-3353 VOLUME 41 NUMBER 12 MARCH 1922

Introduction. Construction in public sector accounts for almost half of the national outlay. The works are generally executed through contracts and hence the importance of contract management. While the contract agency tries to execute the work in the most economical manner as to earn maximum profit for the party, the department tries to get the best work within the given specifications. This conflicting approach between the two parties leads to disputes which are very often sorted out through the process of arbitration.

Settlement of Disputes. It has been seen that settlement of disputes through arbitration not only takes a long time but is very often followed by litigation (It may be noted that primary purpose of arbitration was to obtain, quick decision on the one hand to avoid delay on the other hand. It also helps reduce expenditure to be incurred in litigation).

Even though there is no appeal against the award of the arbitrator but the procedure followed by the arbitrator is challengeable. The lawyer of the losing party invariable discovers a loop hole in the procedure followed by the arbitrator which renders the very purpose of arbitration ineffective.

Courts have also held that the contract awarded by the department is not fair and is one sided. For example all the clauses in the contract document bind the contractor to achieve the following:

(*i*) Quality control with respect to specifications.

(*ii*) Cost control with respect to the quantity of work executed, (irrespective of the increase in the cost of material and labour.

(In some of the modern contracts escalation in the cost of material and labour is now being provided).

(*iii*) *Time control.* As far as the user is concerned, the period of completion is specified and is binding on the contractor. The contract or is bound by the 'Time and Progress Chart'. Failure to get the work completed within the specified period renders the contractor to pay compensation generally 1% of the tendered value for each week's delay (upto maximum of 10%). In the case of supply of materials the penalty is 1% per day delay (Upto a maximum of 10%).

The contract documents have been declared by the court as one sided since there is no clause which takes into consideration the contractor's side. For example the contract document does not specify the compensation to be given in case the running/final payments are delayed beyond a reasonable limit.

One of the outstanding provisions of Arbitration Act is the power of the arbitrator is to give award without stating any reason. Normally in Government contracts, the arbitrator is selected by the Government and at times the contractor does not have confidence in him/her. It is therefore necessary that both the contractor and the Government have full faith in the arbitrator. This is generally achieved by forwarding two or three names to the contractor and asking him to choose one of them. Alternately the contractor is asked to give names of three suitable persons which may be acceptable to the Government.

Contract Management and Arbitration. During the sixth and seventh plans billions of rupees were invested in the country and billions have been allocated in the eight plan. Therefore any time wasted due to inefficient contract management/arbitration would adversely affect national interest.

The Indian contract Act itself is an old one and require, redrafting taking the prevailing condition into consideration. Litigation avoidance is possible in many cases if both the parties are alert and active to their obligations—Indian Contract Act of 1872 is more than a century old and needs revision in the present context.

A comparative study of arbitration clauses of various departments such as Railways, CPWD, MES etc. shows that arbitration clause needs redrafting into a single one with no strings attached and any party to the contract should be authorised to demand arbitration.

From the study off supreme court judgements on the subject it is necessary that suitable amendments to the arbitration clauses be incorporated in the contract document on an uniform equitable basis.

In the seminar on contract management in Delhi (Civil Engineering Division of the Institution of Engineers) it has been suggested that Indian Council of Arbitrators should form suitable rules for dealing with arbitration and also maintain a panel Arbitrators.

In one of the pacers it was suggested tenders be called based on calculated quantities of 20% of major items governing 80% of the project cost for major contracts. It was further suggested that the introduction of professional management and human resources development in construction industry be introduced.

Apart from evolving national policy of construction industry there is need for a national committee consisting of highly qualified planners, engineers and contractors to evolve a system to lay down guide lines for construction management.

Glossary of Technical Terms

PART I

A

Activity. An activity is a part of the project denoted by an arrow in a Network or Flow Diagram.

Administrative Approval. Approval by competent Administrative Authority for the execution of any project.

Analysis of Progress. Evaluation of the work done against the various items of the administrative approval with the corresponding expenditure.

B

Backward Pass. The purpose of backward computations is to compare the latest allowable start and finish time for each activity, which will permit the last event to occur at its earliest expected time as compared in the forward pass.

Bar Chart. It is a graphic representation of programme of procurement of materials and a time bound schedule of completion of various elements of the project.

C

Commissioner for Compensation. Commissioner appointed by the Government for workers' compensation. The appointment is notified by the State Government in the Official Gazette.

Contract Labour Act. Acts of the Government such as Factories Act, Minimum Wages Act, Payment of Wages Act,

Compensation Act etc., for the protection of interests and welfare of the workers.

Cost Control. Overall financial control and scrutiny of a value of completed work in relation to the expenditure.

Critical Path. It is the schematic representation of project by means of diagram called **NETWORK**. It depicts the sequence and interplay of various component events that go to form the project.

D

Direct Cost. It is the cost of labour, material and machinery used in the project.

Dummy Activity. It is a fictitious activity with zero duration and no cost used to maintain the sequential order of the activities in the network.

E

EFT (Early Finish Time). It is the earliest possible time for the activity to start without changing the sequence of activities in the network.

EST (Early Start Time). It is earliest possible time for the activity to start without changing the sequence of activities in the network.

EVENT. It is a stage or points where all previous jobs merging in it are completed and all further jobs bursting out are still to be completed.

F

Flow Diagram. It is a diagrammatic representation of the project in the CPM network.

Forward Pass. The forward pass computations give the earliest start and earliest finish times for each activity and also earliest occurrence times for each event.

Free Float. The free float of an activity is the amount of time by which the activity completion time can be delayed without interfering with the start of the succeeding activities.

G

Gantt Chart. Same as BAR CHART. The system of recording progress of works introduced by Henry L. Gantt in 1919.

H

Holding Depot. Depot for storing of materials which have been passed on for storage from the Receipt Depot till such time as the same is required by the Issue Depot.

I

Interfering Float. It is the difference between the total float and the free float.

Issue Depot. Depot in the Store organization from which material is issued for the project/work.

J

Junior Engineer. Subordinate Engineer officer responsible to the Engineer-in-charge for site supervision and other duties assigned by the Engineer-in-charge.

L

LFT (Late Finish Time). It is the latest time by which an activity can be completed without delaying the project.

Log Book. An important document for recording details of plant, equipment, machinery and vehicles as well as to record their consumption and output.

LST (Late State Time). It is the latest time by which an activity can be started without delaying the project.

M

Major Work. Works carried out against specific proposals and allotment of funds by competent financial authority costing between Rupees Twenty Thousand and Rupees One Lakh.

Minor Work. These are works of minor nature costing below Rupees Twenty Thousand.

Muster Roll. Special form for recording attendance and payment of wages of departmentally employed labour.

N

Net Work. See Flow Diagram.

O

Overheads. Indirect expenditure incurred in the project on account of administrative and technical personnel. The cost of directly employed resources (labour, material and machinery used) comes under Direct cost or Prime cost.

P

PERT. The term stands for Periodical Evaluation and Review Table used for exercising control on the activities of the project.

Prime Cost. Same as Direct Cost.

PSMB. (Permanent Service Measurement Books). These contain permanent standard measurements of building for purpose of periodical (Whitewashing, Painting etc.) Services.

Q

Quality Control. Checks exercised in the execution of a project/work to ensure work according to specifications.

Quantity Control. Checks exercise to ensure physical progress of the work according to time schedule.

S

Sample Coding. System based upon alphabetical coding as far as possible. The initial letter designates the main operation.

Schedule of Compensation. Standard schedule on the basis of which compensation to workers is paid in the case of death and permanent and temporary disablement.

Secondary Cost. See indirect cost.

Special System. Other methods of increasing production at comparatively less increase in expenditure such as the system of incentive.

Stages of Construction. Stages of construction from initiation of the proposal upto completion report Part II (closing of accounts after disposal of surplus stores).

T

Technical Sanction. Sanction accorded by Component Engineer Authority incorporating these in all technical details of the work and cost thereof.

T_E (Earliest event occurrence time). It is the earliest time that the even can start.

Tender. Bird from parties for the execution of work in the prescribed form.

T_L (Latest allowable event occurrence time). It is the latest time the event can occur.

Total Float. It is the difference between the maximum time allowed for an activity and its estimated duration.

Trade Union Act. Act passed in 1926 to protect the unprivileged class of people (the workers) from the exploitation by the capitalist. The act has been amended in 1928, 1937, 1942, 1950, 1951. 1960, 1964, and 1970.

U

Usage. Rates fixed for purpose of debiting the project in respect of hire/usage of plant, equipment and machinery.

W

Work Charged Establishment. Establishment of the expenses which are directly debited to the project as different from the basic establishment.

Works Diary. An important authenticated document which gives all the information associated with the work such as progress of work, material consumed, weather condition, etc.

Workman Compensation Act. (See Schedule of Compensation). Act known as Workmens' Compensation Act. 1923. The employer is bound to pay compensation in accordance to the provision of the Act.

Work Study. Data collected and study carried out to analysis the performance of project resources (equipment and labour).

PART II

A

Accounting System. The procedure adopted by any organization which is involved in cash transactions. The main accounting systems are:

(*a*) Civil Accounting System
(*b*) P.W.D. Accounting System
(*c*) Fresh Accounting System

Administrative Approval Allotment of Funds. Primary authority for the project/work based on the estimate of work submitted by the Engineering Authority.

Allotment of Funds. Funds for works allotted for each financial year in consultation with the representative of the finance attached to the Ministry concerned.

B

Budget Provision. Money provided in the budget for the financial year.

C

Casual Labour. Labour employed for employment of urgent works such as road block or breach in a cannel when it is not possible to get sanction for employment of labour on muster roll. In M.E.S. the term denotes such labour whose services are required for a comparatively longer duration.

Check MB. Measurement book issued to AEE/AGE/AE/SDO for carrying out test check in respect of measurement of work carried out by Junior Engineer Overseer.

Construction Accounts. Folios maintained by the sub-divisional officer to maintain expenditure incurred and materials issued.

Cost Control. Check exercised on the expenditure of different items of the works.

Credit Note. Adjustment Voucher the payment of which is adjusted between the concerned Department and Railway Department.

D

Demurrage. It is the penalty charged by the Railways for not unloading the goods within specified time.

Deposit Works. Non-Government works taken in hand by the P.W.D. in the same way, as other Government works. The funds in the execution of the work including department charges are deposited in Government treasury in lump sum.

E

Expenditure Return. Monthly details of expenditure submitted by the drawing disbursing officers (Engineer-in-charge) to the higher engineer and accounts authority.

F

Financial Control. Control on expenditure in respect of any work/ project exercised by the project authorities.

I

Imprest Account. Standing advance sanctioned by the disburing officer to carry out petty purchases for satisfactory execution of work.

L

L.P.C. (Last Pay Certificate). This certificate is given by the previous organization on the basis of which salary is claimed by the individual from the new organization.

M

Material at Site. Construction stores procured for the project and kept segregated from the Divisional Stock.

MES. Abbreviation for Military Engineering Services.

N

NIT Store. Stores notified in tender.

P

Periodical Services. Repairs carried out at regular interval/period such as white-washing, colour washing, painting and distempering.

Piece Works. Work executed by the Engineer-in-charge for carrying out specific petty work without resorting to tender/quotation.

Pink Form. Form used by the goods section of the railways when goods are of strategic importance or when they fare explosives.

Post-tender Action. Action taken after receipt of tenders (procedure for giving out the work).

Pre-audit. Financial check exercised before making payment.

Pre-tender. Action taken before receipt of tender (procedure for inviting and receiving tender).

Q

Quasi Permanent Establishment. Such temporary staff whose work has been found satisfactory for at least three years and there is no likelihood at their being retrenched due to reduction of workload is appointed as Quasi-Permanent.

R

Register of Buildings. Register showing technical details of building such as reference to drawing number, plinth area, brief specification, year of construction and capital cost.

Reserve Stock. It is the maximum limit of amount upto which materials can be kept in a division. The limit for a division is fixed every year.

Road Metal. Construction material such as stone, brick, bajri-bitumen etc., required for road work.

RR. Receipt by the goods section on the basis of which goods are delivered the destination.

Running Account Bill. Bill used when intermediate payment is made to the contractor in respect of the work done.

S

Secured Advance. Payment made for suppliers without recording the same in the Measurement Book but on the certificate of the Engineer-in-charge to the effect that the value of material supplied exceeds the amount of payment being advanced.

Standard MB. Measurement Book containing duty verified measurement in respect of periodical services.

Survey Report. Report prepared for the disposal of articles rendered unserviceable due to fair wear and tear. It is not economical to held such articles on books. The holder of the stock initiates a survey report detailing full reasons for the same.

T

Takvi Works. Works executed by Irrigation Department consisting of lining of water channels to minimise wastage of canal water. The expenditure incurred is recovered from land owner in the form of land revenue.

Tally Card. Identification cards for various items of stock showing day to day transactions and balances.

Three-digit Classification. Scientific system of classification of accounts introduced in 1974-75. Various heads are allotted three digits numbers. There is a difference of 200 between the block numbers of Receipts head and Revenue head as well as between Revenue head and Capital outlay head.

Treasury Challan. Form No. 32-A used to deposit money into government treasury or sub-treasury showing of nature of payment and particulars of the party on whose behalf payment is made.

W

Wharfage. It is a penalty imposed by the railway on account of delay in clearing the siding.

White Form. It is used for booking general merchandise (Forwarding note) when the goods are insured.

Work Order. It is written order to the contractor to start the work on the basis of open tenders invited for the same.

Y

Yellow Form. Used for general merchandise when the value of goods consigned is below rupees five hundred.